The History of
Professional Wrestling:
HOLY GROUND
50 YEARS OF WWE AT
MADISON SQUARE GARDEN

Written by Graham Cawthon
Edited by Grant Sawyer
Cover design by Kristen Allen

Results compiled as of 11/27/14

Printed in the United States of America

Online: TheHistoryofWWE.com

Facebook.com: History of Wrestling

Twitter: @TheHistoryofWWE

Email: TheHistoryofWWE@gmail.com

*To the Mecca, and all the fans
and performers that have made it
The World's Most Famous Arena.*

TABLE OF CONTENTS

March 14, 2004, hours before WrestleMania 20

Everybody has played there. There's a picture of Elvis Presley, Hulk Hogan, John Cena, the Rock, the Rangers, Frank Sinatra, the Knicks. You step into the arena and you see all the championships, or the guys' retired jerseys. They say 'if you can make it there, you'll make it anywhere.'

It's called the Mecca, and I think it's called the Mecca for a reason. It has an atmosphere, and the only other place I've experienced that was the ECW Arena. But to seat 20,000 people and still have that atmosphere...

To me, it's the birthplace of wrestling. The birthplace of WWE. It was the home of WrestleMania. Everything was on the line. The biggest streak of sell outs, Bruno Sammartino. I want to say wrestling put it on the map, because the Rangers and the Knicks certainly didn't.

I saw Andrew Dice Clay there at his hottest. There's all these hot chicks around. But nothing beats wrestling.

In the simplest form: it was a place where you got to put away whatever problems were going on in your life. Cheer for the good and boo for the bad. And, for those three hours, they were some of the best three hours of your life.

I've been blessed to wrestle in a lot of arenas. They close arenas down. So many of those classic arenas have been torn down. The Sportatorium in Dallas, it's gone.

6

There are so few and far between. The Mid-Hudson Civic Center in Poughkeepsie, Monday Night Raw used to be there. There's the AllState Arena in Chicago. Besides that, there's not a whole lot left. And you won't get that small time feel or amazing ambiance anywhere else with such a large crowd.

I went to a Super Bowl one year. I could care less about the teams. If you're a true wrestling fan, you have to make that pilgrimage...just to be part of that ambiance. If you're gonna go there, every seat is a decent seat.

I have been when business was great and when business was bad. But business was always good at Madison Square Garden. If it was the Garden, it didn't matter if it was a live event, Vince McMahon would show up. There were always different celebrities walking around in the back. It's just an amazing place to see professional wrestling. I feel they should do WrestleMania there every 10 years. If there was a 50th, I would hope to still be alive, but I would still go just as a fan.

It's generations to generations. Fathers, my friends, are taking their sons to events.

If my father were still around, I would kill to go to one more wrestling event there with my dad, because I dragged his ass everywhere.

Tommy Dreamer
September 2014

WWE Hardcore Champion Tommy Dreamer makes his way to the ring for a unification match with WWE IC Champion Rob Van Dam during the Aug. 26, 2002 Monday Night Raw held at Madison Square Garden.

I would like to thank each and every person that has helped in making the site what it is today. Without their support, this book would not exist.

Financial Contributers:

Jared Hawkins
Jim Zordani
Andrew Calvert
John Lister
Richard Rollock
Casey Tomten
Gregory Mosorjak
Dante Ramirez
Sean Oliver
Robert Kleeman
Scotty Wampler
Chris Lesinsky
Joseph Hamdan
Alan Complitano
Mike Abitabile
Michael Shoopman
William Newton
Oswald Jackson
Andy Jackson
Patrick A. Riley
Craig Benee
Cherish Wilson
www.profightdb.com
Mike Levay
Grand National Media
Josh Almas
David Colvin
Ryan Schmauch
Bjoern Schnelle
Jason Bishop
Joseph Sauber
Chip Bland
Jonathan McLarty
Danny Bazarsky
Sean Breazeal
Jason Hunsicker
Aaron Smetlzer
Daniel Quinones
Daniele Fusetto
Dale Hicks
Matt Peddycord

Mike Sernoski
Nicholas Morris
John D'Amato
Damon Campagna
Anthony Fullbrook
Gary Merrithew
Angele Cyr
Michael Wilkinson
Chris Harrington
Anthony Miletic
Gregory Leobilla
Ashley Cox
Michael Sempervive

Individuals:

Aaron Cushman
Adam Firestorm
Adam Martin
Adam Roy
Adam Sanders
Adrián Valdivia
Akeem Parsons
Alan Keiper
Alan Timper
Alex Ho
Alex Josephs aka atox
Alex Padrino
Alex Sarti
Allan Robinson
Andrew Calvert
Andrew Christeson
Andrew Gardner
Andrew McRae
Andrew Mollon
Andrew Pritchard
Andy Roberts
Antoine Cagne
Art Jonathan
Ash Purkiss
Becky Taylor
Ben Ivanson
Ben LeDoux
Ben Martin
Ben Temples
Benjamin Puttmann
Bill Wilson
Blackjack Parsons
Bob Johnson
Bobby Adkins
Brad MacDonald
Brad Stutts
Bradley Owen
Brandon Baker
Brett Morgenheim
Brett Wolverton
Brent Hawryluk
Brian Beasley

Brian Dixon
Brian Bingman
Brian Henke
Brian Matheson
Brian Paige
Brian Pickering
Brian Scala
Brock Moore
Candace Hinchey
Carl Campbell
Casey Tomten
Charles Jean
Charles Martin
Charles Short
Charles Wheeler
Cherish Wilson
Chris Berube
Chris Bradshaw
Chris Corridan
Chris Cushman
Chris Dean
Chris Owens
Chris Putro
Chris Skolds
Chris Smith
Chris Tabar
Christian Heintz
Christian Rhode
Christophe Simon
Christopher Fabris
Clayton Carvalho
Clint Halford
Cory Wiatrek
Craig Skennard
Dan Feriolo
Daniel Clemens
Daniel Hill
Daniel Whitehead
Darren Wyse
Dave DeRobbio
Dave Greiser
Dave Layne
David Andre
David Emmell
David Frederick
David Gochenour
David Grebenc
David Grenier
David Hunter
David James
David Taub
David Wallace
Dennis Jackson
Denny Burkholder
Derek Bedard
Derek Bush
Derek Sabato
Derrick Leroux

Devin Cutting
Devin Kelly
Don R. Willhite Jr.
Doug Garrison
Dustin Robinson
Earl Shelley
Ed Demko
Ed Stylc
Eric Cohen
Eric Denton
Eric Ehrhardt
Eric Foster
Eric Larson
Eric Walker
Erik Carlson
Erik Gerlach
Francesco Casto
Fraser Coffeen
Gareth Reed
Gary Robinson
Gary Will
Gerard Bowes
Glenn Newsome
Gordon
Graham Reynolds
Grant Sawyer
Greg Bernard
Greg Houde
Greg Mosorjak
Greg Nugent
Greg Parks
Greg Rufolo
Guillermo Monti
Houston Mitchell
Issacc Cearc
J Michael Kenyon
Jack Van Dyke
Jake Oresick
Jaime Gonzalez
Jake Pappalardo
James Linnebur
James Maxwell
James Trepanier
Jamie Johnson
Jared Hawkins
Jared Insell
Jared Oloffson
Jason Bishop
Jason Dickinson
Jason Kreitzer
Jason Ouimette
Jason Satterfield
Jed Highum
Jeff Barberi
Jeff Bradley
Jeff Fong
Jeffrey Barberi
Jeffrey Jacobson

Jeremy Miles
Jeremy Morgan
Jesse Richardson
Jessica Bullion
Jessica Kuter
Jim Frisk
Jim Zordani
JJ
Joe Jones
Joe Super
Joel Kolsrud
Jon Herman
John Corcoran
John Culbert
John English
John Preston
John Sturm
Johnathan Barton
Jonathan McLarty
Jonathan Raines
Joe Jones
Jordan Claridge
Jose Perez
Joseph Klunk
Josh Eanes
Josh Gaby
Josh Watko
Joshua Morales
JR Jackson
Justin Bailey
Justin Ballard
Justin Domenicucci
Justin Henry
Justin Lijoi
Kavan Hashemian
Keith Brookes
Keith Drabik
Kelly Fairbee
Kenneth McMahon
Kevin Moss
Kevin Barry
Kevin LeClair
Kevin Perry
Kody Hawes
Kris Alvarenga
Kris Levin
Kriss Knights
Kurt Killberg
Kurtis Williams
Larry Stoy
Luis Morales
Luke Hixon
Madison Carter
Maik Burhenne
Mark Davis
Mark Eastridge
Mark Tomol
Mary Blair

Matt Coyle
Matt Davis
Matt Farmer
Matt Henstock
Matt Hern
Matt Jones
Matt Langley
Matt Mattsey
Matt Mauler
Matt Mitchell
Matt O'Brien
Matt Reischl
Matt Wingblad
Matthew Cagle
Max Levy
Michael Bahn
Michael Chilson
Michael Cline
Michael Danilowicz
Michael DeCarolis
Michael Hicks
Michael Rodgers
Michael Motley
Michael Radtke
Michael Schmidt
Michael Silvers
Mike Abitabile
Mike Farro
Mike Labbe
Mike Minadeo
Mike Nice
Mike Noland
Mike DuPree
Mike Sweet
Mister Saint Laurent
Napoleon Santucci
Nick Burgard
Nick Kudreyko
Nick Taylor
Nick West
Noel O'Connor
Pablo Ricca
Pasquale Rulli
Patrick Conkling
Patrick Dailey
Paul Nemer
Paul Zimmerman Jr.
Peter Baird
Peter Tavares
Phil Stenger
Philip Smeltzer
Ramiro Jesus
Escamilla Islas
Raul Garcia
Ray Smith
Ric Gillespie
Ric Smith
Rich Abbott

Rich Jones
Rich Miller
Richard Boscia
Richard Land
Richard J Palladino
Rick Baptist
Rob den Hertog
Rob Thompson
Robert Becker
Robert Hawkins
Robert Portillo
Robert Sandholzer
Robert Sayers
Robert Welch
Robert Wojnarowski
Ron Witmer
Ronald Love
Ronny Kerk
Ross Harris
Rusty Beames
Ryan Droste
Ryan Martinez
Ryan Niemiller
Sam Finley
Sandra Diaz
Scott Douglas
Scott Gold
Scott Thomason
Scott Wojcicki
Sean Watts
Simon Rowley
Stephen Dame
Stephen Gray
Steven Frye
Steve Breech
Steve Dolgosh
Steve Hourdakis
Steve Johnson
Steve Mas
Steve Mueller
Steve Perkins
Steve Nichols
Stephen Lyon
Steven Schera
Steven Smith
Struan Mackenzie
Ted Oliver
Terry Canova
Terry Wall
Thorsten Hogrefe
Tim Johnson
Tim Moysey
Tim Noel
Tim Taylor
Tim Walker
Todd Smith
Tony Bouin
Tom Srbinovski

Trae Wisecarver
Travis Banks
Troy Higgenbotham
Vance Nevada
Wes Kinley
West Potter
Will Bartley
Yair Grinblat
Yasuhiko Morozumi
Anonymous; In
memory of a good
friend

9

Start spreadin' the news, I'm leavin' today
I want to be a part of it
New York, New York

I should start by telling you I am not a native New Yorker.

I've never lived there.

In fact, as I'm writing this, I've visited New York City on only two separate occasions for a total of 10 days.

And yet, like so many others, I've been influenced and captivated by what I've witnessed from the World's Most Famous Arena.

If you're a sports fan, MSG means the Knicks, the Rangers or heavyweight boxing fights like Ali vs. Frazier.

If you're a music fan, it means performances by Elvis Presley, Led Zepplin, Billy Joel, Elton John, John Lennon, and Barbra Streisand, among countless others.

And if you're a pro wrestling fan, it's arguably the center of the universe.

It doesn't matter from what era you became a pro wrestling fan. MSG has played an important role.

In the 1960s and 70s, The Garden belonged to Italian strongman Bruno Sammartino. Sammartino is credited with selling out the venue nearly 200 times, a feat no other single performer comes close to matching. And that includes MSG favorites Billy Joel and Elton John.

As so many wrestling magazines were based in NYC, The Garden became the springboard for men like Sammartino, Andre the Giant, Superstar Billy Graham, Bob Backlund, Ivan Koloff, Capt. Lou Albano and Chief Jay Strongbow to become international stars years before before cable TV or YouTube.

In the 80s, with the onset of cable, it saw the rise of not only Hulkamania but also WrestleMania as the MTV and pop culture world became fascinated with pro wrestling. It was where you would spot celebrities like Regis Philbin, Mr. T, Danny Devito, Joe Piscopo and Cyndi Lauper.

MSG crowds made Canadian Bret Hart a hometown favorite while sometimes turning on traditional good guys like Shawn Michaels and John Cena.

They were witness to not only the TV debut of The Rock and stardom of 'Stone Cold' Steve Austin, but also blink-and-you'll-miss-them appearances by top stars of the territory days: Tommy Rich, Austin Idol, Jay Youngblood, Kevin Von Erich and Gino Hernandez.

And they backed those that once sat alongside them in the stands. Men like Mick Foley, Tommy Dreamer and Zack Ryder, to name a few.

I remember being 12 years old, sitting on my couch in Ashburn, Va., as the mammoth Yokozuna scaled the turnbuckles at WrestleMania X, a prone Bret Hart lying beneath him. I closed my eyes, fearing the worst was about to happen 250 miles away. A loud thud followed, and then the referee's 1-2-3. And 'The Hitman' was the new WWF Champion.

Two years later, I was in Panama City, Fla. and picked up a wrestling magazine with a full-color pictorial spread by famed wrestling photographer George Napolitano on the infamous 'Curtain Call' event at Madison Square Garden. It even included a few close ups of fans you'll hear about in the pages ahead.

Fans like Vladimir Abouzeide and Charlie Adorno.

If you don't know the names, you certainly know the faces. For 20 years, they sat in the same front row seats, month after month, at Madison Square Garden. Vlad, with his glasses and tank top. Charlie, right next to him, sporting his pony tail.

Vlad and Charlie didn't do it for fame. You won't find them on Facebook or Twitter or otherwise trying to market their years of exposure in front of WWE cameras for money. They're just passionate, pure wrestling fans.

In the days before Sign Guy or Tye Dye Guy, or even the ECW regulars like Hat Guy, Vlad and Charlie were among the first wrestling fans to reach celebrity status in the stands. But they weren't *the* first.

Arguably, that title goes to Georgette Kreiger. Kreiger, who died in 1982 at the age of 83, would regularly travel up and down the northeast to follow WWF action. If you're watching a MSG show from the 70s or early 80s, she's the elderly lady taking swipes with her purse at every heel that walks by.

The exploration of this project has been twofold.

One, it was done to put the spotlight on how Madison Square Garden paved the way for the WWE of today. And how WWE honors The Garden in making its events there ... *special*.

Special could be the start of a new era, a new face to lead the company. Special could be surprise guest appearances. Or title changes. Or something that sets the show apart from what could very well be the same line up the night before or the night after in a completely different venue in a completely different city.

It was also done to make the voice of the book you, the fans.

As I said, I'm no New Yorker. I have no business writing 500 pages in my own words about MSG. I've been once. And while I'll never forget the scene of confetti falling at the end of WrestleMania 20 or standing on my chair in the back row of floor seating to see Chris Benoit and Eddie Guerrero celebrating in the ring, that one moment doesn't make me an authority on all things New York City.

The words should be from those who were there.

And in the pages ahead, you'll hear about those who were there. Fans like Vlad, Charlie, and Mary-Kate Grosso. Headliners like Bruno Sammartino himself. And those who made the transition from fan to performer, like Tommy Dreamer and Matt Striker.

It's the World's Most Famous Arena. It helped launch the careers of countless superstars. Some say it is the birthplace of WWE itself.

Maybe, by the end of the book, you'll have some understanding of what makes The Garden The Garden.

I think I do, now.

Graham Cawthon
October 2014

Vladimir Abouzeide, Charlie Adorno and Mary Kate (Grosso) Anthony
at the TNA iMPACT Zone, WrestleMania 24 weekend, 2008.

In addition to the fans and talent represented, we would also like to acknowledge the following, whose works are cited in the pages ahead:

The Place to Be Nation

Titans of Wrestling Podcast

Busted Open Nation

The Steve Corino Show

TitleMatch Wrestling

Sports Illustrated

USA Today

The New York Times

The WWE Network

The Early Years

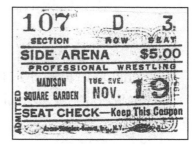

Decades before Hulk Hogan or Bruno Sammartino were born, Madison Square Garden was booming with activity.

But not at the Midtown Manhattan location so many of us associate with the venue.

It would not be until Feb. 11, 1968 that the current building would open its doors. By then, the name Sammartino was already a box office success.

So what about the years before then?

Initially constructed in 1879 at East 26th Street at Madison Avenue, MSG would be rebuilt in 1890. JP Morgan, Andrew Carnegie, and PT Barnum played a part in building the structure and Civil War General William Tecumseh Sherman was among those in attendance for its opening.

In its years of operation, MSG II showcased the first indoor pro football games, introduced Ringling Bros. and Barnum & Bailey Circus and hosted the Westminster Kennel Club's annual dog show.

In 1925, MSG III opened at Eighth Avenue between 49th and 50th streets. In the 43 years that followed, the venue became the home of the New York Rangers and New York Knicks. The venue was dubbed 'The House that Tex Built' due to the $4.75 million put into the construction by boxing promoter and Rangers founder Tex Rickard.

Pro wrestling at MSG dates back to January 19, 1880, less than a year into the first venue's run. A reported 4,000 fans saw William Muldoon defeat Theiband Bauer on that night.

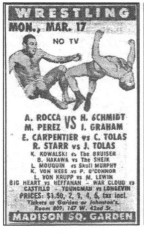
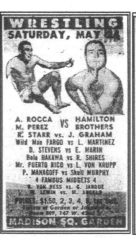
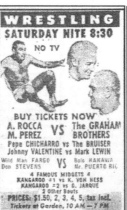

One of the promoters who worked with Rickard was Jess McMahon, grandfather of WWE chairman and CEO Vince McMahon. McMahon would promote wrestling at MSG until his death in 1954, at which time his son Vincent James McMahon would take over the reigns of the Capitol Wrestling Corporation. Vincent James McMahon's success promoting pro wrestling at MSG would eventually lead to his induction into the Madison Square Garden Hall of Fame in 1984, the same year of his death.

At MSG III, names like Gorgeous George, Ed 'Strangler' Lewis, Jim Londos, Verne Gagne, Pat O'Connor, Lou Thesz and Argentina Rocca would regularly draw fans in the door.

But a riot, on Nov. 19, 1957, nearly ended pro wrestling in New York City.

A bout pitting Jerry Graham & Dick the Bruiser against Eduard Carpentier & Argentina Rocca turned bloody. Security tried to intervene, some fans broke bottles and chairs while others swarmed the ring. New York City police officers soon arrived and the wrestlers had to be escorted to the back. In the melee, Graham's $500 robe was stolen. According to newspaper reports, two officers were injured, 300 chairs were damaged and three fans were jailed or fined.

The four wrestlers were brought before the New York State Athletic Commissioner and fined a total of $2,600. In 2014 dollars, that fine equated to $22,024.22.

The riot and its aftermath drew much more media attention than the standard short recap of a wrestling card that was typical for the time. Headlines read 'Matmen carry drama too far,' 'This wasn't in the script' and 'Wrestling script gone awry.' The New York Times regularly featured recaps of wrestling events at MSG, but often with a critical eye toward both the athletes and fans.

As a result of the riot, children under 14 were prohibited from attending, a policy that would remain in effect for more than 20 years.

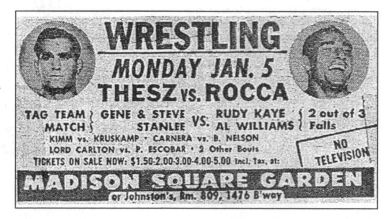

New York City, NY - Madison Square Garden - January 21, 1963 (11,968)

Gordo Chihuahua defeated Gene Kelly at 10:49

Eduard Carpentier defeated Skull Murphy at 10:34

Johnny Barend & the Magnificent Maurice defeated Tony Manousos & Arnold Skaaland in a Best 2 out of 3 falls match at 18:47

Chris & John Tolos fought Pedro Morales & Miguel Perez to a draw in a Best 2 out of 3 falls match at the 30-minute mark

Bobo Brazil & Dory Dixon defeated the Fabulous Kangaroos in a Best 2 out of 3 falls match at 18:55; fall #1: Brazil & Dixon won via disqualification

NWA World Champion Buddy Rogers defeated Killer Kowalski at 18:14

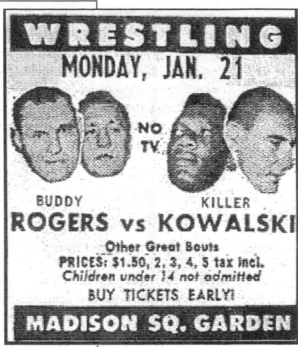

WWWF @ New York City, NY - Madison Square Garden - February 25, 1963 (9,324)

Jerry Colt defeated Gordo Chihuahua at 10:34

Ron Reed defeated Tommy O'Toole at 8:20

Pat Barrett fought Tony Manousos to a 15-minute draw

Tim Woods defeated Miguel Torres at 9:15

Bruno Sammartino & Bobo Brazil defeated Johnny Barend & Magnificent Maurice in a Best 2 out of 3 falls match, 2-0; fall #1: Sammartino & Brazil won at 12:55; fall #2: Sammartino & Brazil won at 8:30

World Champion Buddy Rogers defeated Dory Dixon at 30:57

Skull Murphy & Brute Bernard fought Pedro Morales & Miguel Perez to a curfew draw at 23:50 in a Best 2 out of 3 falls match

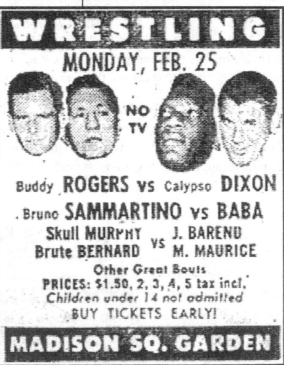

16

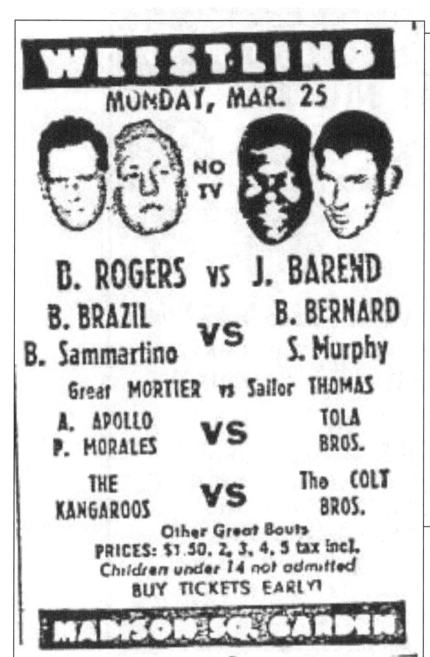

WWWF @ New York City, NY - Madison Square Garden - March 25, 1963 (13,150)

Tim Woods fought Pat Barrett to a 15-minute time-limit draw

The Great Scott defeated Karl Steif at 8:14
Dory Dixon defeated the Magnificent Maurice at 8:31

The Fabulous Kangaroos defeated Jerry & Bobby Colt in a Best 2 out of 3 falls match at 21:17; fall #1: the Kangaroos won; fall #2: the Kangaroos won

Chris & John Tolos fought Pedro Morales & Argentina Apollo to a 30-minute time-limit draw

Hans Mortier defeated Sailor Art Thomas at 5:53

Bruno Sammartino & Bobo Brazil defeated Skull Murphy & Brute Bernard in a Best 2 out of 3 falls match; fall #1: Sammartino & Brazil won via disqualification at 5:50

World Champion Buddy Rogers defeated Johnny Barend at 17:10

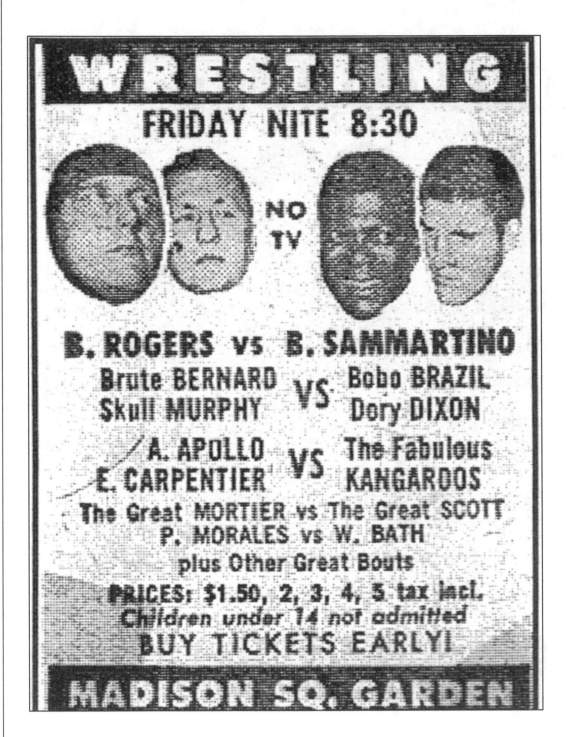

WRESTLING

FRIDAY NITE 8:30

NO TV

B. ROGERS vs B. SAMMARTINO

Brute BERNARD
Skull MURPHY   VS.   Bobo BRAZIL
Dory DIXON

A. APOLLO
E. CARPENTIER   VS   The Fabulous
KANGAROOS

The Great MORTIER vs The Great SCOTT
P. MORALES vs W. BATH
plus Other Great Bouts

PRICES: $1.50, 2, 3, 4, 5 tax incl.
Children under 14 not admitted
BUY TICKETS EARLY!

MADISON SQ. GARDEN

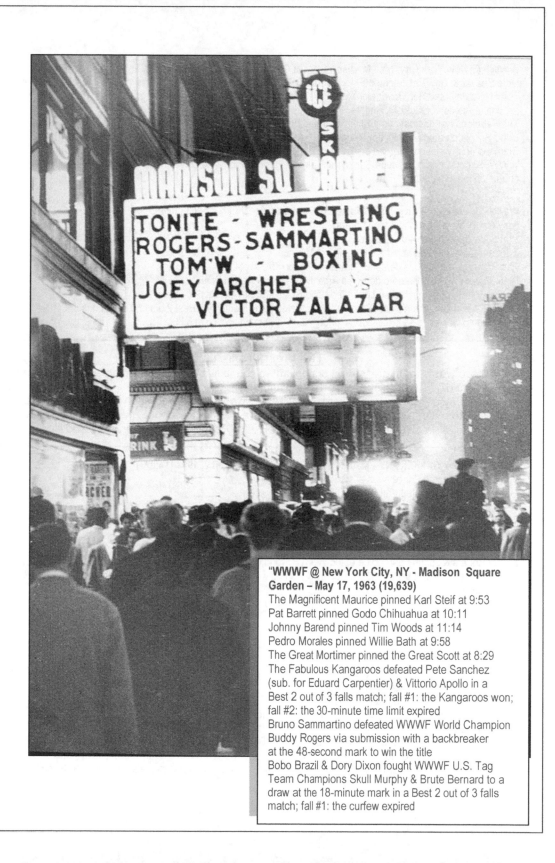

"WWWF @ New York City, NY - Madison Square Garden – May 17, 1963 (19,639)
The Magnificent Maurice pinned Karl Steif at 9:53
Pat Barrett pinned Godo Chihuahua at 10:11
Johnny Barend pinned Tim Woods at 11:14
Pedro Morales pinned Willie Bath at 9:58
The Great Mortimer pinned the Great Scott at 8:29
The Fabulous Kangaroos defeated Pete Sanchez (sub. for Eduard Carpentier) & Vittorio Apollo in a Best 2 out of 3 falls match; fall #1: the Kangaroos won; fall #2: the 30-minute time limit expired
Bruno Sammartino defeated WWWF World Champion Buddy Rogers via submission with a backbreaker at the 48-second mark to win the title
Bobo Brazil & Dory Dixon fought WWWF U.S. Tag Team Champions Skull Murphy & Brute Bernard to a draw at the 18-minute mark in a Best 2 out of 3 falls match; fall #1: the curfew expired

WWWF @ New York City, NY - Madison Square Garden - June 21, 1963 (18,552)
Little Beaver & Tiny Tim defeated Sky Low Low & Billy the Kid in a Best 2 out of 3 falls match at the 22-minute mark
Tony Nero defeated Bob Boyer at 10:59
Argentina Apollo defeated Ox Anderson at 10:31
The Fabulous Kangaroos fought Skull Murphy & Brute Bernard to a draw in a Best 2 out of 3 falls match
Bobo Brazil defeated Magnificent Maurice at 11:44
Diamond Jack & Johnny Barend defeated Pedro Morales & Miguel Perez at 11:12
WWWF World Champion Bruno Sammartino pinned Hans Mortier at 20:36 when the two men fell backward, with the champion landing on top

WWWF @ New York City, NY - Madison Square Garden - July 12, 1963 (14,495)
Jolly Cholly fought Ox Anderson to a draw
Karl Steif fought Tony Nero to a draw
Edouard Carpentier defeated the Magnificent Maurice
The Fabulous Kangaroos defeated Tim Woods & Ron Reed at 23:51
Skull Murphy & Brute Bernard defeated Argentina Apollo & Miguel Perez
Buddy Rogers & Johnny Barend defeated Bobo Brazil & Pedro Morales
WWWF World Champion Bruno Sammartino defeated Hans Mortier in a Best 2 out of 3 falls match, 2-0; fall #1: Sammartino won via disqualification at 11:30; fall #2: Sammartino won at 6:09

The pressure as champion

"There was a lot of pressure. I don't want to sound like I put too much pressure on myself, but I felt a lot of responsibility there. The preliminaries made a lot less (money) and they depended on those pay days. And if you were the headliner, you were looked upon as the guy that was going to make a difference in the paycheck. The bigger the house, the bigger the payoff."
Bruno Sammartino, *TheHistoryofWWE.com interview, 2009*

WWWF @ New York City, NY - Madison Square Garden - August 2, 1963 (14,677)
Tim Woods defeated Prince Nero at 15:36
Gorilla Monsoon defeated Karl Steif at 3:58
Hans Mortier defeated Magnificent Maurice at 7:08
The Fabulous Kangaroos defeated Pete Sanchez & Pedro Morales in a Best 2 out of 3 Falls match, 2-0; fall #1: the Kangaroos won via disqualification at 4:25; fall #2: the Kangaroos won at 18:49
Killer Kowalkski pinned Ron Reed at 1:56
Buddy Rogers & Johnny Barend defeated WWWF World Champion Bruno Sammartino & Bobo Brazil in a Best 2 out of 3 Falls match at 17:53, 2-1; fall #1: Rogers & Barend won; fall #2: Sammartino & Brazil won; fall #3: Rogers & Barend won
Edouard Carpentier & Argentina Apollo fought WWWF U.S. Tag Team Champions Skull Murphy & Brute Bernard to a curfew draw

WWWF @ New York City, NY - Madison Square Garden - August 23, 1963 (19,712)
Tim Woods defeated the Magnificent Maurice at 10:47
Dory Dixon pinned Tony Nero at 9:18
Johnny Barend defeated Karl Steif at 11:16
Gorilla Monsoon pinned Ron Reed at 3:27
Bobo Brazil & Lucas Pestano defeated the Fabulous Kangaroos at 20:33
Buddy Rogers pinned Hans Mortier at the 43-second mark
WWWF World Champion Bruno Sammartino defeated Killer Kowalski at 20:58 via submission with the backbreaker
Argentina Apollo & Pedro Morales defeated Skull Murphy & Brute Bernard in a Best 2 out of 3 falls match, 2-1; fall #1: Apollo & Morales won at 16:08; fall #2: Apollo & Morales won at 19:30 via referee's decision after the curfew

WWWF @ New York City, NY - Madison Square Garden - September 16, 1963 (17,576)
Farmer Pete & Tiny Tim defeated Irish Jackie & Sky Low Low in a Best 2 out of 3 falls match at 24:07
Edouard Carpentier defeated Magnificent Maurice at 8:59
The Fabulous Kangaroos defeated Pedro Morales & Lucas Pestrano in a Best 2 out of 3 falls match at 20: 42
WWWF U.S. Tag Team Champion Brute Bernard fought Tim Wood to a double count-out after the 20-minute mark
Dory Dixon defeated Pedro Rodriguez at 9:37
Argentina Apollo defeated WWWF U.S. Tag Team Champion Skull Murphy at 8:52
Gorilla Monsoon & Hans Mortier (sub. for Buddy Rogers) fought WWWF World Champion Bruno Sammartino & Bobo Brazil to a draw in a Best 2 out of 3 falls match; fall #3: the curfew expired

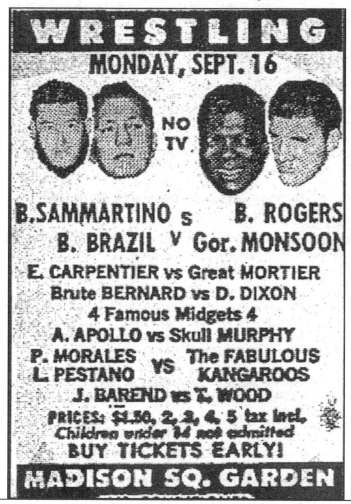

Being hooked as a kid
"I watched TV wrestling when living at home in Maspeth, NY when I was a kid. I marveled at promos plugging upcoming matches at Madison Square Garden with stars like 'Nature Boy' Buddy Rogers, Antonino Rocca, Mark Lewin and Don Curtis, Bobo Brazil, and so many more. I had to wait until I was 13 years old to actually go to a show there as it was a rule from the New York State Athlete Commission that anyone under the age of 13 was not permitted at a wrestling or boxing event."
Bill Apter, *TheHistoryofWWE.com interview, 2014*

WWWF @ New York City, NY - Madison Square Garden - October 21, 1963 (18,969)
Karl Steif defeated Tony Nero at 10:26
Tim Woods defeated Jose Quinosis at 12:38
Pedro Morales defeated WWWF U.S. Tag Team Champion Skull Murphy at 9:07
Edouard Carpentier defeated Hans Mortier via disqualification at 7:19
Miguel Perez defeated Boris Malenko at 6:43
The Fabulous Kangaroos defeated Dory Dixon & George Drake in a Best 2 out of 3 falls match at 23:17; fall #1: the Kangaroos won; fall #2: the Kangaroos won
Argentina Apollo defeated WWWF U.S. Tag Team Champion Brute Bernard at 6:14
WWWF World Champion Bruno Sammartino fought Gorilla Monsoon to a double count-out at 21:11
Killer Kowalksi fought Bobo Brazil to a curfew draw at 14:15

WWWF @ New York City, NY - Madison Square Garden - November 18, 1963 (19,706)
Farmer Pete & Pancho Lopez defeated Fuzzy Cupid & Vito Gonzalez in a Best 2 out of 3 falls match at 15:18
Bobo Brazil defeated Hans Mortier at 13:42
Killer Kowalski defeated Dory Dixon (sub. for Eduard Carpentier) at 9:06
John & Chris Tolos defeated Brute Bernard & Skull Murphy in a Best 2 out of 3 falls match at 18:14
Argentina Apollo defeated Klondike Bill at 7:39
Miguel Perez & Pedro Morales defeated the Fabulous Kangaroos in a Best 2 out of 3 falls match at 18:30
WWWF World Champion Bruno Sammartino defeated Gorilla Monsoon via count-out at 24:52 after the challenger was thrown from the ring

WWWF @ New York City, NY - Madison Square Garden - December 16, 1963 (11,670)
Klondike Bill defeated Tim Woods at 11:17
Dory Dixon defeated Boris Malenko at 9:10
Chris & John Tolos defeated the Fabulous Kangaroos in a Best 2 out of 3 falls match at 23:35; fall #1: the Tolos brothers won via disqualification
Vittorio Apollo defeated Magnificent Maurice at 9:50
Gorilla Monsoon fought Bobo Brazil to a draw
Killer Kowalski defeated Hans Mortier at 8:45
Miguel Perez & Pedro Morales defeated Brute Bernard & Skull Murphy in a Best 2 out of 3 falls match at 12:19; fall #1: Perez & Morales won via disqualification; fall #2: Perez & Morales won
WWWF World Champion Bruno Sammartino defeated Dr. Jerry Graham at 15:47 when the referee stopped the match due to injury after the challenger failed a kneedrop off the top

WWWF @ New York City, NY - Madison Square Garden - January 20, 1964 (17,006)
Tiny Tim & Pancho Lopez defeated Sky Low Low & Fuzzy Cupid in a Best 2 out of 3 falls match at 20:34
Roy Heffernan defeated Gino Brito at 9:57
Tony Marino defeated Al Costello at 8:51
Don McClarity defeated Klondike Bill at 8:09
WWWF U.S. Tag Team Champions Chris & John Tolos defeated Miguel Perez & Pedro Morales in a Best 2 out of 3 falls match at 34:30
Bobo Brazil & Argentina Apollo defeated Gorilla Monsoon & Killer Kowalkski at 11:04 when Kowalski fell on top of Monsoon and the referee counted the pinfall, awarding the win to the opposition
WWWF World Champion Bruno Sammartino pinned Dr. Jerry Graham at 9:10 with a roll up

WWWF @ New York City, NY - Madison Square Garden - February 17, 1964 (14,764)

Sky Low Low & Billy the Kid defeated Sonny Boy Cassidy & Farmer Pete in a Best 2 out of 3 falls match at 26:45

Don McClarity defeated Magnificent Maurice at 8:27

Bill Watts defeated Klondike Bill at 9:31

Hans Mortier defeated Gino Brito at 7:18

Dr. Jerry Graham defeated Tony Marino at 10:20

Bobo Brazil & Argentina Apollo defeated Killer Kowalski & Gorilla Monsoon via disqualification at 15:16 when Monsoon and Kowalski began fighting each other after mistaking the other for their opponents

WWWF World Champion Bruno Sammartino defeated the Giant Baba at 13:38 via submission with the backbreaker

23

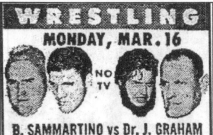

WWWF @ New York City, NY - Madison Square Garden - March 16, 1964 (18,717)
Hans Mortier fought Bobo Brazil to a 20-minute time-limit draw
Ernie Ladd defeated Klondike Bill at 2:17
Miguel Perez defeated Lou Bastien at 15:53
Pedro Morales defeated Bobby Davis via disqualification at 5:08
Bill Watts defeated Luke Graham at 12:52
Tiny Tim & Irish Jackie defeated Sky Low Low & Fuzzy Cupid in a Best 2 out of 3 falls match at 19:45
WWWF World Champion Bruno Sammartino defeated Dr. Jerry Graham at 8:23
Argentina Apollo & Don McClarity defeated the Magnificent Maurice & Boris Malenko in a Best 2 out of 3 falls match at 20:07; fall #1: Apollo & McClarity won; fall #2: Apollo & McClarity won
Gorilla Monsoon fought Killer Kowalski to a no contest; the match was canceled due to the curfew

WWWF @ New York City, NY - Madison Square Garden - May 11, 1964 (16,300)
The scheduled Pedro Morales vs. Duke Miller and Killer Kowalski vs. Don McClarity matches did not take place as advertised
Tony Maniro fought Miguel Perez to a 15-minute draw
Klondike Bill defeated Matt Gilmore at 6:49
Bill Watts defeated Magnificent Maurice at 4:05
The Kentuckians defeated Max & Hans Mortier via disqualification at 9:44
Bobo Brazil & Ernie Ladd defeated Dr. Jerry & Luke Graham at 15:09
WWWF World Champion Bruno Sammartino fought Gorilla Monsoon to a curfew draw at the 70-minute mark

WWWF @ New York City, NY - Madison Square Garden - June 6, 1964 (16,781)
Miguel Perez defeated Lou Albano at 7:45
Pedro Morales defeated Boris Malenko at 10:14
Don McClarity defeated Bulldog Gannon at 5:28
Killer Kowalski fought Bill Watts to a double count-out at 20:20
Jerry & Luke Graham defeated the Kentuckians in a Best 2 out of 3 falls match
Bobo Brazil & Ernie Ladd defeated Max & Hans Mortier at 12:12
WWWF World Champion Bruno Sammartino defeated Gorilla Monsoon in a Best 2 out of 3 falls match; fall #1: Sammartino won at the 24-second mark; fall #2: Monsoon won at 14:12; fall #3: Sammartino scored the pin at 11:36

WWWF @ New York City, NY - Madison Square Garden - July 11, 1964 (18,891)

Miguel Perez fought Red Bastien to a 15-minute time-limit draw

Pedro Morales defeated Magnificent Maurice at 9:46

Bobby Davis defeated Cyclone Soto (sub. for Wild Red Berry) at 1:56

WWWF U.S. Tag Team Champions Jerry & Luke Graham defeated Hans & Max Mortier at 14:03

Gorilla Monsoon & Killer Kowalski defeated Bill Watts & Don McClarity

Bobo Brazil fought Golden Terror to a 20-minute draw

Freddie Blassie defeated WWWF World Champion Bruno Sammartino via disqualification at 23:36 when the champion choked Blassie into unconsciousness

WWWF @ New York City, NY - Madison Square Garden - August 1, 1964 (18,875; sell out)

Cowboy Bradley & Sonny Boy Cassidy defeated Fuzzy Cupid & Billy the Kid at 8:51 in a Best 2 out of 3 falls match; fall #1: Bradley & Cassidy won; fall #2: Bradley & Cassidy won

Red Bastien defeated Hans Mortier at 5:20

Don McClarity fought the Golden Terror (Clyde Stevens) to a 20-minute time-limit draw; Terror wore a mask with the face cut out for the match due to MSG's policy at the time against masked wrestlers

Dr. Jerry & Luke Graham defeated Pedro Morales & Miguel Perez in a Best 2 out of 3 falls match at 23:20

WWWF World Champion Bruno Sammartino defeated Freddie Blassie at 28:00 via submission with a bearhug

Gorilla Monsoon & Killer Kowalski fought Bobo Brazil & Bill Watts to a draw in a Best 2 out of 3 falls match; the curfew ended at 28:41

WWWF @ New York City, NY - Madison Square Garden - August 22, 1964 (16,958)
The scheduled Freddie Blassie vs. Don McClarity match was canceled due to the curfew
Bobby Davis defeated Wild Red Davis at 5:35
Miguel Perez defeated Bull Johnson at 10:31
Red Bastien defeated Lou Albano at 2:47
Bill Watts defeated Klondike Bill at 3:53
Bobo Brazil defeated the Golden Terror at 4:06
Dr. Jerry & Luke Graham defeated Gorilla Monsoon & Killer Kowalski in a Best 2 out of 3 falls match, 2-0; fall #1: the Grahams won at 5:27; fall #2: the Grahams won at 3:32
WWWF World Champion Bruno Sammartino fought Waldo Von Erich to a curfew draw at the 81-minute mark

WWWF @ New York City, NY - Madison Square Garden - September 21, 1964 (14,915)
Arnold Skaaland defeated Lou Albano at 5:36
Robert Duranton defeated Ted Lewin at 5:46
Pedro Morales & Miguel Perez defeated Magnificent Maurice & Klondike Bill in a Best 2 out of 3 falls match at 10:12; fall #1: Morales & Perez won via disqualification; fall #2: Morales & Perez won
Dr. Jerry & Luke Graham defeated Don McLarity & Red Bastien in a Best 2 out of 3 falls match, 2-0, at 10:50
Freddie Blassie fought Bobo Brazil to a draw
Gorilla Monsoon fought Bill Watts to a draw
WWWF World Champion Bruno Sammartino defeated Waldo Von Erich via count-out at 34:25

WWWF @ New York City, NY - Madison Square Garden - October 19, 1964 (18,722)
Klondike Bill fought Steve Stanlee to a 20-minute time-limit draw
Miguel Perez defeated Bobby Davis via disqualification at 1:44
Pedro Morales defeated Robert Duranton at 11:17
Gene Kiniski defeated Magnificent Maurice at 3:32
Haystacks Calhoun & Bobo Brazil defeated Dr. Jerry & Luke Graham at 11:38
WWWF World Champion Bruno Sammartino defeated Waldo Von Erich at 14:57
Freddie Blassie & Gorilla Monsoon fought Bill Watts & McClarity to a curfew draw in a Best 2 out of 3 falls match

WWWF @ New York City, NY - Madison Square Garden - November 16, 1964 (16,816)
The Golden Terror pinned Steve Stanlee at 10:43
Sam Steamboat defeated Boris Malenko at 14:02
Jim Hady defeated Luke Graham via disqualification at 8:33
Bobo Brazil fought Waldo Von Erich to a 20-minute time-limit draw
Freddie Blassie defeated Pedro Morales at 3:08
Miguel Perez & Haystacks Calhoun defeated Bobby Davis & Gorilla Monsoon at 9:46 in a Best 2 out of 3 falls match
Dr. Jerry & Eddie Graham defeated Bill Watts & Don McClarity at 11:53
WWWF World Champion Bruno Sammartino defeated Gene Kiniski via count-out at 17:21

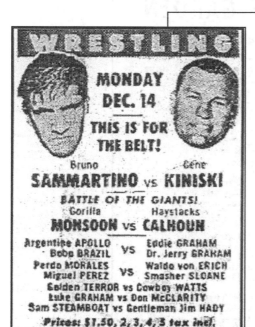

WWWF @ New York City, NY - Madison Square Garden - December 14, 1964 (11,803)

Steve Stanlee defeated Kenny Ackles at 10:06

Don McClarity fought Luke Graham to a 15-minute time-limit draw

Bill Watts defeated the Golden Terror via disqualification at 10:34

Waldo Von Erich & Smasher Sloan defeated Pedro Morales & Miguel Perez at 24:23 in a Best 2 out of 3 falls match

Haystacks Calhoun defeated Gorilla Monsoon via disqualification at 5:14

Dr. Jerry & Luke Graham defeated Bobo Brazil & Jim Hady (sub. for Argentina Apollo) at 9:17

WWWF World Champion Bruno Sammartino defeated Gene Kiniski at 19:24 via submission with a reverse full nelson

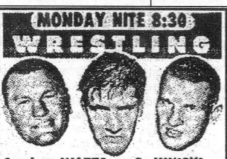

WWWF @ New York City, NY - Madison Square Garden - January 25, 1965 (13,875)

The Golden Terror defeated Steve Stanlee at 15:07

Don McClarity defeated Smasher Sloan at 16:32

Sweet Daddy Siki defeated Luke Graham at 10:23

Wahoo McDaniel defeated Boris Malenko

Dr. Jerry & Eddie Graham defeated Haystacks Calhoun & Miguel Perez at 9:16

Bobo Brazil fought Gorilla Monsoon to a 20-minute time-limit draw

WWWF World Champion Bruno Sammartino & Bill Watts defeated Gene Kiniski & Waldo Von Erich in a Best 2 out of 3 falls match at 25:32; fall #3: Sammaritno & Watts won via disqualification

27

MADISON SQUARE GARDEN

FEBRUARY, 1965

Mon.	Feb.	1	Boxing—Floyd Patterson vs. George Chuvalo
Tues.	"	2	Basketball—Knicks vs. San Francisco—8:30
			Philadelphia vs. St. Louis—6:30
Wed.	"	3	Hockey—Rangers vs. Chicago—7:30
Thurs.	"	4	Basketball—Manhattan vs. Syracuse—7:00
			N. Y. U. vs. Boston University—9:00
Sat..	"	6	Hockey—Rovers vs. Long Island—1:30
Sat..	"	6	Basketball—Knicks vs. Detroit—8:30
Sun.	"	7	Hockey—Rovers vs. Jersey—2:30
Sun.	"	7	Hockey—Rangers vs. Boston—7:30
Tues.	"	9	Basketball—Knicks vs. St. Louis—8:30
Wed.	"	10	Basketball—Iona vs. St. Bonaventure—7:00
			N. Y. U. vs. Holy Cross—9:00
Thurs.	"	11	New York A. C. Track Meet—8:00
Fri.	"	12	Catholic High School Track Meet—9 A.M.
Fri.	"	12	Boxing—8:30
Sat.	"	13	Hockey—Rangers vs. Chicago—2:00
Sat.	"	13	Basketball—Knicks vs. Boston—8:30
			Harlem Magicians—6:45
Sun.	"	14	Hockey—Rovers vs. Greensboro—2:30
Mon.	"	15 }	Westminster Kennel Club Dog Show
Tues.	"	16 }	(Morn., Aft. and Eve.)
Wed.	"	17	Basketball—Knicks vs. Los Angeles—8:30
Thurs.	"	18	Basketball—Manhattan vs. Temple—7:00
			N. Y. U. vs. Georgetown—9:00
Fri.	"	19	Nat'l AAU Track Meet—Aft. 1:30, Eve. 7:30
Sat.	"	20	Nat'l AAU Track Meet—Aft. 12:00, Eve. 7:45
Sun.	"	21	Basketball—Knicks vs. Cincinnati—2:00
Sun.	"	21	Hockey—Rangers vs. Montreal—7:30
Mon.	"	22	Wrestling—8:30
Tues.	"	23	Basketball—Knicks vs. Philadelphia—8:30
			Cincinnati vs. Baltimore—6:30
Wed.	"	24	Basketball—Manhattan vs. Connecticut—7:00
			N. Y. U. vs. Notre Dame—9:00
Thurs.	"	25	Knights of Columbus Track Meet—8:00
Fri.	"	26	Boxing—8:30
Sat.	"	27	Hockey—Rovers vs. Long Island—1:30
Sat.	"	27	Basketball—Knicks vs. Baltimore—8:30
Sun.	"	28	Hockey—Rovers vs. Clinton—2:30
Sun.	"	28	Hockey—Rangers vs. Toronto—7:30

EXPOSITION HALL
National Antique Show
Wednesday, February 24 thru Thursday, March 4

GARDEN ICE SKATING CLUB
Nitely (except Wed.) Mats.: Wed., Sat. and Sun.
Membership Applications Accepted in Iceland
50th Street Entrance

Pamphlets were regularly produced throughout the year to promote every upcoming event at MSG. Wrestling cards typically were held every third or fourth Monday night.

SCHEDULE OF EVENTS

MARCH, 1965

Tues.	Mar.	2	Basketball—Knicks vs. St. Louis—8:30
			Philadelphia vs. Los Angeles—6:30
Wed.	"	3	Hockey—Rangers vs. Boston—7:30
Thurs.	"	4	Basketball—Manhattan vs. Fordham—7:00
			New York U. vs. St. John's—9:00
Fri.	"	5	Basketball—Knicks vs. Los Angeles—8:30
Sat.	"	6	ICAAAA Track Meet—Aft. 12:00—Eve. 6:30
Sun.	"	7	Hockey—Rovers vs. Johnstown—2:30
Sun.	"	7	Hockey—Rangers vs. Detroit—7:30
Mon.	"	8	Home of Old Israel Benefit Show—8:00
Tues.	"	9	Basketball—Knicks vs. Philadelphia—8:30
Wed.	"	10	Hockey—Rangers vs. Chicago—7:30
Thurs.	"	11	National Invitation Tournament—7:00
Fri.	"	12	Boxing—8:30
Sat.	"	13	National Invitation Tournament—1:00
Sat.	"	13	National Invitation Tournament—7:00
Sun.	"	14	Basketball—Knicks vs. Cincinnati—2:00
Sun.	"	14	Hockey—Rangers vs. Montreal—7:30
Mon.	"	15	National Invitation Tournament—7:00
Tues.	"	16	National Invitation Tournament—7:00
Wed.	"	17	Basketball—Knicks vs. Boston—8:30
Thurs.	"	18	National Invitation Tournament Semi-Finals—7:00
Fri.	"	19	Hockey—Rangers vs. Detroit—7:30
Sat.	"	20	National Invitation Tournament Final—1:00
Sat.	"	20	Basketball—Knicks vs. Baltimore—8:30
Sun.	"	21	Hockey—Rangers vs. Toronto—7:30
Mon.	"	22	New York City Golden Gloves Finals—8:00
Fri.	"	26	Boxing—8:30
Sun.	"	28	Hockey—Rangers vs. Montreal—7:30
Mon.	"	29	Wrestling—8:30

TICKET PRICES
(Tax included)

National Invitation Tournament: $6.50, $6, $5, $4, $3, $2.50, $2.
College Basketball (Regular Season): $5, $3.50, $3, $2.50, $2.

Rangers: $6, $5, $4, $3, $2, $1.50.
Knicks: $5, $3.50, $3, $2.50, $2.
Rovers: $3, $2, $1.

For Ticket Information, Call PLaza 7-8870

MAIL ORDERS PROMPTLY FILLED FOR ALL EVENTS
ADD 25c FOR HANDLING AND MAIL CHARGES

THIS IS OUR LAST SCHEDULE OF THE SEASON

WWWF @ New York City, NY - Madison Square Garden - February 22, 1965 (19,101)
Kenny Ackles pinned Steve Stanlee at 9:07
Haystacks Calhoun pinned the Magnificent Maurice at 4:54
Miguel Perez pinned Smasher Sloan at 14:22
Don McClarity pinned Sweet Daddy Siki at 5:41
Bobo Brazil fought Gorilla Monsoon to a 20-minute time-limit draw
Wahoo McDaniel pinned the Golden Terror at 9:19
WWWF U.S. Tag Team Champions Gene Kiniski & Waldo Von Erich defeated Jerry & Eddie Graham via submission at 10:51
Bill Watts defeated WWWF World Champion Bruno Sammartino via disqualification at 19:46 when the champion repeatedly kicked his opponent and shoved referee Dick Kroll to the mat

WWWF @ New York City, NY - Madison Square Garden - March 29, 1965 (19,614; new wrestling attendance record)

Sonny Boy Cassidy & Pancho Lopez defeated Fuzzy Cupid & Billy the Kid at 23:40 in a Best 2 out of 3 falls match

Miguel Perez defeated the Golden Terror via disqualification at 11:19

Argentina Apollo pinned Smasher Sloan at 9:08

Gorilla Monsoon pinned Don McClarity

Wahoo McDaniel pinned Dr. Jerry Graham at 11:33

WWWF World Champion Bruno Sammartino defeated Bill Watts via disqualification at 15:48

WWWF U.S. Tag Team Champions Gene Kiniski & Waldo Von Erich fought Bobo Brazil & Haystacks Calhoun to a curfew draw in a Best 2 out of 3 falls match

30

WWWF @ New York City, NY - Madison Square Garden - May 17, 1965 (12,984)
Wahoo McDaniel vs. Gorilla Monsoon was canceled

Arnold Skaaland defeated Tony Newberry at 16:49

Miguel Perez defeated Steve Stanlee at 12:34

Don McClarity defeated Magnificent Maurice at 16:53

Haystacks Calhoun & Argentina Apollo fought Dr. Jerry Graham & the Goden Terror to a no contest in a Best 2 out of 3 falls match at 24:14

Chief Big Heart & White Owl defeated Waldo Von Erich & Smasher Sloan in a Best 2 out of 3 falls match at 14:10

WWWF World Champion Bruno Sammartino defeated Bill Watts in a Best 2 out of 3 falls match when the challenger was deemed unable to continue at 22:08

WWWF @ New York City, NY - Madison Square Garden - July 12, 1965 (17,134)
Bobo Brazil & Sailor Art Thomas vs. Bill Watts & Gorilla Monsoon was canceled due to the curfew

Fuzzy Cupid & Sky Low Low defeated the Jamaica Kid & Pancho Lopez in a Best 2 out of 3 falls match at 19:56

Chief Big Heart fought the Golden Terror to a 15-minute time-limit draw

Argentina Apollo & Miguel Perez defeated the Sheik & Smasher Sloan at 15:54

Dr. Jerry Graham defeated Haystacks Calhoun via disqualification at 6:09

Waldo Von Erich pinned Wahoo McDaniel at 6:42 after McDaniel hit the ringpost

WWWF World Champion Bruno Sammartino defeated Bill Miller via referee's decision when the match was stopped due to the curfew at the 60-minute mark

WWWF @ New York City, NY - Madison Square Garden - August 2, 1965 (15,064)
Arnold Skaaland pinned Gus Kalas at 4:36
Chief Big Heart pinned Steve Stanlee at 7:53
Smasher Sloan defeated Chief White Owl
Argentina Apollo defeated the Golden Terror at 7:35
Miguel Perez pinned Bob Boyer at 10:39
Waldo Von Erich fought Johnny Valentine to a 15-minute draw
Bobo Brazil & Sailor Art Thomas defeated Bill Watts & Gorilla Monsoon in a Best 2 out of 3 falls match, 2-1; fall #3:
Brazil & Thomas won via disqualification
Bill Miller defeated WWWF World Champion Bruno Sammartino via count-out at 30:03

Bruno Sammartino's legendary run as a MSG headliner was touted as early as the mid 1960s,
as noted by this poster. It didn't matter who the opponent was, the name Sammartino sold tickets.

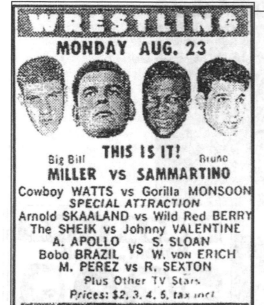

WWWF @ New York City, NY - Madison Square Garden - August 23, 1965 (16,113)

Arnold Skaaland defeated Wild Red Berry at the 41-second mark

Miguel Perez defeated Rick Sexton at 13:24

Chief Big Heart defeated the Magnificent Maurice at 11:36

Tarzan Tyler defeated Chief White Owl at 11:28

Johnny Valentine defeated the Golden Terror (sub. for the Sheik) at 13:44

Bobo Brazil & Argentina Apollo defeated Waldo Von Erich & Smasher Sloan in a Best 2 out of 3 falls match

Bill Watts defeated Gorilla Monsoon at 6:20
WWWF World Champion Bruno Sammartino defeated Bill Miller at the 48-second mark

WWWF @ New York City, NY – Madison Square Garden – September 27, 1965 (13,000+)
Angelo Savoldi defeated Herbie Starr
The Magnificent Maurice defetead Pete Sanchez
Chief Big Heart defeated Frank Martinez
Johnny Valentine fought Bill Miller to a draw
Argentina Apollo & Miguel Perez defeated Waldo Von Erich & Smasher Sloan
Bobo Brazil fought Bill Watts to a draw
WWWF World Champion Bruno Sammartino defeated Tarzan Tyler; according to newspaper reports, Sammartino's belt was stolen from a locked car later that night while Sammartino was celebrating at a restaurant in Times Square

WWWF @ New York City, NY – Madison Square Garden – October 20, 1965 (13,624)
Tiny Tim & the Jamaica Kid defeated Cowboy Bradley & Pancho Lopez in a Best 2 out of 3 falls match
Arnold Skaaland defeated the Golden Terror at 7:39
Argentina Apollo defeated Gino Brito at 7:28
Tarzan Tyler defeated Chief Big Heart at 7:20
Bobo Brazil & Miguel Perez defeated Waldo Von Erich & Smasher Sloan in a Best 2 out of 3 falls match
WWWF World Champion Bruno Sammartino defeated Bill Watts at 21:49
Johnny Valentine fought Bill Miller to a curfew draw at the 28-minute mark

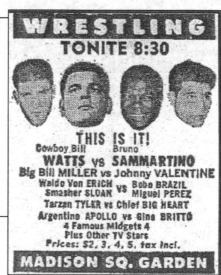

WWWF @ New York City, NY - Madison Square Garden - November 15, 1965 (13,913)
Tony Newberry defeated Steve Stanlee at 9:14
Angelo Savoldi defeated Tomas Marin at 9:56
Smasher Sloan defeated Pete Sanchez at 11:23
Dr. Bill & Dan Miller defeated WWWF World Champion Bruno Sammartino & Johnny Valentine at 32:58
Baron Mikel Scicluna defeated Chief White Owl at 7:41
Chief Big Heart defeated Magnificent Maurice at 11:16
Tarzan Tyler defeated Miguel Perez at 11:29
Bobo Brazil fought Waldo Von Erich to a draw when the bout was stopped due to the curfew at 13:44

WWWF @ New York City, NY - Madison Square Garden - December 13, 1965 (10,090)
The scheduled Bobo Brazil vs. Tarzan Tyler match was canceled
Lord Littlebrook & Rollie the Hawk defeated Sky Low Low & Fuzzy Cupid in a Best 2 out of 3 falls match
Angelo Savoldi pinned Gino Brito at 21:02
Miguel Perez defeated the Magnificent Maurice at 18:09
Chief Big Heart defeated Smasher Sloan
Baron Mikel Scicluna defeated Waldo Von Erich at 18:09
WWWF World Champion Bruno Sammartino & Johnny Valentine defeated Dr. Bill & Dan Miller at 30:52

WWWF @ New York City, NY - Madison Square Garden - January 24, 1966 (12,345)
Angelo Savoldi fought Pete Sanchez to a 20-minute draw
Antonio Pugliese defeated Smasher Stone at 14:56 via submission with a Boston crab (Pugliese's MSG debut)
Tarzan Tyler pinned Miguel Perez at 13:38
WWWF World Champion Bruno Sammartino defeated Baron Mikel Scicluna via disqualification at 25:47 when referee Danny Bartfield was struck by Sammartino's legs as the challenger had Sammartino in a hangman neckbreaker; the referee awarded the match to the champion, citing he was struck because of Scicluna's hold
Prince Iaukea defeated Magnificent Maurice at 4:23 (Iaukea's MSG debut)
The Beast (sub. for the Mongolian Stomper) defeated Chief Big Heart at 5:41 (the Beast's MSG debut)
Bobo Brazil & Johnny Valentine defeated U.S. Tag Team Champions Dan & Bill Miller via referee's decision at 12:20 when the match was stopped due to the curfew

WWWF @ New York City, NY – Madison Square Garden – February 21, 1966 (14,303)
Magnificent Maurice pinned Johnny Carr at 13:41
Smasher Sloan defeated Ronnie Etchison at 17:39
The Best pinned Miguel Perez at 7:10
Prince Iaukea pinned Chief Big Heart at 2:49
Johnny Valentine & Antonio Pugliese defeated WWWF U.S. Tag Team Champions Dan & Dr. Bill Miller to win the titles
Argentina Apollo pinned Tarzan Tyler at 20:00
WWWF World Champion Bruno Sammartino defeated Baron Mikel Scicluna at 17:51 via submission with the backbreaker

WWWF @ New York City, NY - Madison Square Garden - March 28, 1966
Miguel Perez defeated Angelo Savoldi
Chief Big Heart defeated the Magnificent Maurice
The Beast defeated Johnny Carr
The Sheik defeated Ronnie Etchison
Argentina Apollo defeated Smasher Sloan
Bobo Brazil fought Baron Mikel Scicluna to a draw
Johnny Valentine & Tony Pugliese defeated Bill & Dan Miller
WWWF World Champion Bruno Sammartino defeated Curtis Iaukea

WWWF @ New York City, NY - Madison Square Garden - November 7, 1966 (14,159)
El Toro defeated Miguel Perez at 4:18
Argentina Apollo defeated Roberto Gonzalez at 7:57
Tank Morgan defeated Ricky Sexton at 5:28
Mr. Kleen defeated Tony Nero at 4:13
Little Beaver & the Jamaica Kid defeated Sky Low Low & Billy the Kid at 25:52
Bobo Brazil fought Bill Miller to a draw
WWWF US Tag Team Champions Baron Mikel Scicluna & Smasher Sloan defeated Antonio Pugliese & Louis Cerdan
WWWF World Champion Bruno Sammartino defeated Bulldog Brower via submission with the backbreaker at 11:58

36

WWWF @ New York City, NY – Madison Square Garden – December 12, 1966 (12,029)
Televised on WOR Channel 9 in New York
Angelo Savoldi defeated Roberto Gonzalez at 11:53
Arman Hussian defeated Tony Nero at 6:36 with an Arabian crab hold
The Sheik defeated Ricky Sexton at 5:02
Spiros Arion defeated Smasher Sloan at 5:40 with a backbreaker
Luke Graham defeated Louis Cerdan at 9:18
Bulldog Brower defeated Miguel Perez at 8:22
Bobo Brazil, Argentina Apollo, & Antonio Pugliese defeated Bill Miller, Bull Ortega, & Baron Mikel Scicluna via disqualification at 18:44
WWWF World Champion Bruno Sammartino defeated Tank Morgan in a Best 2 out of 3 falls match, 2-0

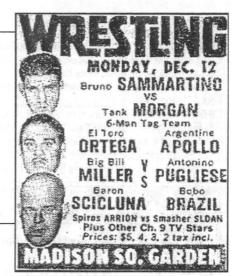

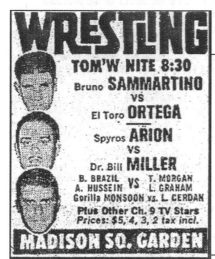

WWWF @ New York City, NY - Madison Square Garden - January 30, 1967 (14,760)
Ricky Sexton defeated Tony Nero via disqualification
Arman Hussian & Bobo Brazil defeated Tank Morgan & Luke Graham
Baron Mikel Scicluna fought Antonio Pugliese to a draw
Spiros Arion defeated Bill Miller at 6:09 with a backbreaker
The Ox (Ox Baker) defeated Smasher Sloan at 5:57 via submission with a bearhug (Baker's MSG debut)
Gorilla Monsoon defeated Lou Albano (sub. for Louis Cerdan) at the 23-second mark
The Sheik defeated Miguel Perez at 8:41 via submission with an Arabian backbreaker
WWWF World Champion Bruno Sammartino pinned Bull Ortega at 4:19

WWWF @ New York City, NY – Madison Square Garden – February 27, 1967
Tony Nero defeated Miguel Perez
Antonio Pugliese, Bobo Brazil, & Arman Hussian defeated Bill Miller, Luke Graham, & Baron Mikel Scicluna
Spiros Arion defeated Bull Ortega at 4:49
Louis Cerdan defeated Angelo Savoldi (sub. for the Sheik)
Ox Baker defeated Tank Morgan at 7:09
Lou Albano defeated Ricky Sexton at 15:28
Gorilla Monsoon defeated WWWF World Champion Bruno Sammartino via count-out at 13:21

WWWF @ New York City, NY – Madison Square Garden – March 27, 1967 (17,395)
The scheduled Ox Baker vs. Luke Graham match was cancelled
Smasher Sloan defeated Tony Nero
Spiros Arion defeated Baron Mikel Scicluna at 9:02
Ray Stevens defeated Miguel Perez at 8:04
Arman Hussian & Bobo Brazil defeated Bull Ortega & Bill Miller
Antonio Pugliese defeated Tank Morgan at 8:04
Prof. Toru Tanaka defeated Ricky Sexton at 4:04
The Sheik defeated Louis Cerdan at 5:18
WWWF World Champion Bruno Sammartino fought Gorilla Monsoon to a curfew draw at 39:52

WWWF @ New York City, NY - Madison Square Garden - May 15, 1967
Bill Miller was scheduled to appear but could not make the show
Arnold Skaaland defeated Smasher Sloan at 18:21
Irish Jackie & Billy the Kid defeated Little Brutus & Fuzzy Cupid
Prof. Toru Tanaka defeated the Ox via submission with a sleeper
Bobo Brazil pinned Bull Ortega at 7:23
Sprios Arion & Antonio Pugliese defeated Luke Graham & Baron Mikel Scicluna in a Best 2 out of 3 falls match, 2-0; both falls were earned respectively by Arion and Pugliese using backbreakers
WWWF World Champion Bruno Sammartino pinned Gorilla Monsoon by kicking off the ropes while caught in a bearhug and falling backwards ontop of the challenger for the pin

WWWF @ New York City, NY – Madison Square Garden – June 19, 1967
Miguel Perez fought Tank Morgan to a draw
Arman Hussein defeated Ricky Sexton
The Sheik defeated Smasher Sloan
Bull Ortega pinned the Ox
Spiros Arion fought Gorilla Monsoon to a draw
Edouard Carpentier, Bobo Brazil, & Antonio Pugliese defeated Bill Miller, Baron Mikel Scicluna, & Luke Graham in a Best 3 out of 5 falls match; fall #1: the heels won; fall #2: the faces won; fall #3: the faces won; fall #4: the heels won; fall #5: the faces won
WWWF World Champion Bruno Sammartino defeated Prof. Toru Tanaka via disqualification at 19:37 when the challenger threw salt into Sammartino's eyes

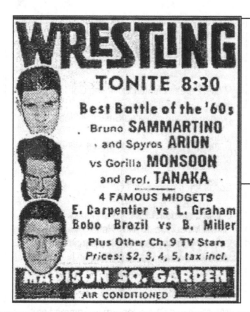

WWWF @ New York City, NY - Madison Square Garden - July 31, 1967
Johnny Rodz defeated Frank Holtz
Guillotine Gordon defeated Bob Taylor
Bobo Brazil fought Bill Miller to a draw
Edouard Carpentier defeated Luke Graham
Irish Jackie & the Jamaica Kid defeated Sky Low Low & Little Brutus
Gorilla Monsoon & Prof. Toru Tanaka defeated WWWF World Champion Bruno Sammartino & Spiros Arion via disqualification

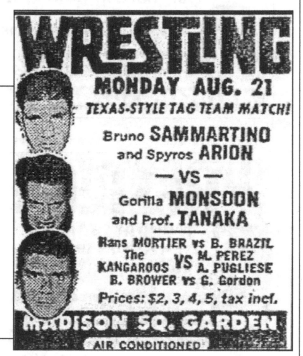

WWWF @ New York City, NY - Madison Square Garden -
August 21, 1967
Arnold Skaaland defeated Tony Altimore
The Sheik defeated Pete Sanchez
Baron Mikel Scicluna defeated Smasher Sloan
Bulldog Brower pinned Guillotine Gordon
Edouard Carpentier & Miguel Perez defeated the Fabulous Kangaroos via disqualification
Hans Mortier defeated Bobo Brazil at the 56-second mark with a full nelson
WWWF World Champion Bruno Sammartino & Spiros Arion defeated Gorilla Monsoon & Prof. Toru Tanaka in a Best 2 out of 3 falls match, 2-1; fall #1: Tanaka pinned Arion at 16:35; fall #2: Arion pinned Tanaka at 3:02; fall #3: referee Terri Taranova stopped the bout at 4:05, awarding the fall to Sammartino & Arion

WWWF @ New York City, NY - Madison Square Garden - September 25, 1967
The Kangaroos defeated Smasher Sloan & Riki Sexton in a Best 2 out of 3 falls match
Gorilla Monsoon defeated Dr. Bill Miller at 6:29
Baron Mikel Scicluna defeated Gil Gordon at 8:36
Bobo Brazil defeated Luke Graham at 7:38 with the Coco Butt
Bulldog Brower defeated Miguel Perez at 6:14
Spiros Arion defeated Prof. Toru Tanaka via disqualification at 6:07 when Tanaka rubbed salt into Arion's eyes
Edouard Carpentier fought the Sheik to a draw
WWWF World Champion Bruno Sammartino fought Hans Mortier to a 40-minute draw

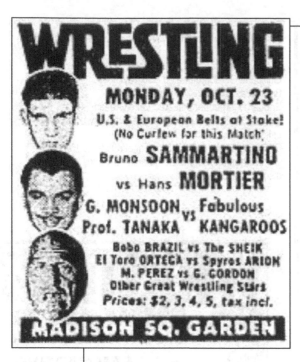

WWWF @ New York City, NY – Madison Square Garden – October 23, 1967
Tony Altimore defeated Pete Sanchez at 15:34

Miguel Perez defeated Guillotine Gordon at 15:46

Bulldog Brower defeated Smasher Sloan at 5:26

Dominic DeNucci defeated Baron Mikel Scicluna at 16:43

Spiros Arion pinned Bull Ortega at 5:19

Gorilla Monsoon & Prof. Toru Tanaka defeated Dr. Bill Miller (sub. for Roy Heffernan) & Al Costello in a Best 2 out of 3 falls match; fall #1: Monsoon pinned Miller by falling on him; fall #2: Costello defeated Tanaka; fall #3: Tanaka pinned Costello after applying a nerve hold

WWWF World Champion Bruno Sammartino pinned Hans Mortier at 28:29 by kicking off the ropes while caught in a full nelson and falling backwards onto Mortier

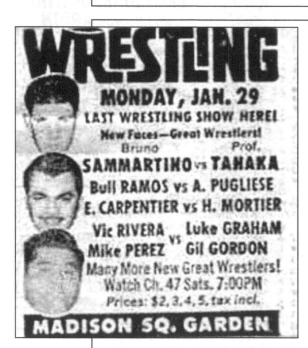

WWWF @ New York City, NY - Madison Square Garden - January 29, 1968
The final show held at the old MSG which had been running wrestling shows for the previous 42 years

Victor Rivera & Miguel Perez fought Luke Graham & Guillotine Gordon to a draw

Bull Ramos pinned Antonio Pugliese at 12:35

Hans Mortier fought Edouard Carpentier to a draw

Dominic DeNucci pinned Smasher Sloan at 9:51

Louis Cerdan pinned Mario Fratarolli at 10:07

Earl Maynard pinned Johnny Rodz at 7:36

Angelo Savoldi pinned Wes Hutchins

WWWF World Champion Bruno Sammartino pinned Prof. Toru Tanaka

This promotional publication touted the upgrades that the *new* and current MSG building offered when it opened in the late 1960s.

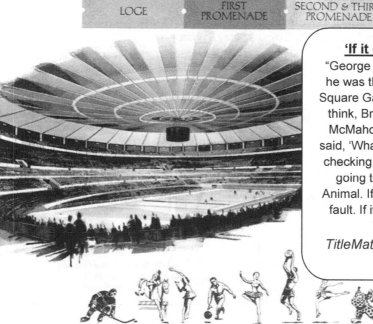

THE NEW AND EXCITING
MADISON SQUARE GARDEN
SPORTS AND
ENTERTAINMENT CENTER

THE INTERNATIONAL LANDMARK IN 1967

| LOGE | FIRST PROMENADE | SECOND & THIRD PROMENADE | MEZZANINE |

SPECIAL SPORTS AND ENTERTAINMENT EVENTS

'If it doesn't sell out...'

"George Steele told me one time, he was the main bout at Madison Square Garden. He was wrestling, I think, Bruno. He went out. Vince McMahon Sr. was there, and he said, 'What are you looking at?' 'I'm checking to see what the house is going to be like.' 'Don't worry, Animal. If it doesn't sell out, it's my fault. If it sells out, it's my fault.'"

Tito Santana,
TitleMatchWrestling interview, 2000

Feb. 11, 1968: The fourth, and current, Madison Square Garden opened. Construction costs were $123 million ($805 million in 2014 dollars). The structure was one of the first of its kind to be built above an active railroad station. The new venue included the Felt Forum, which can seat between 2,000 and 5,600.

WWWF @ New York City, NY - Madison Square Garden - February 19, 1968 (12,989)
1st card held at the new MSG
Magnificent Maurice defeated Karl Steif
Virgil the Kentucky Butcher defeated Edouard Carpentier
Victor Rivera defeated Hans Mortier
Prof. Toru Tanaka fought Dominic DeNucci to a draw
Miguel Perez defeated Gil Gordon
The Sheik defeated Louis Cerdan
Earl Maynard defeated Luke Graham with a West Indian backbreaker
Little Beaver & Little Jackie defeated Sky Low   Low & Little Brutus
WWWF World Champion Bruno Sammartino defeated Bull Ramos via submission with the backbreaker at 12:43

WWWF @ New York City, NY - Madison Square Garden - March 11, 1968 (13,148)
Miguel Perez defeated Luke Graham
Crybaby Cannon defeated Johnny Rodz
Lou Cerdan defeated Bull Johnson
Edouard Carpentier, Dominic DeNucci, & Earl Maynard defeated Dr. Bill Miller, Hans Mortier, & Bull Ramos
Victor Rivera defeated Professor Toru Tanaka via disqualification when Tanaka threw salt into his opponent's eyes
WWWF World Champion Bruno Sammartino defeated Virgil the Kentucky Butcher with a backward flip press

WWWF @ New York City, NY - Madison Square Garden - May 20, 1968 (10,506)
Cowboy Bradley & Irish Jackie defeated Frenchy Lamont & Sonny Boy Cassidy
Baron Mikel Scicluna defeated Louis Cerdan
Hans Mortier fought Bull Ramos to a double disqualification
Ernie Ladd defeated Mike Paidousis (Ladd's MSG debut)
Victor Rivera defeated George Cannon
Gorilla Monsoon & Prof. Toru Tanaka defeated Bobo Brazil & Earl Maynard in a Best 2 out of 3 falls match
WWWF World Champion Bruno Sammartino fought George Steele to a curfew draw at 50:51

While MSG pro wrestling events typically drew strong crowds, they rarely received love through the local media. Recaps of events in the New York Times usually had a critical spin to them, often mocking the crowd or the wrestlers.

"One reason for the thin crowd might have been the imposing newness and unfamiliarity of the new Garden for the fans. Another might have been the lack of television build-up. A third must have been the sameness of Bruno in his five 'championship' years."
Robert Lipsyte, *New York Times, May 23, 1968*

WWWF @ New York City, NY - Madison Square Garden - June 22, 1968
Virgil the Kentucky Butcher defeated Crybaby Cannon
Bull Ramos defeated Louis Cerdan
Gorilla Monsoon & Professor Toru Tanaka fought Victor Rivera & Bobo Brazil to a draw
Johnny Rodz defeated Carlos Colon
Angelo Savoldi defeated Lenny Solomon
Edouard Carpentier defeated Hans Mortimer
WWWF World Champion Bruno Sammartino defeated George Steele at 24:44
Ernie Ladd defeated Earl Maynard; after the bout, Ladd refused to leave the ring until he was promised a title shot against Sammartino; the champion then made his way to the ring and both wrestlers signed a contract to meet at the following month's card; they actually signed a program sheet, not a contract

WWWF @ New York City, NY – Madison Square Garden – July 13, 1968 (9,783)
Little Beaver & Irish Jackie defeated Sky Low Low & Little Brutus
Johnny Rodz defeated Pete Sanchez at 9:03
Virgil the Kentucky Butcher defeated Carlos Colon at 4:58
Earl Maynard defeated Bull Ramos at 4:44
Edouard Carpentier fought George Steele to a 20-minute time-limit draw
Bobo Brazil & Victor Rivera defeated Prof. Toru Tanaka & Gorilla Monsoon via disqualification when Tanaka hit a low blow on Brazil; after the bout, a fan ran into the ring with a chair and knocked over a policeman; after the fan was stopped, another fan threw eggs at Tanaka & Monsoon
WWWF World Champion Bruno Sammartino defeated Ernie Ladd via count-out at 17:01

WWWF @ New York City, NY - Madison Square Garden - August 17, 1968
Irish Jackie & the Jamaica Kid defeated Sky Low Low & Little Brutus
Arnold Skaaland defeated Frank Hickey
Argentina Apollo defeated Bull Ramos
Dick Steinborn fought Earl Maynard to a draw
Bobo Brazil defeated Virgil the Kentucky Butcher
WWWF World Champion Bruno Sammartino & Victor Rivera defeated Gorilla Monsoon & Prof. Toru Tanaka

WWWF @ New York City, NY – Madison Square Garden – September 23, 1968
Earl Maynard fought Baron Mikel Scicluna to a draw
Tony Altimore & Lou Albano defeated Arnold Skaaland & Pete Sanchez in a Best 2 out of 3 falls match
Bull Ramos defeated Lenny Solomon at 9:54
Johnny Rodz defeated Chuck Adcox at 8:11
Spiros Arion defeated Virgil the Kentucky Butcher at 9:40
Victor Rivera pinned George Steele at 10:41
Gorilla Monsoon fought Bobo Brazil to a double count-out at 11:43 when Brazil headbutted Monsoon out of the ring and followed him out, with neither man returning in time
WWWF World Champion Bruno Sammartino defeated Rocky Fitzpatrick (Bob Orton Sr.) via submission with the backbreaker at 8:37

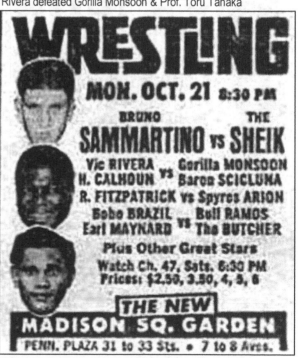

WWWF @ New York City, NY - Madison Square Garden - October 21, 1968 (10,443)
Pete Sanchez defeated Chuck Adcox at 10:31
Tony Altimore defeated Johnny Rodz
Lou Albano defeated Lenny Solomon at 14:59
Bobo Brazil & Ernie Lassiter defeated the Kentucky Butcher & Bull Ramos
Victor Rivera & Haystacks Calhoun defeated Gorilla Monsoon & Baron Mikel Scicluna
Spiros Arion defeated Rocky Fitzpatrick at 7:54
The Sheik defeated WWWF World Champion Bruno Sammartino via count-out at 12:16 when, after pushing the challenger into the ring, Sammartino could not meet the referee's count

WWWF @ New York City, NY - Madison Square Garden - November 18, 1968 (12,000+)
Lou Albano defeated Angelo Savoldi
Tony Altimore defeated Lenny Solomon
Johnny Rodz defeated Chuck Adcock via disqualification
Pete Sanchez defeated Bull Ramos via disqualification
Rocky Fitzpatrick defeated Ernie Lassiter
Haystacks Calhoun, Spiros Arion, & Victor Rivera defeated Gorilla Monsoon, Virgil the Kentucky Butcher & Baron Mikel Scicluna
WWWF World Champion Bruno Sammartino defeated the Sheik via disqualification at 6:14 when the Sheik began biting Sammartino's nose; prior to the bout, the Sheik and Abdullah Farouk attacked Dominic DeNucci; DeNucci then threw the Sheik to the floor and went after Farouk

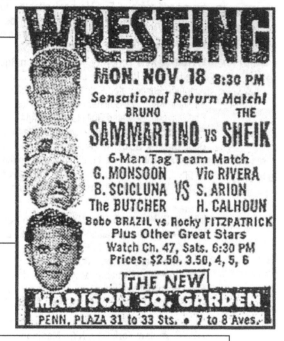

WWWF @ New York City, NY - Madison Square Garden - December 9, 1968 (10,943)
Victor Rivera defeated Rocky Fitzpatrick
Dominic DeNucci defeated Bull Ramos
Baron Mikel Scicluna defeated Chuck Adcox
Gorilla Monsoon fought Haystacks Calhoun to a no contest
Spiros Arion defeated Virgil the Kentucky Butcher
Carlos Colon defeated Lou Albano
Tony Altimore defeated Pete Sanchez
Johnny Rodz defeated Lenny Solomon
Killer Kowalski defeated Tony Pugliese
WWWF World Champion Bruno Sammartino defeated the Sheik in a Texas Death Match at 9:58 after Sammartino took a pen away from the challenger and used it to jab at the challenger's arm until it became bloody and the challenger submitted

44

WWWF @ New York City, NY - Madison Square Garden - January 27, 1969 (11,568)
The Jamaica Kid & Joey Russell defeated Billy the Kid & Cowboy Bradley in a Best 2 out of 3 falls match
Lou Albano defeated Ron Sanders at 10:59
Tony Altimore defeated Bob Harmon at 7:16
Johnny Rodz defeated Carlos Colon at 14:49
Bull Ramos defeated Louis Cerdan at 7:11
Spiros Arion fought Baron Mikel Scicluna to a draw
Haystacks Calhoun defeated the Sheik via disqualification at 6:20 after taking a camera away from a ringside photographer and smashing it to the mat; a small riot took place as Sheik made his way backstage after the bout which resulted in an old woman in attendance being trampled; as a result of the incident, the Sheik was banned from MSG
Killer Kowalski & Gorilla Monsoon defeated WWWF World Champion Bruno Sammartino & Victor Rivera in a Best 2 out of 3 falls match, 2-1; fall #3: Kowalski pinned Sammartino at 10:15 after both he and Monsoon punched and kicked the champion

WWWF @ New York City, NY - Madison Square Garden - February 17, 1969 (9,639)
Arnold Skaaland defeated Bob Harmon at 5:06
Carlos Colon & Pete Sanchez defeated Tony Altimore & Lou Albano in a Best 2 out of 3 falls match
John L Sullivan defeated Johnny Rodz at 10:35
Dominic DeNucci defeated Angelo Savoldi at 8:51
Victor Rivera & Haystacks Calhoun defeated Gorilla Monsoon & Baron Mikel Scicluna in a Best 2 out of 3 falls match, 2-0
WWWF World Champion Bruno Sammartino fought Killer Kowalski to a double disqualification at 17:31

WWWF @ New York City, NY - Madison Square Garden - March 7, 1969
Little Beaver & Irish Jackie defeated Sky Low Low & Little Brutus in a Best 2 out of 3 falls match
Thunderbolt Patterson defeated Tom Branden at 10:52
Bulldog Brower defeated Louis Cerdan at 12:46
Johnny Rodz defeated Bob Harmon at 11:53
Baron Mikel Scicluna fought John L. Sullivan to a draw
WWWF World Champion Bruno Sammartino defeated Killer Kowalski via count-out at 16:59

45

WWWF @ New York City, NY - Madison Square Garden - May 14, 1969
Lou Albano defeated Buster Gordon at 10:41
Bulldog Brower defeated Duke Savage at 9:11
Baron Mikel Scicluna fought John L. Sullivan to a draw
Dominic DeNucci defeated Luke Graham at 11:43
Sky Low Low & Little Brutus defeated Pee Wee Russell & Cowboy Bradley in a Best 2 out of 3 falls match
Haystacks Calhoun defeated Dr. Bill Miller at 5:16
WWWF World Champion Bruno Sammartino & Victor Rivera defeated Killer Kowalski & Prof. Toru Tanaka in a Best 2 out of 3 falls match; Rivera pinned Tanaka at 6:23 to win the deciding fall

WWWF @ New York City, NY - Madison Square Garden - June 30, 1969

Little Beaver, the Jamaica Kid, & Cowboy Bradley defeated Sky Low Low, Billy the Kid, & Little Bruiser in a Best 3 out of 5 falls match

Luke Graham fought John L. Sullivan to a draw

Antonio Pugliese defeated Baron Scicluna via disqualification

Killer Kowalski fought Dominic DeNucci to a draw
Bill Miller defeated Angelo Savoldi (sub. for Bulldog Brower)

Prof. Toru Tanaka & Mitsu Arakawa defeated Victor Rivera & Haystacks Calhoun in a Best 2 out of 3 falls match

WWWF World Champion Bruno Sammartino pinned George Steele at 12:11 after sending him into the corner

The scheduled card for July 21, 1969 was cancelled for an unknown reason.

WWWF @ New York City, NY - Madison Square Garden - October 1, 1969
The Jamaica Kid defeated Little Brutus
Joe Cox defeated Magnificent Maurice
Dominic DeNucci defeated Larry Tyler
Baron Mikel Scicluna defeated Chuck Adcox
Ernie Ladd defeated Bill Miller
Killer Kowalski defeated Bulldog Brower
WWWF International Tag Team Champions Prof. Toru Tanaka & Mitsu Arakawa fought Victor Rivera & Antonio Pugliese to a draw
Waldo Von Erich defeated WWWF World Champion Bruno Sammartino via disqualification

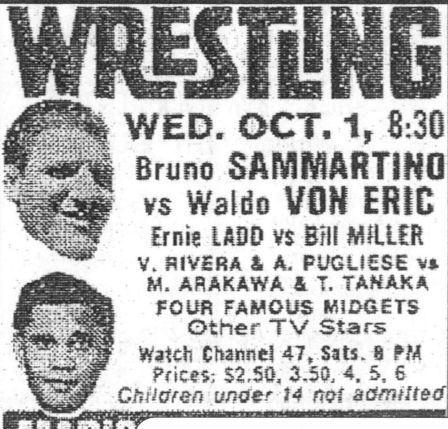

A member of the working press
"A photographer with the top part of my torso leaning on the ring apron and the lower half on the floor. The Garden had perhaps the longest ring apron and it was almost painful to work an entire night clicking away with my Nikon. The atmosphere was electric of course. It was the Garden -- and electric atmosphere was always present. There was nothing in any other arena that could equal the feel of being at the Garden. Nearly once a month, the WWWF ran shows, mostly on Monday nights. For some reason, it rained almost every Monday there was a Garden wrestling show. I can't explain that one."
Bill Apter, *TheHistoryofWWE.com interview, 2014*

WWWF @ New York City, NY - Madison Square Garden - October 27, 1969
 (11,128; new attendance record for wrestling at the new MSG)
Jean DuBois pinned Lou Albano at 9:18
WWWF International Tag Team Champions Mitsu Arakawa & Professor Toru
Tanaka defeated Antonio Pugliese & Dominic DeNucci
Victor Rivera pinned Joe Cox at 11:10
Gorilla Monsoon pinned Killer Kowalski at 10:27
Ernie Ladd pinned Baron Mikel Scicluna at 6:17
WWWF World Champion Bruno Sammartino defeated Waldo Von Erich

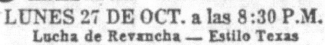

LUCHA LIBRE

LUNES 27 DE OCT. a las 8:30 P.M.
Lucha de Revancha — Estilo Texas

Bruno SAMMARTINO
vs. Waldo VON ERICH

K. KOWALSKI VS. G. MONSOON

B. SCICLUNA Vs. ERNIE LADD	J. COX Vs. VICTOR RIVERA

M. ARAKAWA y T. TANAKA	VS.	A. PUGLIESE y D. DE NICCI

· Además otros grandes encuentros
Vean el Canal 47 los Sábados 4:00 P.M.
Precios: $2.50, $4, $5, $6.
No aceptamos niños menores de 14 años.

MADISON SQ. GARDEN

This Spanish newspaper advertisement spoke to the high hispanic population that regularly filled MSG wrestling events.

WWWF @ New York City, NY - Madison Square Garden - December 9, 1969
Eric the Red pinned Louis Cerdan at 9:23
Baron Mikel Scicluna pinned Jean DuBois at 9:31
Little Beaver pinned Frenchy Lamont at 10:06
Gorilla Monsoon pinned Ernie Ladd at 6:57
Waldo Von Erich pinned Antonio Pugliese at 10:26
Killer Kowalski defeated Dominic DeNucci via count-out
Victor Rivera & Tony Marino defeated WWWF International Tag Team Champions Prof. Toru Tanaka & Mitsu Arakawa in a Best 2 out of 3 falls match, 2-0, to win the titles
Ivan Koloff defeated WWWF World Champion Bruno Sammartino when the match was stopped due to blood at 21:34

WWWF @ New York City, NY - Madison Square Garden - January 19, 1970 (16,858)
Cowboy Bradley & Little Beaver defeated Sky Low Low & Little Brutus in a Best 2 out of 3 falls match
Eric the Red defeated Jack Vansky at 9:25
Mario Milano pinned Willie Farkus at 10:20
Bob Ellis pinned Prof. Toru Tanaka at 3:00
Karl Kovacs pinned Jean Dubois at 4:25
Gorilla Monsoon fought Ernie Ladd to a time-limit draw
WWWF International Tag Team Champions Victor Rivera & Tony Marino defeated Killer Kowalski & Waldo Von Erich in a Best 2 out of 3 falls match
WWWF World Champion Bruno Sammartino pinned Ivan Koloff at 18:10 after a double reverse back flip body-hold

Ernie Ladd, captured playing poker backstage at The Garden.

49

WWWF @ New York City, NY - Madison Square Garden - March 9, 1970 (14,328)
Sky Low Low & Little Brutus defeated Joey Russell & Don Harvey in a Best 2 out of 3 falls match
Joe Turco pinned Jack Vansky at 10:04
Eric the Red pinned Jean Dubois at 10:05
Killer Kowalski fought Waldo Von Erich to a time-limit draw at 8:34
Gorilla Monsoon & Mario Milano defeated Ernie Ladd & Prof. Toru Tanaka in a Best 2 out of 3 falls match; fall #1: Milano & Monsoon won; fall #2: Ladd & Tanaka won; fall #3: Milano & Monsoon won
Ivan Koloff fought Victor Rivera to a 20-minute draw
WWWF World Champion Bruno Sammartino defeated Karl Kovacs at 16:45; the match reportedly ended a minute before the time limit

WWWF @ New York City, NY - Madison Square Garden - June 15, 1970 (20,819; sell out; new attendance record)
Akim Manuka pinned Lee Wong at 16:50
John L. Sullivan defeated George Steele via disqualification
Mario Milano defeated Mike Conrad at 10:44
Dominic DeNucci pinned Joe Turco at 10:35
Prof. Toru Tanaka defeated Red Bastien at 12:45
Gorilla Monsoon defeated Karl Kovacs at 21:35
Beepo & Gito Mongol defeated WWWF International Tag Team Champions Victor Rivera & Tony Marino to win the titles in a Best 2 out of 3 falls match (the Mongols' MSG debut)
Crusher Verdu (w/ Lou Albano) defeated WWWF World Champion Bruno Sammartino at 22:43 when referee Edward Gersh stopped the bout as a result of a gash over Sammartino's eye

WWWF @ New York City, NY - Madison Square Garden - July 10, 1970 (20,982; sell out; new attendance record)
Little Beaver & Jamaica Kid defeated Billy the Kid & Frenchy Lamont
Jose Rivera defeated Mike Conrad at 9:44
Chief Jay Strongbow defeated Joe Turco
Victor Rivera defeated Johnny Rodz at 10:34
Mario Milano fought George Steele to a 20-minute draw
WWWF International Tag Team Champions Beepo & Gito Mongol defeated Gorilla Monsoon & Dr. Bill Miller
WWWF World Champion Bruno Sammartino defeated Crusher Verdu at 15:11

WWWF @ New York City, NY - Madison Square Garden - August 1, 1970 (17,864)
Sky Low Low & Little Brutus defeated the Jamaica Kid & Billy the Kid (*Best of the WWF Vol. 2*)
Manuel Soto defeated Joe Turco at 12:54
John L. Sullivan defeated Johnny Rodz at 10:39
Prof. Toru Tanaka fought Chief Jay Strongbow to a 20-minute draw
Mario Milano defeated George Steele at 11:14
Crusher Verdu defeated Gorilla Monsoon via count-out at 4:56
WWWF World Champion Bruno Sammartino & Victor Rivera defeated WWWF International Tag Team Champions the Mongols via disqualification at 10:22

May 8, 1970: The New York Knicks won the NBA championship
by defeating the LA Lakers, 4 games to 3. The series aired on ABC.

WWWF @ New York City, NY - Madison Square Garden - September 14, 1970 (17,232)
John L. Sullivan defeated the Black Demon via disqualification at 9:36
Jack Brisco defeated Joe Turco
Prof. Toru Tanaka defeated Manuel Soto
Eddie Graham fought Baron Mikel Scicluna to a draw
Gorilla Monsoon defeated Darrell Cochran at 10:34
Ivan Koloff defeated Dr. Bill Miller at 7:29
Victor Rivera fought WWWF International Tag Team Champion Gito Mongol to a 20-minute draw
Crusher Verdu defeated Marino Milano at 10:18
WWWF International Tag Team Champion Bepo Mongol defeated WWWF World Champion Bruno Sammartino via count-out at 14:24

WWWF @ New York City, NY - Madison Square Garden - October 23, 1970 (17,491)
Sky Low Low & Little Brutus defeated the Jamaica Kid & Sonny Boy Hayes in a Best 2 out of 3 falls match at 16:07
Tony Marino fought Baron Mikel Scicluna to a 20-minute draw
Eddie Graham & Jack Brisco defeated Johnny Rodz & Carlos Peredes in a Best 2 out of 3 falls match, 2-0, at 14:45
Ivan Koloff defeated Gorilla Monsoon via count-out at 6:05
WWWF International Tag Team Champion Gito Mongol defeated Victor Rivera via count-out at 13:37 when Rivera failed to meet the referee's 20-count
Chief Jay Strongbow defeated Crusher Verdu at 4:35
WWWF World Champion Bruno Sammartino defeated WWWF International Tag Team Champion Bepo Mongol at 14:30 in a Texas Death Match

WWWF @ New York City, NY - Madison Square Garden - November 16, 1970 (15,107)
The Jamaica Kid & Joey Russell defeated Sky Low Low & Little Brutus
WWWF International Tag Team Champions Bepo & Gito Mongol fought Victor Rivera & Chief Jay Strongbow to a draw
Manuel Soto fought the Black Demon to a draw
Gorilla Monsoon defeated Johnny Rodz & Vincenti Pometti in a handicap match
Ivan Koloff defeated Tony Marino
Crusher Verdu defeated John L. Sullivan
WWWF World Champion Bruno Sammartino defeated Bulldog Brower at 18:55 when referee Dick Kroll stopped the bout due to a cut on the challenger's forehead

51

"I ended up going to Australia. I was there about 10 weeks for Jim Barnett. I got a call when I was in Hawaii, on the way back. Met up with one of the guys from the office. They told me that Vince wanted me to come back and wrestle Bruno again. I guess Pedro (Morales) was the guy there they had their eye on for down the road. I didn't know how serious all that was. At that point, I just knew they wanted me to come back. From talking to them on the phone from Hawaii, it sounded like I was going in for a year. I went with that assumption. Went there, found out it wasn't quite that way. They felt that Pedro needed to win the belt real fast to really have credibility with the people, I guess. I really think Bruno, at that point, had some physical injuries. I remember one time Bruno complained to me about when I came off the top. It wasn't that I laid it in so hard, because I'm a three-hundred pounder and I can only stop so much. When I landed on his stomach, it tore his stomach muscles and he had to go to the hospital."

Ivan Koloff, *Titans of Wrestling interview, 2014*

"After eight years, I was the one that was looking to get out. Not the promoters, they didn't want me out. I wanted out for a number of reasons. Number one, wrestling every single day had taken a toll on me, physically. We had those boxing rings and they were concrete, those darn things. And when you're throwing your body around every night, six or seven nights a week, sometimes twice in one day, it catches up. I was the type of guy, I wouldn't even take an aspirin, much less a painkiller or anything like that. As time went on and on, I was hurting more and more. ...I just felt the public wasn't getting their money's worth. I felt I wasn't able to give like I used to. And I just felt some changes should be made. I approached McMahon right around the seventh year and I told him how I felt, I told him I was hurting, and I told him how difficult it was, that schedule every night. And I told him it was time for him to start looking for somebody to carry on. He kept stalling and stalling me, but finally I reached the point where I said, 'Vince, you better find somebody or I'm going to go on a sabbatical for six months, whatever, because I am hurting a lot.' So finally, he understood that I meant business. And they went and they got (Ivan) Koloff, who took the title from me. And (Pedro) Morales off of him."

Bruno Sammartino, *TheHistoryofWWE.com interview, 2009*

WWWF @ New York City, NY - Madison Square Garden - January 18, 1971 (21,666; new wrestling attendance record)
Jean DuBois defeated Joe Turco at 14:06
Vincenti Pometti defeated the Black Demon
Manuel Soto defeated Mike Conrad
Blackjack Mulligan defeated Jose Luis Rivera at 5:35
Bulldog Brower defeated Tony Marino at 7:19
Pedro Morales defeated the Wolfman at 5:41
Chief Jay Strongbow & Gorilla Monsoon fought WWWF International Tag Team Champions the Mongols to a draw in a Best 2 out of 3 falls match
Ivan Koloff pinned WWWF World Champion Bruno Sammartino with a bodyslam and knee drop off the top rope to win the title at 14:55 after kicking the champion in the face as he charged into the corner

WRESTLING

TOMORROW, JAN. 18th
IVAN KOLOFF
vs. BRUNO
SAMMARTINO

THE MONGOLS	V S	STRONGBOW & MONSOON

MORALES vs WOLFMAN

BROWER vs MARINO

MULLIGAN vs RIVERA

3 TITLE MATCHES—OTHER BOUTS

PRICES
$2.50-4-5-6
CHILDREN

madis

A shocking reaction

"What an experience that was, winning the belt at Madison Square Garden. People got so quiet you could hear a pin drop. ...He was a legend, he was my hero. I felt bad there for about 5 seconds after I defeated him."
Ivan Koloff, *Titans of Wrestling interview, 2014*

"The loudest single reaction was a very quiet one. It was the night Bruno Sammartino lost the WWWF title to Ivan Koloff. Everyone was in shock. It was like being at a huge funeral. I had never seen a reaction like that and it didn't happen again until the Undertaker had his streak ended by Brock Lesnar."
Bill Apter, *TheHistoryofWWE.com interview, 2014*

The crowd wants blood

"...I knew there was trouble. I said, 'Let me get out of here.' I didn't bother showering or anything. I just grabbed my things and tried to make it out. But there were kids outside; they couldn't get in the thing but they knew it was going on. And people started coming out and they were kinda ticked. They caught me outside. It was raining. And they had those flower pots outside the Garden at that time, with dirt and mud in them. As I go out, they're throwing stuff at me so I go and run into the bar. ...Cost McMahon who knows how much because it almost wrecked the Garden. I couldn't get out of the Garden. They broke the window in the bar downstairs, Charlie O's. I jumped in the cab. They smashed the windows in the cab. "
Capt. Lou Albano, *TitleMatchWrestling interview, 2000*

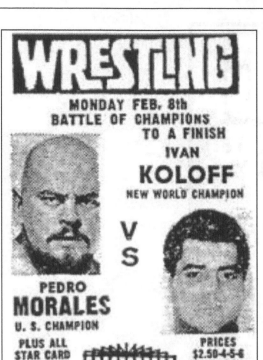

WWWF @ New York City, NY - Madison Square Garden - February 8, 1971
Vincenti Pometti defeated Lee Wong at 13:34
Jack Evans defeated Jean DuBois at 10:15
Sky Low Low & Little Brutus defeated Little Joey & Frenchy Landau
Blackjack Mulligan defeated Tony Marino at 8:07
Gorilla Monsoon fought WWWF International Tag Team Champion Bepo Mongol to a double count-out at 4:13
The Canadian Wolfman battled Manuel Soto to a 20-minute draw
Bruno Sammartino (w/ Arnold Skaaland) defeated Geeto Mongol via submission with the backbreaker at 5:27
US Champion Pedro Morales pinned WWWF World Champion Ivan Koloff to win the title at 23:18 kicking off the top turnbuckle as Koloff had him in a waist lock, with both men falling backwards and having their shoulders down, but Morales lifting his at the count of 2; after the bout, Bruno Sammartino came out to congratulate Morales on his win (*History of the WWF Heavyweight Championship, The History of the WWE Heavyweight Championship*)

The title loss to Morales
"The move that ended up with him winning the belt wasn't legit, anyway. His shoulders were more down were mine. The referee supposedly counted mine down and not his. Bruno won the belt back and I went back and wrestled Bruno again later in the 70s."
Ivan Koloff, *Titans of Wrestling interview, 2014*

WWWF @ New York City, NY - Madison Square Garden - March 15, 1971
Sky Low Low & Little Brutus defeated Joey Russell & Sonny Boy Hayes in a Best 2 out of 3 falls match, 2-1, at 19:09
Manuel Soto defeated Johnny Rodz at 7:18
Jose Luis Rivera defeated Jack Evans at 12:24
Tony Marino pinned Mike Conrad at 13:50
Chief Jay Strongbow fought Bulldog Brower to a 20-minute draw
WWWF World Champion Pedro Morales pinned Blackjack Mulligan at 14:12

Coming to New York

"In 1969-70, I was out in Dallas, TX for Fritz Von Erich. He gave me my name as Handsome Jimmy. Vince McMahon Sr. called and he was working for - exact words he later told me - 'New York is looking for a young, good looking kid. That's what they want.' And he said 'I got one here, Handsome Jimmy Valiant.' And they called me in the office. Years ago they swapped talent. And I went up there and, man, Vince gave me my break. And at that time all the publicity was out in New York as far as the magazines. This was before cable so I was very fortunate; I was just a young kid and got my initial break in New York."
Jimmy Valiant, *TheHistoryofWWE.com interview, 2004*

WWWF @ New York City, NY - Madison Square Garden - May 24, 1971
Sonny Boy Hayes & the Tahiti Kid defeated
Sky Low Low & Little Brutus in a Best 2 out of 3 falls match at 15:59, 2-0; fall #2: Hayes & Kid won when their opponents were disqualified for illegal double teaming
Jimmy Valiant defeated Vincente Pometti at 12:28 via submission with a backbreaker (Valiant's MSG debut)
Manuel Soto defeated Juan Caruso at 11:32
Beautiful Bobby defeated Mike Pappas at 5:26
Bob Roop defeated Akim Manuka at 5:24
Eddie Graham fought Chief Jay Strongbow to a 20-minute draw
Luke Graham defeated Gorilla Monsoon via count-out at 7:56
WWWF World Champion Pedro Morales pinned Tarzan Tyler at 14:12

WWWF @ New York City, NY - Madison Square Garden - June 21, 1971
Beautiful Bobby fought Jimmy Valiant to a 15-minute time limit draw
Dory Funk Sr. defeated Bill White at 7:54
Al Costello & Don Kent defeated Akim Manuka & Mike Pappas in a Best 2 out of 3 falls match at 17:20, 2-0
Bob Roop defeated Manuel Soto at 10:18
Chief Jay Strongbow defeated Eddie Graham
Tarzan Tyler fought Gorilla Monsoon to a 20-minute draw
WWWF World Champion Pedro Morales pinned Luke Graham at 15:28

March 8, 1971 - The Fight of the Century: Heavyweight Champion Joe Frazier (26-0, 23 KOs) faced Muhammad Ali (31-0, 25 KOs) in one of the most hyped fights in history. The battle of the two undefeated boxers ended with Frazier winning via unanimous decision. Frank Sinatra, who was reportedly unable to secure a ringside seat, took photographs of the fight for Life magazine.

WWWF @ New York City, NY - Madison Square Garden - July 24, 1971 (21,912; sell out; new attendance record)
The first ever $100,000 wrestling gate in New York
Little Beaver defeated Joey Russell at 10:24
Mike Pappas defeated Jack Evans at 7:25
The Fabulous Kangaroos defeated Manuel Soto & Bill White at 29:21 in a Best 2 out of 3 falls match; fall #1 - Costello pinned Soto; fall #2 - Soto pinned Kent; fall #3 - Kent pinned White
Jimmy Valiant defeated the Black Demon at 8:17
Chief Jay Strongbow defeated Beautiful Bobby at 7:04
Bruno Sammartino pinned Blackjack Mulligan at 1:04 after a series of bodyslams
WWWF World Champion Pedro Morales & Gorilla Monsoon defeated WWWF International Tag Team Champions Luke Graham & Tarzan Tyler in a Best 2 out of 3 Falls match at 20:13; fall #1: the champions were disqualified; fall #2: Tyler pinned Monsoon; fall #3: Morales pinned Tyler

WWWF @ New York City, NY - Madison Square Garden - August 30, 1971
Joey Russell defeated Frenchy Lamont at 4:16
Jimmy Valiant defeated Mike Pappas at 5:29
Manuel Soto fought Mike Monroe to a 20-minute draw
Karl Gotch defeated the Black Demon at 10:59
Tarzan Tyler & Luke Graham defeated Gorilla Monsoon & Chief Jay Strongbow via count-out
Stan Stasiak defeated WWWF World Champion Pedro Morales at 19:51 when referee Danny Bartfield stopped the bout due to blood
Terry & Dory Funk Sr. fought Al Costello & Don Kent to a 45-minute curfew draw

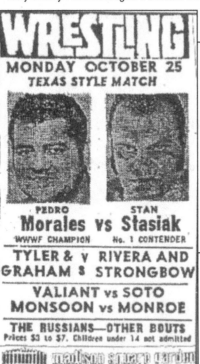

WWWF @ New York City, NY – Madison Square Garden - October 25, 1971
Rene Goulet defeated Juan Caruso at 9:15
Jimmy Valiant defeated Manuel Soto at 7:39
Karl Gotch defeated Beautiful Bobby
The Rugged Russians defeated Mike Pappas & Mike Conrad in a Best 2 out of 3 falls match, 2-0
Gorilla Monsoon defeated Mike Monroe at 7:09
Chief Jay Strongbow & Victor Rivera defeated Tarzan Tyer & Luke Graham in a Best 2 out of 3 falls match, 2-0, at 13:35
WWWF World Champion Pedro Morales pinned Stan Stasiak at 12:45 in a Texas Death Match

Aug. 1, 1971: George Harrison held his Concert for Bangladesh. It is regarded as the first special benefit concert to raise funds for a charity. The two concerts (one at 2:30 p.m., the other at 7 p.m.) included such artists as Harrison, Ravi Shankar, Eric Clapton, Bob Dylan, Ringo Starr, Billy Preston and Klaus Voormann.

Karl Gotch backstage at Madison Square Garden.

WWWF @ New York City, NY - Madison Square Garden - November 15, 1971
The Black Demon defeated Chuck Richards at 8:27
Rene Goulet fought Manuel Soto to a 20-minute draw
Karl Gotch defeated Mike Monroe at 11:05
The Rugged Russians defeated Jimmy Valiant & Beautiful Bobby
Gorilla Monsoon defeated Stan Stasiak at 9:51
Chief Jay Strongbow & Victor Rivera defeated Tarzan Tyler & Luke Graham via disqualification at 24:45
WWWF World Champion Pedro Morales defeated Pacific Coast Champion Freddie Blassie when referee Terry Terranova stopped the match due to blood at 8:24

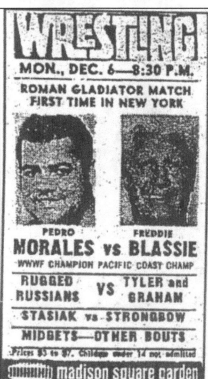

WWWF @ New York City, NY - Madison Square Garden - December 6, 1971 (sell out)
Manuel Soto defeated Mike Monroe at 10:47
Farmer Jerome & Sonny Boy Haynes defeated Sky Low Low & Little Brutus in a Best 2 out of 3 Falls match, 2-0 winning the second fall via disqualification, at 21:09
Stan Stasiak fought Chief Jay Strongbow to a 20-minute time-limit draw
Victor Rivera defeated Jimmy Valiant at 12:16
The Fabulous Kangaroos fought the Rugged Russians to a time-limit draw in a Best 2 out of 3 falls match
Karl Gotch & Rene Goulet defeated WWWF Tag Team Champions Luke Graham & Tarzan Tyler to win the titles in a Best 2 out of 3 falls match, 2-0, at 17:20
WWWF World Champion Pedro Morales defeated Pacific Coast Champion Freddie Blassie at 7:14 in a Roman Gladiator match when the challenger was deemed unable to continue

WWWF @ New York City, NY - Madison Square Garden - January 31, 1972
King Curtis defeated Tomas Marin
Victor Rivera defeated Stan Stasiak
Karl Gotch & Rene Goulet defeated the Rugged Russians in a Best 2 out of 3 falls match, 2-0
Pampero Firpo defeated Manuel Soto
Sonny King & Gorilla Monsoon defeated Jimmy Valiant & Ernie Ladd
Chief Jay Strongbow defeated Freddie Blassie
via disqualification
WWWF World Champion Pedro Morales defeated Professor Toru Tanaka via disqualification when the challenger attempted to throw salt into Morales' eyes but instead hit the referee by mistake

Another night doing my trade
"Back then, of course you know, we wrestled every night, seven days a week. Of course it's a thrill but, and I didn't take anything for granted and everybody in professional wrestling wanted to wrestle at Madison Square Garden and I was in my early 20s up there in the Garden. But it didn't affect me as far as anything else. It was just another night doing my trade but - and I'm not trying to say this loosely - but it was just another night at my trade. If I was in North Attleboro for Vince McMahon, for the WWWF on a Friday night at the Witschi's Arena, or if I was in Madison Square Garden - what I'm saying is that I would go in there if there was only 200 people in Attleboro, MA, I would go in there like it was Madison Square Garden and give 112%, man. Everything I had for them, 10-15 minutes in the ring from the time the door opened from the dressing room till the time the door shut. I would just do everything I could and go in wide open, you know."
Jimmy Valiant, *TheHistoryofWWE.com interview, 2004*

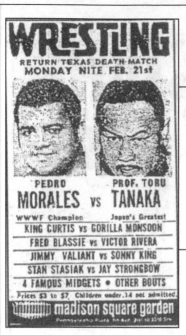

WWWF @ New York City, NY - Madison Square Garden - February 21, 1972
Joey Russell & Farmer Jerome defeated Sky Low Low & Frenchy Lamont
Pompero Firpo defeated Rene Goulet
Victor Rivera defeated Juan Caruso
Baron Mikel Scicluna defeated Manuel Soto
King Curtis defeated Gorilla Monsoon via count-out
WWWF World Champion Pedro Morales pinned Prof. Toru Tanaka after coming off the top
Sonny King pinned Jimmy Valiant
Chief Jay Strongbow defeated Stan Stasiak

WWWF @ New York City, NY - Madison Square Garden - March 13, 1972
Jimmy Valiant fought Joe Nova to a draw
Pampero Firpo beat Ben Justice
Prof. Toru Tanaka defeated Rene Goulet at 7:45
Ernie Ladd fought Sonny King to a draw
Chief Jay Strongbow & Victor Rivera defeated the Rugged Russians in a Best 2 out of 3 falls match, 2-0
King Curtis (w/ Lou Albano) defeated Gorilla Monsoon when the match was stopped due to blood loss
Bruno Sammartino defeated Smasher Sloan at 9:53 via submission with the backbreaker
WWWF World Champion Pedro Morales pinned Baron Mikel Scicluna (w/ Lou Albano) at 11:34

WWWF @ New York City, NY - Madison Square Garden - April 17, 1972
Sky Low Low & Little Brutus defeated the Tahiti Kid & Sonny Boy Hayes
Manuel Soto defeated the Black Demon
Don Curtis defeated Mike Padiousis
Baron Mikel Scicluna defeated Rene Goulet
Sonny King defeated Smasher Sloan
Ernie Ladd pinned Jimmy Valiant
Pampero Firpo defeated Chief Jay Strongbow via count-out
Victor Rivera fought Prof. Toru Tanaka to a draw
WWWF World Champion Pedro Morales pinned King Curtis after coming off the top

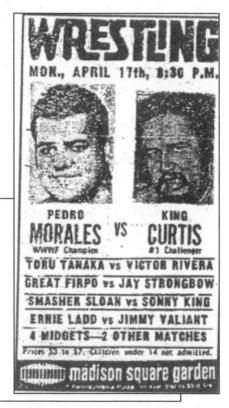

March 15, 1972: The 14th annual Grammy Awards was held at the Felt Forum and aired on ABC.
Top award winners included Carole King, the Carpenters,
James Taylor, Carly Simon, Bill Cosby and Kris Kristofferson.

Those who shot photographs at ringside during WWWF events, including Bill Apter, George Napolitano and even Paul Heyman, would have press passes - like the one pictured - to get in the door.

WORKING PRESS

2 ROW   72 SEAT

ALL STAR WRESTLING 8:30 P.M.   MON. EVE. APR. 24 1972

MADISON SQUARE GARDEN PENNSYLVANIA PLAZA, N.Y.

ALL STAR WRESTLING

WORKING PRESS

N. Y. State Law - Children Under 14 Yrs. of Age NOT ADMITTED

N° 0072

ALL STAR WRESTLING

MONDAY EVENING APR. 24, 1972 8:30 P.M.

WORKING PRESS

APR 17 1972

NOTICE and AGREEMENT

THIS ticket is sold and purchased upon the express understanding that it is and shall be a personal license, not transferable, and good only to admit the person who purchased the same. This corporation hereby reserves the right to cancel the privilege of this ticket and refund the money to its purchaser for any act considered in violation of any of the rules of the New York State Athletic Commission after due notice that such rule or regulation has been violated.

THIS TICKET IS SOLD AND PURCHASED AND IF HONORED, IS TO BE HONORED UPON THE EXPRESS AGREEMENT THAT NO FILM OR TELEVISION PICTURES OF THE EXHIBITION HEREIN REFERRED TO, OR OF ANY OTHER WRESTLING EXHIBITION ON THE SAME CARD WILL BE TAKEN AND NO BROADCASTING THEREOF EFFECTED BY THE PURCHASER OR HOLDER OF THIS TICKET, EXCEPT THAT MAY BE AUTHORIZED BY THE PROMOTER IN WRITING.

STATE OF NEW YORK

Picking up the press pass

"Before the show I would go to the Holland Hotel on 42nd Street and Ninth Avenue to pick up my press ticket at the WWWF's dinky little office. I would knock on the door and Arnold Skaaland would come to the door, cigar smoke coming right at my face, and give me my ticket.

He would invite me in for a moment where he, Gorilla Monsoon, promoter Willie Gilzenberg, Vince McMahon Sr., and others were conducting business and usually a poker game. After the show, I took the subway back to where I lived and always stopped for a slice or two of pizza.

In the early days, my dad Nat Apter accompanied me to the matches. They even let him sit in the press section. And that pizza became a regular routine for both of us. I still look for a good pizza place after the matches these days. Sometimes before the matches, too."
Bill Apter, *TheHistoryofWWE.com interview, 2014*

WWWF @ New York City, NY - Madison Square Garden - May 22, 1972
Tony Cantellis defeated the Blue Demon via disqualification
Prof. Toru Tanaka defeated Manuel Soto
King Curtis defeated Smasher Sloan
Eddie Graham defeated Jimmy Valiant
Ernie Ladd defeated Rene Goulet
Chief Jay Strongbow defeated Cpt. Lou Albano
Chief Jay Strongbow & Sonny King defeated WWWF Tag Team Champions Baron Mikel Scicluna & King Curtis to win the titles in a Best 2 out of 3 falls match, 2-0
WWF World Champion Pedro Morales pinned Pampero Firpo at 15:21

WWWF @ New York City, NY - Madison Square Garden - June 2, 1972
The Black Demon defeated Jack Evans
The Fabulous Kangaroos defeated Mike Pappas & Akim Manuka in a Best 2 out of 3 falls match
Dory Funk Sr. defeated Bill White
Bob Roop defeated Manuel Soto
Beautiful Bobby fought Jimmy Valiant to a draw
Chief Jay Strongbow defeated Eddie Graham
Tarzan Tyler fought Gorilla Monsoon to a draw
WWWF World Champion Pedro Morales defeated Luke Graham

WWWF @ New York City, NY - Madison Square Garden - July 1, 1972 (19,512)
Fred Curry defeated Joe Nova at 6:43
Mike Graham defeated Juan Caruso at 5:19
Chief Jay Strongbow & Sonny King defeated Ernie Ladd & WWWF Tag Team Champion Prof. Toru Tanaka in a Best 2 out of 3 falls match; fall #1: Strongbow & King won; fall #2: Ladd & Tanaka won; fall #3: Strongbow & King won via disqualification
The Fabulous Moolah defeated Vicki Williams (first women's match in New York history)
Terry & Dory Funk Sr. defeated King Curtis Iaukea & Luke Graham
Gorilla Monsoon defeated the Black Demon at 4:17
WWWF World Champion Pedro Morales pinned George Steele at 14:59

WWWF @ New York City, NY - Madison Square Garden - July 29, 1972
Chuck O'Conner defeated Thomas Marin
El Olympico defeated the Blue Demon
Manuel Soto defeated Juan Caruso
Women's Champion the Fabulous Moolah pinned Susan Green at 5:44
George Steele defeated Gorilla Monsoon via count-out after Monsoon was knocked down on the apron
Paul Jones defeated Jerry Brisco
WWWF Tag Team Champions Prof. Toru Tanaka & Mr. Fuji
fought Chief Jay Strongbow & Sonny King to a 60-minute draw
WWWF World Champion Pedro Morales pinned the Spoiler with a crossbody off the top after a backdrop; prior to the bout, Capt. Lou Albano escorted the challenger to the ring

May 11, 1972: The Boston Bruins defeated the New York Rangers to win the Stanley Cup, 4 games to 2.
June 9-12, 1972: Elvis Presley performed his first concerts in New York City since the 1950's by becoming the first entertainer to draw four consecutive sell-outs at Madison Square Garden (attracting approximately 80,000 fans). Among those in attendance for the performances were George Harrison, Art Garfunkel, Bruce Springsteen, David Bowie, Led Zeppelin, Paul Simon and Bob Dylan. Paul Stanley, who would later gain fame as a member of KISS, drove several customers to MSG during those nights while working as a cab driver. The June 10 performance was released by RCA a week later as a live album and went on to be certified 3x Platinum in 1999.

WWWF @ New York City, NY - Madison Square Garden - September 2, 1972 (21,819)
Chuck O'Connor defeated Joe Nova
El Olympico pinned Joe Turco at 13:51
Sonny King defeated the Black Demon
WWWF Tag Team Champions Mr. Fuji & Professor Toru Tanaka defeated Gorilla Monsoon & Manuel Soto in a Best 2 out of 3 Falls match
The Spoiler fought Chief Jay Strongbow to a draw
WWWF World Champion Pedro Morales pinned Ernie Ladd at 15:50
Bruno Sammartino defeated George Steele at 12:29; after the bout, it was announced that Sammartino would face Pedro Morales for the title at Shea Stadium on Sept. 30 (Sammartino's MSG return after more than a year)

WWWF @ New York City, NY - Madison Square Garden - October 16, 1972
The Black Demon defeated Joe Turco
Little Beaver & Little Louie defeated Frenchy Lamont & Sonny Boy Hayes
Buddy Wolfe defeated Blackjack Slade
WWWF World Champion Pedro Morales & Bruno Sammartino defeated WWWF Tag Team Champions Prof. Toru Tanaka & Mr. Fuji in a Best 2 out of 3 falls match, 2-0; fall #2: the challengers won via disqualification
The Spoiler fought Sonny King to a draw
Ray Stevens defeated El Olympico
Toni Rose & Donna Christianello defeated Vicki Williams & Joyce Grable in a Best 2 out of 3 falls match
Chief Jay Strongbow defeated Chuck O'Conner

WWWF @ New York City, NY - Madison Square Garden - November 27, 1972
El Olympico defeated Joe Turco
Tony Garea defeated Chuck O'Conner
Black Gordman defeated Sonny King
WWWF World Champion Pedro Morales defeated Ray Stevens at 11:58 when referee Danny Bartfield stopped the bout, ruling the challenger could not continue
Eddie Graham defeated Blackjack Slade
Victor Rivera fought the Spoiler to a 20-minute draw
Verne Gagne defeated Buddy Wolfe
WWWF Tag Team Champions Prof. Toru Tanaka & Mr. Fuji fought Gorilla Monsoon & Chief Jay Strongbow to a 20-minute draw

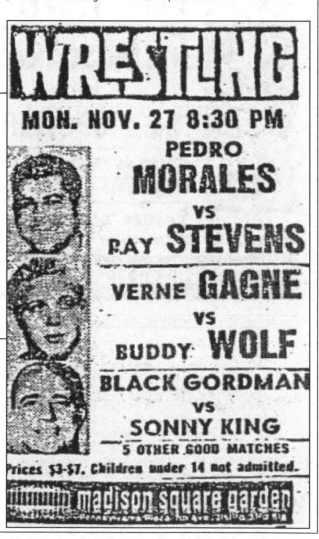

WWWF @ New York City, NY - Madison Square Garden - December 18, 1972

Joe Turco defeated Blackjack Slade at 9:10

Tony Garea defeated Bull Pometti at 10:54

The Great Goliath defeated Manuel Soto at 7:00

Sonny King fought Buddy Wolfe to a 20-minute draw

Gorilla Monsoon defeated Chuck O'Connor at 6:17

El Olympico & Victor Rivera defeated Dory Funk Sr. & Terry Funk in a Best 2 out of 3 falls match at 15:03; fall #1 - Dory forced a submission from Olypico with the spinning toe hold after Olypico sustained an atomic drop from Terry; fall #2 - the Funks were disqualified for tossing Rivera over the top and double teaming Olympico; fall #3 - Rivera pinned Dory with a misile dropkick and a fast count from the referee

Mil Mascaras pinned the Spoiler at 7:20 with a flying bodypress; this was the first appearance of a masked wrestler at MSG; there was a previous ban on masked wrestlers following a ruling from the New York State Athletic Association Commission (Mascaras' MSG debut)

WWWF World Champion Pedro Morales pinned Ray Stevens with a sunset flip at 14:10 after the challenger thought he had won the bout with a Boston Crab

The ban on women, masks

"I was in the elevator going from ground level to the arena level. One night in that elevator was New York State Athletic Commissioner Edwin Dooley. At this time in the early 70s, there was a ban on masked wrestlers and women competitors in pro wrestling anywhere in the state. I decided to ask him -- in front of many people in the elevator, "Mr. Dooley, when will you allow women and masked wrestlers to wrestle here?" His face turned red, he puffed on a cigar, and looked me directly in the eye and said, "Mister Reporter. If you want to keep covering wrestling here at Madison Square Garden you'll be a lot more careful about asking stupid questions like that!" For some reason everyone except me, and my dad, laughed. The elevator door opened, they all got out, and that was it. I never forgot that very uncomfortable moment."

Bill Apter, *TheHistoryofWWE.com interview, 2014*

WWWF @ New York City, NY - Madison Square Garden - January 15, 1973
Sky Low Low & Little Brutus defeated Little Beaver & Joey Russell
The Fabulous Moolah defeated Joyce Grable
Mad Dog & Butcher Vachon defeated Lee Wong & Ben Ortiz in a Best 2 out of 3 falls match, 2-0
Black Gordman defeated El Olympico
Victoria Rivera fought Mr. Fuji to a 20-minute draw
Ray Stevens defeated Sonny King
Bruno Sammartino defeated Prof. Toru Tanaka
WWWF World Champion Pedro Morales pinned Moondog Mayne with a flying bodypress

WWWF @ New York City, NY - Madison Square Garden - February 26, 1973
Susan Green & Lily Thomas defeated Peggy Patterson & Paula Kaye at 18:12
Tony Garea defeated Mike Conrad at 15:05
Mike Graham defeated Joe Turco at 5:42
Terry Funk defeated Chuck Richards at 10:55
Victor Rivera defeated Dory Funk Sr. at 11:45
Mil Mascaras defeated Buddy Wolfe at 9:46
AWA World Champion Verne Gagne defeated Eddie Graham (sub. for Ray Stevens) at 14:35 (Graham's last MSG appearance)
WWWF World Champion Pedro Morales defeated King Curtis at 5:37

Legends share the card
"I have been privileged to work in wrestling, being one of the architects of GLOW - Gorgeous Ladies Of Wrestling, as well as W.O.W. and Wrestlicious. But first and foremost I am a fan. For me, Madison Square Garden was the place to be. It was called the Mecca of wrestling and it truly was. All the major stars passed through its hallowed halls. I remember one card had legends grappling in almost every match. There was Dory Funk Sr., Terry Funk, Eddie Graham, Mike Graham, AWA Champion Verne Gagne, Mil Mascaras in his second Garden appearance, and Pedro Morales defending the WWWF championship against King Curtis in the Main Event. There was also a women's tag team match. I had the pleasure of spending an evening with Verne Gagne some 27 years later, and had him sign that program."
Steven Blance, *Flushing, NY*

Jan. 30, 1973: The 26th NHL All-Star Game was held, with the East defeating the West, 5-4.

Andre the Giant makes his Madison Square Garden debut. He would quickly become a major attraction at MSG and would appear at MSG wrestling events for the next 18 years.

WWWF @ New York City, NY - Madison Square Garden - March 26, 1973
El Olympico defeated Joe Turco
Tony Garea defeated Frank Valois
Mad Dog & Butcher Vachon defeated Curtis Iaukea & Louie Tillet
Victor Rivera fought the Giant Goliath to a draw
Mr. Fuji defeated Sonny King
Gorilla Monsoon fought Prof. Toru Tanaka to a draw
Chief Jay Strongbow fought Moondog Mayne to a draw
Andre the Giant defeated Buddy Wolfe (Andre's MSG debut)
WWWF World Champion Pedro Morales defeated Fred Blassie
when the challenger was deemed unable to continue

WWWF @ New York City, NY - Madison Square Garden - April 30, 1973
El Olympico defeated Frank Valois
Mike McCord defeated Joe Turco
Curtis Iaukea defeated Juan Caruso
Moondog Mayne defeated Manuel Soto
Gorilla Monsoon defeated Buddy Wolfe
Andre the Giant defeated Prof. Toru Tanaka
Chief Jay Strongbow fought Freddie Blassie to a draw
WWWF World Champion Pedro Morales defeated Don Leo Jonathan (w/ the Grand Wizard) when referee Eddie Gersh stopped the bout due to blood following a right hand punch from the champion that opened up the challenger's forehead

Don Leo's robe
"Often when a guy was debuting like IWE former great Japan champ, Shozo "Strong" Kobayashi at MSG, Skoaland or one of Mr. McMahon Sr's people would bring him out for us to pose against the great blue curtain. Also did that when Don Leo Jonathon debuted and he said, 'Hey fellas, wait'll you get a loada my robe. Had it specially made. Well, in Montreal for here.' He came out and it was a magnificent royal blue thick colored material like satin on the outside. When he and The Wiz opened it up and he spread it out and spun around, it had super shiny silver and blue with almost fake crystals gleaning on the inside. Just shiny and spectacular. He was fresh from Montreal/Grand Prix like the returning Killer Walt Kowalski and it was a dream match for myself and others to shoot in Don Leo vs. Bruno sometime later. Sort of like the dream Bruno vs. Billy Graham match when that occurred there. And always first, as everyone knows, at MSG. The heels, first paired with one of the big three on TV, even if the heel was an excellent talker, would slowly beat jobbers and upper tier journeymen like the Manny Sotos, then Vic Rivera. Then maybe Strongbow after Monsoon. And after slowly building them up time after time, they'd finally get the Bruno title match. And again, always for the first time at MSG. Well before Nassau Coliseum, Boston Gardens, the Spectrum, Cap Center or the beloved smaller arenas if they got those major matches at all: Sunnyside Gardens, RollaRama."
Mike Lano, *Alameda, CA*

WWWF @ New York City, NY –
Madison Square Garden - June 4, 1973
The Fabulous Moolah fought Jan Sheridan to a draw
Iron Mike McCord fought El Olympico to a 20-minute draw
Moondog Mayne fought Tony Garea to a 20-minute draw
Blackjack Lanza defeated Manuel Soto
Victor Rivera defeated Giant Goliath
Gorilla Monsoon & Haystacks Calhoun defeated Prof. Toru
Tanaka & Mr. Fuji in a Best 2 out of 3 falls match, 2-0
Chief Jay Strongbow defeated Freddie Blassie via count-out
in a Texas Death Match
WWWF World Champion Pedro Morales pinned Don Leo
Jonathan (w/ the Grand Wizard) with a reverse cradle as the
challenger attempted a backdrop

Little merch, no masked men

"Back then in the 60's and 70's, the WWWF wasn't the merchandising juggernaut it is today. There were no giant foam fingers, replica two by fours, urns, or hats or t-shirts. You bought a program for 50 cents that had the night's line-up of matches, pictures of the stars and an article or two. It was like gold. Even though the matches wouldn't begin until 8:30 PM, you arrived early, full of anticipation. About a minute before start time, the crowd would start to whistle and hoot. When the house lights would go down and spotlights above the ring illuminated the mat, the fans would cheer. Suddenly the outside world disappeared and you were captivated by the spectacle. Believe it or not, masked wrestlers were not allowed to compete with their head fully covered. They had to wear a hood. So now you could actually see the faces of El Olympico and the Rugged Russians that were masked on TV. The rules were suspended for Mil Mascaras, who ironically battled the Spoiler in his first Garden appearance. The Spoiler, who wore a mask in every territory he wrestled in, worked bare faced in the WWWF. After Mascaras, other grapplers were allowed to wrestle fully masked."
Steven Blance, *Flushing, NY*

WWWF @ New York City, NY - Madison Square Garden - June 30, 1973
Televised on HBO - featured Vince McMahon on commentary:
Blackjack Lanza defeated Lee Wong via submission with the claw at 5:05
Prof. Toru Tanaka pinned El Olympico with a chop to the throat at 9:34
Gorilla Monsoon defeated Lou Albano via count-out at 2:58 after Monsoon knocked Albano over the top to the floor
and Albano walked backstage (*Villains of the Squared Circle*)
Victor Rivera pinned Black Gordman with a small package at 11:34
Joyce Grable & Jan Sheridan defeated Peggy Patterson & Dottie Downs in a Best 2 out of 3 falls match at 20:47; fall
#1: Sheridan pinned Downs with a dropkick at 12:17; fall #2: Downs pinned Grable by grabbing the tights for
leverage after Grable missed a dropkick at 6:21; fall #3: Grable pinned Patterson with a victory roll at 2:09
WWWF World Champion Pedro Morales defeated George Steele when the match was stopped due to blood at 8:16
after Morales repeatedly rammed Steele's face into the turnbuckles and punched him; after the bout, Steele attacked
the champion until Morales gained the upper hand and chased Steele from ringside (*Villains of the Squared Circle*)
Chief Jay Strongbow pinned Mr. Fuji with a double tomahawk chop to the face at 13:58
Haystacks Calhoun pinned Moondog Mayne with a splash at 6:03

WWWF @ New York City, NY - Madison Square Garden - July 23, 1973
Televised on HBO - featured Vince McMahon on commentary
Little Boy Blue & Pee Wee Adams defeated Sonny Boy Hayes & Little Louie
Manuel Soto defeated Joe Turco
Blackjack Lanza defeated El Olympico
Chief Jay Strongbow defeated Mike McCord
Victor Rivera defeated Freddie Blassie
WWWF Tag Team Champions Haystacks Calhoun & Tony Garea defeated Mr. Fuji & Prof. Toru Tanaka in a Best 2
out of 3 falls match; fall #1: Tanaka pinned Garea with a kick to the midsection; fall #2: the challengers were
disqualified for choking Haystacks; fall #3: Haystacks pinned Tanaka with a splash (*Best of the WWF Vol. 7*)
WWWF World Champion Pedro Morales defeated George Steele; Joe Louis was the special referee for the bout

WWWF @ New York City, NY - Madison Square Garden - August 27, 1973
Televised on HBO - featured Vince McMahon on commentary
Farmer Jerome & Little Louie defeated Little Brutus & Pee Wee Adams
Manuel Soto fought El Olympico to a 20-minute draw
Victor Rivera defeated Mr. Fuji
Chief Jay Strongbow pinned Prof. Toru Tanaka at 13:01
Gorilla Monsoon defeated George Steele via count-out (*George 'The Animal' Steele*)
WWWF World Champion Pedro Morales defeated Stan Stasiak via judges desicion at the 52 minute mark (*History of
the WWF Heavyweight Championship*)

WWWF @ New York City, NY - Madison Square Garden - October 15, 1973
Vicki Williams & Joyce Grable defeated Toni Rose & Donna Christianello at 17:07
El Olympico fought Mike Pappas to a draw at 13:33
Manuel Soto defeated Tony Altimore at 8:07
Jose Gonzalez defeated Pancho Valdez at 10:27
Ron Fuller defeated Frank Valois at 9:02
Tony Garea defeated Mr. Fuji at 3:54
Victor Rivera defeated Mike McCord at 1:35
Andre the Giant defeated Blackjack Lanza at 10:51
Dean Ho defeated Prof. Toru Tanaka at 11:30
Chief Jay Strongbow fought Don Leo Jonathan to a 20-minute time-limit draw
WWWF World Champion Pedro Morales defeated Stan Stasiak in a Texas Death Match at 7:36

WWWF @ New York City, NY - Madison Square Garden - November 12, 1973
Jose Gonzalez defeated El Olympico at 15:22
Dick Slater defeated Mike Pappas at 6:20
Iron Mike McCord fought Manuel Soto to a 20-minute draw
Dean Ho defeated Pancho Valdez
Don Leo Jonathan defeated Tony Garea at 18:45
Verne Gagne defeated Mr. Fuji at 12:16
Chief Jay Strongbow & Andre the Giant defeated Blackjack Lanza & Stan Stasiak in a Best 2 out of 3 falls match, 2-0
WWWF World Champion Pedro Morales defeated Larry Hennig at 12:45 when the match was stopped due to blood

These rare images capture one of Andre the Giant's first major challenges at MSG, Blackjack Lanza. While pro wrestling events at MSG were often televised during this time on the MSG Network or fledging HBO, this particular card from October 15, 1973 never was.

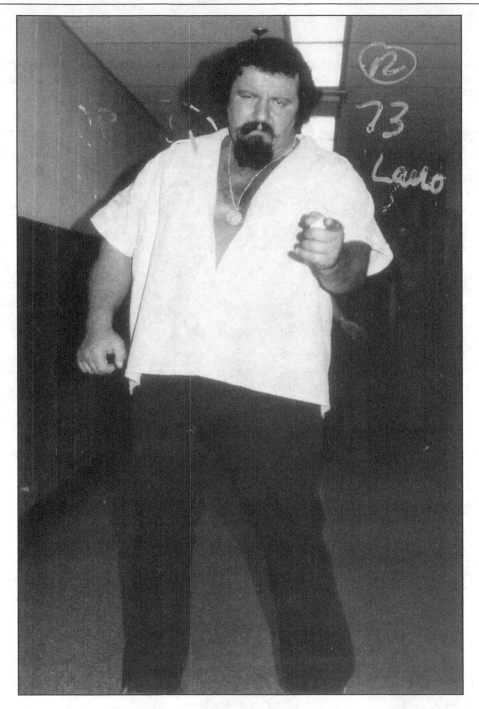

Capt. Lou Albano, backstage at MSG. Albano regularly managed champions in the 1970s and 80s and became a central figure during the WWF's partnership with MTV in the mid 1980s. That partnership included airing two live MSG wrestling events on MTV.

The crowd went wild

"Back in the 70's, titles mostly changed hands on TV or at the Garden. I was lucky enough to watch Chief Jay Strongbow and Sonny King defeat Baron Scicluna and King Curtis for the tag team titles in two straight falls. I also saw the Lumberjacks take the belts from Dominic Denucci and Dino Bravo. Plus, I was there when Bruno Sammartino won the WWWF title a second time by downing Stan Stasiak. Madison Square Garden never stopped giving the fans thrills. Stan Stasiak defeated Pedro Morales for the title in Philadelphia on Dec. 1, 1973. I'm sure this was done out of town as a result of rioting outside of the Garden after Ivan Koloff defeated Sammartino for the belt January 1971. In those days, there was no internet, and wrestling events beyond Madison Square Garden weren't covered in the newspapers. The only way to hear about championship changes was on the WWWF TV program. It was announced that Bruno would meet the new champ nine days later at Madison Square Garden. I had to be there. There was a buzz in the arena all night long. Pedro wrestled earlier on the card, upending Larry Hennig. When the main event began, you could feel the electricity in the air. Bruno would down Stasiak with a series of arm drags and the crowd would cheer each one and then applaud when he would keep the champ down with an armlock. His opponent made a comeback and set Sammartino up for the feared heart punch. Bruno kicked him in the mid section before the hit could be delivered. The crowd when wild. At that point the end was a foregone conclusion. When Sammartino pinned Stasiak and was awarded the belt, the scene was euphoric. The King had returned and reclaimed his throne."

Steven Blance, *Flushing, NY*

WWWF @ New York City, NY - Madison Square Garden - December 10, 1973
El Olympico pinned Tony Altamore at 8:55
Jose Gonzalez pinned Joe Turco at 10:35
Dean Ho defeated Pancho Valdez at 7:05
Tony Garea pinned Mike McCord at 12:35
Chief Jay Strongbow defeated Blackjack Lanza at 7:15
Don Leo Jonathan defeated Manuel Soto at 17:10 when the match was stopped due to blood
John Tolos fought Victor Rivera to a 20-minute draw
Pedro Morales defeated Larry Hennig in a lumberjack death match with the Boston Crab
Bruno Sammartino pinned WWWF World Champion Stan Stasiak at 12:35 to win the title after three consecutive bodyslams; prior to the bout, Sammartino was escorted to the ring by Arnold Skaaland and the Grand Wizard escorted the champion

Initial local advertising for the Dec. 10, 1973 card focused on Pedro Morales as the headliner. That changed once Stan Stasiak upset Morales for the heavyweight crown days earlier and Sammartino became the challenger for the title.

WWWF @ New York City, NY - Madison Square Garden - January 14, 1974

Butcher Brannigan defeated Mike Pappas

Otto Von Heller defeated Tony Altimore

Jose Gonzalez & Manuel Soto defeated Pancho Valdez & Joe Turco

Chief Jay Strongbow defeated Mr. Fuji via disqualification

Nikolai Volkoff defeated Gorilla Monsoon

WWWF Tag Team Champions Dean Ho & Tony Garea defeated Larry Hennig & Mike McCord

Pedro Morales defeated Stan Stasiak

WWWF World Champion Bruno Sammartino defeated Don Leo Jonathon

WWWF @ New York City, NY - Madison Square Garden - March 4, 1974 (sell out)

The scheduled bout between Don Leo Jonathan and Ed Sullivan did not take place

Donna Christianello & the Fabulous Moolah defeated Peggy Patterson & Dardi Dahl

Mr. Fuji defeated Johnny Rodz at 10:14

Prof. Toru Tanaka defeated Jose Gonzalez at 8:59

Chief Jay Strongbow defeated Lou Albano via disqualification at 4:35

WWWF Tag Team Champions Dean Ho & Tony Garea defeated Larry Hennig & Stan Stasiak at 22:45

Pedro Morales defeated Otto Von Heller

WWWF World Champion Bruno Sammartino fought Nikolai Volkoff to a curfew draw after 53 minutes

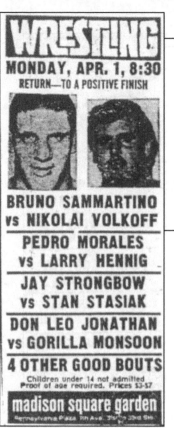

WWWF @ New York City, NY - Madison Square Garden - April 1, 1974 (sell out)
Jumbo Tsuruta pinned Johnny Rodz (Tsuruta's only MSG appearance)
Otto Von Heller fought Jose Gonzalez to a 20-minute time-limit draw
Larry Zbyzsko defeated Ed Sullivan at 7:29 (Zbyszko's MSG debut)
WWWF Tag Team Champions Dean Ho & Tony Garea defeated Prof. Toru Tanaka & Mr. Fuji via disqualification
Gorilla Monsoon pinned Don Leo Jonathan at 14:07
Chief Jay Strongbow defeated Stan Stasiak at 7:15
Pedro Morales pinned Larry Hennig at 11:04 (Hennig's last MSG appearance)
WWWF World Champion Bruno Sammartino pinned Nikolai Volkoff at 13:08

WWWF @ New York City, NY - Madison Square Garden - April 29, 1974
Televised on HBO - *included Vince McMahon on commentary:*
Jose Gonzalez fought Larry Zbyzsko to a draw
Robert Fuller defeated Ed Sullivan at 10:39
Tony Garea defeated Mike Conrad at 17:09
Nikolai Volkoff defeated Dean Ho at 5:22
Pedro Morales pinned Mr. Fuji at 10:29 with two bodyslams after Fuji failed a splash off the top
Chief Jay Strongbow & Andre the Giant defeated Otto Von Heller & Don Leo Jonathan in a Best 2 out of 3 falls match, 2-0
WWWF World Champion Bruno Sammartino (w/ Arnold Skaaland) fought Killer Kowalski to a no contest at 24:15 when the two men began brawling around the ring after the champion began bleeding from the face; after the bout, Chief Jay Strongbow, Pedro Morales, and another wrestler pulled the two men apart *(Bruno Sammartino: Wrestling's Living Legend, The History of the WWE Heavyweight Championship)*

WWWF @ New York City, NY - Madison Square Garden - May 20, 1974
Larry Zbyszko defeated Mike Conrad at 8:35
Jose Gonzalez defeated Lou Albano at 14:20
Dean Ho defeated Tony Altimore at 13:01
Pedro Morales defeated Johnny Rodz at 10:29
Chief Jay Strongbow defeated Nikolai Volkoff at 7:26
Peggy Patterson & the Fabulous Moolah defeated Sharon Brooks &
Debbie Johnson in a Best 2 out of 3 falls match
WWWF World Champion Bruno Sammartino pinned Killer Kowalski
at 18:14 in a Texas Death Match

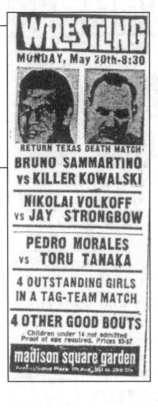

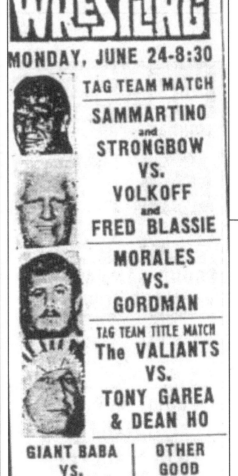

WWWF @ New York City, NY –
Madison Square Garden - June 24, 1974 (sell out)
Jose Gonzalez defeated Tony Altimore at 6:50
WWWF Tag Team Champions Johnny & Jimmy Valiant defeated
Dean Ho & Tony Garea in a Best 2 out of 3 falls match; fall #1 - the
champions won; fall #2 - the challengers won; fall #3 - the
champions won
Haystacks Calhoun & Larry Zbyszko defeated Otto Von Heller &
Killer Kowalski
The Giant Baba defeated Gorilla Monsoon
Pedro Morales defeated Black Gordman at 15:17
WWWF World Champion Bruno Sammartino & Chief Jay
Strongbow defeated Freddie Blassie & Nikolai Volkoff in a Best 2
out of 3 falls match, 2-0; fall #1 - Sammartino & Strongbow won via
disqualification; fall #2 - Sammartino pinned Blassie (Blassie's last
wrestling match at MSG)

WWWF @ New York City, NY -
Madison Square Garden - July 22, 1974
Televised on HBO - featured Vince McMahon on commentary
Gorilla Monsoon defeated Nikolai Volkoff
The Fabulous Moolah defeated Vicki Williams
Dean Ho defeated Prof. Toru Tanaka
WWWF Tag Team Champions Jimmy & Johnny Valiant defeated
Haystacks Calhoun & Chief Jay Strongbow in a Best 2 out of 3 falls
match; fall #1: the champions won at 9:05; fall #2: the challengers
won at 2:24; fall #3: the challengers were disqualified after the 13-
minute mark when WWWF World Champion Bruno Sammartino
interfered and came to Strongbow's aid
Pedro Morales fought Killer Kowalski to a double count-out at 10:27
(*Best of the WWF Vol. 2*)
WWWF World Champion Bruno Sammartino defeated John Tolos
with a backbreaker at 15:29

<u>On Vince McMahon Sr.</u>
"He was the greatest man that I ever met in my life. And I'm telling you the
truth. Everything he told me came true and never once did he tell me
something that didn't happen. He made it happen. He was a gentleman. He
was just a great human being. As a promoter, he was a genius. You know,
of course out east he had the best territory in the world. He had all the New
England cities, the whole eastern seaboard, Madison Square Garden, the
Boston Garden, Philadelphia, Washington DC - he had it all."
Jimmy Valiant,
TheHistoryofWWE.com interview, 2004

WRESTLING

MON. AUG. 26—8:30
TAG-TEAM TITLE MATCH

BRUNO SAMMARTINO AND STRONGBOW
VS
VALIANT BROTHERS

ANDRE the GIANT VS KILLER KOWALSKI

PEDRO MORALES VS NIKOLAI VOLKOFF

STRONG KOBAYASHI VS TONY GAREA

4 OTHER GOOD BOUTS
Children under 14 not admitted
Proof of age required Prices $3-$7

madison square garden
Pennsylvania Plaza 7th Ave 34d to 33rd Sts

WWWF @ New York City, NY - Madison Squre Garden - August 26, 1974
Jose Gonzalez defeated Johnny Rodz
Jack Evans defeated Dean Ho
Haystacks Calhoun defeated Otto Von Heller
Larry Zbyszko defeated Louie Tillet
Tony Garea defeated Strong Kobyashi
Pedro Morales defeated Nikolai Volkoff
Andre the Giant defeated Killer Kowalski via count-out
WWWF World Champion Bruno Sammartino & Chief Jay Strongbow fought WWWF Tag Team Champions Jimmy & Johnny Valiant to a draw when the bout was stopped due to the curfew

WWWF @ New York City, NY - Madison Square Garden - October 7, 1974 (over 22,000)
Larry Zbyszko fought Jose Gonzalez to a 20-minute time-limit draw
Spiros Arion defeated Jack Evans
Tony Garea defeated Johnny Rodz
Dean Ho defeated Bill White
Bobby Duncum defeated Haystacks Calhoun
Andre the Giant & Victor Rivera defeated Killer Kowalski & Strong Kobayashi
WWWF World Champion Bruno Sammartino & Chief Jay Strongbow defeated WWWF Tag Team Champions Jimmy & Johnny Valiant in a Best 2 out of 3falls match; fall #1: the Valiants won; fall #2: the challengers won via disqualification; fall #3: the champions won

WRESTLING

MON. OCT. 7—8:30
TAG-TEAM TITLE MATCH

RETURN MATCH
BRUNO SAMMARTINO and JAY STRONGBOW
VS
VALIANT BROTHERS

Big Bob Duncum vs Haystacks Calhoun

STRONG KOBAYASHI and KILLER KOWALSKI
VS
ANDRE the GIANT and VICTOR RIVERA

4 OTHER GOOD BOUTS
Children under 14 not admitted
Proof of age required Prices $3-$7

madison square garden
Pennsylvania Plaza 7th Ave 34d to 33rd Sts

Oct. 13, 1974: Frank Sinatra performed, to cap his comeback after retirement in 1971, in front of 20,000 fans during a show dubbed 'The Main Event' that was broadcast nationally and internationally.

WWWF @ New York City, NY -
Madison Square Garden - November 18, 1974
Larry Zbyzsko defeated Jack Evans
Jose Gonzalez defeated Tony Atlimore
Spiros Arion defeated Bill White
Dominic DeNucci defeated Johnny Rodz
Mad Dog Vachon defeated Thomas Marin
Chief Jay Strongbow defeated Hans Schroeder
Killer Kowalski & the Valiant Brothers defeated Gorilla Monsoon, Dean Ho, & Tony Garea
Pedro Morales defeated Strong Kobayashi
WWWF World Champion Bruno Sammartino fought Bobby Duncum to a no contest in a Best 2 out of 3 falls match when both men were deemed too bloody to continue

WWWF @ New York City, NY –
Madison Square Garden - December 16, 1974
Televised on HBO - featured Vince McMahon on commentary:
The Fabulous Moolah pinned Joyce Grable by reversing a bodyslam attempt into a cradle (*Best of the WWF Vol. 13*)
Jack Evans defeated SD Jones
Jose Gonzalez fought Bill White to a draw
Larry Zbyszko defeated Johnny Rodz
Chief Jay Strongbow & Spiros Arion defeated Joe Nova & Hans Schroeder
Pedro Morales fought Killer Kowalski to a draw
WWWF Tag Team Champions Jimmy & Johnny Valiant defeated Tony Garea & Dean Ho
WWWF World Champion Bruno Sammartino defeated Bobby Duncum in a Texas Death Match

WWWF @ New York City, NY -
Madison Square Garden - January 20, 1975
Dean Ho defeated Bill White
Tony Garea defeated Hans Schroeder
Butcher Vachon defeated Joe Nova
The Wolfman defeated Johnny Rodz
Spiros Arion defeated Larry Zbyszko
Pedro Morales & Victor Rivera fought Killer Kowalski & Bobby Duncum to a draw
WWWF World Champion Bruno Sammartino & Chief Jay Strongbow defeated WWWF Tag Team Champions Jimmy & Johnny Valiant in a Best 2 out of 3 falls match, winning a fall on a disqualification

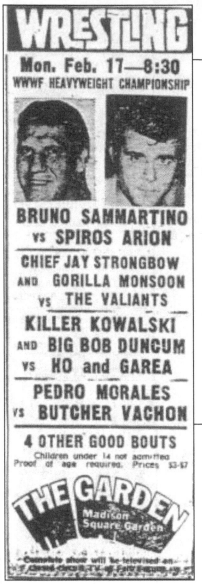

WWWF @ New York City, NY - Madison Square Garden - February 17, 1975

Televised on HBO - featured Vince McMahon on commentary:
Prime Time Wrestling - 2/17/86: Manuel Soto & Pete Sanchez defeated Jack Evans & Johnny Rodz in a Best 2 out of 3 falls match; final fall: Soto pinned Evans with a sunset flip
Joe Nova defeated Bill White at 15:02
Victor Rivera defeated Hans Schroeder at 9:17
Dean Ho & Tony Garea defeated Killer Kowalski & Bubby Duncum via disqualification at 14:17 when Garea was repeatedly double teamed
The Wolfman defeated El Olympico at 3:14
Pedro Morales defeated Butcher Vachon at 4:59
Prime Time Wrestling - 12/17/85: Spiros Arion defeated WWWF World Champion Bruno Sammartino via disqualification at 13:00 when Bruno twice pushed the referee away when he was trying to break the two up from fighting in the corner; after the bout, Bruno had to be held back by several wrestlers including Gorilla Monsoon,
Dean Ho, & Tony Garea
WWWF Tag Team Champions Jimmy & Johnny Valiant fought Gorilla Monsoon & Chief Jay Strongbow to a curfew draw at 19:09 in a non-title match; prior to the bout, Capt. Lou Albano escorted the champions ringside

WWWF @ New York City, NY - Madison Square Garden - March 17, 1975

Televised on HBO - featured Vince McMahon on commentary:
Johnny Rodz pinned Bill White at 11:31 with a stomp from the middle rope after White failed a dropkick attempt
Mike Paidousis pinned Jack Evans at 5:43 with a kneedrop after Evans ran into the ropes when Paidousis moved out of the way
Manuel Soto & Pete Sanchez defeated Joe Nova & Hans Schroeder at 22:05 in a Best 2 out of 3 falls match
Chief Jay Strongbow pinned Butcher Vachon at 9:10 with a Thesz Press
WWWF World Champion Bruno Sammartino (w/ Arnold Skaaland) pinned Spiros Arion at 14:51 in a Texas Death match with a powerslam even though Arion's foot was on the bottom rope during the cover; prior to the bout, Freddie Blassie escorted Arion to the ring before returning to the dressing room
Victor Rivera defeated Killer Kowalski via disqualification at 15:58 after Kowalski began biting at Rivera's head; prior to the bout, the Grand Wizard escorted Kowalski to the ring before returning to the dressing room
All American Wrestling - 5/6/84: Ivan Putski defeated the Wolfman via submission at 6:45 with a bearhug (Putski's MSG debut)
Dean Ho & Tony Garea fought WWWF Tag Team Champions Johnny & Jimmy Valiant to a draw in a Best 2 out of 3 falls non-title match; fall #1: Garea pinned Johnny at 1:49 after throwing him off the top rope; fall #2: Johnny pinned Garea at 4:05 with a sunset flip; fall #3: the bout was stopped due to the curfew at 12:13; prior to the bout, Capt. Lou Albano escorted the Valiants to the ring before returning to the dressing room

WWWF @ New York City, NY - Madison Square Garden - April 14, 1975 (26,000, which included several thousand at Felt Forum)

Televised on HBO - featured Vince McMahon on commentary:
Mike Paidousis pinned Tony Altimore at 13:05 after Altimore missed a running kick and fell onto his back; prior to the match, the ring announcer mispronounced both men's names; after the contest, Altimore confronted Vince McMahon at the ringside table and told him not to air the match

Greg Valentine pinned El Olympico at 7:49 with an elbow to the side of the head followed by an elbow drop; Olympico wore a mask with the face cut out since MSG did not allow wrestlers to wear full masks at the time; the ring announcer mispronounced Valentine's last name (Valentine's MSG debut)

Waldo Von Erich defeated Chief Jay Strongbow via count-out at the 39-second mark after Von Erich attacked Strongbow from behind and threw him over the top rope; immediately after the bout, WWWF World Champion Bruno Sammartino ran out to tend to Strongbow at ringside, with Strongbow and an official then carrying Strongbow backstage; Von Erich remained in the ring until the official decision was announced

Lord Littlebrook & Little Tokyo defeated Midget Tag Team Champions Sonny Boy Hayes & Little Louie in a non-title Best 2 out of 3 falls match at 18:59; fall #1: Tokyo pinned Hayes at 12:01 with a kick and grabbing the tights for leverage; fall #2: Hayes pinned Littlebrook at 4:25 after Tokyo accidentally hit his partner; fall #3: Littlebrook pinned Louie at 3:33 with a shoulderblock; the champions came to the ring in possession of title belts

WWWF World Champion Bruno Sammartino defeated Spiros Arion in a Greek Death match at 14:58 via submission with a half crab after the challenger missed a kneedrop off the top and Sammartino repeatedly stomped the injured leg; stipulations stated the match could only be won via submission; prior to the ring introductions, Vince McMahon briefly spoke with international banker Andrew D'Amato about the previous contest; Freddie Blassie escorted Arion to the ring and Arnold Skaaland escorted Sammartino before the opening bell; after the match, Arion attempted to pull himself up before Sammartino repeatedly stomped him and then stepped on his throat as Arion's head was on the bottom rope; following the commercial break, Arion refused to be taken backstage by a stretcher but was helped backstage by the referee

Edouard Carpentier pinned Joe Nova at 9:16 after three standing sentons; before the match, a brief on-screen graphic mistakenly read "Victor Rivera vs. Big Bob Duncum;" McMahon briefly spoke with Andrew D'Amato again before the contest

WWWF Tag Team Champions Jimmy & Johnny Valiant defeated Manuel Soto & Pete Sanchez in a non-title match when Johnny pinned Soto; the match did not air as part of the telecast

Victor Rivera fought Bobby Duncum to a curfew draw at around the 16-minute mark; prior to the bout, the Grand Wizard escorted Duncum to the ring; the match ended after Rivera prevented Duncum from using a foreign object and knocked him to the mat

81

WWWF @ New York City, NY - Madison Square Garden - May 19, 1975
Televised on HBO - featured Vince McMahon on commentary:
SD Jones defeated Johnny Rodz
Haystacks Calhoun defeated Jack Evans & Hans Schroeder in a handicap match
Baron Mikel Scicluna defeated Bill White
The Wolfman defeated Mike Paidousis
Bobby Duncum defeated Dean Ho
Dominic DeNucci defeated Johnny Valiant
Victor Rivera defeated Greg Valentine
Ivan Putski pinned Butcher Vachon at 5:07 with the Polish Hammer
Chief Jay Strongbow fought Jimmy Valiant to a 20-minute time-limit draw
Spiros Arion defeated Tony Garea
Waldo Von Erich defeated WWWF World Champion Bruno Sammartino when the match was stopped due to blood

WWWF @ New York City, NY - Madison Square Garden - June 16, 1975
Televised on HBO - featured Vince McMahon on commentary
Women's Champion the Fabulous Moolah pinned Susan Green at 10:16 with a splash after Green missed a splash off the top (*WWE's Top 50 Superstars of All Time*)
Pete Sanchez defeated Johnny Rodz
Jack Evans defeated Bill White
Baron Mikel Scicluna defeated Mike Paidousis
WWWF Tag Team Champions Domenic DeNucci & Victor Rivera defeated Bobby Duncum & Butcher Vachon in a Best 2 out of 3 falls match, 2-1; fall #1: Duncum pinned Rivera at 18:21 after Vachon jumped on Rivera's mid-section; fall #2: Rivera pinned Duncum at 2:04 after two somersault splashes; fall #3: DeNucci pinned Vachon at 1:58 with a sunset flip; the ring announcer mispronounced DeNucci's last name
Ivan Putski pinned Johnny Valiant (w/ Capt. Lou Albano) at 4:30 with a sit-down splash following the Polish Hammer; prior to the bout, Capt. Lou Albano escorted Valiant to the ring; after the contest, Putski sent Valiant to the floor (*Best of the WWF Vol. 6*)
Chief Jay Strongbow pinned Jimmy Valiant with the Thesz Press at 15:50
WWWF World Champion Bruno Sammartino (w/ Arnold Skaaland) pinned Waldo Von Erich (w/ Freddie Blassie) at 4:12 with a kick to the midsection as the challenger ran the ropes

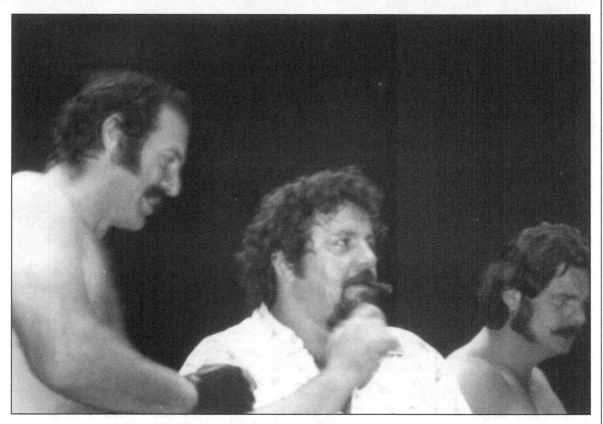

The Blackjacks make their MSG debut, alongside Capt. Lou Albano.

Meeting the Blackjacks

"From my memories of MSG, nearly everyone had their own room. When I interviewed the Blackjacks, for example, the night they debuted, they had me sit while they stood. Mulligan smoking a cigarette. They were very animated and an extremely great and colorful interview, almost shooting. They were talking about dominating various promotions in my taped interview -- old school cassette -- like St Louis for Lanza with Heenan, and Mulligan mentioned Los Angeles, where he worked under his own name of Bob Windham, and the entire WWWF from his solo or first tour there. They also dropped Montreal as both worked there for the Vachon/Grand Prix promotion. And of course they talked about Texas, separately beating everyone in Dallas and then Houston for Paul Boesch who they said was 'the best promoter we've worked for to date other than Muchnick. Paul's a great man. We just destroyed the so-called best team from the West Coast in Black Gordman and Great Goliath there at the Coliseum,' Lanza said. 'Left them in a pool of greasy tacos.' Mulligan added: 'We'll be toying around with Garea and Ho once we get our hands on them...the thing in the magazines with Heenan 'selling our contract to' Lou Albano here was kind of just for the magazines. Bobby works in the Midwest and is tied there. When you come here, you get one of the big three managers automatically. Albano is a former wrestler, he can still don the tights and cause some destruction. We can talk for ourselves, but he adds to the package.' It was kind of a coup at the time because few rarely went on record, with a tape recorder going in 1975, kind of shooting."

Mike Lano, *Alameda, CA*

WWWF @ New York City, NY - Madison Square Garden - July 12, 1975
Manuel Soto defeated Mike Paidousis
Baron Mikel Scicluna fought Pete Sanchez to a draw
Blackjack Mulligan & Blackjack Lanza defeated Tony Garea & Dean Ho in a Best 2 out of 3 falls match
Spiros Arion defeated Bill White
WWWF Tag Team Champions Victor Rivera & Dominic DeNucci defeated Jimmy & Johnny Valiant in a Best 2 out of 3 falls match
Andre the Giant defeated Butcher Vachon
WWWF World Champion Bruno Sammartino fought George Steele to a curfew draw at 46:11

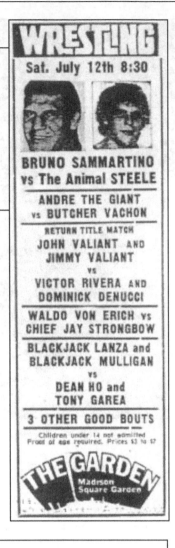

WWWF @ New York City, NY - Madison Square Garden - August 9, 1975
Baron Mikel Scicluna defeated Manuel Soto
Chief Jay Strongbow fought Waldo Von Erich to a draw
Spiros Arion defeated Dean Ho
Victor Rivera defeated Butcher Vachon
Bugsy McGraw defeated Tony Garea
WWWF Tag Team Champions Pat Barrett & Dominic DeNucci defeated the Blackjacks
Andre the Giant & Verne Gagne defeated Johnny & Jimmy Valiant in a Best 2 out of 3 falls match, 2-0
WWWF World Champion Bruno Sammartino defeated George Steele

WWWF @ New York City, NY - Madison Square Garden - September 6, 1975
Joyce Grable defeated Dottie Downs
Pete Sanchez defeated Jack Evans
Manuel Soto defeated Johnny Rodz
Mike Graham defeated Tony Altimore
Haystacks Calhoun defeated Hans Schroder
Waldo Von Erich defeated Dominic DeNucci
Spiros Arion defeated Pat Barrett
Ivan Putski defeated Baron Mikel Scicluna
Francisco Flores & Andre the Giant fought Blackjack Mulligan & Blackjack Lanza to a draw
WWWF World Champion Bruno Sammartino defeated Buggsy McGraw & Lou Albano in a handicap match at 18:23

Aug. 4, 1975: Black Sabbath performed at MSG for the first time.

WWWF @ New York City, NY - Madison Square Garden - October 13, 1975

Televised on HBO - featured Vince McMahon on commentary:

Pat Barrett defeated Davey O'Hannon

Manuel Soto defeated Jack Evans at 14:55

Francisco Flores defeated Johnny Rodz at 11:36

Pete Sanchez fought Frank Monte to a 20-minute time-limit draw

Louis Cerdan & Tony Parisi defeated Spiros Arion & Waldo Von Erich in a Best 2 out of 3 falls match, 2-0, at 12:16

Dominic DeNucci defeated Baron Mikel Scicluna at 7:05

WWWF World Champion Bruno Sammartino fought Ivan Koloff to a draw when the match was stopped due to blood at 21:59; after the bout, the two men were held apart by Gorilla Monsoon, the Blackjacks, Dominic DeNucci, Tony Parisi, and several others (*Grudge Matches*)

Gorilla Monsoon, Ivan Putski, & Haystacks Calhoun defeated Bugsy McGraw, WWWF Tag Team Champions Blackjack Mulligan & Blackjack Lanza in a Best 3 out of 5 falls match at 14:37; fall #1: Putski pinned Mulligan with a kneedrop at 5:56; fall #2: the bout was stopped due to the curfew at 8:41

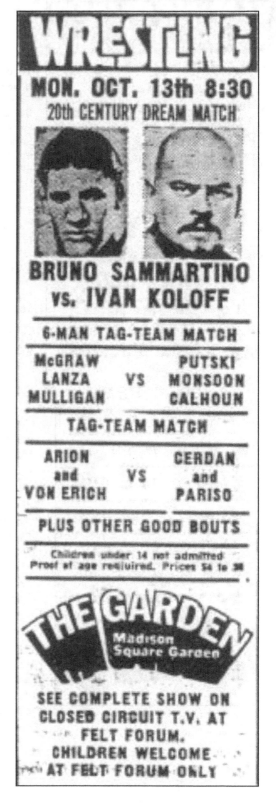

WWWF @ New York City, NY - Madison Square Garden - November 17, 1975
Televised on HBO - featured Vince McMahon on commentary:
Manuel Soto defeated Davey O'Hannon
Francisco Flores defeated Frank Monte
Kevin Sullivan fought Pete Sanchez to a 20-minute draw
Pat Barrett defeated Baron Mikel Scicluna
Billy Robinson defeated Johnny Rodz
Dominic DeNucci defeated Spiros Arion via disqualification
Ivan Putski defeated Bugsy McGraw
WWWF World Champion Bruno Sammartino defeated Ivan Koloff via disqualification at 21:14; Gorilla Monsoon was the special referee for the bout (*Grudge Matches*, *The History of the WWE Heavyweight Championship*)
Ernie Ladd defeated Haystacks Calhoun via count-out at 8:40 after a running shoulderblock knocked Calhoun through the ropes to the floor
Tony Parisi & Louis Cerdan defeated WWWF Tag Team Champions Blackjack Mulligan & Blackjack Lanza in a Best 2 out of 3 falls match at 10:08; fall #1: Parisi pinned Mulligan at 5:42 with an elbow drop following a double slam; fall #2: the bout was stopped due to the curfew at 4:26

Attending underage

"I was 8 years old. My first show was Nov. 17, 1975, when we lived in Brooklyn. One time, my mother went out with friends and we stayed with their older son until midnight. That's back when the WWWF would come on, on Channel 9. I was watching it, I was hooked on watching it. The people that my mother was hanging out with had season tickets, on the 4th row where the wrestlers were coming out. She said, 'If you ever have an extra ticket, my son would love to go.' Back then, you couldn't go if you were under 14. But they had season tickets and they knew the ushers, and they said I was older. The first main event was Bruno against Ivan Koloff. When I was little, I liked Bruno a lot. I turned into a heel fan. The fans were very into it, especially with Bruno. It was very exciting. The matches, you go back and watch now, the fans today aren't going to buy it. At 8-9 years old, I'm the only kid that knows anything about wrestling. No one had a clue, everyone was into baseball, football, stuff like that. I stuck out among the adults. For the most part, I was the smallest one there. You could smoke, the building is full of smoke. Most of the fans were 40s and up. You don't see a lot of 50, 60-year-old fans today."
Charlie Adorno, *Brooklyn, NY*

Ivan Koloff returned in 1975 to once again challenge Bruno Sammartino for the title. Their feud led to the first steel cage match in the history of MSG.

Bruno vs. Ivan

"I felt so comfortable with Bruno. He wasn't a selfish type of guy. He knew what it would take to draw was people believing in him. If all you ever do is beat everybody up, you're stronger than them, you're a better wrestler than them, you always get your hand raised...that was the way it was with Bruno throughout his career. But he had to show the guy had a chance, a big chance, against him for them to come back and see it again. Hats off to Bruno to his ability to do that. Bruno could mix it up."
Ivan Koloff, *Titans of Wrestling interview, 2014*

"I've been criticized for being too much of a brawler. They might see me wrestle (Ivan) Koloff, and see pretty much a brawling match. But what they don't know is this was the third match, or what we call a blowoff match. The first match was a lot of wrestling and high spots. But then it ended a little rough, which led to the second match. And in the second match, we did high spots and some wrestling but then it got more violent, to where the brawling came into it. And then, by the time of the third match, it was such a heated situation that this isn't going to be a wrestling match, it's going to be an all out war."
Bruno Sammartino, *TheHistoryofWWE.com interview, 2009*

WWWF @ New York City, NY - Madison Square Garden - December 15, 1975

Televised on HBO - featured Vince McMahon on commentary:

Pete Sanchez defeated Johnny Rodz

Pat Barrett defeated Manuel Soto at 10:25

Antonio Inoki defeated Frank Monte at 8:41

Tony Parisi & Louis Cerdan defeated Spiros Arion & Baron Mikel Scicluna

Ivan Putski defeated Blackjack Lanza at 11:50

Superstar Billy Graham defeated Dominic DeNucci at the 9 second mark (Graham's debut)

Ernie Ladd & Bugsy McGraw defeated Kevin Sullivan & Haystacks Calhoun

WWWF World Champion Bruno Sammartino defeated Ivan Koloff in a steel cage match by escaping through the door at 9:39 after sending the challenger into the corner of the cage (the first cage match held at MSG) (*Bloodbath: Wrestling's Most Incredible Steel Cage Matches*)

WWWF @ New York City, NY - Madison Square Garden - January 12, 1976

Televised on HBO - featured Vince McMahon on commentary:

Dominic DeNucci defeated Bugsy McGraw via disqualification at 11:35

Kevin Sullivan fought Frank Monte to a 20-minute draw

Baron Mikel Scicluna defeated Francisco Flores at 11:45

Ernie Ladd defeated Gorilla Monsoon via referee's decision at 8:25 when the match was stopped due to excessive blood loss on Monsoon

Superstar Billy Graham (w/ the Grand Wizard) defeated WWWF World Champion Bruno Sammartino (w/ Arnold Skaaland) via count-out after the two collided head-first in the ring, sending the champion to the floor; after the bout, Sammartino sent the challenger out of the ring (*The History of the WWE Heavyweight Championship*)

Pat Barrett fought Pete Sanchez to a 20-minute draw

Ivan Putski pinned Crusher Blackwell at 7:03 with the Polish Hammer

WWWF Tag Team Champions Tony Parisi & Louis Cerdan vs. Spiros Arion & Ivan Koloff

88

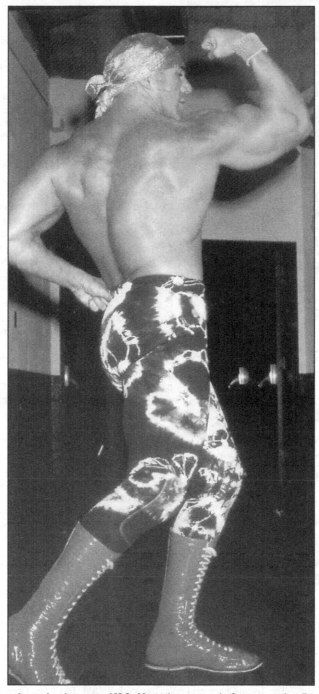

Superstar Billy Graham shown backstage at MSG. More than a year before upsetting Bruno Sammartino for the heavyweight crown, Graham challenged Sammartino in a series of title bouts at Madison Square Garden.

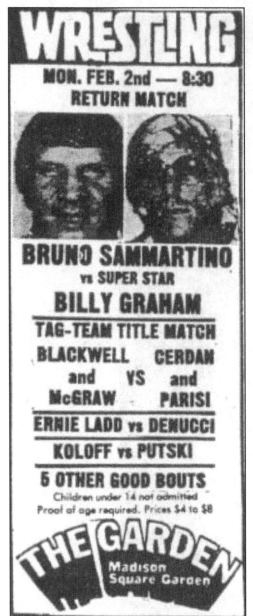

WWWF @ New York City, NY - Madison Square Garden - February 2, 1976

Televised on HBO - featured Vince McMahon on commentary:

Frank Monte defeated Pete Sanchez at 9:21

Louis Cyr pinned Francisco Flores at 9:16 with a shoulderbreaker; prior to the bout, Cyr was escorted to the ring by Freddie Blassie; after the match, Cyr knocked Flores to the floor

Spiros Arion (sub. for Pat Barrett) pinned Kevin Sullivan at 6:44 with an atomic drop; prior to the bout, the ring announcer promoted the wrestling broadcasts on channel 47; following the match, the ring announcer promoted the March 1 event

Ernie Ladd pinned Dominic DeNucci at 11:55 by putting his feet on the top rope for leverage after a thumb strike to the throat; as Ladd left ringside, an elderly woman had to be restrained from trying to hit Ladd with her purse

Ivan Putski fought Ivan Koloff to a time-limit draw at around the 11-minute mark as both men brawled on the ring apron; Capt. Lou Albano escorted Koloff to the ring before the contest; after the bout, Putski held up a T-shirt featuring him and asked the fans who won the match, with the crowd cheering for him

Little Louie & the Cocoa Kid defeated Billy the Kid & Little Johnny in a Best 2 out of 3 falls match, 2-0; fall #1: Cocoa pinned Johnny with a leg roll up at 12:02; fall #2: Louie pinned Billy at 6:27 after catapulting him into Johnny, who came into the ring; the on-screen graphic before the match listed Cocoa as 'Bobo Johnson'

WWWF World Champion Bruno Sammartino (w/ Arnold Skaaland) defeated Superstar Billy Graham at 17:55 when the match was stopped due to blood after Sammartino repeatedly punched a bloody gash on Graham's head; after the decision was announced, Graham took the mic and said he wanted more, with Sammartino then knocking him to the floor; following the match, the ring announcer reminded the fans not to throw anything into the ring or they would be subject to arrest

Baron Mikel Scicluna pinned Pat Barrett (sub. for Bobo Brazil) at 6:44 after throwing him head-first into the corner; during the bout, Vince McMahon said WWWF Tag Team Champion Louis Cerdan had been in an accident and Brazil would replace him in the final match; following the bout, ring announcer Buddy Wagner was handed the next month's card from WWWF President Willie Gilzenberg which featured Davey O'Hannon vs. Johnny Rivera, Ric Flair vs. Pete Sanchez in Flair's MSG debut, Baron Mikel Scicluna vs. Dominic DeNucci, Louis Cyr vs. Pat Barrett, Crusher Blackwell vs. Bobo Brazil, Fabulous Moolah vs. Susan Green, WWWF Tag Team Champions Louis Cerdan & Tony Parisi vs. Ivan Koloff & Superstar Billy Graham, and Ernie Ladd vs. WWWF World Champion Bruno Sammartino

Bobo Brazil (sub. for WWWF Tag Team Champion Louis Cerdan) & WWWF Tag Team Champion Tony Parisi defeated Crusher Blackwell & Bugsy McGraw in a Best 2 out of 3 falls match, 2-0; fall #1: Blackwell & McGraw were disqualified at 7:13 when McGraw choked Bobo with the tag rope; fall #2: Parisi pinned Blackwell at 4:21 with a bodyslam and jumping off the top; prior to the match, the ring announcer said Cerdan was grounded at the Montreal airport and could not make it to the show

WWWF @ New York City, NY - Madison Square Garden - March 1, 1976
Televised on HBO - featured Vince McMahon on commentary
Rocky Tamayo defeated Johnny Rivera
Dominic DeNucci defeated Baron Mikel Scicluna
Ric Flair pinned Pete Sanchez at 10:05 with a suplex (Flair's MSG debut) (*The Ultimate Ric Flair Collection*)
Louis Cyr pinned Pat Barrett at 11:05 with a backbreaker
Superstar Billy Graham & Ivan Koloff defeated WWWF Tag Team Champions Tony Parisi & Louis Cerdan in a Best 2 out of 3 falls match at around the 18-minute mark; fall #1: both teams were disqualified at 11:58 when all four men began fighting in the ring and the champions attempted to make double pins; fall #2: the champions were disqualified when Bruno Sammartino interfered and attacked both challengers, clearing them from the ring; prior to the bout, the Grand Wizard escorted Graham to the ring while Capt. Lou Albano did the same for Koloff; during the contest, Graham & Koloff "injured" Cerdan's leg, with the challengers then double teaming Parisi until Parisi's cousin, Sammartino, made the save
WWWF World Champion Bruno Sammartino pinned Ernie Ladd at 11:25 after the challenger missed a splash off the top; prior to the bout, the champion was escorted to the ring by Arnold Skaaland
Susan Green pinned Kitty Adams (sub. for Women's Champion the Fabulous Moolah) at 9:21; Moolah was deemed unable to compete after breaking her collerbone the previous night in Toronto
US Champion Bobo Brazil pinned Crusher Blackwell with the Coco Butt at 8:22

WWWF @ New York City, NY - Madison Square Garden - March 29, 1976
Pat Barrett defeated Johnny Rodz at 12:35
Jose Gonzalez defeated Gene Dundee at 13:10
Chris Taylor defeated Baron Mikel Scicluna at 9:44
Kevin Sullivan defeated Pete Sanchez
Dominic DeNucci defeated Crusher Blackwell at 14:29
Bobo Brazil defeated Louis Cyr at 14:59
Andre the Giant & Ivan Putski defeated Ernie Ladd & Bugsy McGraw at 13:25
WWWF World Champion Bruno Sammartino & WWWF Tag Team Champion Tony Parisi defeated Superstar Billy Graham & Ivan Koloff in a Best 2 out of 3 falls match at 26:57; fall #3 - Sammartino & Parisi won via count-out

WRESTLING
Mon., Mar. 1 — 8:30
4 TITLE MATCHES

BRUNO SAMMARTINO
VS.
KING ERNIE LADD

KOLOFF   CERDAN
AND   VS.   AND
GRAHAM   PARISI

BLACKWELL VS. BRAZIL
MOOLAH VS. SUSAN GREEN

4 OTHER GOOD BOUTS
Children under 14 not admitted
Proof of age required. Prices $4 to $8

THE GARDEN
Madison Square Garden

WWWF @ New York City, NY -
Madison Square Garden - April 26, 1976
Televised on HBO - included Vince McMahon on commentary:
Louis Cerdan defeated Johnny Rodz
Tony Parisi defeated Baron Mikel Scicluna
Ric Flair defeated Frankie Williams
Stan Hansen defeated WWWF World Champion Bruno Sammartino
via referee's decision when the match was stopped due to blood
moments after Hansen hit the lariat after putting a foreign object in his
elbow pad; after the bout, Bruno continued to attack Hansen; it was
during the bout that Bruno sustained a broken neck from a bodyslam,
though it was Hansen's lariat which was credited for causing the injury
Bobo Brazil pinned Rocky Tomayo at 10:49 with the Coco Butt
Dominic DeNucci defeated Louis Cyr
Superstar Billy Graham & Ivan Koloff defeated Haystacks Calhoun &
Pat Barrett via count-out
Prime Time Wrestling - 2/3/86: Andre the Giant defeated Ernie Ladd
via count-out at 12:28 when Ladd walked out of the match after
avoiding a splash from Andre (*Villains of the Squared Circle*)

WWWF @ New York City, NY - Madison Square Garden - May 17, 1976
Vivian St. John defeated Paula Kaye at 7:10
The Fabulous Moolah defeated Susan Green at 11:14
Baron Mikel Scicluna fought Jose Gonzalez to a draw
Tony Parisi defeated Rocky Tamayo at 6:09
Scandor Akbar defeated Louis Cerdan at 5:09
Billy White Wolf defeated Crusher Blackwell at 8:46
The Executioners defeated Pat Barrett & Kevin Sullivan at 11:43
Gorilla Monsoon, Haystacks Calhoun, & Bobo Brazil defeated Superstar
Billy Graham, Ivan Koloff, & Ernie Ladd
Stan Hansen defeated Ivan Putski
(sub. for WWWF World Champion Bruno Sammartino) via count-out

July 12-15, 1976: The Democratic National Convention was held at MSG, with Jimmy Carter
named the presidential nominee and Walter Mondale the vice president.

WWWF @ New York City, NY - Madison Square Garden - August 7, 1976 (22,000)
Televised on the MSG Network - featured Vince McMahon on commentary:
Johnny Rivera pinned Jose Cadiz at 10:41 with a flying bodypress off the top
SD Jones pinned Johnny Rodz at 8:12 after kicking from the turnbuckle and falling back on Rodz as Rodz attempted a German suplex and lifting his left shoulder when both were on the mat
WWWF Tag Team Champions the Executioners defeated Jose Gonzalez & Dominic DeNucci (sub. for Haystacks Calhoun) in a Best 2 out of 3 falls match at 22:54, 2-1; fall #1: Executioner #1 pinned DeNucci at 10:11 following a double backbreaker; fall #2: DeNucci pinned Executioner #1 at 7:29 following an airplane sping; fall #3: Executioner #2 pinned Gonzalez at 5:14 after Executioner #1 kicked his partner's back as Gonzalez lifted him up for a bodyslam so that he would land on top of Gonzalez for the pin
Bruiser Brody defeated Kevin Sullivan via submission at 2:29 with the backbreaker; prior to the bout, Brody was escorted to the ring by the Grand Wizard (Brody's MSG debut)
Chief Jay Strongbow & Billy White Wolf defeated Baron Mikel Scicluna & Rocky Tomayo at 5:58 when White Wolf pinned Tomayo with a double chop
WWWF World Champion Bruno Sammartino defeated Stan Hansen in a steel cage match at 11:11 by escaping the cage through the door after continually beating on Hansen with Hansen's own loaded elbow pad that he Bruno had ripped off Hansen's arm
Bobo Brazil defeated Doug Gilbert via count-out at the 35-second mark when Gilbert left ringside after receiving Brazil's Coco Butt
Ivan Putski pinned Skandor Akbar at 2:56 with the Polish Hammer

WWWF @ New York City, NY - Madison Square Garden - September 4, 1976
Johnny Rivera defeated Johnny Rodz
SD Jones defeated Davey O'Hannon
Kevin Sullivan fought Jose Gonzalez to a draw
Ivan Putski defeated Doug Gilbert
Nikolai Volkoff defeated Manuel Soto
Rocky Tamayo defeated Ted Adams (sub. for Victor Rivera)
Andre the Giant, Chief Jay Strongbow, & Billy White Wolf defeated Stan Hansen & the Executioners in a Best 3 out of 5 falls match
WWWF World Champion Bruno Sammartino defeated Bruiser Brody via disqualification at 16:19 when the referee caught Brody with his feet on the ropes for leverage during a pin attempt

On Vince McMahon Sr.
"If you met him, he was a gentleman. I used to meet with him once a week to discuss different opponents and different things. We had our differences. Sometimes he'd want me to go wrestle for a promoter I didn't care for. But, overall, we had a very good relationship. I was not a guy that would keep my mouth shut if there was something I believed in."
Bruno Sammartino, *TheHistoryofWWE.com interview, 2009*

WRESTLING

SAT. SEPT. 4 — 8:30

WWWF HEAVYWEIGHT CHAMPIONSHIP

BRUNO SAMMARTINO

vs.

BRUISER BRODY

**6 MAN TAG TEAM MATCH
EXECUTIONEER #1
EXECUTIONEER #2
STAN HANSEN**

vs.

**CHIEF JAY STRONGBOW
BILLY WHITE WOLF
ANDRE THE GIANT**

GILBERT vs. PUTSKI

VOLKOFF vs. SOTO

4 OTHER GOOD BOUTS

Children under 14 not admitted
Proof of age required. Prices $4 to $8

THE GARDEN
Madison Square Garden

Studying the opponent
"What I would try to do different is I would study my opponent if I got to see him wrestle, and I would see what was his style and what was he best at. ...For example, if I wrestled Ray Stevens, you'd get a lot of great wrestling and high spotting and all that kind of stuff. If you wrestled Bruiser Brody, you better go out there and be a pretty darn good brawler because that's what he was best at. And I honestly believe to this day that's one of the reasons I lasted for so many years as a headliner, because people didn't come to The Garden or any other place and predict everything that I was going to be doing that night."
Bruno Sammartino,
TheHistoryofWWE.com interview, 2009

Spotting the stars
"Living in Queens, traveling to Madison Square Garden meant taking a bus and the subway. The E train actually stopped under the building. My father would take me to the matches when I was young, later I would travel with a gang of friends or on rare occasions, a girlfriend that actually liked wrestling. My dad worked at the Post Office across the street. When he was going home, he would sometimes see the wrestlers heading to the Garden. Once, he told me the Valiant Brothers seemed like typical tourists, looking up at the skyscrapers. Another time, thanks to him, I knew the masked Executioners' identities before anyone else. He reported seeing Killer Kowalski and Chuck O'Connor (later John Studd) talking to Lou Albano outside the building."
Steven Blance, *Flushing, NY*

Sept. 10, 1976: ZZ Top performed at MSG for the first time.

WWWF @ New York City, NY - Madison Square Garden - October 4, 1976
Pete Sanchez defeated Johnny Rodz
SD Jones defeated Pete Doherty at 8:30
Jose Gonzalez defeated Tony Altimore at 10:11
Manuel Soto fought Johnny Rivera to a draw
Kevin Sullivan defeated Rocky Tamayo at 6:20
Victor Rivera defeated Doug Gilbert at 8:45
Bobo Brazil defeated Baron Mikel Scicluna at 10:05
Chief Jay Strongbow & Billy Whitewolf defeated the Executioners in a Best 2 out of 3 falls match; fall #1 - Strongbow & White Wolf win via disqualification
Stan Hansen & Nikolai Volkoff defeated Ivan Putski & Gorilla Monsoon via count-out at 7:15
WWWF World Champion Bruno Sammartino pinned Bruiser Brody in a Texas Death match at 14:45

WWWF @ New York City, NY - Madison Square Garden - October 25, 1976
Televised on the MSG Network - included Vince McMahon on commentary:
Manuel Soto pinned Johnny Rodz at 11:45 with a flying bodypress; after the bout, Soto cleared Rodz from the ring
Kevin Sullivan fought Pete Sanchez to a 20-minute time-limit draw
Bobo Brazil pinned Doug Gilbert at 8:04 with the Coco Butt
Tor Kamata pinned Jose Gonzalez at 11:36 with a shoulderblock and kneedrop
Ivan Putski defeated Stan Hansen via disqualification at 6:26 after Hansen crotched Putski on the top rope; Gorilla Monsoon was the guest referee for the bout; Hansen attacked Monsoon after the bout but Monsoon quickly chased him away; the ring announcer mistakingly announced the time as 10:26
Prime Time Wrestling - 4/21/86: WWWF World Champion Bruno Sammartino (w/ Arnold Skaaland) pinned Nikolai Volkoff at 19:44 with a roll up after the challenger hit the corner; prior to the bout, Capt. Lou Albano escorted Volkoff to the ring (*Bruno Sammartino: Wrestling's Living Legend*)
Victor Rivera pinned Baron Mikel Scicluna at 6:15 after using Scicluna's own foreign object against him
Andre the Giant, Chief Jay Strongbow, & Billy White Wolf defeated Bruiser Brody & the Executioners in a Best 3 out of 5 falls match, 3-1 at 20:34; fall #1: Executioner #1 pinned Wolf at 10:50 with a boot to the chest and two kneedrops; fall #2: Wolf pinned Executioner #1 at 2:29 with a double chop; fall #3: Brody & the Executioners were disqualified at 3:10 even though all 6 wrestlers were brawling in the ring at the same time; fall #4: Andre pinned Executioner #2 at 4:05 with a boot to the face and a splash

WWWF @ New York City, NY - Madison Square Garden - November 22, 1976

Televised on the MSG Network - included Vince McMahon on commentary:

Prime Time Wrestling - 5/19/86: Bobo Johnson & Cowboy Colt defeated Billy the Kid & Little John in a Best 2 out of 3 falls match, 2-0; fall #2: Bobo pinned John with a sunset flip

Women's Champion the Fabulous Moolah pinned Joyce Grable at 4:40 by reversing a powerslam attempt into a cradle

Billy White Wolf defeated Baron Mikel Scicluna

Doug Gilbert defeated Pete Sanchez

Victor Rivera defeated Executioner #2

Chief Jay Strongbow defeated Executioner #1 via disqualification

Chavo Guerrero defeated Rocky Tamayo

Ivan Putski defeated Tor Kamata via disqualification

Bobo Brazil fought Bruiser Brody to a 20-minute time-limit draw

Stan Stasiak defeated WWWF World Champion Bruno Sammartino via count-out at 20:44

Prime Time Wrestling - 3/10/86: Stan Hansen fought Gorilla Monsoon to a curfew draw at 4:28

WWWF @ New York City, NY - Madison Square Garden - December 20, 1976

Bobo Brazil defeated Baron Mikel Scicluna

Jose Gonzalez defeated Jack Veneno

Billy White Wolf defeated Rocky Tamayo

Bruiser Brody defeated Manuel Soto

Doug Gilbert defeated SD Jones

Chavo Guerrero defeated Johnny Rodz

Chief Jay Strongbow defeated Nikolai Volkoff

Andre the Giant & Dominic DeNucci defeated the Executioners

Ivan Putski defeated Tor Kamata

WWWF World Champion Bruno Sammartino defeated Stan Stasiak in a Sicilian Stretcher match at 17:12

WWWF @ New York City, NY -
Madison Square Garden - January 17, 1977
Televised on the MSG Network -
featured Vince McMahon on commentary;
Howard Finkel's MSG debut as ring announcer:
Jose Gonzalez fought Pete Sanchez to a draw
Doug Gilbert defeated Don Serrano

North American Champion Pat Patterson pinned Baron Mikel Scicluna with a sunset flip at 11:15; after the bout, Patterson cleared Scicluna from the ring after he had attacked hi from behind (Patterson's MSG debut)
Greg Gagne defeated Johnny Rodz
Tor Kamata & Nikolai Volkoff defeated Dominic DeNucci & Manuel Soto
Ken Patera defeated WWWF World Champion Bruno Sammartino (w/ Arnold Skaaland) via count-out at 19:54 after hitting Bruno with a chair as he was climbing onto the apron after they briefly fought on the floor; prior to the bout, Capt. Lou Albano escorted Patera to the ring and also Larry Zbyszko was introduced to the crowd as Bruno's protege, and that he would be wrestling at MSG on 2/7 against Executioner #1 (Patera's MSG debut)
WWWF Tag Team Champions Chief Jay Strongbow & Billy Whitewolf defeated the Executioners in a Best 2 out of 3 falls match, 2-1; fall #1: Strongbow scored the pin at 5:14 with a double chop to the chest; fall #2: Whitewolf was pinned at 4:55 following a double bodyslam and kneedrop; fall #3: Whitewolf scored the pin at 4:38 after Strongbow hit a shoulderblock, sending the Executioner falling backwards over Whitewolf, who was on his knees behind him
Ivan Putski fought Bruiser Brody to a double disqualification at 6:10 when both men ignored the referee and kept brawling in the corner
Bobo Brazil defeated Stan Stasiak via disqualification at the 5-minute mark when Stasiak refused to stop choking Brazil in the corner; prior to the bout, the Grand Wizard escorted Stasiak to ringside

WWWF @ New York, NY - Madison Square Garden - February 7, 1977
Mil Mascaras defeated Doug Gilbert
Larry Zbyzsko defeated Executioner #1
WWWF Tag Team Champions Chief Jay Strongbow & Billy Whitewolf defeated Nikolai Volkoff & Tor Kamata
Carlos Rocha defeated Moose Monroe
Stan Stasiak defeated Manuel Soto
Jose Gonzalez defeated Baron Mikel Scicluna via disqualification
Johnny Rodz fought Pete Sanchez to a draw
WWWF World Champion Bruno Sammartino fought Ken Patera to a draw in a Texas Death Match after the referee was knocked out

WWWF @ New York City, NY - Madison Square Garden - March 7, 1977
Don Kent fought Jose Gonzalez to a draw
Gino Hernandez defeated Johnny Rodz (Hernandez's only MSG appearance)
Larry Zbyzsko defeated Doug Gilbert
Bobo Brazil defeated Jan Nelson
Carlos Rocha defeated Executioner #2
Ivan Putski defeated Executioner #1
Tony Garea defeated Baron Mikel Scicluna
Dusty Rhodes pinned Rocky Tomayo with the Bionic elbow drop (Rhodes' MSG debut)
WWWF Tag Team Champions Chief Jay Strongbow & Billy Whitewolf defeated Stan Stasiak & Tor Kamata
WWWF World Champion Bruno Sammartino defeated Ken Patera when guest referee Gorilla Monsoon stopped the match due to blood loss

Feb. 5, 1977: Queen performed at MSG for the first time.
Feb. 18, 1977: KISS performed at MSG for the first time.

WWWF @ New York City, NY -
Madison Square Garden - March 28, 1977
Televised on the MSG Network - featured Vince McMahon on commentary
Johnny Rodz fought Jan Nelson to a draw
Jose Gonzalez fought SD Jones to a draw
Carlos Rocha defeated Baron Mikel Scicluna
WWWF Tag Team Champion Chief Jay Strongbow defeated Executioner #2
The Hillbilly Kid & the Haiti Kid defeated Little Johnny & Billy the Kid
WWWF World Champion Bruno Sammartino defeated Baron Von Raschke via disqualification at 17:35 when the challenger brought a steel chair into the ring, as Sammartino had his leg tied in the ring ropes, and hit him with the weapon; prior to the bout, the challenger was escorted to the ring by Freddie Blassie while Sammartino was escorted down by Arnold Skaaland; after the match, Von Raschke applied the claw on the champion, as he was tied in the ropes, and threw down the referee until Tony Garea, Larry Zbyzsko, and another wrestler came out to pull Von Raschke from the ring as Skaaland checked on the champion (*Bruno Sammartino: Wrestling's Living Legend*)
Tony Garea defeated Doug Gilbert
WWWF Tag Team Champion Billy Whitewolf defeated Executioner #1 via disqualification
Championship Wrestling - 9/17/77: Dusty Rhodes pinned Tor Kamata with the Bionic elbow drop
Ivan Putski & Larry Zbyzsko fought Ken Patera & StanStasiak to a draw

WWWF @ New York City, NY -
Madison Square Garden - April 25, 1977
Carlos Rocha defeated Rocky Tomayo
Larry Zbyzsko defeated Baron Mikel Scicluna
WWWF Tag Team Champion Billy Whitewolf defeated Doug Gilbert
Ivan Putski defeated Tor Kamata
Gorilla Monsoon defeated Nikolai Volkoff
WWWF Tag Team Champion Chief Jay Strongbow fought Stan Stasiak to a draw
Ken Patera defeated Tony Garea via count-out
Bob Backlund defeated Executioner #2
WWWF World Champion Bruno Sammartino defeated Baron Von Raschke

Baron Von Raschke backstage at MSG.

99

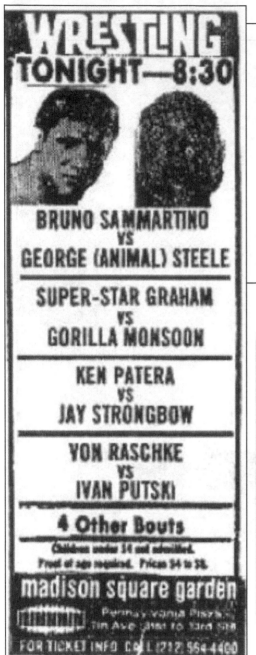

WWWF @ New York City, NY - Madison Square Garden - May 16, 1977
Carlos Rocha defeated Jan Nelson
Ron Mickolajoka defeated Doug Gilbert
Baron Mikel Scicluna fought Ivan Putski to a draw
Ken Patera fought WWWF Tag Team Champion Chief Jay Strongbow to a draw
WWWF Tag Team Champion Billy Whitewolf defeated Rocky Tamoyo
Tony Garea & Larry Zbyzsko defeated Stan Stasiak & Nikolai Volkoff
Bruno Sammartino defeated George Steele when the match was stopped due to blood
WWWF World Champion Superstar Billy Graham (w/ the Grand Wizard) pinned Gorilla Monsoon with a knee drop off the top after repeatedly ramming the challenger into the steel barrier on the floor (*History of the WWF Heavyweight Championship*)

Little advertising for big house

"Back in the 60's and early 70's, the WWWF was only seen on UHF TV, channel 47 in New York. It was the only English program on an all Spanish network. You really had to play with the antenna to get the station in. The upcoming Garden shows were hyped during interview segments between matches. There would also be an ad printed in the Daily News the day of the event, about two inches by four inches. That was basically all the promotion and still the Garden regularly drew crowds over 22,000. During Bruno's second reign, they would actually open the Felt Forum, a smaller arena in the same building and show the matches on closed circuit TV, seating another 5,000 fans."
Steven Blance, *Flushing, NY*

June 7-8, 10-11, 13-14, 1977: Led Zeppelin performed six sold-out concerts. The band reportedly spent no money on advertising and instead relied on street demand.

WWWF @ New York City, NY - Madison Square Garden - June 27, 1977 (22,090; 4,000 in Felt Forum)
Televised on the MSG Network - included Vince McMahon on commentary:
Jose Gonzalez pinned Jan Nelson at 9:46 with a dropkick
Larry Zbyszko pinned Rocky Tamayo with a small package at 7:31
Tony Garea defeated George Steele via disqualification at 7:28 after using a foreign object; after the bout, Steele continued to attack Garea with the object until Garea was able to fight, attack Steele with the object, and clear him from the ring
Andre the Giant & Chief Jay Strongbow defeated Nikolai Volkoff & Ken Patera in a Best 2 out of 3 falls match at 16:25, 2-0; fall #1: Volkoff & Patera were disqualified at 13:46 when Patera hit a knee to Strongbow's back; fall #2: Andre pinned Volkoff at 2:39 with a splash after Patera walked out on his partner
Stan Stasiak pinned Lenny Hurst at 8:21 with the heart punch
WWWF World Champion Superstar Billy Graham fought Bruno Sammartino to a double disqualification at 18:39; prior to the bout, Graham was escorted to the ring by the Grand Wizard while Sammartino was escorted by Arnold Skaaland
Ivan Putski fought Baron Von Raschke to a 30-minute time-limit draw; prior to the bout, Von Raschke was escorted ringside by Freddie Blassie
Peter Maivia pinned Baron Mikel Scicluna at 2:09 (Maivia's MSG debut)
Prof. Toru Tanaka & Mr. Fuji defeated Haystacks Calhoun & Dominic DeNucci in a Best 2 out of 3 falls match; fall #1: Fuji pinned DeNucci at 3:06; fall #2: the bout was stopped due to the curfew; Calhoun was never tagged into the match

WWWF @ New York City, NY - Madison Square Garden - August 1, 1977
Televised on HBO - featured Vince McMahon on commentary:
Prime Time Wrestling - 4/28/86: Prof. Toru Tanaka & Mr. Fuji defeated Jose Gonzalez & Lenny Hurst in a Best 2 out of 3 falls match, 2-0; fall #1: Fuji pinned Gonzalez with a clothesline; fall #2: Tanaka pinned Hurst after applying a cobra clutch and then shoving Hurst to the mat
Carlos Colon pinned Johnny Rodz at 6:50 with a victory roll
Ken Patera defeated Chief Jay Strongbow via count-out at 7:04 after pushing Strongbow over the top rope after breaking Strongbow's sleeper hold; prior to the bout, Capt. Lou Albano escorted Patera to the ring with Strongbow clearing Albano from ringside with his own shoe
Bruno Sammartino (w/ Arnold Skaaland) fought WWWF World Champion Superstar Billy Graham (w/ the Grand Wizard) to a draw at 13:05 when both men were too bloody to continue; Gorilla Monsoon was the special referee for the bout; after the match, Bruno continued to attack the champion, despite Monsoon trying to hold him back (*Grudge Matches*)
Ivan Putski defeated Baron Von Raschke
Peter Maivia pinned Nikolai Volkoff at 16:35 with a roll up
Tony Garea & Larry Zbyzsko defeated George Steele & Stan Stasiak via referee's decision in a Best 2 out of 3 falls match after the match went to curfew; there were no falls in the 29 minutes the match lasted until the curfew with the referee awarding the match to Garea & Zbyszko at the end

Superstar Billy Graham backstage at MSG. Graham regularly drew big houses to The Garden as he fended off challenges from Bruno Sammartino, Dusty Rhodes and Mil Mascaras.

WWWF @ New York City, NY -
Madison Square Garden - August 29, 1977
Televised on the MSG Network and HBO - featured Vince McMahon on commentary:
Lenny Hurst defeated Rocky Tomayo
Johnny Rivera defeated Joe Turco at 10:51
SD Jones defeated Jack Evans at 8:19
Peter Maivia defeated Stan Stasiak at 7:35 via count-out after Maivia avoided the Heart Punch on the floor and Stasiak accidentally hit the ringpost; prior to the bout, Vince McMahon interviewed Maivia on the ring apron
Tony Garea & Larry Zbyzsko defeated George Steele & Baron Mikel Scicluna in a Best 2 out of 3 falls match, 2-0; fall #1: Steele & Scicluna were disqualified after Steele shoved the referee; fall #2: Garea pinned Scicluna with a sunset flip off the top
WWWF World Champion Superstar Billy Graham defeated Ivan Putski via count-out at 18:01 after the challenger was backdropped to the floor; prior to the bout, McMahon interviewed the champion inside the ring; the Grand Wizard escorted the champion to the ring before the match (*20 Years Too Soon: The Superstar Billy Graham Story*)
Bruno Sammartino (w/ Arnold Skaaland) pinned Ken Patera in a Texas Death Match at 12:13 by kicking off the corner, as Patera had a full nelson applied, and falling backwards onto his opponent; prior to the bout, Capt. Lou Albano escorted Patera to the ring (*Bruno Sammartino: Wrestling's Living Legend*)
Verne Gagne pinned Nikolai Volkoff at 7:10 with a roll up as Volkoff attempted an over-the-knee backbreaker
Chief Jay Strongbow fought Mr. Fuji to a curfew draw at around the 6-minute mark; prior to the bout, Freddie Blassie & Prof. Toru Tanaka escorted Fuji to the ring, with Tanaka on crutches and announced as being unable to compete

July 1-4, 1977: Pink Floyd performed at MSG for the first time, with four consecutive sell-out shows.

WWWF @ New York City, NY - Madison Square Garden - September 26, 1977 (22,102, which included 3,000 in Felt Forum)

Televised on the MSG Network - included Vince McMahon on commentary:

Cowboy Lang & the Haiti Kid defeated Little John & Little Tokyo in a Best 2 out of 3 falls match, 2-0; fall #1: Haiti pinned John with a leg roll up at 7:31; fall #2: Lang pinned Tokyo with a roll up at 9:11

Prof. Toru Tanaka pinned Johnny Rivera at 10:09 with a chop to the neck after Rivera missed a dropkick

Baron Mikel Scicluna fought Jack Evans to a double count-out at 7:29 when both men began fighting on the ring apron and Scicluna's arms became stuck in the ropes; after the match, the ring announcer said the match was a double disqualification

Mr. Fuji pinned Lenny Hurst at 6:19 with a clothesline; prior to the bout, Freddie Blassie escorted Fuji to the ring

Bob Backlund pinned Larry Sharpe at 9:04 with the atomic drop; prior to the bout, Vince McMahon conducted an interview with Backlund on the ring apron about his undefeated streak not only at MSG but throughout the country

Dusty Rhodes defeated WWWF World Champion Superstar Billy Graham via count-out at 15:55 after Graham was backdropped over the top to the floor; prior to the bout, Graham was escorted to the ring by the Grand Wizard; after the match, Rhodes celebrated with the title belt and put it around his waist until it was taken away by the referee; after the decision was announced, the crowd chanted "Bullshit" until Rhodes grabbed the mic and said "Superstar, I came a long way to whip your ass. Now come out here, baby!" (*American Dream: The Dusty Rhodes Story*, *WWE's Top 50 Superstars of All Time*)

Peter Maivia defeated George Steele via count-out at 13:19 when Steele's legs became entangled in the ring ropes; after the bout, Maivia cleared Steele from the ring with Steele's own foreign object

Chief Jay Strongbow, Tony Garea, & Larry Zbyszko defeated Ken Patera, Stan Stasiak, & Capt. Lou Albano via in a Best 3 out of 5 falls match; fall #1: Strongbow pinned Stasiak with a double chop to the throat at 10:40; fall #2: Patera pinned Zbyszko with a double axe handle off the top at 5:21; the match then went to the 11 pm curfew as Patera assaulted Zbyszko; following the bell, the referee awarded the contest to Strongbow, Garea, & Zbyszko

The Dream vs. The Superstar

"I'm 9 years old. I'm doing chores around the house to get a little allowance. What did I spend every penny on? Wrestling magazines. If you went into the newsstands back in the day, there were tons of magazines. They were maybe a dollar. Inside Wrestling, The Wrestler, Wrestling World, PWI. I'm reading all about different people, like Dusty Rhodes, Harley Race, Jack Brisco. I remember when 1977 came around, two months in a row was (Superstar Billy) Graham vs. Dusty. I had seen Dusty maybe once on WWWF television. I became a huge Billy Graham fan. When Dusty came out, people went crazy. Billy Graham was the heel, was the champion, but half the building was cheering him."

Charlie Adorno, *Brooklyn, NY*

WWWF @ New York City, NY - Madison Square Garden - October 24, 1977
Televised on the MSG Network - featured Vince McMahon on commentary:
Larry Zbyzsko pinned Johnny Rodz with a small package at 9:29
Tony Garea defeated Baron Mikel Scicluna
Larry Sharpe pinned Johnny Rivera at 10:22 after a suplex
Butcher Vachon defeated Lenny Hurst via submission at 5:59 with the hangman hold; prior to the bout, Capt. Lou Albano escorted Vachon to the ring
Kitty Adams & Leilani Kai defeated Wenona Little Heart & Vivian St. John at 10:43 when Adams pinned Little Heart following a double bodyslam (Kai's MSG debut)
WWWF World Champion Superstar Billy Graham pinned Dusty Rhodes in a Texas Death Match at 9:12 by placing one hand on the challenger's chest after both men collided; prior to the bout, Vince McMahon interviewed Rhodes inside the ring; the Grand Wizard escorted the champion to the ring before the match; after the contest, Rhodes hit three Bionic Elbows on Graham and threw him to the floor, not realizing the match had ended (*20 Years Too Soon: The Superstar Billy Graham Story*)
Mil Mascaras pinned Jack Evans at 8:17 with a flying bodypress off the top
WWWF Tag Team Champions Prof. Toru Tanaka & Mr. Fuji (w/ Freddie Blassie) fought Peter Maivia & Chief Jay Strongbow to a draw in a Best 2 out of 3 falls match at 23:06; fall #1: Maivia pinned Fuji at 18:14 with a headbutt and splash; fall #2: the champions were awarded the fall at 2:08 when the referee stopped the match based on advice of a doctor, saying that Maivia's cut on his forehead was too severe for him to continue; Maivia then went backstage for treatment, and Strongbow worked the third fall by himself; fall #3: the referee stopped the match at 2:44 when Maivia returned to the ring and attacked the champions, with the referee then declaring the match a draw
Ivan Putski defeated Stan Stasiak via count-out at 2:03 when Stasiak left ringside after Putski hit the Polish Hammer knocking Stasiak to the floor

WWWF @ New York City, NY - Madison Square Garden - November 21, 1977 (17,914)
Ken Patera defeated Dewey Robertson at 12:25
Stan Stasiak pinned Dominic DeNucci at 15:16
Baron Mikel Scicluna defeated Johnny Rivera at 10:31
Dusty Rhodes defeated Butcher Vachon at 6:39
Mil Mascaras pinned Larry Sharpe at 11:29
WWWF Tag Team Champions Mr. Fuji & Prof. Toru Tanaka defeated Tony Garea & Larry Zbyzsko
WWWF World Champion Superstar Billy Graham defeated Peter Maivia via count-out

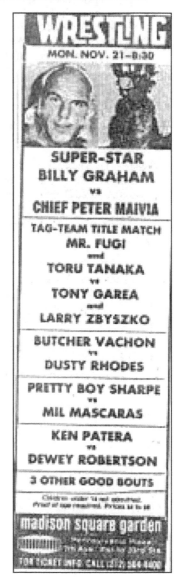

104

Wrestling programs available to purchase at MSG events regularly included this warning to fans about what might happen if they got too wrapped up in the action.

YOUR ATTENTION PLEASE

THROWING OBJECTS AT A SPORTING EVENT IS A COWARDLY ACT, AND ANYONE CAUGHT WILL BE ARRESTED AND PROSECUTED BY THE WRESTLING CLUB. THE THROWING OF ANYTHING, REGARDLESS OF HOW SMALL, CAN INJURE SOMEONE. FANS ARE URGED TO CLAP HANDS, TO HOLLAR, TO CHEER, TO EVEN BOO, BUT NOT TO THROW ANYTHING. PLEASE REMEMBER THIS, FANS, AND RESTRAIN YOURSELVES IN THE FUTURE.

FOR YOUR OWN SAFETY AND PROTECTION PLEASE AVOID PHYSICAL CONTACT WITH THE WRESTLERS. PLEASE REMAIN IN YOUR SEATS AND KEEP THE AISLES CLEAR WHEN THE WRESTLERS ARE WALKING TO AND FROM THE RING. THE POLICE OFFICERS IN ATTENDANCE WILL STRICTLY ENFORCE THIS RULE AND VIOLATORS WILL BE PROSECUTED.

TO INSURE GETTING THE SEAT LOCATION OF YOUR CHOICE WE SUGGEST THAT YOU BUY YOUR WRESTLING TICKETS IN ADVANCE. SEASON TICKET RESERVATIONS CAN BE MADE SO THAT YOU RECEIVE THE SAME CHOICE LOCATION FOR EVERY WRESTLING CARD. CONTACT YOUR BOX OFFICE OR ADVANCE TICKET OUTLET FOR COMPLETE DETAILS.

LUCHA LIBRE

MON. DEC. 19 - 8:30

**SUPER-STAR
BILLY GRAHAM
VS
MIL MASCARAS**

**MR FUJI
VS
BOB BACKLUND**

**STAN STASIAK
VS
DUSTY RHODES**

**5 OTHER GREAT BOUTS
PLUS
BATTLE OF THE MANAGERS
CAPT LOU ALBANO
VS
ARNOLD SKAALAND**

Children under 14 not admitted. Proof of age required. Prices $4-$8

madison square garden

FOR TICKET INFO CALL (212) 564-4400

WWWF @ New York City, NY - Madison Square Garden - December 19, 1977 (22,085)

Televised on the MSG Network - featured Vince McMahon on commentary; Debra Harry of Blondie and Andy Kauffman were in attendance for the card; the scheduled bout between Peter Maivia and Ken Patera was canceled

Baron Mikel Scicluna fought SD Jones to a 15-minute time-limit draw at 14:49; the match ended as Scicluna stomped Jones against the ropes; after the bout, Jones landed several headbutts until Scicluna backed away

Dominic DeNucci fought the Golden Terror to a double count-out; the match was not televised; instead, footage of NWA World Champion Harley Race vs. Rick Martel in Australia aired in its place; prior to Race vs. Martel, there was an introduction from Sydney, Australia; Race pinned Martel at 5:13 with a delayed suplex

Butcher Vachon pinned Johnny Rivera (sub. for Victor Rivera) at 6:04 with a double stomp after avoiding a dropkick; prior to the bout, Howard Finkel said Rivera could not appear due to transportation issues

Arnold Skaaland defeated Lou Albano via count-out at 4:35 when Albano walked out of the match after losing his foreign object and being bloodied by Skaaland (*Best of the WWF Vol. 7, The World's Greatest Wrestling Managers*)

Bob Backlund pinned WWWF Tag Team Champion Mr. Fuji (w/ Freddie Blassie) with the atomic drop at 11:40; prior to the match, the referee had to force Blassie to leave the ring, but Blassie remained ringside for the bout

Mil Mascaras (w/ Bob Backlund) defeated WWWF World Champion Superstar Billy Graham (w/ the Grand Wizard) via referee's decision at 16:24 when referee John Stanley stopped the match due to a cut on the champion's forehead; following the ring introductions, Howard Finkel announced that the Grand Wizard would be allowed ringside as long as he didn't interfere; moments later, Mascaras left ringside and returned with Backlund to be in his corner; the bell rang just before Mascaras made a cover after ramming Graham's bloody head into the turnbuckle

Dusty Rhodes pinned Stan Stasiak with the Bionic elbow at 11:22 (*American Dream: The Dusty Rhodes Story*)

Prime Time Wrestling - 3/17/86: Chief Jay Strongbow defeated WWWF Tag Team Champion Prof. Toru Tanaka via disqualification at 11:23 after Tanaka threw salt into the referee John Stanley's eyes as Strongbow had the sleeper applied; after the bout, Strongbow went to reapply the hold before Tanaka escaped from the ring

Tony Garea & Larry Zbyzsko defeated Larry Sharpe & Jack Evans in a Best 2 out of 3 falls match, 1-0; fall #1: Zbyzsko pinned Evans with a kneedrop at 7:45; fall #2: the curfew ended the match at 12:39; the match ended as Garea and Evans traded punches

> ### Meeting Andy Kaufman
> "I wound up introducing Andy to Jerry Lawler. And it was backstage at The Garden where Andy and I became friends."
> **Bill Apter,** *TheHistoryofWWE.com interview, 2014*

106

WWWF @ New York City, NY - Madison Square Garden - January 23, 1978
Dusty Rhodes defeated the Golden Terror
Carlos Colon defeated Jack Evans at 1:51
Butcher Vachon fought SD Jones to a 20-minute draw
Steve Kiern defeated Larry Sharpe at 4:58
Spiros Arion defeated Dominic DeNucci via count-out at 11:06
Ken Patera defeated Chief Jay Strongbow via count-out at 5:26
Bob Backlund, Peter Maivia, Tony Garea, & Larry Zbyszko defeated WWWF Tag Team Champions Prof. Toru Tanaka & Mr. Fuji, Stan Stasiak, & Baron Mikel Scicluna in an elimination match; Backlund defeated Fuji and Tanaka to win the bout
Televised in Japan: Tatsumi Fujinami pinned WWWF Jr. Heavyweight Champion Jose Estrada to win the title at 11:31 with a Dragon suplex into a bridge; after the bout, Fujinami was interviewed in the ring by the Japanese TV announcer
WWWF World Champion Superstar Billy Graham (w/ the Grand Wizard) defeated Mil Mascaras (w/ Bob Backlund) via disqualification at 13:19 when Backlund and the champion began brawling after Backlund twice prevented Graham from getting the pin with his feet on the ropes

WWWF @ New York City, NY - Madison Square Garden - February 20, 1978 (22,092; sell out)
Televised on the MSG Network - featured Vince McMahon on commentary; the first MSG show to allow children under 14 to attend; children ages 8 to 14 were admitted with an adult
SD Jones defeated Baron Mikel Scicluna via disqualification at 13:04 after continually kicking Jones when he was caught on the ring apron and not allowing him back in the ring
Spiros Arion defeated Chief Jay Strongbow via referee's decision at 1:49 after Arion attacked Strongbow's bandaged right knee and the referee deemed Strongbow unable to continue
Dusty Rhodes pinned WWWF Tag Team Champion Prof. Toru Tanaka at 8:09 with the Bionic elbow drop
Ken Patera defeated Peter Maivia via count-out at 13:14 after Patera dumped Maivia over the top rope and was only able to get to the apron before the 10-count
Mil Mascaras pinned WWWF Tag Team Champion Mr. Fuji at 10:05 with a headscissors into a cradle
WWF Jr. Heavyweight Champion Tatsumi Fujinami pinned Ted Adams with a German suplex into a bridge at 15:06 (*Best of the WWF Vol. 15*)
Bob Backlund pinned WWWF World Champion Superstar Billy Graham to win the title at 14:51 with the atomic drop, even though the champion's foot was on the bottom rope during the pinfall; voted Pro Wrestling Illustrated's Match of the Year (*History of the WWF Heavyweight Championship*, *The History of the WWE Heavyweight Championship*)
Wee Willie Wilson & Hillbilly Pete defeated Little John & Billy the Kid in a Best 2 out of 3 falls bout at 11:39; 2-0; fall #1: Pete pinned Kid at 5:15; fall# 2: Wilson pinned John at 6:24
Tony Garea & Larry Zbyszko defeated Butcher Vachon & Stan Stasiak in a Best 2 out of 3 falls bout at 3:39; 2-0; fall #1: Stasiak was disqualified at 2:30 for choking Garea with the ropes; fall #2: Garea pinned Vachon at 1:09

MADISON SQUARE GARDEN

★★
For the WORLD WIDE WRESTLING FEDERATION
HEAVYWEIGHT CHAMPIONSHIP BELT

SUPERSTAR BILLY GRAHAM	vs.	**BOB BACKLUND**
Paradise Valley, Arizona		Princeton, Minnesota
"Challenger"		"Champion"

★★
SPECIAL SIX MAN TAG TEAM MATCH — Two Out Of Three Falls

MR. FUJI		**DUSTY RHODES**
Japan		Texas
and		and
TORU TANAKA	vs.	**MIL MASCARAS**
Japan		Mexico
and		and
KEN PATERA		**ANDRE THE GIANT**
Portland, Oregon		Paris, France

★★
SPIROS ARION	vs.	**TONY GAREA**
Greece		New Zealand

★★
BUTCHER VACHON	vs.	**CHIEF PETER MAIVIA**
Montreal		Samoa

★★
STAN STASIAK	vs.	**LARRY ZBYSZKO**
Buzzard Creek, Oregon		Pittsburgh

★★

★★★★★★★★★★★★★★★★★★★★★★★★★★★★★★★★★★★★★★
THE NEXT SPECTACULAR
MADISON SQUARE GARDEN
WRESTLING CARD WILL BE ON
MONDAY, APRIL 24TH, 1978
AT 8:30 P.M.
★★★★★★★★★★★★★★★★★★★★★★★★★★★★★★★★★★★★★★

 madison square garden
Pennsylvania Plaza, 7th Ave., 31st to 33rd Sts.

VINCE McMAHON, PROMOTER
MONDAY, MARCH 20TH, 1978
square garden
W.W.W.F. CHAMPIONSHIP
WRESTLING
SANCTIONED BY THE WORLD WIDE WRESTLING FEDERATION
Willie Gilzenberg, President
AL PROGRAM
PRICE: $1.00

The Box Office at Madison Square Garden is open daily, from 10 to 8.

WWWF @ New York City, NY - Madison Square Garden - March 20, 1978
Dick Slater pinned Baron Mikel Scicluna
Steve Keirn & Mike Graham defeated Butcher Vachon & the Golden Terror via disqualification
Spiros Arion pinned Larry Zbyszko
Peter Maivia pinned Stan Stasiak
Superstar Billy Graham defeated WWWF World Champion Bob Backlund at 18:31 when the match was stopped due to cuts over the champion's left eye
Seiji Sakaguchi defeated Wilhelm Ruska via disqualification in a judo match
WWWF Jr. Heavyweight Champion Tatsumi Fujinami pinned Frank Rodriguez
Dusty Rhodes, Mil Mascaras, & Andre the Giant defeated Mr. Fuji, Prof. Toru Tanaka, & Ken Patera in a Best 2 out of 3 falls match

108

WWWF @ New York City, NY - Madison Square Garden - April 24, 1978
Televised on the MSG Network - featured Vince McMahon on commentary:
Strong Kobayashi pinned Steve King at 5:07 with a back suplex
Luke Graham pinned SD Jones at 8:11 with a thumb to the throat
Spiros Arion fought Dusty Rhodes to a 20-minute time-limit draw at 19:17; Freddie Blassie escorted Arion to the ring before the match, then returned backstage
Ken Patera defeated Larry Zbyszko via submission with the full nelson at 12:45
WWWF Tag Team Champions Dino Bravo & Dominic DeNucci defeated Stan Stasiak & Johnny Rodz at 11:31 in a Best 2 out of 3 falls bout; 2-0; fall #1: the champions won via disqualification after Stasiak was caught choking Bravo with the tag rope; fall #2: Bravo pinnd Rodz following a double dropkick
Shown on Japanese TV: WWWF World Champion Bob Backlund defeated Superstar Billy Graham in a steel cage match at 14:28 by escaping through the door after the challenger's foot became entagled in the cage
Mil Mascaras pinned the Golden Terror at 6:18 with a flying bodypress; after the bout, Mascaras unmasked Terror, who was actually Davey O'Hannon
Peter Maivia pinned Butcher Vachon at 2:54

WWWF @ New York City, NY - Madison Square Garden - May 22, 1978
SD Jones pinned Strong Kobayashi at 8:55
Luke Graham pinned Tank Patton at 8:47 after using a foreign object
Spiros Arion pinned Peter Maivia at 12:46 after Maivia charged into the turnbuckle when Arion moved out of the way
The Yukon Lumberjacks defeated Larry Zbyszko & Haystacks Calhoun in a Best 2 out of 3 falls match at 24:07; 2-1; fall #1: Zbyszko pinned Pierre at 14:02 with a rollover cradle; fall #2: Calhoun was counted out at 6:20 after being knocked to the floor; fall #3: Pierre pinned Zbyszko at 3:45 after Eric tripped Zbyszko from the outside as he had Pierre up for a powerslam
Superstar Billy Graham fought Gorilla Monsoon (sub. for Dusty Rhodes) to a double count-out at 8:47 after Monsoon had hit an airplane spin on Graham he fell out of the ring to the floor with Graham following him out when he had recovered
WWWF World Champion Bob Backlund pinned Ken Patera at 21:06 with an inside cradle

Mil Mascaras pinned Stan Stasiak at 8:07 after Mascaras blocked a bodyslam attempt and fell on top for the pin
WWWF Tag Team Champions Dino Bravo & Dominic DeNucci defeated Florida Tag Team Champions Mr. Sato & Mr. Saito in a Best 2 out of 3 falls match at 8:40, 2-0; fall #1: Sato & Saito were disqualified for double-teaming DeNucci; fall #2: Bravo pinned Sato after Saito accidentally hit his own partner when Bravo ducked

WWWF @ New York City, NY - Madison Square Garden - June 26, 1978
Televised on the MSG Network - featured Vince McMahon on commentary:
Chief Jay Strongbow pinned Baron Mikel Scicluna at 9:15 with a tomahawk chop
George Steele pinned Tony Garea at 5:02 after hitting him with a foreign object
The Yukon Lumberjacks defeated WWWF Tag Team Champions Dino Bravo & Dominic DeNucci to win the titles at 15:21 when Pierre pinned DeNucci following a double chop behind the referee's back (*Tag Team Champions*)
Stan Stasiak pinned SD Jones at 10:21 with the heart punch
Championship Wrestling - 6/6/81: WWWF World Champion Bob Backlund pinned Spiros Arion at 19:24 with the atomic kneedrop
Andre the Giant & Ivan Putski (& Dusty Rhodes) defeated Luke & Superstar Billy Graham in a Best 2 out of 3 falls match at 16:15, 2-1; fall #1: the Graham's were disqualified at 9:40 for double-teaming Putski; fall# 2: the Grahams were awarded the fall at 5:11 after Putski was deemed unable to continue after ramming his head in the ring post; fall #3: Andre was given permission to find a replacement partner for the final fall and brought out Dusty Rhodes which led to Andre pinning Luke at 1:24; after the bout, Rhodes challenged Superstar Billy Graham to a match which was confirmed for next month later in the card
Jack Brisco pinned Butcher Vachon at 4:29 with a sunset flip
Mil Mascaras fought Ken Patera to a curfew draw

WWWF @ New York City, NY - Madison Square Garden - July 24, 1978
Baron Mikel Scicluna pinned Tony Russo at 8:39 with a boot to the face
Luke Graham defeated Dominic DeNucci via count-out at 11:14 after both collided mid-ring with DeNucci falling to the outside
Jack Brisco pinned Stan Stasiak at 9:02 with a victory roll
Superstar Billy Graham defeated Dusty Rhodes via disqualification at 6:10 when Rhodes struck the referee
Dino Bravo pinned Butcher Vachon at 4:01 with an airplane spin
WWWF World Champion Bob Backlund pinned George Steele at 7:21 after ramming Steele throat first into the corner
Tony Garea fought Victor Rivera to a 20-minute time-limit draw
Ivan Putski defeated Spiros Arion via disqualification at 11:15 after Arion choked Putski with the top rope
WWWF Tag Team Champions the Yukon Lumberjacks defeated SD Jones & Gorilla Monsoon at 7:28 when Pierre pinned Jones after Eric tripped him from the outside

WWWF @ New York City, NY - Madison Square Garden - August 28, 1978 (announced at 22,000 with 4,000 at Felt Forum)
Televised on the MSG Network - featured Vince McMahon on commentary; included a look at how pro wrestlers were raising money for the Juvenile Diabetes Foundation:
Stan Stasiak fought Dominic DeNucci to a 20-minute time-limit draw at 19:48; the match ended just as DeNucci knocked Stasiak to the mat with a flurry of jabs
Haystacks Calhoun pinned Baron Mikel Scicluna at 7:12 with a splash, even though Scicluna clearly kicked out before the 3-count
Victor Rivera pinned SD Jones at 10:21 with a suplex after Jones ran shoulder-first into the ring post when Rivera moved out of the way; prior to the bout, Freddie Blassie escorted Rivera to the ring
Ivan Koloff defeated WWWF World Champion Bob Backlund via referee's decision at 30:11 when the referee deemed Backlund unable to continue due to facial cuts; prior to the bout, Backlund was escorted to the ring by Arnold Skaaland while Capt. Lou Albano came out with the challenger; after the bout, Backlund hit the atomic drop, which sent the challenger out of the ring, and then got on the microphone to challenge him to come back out, which Koloff failed to do
Prime Time Wrestling - 4/8/86: Peter Maivia defeated Luke Graham via disqualification at 14:02 after Graham continuously punched Maivia in the throat; during the bout, bodybuilder Dan Lurie briefly joined Vince McMahon on commentary, discussed the Sept. 9 Lincoln Center bodybuilding competitions, and said Ivan Putski would be inducted into the hall of fame; after the contest, Maivia attacked Graham and knocked him to the floor
Dusty Rhodes defeated Superstar Billy Graham in a No DQ bullrope match at 6:28 via count-out after Rhodes hit Graham with the cowbell knocking him to the floor; Chief Jay Strongbow was the special referee for the bout and gave Graham a fast 8-count after he fell outside the ring; the stipulations for the bout said the wrestlers had an 8-count to return to the ring instead of the usual 10 or 20; prior to the match, Graham was escorted to the ring by the Grand Wizard (*American Dream: The Dusty Rhodes Story*)
Women's Champion the Fabulous Moolah pinned Vicki Williams at 5:20 after reversing a monkey flip into a roll up
Andre the Giant, Tony Garea, & Dino Bravo defeated Spiros Arion, WWWF Tag Team Champions the Yukon Lumberjacks in a Best 2 out of 3 falls match, 2-0, at 6:14; fall #1: Arion & the Lumberjacks were disqualified at 2:52 for illegally triple teaming Garea in their corner; fall #2: Andre pinned Pierre with a boot to the face and a splash at 3:22 (*Best of the WWF Vol. 14*)

WWWF @ New York City, NY - Madison Square Garden - September 25, 1978
Stan Stasiak pinned Baron Mikel Scicluna at 10:21
Victor Rivera pinned Larry Zbyszko at 6:28 after Rivera blocked a powerslam attempt by grabbing the top rope and caused himself to fall on top for the pin
Luke Graham defeated Dominic DeNucci via count-out at 8:10 after a collision mid-ring caused DeNucci to fall out to the floor
Crusher Blackwell pinned SD Jones at 9:11 with a powerslam
Dino Bravo defeated WWWF Tag Team Champion Pierre the Lumberjack via count-out at 8:49 after a dropkick knocked Pierre out to the floor
Superstar Billy Graham pinned Chief Jay Strongbow at 4:01 with an elbow drop even though Strongbow put his foot on the ropes at the 2-count which was not seen by the referee
WWWF World Champion Bob Backlund pinned Ivan Koloff at 17:09 with the atomic kneedrop
Dusty Rhodes pinned WWWF Tag Team Champion Eric the Lumberjack at 5:18 with a shoulderblock
Coconut Willie & Cowboy Lang defeated Billy the Kid & Little Tokyo at 5:11 when Willie pinned Kid
Peter Maivia pinned Butcher Vachon at 1:03
Spiros Arion fought Tony Garea to a curfew draw

Fast talking into a job

"I was a huge fan of the product. On Sunday, my parents would go to the lower east side of Manhattan because my Mother likes to shop there and my Father and I would bum around before we picked up my Mother. One of the things my Father liked to do was we would pick up these radical lower New York free newspapers with their own social agenda, because their writing was always very passionate. Whether we agreed with their politics or not doesn't matter, you would find great emotions in the writing. In one of these papers was a sports column and it was more of a sports gossip column and the writer mentioned that after Madison Square Garden, Vincent J. McMahon would take his inner circle to lunch at Ben Benson's Steakhouse in midtown Manhattan. Now I don't know the readership of this article, so I don't know if a lot of old WWWF fans got to see this, so I figured this was some inside information. I found out that the office was at the Cape Cod Coliseum which was owned by Vincent J. McMahon, so I called and said 'My name is Paul Heyman. I was told to call by Vince McMahon to get my press pass for Madison Square Garden'. I'm put through three or four assistants until I got patched through to Vincent J. McMahon. I said, 'This is Paul Heyman from the Wrestling Times,' because we have The New York Times. I said, 'I was talking to you at Ben Benson's and you said to call you about a press pass at Madison Square Garden.' He said, 'I did?!' I said, 'Yeah, you did.' Because who else would know he dines at Ben Benson's and who would tell him that he was in a radical newspaper in the lower east side of New York with a readership of a couple hundred, so I must have been real. He said 'Go to the Holland Hotel at 42nd St. and 8th Ave. and talk to Gorilla Monsoon and Arnold Skaaland and I look forward to seeing you at the Garden.' I got a ride down to the Holland Hotel and I saw Monsoon and Skaaland playing pinochle with a bottle of booze. I got my press pass, BS'd my way into Madison Square Garden with my press pass and got in Vince Sr.'s good graces by snapping some photos with him and Andre the Giant and bringing him some 8x10s the next month. For the rest of the time he was in charge, I would bring pictures they could use in their programs or on posters and they would give me $50 for my transportation and trouble. I've always found that honesty is dramatically overrated."

Paul Heyman, *Busted Open Nation, 2014*

Superstar Billy Graham on facing Bruno Sammartino

"Can't believe it. It's actually true. Actually a fact of life, this match. After laying dormant for some time, Bruno Sammartino stepping back in to the limelight. And I'm curious, just like the rest of the world - and I know you're (Vince McMahon) curious, has this man lost anything? Most of all, has he lost his power? We know when a man gets older, he loses speed. But has he lost brute, physical strength? That will be the test on this night. It will not be for a belt, that's up to Bob Backlund and Ernie Ladd to decide the belt. This will be a match of pride. Who is the better man? Who is the better human being?"

WWWF World Champion Bob Backlund on facing Ernie Ladd

"There's a lot of people interested in the match. They talked to me about it on the way home and I'm excited about it, too. It's my pleasure to wrestle the man. He's a big man. I know I'm going to have my hands full. I know he and the Grand Wizard think that he has this belt wrapped around his waist. Well, Ladd, I've worked for this belt since I was 10 years old. I've worked all the way through high school, all the way through college. And now I'm a professional wrestler, now I'm the champion. I'm very proud of this belt. You're going to have to something very desperate to win this, because I'll do anything to keep it. I'm going to wrestle you hard and wrestle you strong and wrestle you any way I can to keep it."

WWWF @ New York City, NY - Madison Square Garden - October 23, 1978 (announced at 22,000)
Televised on the MSG Network - featured Vince McMahon on commentary; included Howard Finkel promoting the weekly WWWF TV airing in the New York City market; featured McMahon hosting an in-ring presentation where Gorilla Monsoon presented a check to the President of the Juvenile Diabetes Foundation of $17,005.89 which had been raised by the WWWF; included an in-ring segment in which Finkel promoted the Nov. 20 show with Luke Graham vs. Mike Paidousis, Tony Russo vs. Roddy Piper, Spiros Arion vs. SD Jones, Victor Rivera vs. Chief Jay Strongbow, Dominic DeNucci vs. Crusher Blackwell, WWWF Tag Team Champions the Yukon Lumberjacks & Ivan Koloff vs. Tony Garea, Larry Zbyszko, & Gorilla Monsoon in a Best 2 out of 3 falls match, Superstar Billy Graham vs. Dino Bravo, WWWF World Champion Bob Backlund vs. Peter Maivia, and Ernie Ladd vs. Andre the Giant; following the announcements, McMahon said the show would not air on TV and could only be seen live:
Johnny Rodz pinned Del Adams (Jim Ray) at 9:39 with a double underhook suplex after Adams missed a running shoulderblock into the turnbuckle
Baron Mikel Scicluna fought SD Jones to a 20-minute time-limit draw; the match ended just after Jones kicked out of a pin attempt; after the contest, the two continued to fight before the referee intervened
WWWF Tag Team Champions the Yukon Lumberjacks defeated Peter Maivia & Chief Jay Strongbow when Eric pinned Strongbow with a boot to the chest at 3:57; Maivia was booed upon his entrance to the ring; Strongbow and Maivia argued throughout the contest; Maivia was never legally in the match and there was no physicality until Maivia attacked his partner and left ringside
Crusher Blackwell pinned Tony Russo with a bodyslam and splash off the bottom rope at 4:39
WWF World Champion Bob Backlund pinned Ernie Ladd with the atomic drop at 17:24 after the challenger failed a splash; prior to the bout, the champion was escorted ringside by Arnold Skaaland while Ladd was escorted by the Grand Wizard
Larry Zbyszko defeated Spiros Arion via disqualification at 6:12 after Arion ignored the referee's instructions to stop ramming Zbyszko's head into the turnbuckle; prior to the bout, Freddie Blassie escorted Arion to the ring
Bruno Sammartino defeated Superstar Billy Graham when the referee stopped the match due to Graham bleeding from the face at 12:19 after repeated punches and kicks to the head from Sammartino; late in the match, Sammartino went to cover Graham but sat up at 2, opting to continue to punish his opponent instead of gain the pinfall (Sammartino's MSG return after a 14-month absence)
Ivan Koloff pinned Tony Garea at 2:39 with a roll over and grabbing the tights for leverage
Victor Rivera pinned Dominic DeNucci at 4:11 after kicking off the turnbuckle and falling back on DeNucci as DeNucci attempted a full nelson
Dino Bravo pinned Luke Graham at 3:46 with a dropkick that sent Graham into the corner after Graham thought he won the match

Andre the Giant straps the title belt on Bob Backlund at MSG.

WWWF @ New York City, NY - Madison Square Garden - November 20, 1978
Jose Estrada (sub. for Roddy Piper) pinned Tony Russo at 9:48 with a legdrop
Luke Graham pinned Mike Paidousis at 11:15 after using a foreign object
WWWF Tag Team Champions the Yukon Lumberjacks & Ivan Koloff defeated Tony Garea, Larry Zbyszko, & Gorilla Monsoon in a Best 2 out of 3 falls match at 23:26; fall #1: Zbyszko pinned Lumberjack Pierre at 11:20 with a roll over; fall #2: Lumberjack Eric pinned Garea at 7:39 with a running knee; fall #3: Koloff pinned Zbyszko at 4:27 with a kneedrop off the top
Spiros Arion pinned SD Jones at 5:31 with a boot to the chest
Dino Bravo fought Superstar Billy Graham to a double disqualification at 12:11 after both men shoved the referee down
Peter Maivia defeated WWWF World Champion Bob Backlund via count-out at 9:18 after the champion received a headbutt on the floor
Andre the Giant pinned Ernie Ladd at 7:45 with a splash after Ladd failed a powerslam attempt
Crusher Blackwell pinned Dominic DeNucci at 12:16 with a splash from the bottom turnbuckle
Victor Rivera fought Chief Jay Strongbow to a curfew draw

WWWF @ New York City, NY - Madison Square Garden - December 18, 1978
Televised on the MSG Network - included Vince McMahon on commentary:
SD Jones defeated Crusher Blackwell via disqualification at 7:09 when Blackwell began choking Jones across the bottom rope
Chief Jay Strongbow fought Spiros Arion to a 20-minute time-limit draw
WWWF Martial Arts Champion Antonio Inoki pinned Texas Red (Red Bastien) at 16:27 with a German suplex
NWA World Champion Harley Race pinned WWWF Tag Team Champion Tony Garea at 8:57 with a suplex
WWWF World Champion Bob Backlund fought Peter Maivia to a double count-out at 21:45
Ernie Ladd pinned WWWF Tag Team Champion Larry Zbyszko at 3:47 with a legdrop
WWWF Jr. Heavyweight Champion Tatsumi Fujinami pinned Jose Estrada at 10:59 with a German suplex
Johnny Rodz defeated Tony Russo
Ivan Koloff, Victor Rivera, & Lumberjack Pierre defeated Dino Bravo, Dominic DeNucci, & Dusty Rhodes at 5:54 when Koloff pinned DeNucci

NWA World Champion Harley Race backstage at MSG. Race made a handful of appearances at Madison Square Garden as NWA World Champion before returning under 'The King' gimmick in the mid 1980s.

Jan. 7, 1979: The Grateful Dead played their first of 52 performances at MSG.

This special advertising publication in 1979 noted 100 years of Madison Square Garden, throughout its various venue locations.

MADISON SQUARE GARDEN

AT THE HUB OF
THE METROPOLITAN AREA'S
MASS TRANSIT SYSTEM — EASY TO GET TO
FROM ANY DIRECTION...BY ANY MEANS.

SUBWAY

IRT - Seventh Ave. at 34th St. - 1-2-3
IND - Eighth Ave. at 34th St. - A-AA-CC-E
IND - Sixth Ave. at 34th St. - B-D-F
BMT - Sixth Ave. at 34th St. - N-RR-QB

RAILROAD

Long Island Railroad - Penn Station
Amtrak - Penn Station
PATH - Sixth Ave. at 34th St.

N.Y.C. BUSES

Seventh Ave. (downtown) - 10
Eighth Ave. (uptown) - 10
Sixth Ave. (uptown) - 5-6-7
Ninth Ave. (downtown) - 11
Thirty-fourth St. (crosstown) - 16

Port Authority Bus Terminal serving New York,
New Jersey & Connecticut is just eight blocks north
at 41st St. & Eighth Ave.

TAXI

Stands on Seventh Ave., Eighth Ave.,
Penn Station underpass

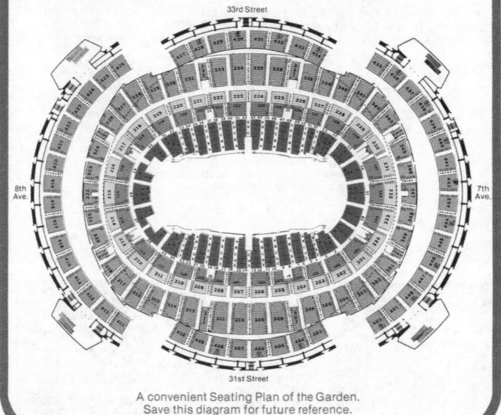

A convenient Seating Plan of the Garden.
Save this diagram for future reference.

PARKING & DINING GUIDE TO MADISON SQUARE GARDEN

100 ... **100**

SOME OF THE CONVENIENT PARKING LOCATIONS IN THE GARDEN NEIGHBORHOOD
● See Map For Locations ●

A- **PARK/FAST**
9th Ave. & 35th St.

B- **PARK/FAST**
9th Ave. & 34th St.

C- **PARK/FAST**
9th Ave. & 33rd St.

D- **PARK/FAST**
440 W. 33rd St., bet. 9th & 10th Aves.

E- **PARK/FAST**
28th-29th St., bet 7th & 8th Aves.

F- **KINNEY**
114 W. 31st St., bet. 6th & 7th Aves.

G- **PARK/FAST**
433 W. 33rd St., bet. 9th & 10th Aves.

H- **MEYERS PARK 'N LOCK**
225 W. 30th St. & 220 W. 31st St.

I- **1 PENN PLAZA PARKING**
33rd St.,bet 7th & 8th Aves.

J- **SHARON'S GARAGE INC.**
148 W. 31st St., bet. 6th & 7th Aves.

K- **SYLVAN WEST PARKING**
406 8th Ave.,bet. 30th & 31st Sts.

L- **TERM W. 31 GARAGE**
340 W. 31st St.,bet. 8th & 9th Aves.

M- **SQUARE PARKING**
839 6th Ave. - 30th St.

N- **SQUARE PARKING**
425 W. 31st St.,bet. 9th & 10th Aves.

O- **SQUARE PARKING**
308 W. 31st St. - 8th Ave.

P- **EXHIBITION PARKING**
305 W. 33rd St., bet. 8th & 9th Aves.

Q- **LISA PARKING** 313 W. 33rd St. bet. 8th & 9th Aves.

BEFORE OR AFTER THE GARDEN YOU CAN ENJOY THESE RESTAURANTS IN THE AREA
● See Map For Locations ●

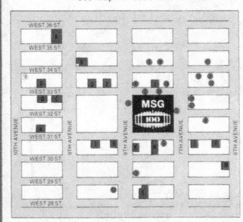

1- **FAN CLUB RESTAURANTS**
Madison Square Garden,
8th Fl. of Arena

2- **CHARLEY O'S**
33rd St. at the Garden, 947-0222

3- **CLUBHOUSE**
225 W. 34th St., 736-0404

4- **DINO & HENRY'S**
132 W. 32nd St., 695-7995

5- **ESTORIL SOL**
382 8th Ave. & 29th St., 947-1043

6- **GOOD OLD DAYS**
33rd St. & 8th Ave., 695-8276

7- **IRON HORSE RESTAURANT & BAR**
Penn Station, 298-1267

8- **PADDY'S CLAM HOUSE**
215 W. 34th St., 244-9123

KOUKLA
9- 220 W. 31st St.,bet. 7th & 8th Aves., 594-7108

10- **MC ANN'S RESTAURANT & BAR**
157 W. 33rd St., 594-1210

11- **NEW HANKOW**
132 W. 34th St., 695-4972

12- **P J CLARKE'S AT MACY'S**
135 W. 34th St., 564-5690

13- **SAN REMO WEST**
393 8th Ave. & 29th St., 564-1819

14- **STEER PALACE**
2 Penn Plaza at the Garden, 947-3060

15- **TAD'S STEAKS**
154 W. 34th St., 244-4085

16- **TOOTS SHOR**
233 W. 33rd St.,bet. 7th & 8th Aves., 279-8150

17- **BREW BURGER**
7th Ave. & 32nd St.

18- **FORO ITALICO**
455 W. 34th St., 564-6619

19- **HAYMARKET**
Statler Hilton Hotel, 7th Ave. & 32nd St., 736-5000

OTHER RESTAURANTS IN THE AREA

ACT 1
1 Times Square, 695-1880

ALGONQUIN
59 W. 44th St., 840-6800

BEEFSTEAK CHARLIE'S
221 W. 46th St., 265-0480

CAFE COCO
555 7th Ave. & 39th St., 354-0210

CHEERS
120 W. 41st St., 840-8811

GALLAGHER'S STEAK HOUSE
228 W. 52nd St.,bet. B'way & 8th Ave., 245-5336

GIORDANO
409 W. 39th St.,bet. 9th & 10th Aves., 947-3883

JOE'S PIER 52
144 W. 52nd St.,bet. 6th & 7th Aves., 245-6652

LANDMARK TAVERN
626 11th Ave. & 46th St., 757-8595

LINO'S
147 W. 36th St., 695-6444

LONGCHAMPS
1450 B'way & 41st St., 279-7216

LUCHOW'S
110 E. 14th St., 477-4860

MAMMA LEONE'S
239 W. 48th St.,bet. B'way & 8th Ave., 586-5151

MANUCHE'S
150 W. 52nd St., 582-5483

PAMPLONA
822 Ave. of the Americas,bet. 28th & 29th St., 683-4242

SARDI'S
234 W. 44th St., 221-8440

U.S. STEAKHOUSE
120 W. 51st St., 757-8800

FIRST (Sept. 1, 1976) there was marvelous MEADOWLANDS RACETRACK. It quickly became the Nation's leading harness track, and the only racing plant in the area offering Thoroughbred racing at night.

RIGHT BEHIND (Oct. 10, 1976) came spectacular GIANTS STADIUM. It's home to The Giants of the National Football League and The Cosmos of the North American Soccer League. It is the field on which soccer came of age in the United States.

AND SOON THERE WILL BE 3

MEADOWLANDS ARENA, an incredibly versatile indoor arena, scheduled to open its doors next to Meadowlands Racetrack and Giants Stadium in December, 1980. Three fabulous facilities grouped together at the most convenient* sports and entertainment address in the world...

The New Jersey Meadowlands Sports & Exposition Complex

*More than 18 million sports and entertainment-minded people live, work and play within a one hour drive of the complex, located in the heart of the North Jersey/New York metropolitan area. And millions more visit the region each year. If your event would be at home among that kind of numerous, enthusiastic, appreciative audience, there could be a home for it — indoor or out — at The Meadowlands.

For information on New Jersey Meadowlands facilities – present or future – please direct inquiries to:
General Manager/Stadium and Arena
New Jersey Sports & Exposition Authority • East Rutherford, New Jersey 07073 • (201) 935-8500

The anniversary publication also noted the upcoming opening of the Meadowlands in nearby East Rutherford, NJ. The Meadowlands Arena, now IZOD Center, has its own long history with pro wrestling.

WWWF @ New York City, NY - Madison Square Garden - January 22, 1979
The scheduled match with WWWF Jr. Heavyweight Champion Tatsumi Fujinami vs. Johnny Rodz did not take place as scheduled; this card was not televised
Chief Jay Strongbow (sub. for SD Jones who appeared with a cast on his leg) pinned Baron Mikel Scicluna at 3:26
Roddy Piper pinned Frankie Williams at 12:17 with a neckbreaker (Piper's MSG debut)
Ivan Koloff defeated Ivan Putski via count-out at 17:18 after Koloff knocked him out of the ring after Putski had just woke the referee who had been knocked down just before Putski had hit the Polish Hammer; Dusty Rhodes made the save after the bout
Dusty Rhodes pinned Lumberjack Pierre at 7:02 after missing a kick
WWWF World Champion Bob Backlund defeated Peter Maivia in a steel cage match by escaping the cage at 20:46 by escaping over the top after knocking Maivia off the top of the cage back into the ring as both were fighting up there
Women's Champion the Fabulous Moolah & Suzette Ferrara defeated Joyce Grable & Wenonah Little Heart at 8:04 when Moolah pinned Grable
WWWF Tag Team Champions Tony Garea & Larry Zbyszko defeated Stan Stasiak (sub. for Spiros Arion) & Victor Rivera at 9:49 when Garea pinned Stasiak with a powerslam

'You could cut the energy with a knife'

"I lived in the suburbs. The city in the 70s, early 80s wasn't the nicest place. But once you got to the Garden, there was always a buzz. You could always see the billboard. I remember walking up the first set of steps. I could not tell you the awesome feeling of riding up the escalators to go into the building. Just walking into that place, it became cliche. You could cut the energy with a knife. I've attended basketball games there, I've attended hockey games, but wrestling always had that buzz back then. It wasn't as mainstream as it was now. But you always had sell outs."
Tommy Dreamer, *TheHistoryofWWE.com interview, 2014*

WWWF @ New York City, NY - Madison Square Garden - February 19, 1979
Televised on the MSG Network - included Vince McMahon on commentary; the scheduled match between Chief Jay Strongbow & Dominic DeNucci vs. Johnny & Jimmy Valiant did not take place due to time constraints:
Allen Coage pinned Frankie Williams at 6:38 with a clothesline (Coage's MSG debut)
Ivan Putski defeated Victor Rivera via count-out at 8:45 after Putski backdropped Rivera over the top
WWWF World Champion Bob Backlund (w/ Arnold Skaaland) fought Greg Valentine to a 60-minute time-limit draw at 59:18; after the match, Skaaland saved Backlund from the figure-4 by hitting Valentine with the world title belt (Valentine's MSG return after a 4-year absence)
Steve Travis pinned Baron Mikel Scicluna at 8:50 with an inside cradle (Travis' MSG debut)
WWWF Jr. Heavyweight Champion Tatsumi Fujinami pinned Tony Russo at 5:58 following two dropkicks
WWWF Tag Team Champions Tony Garea & Larry Zbyszko defeated Stan Stasiak & Peter Maivia at 5:52 when Zbyszko pinned Stasiak after Garea dropkicked his partner as he was being held up for a powerslam so he fell on top of Stasiak for the pin
Ivan Putski (sub. for Bruno Sammartino who was snowbound in Pittsburgh and unable to get a flight to New York) fought Ivan Koloff to a curfew draw at around the 7:30 mark; during the bout, Jimmy, Johnny, & Jerry Valiant walked around ringside

VINCE McMAHON, PROMOTER · MONDAY, MARCH 26th, 1979
W.W.F. CHAMPIONSHIP
WRESTLING
SANCTIONED BY THE WORLD WRESTLING FEDERATION
HISASHI SHINMA, PRESIDENT
UNDER SUPERVISION OF THE NEW YORK STATE ATHLETIC COMMISSION
OFFICIAL PROGRAM MAGAZINE #19   **PRICE: $1.00**

W.W.F.
THE WORLD WRESTLING FEDERATION
HISASHI SHINMA, PRESIDENT

W.W.F. HEADQUARTERS
7-13 MINAMI-AOYAMA 6-CHOME
MINATO-KU, TOKYO, JAPAN 107

Fred Curry defeated Victor Rivera via count-out at 6:04 after getting his leg tied in the ropes

Bruno Sammartino defeated Ivan Koloff via count-out at 12:14 after backdropping Koloff over the top rope to the floor; prior to the bout, Howard Finkel introduced WWWF North American Champion Ted DiBiase to the crowd and announced he would be appearing on the 4/30 card

Capt. Lou Albano, WWWF Tag Team Champions Johnny & Jerry Valiant defeated Dusty Rhodes, Larry Zbyszko, & Tony Garea in a Best 2 out of 3 falls match at 18:04; fall #1: Jerry pinned Garea at 12:37 with a clothesline; fall #2: Garea defeated Jerry via submission with an abdominal stretch at 2:08; fall #3: Johnny pinned Zbyzsko at 3:59 with a piledriver

Ivan Putski defeated Peter Maivia via referee's decision at 9:13 when the bout was stopped due to curfew; prior to the bout, Freddie Blassie escorted Maivia to ringside

WWWF @ New York City, NY - Madison Square Garden - March 26, 1979
Televised on the MSG Network - featured Vince McMahon on commentary:
Dominic DeNucci pinned Baron Mikel Scicluna at 4:35 with a backslide
Allen Coage pinned SD Jones at 4:02 with a clothesline
Steve Travis pinned Mike Hall at 5:32 with a boot to the chest
Dick Murdoch pinned Johnny Rodz at 1:20 with a suplex (Murdoch's MSG debut; his last MSG appearance for 5 years)
WWWF World Champion Bob Backlund pinned Greg Valentine in a No Time Limit match at 30:56 with the atomic kneedrop; prior to the bout, Arnold Skaaland and the Grand Wizard escorted their respective wrestlers to ringside

MADISON SQUARE GARDEN		MONDAY, MARCH 26th, 1979
Main Event Return Match For The		
World Wrestling Federation Heavyweight Championship		
GREG VALENTINE	vs.	**BOB BACKLUND**
Seattle, Washington	30:56	Princeton, Minnesota
"Challenger"		"Champion"
No Curfew - No Time Limit - To A Positive Finish		
Main Event		
Battle Of The Former W.W.F. Heavyweight Champions		
IVAN KOLOFF	vs.	**BRUNO SAMMARTINO**
U.S.S.R.	7 12:14	Abruzzi, Italy
"The Russian Bear"		"The Living Legend"
One Fall With A One Hour Time Limit		
Six Man Tag Team Match - Two Out Of Three Falls		
"LUSCIOUS" JOHNNY VALIANT		**TONY GAREA**
New York City	1) 12:37 2) 2:08	New Zealand
and		and
"HANDSOME" JIMMY VALIANT	vs.	**LARRY ZBYSZKO**
New York City	3) 8	Pittsburgh, Pa.
and		and
CAPT. LOU ALBANO	total 18:04	**DUSTY RHODES**
Mount Vernon, New York		Dallas, Texas
CHIEF PETER MAIVIA	vs. won	**IVAN PUTSKI**
Samoa	X	Krakow, Poland
VICTOR RIVERA	count out vs. 6 6:04	**"FLYING" FRED CURRY**
Puerto Rico		Texas
DICK MURDOCH	1:20 vs. 4	**JOHNNY RODZ**
Waxahatchie, Texas		New York City
MIKE HALL	vs. 3 5:32	**STEVE TRAVIS**
Cleveland, Ohio		Charlotesville, Virginia
ALLEN COAGE	4:02 vs. 2	**S. D. JONES**
New Jersey		Philadelphia, Pa.
BARON MIKEL SCICLUNA	vs. 4:35	**DOMENIC DeNUCCI**
Isle Of Malta	1	Italy
FIRST BOUT STARTS AT 8:30 P.M.		

The night's line up page found in the monthly programs often lent itself to a scorecard, with fans noting winners, losers and the time of the match.

122

> **Capt. Lou Albano**
> "This is your master. This is a man that will defeat, in Madison Square Garden, will humiliate, will humble, will hurt, will maim..."
>
> **Bulldog Brower**
> "Backlund, I'm going to get you, Backlund. I want you, Backlund. I'm going to take you apart."
>
> **WWF World Champion Bob Backlund**
> "I was up on the monitor watching that. I'm going to do all I can do to keep the belt around my waist and keep representing all the people out there. ...You can't predict what he's going to do. I'm going to have to fight fire with fire. I'm going to have to go in there and wrestle his type of match."
> *Localized TV promos*

WWF @ New York City, NY - Madison Square Garden - April 30, 1979
This card was not televised
Johnny Rodz pinned Frank Williams at 9:42 with a suplex and elbow drop
Allen Coage pinned Jose Estrada (sub. for Dominic DeNucci) at 4:19 with a clothesline
Roddy Piper pinned Steve King at 9:37 with a neckbreaker
Cowboy Lang & Tiny Thumb defeated Little Tokyo & Butch Cassidy at 14:31 when Lang pinned Tokyo with a reverse roll up
WWF World Champion Bob Backlund pinned Bulldog Brower at 11:08 with the atomic kneedrop
Verne Gagne defeated Mr. X (Jack Evans) via submission with the sleeper at 12:05
Ivan Putski (sub. for Dusty Rhodes) fought Greg Valentine to a 20-minute time-limit draw
NWA World Champion Harley Race pinned Steve Travis at 5:14 with a suplex
Andre the Giant, WWF North American Champion Ted DiBiase, & Dominic DeNucci (sub. for Fred Curry) defeated Jimmy, WWF Tag Team Champions Johnny & Jerry Valiant in a Best 2 out of 3 falls match at 8:32, 2-1; fall #1: DeNucci pinned Jerry at 3:02; Jerry pinned DeNucci at 3:31 with a neckbreaker; fall #3: Andre pinned Jimmy at 1:59 with a boot to the face and a splash

WWF @ New York City, NY - Madison Square Garden - June 4, 1979
Televised on the MSG Network - featured Vince McMahon on commentary:
Tito Santana defeated Jose Estrada (Santana's MSG debut)
Hussein Arab won a 20-man $10,000 battle royal at 8:17 by last eliminating Dominic DeNucci & Jimmy Valiant; other participants included: Gorilla Monsoon, Greg Valentine, Ivan Putski, Haystacks Calhoun, Nikolai Volkoff, Steve Travis, Jose Estrada, Gypsy Rodriguez, SD Jones, Mr. X, Johnny Rodz, Baron Mikel Scicluna, Tito Santana, WWF Tag Team Champions Johnny & Jerry Valiant, Bulldog Brower, & WWF North American Champion Ted DiBiase; order of elimination: Calhoun by several wrestlers; Rodriguez by several wrestlers; Putski by several wrestlers; Volkoff by several wrestlers; Brower by a Valiant; Estrada by Jones; Jones by several wrestlers; Scicluna by Arab; Rodz by Monsoon; Valentine by Johnny & Jerry Valiant; Johnny & Jerry Valiant by DiBiase & Santana with simultaneous dropkicks; DiBiase by Jimmy Valiant; Travis by Arab; Santana by Jimmy Valiant; X by DeNucci; Monsoon eliminated himself after grabbing Jimmy Valiant by the legs and spinning him round with the momentum knocking Monsoon over the top; stipulations stated the winner would earn a WWF World Title match later in the show (the first battle royal held at MSG)
Nikolai Volkoff pinned SD Jones at 6:50 after hoisting him up in a gorilla press slam and dropping him across his knee
Greg Valentine pinned Dominic DeNucci at 9:07 after reversing a monkey flip into a cover; prior to the bout, the Grand Wizard escorted Valentine ringside
Bulldog Brower pinned Mr. X at the 3-minute mark with an elbow drop
WWF World Champion Bob Backlund pinned Hussein Arab at 30:40 with an atomic drop; prior to the bout, Arnold Skaaland & Capt. Lou Albano (sub. for Freddie Blassie) accompanied Backlund and Arab, respectively, to ringside; as Albano went to leave ringside, he went up to Vince McMahon who threw his drink in Albano's face
Ivan Putski pinned Baron Mikel Scicluna at 4:28 after pushing him into the corner
WWF North American Champion Ted DiBiase fought Jimmy Valiant to a 15-minute time-limit draw in a non-title match
WWF Tag Team Champions Johnny & Jerry Valiant defeated Haystacks Calhoun & Steve Travis at 6:25 in a non-title match when Johnny pinned Travis with an elbow to the back off the top as Travis had Jerry in an abdominal stretch

The Curfew

"The matches usually ended before 11 o'clock. There was an antiquated curfew in effect back then, and sometimes matches would have to be stopped and declared a draw. I saw that happen when Ken Patera battled Mil Mascaras. During Hulk Hogan's first run in New York as a heel, he was feuding with Andre the Giant, having bloodied him at Shea Stadium The rematch was held at the Garden with Gorilla Monsoon as the special referee. They entered the ring at about five minutes to 11. I'm thinking the introductions will barely be finished when the curfew will end things. Suddenly the ring announcer declares "For the first time in history, Governor Hugh Carey has waived the 11 o'clock curfew, and this match will go on to a finish." The crowd went nuts."

Steven Blance, *Flushing, NY*

WWF @ New York City, NY - Madison Square Garden - July 2, 1979
This card was not televised
Johnny Rivera fought Mr. X to a time-limit draw
Tito Santana pinned Baron Mikel Scicluna with a cradle
Nikolai Volkoff defeated SD Jones via submission with a bearhug
Greg Valentine defeated Chief Jay Strongbow via count-out at 9:11 after preventing Strongbow from getting back in the ring
Hussein Arab pinned Dominic DeNucci after kicking him with his loaded boot

VINCE McMAHON, PROMOTER   MONDAY, JULY 2nd, 1979

W.W.F. CHAMPIONSHIP
WRESTLING

madison square garden

SANCTIONED BY THE WORLD WRESTLING FEDERATION
HISASHI SHINMA, PRESIDENT
UNDER SUPERVISION OF THE NEW YORK STATE ATHLETIC COMMISSION
OFFICIAL PROGRAM MAGAZINE #22   PRICE: $1.00

THE BOX OFFICE
AT MADISON SQUARE
GARDEN IS OPEN
DAILY FROM 10 to 8

THE CHIEF RETURNS

WWF North American Champion Pat Patterson defeated WWF World Champion Bob Backlund when the match was stopped due to excessive blood loss from the champion at 15:21
Jimmy, WWF Tag Team Champions Jerry & Johnny Valiant defeated Steve Travis, Ted DiBiase, & Haystacks Calhoun in a Best 2 out of 3 falls match, 2-1; fall #1: DiBiase pinned Jerry with an elbow drop after he collided with one of his own partners, fall #2: Jerry pinned DiBiase with an elbow drop after DiBiase missed a charge into the corner; fall #3: Jimmy pinned Travis after Travis ran into the turnbuckle
Ivan Putski pinned Bulldog Brower

MADISON SQUARE GARDEN
TONIGHT'S OFFICIAL LINE-UP
MONDAY, JULY 2nd, 1979

Main Event - One Fall or One Hour - For The World Wrestling Federation Heavyweight Championship

BOB BACKLUND   vs.   PAT PATTERSON M
Princeton, Minnesota   San Francisco, California
"Champion"   "Challenger"

GREG VALENTINE   vs.   CHIEF JAY STRONGBOW
Seattle, Washington   Pawhuska, Oklahoma

"BULLDOG" BROWER   vs.   IVAN PUTSKI
Toronto, Ontario, Canada   Krakow, Poland

Six Man Tag Team Match - Two Out Of Three Falls

"HANDSOME" JIMMY VALIANT   STEVE TRAVIS
New York City   Charlottesville, Virginia
and   and
"GENTLEMAN" JERRY VALIANT vs.   TED DiBIASE
New York City   Omaha, Nebraska
and   and
"LUSCIOUS" JOHNNY VALIANT   HAYSTACKS CALHOUN
New York City   Morgans Corners, Arkansas

HOSSIEN THE GREAT   vs.   S. D. JONES
Iran   Philadelphia

NIKOLAI VOLKOFF   vs.   DOMENIC DeNUCCI
Mongolia, U.S.S.R.   Italy

BARON MIKEL SCICLUNA vs.   TITO SANTANA
Isle of Malta   Mexico

MR. "X"   vs.   JOHNNY RIVERA
???????????????????   Puerto Rico

FIRST BOUT STARTS AT 8:30 P.M.

WWF North American Champion Pat Patterson, with the Grand Wizard
"You know, over the years Bob Backlund has beaten a lot of wrestlers. A lot of great wrestlers. There's one man he couldn't beat and it's Pat Patterson. ...When I get done with you, I will have not one but two championship belts. I know you're afraid of me. Backlund, I'm taking the championship away from you. You didn't look like a champion last time. You were covered in blood. Backlund, I know you're running scared. And I'll tell you one thing, I'm taking the belt away from you, you punk."
Localized TV promo

VINCE McMAHON, PROMOTER   MONDAY, JULY 30th, 1979

W.W.F. CHAMPIONSHIP
WRESTLING

madison square garden

SANCTIONED BY THE WORLD WRESTLING FEDERATION
HISASHI SHINMA, PRESIDENT
UNDER SUPERVISION OF THE NEW YORK STATE ATHLETIC COMMISSION
OFFICIAL PROGRAM MAGAZINE #23   PRICE: $1.00

W.W.F.
THE WORLD WRESTLING FEDERATION
HISASHI SHINMA, PRESIDENT

W.W.F. HEADQUARTERS
7 13 MINAMI-AOYAMA 6-CHOME
MINATO-KU, TOKYO, JAPAN 107

WWF @ New York City, NY - Madison Square Garden - July 30, 1979
Televised on the MSG Network - included Vince McMahon on commentary:
Roddy Piper pinned Johnny Rodz at 2:49 with a knee to the stomach as Rodz jumped off the ropes
Ted DiBiase fought Hussein Arab to a 20-minute time-limit draw
Nikolai Volkoff pinned Jose Estrada (sub. for Baron Mikel Scicluna) at 2:57 with a backbreaker over the knee
WWF World Champion Bob Backlund (w/ Arnold Skaaland) fought WWF North American Champion Pat Patterson to a double standing count-out at 28:22 when, after Patterson hit Backlund with brass knuckles, Skaaland climbed on the ring apron and hit Patterson with the title belt

MADISON SQUARE GARDEN _____ MONDAY, JULY 30th, 1979
****
Main Event - One Fall or One Hour - Return Match For
World Wrestling Federation Heavyweight Championship

BOB BACKLUND   **PAT PATTERSON**
Princeton, Minnesota   vs.   San Francisco, California
"Champion"   DIAN 4   "Challenger"
****
Return Bout - Indian Strap Match

CHIEF JAY STRONGBOW   **GREG VALENTINE**
Pawhuska, Oklahoma   vs.   Seattle, Washington
                     DIAN 7
****
Eight Man Tag Team Match - Three Out Of Five Falls

"HANDSOME" JIMMY VALIANT   **TITO SANTANA**
New York City   Mexico
and   and
"GENTLEMAN" JERRY VALIANT   **DOMENIC DeNUCCI**
New York City   Italy
and   vs.   and
"LUSCIOUS" JOHNNY VALIANT   **IVAN PUTSKI**
New York City   Krakow, Poland
and   and
"CAPTAIN" LOU ALBANO   **ANDRE THE GIANT**
Mount Vernon, New York   Paris, France
****
Preliminary Matches - One Fall or Twenty Minutes

THE GREAT HOSSIEN   **TED DiBIASE**
Iran   vs.   Omaha, Nebraska
****
~~BULLDOG BROWER~~   **STEVE TRAVIS**
Toronto, Ontario, Canada vs. Charlottesville, Virginia
****
NIKOLAI VOLKOFF   ~~BARON MIKEL SCICLUNA~~
Mongolia, U.S.S.R.   vs.   Isle of Malta
****
JOHNNY RODZ   **RODDY PIPER**
New York City   vs.   Glasgow, Scotland
****
Four Girl Tag Team Match

JOYCE GRABEL   **KITTY ADAMS**
Griffin, Georgia   Long Island, New York
and   vs.   and
VIVIAN ST. JOHN   **THE FABULOUS MOOLAH**
Ft. Lauderdale, Florida   Columbia, South Carolina
****

Women's Champion the Fabulous Moolah & Kitty Adams defeated Joyce Grable & Vivian St. John in a Best 2 out of 3 falls match at 17:47, 2-1; fall #1: Adams pinned Grable at 7:54 after Moolah dropkicked Adams onto Grable as Grable held Adams up for a powerslam; fall #2: Grable pinned Adams at 6:20 after reversing a powerslam attempt into a small package; fall #3: Moolah pinned St. John at 3:33 after Grable accidentally dropkicked her partner when Moolah moved out of the way
Steve Travis pinned Baron Mikel Scicluna (sub. for Bulldog Brower) at 5:08 with a sunset flip
Greg Valentine fought Chief Jay Strongbow to a double disqualification at 7:46 in an Indian Strap Match when referee Jack Lotz was knocked down; after the match, the two men had to be held apart by Ivan Putski, Tito Santana, Dominic DeNucci, and Gorilla Monsoon (first strap match held at MSG) (*The WWF's Most Unusual Matches*)
Andre the Giant, Ivan Putski, Tito Santana, & Dominic DeNucci defeated Jimmy, WWF Tag Team Champions Jerry & Johnny Valiant, & Capt. Lou Albano in a Best 3 out of 5 falls match, 2-1; fall #1: Johnny pinned Santana at 3:02; fall #2: Santana pinned Johnny at 3:04; fall #3: Andre pinned Jerry at 4:02; fall #4: the bout was stopped due to the curfew (first eight-man tag held at MSG)

WWF @ New York City, NY - Madison Square Garden - August 27, 1979

Televised on the MSG Network - featured Vince McMahon on commentary:

SD Jones pinned Frank Rodriguez at 6:02

WWF Tag Team Champion WWF Tag Team Champion Johnny Valiant defeated Dominic DeNucci via count-out at 8:31 after a collision caused DeNucci to fall out of the ring

Greg Valentine pinned Steve Travis at 11:39 with an elbow drop

Ivan the Terrible & Billy the Kid defeated Butch Cassidy & Tiny Tom at 6:56 when Kid pinned Cassidy (*Biggest, Smallest, Strangest, Strongest*)

WWF Intercontinental Champion Pat Patterson defeated WWF World Champion Bob Backlund via count-out at 14:29 after Patterson used brass knuckles while the referee was knocked out and then beat Backlund back inside the ring; prior to the bout, Patterson was escorted to the ring by the Grand Wizard while Arnold Skaaland escorted Backlund

Tito Santana fought Hussein Arab to a 20-minute time-limit draw; after the bout, Vince McMahon conducted an interview with Debbie Harry, lead singer of Blondie, who remained at ringside to watch the remainder of the show

Bruno Sammartino pinned Nikolai Volkoff at 6:21 after hitting him with a chair Volkoff had brought into the ring; prior to the bout, Freddie Blassie escorted Volkoff to the ring

Ted DiBiase fought Jimmy Valiant to a double count-out at 6:19 as both men brawled on the ring apron

Andre the Giant pinned WWF Tag Team Champion Jerry Valiant at 3:43 with a boot to the face and splash; prior to the bout, Valiant was escorted to the ring by Capt. Lou Albano

Chief Jay Strongbow pinned Bulldog Brower at 4:53 after missing a kneelift and hitting the turnbuckle

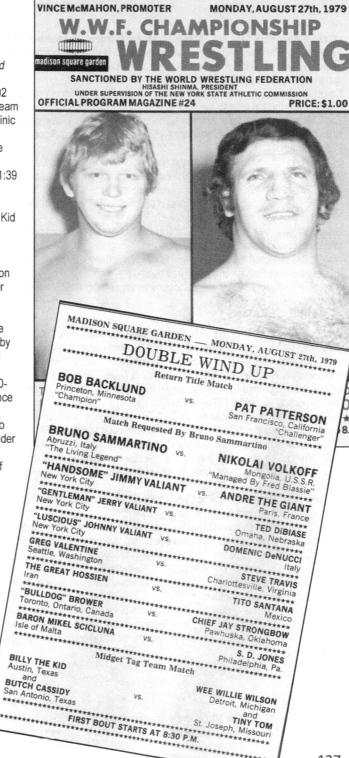

VINCE McMAHON, PROMOTER   MONDAY, AUGUST 27th, 1979

W.W.F. CHAMPIONSHIP
WRESTLING

madison square garden

SANCTIONED BY THE WORLD WRESTLING FEDERATION
HISASHI SHINMA, PRESIDENT
UNDER SUPERVISION OF THE NEW YORK STATE ATHLETIC COMMISSION

OFFICIAL PROGRAM MAGAZINE #24   PRICE: $1.00

MADISON SQUARE GARDEN — MONDAY, AUGUST 27th, 1979

DOUBLE WIND UP
Return Title Match

BOB BACKLUND
Princeton, Minnesota
"Champion"
vs.
PAT PATTERSON
San Francisco, California
"Challenger"

Match Requested By Bruno Sammartino

BRUNO SAMMARTINO
Abruzzi, Italy
"The Living Legend"
vs.
NIKOLAI VOLKOFF
Mongolia, U.S.S.R.
"Managed By Fred Blassie"

"HANDSOME" JIMMY VALIANT
New York City
vs.
ANDRE THE GIANT
Paris, France

"GENTLEMAN" JERRY VALIANT
New York City
vs.
TED DiBIASE
Omaha, Nebraska

"LUSCIOUS" JOHNNY VALIANT
New York City
vs.
DOMENIC DeNUCCI
Italy

GREG VALENTINE
Seattle, Washington
vs.
STEVE TRAVIS
Charlottesville, Virginia

THE GREAT HOSSIEN
Iran
vs.
TITO SANTANA
Mexico

"BULLDOG" BROWER
Toronto, Ontario, Canada
vs.
CHIEF JAY STRONGBOW
Pawhuska, Oklahoma

BARON MIKEL SCICLUNA
Isle of Malta
vs.
S. D. JONES
Philadelphia, Pa.

Midget Tag Team Match

BILLY THE KID
Austin, Texas
and
BUTCH CASSIDY
San Antonio, Texas
vs.
WEE WILLIE WILSON
Detroit, Michigan
and
TINY TOM
St. Joseph, Missouri

FIRST BOUT STARTS AT 8:30 P.M.

127

WWF @ New York City, NY - Madison Square Garden - September 24, 1979
Televised on the MSG Network - featured Vince McMahon on commentary:
Johnny Rivera pinned Gypsy Rodriguez at 10:23 with a backslide
Johnny Rodz pinned Steve King at 8:08 with a suplex
Baron Mikel Scicluna defeated SD Jones (sub. for Frank Williams) via count-out at 7:09 after Jones missed a charge and fell over the top rope to the floor
Ted DiBiase defeated Jose Estrada (sub. for Bulldog Brower) via submission at 9:42 with an abdominal stretch
Hussain Arab pinned Pete Sanchez at 3:57 with a butterfly suplex; prior to the bout, Arab was escorted to the ring by Freddie Blassie
WWF World Champion Bob Backlund (w/ Arnold Skaaland) defeated WWF Intercontinental Champion Pat Patterson in a steel cage match at 16:43 by kicking Patterson off him and escaping through the door (*Inside the Steel Cage, Bloodbath: Wrestling's Most Incredible Steel Cage Matches, The Greatest Cage Matches of All Time*)
Andre the Giant & Tito Santana defeated Jimmy & WWF Tag Team Champion Jerry Valiant at 6:04 when Andre pinned Jimmy with a headbutt and splash
Greg Valentine defeated Dominic DeNucci via submission with the figure-4 at 10:46; prior to the bout, the Grand Wizard escorted Valentine to the ring
Ivan Putski defeated WWF Tag Team Champion Johnny Valiant via disqualification at 6:53 when Valiant punched the referee after Putski caught him in a bearhug
Nikolai Volkoff fought Chief Jay Strongbow to a draw after the 5-minute mark when the match was stopped due to the curfew

WWF @ New York City, NY - Madison Square Garden - October 22, 1979
Televised on the MSG Network - featured Vince McMahon on commentary
Johnny Rivera fought Johnny Rodz to a 20-minute time-limit draw
Ivan Putski & Tito Santana defeated WWF Tag Team Champions Johnny & Jerry Valiant at 13:39 to win the titles when Santana pinned Johnny, the illegal man, with a crossbody after the champions collided in the ring, with Jerry being knocked to the floor (*Tag Team Champions*)
Nikolai Volkoff pinned Moose Monroe a 3:56 with a boot to the face and a stomp; after the bout, Vince McMahon interviewed Andy Kaufman at ringside; Kaufman appeared the previous Saturday on "Saturday Night Live" with his inter-gender wrestling challenge and challenged any woman at MSG $500 if they could beat him
WWF World Champion Bob Backlund pinned Swede Hanson at 16:28 with the atomic drop after Hansen missed a move off the top; prior to the bout, Freddie Blassie escorted Hansen and Arnold Skaaland escorted Backlund ringside
Hussein Arab defeated Dominic DeNucci via count-out at 6:31 after DeNucci attempted an airplane spin but Arab grabbed the ropes, with both men falling to the floor
Bruno Sammartino defeated Greg Valentine when the referee stopped the match due to excessive bleeding at 15:10 after Sammartino slammed Valentine's head into the metal part of the turnbuckle; prior to the bout, the Grand Wizard escorted Valentine ringside
Dusty Rhodes pinned Jimmy Valiant at 5:27 with the Bionic Elbow
Larry Zbyszko defeated Bulldog Brower via disqualification at 3:49 after Brower kicked Zbyszko low and would not follow the referee's instructions
WWF Intercontinental Champion Pat Patterson pinned Ted DiBiase at 7:54 by putting his leg on the middle rope for leverage after DiBiase attempted to hit Patterson with the champion's own foreign object; during the bout, music industry pioneer Kal Rudman briefly joined Vince McMahon on commentary (*History of the Intercontinental Championship*)

Sept. 19-23, 1979: The 'No Nukes' concert series was held, with performances by Jackson Browne, Bonnie Raitt, Bruce Springsteen, the Doobie Brothers, Carly Simon, James Taylor, Chaka Khan, and Crosby, Stills and Nash.

WWF @ New York City, NY - Madison Square Garden - November 19, 1979
This card was not televised
Larry Zbyszko defeated Johnny Rodz at 9:21
David Von Erich defeated Davey O'Hannon at 8:47
Hussein Arab defeated Chief Jay Strongbow at 2:51
Capt. Lou Albano pinned Jimmy Valiant at 2:07
Dusty Rhodes defeated Swede Hanson
WWF World Champion Bob Backlund fought Bobby Duncum to a draw at 18:32 when both men were deemed too bloody to continue
Dominic DeNucci defeated Bulldog Brower via disqualification at 15:03
WWF Tag Team Champions Ivan Putksi & Tito Santana defeated Johnny & Jerry Valiant at 22:58
WWF Intercontinental Champion Pat Patterson defeated Ted DiBiase at 15:04

WWF @ New York City, NY - Madison Square Garden - December 17, 1979
Televised on the MSG Network and in Japan - featured Vince McMahon on commentary; the 11 p.m. curfew was waived by the New York State Athletic Commission for the event
Larry Zbyszko pinned Bulldog Brower at 4:43 when Zybszko caused Brower to fall over while attempting a bodyslam
Riki Choshu & Seji Sakaguchi defeated Bad News Allen Coage & Jo Jo Andrews at 9:44 when Andrews submitted to Sakaguchi's Boston Crab; the bout was announced as being for the Japanese tag team titles but the championship Choshu & Sakaguchi held at the time was actually the NWA North American Tag Team Titles
Mike Graham defeated Johnny Rodz via submission at 5:03 with a figure-4
Hulk Hogan defeated Ted DiBiase via KO at 11:12 with a bearhug; prior to the bout, Hogan was escorted to the ring by Freddie Blassie (DiBiase's last appearance for almost 8 years) (Hogan's MSG debut) (*Hulk Still Rules*)
Bob Backlund defeated Bobby Duncum in a Texas Death Match to win the vacant WWF World Title at 17:18; Backlund did not come to the ring with the belt, rather WWF President Hisashi Shima was in possession of it and was introduced to the crowd before the match; Backlund was not introduced as champion however the title being vacant was not mentioned to the US audience but was known by the Japanese audience since the title controversy took place there; in commentary, Vince McMahon continued to refer to Backlund as the title holder
Antonio Inoki pinned Hussein Arab at 14:59 with the enzuiguri; the match was announced as being for Inoki's Japanese Heavyweight Title but the belt Inoki actually held at the time was the NWF title; following the ring entrances, Arab took the mic and cut a promo on the fans; after the match, Arab knocked the referee out with his loaded boot (*WrestleMania 26 Collector's Edition*)
NWA World Champion Harley Race defeated Dusty Rhodes when the referee stopped the match at 13:18 after Rhodes began bleeding from the forehead and lost his vision to the point that he fell out of the ring; after the match, the fans chanted "bullshit" before Race hit Rhodes in the head with the title belt (*American Dream: The Dusty Rhodes Story*)
WWF Intercontinental Champion Pat Patterson defeated Dominic DeNucci by turning a monkey flip attempt into a roll up at 6:31 (*History of the Intercontinental Title*)
WWF Jr. Heavyweight Champion Tatsumi Fujinami pinned Johnny Rivera at 10:17 with a back suplex
WWF Tag Team Champions Ivan Putski & Tito Santana defeated Victor Rivera & Swede Hanson at 6:57 when Santana pinned Hanson with a crossbody off the top

VINCE McMAHON, PROMOTER   MONDAY, JANUARY 21st, 1980

W.W.F. CHAMPIONSHIP
WRESTLING

madison square garden

SANCTIONED BY THE WORLD WRESTLING FEDERATION
HISASHI SHINMA, PRESIDENT
UNDER SUPERVISION OF THE NEW YORK STATE ATHLETIC COMMISSION

OFFICIAL PROGRAM MAGAZINE #29   PRICE: $1.00

W.W.F. HEAVYWEIGHT CHAMPION   WORLD'S STRONGEST HUMAN
BOB BACKLUND vs. **KEN PATERA**
TONIGHT IN THE GARDEN FOR THE TITLE!

The Box Office At Madison Square Garden Is Open Daily From 10 to 8.

WWF @ New York City, NY - Madison Square Garden - January 21, 1980 (20,000+)
Televised on the MSG Network - featured Vince McMahon on commentary:
Davey O'Hannon pinned Angelo Gomez at 10:21 with a neckbreaker
Kevin Von Erich pinned Johnny Rodz with a Thesz Press at 8:28 (Von Erich's only MSG appearance)
Larry Zbyszko defeated Hussein Arab via disqualification at 10:29 when Arab accidentally hit an elbow drop on referee Terry Terranova when Zbyzsko moved out of the way after Arab had pushed Zbyszko onto the referee when kicking out of a pin attempt; after the bout, Zbyszko cleared Arab from the ring
Hulk Hogan pinned Dominic DeNucci at 7:34 with the legdrop after dropping DeNucci throat-first across the top rope; prior to the bout, Freddie Blassie escorted Hogan to the ring before returning backstage when the match began

The Wild Samoans defeated WWF Tag Team Champions Ivan Putski & Tito Santana via count-out at 12:46 after Samoan #2 crotched Santana on the top rope, with Santana then falling out to the floor; after the bout, Santana was taken backstage on a stretcher (the Samoans' MSG debut)
Rene Goulet pinned Baron Mikel Scicluna at 4:59 with a sunset flip; during the bout, Vince McMahon interviewed Mike Weppner from Front Line Management in NYC, & Kal Rudman about their experience being here at MSG (Goulet's return to MSG after an 8-year absence)
WWF World Champion Bob Backlund (w/ Arnold Skaaland) fought Ken Patera to a draw at 25:52 when, after Patera threw Backlund into referee Jack Lotz, referee Terry Terranova called for the bell; after the bout, Lotz was taken backstage on a stretcher; prior to the bout, the Grand Wizard escorted Patera to the ring before returning backstage when the match began; after the bout, both men continued brawling until they were eventually separated by several other wrestlers and referees
WWF Intercontinental Champion Pat Patterson defeated Capt. Lou Albano via count-out at 6:11 in a non-title match after Patterson hit Albano with his own foreign object, causing Albano to bleed, with Albano then running backstage
Bobby Duncum pinned Mike Masters at 1:29 with a bulldog
Tony Atlas pinned Swede Hanson at 2:17 with a headbutt off the top (Atlas' MSG debut)

VINCE McMAHON, PROMOTER MONDAY, FEBRUARY 18th, 1980

W.W.F. CHAMPIONSHIP
WRESTLING

madison square garden

SAN ... THE WORLD WRESTLING FEDERATION
ISASHI SHINMA, PRESIDENT
UN ... F THE NEW YORK STATE ATHLETIC COMMISSION
OFFICIAL ... AZINE #30   PRICE: $1.00

THE WORLD'S STRONGEST HUMAN

KEN PATERA SAYS HE'LL DESTROY BACKLUND TONIGHT IN GARDEN!

WWF @ New York City, NY - Madison Square Garden - February 18, 1980
Austin Idol defeated Jose Estrada at 7:26 (Idol's only MSG appearance)
Tommy Rich defeated Johnny Rodz at 7:41 (Rich's only MSG appearance)
Hulk Hogan defeated WWF Tag Team Champion Tito Santana via count-out at 10:48
Sika defeated WWF Tag Team Champion Ivan Putski via count-out at 5:28
Bobby Duncum defeated Dominic DeNucci at 11:21
WWF World Champion Bob Backlund defeated Ken Patera via count-out at 15:37; Pat Patterson was the special referee for the bout
Afa defeated Rene Goulet at 9:18
Cowboy Lang & Lone Eagle defeated Little Tokyo & Dirty Morgan at 6:55
Tony Atlas defeated Hussein Arab at 12:18

... SQUARE GARDEN   MONDAY, FEBRUARY 18th, 1980

...IGHT'S OFFICIAL LINE-UP
****
... Wrestling Federation Heavyweight Championship

BOB BACKLUND	vs.	**KEN PATERA**
Princeton, Minnesota		Portland, Oregon
"Champion"		"Challenger"

RETURN MATCH — SPECIAL REFEREE: PAT PATTERSON
****

THE SAMOAN #2	vs.	**IVAN PUTSKI**
Samoa		Krakow, Poland

****
Special Attraction

THE FABULOUS HULK HOGAN	vs.	**TITO SANTANA**
Venice Beach, California		Mexico

****

THE SAMOAN #1	vs.	**RENE GOULET**
Samoa		Nice, France

****

THE GREAT HOSSIEN ARAB	vs.	**TONY ATLAS**
Iran		Atlanta, Georgia

****

JOHNNY RODZ	vs.	**"WILDFIRE" TOMMY RICH**
New York City		Tennessee

****

"BIG BAD" BOBBY DUNCUM	vs.	**DOMENIC DeNUCCI**
Austin, Texas		Italy

****

AUSTIN IDOL	vs.	**JOSE ESTRADA**
Texas		Puerto Rico

****
Midget Tag Team Match

COWBOY LONG		**LITTLE TOKYO**
Texas		Japan
and	vs.	and
LONG EAGLE		**DIRTY MORGAN**
Arizona		Louisiana

****
FIRST BOUT STARTS AT 8:30 P.M.
****

WWF @ New York City, NY - Madison Square Garden - March 24, 1980 (26,102 which included 4,000 in Felt Forum)
Televised on the MSG Network - featured Vince McMahon on commentary
Bulldog Brower pinned Frank Williams at 8:53 with an elbow drop following a running back elbow
Kerry Von Erich pinned Jose Estrada at 10:49 with a sunset flip out of the corner (Kerry's MSG debut)
Tor Kamata pinned Mike Masters at 5:46 with a jumping kick and a kneedrop
Larry Zbyszko defeated Bruno Sammartino (w/ Arnold Skaaland) via disqualification at 15:31 when Sammartino failed to release a choke; Sammartino was eventually pulled away by Skaaland and referee Dick Kroll while Zbyzsko escaped
Afa pinned Dominic DeNucci at 9:42 with a jumping headbutt
WWF World Champion Bob Backlund pinned Sika at 18:32 after throwing the challenger off the top as Sika attempted a diving headbutt
Andre the Giant & WWF Intercontinental Champion Pat Patterson defeated Bobby Duncum & Ken Patera at 11:04 when Andre pinned Duncum with a splash as Patterson had Duncum in the figure-4
Rene Goulet pinned Baron Mikel Scicluna with a sunset flip at 6:11
Hulk Hogan pinned WWF Tag Team Champion Tito Santana at 8:12 with a suplex and grabbing the tights for leverage; prior to the bout, Hogan was escorted to the ring by Freddie Blassie (*Hulk Hogan: The Ultimate Anthology* Wal-Mart exclusive 4th disc)

WWF @ New York City, NY - Madison Square Garden - April 21, 1980 (20,000+)
Televised on the MSG Network - featured Vince McMahon on commentary:
Larry Sharpe defeated Mike Masters at 8:11 with a piledriver
Greg Gagne pinned Jose Estrada at 8:53 following two dropkicks (Gagne's return to MSG after 3 years and his final appearance)
Ken Patera defeated WWF Intercontinental Champion Pat Patterson to win the title at 20:48 with a knee drop off the middle turnbuckle to the champion's back; the referee, still groggy from a collision with Patterson moments prior, did not notice that the champion's foot was on the bottom rope during the cover; prior to the bout, the Grand Wizard escorted Patera to ringside before returning backstage when the match began (*History of the Intercontinental Title, The Ken Patera Story*)
WWF Tag Team Champion Sika defeated Dominic DeNucci via count-out at 9:27 after DeNucci missed a right hand punch and Sika back dropped him to the floor; during the bout, Vince McMahon interviewed Peter Patton, general manager of the Cape Cod Coliseum about his experience here at MSG
Bruno Sammartino (w/ Arnold Skaaland) defeated Larry Zbyszko via count-out at 11:53 when Zbyszko left ringside after Sammartino kept preventing Zbyszko from trying to re-enter the ring
Ricky Steamboat & Jay Youngblood defeated Tor Kamata & Bulldog Brower at 13:11 when Youngblood pinned Brower after Steamboat dropped his partner on top of him from a gorilla press position (Steamboat's MSG debut; Youngbloods' only MSG appearance)
WWF World Champion Bob Backlund (w/ Arnold Skaaland) pinned WWF Tag Team Champion Afa at 16:34 with a reverse roll up into a bridge; prior to the bout, Capt. Lou Albano escorted Afa to ringside before returning backstage when the match began
Hulk Hogan pinned Rene Goulet at 3:14 with the legdrop; prior to the bout, Freddie Blassie escorted Hogan to ringside before returning backstage when the match began
Andre the Giant pinned Bobby Duncum at 2:51 with a suplex and sit-down splash

WWF @ New York City, NY - Madison Square Garden - May 19, 1980 (near capacity crowd)
Televised on the MSG Network - featured Vince McMahon on commentary
Rick McGraw defeated Jose Estrada at 10:38 (McGraw's MSG debut)
Larry Zbyszko won a 16-man $15,000 battle royal at 11:25 by last eliminating Dominic DeNucci and Bobby Duncum
at the same time when, as DeNucci had Duncum in an airplane spin, Zbyzsko dropkicked them both to the floor;
order of elimination: Frankie Williams by Baron Mikel Scicluna, Ivan Putski by Peter Maivia, Maivia by Putski via
pulling him out from the outside, Scicluna by Tony Atlas, Atlas by the Wild Samoans, Johnny Rodz by DeNucci,
Rene Goulet by Duncum, Samoan #2 by Samoan #1 following an accidental headbutt, Samoan #1 by Gorilla
Monsoon, Tor Kamata by Pat Patterson, Monsoon by Zbyzsko & Duncum, Patterson by Zbyzsko & Duncum; due to
pre-match stipulations, Zbyszko earned a world title shot for the next show at MSG
Larry Sharpe defeated Frankie Williams at 8:24
Larry Zbyszko pinned Dominic DeNucci at 7:08 following a kick to the face as DeNucci charged the corner
Tor Kamata pinned Johnny Rodz at 7:58 after a double karate chop to the throat
WWF World Champion Bob Backlund pinned WWF Intercontinental Champion Ken Patera in a Texas Death Match
at 22:56 with a crossbody off the top; prior to the bout, the Grand Wizard escorted Patera to the ring and Arnold
Skaaland escorted Backlund; named Wrestling Observer's Match of the Year
Gorilla Monsoon pinned Baron Mikel Scicluna (sub. for Hulk Hogan) at 3:11 with a chop and splash
Bobby Duncum defeated Rene Goulet at 5:42
Tony Atlas, Ivan Putski, & Pat Patterson defeated Peter Maivia & WWF Tag Team Champions the Wild Samoans in
a Best 2 out of 3 falls match at 16:25; fall #1: Patterson pinned Maivia with a roll up at 8:26; fall #2: Maivia pinned
Patterson after a double team from the Samoans
at 4:31; fall #3: Atlas pinned Samoan #1 with a
splash after the Samoans accidentally headbutted
each other at 3:28; prior to the bout, Capt. Lou
Albano escorted the Samoans ringside

**WWF @ New York City, NY - Madison Square
Garden - June 16, 1980 (20,000+)**
Johnny Rodz defeated Steve King
Bobby Duncum defeated Rick McGraw
Hulk Hogan defeated Gorilla Monsoon
Larry Zbyszko defeated WWF World Champion
Bob Backlund when the bout was stopped due to
blood at 27:39
Ivan Putski (sub. for Dusty Rhodes) defeated Tor
Kamata
WWF Intercontinental Champion Ken Patera
defeated Pat Patterson
Rene Goulet defeated Larry Sharpe via
disqualification
WWF Tag Team Champions the Wild Samoans
defeated Dominic DeNucci & Ivan Putski

VINCE McMAHON, PROMOTER   MONDAY JUNE 16th, 1980
W.W.F. CHAMPIONSHIP
madison square garden **WRESTLING**
SANCTIONED BY THE WORLD WRESTLING FEDERATION
HISASHI SHINMA, PRESIDENT
UNDER SUPERVISION OF THE NEW YORK STATE ATHLETIC COMMISSION
OFFICIAL PROGRAM MAGAZINE #34   PRICE: $1.00

BOB BACKLUND
DEFENDS HIS W.W.F.
CHAMPIONSHIP VS.
BATTLE ROYAL WINNER
LARRY ZBYSZKO IN
M.S.G. RING TONIGHT

PAT PATTERSON GETS A
RETURN MATCH WITH
KEN PATERA FOR THE
INTER-CONTINENTAL
HEAVYWEIGHT TITLE

SAMOANS DEFEND THE
W.W.F. TAG TEAM TITLE
VERSUS DeNUCCI AND
"POLISH POWER" PUTSKI

HULK HOGAN VERSUS
GORILLA MONSOON IN A
BATTLE OF THE SUPER
HEAVYWEIGHTS

"AMERICAN DREAM"
DUSTY RHODES VS.
WILY TOR KAMATA

EIGHT BIG MATCHES

THE BOX OFFICE AT MADISON SQUARE GARDEN IS OPEN DAILY FROM 10 TO 8

Aug. 11-14, 1980: The Democratic National Convention was held at MSG, with incumbent President Jimmy
Carter and Vice President Walter Mondale named the respective nominees for the party.

WWF @ New York City, NY - Madison Square Garden - September 22, 1980 (20,000+)
Televised on the MSG Network - featured Vince McMahon & Kal Rudman on commentary; included the Fujinami /
Guerrero, Patterson / Kamata, Moolah & Shade / Lee & Malloy and Inoki / Sharpe matches from the Aug. 9 Shea
Stadium show, with McMahon & Rudman doing live commentary from MSG as there was no original English
commentary for the show; the matches were shown in the place of the Harley Race / Bob Backlund match and the
introductions and crowd noise could be heard as the Shea bouts were shown:
NWA Jr. Heavyweight Champion Les Thornton pinned Jose Estrada at 7:02 with a backbreaker (Thornton's MSG
debut)
Pat Patterson pinned Johnny Rodz at 8:04 with a sunset flip
The Hangman pinned Dominic DeNucci at 10:15 when the Hangman fell on top of DeNucci after holding onto the top
rope while in the middle of an airplane spin; after the bout, DeNucci hung the Hangman over the top rope with his
own noose (Hangman's MSG debut)
Larry Zbyszko defeated Tony Garea via disqualification at 12:15 when Garea failed to release an abdominal stretch
after Zbyszko reached the ropes (Garea's MSG return after an 18-month absence)
Rick Martel pinned Rick McGraw at 6:47 with a backslide (Martel's MSG debut)
Pedro Morales pinned Afa at 3:34 by reversing a bodyslam into the ring and falling on top for the win; prior to the
bout, Capt. Lou Albano escorted Afa to the ring
WWF Intercontinental Champion Ken Patera pinned Rene Goulet at 1:04 with a small package; prior to the bout, the
Grand Wizard escorted Patera ringside
WWF World Champion Bob Backlund defeated NWA World Champion Harley Race via disqualification at 35:14
when Race pulled the referee into Backlund as the NWA title holder was caught in a sleeper; this bout was not
televised with the rest of the show, rather four matches from the Aug. 9 Shea Stadium show aired in its place
Tony Atlas pinned Sika at 5:32 with an elbow drop
All American Wrestling - 9/11/83: Andre the Giant pinned Hulk Hogan at 12:18 when Hogan failed a slam attempt
and guest referee Gorilla Monsoon made a fast count; prior to the match, Hogan was escorted ringside by Freddie
Blassie; just before the finish, Hogan successfully slammed Andre; the match was not televised and the MSG
broadcast went off the air immediately following the Atlas / Sika bout (*Hulk Hogan: The Unreleased Archives*)

WWF @ New York City, NY - Madison Square Garden - October 20, 1980
Televised on the MSG Network - featured Vince McMahon on commentary:
Terry Taylor pinned Jose Estrada with an abdominal stretch into a roll up at 9:59
Rene Goulet pinned Johnny Rodz after Rodz hit the corner at 8:41
The Hangman defeated Rick McGraw via submission to a backbreaker at 7:19
Pedro Morales fought WWF Intercontinental Champion Ken Patera to a double disqualification at 16:19 after both
men attacked the referee and used illegal holds; after the bout, the two men had to be held apart by a number of
wrestlers including Pat Patterson, Dominic DeNucci, Rick Martel, and several others (*History of the Intercontinental
Title, History of the Intercontinental Championship*)
Dominic DeNucci pinned Larry Sharpe with an inside cradle at 8:38
Sgt. Slaughter defeated WWF World Champion Bob Backlund via disqualification at 16:33 when Arnold Skaaland hit
Slaughter in the head, following a confrontation on the floor, as Backlund was trapped in the Cobra Clutch
Rick Martel pinned Baron Mikel Scicluna with a sunset flip at 3:34
Tony Garea defeated Larry Zbyszko via disqualification at 4:58 after Zbyszko shoved the referee
Dusty Rhodes & Pat Patterson defeated WWF Tag Team Champions the Wild Samoans in a Best 2 out of 3 Falls
match via referee's decision; fall #1: Rhodes pinned Sika with an elbow at 11:47; fall #2: the curfew expired

WWF @ New York City, NY - Madison Square Garden - December 8, 1980 (20,011)
This card was not televised; John Lennon was shot and killed in NYC this same night
Johnny Rodz defeated Sylvano Sousa at 10:49
The Moondogs defeated Rick McGraw & Angel Marvilla at 11:37
Larry Zbyszko defeated Dominic DeNucci via count-out at 12:42
WWF Tag Team Champions Rick Martel & Tony Garea defeated the Wild Samoans in a Best 2 out of 3 falls match at 26:27, 2 falls to 1
Ernie Ladd fought Tony Atlas to a double count-out at 5:24
Pedro Morales defeated WWF Intercontinental Champion Ken Patera to win the title at 18:51; Pat Patterson was the guest referee for the bout
Bruno Sammartino defeated Sgt. Slaughter via count-out at 18:38

'John Lennon is dead'
"I remember Rick Martel told me one story. In 1980, they used to go afterwards to the Ramada Inn, it had a bar a couple blocks away from Madison Square Garden. They're all drinking and doing whatever they do. And someone comes in and says, 'John Lennon is dead.'"
Lanny Poffo, *TheHistoryofWWE.com interview, 2014*

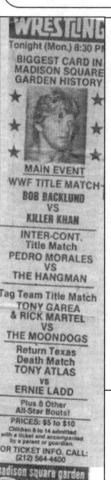

WWF @ New York City, NY - Madison Square Garden - December 29, 1980 (19,000)
Televised on the MSG and USA networks and in Japan - featured Vince McMahon on commentary:
Yoshiaki Yatsu pinned Jose Estrada at 8:47 with a belly to belly suplex
Seiji Sakaguchi fought Sika (w/ Afa) to a draw at 5:34 when both Afa, who switched places with Sika during the bout, and Antonio Inoki, who made the save for Sakaguchi, interfered
WWF Jr. Heavyweight Champion Tatsumi Fujinami pinned Don Diamond with a back suplex into a bridge at 10:28
Hulk Hogan pinned Dominic DeNucci at 4:38 with a powerslam
WWF World Champion Bob Backlund pinned Killer Khan at 12:23 with a back suplex into a bridge
WWF Tag Team Champions Tony Garea & Rick Martel defeated the Moondogs via disqualification at 13:16 when, as Garea had King in an abdominal stretch, Rex hit Garea in the back with one of the challengers' bones
NWF Champion & World Martial Arts Champion Antonio Inoki pinned Bobby Duncum at 12:47 with an enzuiguri; only the Martial Arts title was at stake but Inoki came to the ring wearing the NWF belt
Women's Champion the Fabulous Moolah & Joyce Grable defeated Candy Malloy & Peggy Lee when Moolah pinned Lee following a double clothesline at 5:09
WWF Intercontinental Champion Pedro Morales pinned the Hangman at 7:07 with a roll up after the Hangman hit the corner
Pat Patterson defeated Ken Patera via disqualification at 8:12 when Patera refused to break on the ropes
Untelevised matches:
Ivan Putski pinned Afa at 2:34
Tony Atlas pinned Ernie Ladd at 9:24 in a Texas Death match

Jan. 10, 1981: The Police performed at MSG for the first time.

VINCE McMAHON, PROMOTER

MONDAY, DECEMBER 29, 1980

W.W.F. CHAMPIONSHIP
WRESTLING

madison square garden

SANCTIONED BY THE WORLD WRESTLING FEDERATION
HISASHI SHINMA, PRESIDENT
UNDER SUPERVISION OF THE NEW YORK STATE ATHLETIC COMMISSION

OFFICIAL PROGRAM MAGAZINE #38   PRICE: $1.00

W.W.F.
THE WORLD WRESTLING FEDERATION
HISASHI SHINMA, PRESIDENT

W.W.F. HEADQUARTERS

BOB BACKLUND PUTS TITLE UP AGAINST TOUGH KILLER KAHN

PEDRO MORALES RISKS INTER-CONTINENTAL HEAVYWEIGHT TITLE AGAINST THE HANGMAN

ANTONIO INOKI FACES BOBBY DUNCUM

TONY "MR. U.S.A." ATLAS VS. ERNIE "CAT" LADD IN A SPECIAL RETURN TEXAS DEATH MATCH

IVAN PUTSKI RETURNS VS. SAMOAN #1

TONY GAREA & RICK MARTEL DEFEND TAG TEAM TITLE AGAINST THE MOONDOGS

TATSUMI FUJINAMI DEFENDS JUNIOR HEAVYWEIGHT CROWN

THE BOX OFFICE AT MADISON SQUARE GARDEN IS OPEN DAILY FROM 10 TO

136

WWF @ New York City, NY - Madison Square Garden - February 16, 1981 (20,808)
Televised on the MSG Network - featured Vince McMahon on commentary:
Yoshiaki Yatsu defeated Johnny Rodz at 11:12
Hulk Hogan defeated Rick McGraw at 1:31
The Hangman defeated Frank Savage at 10:58
SD Jones defeated Baron Mikel Scicluna at 8:44
WWF Intercontinental Champion Pedro Morales defeated Sgt. Slaughter via disqualification at 22:40 after the challenger used a pair of brass knuckles; after the bout, Morales used the brass knuckles to pound on Slaughter all the way back to the dressing room
WWF World Champion Bob Backlund fought Stan Hansen to a draw at 18:22 when the referee deemed both men too bloody to continue; after the bout, the two continued to brawl back to the dressing room where they were eventually separated by security guards
Killer Khan pinned Dominic DeNucci at 7:46 with a kneedrop from the middle turnbuckle
Pat Patterson, WWF Tag Team Champions Rick Martel & Tony Garea defeated the Moondogs & Capt. Lou Albano in a Best 2 out of 3 falls match, 2-1, at 9:47; fall #1: Martel pinned Rex at the 51-second mark with a flying bodypress; fall #2: Rex pinned Martel at 4:02 with a backbreaker after King kneed Martel in the back from the apron; fall #3: the Moondogs & Albano were counted-out at 4:55

Vince McMahon

"The big question is whether you will be successful against Andre the Giant."

Sgt. Slaughter

"In what, a wrestling match or the Cobra Clutch? You mean whether I'll still have the $5,000 after I put the Cobra Clutch on Andre the Giant right in the middle of Madison Square Garden? ...First off, Andre the Giant, I'm going to have to wear you down. I'm going to pick up your big body and I'm going to slam it onto that mat. Number eight on the Richter Scale is going to come up and that will be the end of you, Andre the Giant."
Localized TV promo

WWF @ New York City, NY - Madison Square Garden - March 16, 1981 (21,000+)
Televised on the MSG Network and USA Network - featured Vince McMahon on commentary:
Yoshiaki Yatsu pinned Baron Mikel Scicluna at 8:39 with a small package
SD Jones pinned Johnny Rodz at 9:41 with a diving headbutt after Rodz missed a move off the middle turnbuckle
Moondog Rex pinned Rick McGraw at 6:38 with a shoulderbreaker after avoiding a charge in the corner
Dominic DeNucci pinned Larry Sharpe at 6:53 with a small package
Stan Hansen defeated WWF World Champion Bob Backlund (w/ Arnold Skaaland) via count-out at 12:02 after the champion suffered the loaded lariat on the ring apron, knocking him to the floor; prior to Hansen's entrance, Pat Patterson entered the ring, issued a public challenge to Sgt. Slaughter over the house microphone, and shook the hands of Howard Finkel, Arnold Skaaland, and the champion; prior to the match, Freddie Blassie escorted Hansen to the ring; after the bout, Backlund cleared the ring of his opponent
WWF Intercontinental Champion Pedro Morales pinned Moondog King at 4:48 with a roll up as King charged at him; prior to the bout, Capt. Lou Albano escorted King ringside
Andre the Giant defeated Sgt. Slaughter via disqualification at 7:58 when Slaughter grabbed the referee and used him as a shield when Andre charged at him; prior to the bout, the Grand Wizard escorted Slaughter ringside
WWF Tag Team Champion Rick Martel pinned the Hangman at 15:37 with a flip and roll up
WWF Tag Team Champion Tony Garea pinned Bulldog Brower at 10:56 with a roll up
Tony Atlas pinned Hulk Hogan at 7:08 after crotching Hogan on the top rope; Hogan had his foot on the middle rope during the cover but the referee failed to notice; after the bout, Hogan attacked referee Dick Kroll, bodyslammed him, and gave him a legdrop

WWF @ New York City, NY - Madison Square Garden - April 6, 1981 (25,302 including 3,334 in Felt Forum)
Televised on the MSG Network - featured Vince McMahon on commentary:
Yoshiaki Yatsu pinned Terry Gunn at 5:11 with a belly to belly suplex
Killer Khan (w/ Freddie Blassie) pinned Dominic DeNucci at 5:19 with a kneedrop
WWF Intercontinental Champion Pedro Morales pinned WWF Tag Team Champion Moondog Rex (w/ Capt. Lou Albano) at 9:33 with a small package
Pat Patterson fought Sgt. Slaughter (w/ the Grand Wizard) to a double disqualification at 13:36 after both men abused referee Jack Lotz
All American Wrestling - 11/6/83: Mil Mascaras pinned Moondog King (w/ Capt. Lou Albano) at 8:14 with a crossbody off the top
WWF World Champion Bob Backlund defeated Stan Hansen in a steel cage match by escaping through the door at 8:59 (*Bloodbath: Wrestling's Most Incredible Steel Cage Matches*)
SD Jones pinned Baron Mikel Scicluna at 8:53 with a sunset flip
Women's Champion the Fabulous Moolah & Lelani Kai defeated Jill Fontaine & Suzette Ferriera at 7:08 when Moolah pinned Fontaine following a flapjack
Tony Garea & Rick Martel defeated Johnny Rodz & Larry Sharpe at 7:38 when Martel pinned Rodz with a double leg cradle

WWF @ New York City, NY - Madison Square Garden - May 4, 1981 (near capacity)
Televised on the MSG Network - featured Vince McMahon on commentary; prior to the show, it was announced to the crowd Andre the Giant had sustained a broken ankle:
SD Jones defeated Johnny Rodz at 15:36
Yoshiaki Yatsu defeated the Hangman at 10:31; the bout was originally scheduled for Yatsu & Antonio Inoki vs. Hangman & Frank Savage
Dominic DeNucci pinned Baron Mikel Scicluna at 6:53 with a backslide
Peter Maivia pinned Rick McGraw at 7:08 with a backbreaker
Angelo Mosca defeated WWF World Champion Bob Backlund via disqualification at 13:51 when Backlund accidentally punched the referee when Mosca ducked the blow; after the bout, Mosca ran backstage with the title belt (Mosca's MSG debut)
Pat Patterson defeated Sgt. Slaugther (w/ the Grand Wizard) in an alley fight at 14:25 when the Grand Wizard, who escorted Slaughter to the ring before the match, returned ringside and threw in the towel after Slaughter had been beaten a bloody mess; voted Match of the Year by the Wrestling Observer Newsletter (*WWE Hall of Fame 2004, Falls Count Anywhere: The Greatest Street Fights and other Out of Control Matches*)
Tony Garea, Rick Martel, & Gorilla Monsoon (sub. for Andre the Giant) defeated Stan Hansen, WWF Tag Team Champion Moondog Rex, & Capt. Lou Albano (sub. for Moondog King) in a Best 2 out of 3 falls match at 14:01, 2-0; fall #1: Monsoon's team won via disqualification at 11:39 when all three heels began attacking Martel; fall #2: Monsoon pinned Rex at 2:22 with a splash (Hansen's final MSG appearance; Monsoon's final MSG appearance as a wrestler)
The Carolina Kid & Farmer Jerome defeated Sky Low Low & Kid Chocolate at 11:23 when Carolina pinned Chocolate following an airplane spin
WWF Intercontinental Champion Pedro Morales defeated Killer Khan at 4:26

The Alley Fight
"I've been in this industry for more than 55 years, and I am so proud of that match. I think it was instrumental in the molding and thinking of what we have in the matches like it today."
Pat Patterson, *WWE.com interview, 2014*

WWF @ New York City, NY - Madison Square Garden - June 8, 1981 (near capacity)

Televised on the MSG Network and USA Network - featured Vince McMahon on commentary; included McMahon conducting a ringside interview with Andre the Giant regarding Killer Khan and Andre's broken ankle:

Larry Sharpe pinned Rick McGraw at 9:06 after falling on top when both men collided with a double shoulderblock

Curt Hennig pinned Johnny Rodz at 9:45 with a running forearm smash followed by an elbow drop (Hennig's MSG debut)

Don Muraco (w/ the Grand Wizard) defeated Rick Martel via count-out at 10:27 after crotching Martel on the top rope (Muraco's MSG debut)

SD Jones pinned Frank Savage at 6:17 with a swinging neckbreaker

Dusty Rhodes defeated Killer Khan via disqualification at 11:45 when Khan kept attacking Rhodes against the ropes for longer than the referee's 5-count; prior to the bout, Khan was escorted to the ring by Freddie Blassie

Tony Garea pinned Man Mountain Cannon (King Kong Bundy) at 6:23 with a powerslam; prior to the bout, Howard Finkel introduced Andre the Giant, who came ringside on crutches and was interviewed by Vince McMahon and remained ringside for this and the next match where McMahon continued to interview him

WWF World Champion Bob Backlund (w/ Arnold Skaaland) pinned Angelo Mosca at 10:31 with a crossbody when guest referee Pat Patterson made a fast count while Mosca's foot was also on the bottom rope during the cover after Mosca had shoved Patterson moments earlier; prior to the bout, Capt. Lou Albano escorted Mosca to ringside; after the bout, Mosca attacked Patterson and kicked him out of the ring

Yoshiaki Yatsu & WWF Jr. Heavyweight Champion Tatsumi Fujinami defeated WWF Tag Team Champions the Moondogs in a Best 2 out of 3 falls match at 22:15, 2-0; fall #1: the champions were disqualified at 15:44 when Spot used his rope belt to choke out Fujinami; fall #2: Fujinami pinned Spot after Rex accidentally hit an elbow drop on his partner; prior to the bout, Strong Kobyashi was introduced alongside the challengers; after the bout, Fujinami announced that he was engaged and his fiancee, Miss Kayori, was escorted to the ring

WWF Intercontinental Champion Pedro Morales defeated Sgt. Slaughter via disqualification at 6:53 after the challenger punched referee Dick Kroll in the face after Morales repeatedly punched the challenger; prior to the match, the Grand Wizard escorted Slaughter to the ring; after the bout, Morales and Slaughter continued to fight until Morales knocked Slaughter to the floor; moments later, Slaughter came up behind Kroll and put him in the Cobra Clutch while on the apron until Morales fought him off and stalked him backstage

WWF @ New York City, NY - Madison Square Garden - July 20, 1981 (22,091)
Johnny Rodz defeated Terry Gunn at 9:31
SD Jones defeated Baron Mikel Scicluna at 9:18
Curt Hennig defeated Strong Kobayashi at 5:44
Sgt. Slaughter defeated Dominic DeNucci at 8:39
WWF World Champion Bob Backlund defeated George Steele at 7:11
Pat Patterson defeated Angelo Mosca via disqualification at 11:08
WWF Intercontinental Champion Don Muraco fought Pedro Morales to a 20-minute draw
Andre the Giant fought Killer Khan to a double disqualification
Tony Garea & Rick Martel fought WWF Tag Team Champions the Moondogs to a curfew draw at the 10-minute mark

July 17, 1981: Van Halen performed at MSG for the first time.

WWF @ New York City, NY - Madison Square Garden - August 24, 1981 (22,000)
Curt Hennig defeated Baron Mikel Scicluna at 6:42
Dominic DeNucci defeated Frank Savage at 5:16
SD Jones defeated Johnny Rodz at 5:53
El Canek defeated Jose Estrada at 14:31
WWF World Champion Bob Backlund fought WWF Intercontinental Champion Don Muraco to a 60-minute time-limit draw
Pedro Morales defeated Angelo Mosca via disqualification at 10:49
Andre the Giant defeated Killer Khan in a Texas Death Match at 6:48; both Pat Patterson & Gorilla Monsoon were special referees for the bout
WWF Tag Team Champion Tony Garea defeated Bulldog Brower at 5:16
WWF Tag Team Champion Rick Martel defeated Moondog Spot at 3:27
Tony Atlas defeated Moondog Rex at 5:02

WWF @ New York City, NY - Madison Square Garden - September 21, 1981 (20,920)
Televised on the MSG Network and USA Network - featured Vince McMahon on commentary:
Yoshiaki Yatsu pinned Baron Mikel Scicluna at 9:37 with a sunset flip
Mr. Saito and Mr. Fuji co-won a $10,000 20-man battle royal by last eliminating WWF Tag Team Champion Rick Martel at 18:24; order of elimination: Bulldog Brower, Ron Shaw, Curt Hennig, Baron Mikel Scicluna, Steve O, Jose Estrada, Yoshiaki Yatsu, Mil Mascaras, Pedro Morales, Angelo Mosca, Killer Khan, Johnny Rodz, Roberto Soto, Larry Sharpe, WWF Tag Team Champion Tony Garea, SD Jones, Dominic DeNucci, and Martel (Steve O's MSG debut)
Steve O pinned Ron Shaw at 6:52 after an axe handle off the top
Mr. Fuji pinned Curt Hennig at 7:14 with a Samoan Drop; prior to the bout, Capt. Lou Albano escorted Fuji to the ring
Killer Khan pinned Dominic DeNucci at 4:03 after avoiding a charge in the corner; prior to the bout, Freddie Blassie escorted Khan to the ring
Mr. Saito pinned Roberto Soto at 6:54 with a kick to the chest; prior to the bout, Capt. Lou Albano escorted Saito to the ring
WWF World Champion Bob Backlund pinned WWF Intercontinental Champion Don Muraco in a Texas Death Match at 31:35 after reversing a suplex attempt into a backdrop; Muraco's foot was on the bottom rope during the cover but the referee failed to notice; prior to the bout, the Grand Wizard escorted Muraco to the ring
Pedro Morales pinned Larry Sharpe at 6:28 with a backslide
Mil Mascaras pinned Bulldog Brower at 2:41 with a crossbody and splash
WWF Tag Team Champions Tony Garea & Rick Martel defeated Johnny Rodz & Jose Estrada at 12:15 when Martel pinned Estrada with a sunset flip

December 2, 1981: AC/DC performed at MSG for the first time.

WWF @ New York City, NY - Madison Square Garden - October 19, 1981 (18,120)
Televised on the MSG Network and USA Network - featured Vince McMahon on commentary:
Curt Hennig pinned Joe Cox with a sunset flip at 9:14
Tony Garea & Rick Martel defeated WWF Tag Team Champions Mr. Fuji & Mr. Saito via disqualification at 11:44 when referee John Stanley stopped the bout for excessive double teaming of Garea after Martel was thrown to the floor
Pedro Morales defeated WWF Intercontinental Champion Don Muraco at 18:46 when referee Jack Lotz stopped the bout due to Muraco's bleeding (*History of the Intercontinental Title*)
Dusty Rhodes pinned Ron Shaw at 1:28 with the Bionic Elbow
WWF World Champion Bob Backlund fought Greg Valentine to a no contest at 19:32; Backlund scored the pin when Valentine fell over after putting Backlund in an airplane spin but dazed referee John Stanley gave the title to Valentine and raised his hand as the winner after Backlund's leg knocked Stanley out during the airplane spin and Stanley thought Valentine had scored the pin, since both wore black tights; after the bout, several officials and NY State Athletic commissioners came to the ring and it was announced no decision would be rendered and the title would be held up pending further investigation; the title controversy was only a factor in NYC as Backlund continued to defend the title until the following month's Texas Death Match rematch
Pat Patterson pinned Angelo Mosca at 9:18 when Patterson lifted his shoulder out of a back suplex and bridge
Dominic DeNucci & SD Jones defeated Jose Estrada & Johnny Rodz at 11:29 when Jones pinned Estrada with a sunset flip
All American Wrestling - 10/30/83: Tony Atlas defeated Killer Khan via count-out at 9:49 when Khan walked out of the match after sustaining a gorilla press slam

December 2, 1981: AC/DC performed at MSG for the first time.

WWF @ New York City, NY - Madison Square Garden - November 23, 1981 (21,104)

Televised on the MSG Network & USA Network - featured Vince McMahon on commentary:

WWF Tag Team Champion Mr. Saito pinned SD Jones at 7:37 after a kneedrop from the middle turnbuckle; prior to the bout, Capt. Lou Albano escorted Saito to the ring

Tony Garea pinned Baron Mikel Scicluna at 11:39 with a sunset flip

Dominic DeNucci & Curt Hennig defeated Johnny Rodz & Jose Estrada at 11:26 when DeNucci pinned Estrada after dropkicked DeNucci in the back as Estrada held DeNucci in a powerslam position

Rick Martel pinned Hans Schroeder with a roll up at 13:11

Pedro Morales pinned WWF Intercontinental Champion Don Muraco in a Texas Death Match to win the title after hitting Muraco with his own foreign object at 13:36 (*History of the Intercontinental Title*)

The Haiti Kid pinned Little Boy Blue at 8:33

Bob Backlund (w/ Arnold Skaaland) pinned Greg Valentine to win the vacant WWF World Heavyweight title at 15:36 with a German suplex into a bridge after avoiding a punch; in a move that was only recognized in the NYC area, the championship was vacated the previous month when the referee accidentally handed Valentine the title following his loss to Backlund; prior to the bout, the Grand Wizard escorted Valentine to the ring

Dusty Rhodes defeated Angelo Mosca via count-out at 7:24 when, as both men were fighting on the apron, Rhodes missed a punch and fell back into the ring to break the count

Mil Mascaras pinned the Executioner (Ron Shaw) at 2:36 with a crossbody off the top

Tony Atlas pinned WWF Tag Team Champion Mr. Fuji at 8:16 following a gorilla press slam; prior to the bout, Capt. Lou Albano escorted Fuji to the ring

142

WWF @ New York City, NY - Madison Square Garden - January 18, 1982 (18,301)
Televised on the MSG Network and USA Network - featured Vince McMahon on commentary:
Davey O'Hannon pinned Manuel Soto at 9:52 with a neckbreaker
Larry Sharpe pinned Jose Estrada at 8:41 after holding onto the ropes to avoid a dropkick from Estrada
Charlie Fulton pinned Johnny Rodz at 9:28 after avoiding a splash
Greg Valentine defeated WWF Intercontinental Champion Pedro Morales via disqualification at 14:43 after the champion hit Valentine with Valentine's own foreign object
Jesse Ventura pinned Dominic DeNucci at 10:26 with an elbow drop; after the bout, there was an in-ring announcement made regarding the New Japan Pro Wrestling IWGP Tournament with Vince McMahon Sr., WWF President Hisashi Shima, Frank Tunney, and NWA President Jim Crockett Jr.; on the broadcast, McMahon Jr. talked over the announcement as it was going on and hyped the world title match later in the card (Ventura's MSG debut)
Adrian Adonis defeated WWF World Champion Bob Backlund when the referee stopped the match at 30:54 due to excessive blood loss
Rick Martel & Tony Garea defeated WWF Tag Team Champions Mr. Fuji & Mr. Saito via disqualification at 8:58 when Fuji threw salt in the face of guest referee Pat Patterson as Martel had Saito in a sleeper
Tony Atlas pinned the Executioner (Hans Schroeder) at 2:57 with a headbutt off the middle turnbuckle and a splash
Ivan Putski defeated Killer Khan via referee's decision after the curfew expired at 2:29

WWF @ New York City, NY - Madison Square Garden - February 15, 1982 (22,034)
Johnny Rodz fought Davey O'Hannon to a 20-minute time limit draw
Capt. Lou Albano, WWF Tag Team Champions Mr. Fuji & Mr. Saito defeated Pat Patterson, Tony Garea, & Rick Martel in a Best 3 out of 5 falls match at 15:31
Jesse Ventura defeated SD Jones at 5:43
WWF World Champion Bob Backlund pinned Adrian Adonis in a Texas Death Match via a backflip pin at 16:33; Ivan Putski was the special referee for the bout
Pierre Martel defeated Larry Sharpe via disqualification at 9:51
Steve Travis defeated Charlie Fulton at 6:33
Rick McGraw defeated Jose Estrada at 8:24
WWF Intercontinental Champion Pedro Morales defeated Greg Valentine in a Brass Knuckles Alley Fight at 14:10; Ivan Putski was the guest referee for the bout
Tony Atlas fought Killer Khan to a curfew draw

WWF @ New York City, NY - Madison Square Garden - March 14, 1982 (matinee)
Televised on the MSG Network and USA Network - featured Vince McMahon on commentary:
Steve Travis pinned Jose Estrada at 10:06 with a roll up
Women's Champion the Fabulous Moolah & Wendi Richter defeated Velvet McIntyre & Princess Victoria at 11:56
when Moolah pinned Victoria with a powerbomb after Victoria failed a hurricanrana attempt
Greg Valentine pinned SD Jones at 9:48 with a clothesline and elbow drop; prior to the bout, the Grand Wizard
escorted Valentine to the ring
All American Wrestling - 9/11/83: Rick McGraw & Andre the Giant defeated WWF Tag Team Champions Mr. Saito &
Mr. Fuji in a Best 2 out of 3 falls match, 2-0 at 13:02; fall #1: the challengers won via disqualification at 11:24 after
Fuji critched McGraw on the top turnbuckle; fall #2: Andre pinned Fuji at 1:38 with a boot to the face and sit-down
splash; because the first fall was won via disqualification, the title did not change hands
WWF World Champion Bob Backlund (w/ Arnold Skaaland) pinned Jesse Ventura (w/ Freddie Blassie) at 9:21 with a
roll up into a bridge and a fast count from guest referee Ivan Putski; after the bout, an enraged Ventura attacked
Putski until Backlund and Putski together sent him out of the ring (*History of the WWF Heavyweight
Championship, WWE Hall of Fame 2004*)
WWF Intercontinental Champion Pedro Morales pinned Adrian Adonis at 10:47 by lifting his shoulder out of a suplex
in which both men's shoulders were down (*Best of the WWF Vol. 8*)
Pat Patterson defeated Capt. Lou Albano via count-out at 1:59 after Patterson hit Albano with his own foreign object,
causing Albano to bleed, with Albano then running backstage (*Best of the WWF Vol. 8*)
Tony Garea & Rick Martel defeated Charlie Fulton & the Executioner (Baron Mikel Scicluna) at 7:28 when Garea
pinned Fulton with a sunset flip

@ New York City, NY - Madison Square Garden - April 26, 1982
Johnny Rodz defeated Baron Mikel Scicluna via disqualification at 5:52
Bob Orton Jr. defeated Rick McGraw when the match was stopped due to blood at 7:06 (Orton's MSG debut)
Blackjack Mulligan defeated Steve Travis at 12:49
Jimmy Snuka defeated WWF World Champion Bob Backlund via disqualification at 10:42 when Backlund refused to break a choke; after the match, Snuka hit the splash off the top and the champion had to be taken from the ring on a stretcher (Snuka's MSG debut)
Tony Garea defeated Charlie Fulton at 13:02
Tony Atlas pinned Jesse Ventura at 15:09
Adrian Adonis defeated Pete Sanchez at 6:10
Ivan Putski, WWF Intercontinental Champion Pedro Morales, & Andre the Giant defeated Greg Valentine, WWF Tag Team Champions Mr. Fuji & Mr. Saito in a Best 2 out of 3 falls match at 23:40, 2-0; the 1st fall was decided via disqualification

W.W.F. CHAMPIONSHIP
WRESTLING
madison square garden

MONDAY, APRIL 26th, 1982
VINCE McMAHON, PROMOTER

SANCTIONED BY THE WORLD WRESTLING FEDERATION
HISASHI SHINMA, PRESIDENT
UNDER SUPERVISION OF THE NEW YORK STATE ATHLETIC COMMISSION

OFFICIAL PROGRAM MAGAZINE #52 - PRICE: $2.00
PUBLISHED BY THE WRESTLING NEWS™ DIVISION OF PRO WRESTLING ENTERPRISES
NORMAN H. KIETZER, PUBLISHER — JAMES C. MELBY, EDITOR

W.W.F.
THE WORLD WRESTLING FEDERATION
HISASHI SHINMA, PRESIDENT

W.W.F. HEADQUARTERS
7-13 MINAMI-AOYAMA 6-CHOME
MINATO-KU, TOKYO, JAPAN 107

BOB BACKLUNDS DEFENDS W.W.F. CHAMPIONSHIP
AGAINST JIMMY "SUPERFLY" SNUKA

TONY "Mr USA" ATLAS VS. JESSE "THE BODY" VENTURA

ANDRE THE GIANT, PEDRO MORALES, AND "POLISH POWER"
IVAN PUTSKI UNITE FOR SIX MAN TAG TEAM MATCH VERSUS
MR. FUJI, MR. SAITO, AND GREG "THE HAMMER" VALENTINE

BLACK JACK MULLIGAN BATTLES STEVE TRAVIS

COWBOY BOB ORTON DEBUTS AGAINST RICK McGRAW

"GOLDEN BOY" ADRIAN ADONIS VS. PETE SANCHEZ

CHARLIE FULTON VS. TONY GAREA

BARON MIKEL SCICLUNA VS. JOHNNY RODZ

THE BOX OFFICE AT MADISON SQUARE GARDEN
IS OPEN DAILY FROM 10:00 A.M. TO 8:00 P.M.

PEDRO MORALES

'Do you want to see someone fly?'

"My parents were divorced and the weekends I spent with my father. I'm 7 years old and he came to get me. We were going to go see a movie, and he asks me, 'Do you want to see someone fly?' And of course I say yes. He turns on wrestling and 'Superfly' Jimmy Snuka is there. 'Watch this guy.' We watch him and he jumps off the top rope and I'm mesmerized. Suffice it to say, we never made it to the movie that day. We spent the entire day talking about wrestling. He told me all about watching wrestling with his dad. That Wednesday, my father shows up at my mother's house and he had three wrestling magazines for me. That next month is my birthday. June 1982, my father takes me to my first wrestling show at Madison Square Garden. My father worked around the corner of Madison Square Garden and lived on Long Island. It turned out, every month we went. Back then, they ran on Monday nights. I only saw my dad on the weekends but now I'm getting to see him Mondays as well. From there, it just became something that he and I bonded over. It was our thing. It was our place. The only person screaming louder than me at Madison Square Garden on those nights was my dad, throwing his fist in the air. It was a complete bond and connection. I started to like the rule breakers and he liked the good guys."

Matt Striker, *TheHistoryofWWE.com interview, 2014*

WWF @ New York City, NY - Madison Square Garden - June 5, 1982
Televised on the MSG Network and USA Network - featured Vince McMahon on commentary:
Jose Estrada pinned Laurent Soucie at 10:28 with a flying back elbow
Ivan Putski pinned WWF Tag Team Champion Mr. Saito at 8:37 with the Polish Hammer
Tony Atlas fought Greg Valentine to a double count-out at 8:24 when both men were brawling on the floor; prior to the bout, the Grand Wizard escorted Valentine to the ring
Bob Orton Jr. pinned Steve Travis at 9:42 with the superplex; prior to the bout, the Grand Wizard escorted Orton to the ring
Tony Garea defeated Swede Hanson via disqualification at 7:31 after Hanson ignored the referee's 5-count and kept beating on Garea in the corner where he had hung him upside down
Jimmy Snuka defeated WWF World Champion Bob Backlund (w/ Arnold Skaaland) via count-out at 20:53 after Snuka beat on Backlund on the floor and rammed Backlund's head into a chair; prior to the bout, Capt. Lou Albano escorted Snuka to the ring; after the bout, a bloodied Backlund attacked Snuka and eventually cleared him from the ring
WWF Intercontinental Champion Pedro Morales pinned WWF Tag Team Champion Mr. Fuji at 5:39 with a sunset flip out of the corner
Chief Jay & Jules Strongbow defeated Jesse Ventura & Adrian Adonis at 11:19 when Jay pinned Adonis with a Thesz Press even though Adonis had his foot on the middle ropes during the cover
Rick McGraw pinned Charlie Fulton at 2:21 with a small package
Women's Champion the Fabulous Moolah & Sherri Martel defeated Judy Martin & Penny Mitchell at 3:30 when Moolah pinned Martin with a roll up
Andre the Giant fought Blackjack Mulligan to a double count-out at 9:34 when both men were brawling on the floor and Mulligan applied the claw hold; prior to the bout, Freddie Blassie escorted Mulligan to the ring; after the bout, a bloodied Andre attacked Mulligan and threw several chairs into the ring which scared Mulligan off

WWF @ New York City, NY - Madison Square Garden - June 28, 1982
Televised on the MSG and USA networks - featured Vince McMahon on commentary:
Johnny Rodz pinned Rick McGraw at 10:32 with a legdrop from the middle turnbuckle
Swede Hanson pinned Laurent Soucie at 3:24 with a kneedrop to the throat
Salvatore Bellomo pinned Baron Mikel Scicluna at 4:19 with a dropkick and splash
Bob Orton Jr. defeated WWF Intercontinental Champion Pedro Morales via disqualification at 14:38 when Morales threw referee Dick Kroll to the mat; prior to the bout, the Grand Wizard escorted Orton to the ring
Blackjack Mulligan pinned SD Jones at 7:44 after avoiding a move off the turnbuckle and hitting an elbow drop; prior to the bout, Freddie Blassie escorted Mulligan to the ring
Steve Travis pinned Charlie Fulton at 5:41 with a small package
All American Wrestling - 9/4/83: WWF World Champion Bob Backlund defeated Jimmy Snuka in a steel cage match at 15:10 by avoiding a lunge from the challenger and escaping through the door after Snuka missed a splash off the top of the cage; prior to the match, Vince McMahon conducted ringside interviews with Steve Travis and Freddie Blassie and announced Andre the Giant would face Blackjack Mulligan the following month in a Texas Death Match; before the bout, Capt. Lou Albano escorted Snuka and Arnold Skaaland escorted Backlund to the ring; after the bout, the champion was interviewed at ringside by McMahon regarding the match as well as his next challenge, Bob Orton Jr.; rules for the bout stated the winner could only win by escaping through the door; voted Pro Wrestling Illustrated's Match of the Year (*The Greatest Wrestling Stars of the 80s, Legends of Wrestling: Hulk Hogan and Bob Backlund, The Greatest Cage Matches of All Time*)
Chief Jay & Jules Strongbow defeated WWF Tag Team Champions Mr. Fuji & Mr. Saito to win the titles at 9:48 when Jules pinned Fuji after Fuji missed a dive in the ring; the decision was later overturned when the replay showed Fuji's foot on the bottom rope during the pin and the titles were declared vacant; Ivan Putski was the guest referee for the bout; prior to the match, Fuji & Saito were escorted to the ring by Capt. Lou Albano (*Tag Team Champions*)
Tony Garea defeated Adrian Adonis via disqualification at 8:35 when Adonis shoved referee Mike Torres as Torres attempted to break Adonis' sleeper
Tony Atlas defeated Greg Valentine via count-out at 3:02 when Valentine left ringside after sustaining several headbutts; prior to the bout, Valentine was escorted to the ring by the Grand Wizard

WWF @ New York City, NY - Madison Square Garden - August 2, 1982 (22,000; sell out)
Women's Champion the Fabulous Moolah & Leilani Kai defeated Vivian St. John & Peggy Lee at 7:13
Johnny Rodz fought Pete Sanchez to a double disqualification
Tony Garea fought Steve Travis to a draw at 13:32
Salvatore Bellomo defeated Jose Estrada at 4:14
SD Jones defeated Swede Hanson at 2:36
Ivan Putski (sub. for Tony Atlas) defeated WWF Tag Team Champion Mr. Saito at 10:18
Ivan Putski defeated WWF Tag Team Champion Mr. Fuji via disqualification at 2:58
Chief Jay & Jules Strongbow defeated the Masked Demons at 5:06
Jimmy Snuka defeated WWF Intercontinental Champion Pedro Morales via count-out at 9:18
Andre the Giant defeated Blackjack Mulligan at 14:41 in a Texas Death Match
WWF World Champion Bob Backlund defeated Bob Orton Jr. at 23:38

WWF @ New York City, NY - Madison Square Garden - August 30, 1982 (19,908)
Televised on the MSG and USA networks - included Vince McMahon on commentary
Tony Garea pinned Charlie Fulton at 6:39 with a crossbody off the top
Killer Khan pinned Steve Travis at 5:31 with a kneedrop from the middle turnbuckle
Bob Orton Jr. defeated Pat Patterson via count-out at 9:28 after crotching Patterson on the top, causing him to fall to the floor
WWF Jr. Heavyweight Champion Tiger Mask pinned the Dynamite Kid at 6:34 with a suplex and moonsault after the challenger failed a diving headbutt (Tiger Mask and Dynamite's MSG debut)
WWF Intercontinental Champion Pedro Morales fought Jimmy Snuka to a double disqualification at 17:55 after both men refused to break choke holds, with Snuka also hitting a headbutt on guest referee Ivan Putski; prior to the bout, Capt. Lou Albano escorted Snuka to the ring
Tiger Jackson & Little Beaver defeated Sky Low Low & Sonny Boy (w/ Thomas Charles Cassidy) in a Best 2 out of 3 falls match, 2-0; fall #1: Jackson pinned Sonny Boy at 4:46 wit a forearm to the chest; fall #2: Beaver pinned Sky Low Low at 1:17 with a gorilla press slam
Tatsumi Fujinami pinned WWF International Champion Gino Brito with a suplex at 11:34 to win the title; prior to the bout, WWF President Hisashi Shinma was introduced to the crowd
Salvatore Bellomo pinned Swede Hanson at 3:26 with a roll up after Hanson hit the corner; prior to the bout, Freddie Blassie escorted Hanson to the ring
WWF World Champion Bob Backlund defeated Buddy Rose via submission with the Crossface Chicken Wing at 20:24 after reversing an attempt at a back suplex; prior to the bout, Backlund was escorted to the ring by Arnold Skaaland while Rose was escorted to the ring by the Grand Wizard, Sherri Martel, & ? (*Legends of Wrestling: Hulk Hogan and Bob Backlund*)
Women's Champion the Fabulous Moolah defeated Penny Mitchell at 4:49 after the challenger missed a crossbody from the middle turnbuckle
Andre the Giant, Chief Jay & Jules Strongbow defeated Blackjack Mulligan, WWF Tag Team Champions Mr. Fuji & Mr. Saito in a Best 2 out of 3 falls match, 2-1; fall #1: Fuji pinned Jay at 8:16 with a karate chop to the throat; fall #2: Jay pinned Fuji at 3:26 with a forearm blow; fall #3: Jules pinned Saito at 2:21 after releasing a sleeper hold; after the bout, Andre applied a claw on Mulligan for several minutes while wearing a black glove similar to Mulligan's

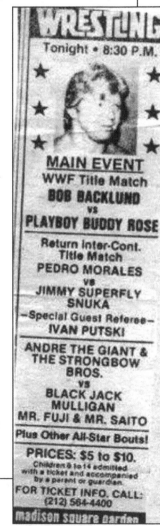

WWF @ New York City, NY - Madison Square Garden - October 4, 1982 (22,101)
Baron Mikel Scicluna defeated Pete Sanchez at 9:23
SD Jones defeated Mac Rivera at 5:41
Salvatore Bellomo defeated Johnny Rodz at 9:54
Ivan Putski defeated Swede Hanson at 10:43
Tony Garea & Curt Hennig defeated the Black Demon (Charlie Fulton) & the White Angel at 13:36
Chief Jay & Jules Strongbow defeated WWF Tag Team Champions Mr. Saito & Mr. Fuji in a Best 2 out of 3 falls match at 8:58, 2-1; fall #1: Jules pinned Fuji at 5:22; fall #2: Fuji pinned Jules at 1:09; fall #3: Fuji & Saito were disqualified at 2:27
Andre the Giant defeated Bob Orton Jr. at 9:26
Buddy Rose fought WWF Intercontinental Champion Pedro Morales to a 20-minute time-limit draw
Superstar Billy Graham defeated WWF World Champion Bob Backlund via disqualification at 15:10

WWF @ New York City, NY - Madison Square Garden - November 22, 1982
Televised on the MSG Network and USA Network - featured Vince McMahon & Gorilla Monsoon on commentary:
Curt Hennig fought Eddie Gilbert to a 20-minute time-limit draw at 14:22 as Hennig had Gilbert covered following an elbow drop; prior to and after the bout, the two shook hands (Gilbert's MSG debut) (*The Life and Times of Mr. Perfect*)
SD Jones defeated Swede Hanson via disqualification at 9:20 after hanging Jones upside down in the corner and refusing to break for the referee; prior to the match, Nigerian promoter Power Mike was introduced to the crowd
WWF Jr. Heavyweight Champion Tiger Mask pinned Jose Estrada at 9:42
Little Beaver & Sonny Boy Hayes defeated Sky Low Low & Butch Cassidy in a Best 2 out of 3 falls match, 2-0; fall #1: Beaver pinned Low Low at 4:43 after a press slam; fall #2: Beaver pinned Cassidy at 3:44 after a slingshot into Low Low
WWF World Champion Bob Backlund fought Superstar Billy Graham to a double disqualification at 10:14 when referee Danny Davis threw the match out after being knocked down by the participants, with both men brawling their way backstage moments thereafter; prior to the bout, Graham was accompanied to the ring by the Grand Wizard and Backlund by Arnold Skaaland (*20 Years Too Soon: The Superstar Billy Graham Story*)
Salvatore Bellomo defeated Mr. Fuji via disqualification at 7:11 when Fuji continued to assault Bellomo as Fuji was on the ring apron, despite the referee's order to break
WWF Intercontinental Champion Pedro Morales pinned Buddy Rose at 11:29 with a sunset flip into the ring as Rose charged the champion
Jimmy Snuka (w/ Buddy Rogers) defeated Capt. Lou Albano at 5:59 when referee Gilberto Roman stopped the match, deeming Albano was too bloody to continue; after the match, Snuka hit the top rope splash onto Albano
Ray Stevens (w/ Freddie Blassie) pinned WWF Tag Team Champion Chief Jay Strongbow at 1:02 with a piledriver; after the match, Strongbow was taken backstage on a stretcher
WWF Tag Team Champion Jules Strongbow pinned Charlie Fulton at 4:36 after several tomahawk chops
Rocky Johnson & Tony Garea defeated Riki Choshu & Mr. Saito in a Best 2 out of 3 falls match at 9:13, 2-1; fall #1: Garea pinned Saito at 4:33 with an abdominal stretch into a roll up; fall #2: Saito pinned Garea with a back suplex at 2:13; fall #3: Johnson pinned Choshu following two dropkicks at 2:32

MADISON SQUARE GARDEN   TUES., DEC. 28, 1982

HAPPY NEW YEAR TO YOU ALL!
TONIGHTS OFFICIAL WRESTLING LINE-UPS

MAIN EVENT
1st TIME IN MADISON SQUARE GARDEN
LUMBERJACK MATCH
RE-MATCH FOR THE WORLD WRESTLING FEDERATION
HEAVYWEIGHT CHAMPIONSHIP
Special Guest Referee: Swede Hansen

BOB BACKLUND	vs.	SUPERSTAR BILLY GRAHAM
234 Princeton, Minn		260 Paradise Valley, Arizona
Champion		Challenger

GRUDGE MATCH

CRIPPLER		
RAY STEVENS	vs.	JIMMY "SUPERFLY" SNUKA
238 lbs San Francisco		250 Fiji Islands

INTER-CONTINENTAL HEAVYWEIGHT CHAMPIONSHIP
PEDRO MORALES	vs.	MAGNIFICENT MURACO
240 lbs Culebra, P.R.		Hawaii
Champion		Challenger

WORLDWIDE WRESTLING FEDERATION TAG TEAM TITLE
TEXAS DEATH MATCH

JAY & JULES STRONGBOW	vs.	MR. FUJI & MR. SAITO
235 lbs, 248 lbs, Pawhuska, OK		275 lbs Osaka 268 Tokyo, Japan
Champions		Challengers

PLAYBOY BUDDY ROSE	vs.	IVAN PUTSKI
256 Las Vegas, Nevada		235 lbs Krakaw, Poland

ROCKY JOHNSON	vs.	THE BLACK DEMON
244 Washington, D.C.		?

JOSE ESTRADA	vs.	SALVATORE BELLOMO
225 lbs N.Y.		253 lbs Italy

TONY GAREA	vs.	JOHNNY RODZ
240 lbs N.Z.		239 lbs N.Y.

LADIES TAG TEAM WRESTLING MATCH

PRINCESS VICTORIA		THE FABULOUS MOOLAH
&	vs.	&
WONDER GIRL SABRINA		WENDY RICHTER

SCIENTIFIC ATTRACTION
S.D. JONES	vs.	EDDIE GILBERT
237 lbs Phila. PA		212 lbs Lexington, Tenn

THE FIRST MATCH STARTS AT 8:00 P.M.

REMEMBER FANS

THE NEXT SPECTACULAR
MADISON SQUARE GARDEN WRESTLING CARD
WILL BE HELD ON
SATURDAY NIGHT, JANUARY 22ND
STARTING AT 8:00 P.M.

WWF @ New York City, NY - Madison Square Garden - December 28, 1982

Televised via closed circuit - featured Vince McMahon & Gorilla Monsoon on commentary; Mel Phillips was the ring announcer for the first two matches as regular announcer Howard Finkel was late arriving to the show, with Finkel taking over when he arrived to announce the result of the third match:

SD Jones fought Eddie Gilbert to a 20-minute time limit draw at 13:44

Tony Garea pinned Johnny Rodz at 9:04 with a sunset flip out of the corner

Buddy Rose defeated Ivan Putski via count-out at 8:33 after Putski knocked Rose back into the ring just before the 10-count when Putski was beating on Rose on the apron

WWF Intercontinental Champion Pedro Morales fought Don Muraco to a double disqualification at 14:25 after both men struck the referee; prior to the bout, Capt. Lou Albano escorted Muraco to the ring; after the contest, both men continued to brawl in and out of the ring until Muraco left ringside (*History of the Intercontinental Championship*)

Salvatore Bellomo pinned Jose Estrada at 8:46 with a reverse flying bodypress from the middle turnbuckle

WWF World Champion Bob Backlund (w/ Arnold Skaaland) defeated Superstar Billy Graham via submission with the Crossface Chicken Wing in a lumberjack match at 12:33; Swede Hansen was the special referee for the match; prior to the match, Graham was escorted to the ring by the Grand Wizard; after the bout, Graham argued the decision with Hanson with the two men eventually coming to blows and Swede eventually clearing the ring of Graham; lumberjacks for the match included Mr. Fuji, Buddy Rose, Mr. Saito, Jules Strongbow, Salvatore Bellomo, the Black Demon, Johnny Rodz, Tony Garea, Chief Jay Strongbow, Eddie Gilbert, Rocky Johnson, and Jose Estrada

Wendi Richter & Women's Champion the Fabulous Moolah defeated Elizabeth Chase & Princess Victoria when Moolah pinned Victoria at 9:11 following a legdrop from the middle turnbuckle by Richter

All American Wrestling - 9/4/83: Jimmy Snuka defeated Ray Stevens via count-out at 6:50 after Snuka threw Stevens into the corner, with Stevens then falling out to the floor and not being able to meet the referee's 10-count; prior to the bout, Capt. Lou Albano and Freddie Blassie escorted Stevens to the ring and after the refused to leave the ring, Snuka went back to the locker room and brought Buddy Rogers out with him to offset Albano & Blassie; after the bout, Snuka again knocked Stevens to the floor (*Best of Confidential Vol. 1*)

Rocky Johnson pinned the Black Demon at 5:13 with a sunset flip following two dropkicks

Prime Time Wrestling - 1/14/86: WWF Tag Team Champions Chief Jay & Jules Strongbow defeated Mr. Fuji & Mr. Saito in a Texas Death Match at 8:47 when Jules pinned Saito following a double elbowsmash

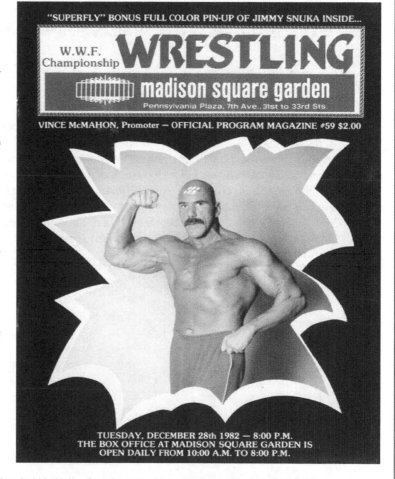

"SUPERFLY" BONUS FULL COLOR PIN-UP OF JIMMY SNUKA INSIDE...

W.W.F. Championship **WRESTLING**

madison square garden

Pennsylvania Plaza, 7th Ave., 31st to 33rd Sts.

VINCE McMAHON, Promoter — OFFICIAL PROGRAM MAGAZINE #59 $2.00

TUESDAY, DECEMBER 28th 1982 — 8:00 P.M.
THE BOX OFFICE AT MADISON SQUARE GARDEN IS
OPEN DAILY FROM 10:00 A.M. TO 8:00 P.M.

December 31, 1982: Billy Joel ended his Nylon Curtain tour with a sell out New Year's Eve performance

WWF @ New York City, NY - Madison Square Garden - January 22, 1983
Televised on the MSG Network and the USA Network - featured Vince McMahon & Gorilla Monsoon on commentary:
Johnny Rodz pinned Pete Sanchez at 8:42 with a small package
SD Jones pinned Baron Mikel Scicluna with a headbutt at 6:36
Superstar Billy Graham (w/ the Grand Wizard) pinned Swede Hanson after hitting him in the throat with a foreign object hidden in his boot at 3:29
Championship Wrestling - 1/29/83; All American Wrestling - 10/2/83: Don Muraco pinned WWF Intercontinental Champion Pedro Morales to win the title at 11:34 when the champion's injured knee gave out as he attempted a slam, with Morales falling on top for the pin (Morales' first pinfall loss at MSG in 18 years) (*Best of the WWF Vol. 2, History of the Intercontinental Title*)
The Wild Samoans (w/ Capt. Lou Albano) defeated Tony Garea & Eddie Gilbert at 9:23 when Sika pinned Garea after Afa connected with a flying axe handle to the back as Garea had Sika in an abdominal stretch
Ray Stevens pinned WWF Tag Team Champion Jules Strongbow with a piledriver at 7:51
WWF World Champion Bob Backlund (w/ Arnold Skaaland) pinned Big John Studd (w/ Freddie Blassie) at 7:17 by backdropping out of an overhead backbreaker after kicking off the top turnbuckle and landing on top for the win, despite the replay showing Studd may have lifted his shoulder before the 3-count; before the bell rang, Studd reapplied the hold, giving some the impression Backlund had submitted
Curt Hennig pinned Mac Rivera with a missile dropkick at 8:29
All American Wrestling - 10/16/83: Jimmy Snuka (w/ Buddy Rogers) pinned Buddy Rose (w/ Capt. Lou Albano) at 15:26 with the splash off the top
Salvatore Bellomo pinned Charlie Fulton with a high crossbody at 3:33
Rocky Johnson pinned Mr. Fuji with a small package at 6:28 as Fuji attempted a bodyslam

Merchandising

"From when I started going, '75 to '82 maybe, the most you could find: you get your monthly program, they sold buttons, sometimes they sold photos. Pretty much, that was it. It wasn't until '82 that the WWF made a couple of shirts. I still have a bunch of them. Bob Backlund, Jimmy Snuka, and a Don Muraco shirt. It was pretty limited. While I'm going to Garden shows, before the expansion, they used to have WWF shows at high school gyms, in church basements here in Brooklyn. And even there, I'd seek out George Napolitano and he would sell 8x10s of all the wrestlers. George became one of my best friends later down the road."
Charlie Adorno, *Brooklyn, NY*

MADISON SQUARE GARDEN
8 P.M.

FRIDAY, FEB. 18th 1983

MAIN EVENT
FOR THE WORLD WRESTLING FEDERATION TITLE — ONE FALL
60 MINUTE TIME LIMIT

BOB BACKLUND
Champion
234 Princeton, Minn.

VS.

MAGNIFICENT MURACO
Challenger
275 Sunset Beach, Hawaii

Won By:_____

SPECIAL TAG TEAM WRESTLING MATCH

THE WILD SAMOANS
Afa & Sika
598 lbs
Island of Samoa

VS.

ANDRE THE GIANT
500 Grenoble, France
JIMMY "SUPERFLY" SNUKA
250 Fiji Islands

Won By:_____

SUPER GRUDGE RE-MATCH

RAY "THE CRIPPLER" STEVENS
238 San Francisco, Ca.

VS.

CHIEF JAY STRONGBOW
235 Pawhuska, Oklahoma

Won By:_____

SPECIAL CHALLENGE BOUT
One Fall — One Hour

PEDRO MORALES
240 Culebra, P.R.

VS.

PLAYBOY BUDDY ROSE
256 Las Vegas, Nev.

Won By:_____

EXTRA ADDED ATTRACTION

SUPERSTAR BILLY GRAHAM
260 Paradise Valley, Ar.

VS.

ROCKY JOHNSON
244 Washington D.C.

Won By:_____

JULES STRONGBOW
248 Pawhuska, Oklahoma

VS.

BIG JOHN STUDD
364 Los Angeles, Ca.

Won By:_____

MR. FUJI
275 Osaka, Japan

VS.

TONY GAREA
240 New Zealand

vs.

Won By:_____

SALVATORE BELLOMO
253 Italy

VS.

STAN HANSON
312 Slaughter Creek, N.C.

Won By:_____

EDDIE GILBERT
212 Lexington, Tenn.

VS.

CHARLIE FULTON
260 Marion, Ohio

Won By:_____

BARON MIKEL SCICLUNA
273 Isle of Malta

VS.

JOHNNY RODZ
239 New York City

Won By:_____

REMEMBER FANS

HERE IN MADISON SQUARE GARDEN
SUNDAY AFTERNOON MARCH 20th FOR THE ENTIRE FAMILY
A SPECIAL DAYTIME WRESTLING SPECTACULAR
STARTING AT 1:00 P.M.

INSIDE — BONUS COLOR PIN-UP OF THE 8TH WONDER OF WRESTLING — ANDRE THE GIANT

W.W.F. Championship WRESTLING

madison square garden
Pennsylvania Plaza, 7th Ave., 31st to 33rd Sts.

OFFICIAL PROGRAM MAGAZINE #61 $2.00

AFTER VALENTINE'S DAY MASSACRE WORLD WRESTLING FEDERATION TITLE

BLOOD WAR

BOB BACKLUND
CHAMPION

MAGNIFICENT MURACO
CHALLENGER

WWF @ New York City, NY - Madison Square Garden - February 18, 1983
Televised on the MSG Network and the USA Network - featured Vince McMahon & Gorilla Monsoon on commentary; included pretaped footage of McMahon conducting interviews with WWF Intercontinental Champion Don Muraco in the locker room and WWF World Champion Bob Backlund, shown just before their match; included a preataped interview of McMahon with Andre the Giant & Jimmy Snuka, shown prior to their match with the Wild Samoans:
Jose Estrada pinned Curt Hennig at 13:25 with a flying back elbow
Johnny Rodz pinned Baron Mikel Scicluna at 4:59 with a splash
Mr. Fuji pinned Tony Garea at 8:26 after falling on top of Garea as Garea attempted to suplex Fuji into the ring from the apron; after the bout, Kal Rudman interviewed Fuji backstage about his victory
Big John Studd defeated WWF Tag Team Champion Jules Strongbow via submission at 2:40 with the backbreaker; prior to the bout, Freddie Blassie escorted Studd to the ring; after the bout, Kal Rudman interviewed Studd in the hallway about his victory
Ray Stevens pinned WWF Tag Team Champion Chief Jay Strongbow at 9:26 after reversing Strongbow's suplex attempt into a small package; prior to the bout, Freddie Blassie escorted Stevens to the ring
WWF Intercontinental Champion Don Muraco defeated WWF World Champion Bob Backlund (w/ Arnold Skaaland) via disqualification at 21:19 when Backlund shoved the referee down after Muraco reached the ropes as the champion had the Crossface Chicken Wing was applied; prior to the bout, Capt. Lou Albano escorted Muraco to the ring; after the bout, Backlund attacked Muraco as the Intercontinental Champion was being interviewed in the hallway by Kal Rudman; only Backlund's title was on the line
Rocky Johnson defeated Superstar Billy Graham via count-out at 3:46 when Graham walked out of the match after sustaining three dropkicks from Johnson; prior to the bout, the Grand Wizard escorted Graham to ringside
All American Wrestling - 10/2/83: Andre the Giant & Jimmy Snuka defeated the Wild Samoans at 12:51 when Snuka pinned Sika with a splash off Andre's shoulders following a boot to the face by Andre; prior to the bout, Capt. Lou Albano escored the Samoans to the ring while Buddy Rogers escorted Snuka & Andre (*Andre the Giant* VHS, *Andre the Giant* DVD)
Eddie Gilbert pinned Charlie Fulton at 9:20 with a kneelift as Fulton had his head down ready to hit a back body drop
Salvatore Bellomo pinned Swede Hanson at 4:51 after Hanson ran into the ropes when Bellomo moved out of the way
Pedro Morales pinned Buddy Rose at 11:36 after reversing Rose's attempt at a backbreaker over the knee into a pinning combination

154

WWF @ New York City, NY - Madison Square Garden - March 20, 1983 (matinee) (26,109 including a sold out Felt Forum)

Televised on the MSG Network and the USA Network - featured Gorilla Monsoon on commentary; included the playing of the national anthem to begin the broadcast; included pretaped backstage interviews with Salvatore Bellomo, WWF Intercontinental Champion Don Muraco, Big John Studd, all aired just prior to their matches:
Mac Rivera pinned Baron Mikel Scicluna at 8:46 with a sunset flip; prior to the bout, Howard Finkel announced that Sika would be unable to compete in the six-man tag later in the show due to injury and that Capt. Lou Albano had demanded to replace him in the match
Swede Hanson pinned Pete Sanchez at 6:35 with a kneedrop following a powerslam and elbow drop
Tony Garea pinned Johnny Rodz at 10:09 with a reverse roll up
Superstar Billy Graham pinned Jules Strongbow following a karate thrust to the throat at 9:42; prior to the bout, the Grand Wizard escorted Graham to the ring; after the bout, Mel Phillips interviewed Graham and the Wizard in the hallway about Graham's victory
Salvatore Bellomo fought Ray Stevens to a double count-out at 9:28 when both men began fighting on the ring apron
WWF World Champion Bob Backlund (w/ Arnold Skaaland) pinned WWF Intercontinental Champion Don Muraco in a Texas Death Match at 19:51 with a back suplex into a bridge; only Backlund's title was on the line; after the bout, Mel Philips interviewed Backlund in the hallway about his victory
Andre the Giant, Rocky Johnson, & Jimmy Snuka defeated Big John Studd, WWF Tag Team Champion Afa, & Capt. Lou Albano (sub. for Sika) in a Best 3 out of 5 falls match at 9:36, 3-0; fall #1: the heels were disqualified at 6:43 after Albano & Afa entered the ring and pushed Studd on top of Andre as Andre had Studd picked up for a bodyslam; fall #2: Snuka pinned Afa at 1:38 with a splash off the top; fall #3: Andre pinned Albano with a sit-down splash at 1:15; prior to the bout, Freddie Blassie escorted Studd to the ring; after the bout, Mel Phillips interviewed Andre in the hallway saying he had signed an open contract to face Studd
SD Jones pinned Jose Estrada at 4:14 with a crossbody
All American Wrestling - 10/16/83: Sonny Boy Hayes & Pancho Boy defeated Tiger Jackson & Butch Cassidy at 7:40 when Sonny pinned Cassidy after Jackson accidentally dropkicked his partner when Sonny moved out of the way

WWF @ New York City, NY - Madison Square Garden - April 25, 1983

Included Gorilla Monsoon & Pat Patterson on commentary:
Salvatore Bellomo defeated Baron Mikel Scicluna at 9:43
Mr. Fuji pinned SD Jones at 11:34 with a belly to belly suplex as Jones ran off the ropes
Iron Mike Sharpe defeated Johnny Rodz at 9:31 (Sharpe's MSG debut)
Prime Time Wrestling - 1/20/86: Ray Stevens pinned Tony Garea at 10:17 when the momentum of a crossbody by Garea put Stevens on top; after the bout, Garea cleared Stevens from the ring
Rocky Johnson defeated WWF Intercontinental Champion Don Muraco via count-out at 14:20
WWF World Champion Bob Backlund (w/ Arnold Skaaland) defeated Ivan Koloff via submission at 28:36 with the Crossface Chickenwing
Jimmy Snuka pinned Superstar Billy Graham at 3:28 (Graham's last match at MSG for 4 years)
Pedro Morales pinned Swede Hanson at 4:39
Eddie Gilbert defeated Jose Estrada at 5:58
Samula (sub. for Sika) & WWF Tag Team Champion Afa defeated Chief Jay & Jules Strongbow in a Best 2 out of 3 falls match, 2-1 at 11:55; fall #1: Jay pinned Samula at 4:40; fall #2: Afa pinned Jay at 4:07; fall #3: Afa pinned Jules at 3:08
Andre the Giant defeated Big John Studd via count-out at 8:22 when Studd left ringside after narrowly avoiding a bodyslam from Andre (*WWE Hall of Fame 2004*)

On challenging Bruno, Pedro, and Backlund

"Bruno and Backlund did a lot of strong stuff. Those two, they could do it all. They could wrestle, the highspots. Armdrag, dropkick you or whatever. Pedro, he was good with all that stuff also, but he pretty well stayed away from the strong stuff. But he was a fiery guy. That made it easy. I enjoyed wrestling with all of them because they're really great pros."
Ivan Koloff, *Titans of Wrestling interview, 2014*

MADISON SQUARE GARDEN MONDAY NIGHT, MAY 23rd 1983 8:00 P.M.
TRIPLE TITLE NIGHT IN THE GARDEN...
MAIN EVENT
For The World Wrestling Federation Heavyweight Championship
One fall — 60 Min.

BOB BACKLUND   VS.   **SGT. SLAUGHTER**
234 lbs., Princeton, Minn.   296 lbs., South Carolina
Champion   Challenger
                        won by:_____

Inter-Continental Heavyweight Title Re-Match
MAGNIFICENT MURACO   VS.   **ROCKY JOHNSON**
248 lbs., Sunset Beach, Hawaii   244 lbs., Washington D.C.
Champion   Challenger
                        won by:_____

Ladies World Wrestling Championship
FABULOUS MOOLAH   VS.   **PRINCESS VICTORIA**
Champion   Challenger
                        won by:_____

SPECIAL EVENTS
WILD SAMOAN #1   VS.   **JIMMY "SUPERFLY" SNUKA**
302 lbs., Samoa   250 lbs., Fiji Islands
                        won by:_____

DUSTY RHODES   **THE WILD SAMOAN #2**
"The American Dream"   320 lbs., Samoa
                        won by:_____

IVAN KOLOFF   VS.   **JULES STRONGBOW**
260 lbs., Moscow, Russia   248 lbs., Pawhuska, Ok.
                        won by:_____

EDDIE GILBERT   VS.   **RAY "THE CRIPPLER" STEVENS**
212 lbs., Lexington, Tenn.   238 lbs., San Francisco, CA.
                        won by:_____

CHIEF JAY STRONGBOW   VS.   **IRON MIKE SHARPE**
251 lbs., Pawhuska, Ok.   280 lbs., Hamilton Ontario, Canada
                        won by:_____

LAI LANI KAI   VS.   **SUSAN STARR**
                        won by:_____

SALVATORE BELLOMO   VS.   **CHARLIE FULTON**
246 lbs., Italy   244 lbs., Marion, Ohio
                        won by:_____

DON KERNODLE   VS.   **BARON MIKEL SCICLUNA**
235 lbs., Burlington, N.C.   270 lbs., Isle of Malta
                        won by:_____

BIG SWEDE HANSON   VS.   **"Opponent to be Named"**
3121lbs., Slaughter Creek, N.C.
                        won by:_____

REMEMBER FANS

HERE IN MADISON SQUARE GARDEN
WRESTLING
FRIDAY NIGHT,
JUNE 17th 1983 8:00 P.M.

WWF @ New York City, NY - Madison Square Garden - May 23, 1983

Televised live on the MSG Network and USA Network - included Gorilla Monsoon on commentary; featured a look at Sgt. Slaughter recently attacking WWF World Champion Bob Backlund on TV; included backstage comments from Backlund about his upcoming title defense against Slaughter; featured backstage comments from Buddy Rogers and Jimmy Snuka about Snuka's upcoming match against Samoan #1, with Capt. Lou Albano; the scheduled Ray Stevens vs. Eddie Gilbert was canceled:

Don Kernodle pinned Baron Mikel Scicluna with a sunset flip at 10:57 (Kernodle's MSG debut)

Mac Rivera pinned Pete Doherty at 10:39 with a running splash

Ivan Koloff (w/ Freddie Blassie) pinned Jules Strongbow at 11:23 with a knee off the top to the back

Salvatore Bellomo pinned Swede Hanson at 10:28 by falling on top of him after Hanson, with Bellomo on his shoulders, rammed himself into the corner to try to shake Bellomo off him; after the match, Bellomo raised Hanson's hand before Hanson left the ring

Chief Jay Strongbow fought Iron Mike Sharpe to a double disqualification at 6:48 when the referee lost control as Strongbow tried to remove Sharpe's forearm brace while Sharpe was caught in the ring ropes; after the contest, Sharpe escaped to the floor and went backstage to keep Strongbow from taking off the brace

WWF World Champion Bob Backlund (w/ Arnold Skaaland) defeated Sgt. Slaughter (w/ the Grand Wizard) via disqualification at 16:53 when Slaughter hit the champion with his riding crop, handed to him by the Grand Wizard, as he was caught in the Crossface Chicken Wing; after the bout, Slaughter shoved referee Dick Kroll to the floor before Backlund sent Slaughter to the floor after a backdrop (*The History of the WWE Heavyweight Championship*)

Dusty Rhodes pinned Samula (w/ Capt. Lou Albano) with a crossbody at 9:10; after the bout, Gorilla Monsoon conducted an interview with Rhodes on the ring apron (Rhodes' MSG return after 18 months)

Susan Starr pinned Leilani Kai at 6:04 when Starr fell on top as Kai attempted a tilt-a-whirl slam

Jimmy Snuka (w/ Buddy Rogers) pinned Samoan #1 (w/ Capt. Lou Albano) at 3:02 with the splash off the top; after the bout, Samoan #1 was taken backstage on a stretcher

Women's Champion the Fabulous Moolah pinned Princess Victoria at 5:27 when the champion avoided a reverse crossbody off the middle turnbuckle

Prime Time Wrestling - 1/20/86: Rocky Johnson fought WWF Intercontinental Champion Don Muraco to curfew draw as Muraco was trapped in a sleeper; the crowd believed Johnson had won the title due to the nature of the finish; the USA Network broadcast ended with the champion in the sleeper and the bell ringing

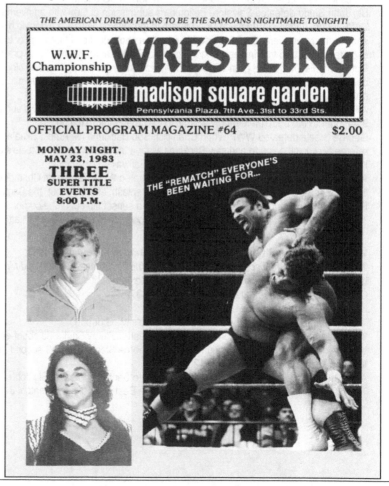

THE AMERICAN DREAM PLANS TO BE THE SAMOANS NIGHTMARE TONIGHT!

W.W.F. Championship **WRESTLING**

madison square garden
Pennsylvania Plaza, 7th Ave., 31st to 33rd Sts.

OFFICIAL PROGRAM MAGAZINE #64 $2.00

MONDAY NIGHT, MAY 23, 1983
THREE SUPER TITLE EVENTS 8:00 P.M.

THE "REMATCH" EVERYONE'S BEEN WAITING FOR...

WWF @ New York City, NY - Madison Square Garden - June 17, 1983
Iron Mike Sharpe pinned SD Jones at 10:39
Swede Hanson defeated Butcher Vachon at 8:33
Salvatore Bellomo defeated Mr. Fuji via disqualification at 11:30
Ivan Koloff (sub. for Iron Mike Sharpe) pinned Tony Garea at 11:41
George Steele defeated Chief Jay Strongbow at 7:13 when the match was stopped due to blood
Ivan Putski, Jimmy Snuka, & Rocky Johnson defeated WWF Intercontinental Champion Don Muraco & the Wild Samoans in a Best 2 out of 3 falls match
Andre the Giant defeated Big John Studd at 8:21 following a bodyslam
Sgt. Slaughter defeated WWF World Champion Bob Backlund via count-out at 19:46

WWF @ New York City, NY - Madison Square Garden - July 30, 1983 (27,000, which included a sold out Felt Forum)
Televised on the MSG Network and USA Network - featured Gorilla Monsoon on commentary; featured pretaped comments from WWF Intercontinental Champion Don Muraco & Jimmy Snuka & Buddy Rogers and WWF World Champion Bob Backlund aired just prior to their matches:
Tony Garea fought Iron Mike Sharpe to a 15-minute time limit draw at 12:06; the time-limit expired as Garea had Sharpe trapped in an abdominal stretch; after the bout, Garea cleared Sharpe from the ring
Ivan Koloff pinned SD Jones at 5:31 by reversing Jones' slam attempt into a cradle
The Invaders defeated Jeff Craney & Frank Rodriguez at 11:27 when Craney was pinned after one Invader hiptossed his partner on top of Craney (The Invaders' MSG debut)
Big John Studd defeated Salvatore Bellomo via submission at 5:09 with an overhead backbreaker
WWF Intercontinental Champion Don Muraco fought Jimmy Snuka to a double disqualification at 12:29 after Muraco shoved the referee and Snuka refused to release a chokehold on Muraco; prior to the bout, Capt. Lou Albano escorted Muraco to the ring and Rogers escorted Snuka; after the match, several wrestlers - including the Invaders, Don Kernodle, Jeff Craney, and Gypsy Rodriguez - attempted to pull the two bloody wrestlers apart but they continued to brawl down the aisle; Snuka was briefly interviewed by Kal Rudman when he made his way back to the hallway
All American Wrestling - 10/9/83: Sgt. Slaughter defeated Swede Hanson via submission with the Cobra Clutch at 9:44; prior to the bout, the Grand Wizard escorted Slaughter to the ring
George Steele defeated WWF World Champion Bob Backlund (w/ Arnold Skaaland) via disqualification at 10:52 after referee Dick Kroll came to and saw Backlund assault the challenger with Steele's own foreign object; after the bout, Kal Rudman interviewed an irate Backlund in the hallway
Andre the Giant, Dusty Rhodes, & Ivan Putski defeated WWF Tag Team Champions the Wild Samoans & Samula at 12:46 when Andre pinned Samula with a sit-down splash; after the bout, the Samoans were cleared from the ring
Rocky Johnson pinned Don Kernodle at 6:15 with a sunset flip out of the corner
Tito Santana pinned Mr. Fuji at 5:39 with a crossbody (Santana's MSG return after a 3-year absence)

WWF @ New York City, NY - Madison Square Garden - August 27, 1983
The card originally had scheduled Salvatore Bellomo vs. Butcher Vachon and Mr. Fuji vs. Chief Jay Strongbow
Ivan Koloff fought Salvatore Bellomo to a 20-minute time-limit draw
Chief Jay Strongbow defeated Butcher Vachon at 3:46
Iron Mike Sharpe pinned Swede Hanson at 10:06
Tiger Chung Lee pinned Tony Garea at 11:24 (Lee's MSG debut)
WWF Intercontinental Champion Don Muraco defeated Jimmy Snuka via count-out at 15:19
WWF World Champion Bob Backlund defeated George Steele at the 39-second mark
Invader #2 pinned Don Kernodle at 12:47
Andre the Giant, Rocky Johnson, Ivan Putski, & Tito Santana defeated Big John Studd, Sgt. Slaughter, WWF Tag Team Champion Sika, & Samula (sub. for Afa) in a Best 3 out of 5 falls match, 3-1 at 12:47

The Grand Wizard, shown managing Dr. Jerry Graham at MSG. The Wizard, who managed Superstar Billy Graham to the WWWF World Title and Don Muraco to the IC title, would pass away on Oct. 12, 1983.

WWF @ New York City, NY - Madison Square Garden - October 17, 1983 (sell out)
Televised on the MSG Network and on the USA Network on 11/16/83 - included Gorilla Monsoon & Pat Patterson on commentary; Mick Foley, Tommy Dreamer, and Bubba Ray Dudley were in attendance for the event; included the playing of the national anthem to begin the broadcast; featured Vince McMahon conducting backstage interviews with Jimmy Snuka, Buddy Rogers and with WWF Intercontinental Champion Don Muraco just prior to Snuka / Muraco steel cage match; included Pat Patterson conducting an interview with pro wrestler Larry O'Dea from Australia, discussing the result of the Muraco / Snuka match; Patterson also interviewed Capt. Lou Albano about the match; included a pretaped interview of McMahon interviewing Andre the Giant in the locker room, aired prior to his match:
Tony Garea pinned Rene Goulet at 12:33 with a sunset flip (Goulet's MSG return after a 3-year absence)
All American Wrestling - 10/23/83: Tiger Chung Lee pinned SD Jones at 8:41 with an enzuiguri; prior to the bout, Freddie Blassie escorted Lee to the ring
Sgt. Slaughter defeated Ivan Putski via disqualification at 10:29 after he accidentally hit referee Dick Kroll when Slaughter ducked out of the way
All American Wrestling - 10/30/83: Tito Santana fought Iron Mike Sharpe to a 20-minute time limit draw at 18:02; after the bout, Santana cleared Sharpe from the ring
The Masked Superstar defeated WWF World Champion Bob Backlund (w/ Arnold Skaaland) via count-out at 16:13 following a corkscrew neckbreaker on the floor; after the bout, both men continued brawling until Backlund cleared Superstar from the ring; after the bout, Pat Patterson interviewed Backlund in the hallway (Superstar's MSG debut)
Mike Graham pinned Bob Bradley at 4:53 with a German suplex into a bridge; after the bout, Pat Patterson interviewed Graham in the hallway (Graham's MSG return after a 4-year absence; Bradley's MSG debut)
WWF Intercontinental Champion Don Muraco defeated Jimmy Snuka in a steel cage match at 6:46 when a flying headbutt from Snuka sent Muraco tumbling out the door; after the bout, Snuka scaled the cage and hit a splash off the top onto the prone champion, 15 feet below; the challenger and champion were escorted to ringside by Buddy Rogers and Capt. Lou Albano, respectively, but the managers returned backstage before the match began (*The WWF's Most Unusual Matches, Inside the Steel Cage, Bloodbath: Wrestling's Most Incredible Steel Cage Matches, History of the Intercontinental Championship*)
Rocky Johnson pinned WWF Tag Team Champion Sika (w/ Capt. Lou Albano) at 1:46 with a sunset flip
The Invaders defeated Israel Matia & Butcher Vachon at 6:58 when Matia was pinned after one Invader hiptossed his partner on top of Matia
Andre the Giant pinned WWF Tag Team Champion Afa at 1:07 with a boot to the face and a sit-down splash

---

'Unless you were there...'

"I was there when Jimmy Snuka dove off the cage and missed Bob Backlund. I was there when Jimmy Snuka dove off the cage and hit Don Muraco. Unless you were there for those special moments, you cannot relate to it. Everybody came together for a common cause. Even in Yankee Stadium, you have fans that are rooting for the other team. But if you go to a wrestling event, everyone's a wrestling fan. Everyone cheered for the good guys and everyone booed for the bad guys, it was so simple. It influenced every single thing that I did."

Tommy Dreamer,
TheHistoryofWWE.com interview, 2014

WWF World Champion Bob Backlund, with Arnold Skaaland, preparing for one of his final title defenses as champion at MSG.

WWF @ New York City, NY - Madison Square Garden - November 21, 1983
Salvatore Bellomo defeated Butcher Vachon
Tito Santana defeated Don Kernodle
WWF Intercontinental Champion Don Muraco pinned Iron Mike Sharpe (w/ Capt. Lou Albano) with a cradle; the champion played the babyface for the bout
The Invaders defeated Mr. Fuji & Rene Goulet (sub. for Tiger Chung Lee)
WWF Tag Team Champions the Wild Samoans defeated Rocky Johnson & SD Jones; the Samoans were recognized as champions since their loss had not yet aired
The Iron Sheik defeated Tony Garea (Sheik's MSG return after a nearly 4-year absence)
Tony Atlas defeated Big John Studd
Jimmy Snuka fought Sgt. Slaughter to a 20-minute time-limit draw when the bell rang as Snuka was caught in the Cobra Clutch
Pat Patterson defeated Ivan Koloff via count-out
WWF World Champion Bob Backlund pinned the Masked Superstar at 17:21 with an inside cradle after avoiding the neckbreaker

CHAMPIONSHIP WRESTLING

Madison Square Garden
Monday, December 26, 1983

Tonight's Official Line-up

Main Event...For the World Wrestling Federation Heavyweight Championship,
One Fall, One-Hour Time Limit

BOB BACKLUND -VS- **THE IRON SHEIK**
Princeton, Minnesota...234 lbs. Iran...247 lbs.
[WWF CHAMPION] [CHALLENGER]

- -

JIMMY "SUPERFLY" SNUKA -VS- **THE MAGNIFICENT MURACO**
Fiji Islands...250 lbs. Sunset Beach, Hawaii...257 lbs.
& &
BUDDY "NATURE BOY" ROGERS **CAPTAIN LOU ALBANO**
New Jersey...225 lbs. Carmel, New York...305 lbs.

- -

THE MASKED SUPERSTAR -VS- **IVAN PUTSKI**
Atlanta...269 lbs. Krakow, Poland...235 lbs.

- -

TONY "MR. U.S.A." ATLAS -VS- **THE WILD SAMOANS**
Roanoke, Virginia...260 lbs. Combined Weight...877 lbs.
&
ROCKY JOHNSON
Washington, D.C...250 lbs.
&
S.D. JONES
Philadelphia, Pennsylvania...245 lbs.

- -

SGT. SLAUGHTER -VS- **CHIEF JAY STRONGBOW**
South Carolina...296 lbs. Pawhuska, Oklahoma...258 lbs.

- -

IVAN KOLOFF -VS- **TITO SANTANA**
Russia...255 lbs. Tocula, Mexico...242 lbs.

- -

Plus other All-Star bouts, featuring Iron Mike Sharpe, Butcher Vachon, The Invaders,
Jose Luis Rivera and Rene Goulet.

TV Wrestling:
WOR-9 Saturdays 10 a.m.
Saturdays Midnight

[We reserve the right to change the order of events]. PROGRAM IS SUBJECT TO CHANGE. The promoter is not responsible if contestants fail to appear in ring because of conditions beyond our control. Whenever possible substitute bouts will be arranged. The practice of using cameras, in any manner, is an infringement of copyright material and is absolutely prohibited.

WWF @ New York City, NY - Madison Square Garden - December 26, 1983 (24,592, which included several thousand in Felt Forum)

Televised on the MSG Network and USA Network - included Gorilla Monsoon & Pat Patterson on commentary; featured Lord Alfred Hayes conducting backstage interviews throughout the night with Jimmy Snuka & Arnold Skaaland following their victory, new WWF World Champion the Iron Sheik & Freddie Blassie, and with Skaaland and former WWF World Champion Bob Backlund, with Backlund upset saying he felt he let the fans down (Hayes' debut):

Jose Luis Rivera pinned Rene Goulet at 10:05 with a botched head scissors into a roll up

Salvatore Bellomo fought Tiger Chung Lee to a 20-minute time-limit draw at 19:30; after the bout, Bellomo cleared Lee from the ring

Jimmy Snuka & Arnold Skaaland (sub. for Buddy Rogers) defeated WWF Intercontinental Champion Don Muraco & Capt. Lou Albano at 10:07 when Snuka pinned Muraco with a crossbody off the top (*The WWF's Most Unusual Matches*)

Sgt. Slaughter pinned Chief Jay Strongbow at 7:42 with a clothesline

The Masked Superstar fought Ivan Putski to a double disqualification at 7:00 after Putski shoved referee Dick Kroll while trying to take off Superstar's mask

All American Wrestling - 1/8/84: The Iron Sheik (w/ Freddie Blassie) defeated WWF World Champion Bob Backlund (w/ Arnold Skaaland) at 11:50 to win the title when Skaaland threw in the towel as Backlund was trapped in the Camel Clutch; moments prior to the finish, Backlund attempted his roll up into a bridge but was unable to keep it applied due to his injured neck (*The WWF's Greatest Matches, History of the WWF Heavyweight Championship, The Greatest Wrestling Stars of the 80s*)

Afa, Sika, & Samula defeated SD Jones, WWF Tag Team Champions Rocky Johnson & Tony Atlas in a Best 2 out of 3 falls match, 2-1 at 20:15; fall #1: both teams were disqualified at 9:36 when all six men were brawling in the ring, awarding each team a fall; fall #2: Afa pinned Jones at 10:39 after a headbutt

All American Wrestling - 2/12/84: Tito Santana pinned Ivan Koloff at 15:46 with an elbow drop off the top (Koloff's last appearance)

The Invaders defeated Iron Mike Sharpe & Butcher Vachon at 4:45 when Vachon was pinned after one Invader hiptossed his partner on top of Vachon

---

Kids crying

"My biggest memory was Dec. 26, 1983 when the Iron Sheik defeated Bob Backlund for the then WWF title. We were in the 9th row and I can remember being stunned that Backlund finally lost. I remember at least one of the kids I was with crying hysterically. I'm 41 and that day, when I was 11, I can remember like it was yesterday."

Matt Turk, *Bakersfield, CA*

WWF @ New York City, NY - Madison Square Garden - January 23, 1984 (26,292 which included 4,000 at Felt Forum)

Televised on the MSG Network - included Gorilla Monsoon & Pat Patterson on commentary; a young Chris Kanyon was in attendance; featured Gene Okerlund conducting a backstage interview with the new WWF World Champion Hulk Hogan regarding his title win, during which Andre the Giant appeared to celebrate and poured champagne over Hogan's head, with Ivan Putski and WWF Tag Team Champion Rocky Johnson appearing moments later; included Okerlund conducting a backstage interview with Hogan's parents Ruth and Pete about Hogan's title win:

Tony Garea pinned Jose Luis Rivera at 6:46 by reversing a crossbody into a cover

The Invaders fought Mr. Fuji & Tiger Chung Lee to a 20-minute time-limit draw at 20:23

The Masked Superstar pinned Chief Jay Strongbow at 7:26 with a clothesline

Sgt. Slaughter defeated Ivan Putski via count-out at 11:29 when Putski knocked Slaughter back in the ring as both men were brawling on the floor; after the bout, Putski continued to attack Slaughter, not realizing the match was over

Paul Orndorff (w/ Roddy Piper) pinned Salvatore Bellomo with a powerslam and the piledriver at 14:06 (Orndorff's MSG debut) (Piper's MSG return after nearly a 5-year absence) (*The Greatest Wrestling Stars of the 80s*)

WWF Intercontinental Champion Don Muraco (w/ Capt. Lou Albano) fought Tito Santana to a double disqualification at 16:03 when both men continually ignored the referee's instructions

The Haiti Kid & Tiger Jackson defeated Dana Carpenter & Pancho Boy in a Best 2 out of 3 falls bout, 2-0; fall #1: Jackson pinned Pancho with a sunset flip at 5:18; fall #2: Haiti pinned Carpenter at 1:35, with the referee seemingly not realizing it was the finish as he hesitated during the pinfall

Hulk Hogan (sub. for Bob Backlund) pinned WWF World Champion the Iron Sheik (w/ Freddie Blassie) at 5:40 with the legdrop to win the title after ramming the champion back-first against the turnbuckle to escape the Camel Clutch; during his entrance, Hogan was seen walking past Vince McMahon in the backstage hallway; after the bout, Gene Okerlund interviewed the new champion backstage in which he was congratulated by Andre the Giant, Rocky Johnson, and Ivan Putski (Hogan's return to MSG after a nearly 3-year absense) (*Hulkamania, History of the WWF Heavyweight Championship, Best of the WWF: Hulkamania, The Hulkster Hulk Hogan, The History of the WWE Heavyweight Championship, Hulk Still Rules, The Greatest Wrestling Stars of the 80s, Hulk Hogan: The Ultimate Anthology*)

Jimmy Snuka pinned Rene Goulet (sub. for Iron Mike Sharpe) at 3:54 with a crossbody off the top

Andre the Giant, WWF Tag Team Champions Rocky Johnson & Tony Atlas defeated Afa, Sika, & Samula when Andre pinned Samula at 5:29 with a boot to the face and sit-down splash

---

Witnessing the birth of Hulkamania

"I was there when the Iron Sheik won the title. That was a shock because Backlund had fought the Iron Sheik before. I figure next month will be the rematch. 'Uh oh, Hulk Hogan's coming.' At the start, I liked Hogan. It was really exciting being in the Garden the night he won the belt. The whole place went nuts. They say it was the start of a new era. Being there, you felt it. It was pretty amazing. Down the road, I was back to cheering for the villains. But to be there was amazing."

Charlie Adorno, *Brooklyn, NY*

The locker room

"The only thing I never liked, the locker room for the wrestlers is so small. If you go back and you watch where Hogan won the title and they're pouring the champagne. That's probably the most amount of people that can fit in there."

Tommy Dreamer,
TheHistoryofWWE.com interview, 2014

WWF @ New York City, NY - Madison Square Garden - February 20, 1984 (26,092, which included 4,000 at Felt Forum)
Televised on the MSG Network and USA Network - featured Gorilla Monsoon & Pat Patterson on commentary; included Vince McMahon conducting a backstage interview with the Iron Sheik and WWF Intercontinental Champion Tito Santana prior to their matches:
Jose Luis Rivera pinned Charlie Fulton at 7:14 with a small package
Iron Mike Sharpe pinned B. Brian Blair at 9:35 by putting his foot on the ropes for leverage (Blair's MSG debut)
Afa (w/ Capt. Lou Albano) pinned Tony Garea at 11:37 with a chop to the throat and headbutt
The Iron Sheik (w/ Freddie Blassie) defeated Eddie Gilbert via submission with the Camel Clutch at 5:48
Roddy Piper & David Schultz defeated the Invaders at 11:17 when Piper pinned Invader #2 after Schultz hit an elbow drop from the middle turnbuckle behind the referee's back (Schultz' MSG debut)
WWF Intercontinental Champion Tito Santana defeated Don Muraco via count-out at 17:20 after Muraco had his head trapped in the ring ropes after Santana hit the champion with a flying forearm
Andre the Giant pinned the Masked Superstar with a boot to the face and splash at 7:46; after the bout, Andre attempted to unmask Superstar but he was able to escape the ring (Bill Eadie's last MSG appearance for 3 years) (*Andre the Giant* VHS, *Andre the Giant* DVD)
All American Wrestling - 3/11/84: WWF World Champion Hulk Hogan defeated Paul Orndorff via count-out at 12:24 after Hogan threw Orndorff over the top rope to the floor
TNT - 7/17/84: Jimmy Snuka pinned Samula at 9:32 with a crossbody off the top (*Wrestling's Highest Flyers*)
Ivan Putski, WWF Tag Team Champions Rocky Johnson, & Tony Atlas defeated Sgt. Slaughter, Mr. Fuji, & Tiger Chung Lee at 6:20 when Putski pinned Fuji with the Polish Hammer after Fuji began yelling at Slaughter; after the bout, Slaughter shook the hands of his opponents and waved an American flag handed to him by someone in the crowd

WWF @ New York City, NY - Madison Square Garden - March 25, 1984 (matinee) (26,092 which included 4,000 at Felt Forum)
This show was not televised on the MSG Network - featured Gorilla Monsoon & Pat Patterson on commentary:
Championship Wrestling - 4/21/84: SD Jones pinned Rene Goulet with a headbutt at 9:23
B. Brian Blair defeated Charlie Fulton at 9:30
All American Wrestling - 4/22/84: *WWF International Championship Tournament Finals*: Akira Maeda defeated Pierre Lefebrve via submission at 4:55 with the abdominal stretch; prior to the bout WWF President Hisashi Shima was introduced to the crowd who then presented Maeda with the belt after the match
The Iron Sheik defeated Ivan Putski at 7:04
Championship Wrestling - 4/21/84: Sgt. Slaughter defeated Mr. Fuji & Tiger Chung Lee in a handicap match at 4:18 when Lee submitted to the Cobra Clutch
Roddy Piper & David Schultz defeated Andre the Giant & Jimmy Snuka via disqualification at 12:20; the match was turned into a handicap match at around the 8-minute mark when Andre was helped backstage by police officers after Piper busted his head open using a foreign object; Snuka argued that the match should continue as a handicap match and Piper & Schultz agreed; the match ended when Andre, his head heavily bandaged, returned to the ring and helped Snuka in assaulting the opposition and eventually clearing them from the ring; since the bout turned into a handicap match, Andre's actions were considered outside interference (*Rowdy Roddy Piper's Greatest Hits*)
WWF Tag Team Champions Tony Atlas & Rocky Johnson fought the Wild Samoans to a double disqualification at 10:02
WWF Intercontinental Champion Tito Santana fought Paul Orndorff to a 20-minute time limit draw
Bob Backlund fought Greg Valentine to a double count-out at 15:00

WWF @ New York City, NY - Madison Square Garden - April 23, 1984 (22,091)
Televised on the MSG Network and USA Network - featured Gorilla Monsoon & Pat Patterson on commentary; included backstage comments from WWF Intercontinental Champion Tito Santana on facing JJ Dillon later in the show; featured Kal Rudman conducting a backstage interview with Santana regarding his win over Dillon; included Rudman interviewing Women's Tag Team Champions Princess Victoria & Velvet McIntyre prior to their bout; featured backstage comments from Greg Valentine and Capt. Lou Albano on Valentine facing Bob Backlund later in the show:
Tiger Chung Lee pinned the Tonga Kid at 8:02 with an elbow drop after dropping Kid throat-first across the top rope
Rene Goulet pinned Jose Luis Rivera at 7:36 with a claw hold
WWF Intercontinental Champion Tito Santana pinned JJ Dillon (sub. for Afa) at 7:46 with a dropkick and the flying forearm (Dillon's MSG debut)
The Iron Sheik defeated Sgt. Slaughter via disqualification at 8:31 when, after Slaughter hit the Slaughter Cannon, Slaughter took off his boot and repeatedly hit Sheik with the weapon until Sheik was knocked to the floor; prior to the bout, Terry Daniels, carrying the American flag, escorted Slaughter to the ring; after the bout, Kal Rudman attempted to conduct a backstage interview with Slaughter until Slaughter jumped the Sheik from behind, with other wrestlers then appearing to break up the fight (*Legends of Wrestling Collection, Legends of Wrestling: Ric Flair and Sgt. Slaughter*)
Salvatore Bellomo pinned Ron Shaw (sub. for the Masked Superstar) at 7:53 with a crossbody
Roddy Piper, Paul Orndorff, & David Schultz defeated Ivan Putski, Rocky Johnson, & Tony Atlas at 5:40 after Piper hit Putski with brass knuckles as he attempted to suplex Piper
B. Brian Blair defeated Samula via referee's decision after the 20-minute time-limit expired at 17:43; after the bout, Samula attacked Blair after hearing the decision
Women's Tag Team Champions Princess Victoria & Velvet McIntyre defeated Peggy Lee & Wendi Richter at 19:02 when McIntyre pinned Lee after avoiding a splash from the middle turnbuckle
Bob Backlund (w/ Arnold Skaaland) pinned Greg Valentine (w/ Capt. Lou Albano) at around 26:05 with a roll up into a bridge; after the match, Valentine knocked down referee Dick Kroll and put Backlund in the figure-4 until Skaaland forced Valentine to break the hold

Who's that?
"Vince used to try guys out at the Garden. Tatsumi Fujianai was at Madison Square Garden and no one knew who he was. JJ Dillon was at Madison Square Garden and no one knew who he was. All these kinda cool things, where it almost made me feel important that my dad would come to me for information. The other fans would ask, 'How do you know who that is?' And he'd go, 'My son told me'"
Matt Striker, *TheHistoryofWWE.com interview, 2014*

WWF @ New York City, NY - Madison Square Garden - May 21, 1984 (25,000 including several thousand at Felt Forum)

This card was not broadcast on the MSG Network; featured Gorilla Monsoon & Gene Okerlund on commentary; the trademark pull-down MSG microphone was not used for the card:

Akira Maeda defeated Rene Goulet at 9:47

Wrestling at the Chase - 5/27/84: Jesse Ventura defeated Salvatore Bellomo via submission with the backbreaker at 4:31; after the bout, Ventura said he wanted WWF World Champion Hulk Hogan and referred to him as a chump and paper champion; Pat Patterson did guest commentary for the bout, replacing Okerlund (Ventura's MSG return after a 2-year absence)

WWF Women's Champion the Fabulous Moolah defeated Wendi Richter via disqualification at 12:20 when the challenger shoved the referee; after the bout, Kal Rudman interviewed Moolah backstage

Mr. Fuji & Tiger Chung Lee defeated B. Brian Blair & Tony Garea at 18:04

The Wild Samoans defeated Bobo Brazil (sub. for Tony Atlas), Rocky Johnson, & SD Jones at 12:00

Jimmy Snuka defeated Greg Valentine via disqualification at 10:05

TNT - 6/12/84: Roddy Piper defeated Ivan Putski via disqualification at 4:07 after Putski hit the referee as both men were brawling in the ring

Paul Orndorff defeated WWF Intercontinental Champion Tito Santana via count-out at 22:26 after Santana fell to the floor after missing the flying forearm and Orndorff pulling down the top rope; after the bout, Santana was placed on a stretcher and attacked by Orndorff after it was announced the title could not change hands via count-out

Sgt. Slaughter fought the Iron Sheik to a double disqualification at 14:47 after both men shoved referee Danny Davis; prior to the bout, Freddie Blassie escorted Sheik to ringside; after the bout, Slaughter continued to try to take Sheik's boot off, and shoved off Rene Goulet, Tony Garea, and B. Brian Blair before doing so; moments later, Goulet helped Sheik regain possession of the boot before both men left ringside; moments later, Slaughter grabbed the microphone and said he would never wrestle in NYC again unless he got to wrestle the Iron Sheik; Slaughter then led the crowd in the Pledge of Allegiance (*The Greatest Wrestling Stars of the 80s*)

Superstars of Wrestling - 6/23/84: George Steele defeated Terry Daniels via submission with the flying hammerlock

WWF World Champion Hulk Hogan pinned David Schultz at 5:46 with a clothesline and the legdrop

---

'It was the hottest ticket in town'

"My father knew an usher and he would always tell us, 'Hey I got a couple tickets.' They were always great seats. My father's a teacher and my father taught his kid. I would probably go to 6 events a year. ...It became the hottest ticket in town. It became trendy. I wasn't bullied but I was made fun of for liking professional wrestling. I defended it all the time to the point where I would fight you or argue it with you. But then it became cool. Wrestling at Madison Square Garden was covered on the local sportscasts. 'The Yankees won, the Mets lost, and at the Garden...' I didn't go every single month. I wish I could have. But if I missed the show, I made sure to stay up to watch the news."

Tommy Dreamer,
TheHistoryofWWE.com interview, 2014

WWF @ New York City, NY - Madison Square Garden - June 16, 1984 (26,092, which included several thousand at Felt Forum)

Televised on the MSG Network and USA Network - included Gorilla Monsoon & Gene Okerlund on commentary:
Don Muraco (w/ Mr. Fuji) pinned Tony Garea at 4:49 with a belly to belly suplex as Garea came off the ropes
George Steele (w/ Mr. Fuji) defeated Jose Luis Rivera via submission with the flying hammerlock at 2:24; prior to the match, the bell was rung and a moment of silence was held in memory of Vincent J. McMahon; after the bout, Steele attacked his opponent with a foreign object
Championship Wrestling - 6/23/84: WWF Tag Team Champions Dick Murdoch & Adrian Adonis fought the Wild Samoans to a draw in a Best 2 out of 3 falls match at 19:51; fall #1: Adonis pinned Afa at 13:02 with a splash following a double elbow drop; after the fall, Capt. Lou Albano came ringside and went to the corner of the champions; fall #2: Afa pinned Murdoch with the Samoan Drop at 2:52; after the fall, Albano went to the corner of the challengers and offered to shake their hands but the Samoans didn't know what to do and Albano left ringside; fall #3: both teams were disqualified at 4:17 when all four men began brawling in the ring and Sika hit the referee; prior to the bout, Albano was introduced to the crowd but left ringside before either team appeared
Jesse Ventura defeated SD Jones via submission at 4:58 with the overhead backbreaker
Greg Valentine defeated WWF Intercontinental Champion Tito Santana via count-out at 14:02 after backdropping Santana out of the ring and then hitting an atomic drop on the floor; prior to the bout, Howard Finkel acknowledged Santana's mother who was in attendance; after the bout, Lord Alfred Hayes interviewed Santana backstage with Santana saying he wants Valentine in the ring again
Andre the Giant pinned David Schultz at 7:05 with a boot to the face and a sit-down splash
Mad Dog Vachon pinned Steve Lombardi at 3:18 with a piledriver; after the bout, Vachon hit a kneedrop from the top onto Lombardi, then threw him to the floor and hit him with a chair (Vachon's MSG return after a near 10-year absence; Lombardi's MSG debut)
Paul Orndorff pinned Salvatore Bellomo with the piledriver at 9:01
Bob Orton Jr. pinned Chief Jay Strongbow with a bomb from the middle turnbuckle at 9:46
Sgt. Slaughter pinned the Iron Sheik in a Bootcamp Match at 16:02 after hitting him with Sheik's own boot; prior to the bout, Freddie Blassie escorted Sheik to ringside; following Slaughter's entrance, Terry Daniels marched at ringside in his USMC uniform with the American flag as "The Halls of Montazmuma" played

Capt. Lou Albano makes his entrance at MSG

June 18, 1984: The band Judas Priest was banned from Madison Square Garden after fans destroyed seats during their performance, causing a reported quarter million dollars in damages.

WWF @ New York City, NY - Madison Square Garden - July 23, 1984 (15,000)

Televised on the MSG Network - featured Gorilla Monsoon & Gene Okerlund on commentary; included Okerlund conducting a backstage interview with WWF Women's Champion Wendi Richter, Cyndi Lauper, Kal Rudman, and David Wolfe regarding the victory over the Fabulous Moolah; moments later, Sgt. Slaughter walked in to congratulate Richter and Lauper on the win, then picked Lauper up in celebration; WWF World Champion Hulk Hogan then walked in, calling Wendi the Marilyn Monroe of wrestling; Capt. Lou Albano then interrupted but was punched in the face by Hogan and then left; moments later, Hogan said Wendi had to replace the photo of Moolah on the belt with a photo of her own:

Sika pinned Ron Shaw at 5:12 with a diving headbutt

Georgia Championship Wrestling - 7/28/84: The Iron Sheik (w/ Freddie Blassie) pinned Tony Garea at 5:35 with a back suplex

All American Wrestling - 8/12/84: WWF Intercontinental Champion Tito Santana fought Bob Orton Jr. to a 20-minute time-limit draw; after the bout, both men continued brawling until the referee was able to pull them apart

Bob Backlund defeated Butcher Vachon (sub. for B. Brian Blair) via submission with the Crossface Chicken Wing at 2:40

WWF World Champion Hulk Hogan pinned Greg Valentine at 10:33 with the legdrop; prior to the bout, Capt. Lou Albano escorted Valentine to ringside

WWF Martial Arts Champion Antonio Inoki pinned Charlie Fulton at 4:10 with an enziguri kick

Georgia Championship Wrestling - 7/28/84: WWF Tag Team Champions Adrian Adonis & Dick Murdoch defeated Sgt. Slaughter & Terry Daniels at 16:52 when Adonis pinned Daniels following a kneedrop off the top by Murdoch as Adonis held Daniels over his knee while the referee was distracted; after the bout, Slaughter cleared the champions out of the ring

The Brawl to End it All - aired live on MTV (9.0): Wendi Richter (w/ Cyndi Lauper) pinned WWF Women's Champion the Fabulous Moolah (w/ Capt. Lou Albano) to win the title at 11:20 after lifting her right shoulder out of a bridged roll up; David Wolfe did guest commentary for the bout; after the bout, Moolah & Albano attacked the referee after hearing the decision (*Best of the WWF Vol. 1, WrestleMania 26 Collector's Edition*)

Georgia Championship Wrestling - 7/28/84: Paul Orndorff pinned Chief Jay Strongbow at 6:05 with a clothesline; Gorilla Monsoon provided solo commentary for this and the final two bouts after Gene Okerlund went backstage to conduct several interviews

Afa pinned Rene Goulet at 5:26 with a Samoan Drop

WWF Martial Arts Champion Antonio Inoki won a 20-man battle royal at 13:23 by last eliminating Rene Goulet; other participants included: Sika, Jose Luis Rivera, Butcher Vachon, Tony Garea, Chief Jay Strongbow, Afa, Steve Lombardi, Bob Orton Jr., Charlie Fulton, Ron Shaw, Terry Daniels, the Iron Sheik, WWF Tag Team Champions Adrian Adonis & Dick Murdoch, WWF Intercontinental Champion Tito Santana, Paul Orndorff, Sgt. Slaughter, and Samula; order of elimination: Lombardi by Slaughter (0:59); Orndorff by Afa & Santana (2:16); Strongbow by Shaw (2:38); Sheik by ? (not shown on camera) (3:56); Vachon by Santana (4:17); Fulton by Slaughter & Daniels (7:48); Adonis by Slaughter after ducking a charge (9:38); Murdoch by Afa & Sika (9:44); Slaughter by Afa & Sika by falling off the apron when Murdoch was eliminated (9:45); Afa by ? (not shown on camera) (10:06); Santana by Inoki (10:42); Sika by ? (not shown on camera) (10:52); Rivera by Shaw with a backdrop (11:04); Daniels by Goulet (11:13); Samula by Inoki after ducking a charge (11:26); Orton by Inoki with an enziguri (12:11); Garea by Shaw & Goulet (12:36); Shaw by Goulet when Inoki moved out of the way (13:17) (*The WWF's Most Unusual Matches*)

WWF @ New York City, NY - Madison Square Garden - August 25, 1984
Televised on the MSG Network - featured Gorilla Monsoon & Lord Alfred Hayes on commentary; included backstage comments from WWF Tag Team Champions Adrian Adonis & Dick Murdoch prior to their title defense; featured backstage comments from Jesse Ventura prior to facing Ivan Putski:
Championship Wrestling - 9/8/84: Kamala (w/ Freddie Blassie & Friday) pinned Chief Jay Strongbow at 2:50 with a splash to the back
Championship Wrestling - 9/8/84: B. Brian Blair fought Iron Mike Sharpe to a double count-out at 13:02
Prime Time Wrestling - 8/13/85: Rick McGraw (sub. for Don Muraco) fought Salvatore Bellomo to a time-limit draw at 18:07
TNT - 10/16/84: WWF Tag Team Champions Dick Murdoch & Adrian Adonis defeated the Wild Samoans via disqualification at the 12-minute mark when the challengers began shoving guest referee Capt. Lou Albano after Albano stopped Afa's cover on Murdoch and went to tell Sika he had to hold onto the tag rope; after the bout, Albano cheap shoted Afa, who was held by the champions, until Sika cleared the ring (*The Life & Times of Capt. Lou Albano*)
Georgia Championship Wrestling - 9/8/84: Ken Patera defeated Pat Patterson via submission with the full nelson at 9:04 (Patera's MSG return after a near 4-year absence)
Jesse Ventura defeated Ivan Putski via count-out at 11:40 after hitting Putski with a foreign object as both men fought on the apron
Georgia Championship Wrestling - 9/8/84: Michael Hayes, Terry Gordy, & Buddy Roberts (w/ David Wolff) defeated Butcher Vachon, Ron Shaw, & Pete Doherty at 8:58 in a Best 2 out of 3 falls match, 2-0; fall #1: Gordy pinned Vachon at 5:39 with a crossbody; fall #2: Roberts pinned Doherty with an elbow drop
Championship Wrestling - 9/29/84: Roddy Piper defeated Jimmy Snuka via count-out at 7:05 when Snuka was dropped across the top rope while attempting a crossbody off the top, then falling to the floor and hitting his back against the apron; after the bout, Piper hit Snuka three times in the back of the neck with a folded steel chair; moments later, Snuka was placed on a stretcher and taken backstage (*Best of the WWF Vol. 1*)
Terry Daniels pinned Fred Marzino (sub. for Rene Goulet) at 3:55 with a reverse roll up; only a small portion of the bout was shown, with the focus being Jimmy Snuka being attended to backstage
WWF Intercontinental Champion Tito Santana pinned Greg Valentine with a crossbody at 7:23; Valentine's leg was on the bottom rope during the pinfall but the referee didn't notice; immediately after the match, Valentine put the champion in the figure-4; Gorilla Monsoon provided solo commentary for most of the match as before the bout Lord Alfred Hayes was backstage with the doctors where Jimmy Snuka was being attended to, with an oxygen mask being put on Snuka's face; later in the match Snuka was shown being taken out of the arena on a stretcher with a neckbrace on; after the bout, Hayes conducted separate backstage interviews with Santana and Valentine with both wanting each other back in the ring (*History of the Intercontinental Title*)

WWF @ New York City, NY - Madison Square Garden - September 22, 1984 (19,000)
Televised on the MSG and USA networks - included Gorilla Monsoon & Gene Okerlund on commentary:
Prime Time Wrestling - 4/16/85: Brutus Beefcake pinned Salvatore Bellomo at 9:56 with a powerslam after catching Bellomo in a crossbody off the top; prior to the bout, Howard Finkel announced Jesse Ventura was hospitalized in San Diego and wouldn't be able to face WWF World Champion Hulk Hogan later in the show but Hogan had agreed to face Big John Studd in Ventura's absence (Beefcake's MSG debut)
Prime Time Wrestling - 4/16/85: Nikolai Volkoff pinned Chief Jay Strongbow at 6:48 with an elbow drop after ramming Strongbow into the corner as he had the sleeper applied
Georgia Championship Wrestling - 9/29/84: David Schultz pinned SD Jones with a dropkick at 6:35
Georgia Championship Wrestling - 9/29/84: Greg Valentine defeated Jose Luis Rivera via submission with the figure-4 at 7:19; after the bout, Valentine reapplied the hold
Prime Time Wrestling - 4/16/85: Big John Studd (sub. for Jesse Ventura) (w/ Bobby Heenan) defeated WWF World Champion Hulk Hogan via count-out at 11:09 when Heenan helped shove the challenger back inside the ring after Studd and Hogan began brawling on the floor; after the bout, Studd & Heenan left ringside with the world title belt (Heenan's surprise debut) (*Hulk Hogan: The Ultimate Anthology*)
Georgia Championship Wrestling - 9/29/84: Ken Patera defeated Rick McGraw via submission with the full nelson at 7:40
Sgt. Slaughter & the Wild Samoans defeated Capt. Lou Albano, WWF Tag Team Champions Dick Murdoch & Adrian Adonis at 20:16 when Slaughter pinned Murdoch after slamming him off the top rope when Albano walked out of the match; after the bout, Murdoch had an altercation with Gorilla Monsoon outside the ring
Prime Time Wrestling - 4/16/85: B. Brian Blair defeated Iron Mike Sharpe via disqualification at 19:46 after Sharpe hit the referee; after the match, Sharpe continued to attack Blair until Blair cleared him from the ring
Prime Time Wrestling - 9/22/86: Kamala (w/ Friday) pinned Pat Patterson with a splash at 5:21

"The grandiloquent gladiators thrilled the throng with backbreakers and flying leg drops, but suddenly Big John had the champ in the terrible grip of a sleeper hold. The crowd thundered, "Hogan! Hogan! Hogan!" and somehow, defying medical science, their hero survived the sleeper, only to be tossed out of the ring, bloodied and counted out by a referee on a technicality.

Boos shook the Garden, torrential debris rained down on the ring, and the referee was surrounded by police officers. June Van Brunt wept openly in the stands on this night that Hulk Hogan lost...

Angel Vilella, who holds a season ticket, had predicted that the Hulk would lose on a disqualification only to return next month to whip Big John. 'I know what's going on,' he said. 'You don't have to believe all of it to have fun.'"
William E. Geist, *New York Times, September 29, 1984*

WWF @ New York City, NY - Madison Square Garden - October 22, 1984 (20,000)
Televised on the MSG Network - included Gorilla Monsoon & Gene Okerlund on commentary:
Georgia Championship Wrestling - 11/4/84: David Schultz pinned Salvatore Bellomo at 4:02 with a suplex
Georgia Championship Wrestling - 11/4/84: Afa fought WWF Tag Team Champion Dick Murdoch to a 20-minute time-limit draw at 19:15; after the bout, Afa cleared Murdoch from the ring after Murdoch challenged Afa to 5 more minutes
Prime Time Wrestling - 1/1/85: Mad Dog Vachon pinned Rick McGraw at 7:24 with a piledriver (*WrestleMania 26 Collector's Edition*)
Georgia Championship Wrestling - 11/4/84: David Sammartino pinned Moondog Spot at 12:23 after reversing a powerslam attempt into a small package; after the bout, Spot attacked Sammartino but David grabbed Spot's bone away with Spot quickly leaving ringside
Prime Time Wrestling - 1/1/85: WWF Intercontinental Champion Greg Valentine (w/ Capt. Lou Albano) defeated Tito Santana via disqualification at 5:52 when Santana threw the referee across the ring
Ken Patera pinned Rocky Johnson at 13:08 with a reverse roll up and grabbing the tights for leverage
Prime Time Wrestling - 1/1/85: Sika defeated WWF Tag Team Champion Adrian Adonis via disqualification at 9:29 when Adonis accidentally hit the referee after putting a foreign object on his hand
Nikolai Volkoff (w/ Freddie Blassie) defeated Sgt. Slaughter via count-out at 15:40 when Slaughter applied the Cobra Clutch while standing on the ring apron
TNT - 10/30/84: Brutus Beefcake (w/ Johnny V) pinned Tony Garea at 5:20 with a running kneelift
Prime Time Wrestling - 1/1/85: WWF World Champion Hulk Hogan pinned Big John Studd (w/ Bobby Heenan) at 7:38 with a lariat; after the bout, Studd backed out of Hogan's challenge to attempt to bodyslam Studd for $15,000; pre-match stipulations stated that Hogan could lose the title via count-out

Hulk and Studd at McDonald's

"My very earliest memory of MSG took place during a match between Hulk Hogan and Big John Studd. At one point in this match, Studd had Hogan in the bear hug, and from where we were sitting, I could clearly see Hulk and Studd talking to each other. I looked up at my dad and asked him, "What do you think Hulk's saying to him?" My dad, with his sarcastic sense of humor, answered, "He probably asked him if he wants go to McDonald's after the match." That was followed by laughter by most people who heard it. I laughed too. I was around 4 or 5 years old at that time and, even at that early age, kinda had a feeling pro wrestlers were playing characters. But hearing my dad say that pretty much sealed the deal on whether I thought it was "real or fake." I knew it was predetermined and that the wrestlers were real life people portraying superhero like characters, and I was perfectly cool with it."
Michael Berlinski, *Edison, NJ*

Nov. 8, 1984: Michael Jordan, as a member of the Chicago Bulls, made his debut at MSG against the New York Knicks. He scored 33 points and a crowd-pleasing dunk during the game would become famous in highlight videos.

WWF @ New York City, NY - Madison Square Garden - November 26, 1984 (22,090)
Televised on the MSG Network - included Gorilla Monsoon & Lord Alfred Hayes on commentary:
Prime Time Wrestling - 1/8/85: SD Jones pinned Charlie Fulton (sub. for Samula) at 10:40 with a headbutt
Prime Time Wrestling - 1/8/85: Moondog Spot pinned Jose Luis Rivera (sub. for Billy Jack) at 9:16 with a clothesline from the middle turnbuckle
Georgia Championship Wrestling - 12/9/84: Bobby Heenan pinned Salvatore Bellomo at 8:56 by blocking a sunset flip into the ring and punching Bellomo in the face (*Best of the WWF Vol. 14, Bobby 'The Brain' Heenan*)
Georgia Championship Wrestling - 12/9/84: Angelo Mosca defeated Mr. Fuji via disqualification at 8:01 when Fuji threw salt into Mosca's eyes as Fuji was caught in the sleeper (Mosca's MSG return after more than 3 years; his final MSG appearance)
Georgia Championship Wrestling - 12/9/84: Bob Orton Jr. pinned Swede Hanson at 8:51 with a reverse splash off the top
Prime Time Wrestling - 1/8/85: Roddy Piper (w/ Bob Orton Jr.) fought the Tonga Kid (w/ Jimmy Snuka) to a double disqualification at 7:03 when both Snuka and Orton interfered; after the bout, Snuka and Tonga cleared the ring
TNT - 12/18/84: Barry Windham pinned Moondog Rex at 12:11 with the bulldog (Windham's MSG debut)
Georgia Championship Wrestling - 12/9/84: Tony Atlas pinned the Executioner at 1:48 with a gorilla press slam and splash
David Schultz pinned Rocky Johnson at 9:25 after reversing a powerslam attempt into a cradle
Prime Time Wrestling - 1/8/85: David Sammartino (w/ Bruno Sammartino) defeated Ken Patera (w/ Capt. Lou Albano) via disqualification at 12:24 when Albano tripped David from the outside; after the bout, Bruno chased Albano in and out of the ring (Bruno's MSG return after a 4-year absence)
Georgia Championship Wrestling - 12/9/84: Tito Santana fought WWF Intercontinental Champion Greg Valentine to a curfew draw at 22:23; after the bout, Santana had to be held back from further attacking the champion (*History of the Intercontinental Title*)

Yesterday's equivalent to Raw

"Everything started or ended at The Garden. Hulk Hogan might wrestle at the Nassau Coliseum and maybe there wouldn't be a clean finish, or they would go to the Meadowlands and there wouldn't be a clean finish. But when they came to The Garden, they would. Because it aired on television, it was a little more important because it was a live show. Watching The Garden was my equivalent to watching Monday Night Raw. It always felt like more of an event. I think a big part of that had to do with Howard Finkel. He would run down the card for the next show. Today, it sounds mad. They would give you the exact same card for everything. But, as he went through the card, he got a little more dramatic. 'The Brooklyn Brawler will face...Jim Powers!' And he would go on and on until he got up to 'Hullllllllllk Hogaaaaaaaaaaaan!' I think that lent a lot to The Garden."
Mike Johnson; *Glendale, NY*

Backstage encounter
"My father greased an attendant to get my friend and I backstage. Both (Jimmy) Snuka and Tonga (Kid) noted my hand sign and high-fived me afterwards. To this day, you will see me throw this sign up in pictures with fans, a direct influence of the night pictured. Special place with special people made for special memories."
Matt Striker, *TheHistoryofWWE.com interview, 2014*

WWF @ New York City, NY - Madison Square Garden - December 28, 1984 (26,092, including several thousand at Felt Forum; sell out for both the arena and Forum)

It was backstage during this event that ABC '20/20' reporter John Stossel was assaulted by David Schultz during an interview in which Stossel asked Schultz if wrestling was fake; as a result of the incident, Stossel filed suit against both the WWF and Schultz

Televised on the MSG Network - included Gorilla Monsoon & Gene Okerlund on commentary; originally announced to appear were Paul Orndorff, Rocky Johnson, Angelo Mosca, and a match between Nikolai Volkoff and Tony Garea; featured Cyndi Lauper being presented an award by the WWF for her contributions over the past year, with Cyndi then giving the WWF a gold platinum record, accepted by WWF World Champion Hulk Hogan and WWF Women's Champion Wendi Richter; moments later, Lauper introduced Capt. Lou Albano and presented him with a record as well for his helping Lauper raise over $4 milliong for multiple sclerosis; eventually, Roddy Piper and Bob Orton Jr. came ringside, with Piper smashing the record over Albano's head, pushing Lauper down, and then bodyslamming David Wolff; Piper then went backstage when Hogan returned to the ring:

Prime Time Wrestling - 2/19/85: Brutus Beefcake (w/ Johnny V) pinned SD Jones at 13:22 with a running kneelift
Salvatore Bellamo pinned Johnny Rodz at 5:36 with a reverse crossbody off the middle turnbuckle; prior to the bout, Howard Finkel introduced Bellomo's parents who were sitting in the crowd
Japanese TV - 1/4/85; Prime Time Wrestling - 2/19/85: World Martial Arts Champion Antonio Inoki pinned David Schultz at 5:16 with an enzuiguri (Schultz and Inoki's last MSG appearance)
Prime Time Wrestling - 2/19/85: The Junkyard Dog pinned Paul Kelly at 3:05 with the powerslam (JYD's MSG debut)
Prime Time Wrestling - 2/19/85; Japanese TV - 1/4/85: The Cobra pinned the Black Tiger to win the vacant WWF Jr. Heavyweight Title at 12:29 with a tombstone and senton bomb off the top; after the bout, the Black Tiger attacked the Cobra after Cobra offered to shake hands; moments later, the Cobra retaliated by hitting Tiger with a steel chair (*Best of the WWF Vol. 1*)
Prime Time Wrestling - 2/19/85: Jimmy Snuka & the Tonga Kid fought Roddy Piper & Bob Orton Jr. to a double disqualification at 14:58 when all four men began brawling in the ring and Snuka shoved the referee to the mat; after the bout, Snuka & Tonga cleared the ring of the opposition (*Rowdy Roddy Piper's Greatest Hits*)
Prime Time Wrestling - 2/19/85: Mike Rotundo pinned Rene Goulet at 10:38 with an airplane spin
WWF Tag Team Champions Adrian Adonis & Dick Murdoch fought Jack & Jerry Brisco to a double count-out at 26:46 when all four men began brawling on the floor; after the match, the challengers put Adonis & Murdoch in simultaneous figure-4 leglocks
Prime Time Wrestling - 2/19/85: Barry Windham pinned Mr. Fuji at the 19-second mark with a bulldog
Japanese TV - 1/4/85; Prime Time Wrestling - 2/19/85: WWF World Champion Hulk Hogan pinned the Iron Sheik (w/ Freddie Blassie) at 3:31 with a powerslam and the legdrop (*WWE's Top 50 Superstars of All Time*)

COMING EVENTS

JANUARY THRU FEBRUARY 1985

madison square gard

ARENA

FELT FORUM • EXPOSITION RO

105
madison square garden

PENNSYLVANIA PLAZA/Seventh Ave., 31st

ARENA

NEW YORK KNICKS
National Basketball Association

Sat., Jan. 5	Chicago Bulls	7:30 p.m.
Mon., Jan. 7	Boston Celtics	8:00 p.m.
Tues., Jan. 15	Philadelphia 76ers	7:30 p.m.
Thurs., Jan. 17	Detroit Pistons	8:00 p.m.
Sat., Jan. 19	Atlanta Hawks	7:30 p.m.
	Burger King T-Shirt Night	
Tues., Jan. 22	Seattle Supersonics	7:30 p.m.
Sat., Jan. 26	Indiana Pacers	7:30 p.m.
Mon., Jan. 28	Los Angeles Clippers	7:30 p.m.
	Getty Player Photo Night	
Thurs., Feb. 14	Houston Rockets	8:00 p.m.
Sat., Feb. 16	New Jersey Nets	7:30 p.m.
	Schick Dad's Appreciation Night	
Tues., Feb. 19	Milwaukee Bucks	7:30 p.m.
Sun., Feb. 24	Los Angeles Lakers	12 noon
Tues., Feb. 26	San Antonio Spurs	7:30 p.m.

NEW YORK RANGERS
National Hockey League

Wed., Jan. 2	Vancouver Canucks	7:30 p.m.
Sun., Jan. 6	New Jersey Devils	7:30 p.m.
Mon., Jan. 14	New Jersey Devils	7:30 p.m.
Wed., Jan. 16	Buffalo Sabres	7:30 p.m.
Thurs., Jan. 24	Detroit Red Wings	7:30 p.m.
Sun., Jan. 27	Minnesota North Stars	7:30 p.m.
Fri., Feb. 15	Edmonton Oilers	7:30 p.m.
Sun., Feb. 17	New York Islanders	7:30 p.m.
Thurs., Feb. 21	Hartford Whalers	7:30 p.m.
Mon., Feb. 25	Winnipeg Jets	7:30 p.m.
Thurs., Feb. 28	Washington Capitals	7:30 p.m.

COLLEGE BASKETBALL

Wed., Jan. 23	South Florida vs. St. Peter's	5:30 p.m.
	St. John's vs. Syracuse	
Wed., Feb. 20	Manhattan vs. Iona	7:00 p.m.
	Notre Dame vs. Fordham	
Wed., Feb. 27	NYU vs. CCNY	6:30 p.m.
	St. John's vs. Georgetown	

SPORTS EVENTS

Sun., Jan. 6	Police-Firemen Hockey Game	12 noon

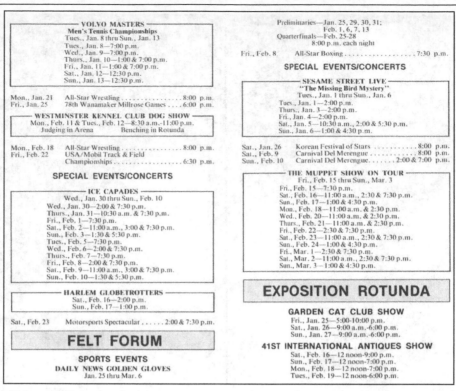

Feb. 18, 1985 saw MTV air a bout between Hulk Hogan and Roddy Piper, live from MSG, which played an integral role in launching the first WrestleMania. You'll see the local advertising listed the show as simply 'All Star Wrestling' at 8 p.m.

WWF @ New York City, NY - Madison Square Garden - January 21, 1985 (16,000)
Televised on the MSG Network - featured Gorilla Monsoon & Gene Okerlund on commentary:
Prime Time Wrestling - 9/22/86: Moondog Rex pinned Terry Gibbs with a reverse neckbreaker at 10:14; prior to the bout, Howard Finkel announced that the Junkyard Dog would be Jimmy Snuka's partner later in the show, substituting for the Tonga Kid
All American Wrestling - 2/24/85: Bret Hart defeated Rene Goulet via submission with a sleeper at 14:32 (Hart's MSG debut)
Prime Time Wrestling - 3/5/85: Jim Neidhart pinned Tony Garea with a powerslam at 12:05 (Neidhart's MSG debut)
Prime Time Wrestling - 3/5/85: Don Muraco (w/ Mr. Fuji) pinned Swede Hanson at 10:54 with the tombstone; prior to the bout, Pedro Morales was introduced to the crowd
Blackjack Mulligan pinned Moondog Spot at 6:40 with a small package; Rita Marie made her debut as referee for the bout and was billed as the first ever female referee
Prime Time Wrestling - 3/5/85: Andre the Giant defeated Ken Patera (w/ Bobby Heenan) via disqualification when Heenan came off the top onto Andre, hitting him with a pair of brass knuckles and causing the referee to be knocked down; moments later, Patera came off the top onto Andre, with Andre lifting his boot into Patera's face before sending both men out of the ring (*Andre the Giant* VHS, *Andre the Giant* DVD)
Prime Time Wrestling - 3/5/85: Big John Studd (w/ Bobby Heenan) pinned George Wells at 7:19 with a backbreaker; the referee made an obvious fast count to end the match
Roddy Piper & Bob Orton Jr. defeated Jimmy Snuka & the Junkyard Dog (sub. for the Tonga Kid) in a Texas Tornado Match at 8:45 when Orton pinned JYD after Piper tripped JYD from the apron (*The WWF's Most Unusual Matches*)
Prime Time Wrestling - 3/5/85: The Spoiler pinned Rick McGraw at 8:59 with a butterfly spulex
Tito Santana defeated WWF Intercontinental Champion Greg Valentine via count-out at 20:21 when a flying forearm from the challenger sent Valentine out of the ring

177

Landing an acting gig

"I got cast in a movie, 'Wise Guys.' They had cast Capt. Lou Albano as a villain in the movie. Joe Piscopo and Danny Devito were at Madison Square Garden. I asked for autographs and they saw that I was jumping up and down (during the matches). They asked my father, 'Would your son like to audition tomorrow for a role in a movie?' The next day, I go in for the audition. They shouted down to us to come back up and I got the role. 'Harry Jr.' They needed a little kid to be Danny Devito's son. At the wrap party, Cyndi Lauper was there and Lou Albano brought Andre the Giant."
Matt Striker, *TheHistoryofWWE.com interview, 2014*

'Holy shit, this is real'

"When Mr. T hopped the guard rail - nowadays you'll see cops arrest guys all the time - but when that happened, everyone was like 'Holy shit, this is real.' It was the closest thing I've ever been to as a riot, before I was in actual riots with the original ECW. Everyone was willing to fight for Mr. T and Hulk Hogan."
Tommy Dreamer, *TheHistoryofWWE.com interview, 2014*

WWF @ New York City, NY - Madison Square Garden - February 18, 1985 (26,092 including several thousand at Felt Forum; sell out)

Televised on the MSG Network - included Gorilla Monsoon & Gene Okerlund on commentary:

Prime Time Wrestling - 3/19/85: Rick McGraw fought Moondog Spot to a 15-minute time-limit draw at 14:32 as McGraw had Spot covered with a superplex

Prime Time Wrestling - 3/19/85: Johnny Rodz pinned Jose Luis Rivera at 11:14 with a diving headbutt after Rivera missed a back elbow drop from the middle rope

All American Wrestling - 3/17/85: Hillbilly Jim defeated Rene Goulet via submission with a bearhug at 7:29; after the bout, Goulet had a verbal confrontation with Mr. T, who was sitting in the front row, until T jumped the guard rail and scared Goulet backstage (Hillbilly's MSG debut) (*Biggest, Smallest, Strangest, Smallest, Wrestling's Country Boys*)

Prime Time Wrestling - 3/5/85: Leilani Kai (w/ the Fabulous Moolah) pinned WWF Women's Champion Wendi Richter (w/ Cyndi Lauper & David Wolff) with a roll up to win the title at 11:49 after Moolah hit the champion with a forearm to the face as Richter was trying to help Lauper on the floor after she was attacked by Moolah; after the bout, Richter and Lauper scared Moolah and Kai from the ring (*The Best of the WWF Vol. 5*)

Prime Time Wrestling - 3/19/85: David Sammartino pinned Moondog Rex at 12:27 with a powerslam

Prime Time Wrestling - 3/19/85: Nikolai Volkoff (w/ Freddie Blassie) pinned Swede Hanson at 5:48 after picking Hanson up and dropping him to the mat

Prime Time Wrestling - 3/19/85: Jimmy Snuka pinned Bob Orton Jr. at 9:59 with a sunset flip into the ring after punching Orton's injured left arm; moments prior to the finish, Orton seriously injured the arm after a missed charge resulted in Orton hitting the steel ring post (*The Greatest Wrestling Stars of the 80s*)

Prime Time Wrestling - 3/19/85: Paul Orndorff pinned Tony Atlas at 6:08 with a German suplex into a bridge

Prime Time Wrestling - 3/19/85: WWF Tag Team Champions Barry Windham & Mike Rotundo (w/ Capt. Lou Albano) defeated the Spoiler & the Assassin at the 36-second mark when Windham pinned the Assassin with a bulldog

Prime Time Wrestling - 3/19/85: Don Muraco (w/ Mr. Fuji) pinned Salvatore Bellomo at 2:41 with the tombstone

The War to Settle the Score - aired live on MTV (9.1) - featured an opening promo by WWF World Champion Hulk Hogan; hosted by Gene Okerlund & MTV's Alan Hunter; included a video package recapping the history of Cyndi Lauper and Capt. Lou Albano, culminating in The Brawl to Settle it All the previous summer on MTV, Lauper's and Albano's friendship since then, and Roddy Piper attacking the two in December at Madison Square Garden; featured pretaped comments by MTV with Bobby Heenan, Paul Orndorff, David Schultz, and Piper about Piper's actions against Lauper and Albano; Gloria Steinem, Jimmy Snuka, Bruno Sammartino, Patty Smyth, Ted Nugent, Dee Snider, Geraldine Ferraro, Dick Clark, and Hogan then commented on Piper's actions; pretaped Okerlund interviews then aired with Piper and Hogan about agreeing to face each other as well as footage of their contract signing, leading to more comments from Kenny Loggins, Adam Taylor, Peter Wolf, Heenan, Adrian Adonis & Dick Murdoch, Freddie Blassie, Tina Turner, the Junkyard Dog, Tony Atlas, Nikolai Volkoff, Greg Kihn, the Iron Sheik, Charles M. Young, Timothy White, Merle Ginsburg, and Vic Garbarini; featured a video package on Piper's background; included a video package on Hogan's background; featured predictions on Hogan vs. Piper from Mr. Fuji, Hillbilly Jim, Brutus Beefcake, Snider, Big John Studd, Little Richard, Blassie, Blackjack Mulligan, Volkoff, Wolf, and Kihn; following the match, Okerlund spoke with Hunter in the locker room, then Hogan, Lauper, David Wolfe, Mr. T, and Albano about what happened earlier; moments later, Okerlund spoke with Andy Warhol about his reaction of what happened; Hunter then brought in Joe Piscopo, who said he loved it and would be back March 17; Okerlund then spoke with Billy Squier and Danny Devito, with Piper then interrupting wearing a towel out of the shower; Piper then claimed Hogan didn't have the guts to face him one-on-one:

WWF World Champion Hulk Hogan (w/ Capt. Lou Albano & Cyndi Lauper) defeated Roddy Piper (w/ Bob Orton Jr.) via disqualification at 7:40 after Paul Orndorff, who came ringside midway through the contest, joined Piper in attacking the champion after the referee was knocked out; moments later, as Piper and Orndorff prepared to knock Cyndi Lauper off the ring apron, Mr. T - who was sitting ringside for the event - came out of his seat and into the ring where he and Hogan faced off against Piper and Orndorff until officials and police swarmed the ring; prior to the bout, Piper came to the ring wearing a Hulk Hogan t-shirt and smashed a guitar in the ring to show what he thought of rock 'n' roll; Orton wore a sling on his arm as a result of his match against Jimmy Snuka earlier in the show; after the match, Hogan took the mic and challenged Piper and Orndorff to get back in the ring; moments later, he celebrated in the ring with Mr. T, Albano, and Lauper; Bob Costas introduced the participants prior to the contest (*Rowdy Roddy Piper's Greatest Hits, The Greatest Wrestling Stars of the 80s, Hulk Hogan: The Ultimate Anthology, Born to Controversy: The Roddy Piper Story, The Top 25 WWE Rivalries*)

Warhol on hand

Gene Okerlund: "Andy Warhol, your impressions of what went down earlier on here?"

Andy Warhol: "Oh, I'm speechless."

Okerlund: "Well, you've got to be. ...I saw jaws drop to the floor."

Warhol: "It's just so exciting, I just don't know what to say."

Okerlund: "Have you ever seen such total bedlam and pandemonium in your entire life?"

Warhol: "Never."

Okerlund: "Your impressions of the Rock 'n' Wrestling Connection? Don't you think that they got together here tonight and stood on firm ground?"

Warhol: "It's the best thing I've ever seen in my whole life, the most exciting thing."

WWF @ New York City, NY - Madison Square Garden - March 17, 1985 (18,700) (matinee)
Televised on the MSG Network - featured Gorilla Monsoon & Gene Okerlund on commentary; included Mr. T as a guest of Piper's Pit, with Bob Orton Jr., Paul Orndorff, WWF World Champion Hulk Hogan, and Jimmy Snuka all present for the segment:
Prime Time Wrestling - 4/9/85: Rocky Johnson pinned Charlie Fulton at 3:51 with a sunset flip
Prime Time Wrestling - 4/9/85: Barry O pinned Rene Goulet at 8:50 with a small package
All American Wrestling - 4/7/85: Jim Neidhart (w/ Jimmy Hart) pinned SD Jones at 6:52 with a powerslam (Jimmy Hart's MSG debut)
Prime Time Wrestling - 4/9/85: King Kong Bundy (w/ Jimmy Hart) pinned Jose Luis Rivera at 2:30 with the Avalanche and an elbow drop
Prime Time Wrestling - 4/9/85: The Iron Sheik & Nikolai Volkoff (w/ Freddie Blassie) defeated George Wells & Bret Hart at 8:45 when Sheik pinned Wells with an elbow drop after a kick to the face
Prime Time Wrestling - 4/9/85: David Sammartino pinned Matt Borne at 8:36 by reversing a powerslam into a cradle
Andre the Giant, Jimmy Snuka, & the Junkyard Dog (w/ Capt. Lou Albano) defeated Big John Studd, Jesse Ventura, & Ken Patera at 11:55 when Snuka pinned Patera with the top rope splash after a boot to the face from Andre (*Best of the WWF Vol. 9*)
Prime Time Wrestling - 4/9/85: Ricky Steamboat pinned Terry Gibbs at 4:36 with a crossbody off the top (Steamboat's MSG return after a 5-year absence)
Prime Time Wrestling - 4/9/85: WWF Intercontinental Champion Greg Valentine (w/ Jimmy Hart) pinned Tito Santana at 10:22 in a lumberjack match after both men collided and the champion fell on top for the win; lumberjacks included King Kong Bundy, Big John Studd, the Junkyard Dog, Barry O, Matt Borne, Ricky Steamboat, Jimmy Snuka, Rocky Johnson, Charlie Fulton, and Terry Gibbs (*The WWF's Most Unusual Matches, The Greatest Wrestling Stars of the 80s, History of the Intercontinental Championship*)

WRESTLEMANIA
Madison Square Garden - March 31, 1985

McMahon's risk vs. reward
"I remember the very first WrestleMania press conference. The New York Times, The Daily News, The New York Post, everybody was there. No one had seen anything like this on the level he had brought it to before this. ...This was the first real move of Vince McMahon's expansion. The promoters were telling wrestlers that if you go to work for him you may not come back here again. The risk for Vince McMahon was his entire life, so to say. He had everything, all his money, down on WrestleMania, betting that this thing would make his business soar."
Bill Apter, *WrestleMania Rewind*, WWE Network

On celebrities in wrestling
"I became pretty good friends with Mr. T. We had some matches later, he refereed in Montreal when I wrestled Pat Patterson and cut his hair. Mr. T was the special referee. So I got to know Mr. T pretty good. It was a great time. Huge, huge crowd. Celebrities were starting to get involved in the wrestling business when they never really had ever before because Hulk had a really innovative thing going. He did that Rocky III film with Mr. T and Stallone and it really broke into the limelight. So it became cool to be around wrestlers."
Brutus Beefcake, *TheHistoryofWWE.com interview, 2005*

On changes in wrestling

"Wrestling had to change with the times. WrestleMania and its success was a no brainer. Vinnie was in the right place at the right time. I really believe Vinnie was the only person that was involved in the wrestling business that could take it to the levels that he has taken the business."

George Steele,
TheHistoryofWWE.com interview, 2009

Concerts America
presents
from Madison Square Garden
on closed circuit T.V.

**W W F
WRESTLING MANIA**

**CYDI LAUPER'S team of
HULK HOGAN**
and
MR. T
vs
ROWDY RODDY PIPER
and
PAUL ORNDORFF

also

Vendy Rictor
vs
Lelani Kai

Guest Referee: MOHAMMED ALI
Time keeper: LIBERACE
Ring Announcer: BILLY MARTIN

SUNDAY, MARCH 31
1:00 PM

Sheraton Washington Ballroom &
Starplex Armory

Tickets at all Ticketron and Ticket Center locations
or charge 499-1800

WrestleMania - New York City, NY - Madison Square Garden - March 31, 1985 (19,121)

Pay-per-view bouts - featured Gorilla Monsoon & Jesse Ventura on commentary; included Gene Okerlund singing the National Anthem; Tommy Dreamer and Nunzio were both in attendance; featured Lord Alfred Hayes introducing the matches from backstage; included pre-taped backstage interviews by Okerlund with both Tito Santana and the Executioner, said to be undefeated, regarding their match on the card; featured Okerlund conducting pre-taped interviews with SD Jones and King Kong Bundy, with Jimmy Hart, regarding their match later in the show; included Okerlund conducting pre-taped backstage interviews with Matt Borne and Ricky Steamboat regarding their match later in the show; featured Okerlund conducting pre-taped backstage interviews with David & Bruno Sammartino and Brutus Beefcake & Johnny V regarding their match later in the show; featured Okerlund conducting pre-taped backstage interviews with WWF Intercontinental Champion Greg Valentine, with Hart, and the Junkyard Dog regarding their match later in the show; included Okerlund conducting pre-taped backstage interviews with Nikolai Volkoff & the Iron Sheik, with Freddie Blassie, and WWF Tag Team Champions Barry Windham & Mike Rotundo, with Capt. Lou Albano, regarding their match later in the show; featured Okerlund conducting backstage interviews with Big John Studd, with Bobby Heenan, about his bodyslam match later in the show against Andre the Giant; included Okerlund conducting backstage interviews with Cyndi Lauper and Wendi Richter and WWF Women's Champion Leilani Kai and the Fabulous Moolah regarding the women's title match later in the show:

Tito Santana defeated the Executioner (Buddy Rose) via submission with the figure-4 at 4:49 after the flying forearm (Rose's last appearance for 5 years)

King Kong Bundy (w/ Jimmy Hart) pinned SD Jones at the 24-second mark with the Avalanche and a splash; the announced time of the match was 9 seconds (*Grand Slams*)

Ricky Steamboat pinned Matt Borne with the crossbody off the top at 4:38

David Sammartino (w/ Bruno Sammartino) fought Brutus Beefcake (w/ Johnny V) to a double disqualification at 11:44 when Johnny slammed David on the floor, with Bruno then chasing Johnny into the ring and all four men then brawling until Johnny and Beefcake were cleared from the ring (*Best of the WWF Vol. 3*)

The Junkyard Dog defeated WWF Intercontinental Champion Greg Valentine (w/ Jimmy Hart) via count-out at 6:55; Valentine originally won the match with both feet on the ropes for leverage at 6:00 but Tito Santana came out and told referee Dick Kroll what happened, with Kroll then continuing the match after Valentine had left the ring, with Valentine refusing to get back inside (*Legends of Wrestling Collection, Legends of Wrestling: Jerry Lawler and the Junkyard Dog*)

Prime Time Wrestling - 4/16/85: Nikolai Volkoff & the Iron Sheik (w/ Freddie Blassie) defeated WWF Tag Team Champions Mike Rotundo & Barry Windham (w/ Capt. Lou Albano) to win the titles at 6:56 when Volkoff pinned Windham after Sheik hit Windham in the back with Blassie's cane; after the bout, Gene Okerlund conducted a backstage interview with Blassie and the new champions (*Tag Team Champions, Legends of Wrestling: Andre the Giant and the Iron Sheik, Allied Powers*)

Andre the Giant defeated Big John Studd (w/ Bobby Heenan) in a bodyslam match at 5:53; pre-match stipulations stated Andre would win $15,000 if he was able to slam Studd and would retire if he couldn't do it within the time-limit; after the bout, Andre began throwing the money into the crowd until Heenan grabbed the money bag and ran backstage; moments later, Gene Okerlund conducted a backstage interview with Andre regarding his win (*Andre the Giant* VHS, *Andre the Giant* DVD)

Prime Time Wrestling - 4/23/85: Wendi Richter (w/ Cyndi Lauper) pinned WWF Women's Champion Leilani Kai (w/ the Fabulous Moolah) to win the title at 6:14 when the momentum of a crossbody off the top by Kai put Richter on top for the win; after the bout, Gene Okerlund conducted a backstage interview with Richter and Lauper, with David Wolfe (*Amazing Managers*)

WWF World Champion Hulk Hogan & Mr. T (w/ Jimmy Snuka) defeated Roddy Piper & Paul Orndorff (w/ Bob Orton Jr.) at 13:33 when Hogan pinned Orndorff after Orton accidentally knocked Orndorff out with a double axe handle off the top, using his arm cast, while refereee Pat Patterson was distracted; Billy Martin served as guest ring announcer for the match; prior to the bout, guest timekeeper Liberace danced in the ring with the Rockettes; Muhammed Ali served as the outside official while Patterson was the referee inside; former boxer Jose Torres was shown in the crowd during the introductions; Piper's team was escorted to the ring by a bagpipe band performing "Scotland the Brave;" after the bout, Piper and Orton left ringside, leaving Orndorff to be helped to his feet by Mr. T; a dazed Orndorff faced off with Hogan and T before eventually leaving the ring himself; moments later, Gene Okerlund conducted a backstage interview with Hogan, T, and Snuka; voted Pro Wrestling Illustrated's Match of the Year

"At the end of the night, we had been partying quite heavily."
Vince McMahon, *WrestleMania Rewind, WWE Network*

Closed circuit feeds of WrestleMania reportedly sold out the Boston Garden, Capital Centre, Spectrum, and Nassau Coliseum in the northeast.

April 1, 1985: U2 performed at MSG for the first time.

On being in the opening match of the first WrestleMania

"I still got a really good pay day. I probably got what Junkyard Dog got, wrestling in the opening match. I think it was George Scott, again, not helping me out, telling me it would take away from a lot of the house shows by doing one big exposure (facing WWF IC Champion Greg Valentine). I don't think I was one of George Scott's favorites."

Tito Santana, *TitleMatchWrestling interview, 2000*

Wrestling becomes mainstream

"I thought that was really cool. Mr. T. Three seats away from me was Danny Devito and Joe Piscopo. Regis Philbin would go to the shows, Dave Winfield from the Yankees. (WrestleMania) was fast to sell out, obviously. A lot of times you could buy your ticket a week later. But when they announced it, it was 'OK, we gotta go to the Garden the first day and get the tickets.' Even waiting in the line to get the tickets, I was 18 years old, it was such a big line. Everybody was just excited to buy the ticket for the show. And then you started to see the merchandise. The celebrity thing added so much to it. It made more people come out. I saw a lot of fans there that I had never seen there. Going to the Garden month after month after month, you'd see the same people. But once Hogan got there, once they got to WrestleMania, now I'm seeing tons of people. And then it started to be a thing with more kids, a lot more teenagers and kids. The matches, if you go back and watch it now, no match is a great match. Everything is good. Nothing is great like Savage-Steamboat. But the whole buildup of it was exciting. Good matches but nothing spectacular but just being there was spectacular. If you put Starrcade '83 up against Wrestlemania, Starrcade obviously is much better. But it was in New York at the Garden, everybody's there. All the newscasters outside, the ringside was flooded by photographers. The next day, you go to school and now everybody's talking about wrestling. When I was a kid, there were very few people that knew about it. Now I'm graduating high school and everybody's talking about it."

Charlie Adorno, *Brooklyn, NY*

WWF @ New York City, NY - Madison Square Garden - April 22, 1985 (18,000)
Televised on the MSG Network - included Gorilla Monsoon & Gene Okerlund on commentary; featured Okerlund conducting backstage interviews with King Kong Bundy & Jimmy Hart and the Junkyard Dog & Tito Santana prior to their matches:
Prime Time Wrestling - 5/14/85: WWF Jr. Heavyweight Champion the Cobra pinned Barry O at 13:20 with a hurricanrana
Prime Time Wrestling - 8/13/85: Tatsumi Fujinami pinned Matt Borne at 11:25 with a German suplex into a bridge
Prime Time Wrestling - 5/7/85: King Kong Bundy (w/ Jimmy Hart) pinned Swede Hanson with an elbow drop following the Avalanche in the corner at 4:27
Prime Time Wrestling - 5/14/85: Davey Boy Smith & the Dynamite Kid defeated Rene Goulet & Johnny Rodz (sub. for Buddy Rose) at 8:16 when Dynamite pinned Rodz with a diving headbutt off Goulet's back, who was held in a fireman's carry by Smith (*Best of the WWF Vol. 3*)
Prime Time Wrestling - 5/14/85: Ricky Steamboat pinned Moondog Spot at 7:24 with a flying bodypress
Prime Time Wrestling - 5/14/85: Don Muraco (w/ Mr. Fuji) defeated WWF World Champion Hulk Hogan via count-out at 13:35 after ramming Hogan into the ring apron when Hogan became distracted by Fuji
Prime Time Wrestling - 5/14/85: Mike Rotundo (w/ Capt. Lou Albano) pinned WWF Tag Team Champion the Iron Sheik (w/ Freddie Blassie) at 14:16 with a roll up after Sheik missed a running kneelift into the corner
Prime Time Wrestling - 5/14/85: Barry Windham (w/ Capt. Lou Albano) defeated WWF Tag Team Champion Nikolai Volkoff (w/ Freddie Blassie) via disqualification at 12:11 when the Iron Sheik interfered; after the bout, Mike Rotundo made the save
Prime Time Wrestling - 11/18/86: Tito Santana & the Junkyard Dog defeated Brutus Beefcake (w/ Johnny V) & WWF Intercontinental Champion Greg Valentine (w/ Jimmy Hart) at 16:03 when Santana pinned Valentine with the flying forearm

Putting back on the tights

"I hated, despised beyond words, to put back on the tights. I was put in a bad situation. My son was in the business, David. I went back. My job was strictly to be a color commentator. My wrestling days were over. Boston wasn't doing well at all and Pittsburgh was way down. So Vince McMahon asks me if I can put back on the tights and give those clubs a shot in the arm. So I said, 'Vince, I'm retired. I'm getting up there in age. My body is feeling pretty good but I'm not at that stage.' So he went to my kid and said, 'Your dad won't put on his tights. Maybe we could do a tag match here and there. That could really boost your career.' I put on my tights but I despised it and was angry. I was angry at McMahon because he created that situation. David became frustrated because he didn't move up the ladder when he was by himself. McMahon knew David had no place else to go so he would ask me to wrestle here and there, and if I didn't then he wouldn't take David back. It was a nightmare. ...I was retired in 1981. And anything after that, it wasn't by choice. It was just circumstances that put me in that situation."

Bruno Sammartino. *TheHistoryofWWE.com interview. 2009*

WWF @ New York City, NY - Madison Square Garden - May 20, 1985 (15,000)
Televised on the MSG Network - included Gorilla Monsoon & Gene Okerlund on commentary for the first 4 bouts, with Lord Alfred Hayes replacing Okerlund for the remainder of the card; featured Okerlund conducting a backstage interviews with Bobby Heenan & the Missing Link, Jesse Ventura, Brutus Beefcake & Johnny V, and Bruno & David Sammartino prior to their matches:
Prime Time Wrestling - 6/11/85: Rocky Johnson pinned Rene Goulet at 10:19 with a reverse roll up (Johnson's last MSG appearance)
Prime Time Wrestling - 6/11/85: Jim Neidhart pinned Ivan Putski at 6:04 after reversing a powerslam attempt from the apron into a small package and grabbing the tights for leverage
Prime Time Wrestling - 6/11/85: Pedro Morales defeated Terry Gibbs via submission at 12:15 with the Boston Crab
WWF World Champion Hulk Hogan defeated Don Muraco (w/ Mr. Fuji) via disqualification at 6:12 when the challenger threw salt into Hogan's eyes after it was handed to him by Fuji; the bell originally sounded at 5:42 when Hogan scored the 3-count after hitting the legdrop but the referee had the contest continue when he noticed Muraco's foot was on the bottom rope during the cover after Fuji put it there (*Grudge Matches*)
Prime Time Wrestling - 6/11/85: Bret Hart pinned Rick McGraw at 8:31 with a fistdrop after sending McGraw into the top turnbuckle
Prime Time Wrestling - 6/11/85: Ken Patera (w/ Bobby Heenan) pinned Tony Atlas at 10:50 with a forearm off the top after Atlas was distracted by Heenan on the ring apron (Patera's last MSG appearance for 2 years)
Barry Windham & Mike Rotundo (w/ Capt. Lou Albano) defeated WWF Tag Team Champions Nikolai Volkoff & the Iron Sheik (w/ Freddie Blassie) via count-out at 11:21 when the challengers were able to get back in the ring before the 10-count after a brawl with the champions on the floor; prior to the bout, Dr. Jerry Graham was introduced to the crowd
All American Wrestling - 6/2/85: The Missing Link (w/ Bobby Heenan) pinned SD Jones at 1:55 with a diving headbutt off the top; prior to the bout, Heenan cut an in-ring promo saying his man would be the one to beat Hulk Hogan (Link's debut)
Prime Time Wrestling - 6/11/85: Jesse Ventura pinned Tony Garea at 10:31 with an elbow drop after causing Garea to hit the corner face-first (*Best of the WWF Vol. 19*)
Bruno & David Sammartino (w/ Arnold Skaaland) defeated Brutus Beefcake & Johnny V when David pinned Johnny V with an inside cradle at 9:07; after the bout, Bruno was double-teamed by Beefcake & Johnny V (Bruno's first match at MSG in 4 and a half years) (*Best of the WWF Vol. 3*)

Hulk Hogan defends the title against Don Muraco at MSG.

Randy & Lanny's debuts

"Naturally, I knew it as the world's most famous arena. I never thought I would get to wrestle there. We just flew in from Lexington, KY. We got in there very early. We watched as they were setting up the cage."

'You know this guy?'

"I remember I was very nervous when I first got there. When I came down the aisle, the fans were receptive and I immediately stopped worrying that it was Madison Square Garden. Afterwards, I took a shower. I thought 'I may never be here again. I may as well go explore.' I went to the Felt Forum, they had a big TV screen. I went in there, didn't pay to get in. And then Randy was facing Rick McGraw, and I got to see him wrestle on the big screen. They didn't know who the hell he was. He got into three arguments on the way to the ring and they figured out he was a heel. 'Man, he's getting over big.' A guy beside me goes, 'You know this guy?' 'Yes, I do.' 'He any good?' 'He certainly is.'

Lanny Poffo,
TheHistoryofWWE.com interview, 2014

WWF @ New York City, NY - Madison Square Garden - June 21, 1985 (19,800)
Televised on the MSG Network - included Gorilla Monsoon & Gene Okerlund on commentary:
Prime Time Wrestling - 7/9/85: Lanny Poffo pinned Terry Gibbs at 6:34 with a moonsault (Poffo's MSG debut)
Prime Time Wrestling - 7/9/85: Tony Atlas pinned Matt Borne at 7:02 with a press slam / splash combo
Prime Time Wrestling - 8/13/85: The Missing Link (w/ Bobby Heenan) pinned Jose Luis Rivera at 1:42 with a headbutt off the middle turnbuckle
Prime Time Wrestling - 7/9/85: Jim Brunzell pinned Moondog Spot with a dropkick at 12:22 (Brunzell's MSG debut)
All American Wrestling - 7/7/85: Randy Savage pinned Rick McGraw at 12:51 with the flying elbowdrop; after the bout, Savage threw McGraw to the floor (Savage's MSG debut) (*Macho Madness: The Ultimate Randy Savage Collection*)
Prime Time Wrestling - 8/13/85: Adrian Adonis (sub. for Ken Patera), Big John Studd, & Bobby Heenan defeated George Steele, WWF Tag Team Champions Barry Windham & Mike Rotundo via disqualification at 9:59 when Steele hit referee Dick Kroll with a chair after chasing Heenan around ringside with it (*Best of the WWF Vol. 3*)
Prime Time Wrestling - 7/9/85: Desiree Peterson pinned Judy Martin with a roll up into a bridge at 16:05
Prime Time Wrestling - 7/9/85: King Kong Bundy (w/ Jimmy Hart) pinned Tony Garea at 6:17 following the Avalanche (*Best of the WWF Vol. 3, Biggest, Smallest, Strangest, Smallest*)
Prime Time Wrestling - 7/9/85: Ricky Steamboat defeated WWF Intercontinental Champion Greg Valentine (w/ Jimmy Hart) via count-out at 14:20 when the champion was unable to get back into the ring after an enzuiguri from the challenger knocked him to the floor; after the bout, Steamboat cleared both Valentine and Hart from the ring (*Ricky "The Dragon" Steamboat*)
Prime Time Wrestling - 8/13/85: B. Brian Blair defeated Barry O via submission with a sleeper at 8:13
WWF World Champion Hulk Hogan defeated Don Muraco (w/ Mr. Fuji) in a steel cage match at 9:05 by escaping through the door moments after the challenger's head became entangled in the ring ropes (*The Hulkster Hulk Hogan*)

Hulk Hogan

"You know, I sure am glad all you people out there are watching the Madison Square Garden Network. Because you apparently know, the best in the WWF, the best in the Worldwide Wrestling Federation, the best in professional wrestling is right here with Hulk Hogan, Hulkamania running wild. It's fun, it's exciting. It's Americana. And these are the largest arms in the world. Whatcha gonna do when the Hulkster runs wild on you?"
TV spot for the MSG Network

190

WWF @ New York City, NY - Madison Square Garden - July 13, 1985 (15,000)
Televised on the MSG Network - featured Gorilla Monsoon & Lord Alfred Hayes on commentary; featured Monsoon conducting backstage interviews with Roddy Piper, Brutus Beefcake & Johnny V, and Paul Orndorff prior to their matches:
Prime Time Wrestling - 7/30/85: Ivan Putski pinned Moondog Spot at 12:58 with the Polish Hammer
The Missing Link (w/ Bobby Heenan) pinned Rick McGraw at 2:25 with a diving headbutt from the middle ropes
Prime Time Wrestling - 8/13/85: Pedro Morales pinned Rene Goulet at 12:56 with a small package
Prime Time Wrestling - 7/30/85: Adrian Adonis (w/ Bobby Heenan) defeated Jose Luis Rivera via submission with a Japanese sleeper hold
Prime Time Wrestling - 7/30/85: The Junkyard Dog defeated Bob Orton Jr. via disqualification at 14:40 when Orton came off the top with his arm cast; after the bout, Orton attempted to attack JYD a second time with the cast but he left the ring after JYD avoided the attack
Prime Time Wrestling - 7/30/85: Terry Funk defeated Lanny Poffo via submission at 13:02 with a sleeper hold; prior to the bout, Funk chased ring attendant Mel Phillips away from ringside after refusing to give him his ring gear and cowboy hat; after the bout, Funk branded Poffo (*Best of the WWF Vol. 6*)
Paul Orndorff defeated Roddy Piper via disqualification at 8:43 when Bob Orton Jr. interfered, pushed Orndorff off the top, and assaulted him with his arm cast; after the bout, Orndorff was bloodied and sustained a double suplex; moments later, Davey Boy Smith & the Dynamite Kid made the save and, after a brief brawl with Piper & Orton, were able to clear the ring (*Best of the WWF Vol. 4*)
Prime Time Wrestling - 7/30/85: The Iron Sheik (w/ Freddie Blassie) pinned Swede Hanson at 2:24 with an elbow drop after kicking him in the face with a loaded boot
Prime Time Wrestling - 7/30/85: George Steele (w/ Capt. Lou Albano) fought Nikolai Volkoff (w/ Freddie Blassie) to a double count-out at 4:18 after Steele left the ring to confront Blassie on the floor, after Blassie assaulted Albano with his cane, which led to a brawl with Steele & Albano against Volkoff & Blassie (*Amazing Managers*)
Prime Time Wrestling - 8/13/85: Brutus Beefcake (w/ Johnny V) pinned George Wells at 7:26 with a running kneelift after Wells was distracted by Johnny V
Prime Time Wrestling - 7/30/85: Davey Boy Smith & the Dynamite Kid fought Bret Hart & Jim Neidhart (w/ Jimmy Hart) to a curfew draw at 13:12 (*Best of the WWF Vol. 3, The Bret Hart Story: The Best There Is, Was, and Ever Will Be*)

Facing Terry Funk
"In June of 1985, I wrestled against Terry Gibbs in the opening match and won with a moonsault. In July, I wrestled Terry Funk. He beat me. He's so great, I got over better losing to Terry Funk than I did beating Terry Gibbs. He didn't believe in the one-way street, and neither did I. He tried to make me look good before he killed me."
Lanny Poffo,
TheHistoryofWWE.com interview, 2014

WWF @ New York City, NY - Madison Square Garden - August 10, 1985 (22,091)
Televised on the MSG Network - included Gorilla Monsoon & Lord Alfred Hayes on commentary:
Prime Time Wrestling - 9/10/85: Paul Roma pinned Charlie Fulton at 10:45 with a sunset fip into the ring
Prime Time Wrestling - 9/10/85: Lanny Poffo fought Iron Mike Sharpe to a 20-minute time-limit draw
Prime Time Wrestling - 9/10/85: The Missing Link (w/ Bobby Heenan) pinned Tony Garea at 4:09 with a headbutt from the middle rope
Prime Time Wrestling - 7/7/86: Pedro Morales pinned Barry O at 5:02 with a backbreaker; after the bout, Barry attacked Morales but was quickly sent to the floor
Uncle Elmer (w/ Hillbilly Jim) defeated Big John Studd (w/ Bobby Heenan) via disqualification at 2:40 when Bobby Heenan interfered as Elmer attempted a bodyslam; after the match, Elmer and Hillbilly Jim chased Studd and Heenan out of the ring (*Wrestling's Country Boys*)
Prime Time Wrestling - 9/10/85: Tony Atlas pinned Les Thornton at 11:32 with a press slam and splash
Andre the Giant & Paul Orndorff defeated Roddy Piper & Bob Orton Jr. at 8:25 when Orndorff pinned Orton after Andre kicked Orton in the face as he attempted a dive from the middle turnbuckle
Prime Time Wrestling - 9/10/85: Randy Savage pinned Jose Luis Rivera (sub. for George Wells who had an eye injury) at 16:14 with the flying elbowsmash
WWF Tag Team Champions Barry Windham & Mike Rotundo (w/ Capt. Lou Albano) defeated Greg Valentine (w/ Jimmy Hart) & Brutus Beefcake (w/ Johnny V) at 24:02 when Windham pinned Valentine with a sunset flip as Valentine attempted to put the figure-4 on Rotundo

Images from the August 1985 MSG event.

192

Images from the August 1985 MSG event.

Hanging out at the Ramada Inn

"There was a Ramada Inn on 8th Avenue at 48th Street. We started to go there after the shows, me and Vladimir. And it would be just a cool environment, no security guards. There was a bar there, there was a restaurant. The wrestlers stayed there because they got a good rate, it was right near the Garden. They would go out to clubs and bars and come back at 1-2 in the morning. The guys would come in and out, you could mark out and get photos. It was just me, Vladimir and maybe 20 other fans. It wasn't a big thing to go to the hotel then. We'd grab our monthly gyro, you'd settle in, watch the show, hop on the a train, take you two stops, and hang out at the Ramada. Even though I'm getting older and I'm liking the villains, it's pretty cool to get a photo with Hogan. He just main evented WrestleMania 1 a few months ago. It's not even like meeting a wrestler, it's like meeting a celebrity, especially in New York. Hogan was everywhere."

Charlie Adorno, *Brooklyn, NY*

WWF @ New York City, NY - Madison Square Garden - September 23, 1985 (18,000)
Televised on the MSG Network - included Gorilla Monsoon & Jesse Ventura on commentary:
Prime Time Wrestling - 10/29/85: Scott McGhee pinned Les Thornton with a reverse roll up into a bridge at 18:20
Prime Time Wrestling - 10/29/85: Adrian Adonis (w/ Bobby Heenan) pinned Rick McGraw at 10:06 with the DDT (McGraw's last MSG appearance)
Prime Time Wrestling - 10/29/85: Randy Savage (w/ Miss Elizabeth) pinned Paul Roma at 6:57 after twice hitting the flying elbowsmash; prior to the bout, Howard Finkel introduced Otto Wanz to the crowd, introduced as the European Heavyweight Champion
Andre the Giant (w/ Capt. Lou Albano) defeated King Kong Bundy (w/ Jimmy Hart) via disqualification at 13:50 when Big John Studd interfered, wearing street clothes, after Andre hit a sit-down splash onto Bundy; following the bout, Andre was double-teamed until he escaped the ring and grabbed a chair, forcing Studd, Bundy, Hart, and Bobby Heenan away from ringside (*Best of the WWF Vol. 4*, *Legends of Wrestling: Andre the Giant and the Iron Sheik*)
Prime Time Wrestling - 10/29/85: Bob Orton Jr. pinned SD Jones (sub. for George Wells) at 12:07 with a reverse splash off the top
Prime Time Wrestling - 10/29/85: Davey Boy Smith & the Dynamite Kid defeated Bret Hart & Jim Neidhart (w/ Jimmy Hart) at 18:31 when Dynamite pinned Bret after after a diving headbutt off the top behind the referee's back as Hart had Smith covered; after the bout, the Harts attacked Dynamite with Jimmy Hart's megaphone (*Best of the WWF Vol. 7*, *Allied Powers*)
Prime Time Wrestling - 10/29/85: The Missing Link pinned Lanny Poffo at 5:59 with a diving headbutt from the middle turnbuckle (Link's last MSG appearance)
Ricky Steamboat defeated Don Muraco (w/ Mr. Fuji) via disqualification at 12:45 when Fuji threw salt into Steamboat's eyes as he prepared to come off the top; after the bout, Muraco attacked Steamboat with Fuji's cane
Prime Time Wrestling - 10/29/85: Cpl. Kirchner pinned Moondog Spot at 2:45 with a Samoan Drop
The Junkyard Dog pinned Terry Funk (w/ Jimmy Hart) at 3:34 with a small package; after the bout, Funk attacked JYD with his branding iron and branded him with it (*Most Embarrassing Moments*)

WWF @ New York City, NY - Madison Square Garden - October 21, 1985 (19,000)

Televised on the MSG Network - featured Gorilla Monsoon & Jesse Ventura on commentary; included Bruno Sammartino as a guest of Piper's Pit in which Sammartino demanded Bob Orton Jr. leave the ring so that Piper could conduct the interview one-on-one; moments later, after receiving a number of insults from Piper, Sammartino shoved him down and was then assaulted by a chair; Sammartino eventually chased Piper away with the chair; prior to Sammartino's appearance, Piper had future WWF referee Tim White and a woman named Stephanie, both from New York, on as guests; Stephanie was forced to leave after saying Paul Orndorff was her favorite wrestler and White was forced to leave after saying Hulk Hogan was his; Sammartino appearing on Piper's Pit was later reshown during Prime Time Wrestling on 11/5/85; featured Gene Okerlund hosting a segment in which Vince McMahon was presented with an outstanding achievement award for the success of WrestleMania; during the segment, it was announced that the video of WrestleMania had gone platinum; Arnold Skaaland, Jim Troy, & George Scott, and the British Bulldogs were present for the presentation:

Prime Time Wrestling - 11/5/85: Steve Gatorwolf pinned Terry Gibbs (sub. for the Masked Superstar) at 7:17 with a double tomahawk chop to the chest

Prime Time Wrestling - 11/5/85: Adrian Adonis (w/ Jimmy Hart) pinned SD Jones at 6:51 with the DDT

Prime Time Wrestling - 11/5/85: Mike Rotundo & Tony Atlas (sub. for Barry Windham) defeated Barry O & Iron Mike Sharpe at 16:45 when Rotundo pinned Barry following the airplane spin; after the bout, Atlas fought off Barry O and threw him onto Jesse Ventura at ringside, leading to a heated verbal confrontation between Barry O and Ventura to set up their match the following month

King Tonga pinned Ron Shaw at 9:25 with a side kick to the face

Prime Time Wrestling - 11/5/85: Pedro Morales pinned Rene Goulet with an inside cradle at 14:03

Andre the Giant & Hillbilly Jim (w/ Capt. Lou Albano) fought Big John Studd & King Kong Bundy (w/ Bobby Heenan) to a double disqualification at 14:08 when all four men began brawling in the ring as Albano and Heenan fought on the floor; after the bout, Andre, Jim, and Albano cleared the opposition from the ring

Prime Time Wrestling - 11/5/85: Paul Orndorff pinned the Spoiler at 12:35 with a clothesline in a $50,000 bounty match; had the Spoiler been able to put Orndorff out of action, he would have won the bounty put on Orndorff's head by Bobby Heenan; prior to the bout, the Crush Girls - Chigusa Nagoya & Lioness Asuka - were introduced to the crowd as the Japanese Women's Tag Team Champions

Prime Time Wrestling - 11/5/85: Davey Boy Smith & the Dynamite Kid defeated the Iron Sheik & Nikolai Volkoff (w/ Freddie Blassie) at 6:46 when Smith dropkicked Volkoff from the top rope, as Volkoff prepared to slam Dynamite, with Dynamite landing on top for the win (*The British Bulldogs*)

Freddie Blassie makes his way ringside at MSG. Blassie, a once MSG headliner, became a ringside regular during his managing days.

WWF @ New York City, NY - Madison Square Garden - November 25, 1985 (16,000)
Televised on the MSG Network - included Gorilla Monsoon & Jesse Ventura on commentary:
All American Wrestling - 12/8/85: Dan Spivey pinned Terry Gibbs with a bulldog at 10:10 (*Best of the WWF Vol. 8*)
King Tonga pinned Mr. X at 8:48 with a diving headbutt
All American Wrestling - 12/15/85: Jesse Ventura defeated Barry O via submission with the backbreaker at 10:21
Hercules pinned Cousin Junior with a reverse roll up at 11:33 (*Best of the WWF Vol. 8*)
Spider Lady pinned WWF Women's Champion Wendi Richter to win the title at 6:38 with a small package even though the champion clearly kicked out before 3; after the bout, Richter continued attacking the challenger and pulled her mask off to reveal her as the Fabulous Moolah, not realizing the match had ended and - once she did - she refused to give up the championship belt; the finish, which Richter was unaware, came as a result of contract disputes with the champion; moments later, Richter whipped Moolah out of the ring with the title belt (Richter's last appearance in the WWF) (*The Best of the WWF Vol. 5*, *The Women of the WWF*)
WWF Intercontinental Champion Tito Santana & Pedro Morales defeated WWF Tag Team Champions Greg Valentine & Brutus Beefcake via disqualification at 15:17 when Santana was double-teamed by the champions as Morales fought with Johnny V on the floor
Don Muraco (w/ Mr. Fuji) defeated Ricky Steamboat via disqualification at 16:37 when the referee saw Steamboat use Mr. Fuji's cane as a weapon, moments after Muraco used it as the referee was knocked out; after the bout, Steamboat broke the cane over Muraco's head before then jabbing him in the head with one of the ends, with Muraco then sliding out to the floor; moments later, Muraco climbed back in the ring and the two men continued to brawl for several minutes, with Steamboat dominating; both men bled from the head during the bout (*The Best of the WWF Vol. 5*)
Terry Funk (w/ Jimmy Hart) pinned Mr. Wrestling II at 13:54 after Wrestling II ran into Funk's knee in the corner; prior to the bout, Funk & Hart chased ring announcer Mel Phillips inside and around the ring until he ran backstage; after the bout, Wrestling II chased Funk out of the ring with a steel chair after Funk failed twice to brand his opponent
Andre the Giant, Hillbilly Jim, & Capt. Lou Albano defeated Big John Studd, King King Bundy, & Bobby Heenan at 12:18 when Andre pinned Heenan following a boot to the face (*The Life & Times of Capt. Lou Albano*)

T-shirt vendors
"I went to with my Dad and three middle school friends. It was cold and we were outside MSG before the card. There were several vendors selling t-shirts for Hogan, Savage, Santana, etc. The t-shirts were in big duffle bags. There were a lot of cops outside. One vendor kept looking around at the cops as my Dad was going through his bag, checking out the shirts. He packed up his bag and ran across the street. My Dad approached another vendor and this time pulled shirts out of his duffle bag and started putting them over the chests of me and my friends to make sure that they fit.

A cop came over and said "I got you now!" and approached my Dad. One of my friends said, "How are we going to get home because Mr. Melniczek is going to jail." The first t-shirt vendor ran back across the street and said "No! No! He is the bad guy." He was referring to the other t-shirt vendor. The cops asked to see the guy's business license. We went into the Garden to see the card."

Eric Melniczek, *High Point, NC*

Randy Savage challenges Hulk Hogan at MSG. Years later, the two would headline WrestleMania V.

WWF @ New York City, NY - Madison Square Garden - December 30, 1985 (20,225; sell out)
Televised on the MSG Network - included Gorilla Monsoon & Lord Alfred Hayes on commentary:
SD Jones pinned Ron Shaw with an inside cradle at 18:36
Prime Time Wrestling - 1/14/86: Jim Neidhart fought B. Brian Blair to a 15-minute time-limit draw; Capt. Lou Albano was introduced prior to the bout as Blair's advisor / manager
All American Wrestling - 1/12/86: Hercules (w/ Freddie Blassie) defeated Jose Luis Rivera via submission with a backbreaker at 9:51
Prime Time Wrestling - 1/20/86: Adrian Adonis pinned Lanny Poffo with a bulldog at 9:02
Randy Savage (w/ Miss Elizabeth) defeated WWF World Champion Hulk Hogan via count-out at 9:55 after Savage jumped from the top rope to the floor, hitting Hogan in the head with the world title belt and then waking the referee up so that he could make the count; after the bout, Savage put the title belt around his waist and left ringside with it until Hogan attacked Savage in the aisle, brought him back into the ring, reclaimed his title belt, and beat up Savage until the challenger was able to escape the ring and run backstage (*Best of the WWF Vol. 6, Macho Madness: The Ultimate Randy Savage Collection*)
Big John Studd pinned Tony Atlas with an elbow drop at 12:15 after avoiding a crossbody attempt
Prime Time Wrestling - 1/20/86: The Haiti Kid pinned Butch Cassidy at 10:32 with a reverse roll up (*Best of the WWF Vol. 6*)
Prime Time Wrestling - 6/30/86: Jim Brunzell pinned Bret Hart at 13:55 with a backslide; after the bout, Hart attacked Brunzell and threw him to the floor
Prime Time Wrestling - 1/20/86: WWF Tag Team Champions Brutus Beefcake & Greg Valentine (w/ Johnny V) defeated Uncle Elmer & Hillbilly Jim at 4:29 when Beefcake pinned Elmer after Valentine came
off the top with a double axehandle as Elmer had Beefcake caught in a bearhug, with Beefcake then falling on top for the win (*WWF's Greatest Matches*)

Hogan vs. Savage

"I remember being so excited seeing the ring set up in the middle of Madison Square Garden. When the lights went down, the huge spotlight shone on the ring, making the wrestlers seem even bigger than they were. I was excited to see my hero, Hulk Hogan. I was not familiar with his opponent that night. He was a very flashy man, with sunglasses, a sparkling cape and bandana wrapped around his long hair. He did not look as big as Hulk Hogan, but he was much more mesmerizing. He'd routinely stick his tongue out and twirl his finger in the air. A beautiful lady accompanied him to the ring. I found myself following his every move during the match. At one point when Hogan chased him around the outside of the ring, this man, Randy "Macho Man" Savage, hid behind his lovely manager. The crowd erupted in boos, but I was grinning from ear to ear. This guy had me hooked. From this night on, I was a fan of the bad guys of professional wrestling. Macho Man did not win that night but I vowed to go to every wrestling event at Madison Square Garden from that day on. Of course, I did not see every card, but I went to over 30 live events over the course of the last 30 years. ...I remember the last match of the night, The Dream Team of Brutus Beefcake and Greg "The Hammer" Valentine had left the Hillbillies lying in the center of the ring. I clearly remember a young boy of about 4 or 5, ask his father in the most depressed, I-think-Grandma-just-died voice "Is Uncle Elmer dead?" Just a few steps ahead on the way out of the Garden, a man so enraged of the Hillbillies' loss slammed his fist into the glass advertisement on the side of the wall, smashing it and probably his hand, into a million little pieces. This was just a sneak peak into the types of people I would be sitting amongst throughout the next 30 years."

Mike Goldberg, *Brooklyn, NY*

WWF @ New York City, NY - Madison Square Garden - January 27, 1986 (20,225; sell out)
Televised on the MSG Network - included Gorilla Monsoon & Jesse Ventura on commentary:
Prime Time Wrestling - 2/17/86: Danny Spivey pinned Rene Goulet with a bulldog at 12:50
Prime Time Wrestling - 2/17/86: Iron Mike Sharpe fought George Wells to a time-limit draw at 18:37; the bell rang as both men were fighting on the floor
Prime Time Wrestling - 2/17/86: Ted Arcidi defeated Tiger Chung Lee via submission with a bearhug at 4:05
Prime Time Wrestling - 6/30/86: Paul Orndorff defeated Big John Studd (w/ Bobby Heenan) via disqualification at 5:26 when Heenan interfered as Orndorff attempted to bodyslam Studd; after the bout, Orndorff cleared Heenan from the ring
Prime Time Wrestling - 2/17/86: Terry Funk (w/ Jimmy Hart) pinned Scott McGhee at 9:44 after blocking a top rope attack by lifting his knees; after the bout, Funk branded McGhee
Randy Savage (w/ Miss Elizabeth) defeated WWF World Champion Hulk Hogan via count-out after Hogan hit the steel ring post shoulder-first at 8:33 when Elizabeth kept blocking Hogan from ramming Savage into the post; after the bout, Hogan put the challenger in a bearhug until officials and other wrestlers broke it up (*Best of the WWF Vol. 7, Macho Man Randy Savage & Elizabeth*)
Prime Time Wrestling - 2/17/86: Pedro Morales pinned Moondog Spot with a reverse roll up at 7:38; prior to the bout, Jesse Ventura interviewed Jack Lanza at ringside, introducing him as a new WWF executive
Prime Time Wrestling - 6/30/86: Sivi Afi pinned Ron Shaw at 6:27 with a flying bodypress; Afi was billed as 'Superfly Afi' for the bout
Adrian Adonis (w/ Jimmy Hart) defeated the Junkyard Dog via disqualification at 3:20 after JYD pushed the referee and hit Adonis with Hart's megaphone
George Steele defeated Barry O via submission with the flying hammerlock at 1:18
WWF Tag Team Champions Greg Valentine & Brutus Beefcake (w/ Johnny V) defeated Davey Boy Smith & the Dynamite Kid (w/ Capt. Lou Albano) at 7:46 when Beefcake pinned Dynamite after Johnny V reversed Dynamite's pin attempt, putting Beefcake on top for the win

WWF @ New York City, NY - Madison Square Garden - February 17, 1986 (20,225; sell out)
Televised on the MSG Network - included Gorilla Monsoon & Lord Alfred Hayes on commentary:
Lanny Poffo pinned Rene Goulet at 12:42 with a moonsault
King Tonga pinned Les Thornton at 9:18 with a diving headbutt off the top
Prime Time Wrestling - 3/3/86: Bret Hart & Jim Neidhart (w/ Jimmy Hart) fought B. Brian Blair & Jim Brunzell to a time-limit draw at 18:48 as Brunzell covered Hart following a dropkick (*Best of the WWF Vol. 8*, *The Bret Hart Story: The Best There Is, Was, and Ever Will Be*)
Prime Time Wrestling - 3/3/86: King Kong Bundy pinned George Wells (sub. for Cousin Luke) with the Avalanche and a splash at 3:17; after the bout, Wells was helped from the ring by several officials after he refused to be taken backstage on a stretcher
Ricky Steamboat (w/ King Tonga) pinned Don Muraco (w/ Mr. Fuji) in a martial arts match at 12:47 after Tonga reversed Muraco's small package as Fuji tended to the referee who had been knocked out moments earlier; prior to the match, Steamboat went backstage and came back with Tonga after Fuji refused to leave ringside; after the bout, Muraco attacked Tonga and dropped him with the tombstone
Tony Atlas pinned Barry O following a gorilla press slam and splash at 4:27; prior to the match, Stu Hart - who was celebrating his 76th birthday - was introduced to the crowd; Hart shook hands with Howard Finkel and both wrestlers before leaving the ring
Adrian Adonis (w/ Jimmy Hart) defeated George Steele (w/ Capt. Lou Albano) via disqualification at 4:04 after Steele used Hart's megaphone as a weapon
Prime Time Wrestling - 6/30/86: The Iron Sheik & Nikolai Volkoff (w/ Freddie Blassie) defeated Cpl. Kirchner & Dan Spivey at 9:41 when Sheik pinned Kirchner with a boot to the sternum
Prime Time Wrestling - 3/3/86: Ted Arcidi defeated Terry Gibbs via submission with a bearhug at 2:37 (*Best of the WWF Vol. 8*)
WWF World Champion Hulk Hogan pinned WWF Intercontinental Champion Randy Savage in a lumberjack match at 7:36 after George Steele tripped Savage, allowing Hogan to hit the legdrop for the win; other lumberjacks included: Lanny Poffo, Danny Spivey, Ricky Steamboat, King Tonga, Tony Atlas, the Iron Sheik, Nikolai Volkoff, Cpl. Kirchner, Les Thornton, Barry O, King Kong Bundy, Don Muraco, Bret Hart & Jim Neidhart; Hogan's ribs were heavily taped for the match following the attack he sustained on Saturday Night's Main Event from Bundy (*Macho Man Randy Savage & Elizabeth*)

WWF @ New York City, NY - Madison Square Garden - March 16, 1986 (matinee) (20,225; sell out)
Televised on the MSG Network - included Gorilla Monsoon & Jesse Ventura on commentary:
Prime Time Wrestling - 3/24/86: Sivi Afi pinned Moondog Spot at 7:07 with a flying bodypress
Prime Time Wrestling - 6/30/86: Hercules (w/ Freddie Blassie) pinned George Wells at 4:11 after Wells missed a running shoulderblock in the corner
Prime Time Wrestling - 3/24/86: Dump Matsumoto & Bull Nakano defeated Linda Gonzalez & Velvet McIntyre when Matsumoto pinned Gonzalez at 10:02 with a diving headbutt
Prime Time Wrestling - 6/30/86: Pedro Morales defeated Bob Orton Jr. via disqualification at 9:19 after Orton hit a suplex from the apron so that Morales landed crotch-first across the top rope
Prime Time Wrestling - 3/24/86: Don Muraco (w/ Mr. Fuji) pinned King Tonga at 8:05 after using Fuji's cane behind the referee's back who was distracted by Fuji on the apron
Prime Time Wrestling - 3/24/86: Lioness Asuka & Chigusa Nagoya defeated Leilani Kai & Penny Mitchell at 7:05 when Nagoya pinned Mitchell with a flying bodypress off the top
Prime Time Wrestling - 6/30/86: King Kong Bundy (w/ Bobby Heenan) pinned Hillbilly Jim at 6:03 with a splash following the Avalanche
Prime Time Wrestling - 3/24/86: Ricky Steamboat pinned Mr. Fuji at 6:09 with a flying crossbody
Prime Time Wrestling - 3/24/86: Jake Roberts pinned Lanny Poffo with the DDT at 6:49; after the bout, Roberts laid Damien on top of Poffo (Roberts' MSG debut) (*Jake "The Snake" Roberts: Pick Your Poison*)
Tito Santana defeated WWF Intercontinental Champion Randy Savage (w/ Miss Elizabeth) via disqualification at 9:28 when the champion grabbed the referee and threw him into Santana as the challenger had the figure-4 applied (*Macho Man Randy Savage & Elizabeth*)
The Haiti Kid pinned Dana Carpenter at 6:51 with a dropkick to the back following an airplane spin
Davey Boy Smith, the Dynamite Kid, & Capt. Lou Albano defeated Johnny V, WWF Tag Team Champions Brutus Beefcake & Greg Valentine at 13:09 when Dynamite pinned Beefcake, the illegal man, with a roll up as Beefcake pounded away at Albano in the corner (*The British Bulldogs*)

'...The most important thing in the world'
"Even before I was born, that was where the title changes happened. That's where Bruno won the belt, that's where Superstar Graham lost to the belt to Backlund. That's where the magic happened. Before WrestleMania was the epicenter of the WWF year, The Garden was the epicenter of the WWF month. The Garden was where all the big shows took place. Before there were a million venues and a million arenas, there was The Garden. It was literally in the heart of Manhattan. Before there was a pay-per-view every month, it was the most important thing in the world."
Mike Johnson; *Glendale, NY*

WWF @ New York City, NY - Madison Square Garden - April 22, 1986 (15,000)

Televised on the MSG Network - included Gorilla Monsoon, Ernie Ladd, & Lord Alfred Hayes on commentary; included Monsoon conducting a backstage interview with Greg Valentine, Brutus Beefcake, & Johnny V about their matches later in the show::

Prime Time Wrestling - 4/28/86: Lanny Poffo pinned Rene Goulet at 13:16 with a somersault splash

Prime Time Wrestling - 4/28/86: Nikolai Volkoff (w/ Freddie Blassie) pinned Tony Garea at 6:54 by lifting him up with a gorilla press and dropping him across his knee

Prime Time Wrestling - 4/28/86: King Tonga pinned Paul Christy at 5:57 with a diving headbutt off the top

Prime Time Wrestling - 4/28/86: Sivi Afi defeated Iron Mike Sharpe via count-out at 13:51 after both men began fighting on the floor; after the bout, Afi was attacked by Sharpe but eventually cleared the ring of his opponent

Prime Time Wrestling - 8/4/86: WWF Tag Team Champion the Dynamite Kid pinned Brutus Beefcake (w/ Johnny V) at 11:18 by blocking a suplex into the ring and reversing it into a roll up; after the bout, Beefcake tied Dynamite upside down in the corner and pounded away at him until Davey Boy Smith made the save (*The British Bulldogs*)

WWF Intercontinental Champion Randy Savage (w/ Miss Elizabeth) pinned Tito Santana in a No DQ match at 12:16 with a roll over and using the tights for leverage; late in the bout, Savage knocked out the referee with a punch; after the contest, Santana cleared Savage from the ring (*Macho Man Randy Savage & Elizabeth*)

Prime Time Wrestling - 8/11/86: Greg Valentine (w/ Johnny V) pinned WWF Tag Team Champion Davey Boy Smith at 9:12 following an axe handle from the middle turnbuckle to the back of the head (*The British Bulldogs*)

Prime Time Wrestling - 4/28/86: Cpl. Kirchner defeated the Iron Sheik (w/ Freddie Blassie & Nikolai Volkoff) via disqualification at 4:56 when Volkoff attacked Kirchner with Blassie's cane on the floor; after the bout, Volkoff & Sheik continued to attack Kirchner in the ring but Kirchner eventually chased them off with a steel chair (*Villains of the Squared Circle*)

Pedro Morales pinned Tiger Chung Lee at 3:52 with a small package

Prime Time Wrestling - 4/28/86: Jake Roberts pinned Scott McGhee with the DDT at 4:07 after Roberts held onto the ropes to avoid a roll up; after the bout, Roberts draped Damien over McGhee's body (*Jake 'The Snake' Roberts, Villains of the Squared Circle*)

WWF World Champion Hulk Hogan & Hillbilly Jim defeated Big John Studd & King Kong Bundy (w/ Bobby Heenan) via disqualification when Heenan interfered at 10:48 and kicked Hogan as Hogan had Studd covered following the legdrop; after the bout, Hogan threw Heenan in the corner just as Bundy was about to hit the Avalanche on Jim, with Bundy hitting Heenan instead (*Hulkamania 2*

The flashy Macho Man battled the likes of Hulk Hogan, Bruno Sammartino, Tito Santana, and Pedro Morales at MSG during his first few years in the WWF.

WWF @ New York City, NY - Madison Square Garden - May 19, 1986

Televised on the MSG Network - included Gorilla Monsoon & Lord Alfred Hayes on commentary; featured Monsoon conducting backstage interviews with WWF Intercontinental Champion Randy Savage & Miss Elizabeth, Ricky Steamboat, Greg Valentine, Brutus Beefcake & Johnny V about their matches later in the show; included Monsoon conducting a backstage interview with New York Yankees players Dave Righetti and Dave Winfield about appearing at the show, with Bobby Heenan and King Kong Bundy interrupting them:

Prime Time Wrestling - 5/26/86: Lanny Poffo pinned Tiger Chung Lee at 11:15 with a hurricanrana

Prime Time Wrestling - 5/26/86: Bret Hart pinned SD Jones at 10:15 with a backbreaker

Prime Time Wrestling - 5/26/86: Hercules (w/ Freddie Blassie) pinned Sivi Afi at 13:07 when the momentum of a crossbody by Afi put Hercules on top for the win

Nikolai Volkoff (w/ Freddie Blassie) pinned Cpl. Kirchner at 11:30 after holding his knees up when Kirchner charged at him in the corner, and holding the top rope for leverage; after the bout, Kirchner cleared Volkoff from the ring

Tito Santana fought WWF Intercontinental Champion Randy Savage (w/ Miss Elizabeth) to a no contest at 13:25 when Adrian Adonis interfered and attacked guest referee Bruno Sammartino before attacking the challenger; moments later, Sammartino attacked Adonis until Savage and Adonis double teamed Sammartino; eventually, Santana made the save with a steel chair (*Macho Man Randy Savage & Elizabeth*)

Prime Time Wrestling - 5/26/86: King Kong Bundy (w/ Bobby Heenan) pinned Tony Atlas at 8:04 with an elbow drop after blocking an attempted splash

Jake Roberts fought Ricky Steamboat to a double disqualification at 7:36 after both wrestlers shoved the referee; after the bout Bret Hart, Tiger Chung Lee, & Paul Christy came out and held back Steamboat, with Jake then able to attack Steamboat; Sivi Afi, SD Jones, & Lanny Poffo then tried to also hold back Roberts, with Roberts and Steamboat eventually brawling back to the locker room (*Best of the WWF Vol. 8*)

Prime Time Wrestling - 5/26/86: Dan Spivey pinned Paul Christy at 3:11 with a bulldog; prior to the bout, Howard Finkel introduced Van Halen lead singer Sammy Hagar to the crowd

Prime Time Wrestling - 5/4/87: Jim Neidhart fought Jim Brunzell to a 20-minute time-limit draw

WWF Tag Team Champions Davey Boy Smith & the Dynamite Kid (w/ Capt. Lou Albano) defeated Greg Valentine & Brutus Beefcake (w/ Johnny V) at 11:54 when Dynamite pinned Valentine with a roll up after Valentine was

celebrating thinking he had pinned Dynamite, but the referee called off the pin after he noticed Johnny V was holding down Dynamite's legs

Ricky Steamboat, who made a brief appearance in MSG while still working for Jim Crockett Promotions years earlier, was a hit with the New York City crowd during the mid 1980s.

202

WWF @ New York City, NY - Madison Square Garden - June 14, 1986 (13,000)
Televised on the MSG Network - included Gorilla Monsoon & Lord Alfred Hayes on commentary; originally scheduled was Jimmy Jack & Dory Funk Jr. vs. SD Jones & George Wells which was changed into two singles matches, with Tony Garea replacing Jones:
All American Wrestling - 6/29/86: Jimmy Jack Funk (w/ Jimmy Hart) pinned Tony Garea with a powerslam at 10:06 (*Best of the WWF Vol. 8*)
Prime Time Wrestling - 6/23/86: Pedro Morales defeated the Iron Sheik via disqualification at 11:16 when Sheik pushed referee Dick Kroll as Morales was trapped in the ropes; after the bout, Morales cleared Sheik from the ring after hitting him in the head with the microphone
Prime Time Wrestling - 6/23/86: Mike Rotundo & Dan Spivey defeated the Moondogs at 11:37 when Rotundo pinned Rex following an airplane spin
Prime Time Wrestling - 6/23/86: Nikolai Volkoff defeated George Steele (w/ Capt. Lou Albano) via disqualification at 6:21 after Albano handed Steele a steel chair, who then used it on his opponent
Prime Time Wrestling - 6/23/86: Cowboy Lang pinned Lord Littlebrook at 10:01 with a spinning roll up (*Best of the WWF Vol. 9*)
WWF Intercontinental Champion Randy Savage (w/ Miss Elizabeth) & Adrian Adonis (w/ Jimmy Hart) defeated Bruno Sammartino & Tito Santana via count-out at 9:40 after Savage dropped a double axe handle off the top onto Sammartino, who was on the floor ramming Adonis into the ring apron; after the contest, Sammartino & Santana scared Savage & Adonis from the ring (*Macho Man Randy Savage & Elizabeth*)
Prime Time Wrestling - 6/23/86: Dory Funk Jr. (w/ Jimmy Hart) pinned George Wells at 9:54 after Dory blocked a splash off the top by lifting his knees
Big John Studd (w/ Bobby Heenan) fought King Tonga to a double count-out at 3:50 when both men were brawling on the floor; both men continued brawling long after the bell on the floor and eventually back in the ring until Tonga cleared Studd from ringside with a headbutt (*Best of the WWF Vol. 8*)
Prime Time Wrestling - 6/23/86: Harley Race (w/ Bobby Heenan) pinned Lanny Poffo with the cradle suplex at 10:56 (Race's MSG return after a 6-year absence) (*Best of the WWF Vol. 8*)
The Junkyard Dog defeated King Kong Bundy (w/ Bobby Heenan) via disqualification at 8:43 when Heenan tripped JYD from the outside allowing Bundy to splash him; after the bout, Heenan slapped JYD in the corner as Bundy prepared to hit the Avalanche but JYD pushed Heenan into Bundy's path (*Best of the WWF Vol. 8*)

Finkel on the mic

"One of my favorite parts of the night would be hearing ring announcer Howard Finkel announce the upcoming card match by match. He did it in such a dramatic fashion that, many times, I'd be begging my dad to buy tickets for the next show before he even got to the main event announcement. Seeing that MSG microphone be lowered from the ceiling into Finkel's hands gave me goosebumps."
Mike Goldberg, *Brooklyn, NY*

WWF @ New York City, NY - Madison Square Garden - July 12, 1986 (16,000)
Televised on the MSG Network - included Gorilla Monsoon & Lord Alfred Hayes on commentary:
Prime Time Wrestling - 7/21/86: Tony Atlas pinned Lanny Poffo with a backslide at 12:35
Jimmy Hart won a 22-man $50,000 battle royal when Greg Valentine and the Junkyard Dog eliminated each other at 12:53; Hart spent the entire match hiding underneath the ring; other participants included: the Junkyard Dog, Harley Race, Billy Jack Haynes, King Kong Bundy, Sivi Afi, Brutus Beefcake, Bobby Heenan, Pedro Morales, Lanny Poffo, Mike Sharpe, Moondog Spot, Jimmy Hart, King Tonga, Big John Studd, the Dynamite Kid, Davey Boy Smith, Greg Valentine, Johnny V, SD Jones, Tony Garea, Moondog Rex, & Tony Atlas; order of elimination: Studd by several wrestlers (0:13), Bundy by several wrestlers (0:19), Heenan by several wrestlers (0:43), SD Jones by Moondog Spot (2:21), Sharpe (3:27), Atlas by Spot (3:35), Johnny V by Morales (3:49), Garea by Valentine (5:05), Race by Morales (5:44), Afi by Beefcake (5:54), the Moondogs by the Bulldogs via simultaneous dropkicks (6:31), Dynamite by Beefcake (7:54), Morales by Valentine after three blows to the chest as Morales was perched upon the top rope (9:20), Beefcake by Smith, Haynes, and Poffo (9:33), Haynes by Valentine via backdrop (9:47), Tonga by Valentine via backdrop (9:54), Davey Boy by Valentine via powerslam over the top (10:36), Poffo by Valentine (10:47); WWF Women's Champion the Fabulous Moolah was originally scheduled to compete in the match as well (*Best of the WWF Vol. 9*)
Prime Time Wrestling - 7/21/86: WWF Tag Team Champions Davey Boy Smith & the Dynamite Kid defeated the Moondogs at 18:23 when Dynamite pinned Spot with a crossbody off the top rope, over the heads of both Davey Boy Smith and Rex (*The British Bulldogs*)
Prime Time Wrestling - 7/28/86: Pedro Morales pinned Iron Mike Sharpe with a small package at 5:54
Prime Time Wrestling - 7/21/86: Billy Jack Haynes defeated Brutus Beefcake (w/ Johnny V) via disqualification at 6:26 when Johnny V tripped Haynes (*Best of the WWF Vol. 10*)
All American Wrestling - 8/24/86: King Kong Bundy & Big John Studd (w/ Bobby Heenan) defeated King Tonga & Sivi Afi when Bundy pinned Tonga after a kneedrop to the chest at 8:33, even though it seemed Bundy wasn't attempting to get the pinfall (*Best of the WWF Vol. 9*)
Prime Time Wrestling - 7/28/86: Harley Race (w/ Bobby Heenan) pinned Tony Garea with a cradle suplex at 2:05
The Junkyard Dog fought Greg Valentine to a double count-out at 13:32; prior to the bout, the referee ordered Johnny V backstage
Prime Time Wrestling - 7/28/86: Bruno Sammartino & Tito Santana defeated WWF IC Champion Randy Savage & Adrian Adonis in a steel cage match at 9:51 when Sammartino left through the door as Santana escaped over the top; prior to the bout, both Jimmy Hart & Miss Elizabeth left ringside (Sammartino's last MSG appearance for 28 years) (*Inside the Steel Cage*)

August 2-3, 1986: Prince & the Revolution performed for the first time at MSG.

WWF @ New York City, NY - Madison Square Garden - August 25, 1986 (22,092)
Televised on the MSG Network - included Gorilla Monsoon & Lord Alfred Hayes on commentary:
Prime Time Wrestling - 9/16/86: Nick Kiniski pinned Les Thornton at 9:49 with a German suplex into a bridge
Prime Time Wrestling - 9/8/86: Jake Roberts pinned Sivi Afi at 16:46 with the DDT
Prime Time Wrestling - 9/8/86: Billy Jack Haynes defeated Hercules (w/ Slick) via count-out at 21:29 after Hercules left ringside with Slick; the match originally went to a time-limit draw at 18:52 but the referee granted them 5 more minutes; Freddie Blassie helped accompany Hercules ringside before the bout but went backstage before the match began
Prime Time Wrestling - 9/8/86: Paul Orndorff (w/ Bobby Heenan) pinned Cpl. Kirchner at 9:42 with the piledriver
King Kong Bundy & Big John Studd (w/ Bobby Heenan) defeated Big & Super Machine (w/ Giant Machine) via disqualification at 9:07 after Giant Machine illegally entered the ring with the referee eventually realizing when he attempted to pin Studd following a double clothesline; after the bout, Giant Machine cleared Studd from the ring; later in the show, Bobby Heenan returned to the ring and challenged Capt. Lou Albano to bring all three Machines to a 6-man tag against Studd, Bundy and himself as he was sick of Albano trying to make a fool out of him, and sick of the Machines
Adrian Adonis pinned Tony Atlas (w/ Jimmy Hart) at 7:20 after catching Atlas in mid-air and dropping him throat first across the top rope; Atlas got up and immediately left ringside after the pinfall (Atlas' last MSG appearance for 4 years)
Prime Time Wrestling - 9/8/86: Nikolai Volkoff & the Iron Sheik (w/ Slick) defeated Dan Spivey & Mike Rotundo at 12:46 when Sheik pinned Spivey after Volkoff hit Spivey with Slick's cane as Spivey attempted a powerslam on Sheik; after the bout, Rotundo eventually cleared Sheik, Volkoff, and Slick from the ring; Freddie Blassie helped accompany Volkoff & Sheik ringside before the bout but went backstage before the match began (*Legends of Wrestling: Andre the Giant and the Iron Sheik*)
Prime Time Wrestling - 9/16/86: Pedro Morales defeated WWF Intercontinental Champion Randy Savage (w/ Miss Elizabeth) via count-out at 7:19 after getting back in the ring just before the 10-count after blocking Savage's attempt to use a chair
WWF Tag Team Champions Davey Boy Smith & the Dynamite Kid (w/ Capt. Lou Albano) defeated Jimmy Jack & Dory Funk Jr. (w/ Jimmy Hart) at 5:27 when Dynamite pinned Jimmy Jack after being thrown by Smith; after the bout, the Funks attempted to hogtie Dynamite until Smith made the save; the Bulldogs then tried to hogtie Jimmy Jack but Dory made the save before the could; prior to the bout, when Howard Finkel was announcing the card for the next MSG show, he introduced Albano who gace Finkel the announcement that he had accepted Bobby Heenan's challenge from earlier in the show and that it would be Big & Super Machine teaming with the Hulk Machine

From Montreal to NYC

"Madison Square Garden was not part of my father or my uncle or my grandfather's wrestling. I started wrestling in 1977. It was only in 1985, when I joined the WWF, that we started going worldwide. We did not follow wrestling in the New York area. When we started hearing about the big leagues is when the WWF came to Montreal. They called my brother Raymond and myself to join them. For me, Madison Square Garden was more of Michael Jackson. It was Madonna. For me, the New York Rangers. That was Madison Square Garden to me. What a great tag team to (debut) against, the Hart Foundation. I had never seen so many taxis in my life. We came in our car, trying to make it to Madison Square Garden. Taking the Lincoln Tunnel from New Jersey. Just making our way in, and seeing New York City in its splendor. The Twin Towers, the Empire State Building. It was like a zoo; walking into a jungle. Every time I'd go, it was a weeknight and it was a zoo. Taking the elevator up to the 5th floor, that was something special. That's where the Rangers played."

Jacques Rougeau,
TheHistoryofWWE.com interview, 2014

WWF @ New York City, NY - Madison Square Garden - September 22, 1986 (12,000)
Televised on the MSG Network - featured Gorilla Monsoon & Lord Alfred Hayes on commentary:
Prime Time Wrestling - 10/9/86: The Islanders defeated the Moondogs when Tama pinned Rex with a splash off the top at 13:17
Prime Time Wrestling - 10/21/86: Nick Kiniski pinned Steve Lombardi with a back suplex into a bridge at 8:57
Prime Time Wrestling - 10/9/86: Bob Orton Jr. (sub. for Adrian Adonis) (w/ Jimmy Hart) pinned Billy Jack Haynes at 9:31 by grabbing the tights for leverage
Prime Time Wrestling - 10/9/86: Jacques & Raymond Rougeau defeated Bret Hart & Jim Neidhart when Jacques, the illegal man, pinned Neidhart with a sunset flip into the ring at 14:52 (the Rougeaus' MSG debut) (*The Hart Foundation*)
Ted Arcidi defeated Tony Garea via submission at 4:30 with the bearhug (Garea's last MSG match)
Prime Time Wrestling - 10/9/86: Steve Regal pinned Jose Luis Rivera with a belly to belly suplex at 7:53
Prime Time Wrestling - 10/9/86: SD Jones pinned Mr. X at 8:09 with a standing headbutt from the middle turnbuckle
Prime Time Wrestling - 10/9/86: King Harley Race (w/ Bobby Heenan) pinned Tito Santana at 12:43 with a reverse roll up after Heenan distracted Santana from the ring apron; after the bout, Santana attacked Race on the floor until Race was able to escape
All American Wrestling - 10/12/86: Sika (w/ the Wizard) pinned Lanny Poffo with the Samoan Drop at 7:28
WWF World Champion Hulk Hogan (as Hulk Machine), Big & Super Machine defeated King Kong Bundy, Big John Studd, & Bobby Heenan at 8:45 when Hogan pinned Studd with a bodyslam and the legdrop (*Hulkamania 2*)

Hulk Machine reveals himself to the crowd.

Oversaturated

"When I look back, I didn't like it when it was trendy. Wrestling's mine. I never liked that. I saw Regis Philbin, Billy Squier, I saw everybody under the sun. Once it started to become mine again, that's when I really enjoyed it. Wrestling's become so oversaturated that the speciality of the Garden is one of the few things that remain."
Matt Striker, *TheHistoryofWWE.com interview. 2014*

Roddy Piper enters the ring at MSG. The once-hated heel that co-headlined WrestleMania 1 was quickly becoming a top fan favorite by the middle of 1986.

WWF @ New York City, NY - Madison Square Garden - October 20, 1986 (13,000; the Wrestling Observer newsletter listed it as 9,800)

Televised on the MSG Network - included Gorilla Monsoon, Lord Alfred Hayes, & Gene Okerlund on commentary; featured an in-ring segment in which Howard Finkel introduced Roddy Piper for a segment of Piper's Pit, with Piper then saying he wasn't used to people cheering for him and he was the "same no good, son of a bitch" he's always been; Piper went on to say the fans wouldn't see the Flower Shop anymore, and he was glad; he went on to note he was about to introduce his tag team partner from WrestleMania 1; moments later, Bobby Heenan joined Piper in the ring, with Piper betting Heenan $10,000 that the New York Mets would win the World Series; Heenan went on to introduce Orndorff, who came to the ring to the tune of "Real American;" Piper went on to say the last time he saw Orndorff at MSG, he was "lying on his face with your ass in the air;" Piper and Orndorff then squared off to fight, with Piper saying Orndorff had no friends and had no one to tag team with; Heenan said he could name 100 people who could be Orndorff's tag team partner, with he and Orndorff stammering on naming just one; eventually, they hugged before Heenan named King Harley Race as someone who could team with Orndorff; Heenan then noted Piper wasn't well liked either and questioned him as to who would tag with him; Piper then motioned to Vladimir the superfan, at ringside, to join him on the apron; Piper then took the mic from Heenan and said the fan had an idea for a tag team partner, with Vladimir saying "Hulk Hogan" to a thunderous applause; Piper then left ringside as an enraged Orndorff threw a fit in the ring:

Prime Time Wrestling - 11/11/86: SD Jones pinned Moondog Spot at 9:33 with a headbutt

Prime Time Wrestling - 11/11/86: Tama pinned Moondog Rex at 8:18 with a crossbody off the top

Prime Time Wrestling - 11/18/86: Brutus Beefcake pinned B. Brian Blair at 9:24 by holding onto the tights for leverage after the momentum of a crossbody by Blair put Beefcake on top

Prime Time Wrestling - 11/11/86: King Kong Bundy pinned Super Machine at 3:17 with the Avalanche; after the match, Bundy briefly grabbed the microphone to speak but the discussion of the commentary team drowned out what he said

Prime Time Wrestling - 11/11/86: WWF Tag Team Champion the Dynamite Kid pinned Jim Neidhart at 5:49 with a roll up

Prime Time Wrestling - 11/11/86: Jacques Rougeau pinned the Iron Sheik at 7:29 with a sunset flip into the ring; prior to the bout, Sheik was escorted to the ring by Nikolai Volkoff

All American Wrestling - 10/26/86: Mike Rotundo fought Jim Brunzell to a double count-out at 9:10 when both men failed to get back into the ring after falling over the top rope to the floor as Brunzell was hoisted into a fireman's carry by Rotundo; prior to the match, the two shook hands

Prime Time Wrestling - 11/11/86: Greg Valentine pinned WWF Tag Team Champion Davey Boy Smith at 12:57 by using the ropes for leverage

Prime Time Wrestling - 11/11/86: Haku pinned Nikolai Volkoff at 4:51 with a roll up after Volkoff missed a clothesline and ran into the corner; during the cover, Volkoff clearly had his shoulders up

Bret Hart pinned Raymond Rougeau at 8:34 with a double leg pickup and putting his feet on the ropes for leverage as Rougeau had Hart cornered (*Best of the WWF Vol. 13*)

Prime Time Wrestling - 5/4/87: The Islanders won a $50,000 tag team battle royal by last eliminating King Kong Bundy & Big John Studd at 10:20; other teams included the Moondogs, SD Jones (sub. for Danny Spivey) & Mike Rotundo, Chief Jay Strongbow & Steve Gatorwolf, WWF Tag Team Champions Davey Boy Smith & the Dynamite Kid, Bret Hart & Jim Neidhart, B. Brian Blair & Jim Brunzell, the Iron Sheik & Nikolai Volkoff, Big & Super Machine, Jacques & Raymond Rougeau, and Greg Valentine & Brutus Beefcake; order of elimination: the Moondogs were eliminated, SD Jones eliminated by ?, Strongbow eliminated by several wrestlers, Sheik eliminated by a Machine, Hart and Dynamite eliminated each other, Brunzell eliminated by Beefcake, Jacques Rougeau eliminated by Studd via backdrop, Beefcake eliminated by a Machine via backdrop, a Machine eliminated by Bundy via clothesline to the back of the head as the Machine attempted to eliminate Big John Studd, Studd eliminted after Bundy accidentally clotheslined his own partner out of the ring (*Even More Unusual Matches*)

Many viewers got their first look at lifelong fan Vladimir Abouzeide when Roddy Piper called him to the ring apron in October 1986 to pick his tag team partner to face Paul Orndorff and 'King' Harley Race. Vladimir answered with an enthusiastic, "Hulk Hogan!"

The dangers of the city

"I'll never forget, one of the first times, we were coming down the street; everything's one way. There's like four or five lanes. On the right hand lane, there's this guy that's beating up this girl on the sidewalk. We had just left the building. It must have been 10:30-11 o'clock at night. I stopped the car, just because I wanted to help the girl. My wife said, 'Don't you get out of this car.' She was so afraid. It was happening in front of a bunch of people but no one was helping. For me, it scarred me for life. In New York, it's 'me, myself and I.' That's what it was for me after that."

Jacques Rougeau, *TheHistoryofWWE.com interview, 2014*

October 31, 1986: Promoter Bill Graham's Crackdown Concert featured the Allman Brothers Band, Crosby, Stills & Nash, Run-D.M.C. and Santana, among others.

WWF World Champion Hulk Hogan does his trademark T-shirt tear in front of the MSG crowd.

WWF @ New York City, NY - Madison Square Garden - November 24, 1986 (19,700 paid; sell out)
Televised live on the MSG Network - included Gorilla Monsoon & Lord Alfred Hayes on commentary:
Prime Time Wrestling - 12/2/86: Billy Jack Haynes fought Bob Orton Jr. (w/ Jimmy Hart) to a double count-out at 13:43; Orton came into the ring wearing a kilt and also a jacket with the words "Hot Bob" on the back; during the match, Jimmy Hart briefly joined the commentary team of Gorilla Monsoon and Lord Alfred Hayes at ringside
Prime Time Wrestling - 12/2/86: Hercules (w/ Bobby Heenan) pinned Pedro Morales with a roll up at 9:07 as Morales was distracted by Heenan; moments earlier, Morales chased Heenan around ringside and into the ring after Heenan prevented Morales' cover following a backbreaker
Kamala (w/ the Wizard & Kimchee) pinned George Steele with a splash off the top at 3:16 following a regular splash after using the Wizard's horn as a weapon; Kamala hit another splash after the match before being restrained by Kimchee and the Wizard; Steele was taken from ringside on a stretcher (*Best of the WWF Vol. 11*)
Prime Time Wrestling - 12/2/86: Lanny Poffo pinned Steve Lombardi with a somersault splash off the top at 9:58
Prime Time Wrestling - 1/5/87: Hillbilly Jim defeated Don Muraco (w/ Mr. Fuji) via disqualification at 7:06 when Fuji interfered as Jim had the bearhug applied on Muraco and attacked Jim with his cane, while ripping his overalls at the same time; Muraco came to the ring wearing a kilt and to Roddy Piper's music (*Best of the WWF Vol. 11*)
WWF World Champion Hulk Hogan & Roddy Piper defeated Paul Orndorff & King Harley Race (w/ Bobby Heenan) when Piper pinned Race at 8:15 after Orndorff accidentally clotheslined his partner; immediately after the match, Piper left ringside while Hogan was double teamed; eventually Hogan cleared the ring of the opponents (*Best of the WWF Vol. 11*)
Prime Time Wrestling - 12/2/86: The Karate Kid & Pepe Gomez defeated Lord Littlebrook & Little Tokyo when Tokyo was pinned at 13:30 after Littlebrook accidentally hit a flying bodypress on his partner, with Karate Kid & Gomez climbing on top of Littlebrook for the pin; after the bout, Hillbilly Jim returned to the ring and challenged Mr. Fuji to a Tuxedo match at the next MSG show, with Howard Finkel later revealing Fuji had accepted when announcing next month's card (*Best of the WWF Vol. 11*)
Prime Time Wrestling - 12/2/86: Koko B. Ware pinned Jimmy Jack Funk with the Ghostbuster at 8:46; before the bout, Capt. Lou Albano joined the commentary table to give an update on the condition of George Steele, with Albano revealing that Steele had escaped the ambulance he was in and was running through Central Park
Prime Time Wrestling - 1/5/87: Greg Valentine & Brutus Beefcake (w/ Johnny V) defeated the Islanders when Beefcake pinned Tama at 13:13 after Valentine dropped Tama crotch first on the top rope behind the referee's back; during the match, Johnny V briefly joined Monsoon and Hayes at ringside

WWF @ New York City, NY - Madison Square Garden - December 26, 1986 (sell out)
Televised live on the MSG Network - included Gorilla Monsoon & Bobby Heenan on commentary:
Prime Time Wrestling - 12/30/86: Paul Roma pinned Terry Gibbs with a sunset flip from the top rope at 9:22
Prime Time Wrestling - 12/30/86: Bret Hart & Jim Neidhart defeated Cpl. Kirchner & Dick Slater when Neidhart pinned Kirchner after the Hart Attack at 12:36
Prime Time Wrestling - 4/27/87: WWF Women's Champion the Fabulous Moolah pinned WWF Women's Tag Team Champion Leilani Kai at 10:10 with a double axe handle and roll up after dropkicking the challenger into the referee (*Best of the WWF Vol. 12*)
Pedro Morales defeated Dino Bravo via disqualification at 14:24 after Bravo accidentally punched referee Dick Kroll when Morales ducked his head
WWF World Champion Hulk Hogan defeated Kamala (w/ the Wizard & Kimchee) via disqualification at 6:39 when the Wizard tripped up Hogan from the outside and then held his legs down for Kamala to splash him twice; Hogan was then triple-teamed and was held down by the Wizard and Kimchee for Kamala to hit a splash off the top but Hogan was able to escape and clear all three from the ring; following the bout, Bobby Heenan interviewed the Wizard, Kimchee, & Kamala backstage until Kamala was attacked by Hogan, with both having to be separated by several wrestlers and officials, including Vince McMahon (*Hulkamania 2*)
Prime Time Wrestling - 12/30/86: Jose Luis Rivera pinned Steve Lombardi with a backslide at 2:37
Prime Time Wrestling - 4/27/87: Hillbilly Jim defeated Mr. Fuji in a tuxedo match at the 4-minute mark (*Best of the WWF Vol. 11*)
Prime Time Wrestling - 12/30/86: The Honky Tonk Man pinned Sivi Afi with the Shake, Rattle, & Roll at 7:02; the match was set for earlier in the evening but Honky attacked his opponent prior to the bout, thus forcing it to be rescheduled for later in the card; after the bout, Honky stayed at ringside, dancing for the fans until Tito Santana came out for his match, where he was attacked from behind by Honky with Santana's knee clipping the ring steps
Prime Time Wrestling - 12/30/86: Hercules (w/ Bobby Heenan) pinned Tito Santana at 15:40 after Santana was distracted by Heenan at 15:40; Heenan was introduced prior the match beginning before rejoining Gorilla Monsoon at the announce table; originally the match ended at 12:46 after Heenan left the commentary position and rang the timekeeper's bell while Santana had the figure-4 applied on Herc, attempting to confuse referee Dick Kroll that the time-limit had expired but the referee ruled there was still time left in the match
Prime Time Wrestling - 2/9/87: Blackjack Mulligan pinned Nikolai Volkoff (w/ Slick) at the 33-second mark with a flying back elbow; prior to the bout, Mulligan attacked Volkoff as he was singing the Russian National Anthem; after the contest, Volkoff attacked Mulligan until he was sent from the ring

The first visit
"It was actually a Christmas gift. My father took my brother and myself. To this day, I vividly remember. I lived in Flushing, Queens at the time. Walking to the Long Island railroad and taking the Long Island railroad for the first time in my life that I ever remember. Walking around and seeing George 'The Animal' Steele t-shirts and things. The first time walking into an arena, and it's The Garden. When you walked into The Garden back then, especially as a kid, you feel like you're walking into a majestic theater. It just felt like there was something different. The microphone would lower down, with the yellow insignia on it. I had seats somewhere in the halfway point in the building. I can remember, when Hogan came out, just the entire building rumbling in a way that I've only seen one other time and that's when Steve Austin came out years later. This feeling of electricity. Oh my god, it's like Superman just flew into the building. There was this incredible energy and people literally living and dying by each punch that was thrown. I'll never forget Kamala hitting the big splash in the middle. The way it happened, and hearing crowd, I'm going 'New champ, new champ! No way!' And when Hogan kicked out, I went, 'No way! I can't believe that happened.' Looking back, it was obvious. There was a magic there that just doesn't come across in pro wrestling today."
Mike Johnson; *Glendale, NY*

The Popcorn match

"Many times I wrestled in the opening match. If it wasn't the opening match, it was the popcorn match, the first match after intermission. That can be very, very difficult to get any heat. It depended on the heel whether I could get the heat. If I could wrestle Nikolai Volkoff after intermission, I couldn't get any heat. If I wrestled the Iron Sheik, he got the people going."
Lanny Poffo, *TheHistoryofWWE.com interview, 2014*

WWF @ New York City, NY - Madison Square Garden - January 19, 1987 (15,500; sell out)
Televised on the MSG Network - included Gorilla Monsoon & Gene Okerlund on commentary; featured Okerlund presenting an award to Howard Finkel to celebrate Finkel's 10th anniversary as the MSG ring announcer:
Prime Time Wrestling - 2/2/87: Brad Reinghans pinned Frenchy Martin with a diving shoulderblock from the middle turnbuckle at 16:49 (Reinghans' debut)
Rick Martel & Tom Zenk defeated Greg Valentine & Brutus Beefcake at 18:36 when Martel pinned Valentine with a springboard splash into the ring, while Valentine had Zenk in the figure-4 (Martel's return to MSG after a 5-year absence; Zenk's MSG debut) (*Best of the WWF Vol. 11*)
Prime Time Wrestling - 2/2/87: Ron Bass pinned SD Jones at 6:56 with the Pedigree (Bass' MSG debut)
Prime Time Wrestling - 2/2/87: Paul Orndorff (w/ Bobby Heenan) defeated George Steele via disqualification at 6:00 when Steele swung a steel chair at the referee; before the bout, Heenan tore up a poster of Miss Elizabeth, distracting George during the match as he attempted to put the remains back together; after the match, Orndorff attacked Steele and was about to hit him with the chair but Steele blocked the move and chased Orndorff away with it (*Best of the WWF Vol. 12*)
Prime Time Wrestling - 2/2/87: Tiger Chung Lee pinned Jerry Allen at 7:34 with an elbow drop after Allen missed a crossbody
WWF World Champion Hulk Hogan pinned Kamala (w/ the Wizard & Kimchee) in a No DQ match at 7:56 with the legdrop after hitting the challenger with the Wizard's horn; after the bout, Andre the Giant came to the ring, picked up the title belt, looked at it, and then tossed it to the champion before leaving the ring (Kamala's last MSG appearance for nearly 6 years)
Prime Time Wrestling - 2/13/87: Lanny Poffo pinned the Red Demon at 14:38 with a somersault splash off the top; prior to the bout, Jimmy Hart came out and announced that if the Hart Foundation could beat Davey Boy Smith later in the show then they would win one-half of the WWF Tag Team Championship
The Junkyard Dog defeated King Harley Race (w/ Bobby Heenan) via count-out at 5:27 after shoving Race into the ringpost; after the bout, Race attacked JYD from behind with his own chain and tied him up, while Heenan slapped JYD and tried to force the unconscious JYD to bow before the King; prior to the bout, a representative of the NY State Athletic Commission came out and ordered Danny Davis to leave ringside after Davis came out and tried to tell the referee he was officiating the match
Prime Time Wrestling - 2/13/87: Billy Jack Haynes (sub. for the Dynamite Kid) & WWF Tag Team Champion Davey Boy Smith defeated Bret Hart & Jim Neidhart (w/ Jimmy Hart) at 9:26 when Bret submitted to Haynes' full nelson; Danny Davis was the original referee for the bout but was knocked out late in the contest, with another referee coming to the ring to stop the match

During Paul Orndorff's feud with Hulk Hogan in 1986-87, he often mocked Hogan's antics and even came out to the 'Real American' theme song.

Bobby Heenan made his MSG debut in 1984. He would go on to become a ringside fixture for the next decade, managing IC and tag team champions as well as top contenders to the world title.

Roddy Piper
"In Madison Square Garden, I've got myself a six man elimination match."

Gene Okerlund
"Let's talk about that."

Piper: "Six man elimination. ...That means that the first time one guy on either side loses, he's gotta go back to the dressing room. Now what does that leave? Am I confusing you, friends? That leaves us with three on one side, two on the other side. ...It could go any kind of way."

Okerlund: "It's concievable that your partners are gone and you have to go against (Harley) Race, (Adrian) Adonis, and (WWF IC Champion Randy) Savage, alone. ...Not a good thought."

Piper: "First of all, Savage. Leave the broad at home, we don't need her. We were smart enough to go with JYD. Not a lot of brains, but he comes with a chain."
Localized TV promo

WWF @ New York City, NY - Madison Square Garden - February 23, 1987 (18,317)
Televised on the MSG Network - featured Gorilla Monsoon & Bobby Heenan on commentary:
Prime Time Wrestling - 3/9/87: Paul Roma pinned Salvatore Bellomo at 12:23 with a powerslam
Prime Time Wrestling - 4/6/87: Demolition defeated the Islanders at 9:13 when Ax pinned Tama following the Decapitation behind the referee's back after Smash hit a clothesline on Tama (*Best of the WWF Vol. 13*)
Prime Time Wrestling - 3/9/87: Koko B. Ware pinned Sika at 4:51 with a roll up following a dropkick to the back after sliding under the ring and coming out the other end; after the bout, Sika attacked Koko and threw him out of the ring
Prime Time Wrestling - 3/9/87: Tito Santana fought Butch Reed (w/ Slick) to a double disqualification at 12:10 when, as Slick attempted to interfere with his cane, Koko B. Ware came out and knocked Slick out of the ring; after the bout, Santana and Koko cleared the ring
WWF Tag Team Champions Bret Hart & Jim Neidhart (w/ Jimmy Hart & Danny Davis) defeated B. Brian Blair & Jim Brunzell at 13:52 when Bret reversed a slam by Brunzell into a small package after Davis attacked Brunzell from behind; during the match, Jimmy Hart briefly joined the commentary team at ringside (*The Hart Foundation*)
Prime Time Wrestling - 3/9/87: Outback Jack pinned Barry O with a bulldog at 3:33
Prime Time Wrestling - 3/9/87: Jake Roberts defeated King Kong Bundy via count-out at 9:17 when Bundy pushed Roberts back inside the ring following a ringside brawl; after the bout, Bundy missed the Avalanche in the corner with Roberts then chasing Bundy, Heenan, and Jimmy Hart - who did guest commentary for the bout - backstage with Damien (*Jake "The Snake" Roberts*)
Prime Time Wrestling - 3/9/87: The Honky Tonk Man (w/ Jimmy Hart) pinned Pedro Morales at 11:58 with his feet on the ropes; Slick did guest commentary for the bout, subbing for Bobby Heenan
Roddy Piper, the Junkyard Dog, & Ricky Steamboat defeated WWF Intercontinental Champion Randy Savage, Adrian Adonis, & King Harley Race in an elimination match at 20:22 when Piper pinned Savage with an inside cradle after Savage missed his flying elbowdrop; Adonis and JYD fought to a double count-out at 7:50; Race pinned Steamboat at 11:42 after Savage interfered behind the referee's back and reversed Steamboat's inside cradle; Piper pinned Race at 15:43 after Savage accidentally hit his partner with a double axe handle; prior to the bout, Jimmy Hart, Miss Elizabeth, and Bobby Heenan left ringside; after the bout, Gorilla Monsoon interviewed Piper backstage (Piper's last appearance at MSG for 2 1/2 years) (*Best of the WWF Vol. 11, WWE's Top 50 Superstars of All Time*)

WWF @ New York City, NY - Madison Square Garden - May 18, 1987 (16,800)
Televised on the MSG Network - included Gorilla Monsoon, Bobby Heenan, & Lord Alfred Hayes on commentary:
Prime Time Wrestling -5/25/87: Sam Houston pinned Terry Gibbs with a bulldog at 7:53
Prime Time Wrestling -5/25/87: Jim Powers & Paul Roma defeated Bob Orton Jr. & Don Muraco at 10:31 when Roma pinned Orton after Muraco accidentally reversed a small package, putting Roma on top of Orton for the pin; after the bout, Muraco & Orton attacked their opponents
Danny Davis (w/ Jimmy Hart) pinned Koko B. Ware at 13:15 after Hart threw a foreign object to Davis who then hit Koko in the face with it (*Best of the WWF Vol. 14*)
Prime Time Wrestling - 6/8/87: Lanny Poffo pinned Dave Barbie with a moonsault at 8:05
WWF World Champion Hulk Hogan pinned King Harley Race (w/ Bobby Heenan) at 7:54 with a roll up after the challenger failed a diving headbutt off the top; after the bout, Race attacked a bloody Hogan with the title belt as the champion posed in the ring; later in the show, Hogan returned ringside and challenged Race to a no holds barred match with the stipulation being that if he couldn't beat Race, he would quit wrestling
Debbie Combs defeated WWF Women's Champion the Fabulous Moolah via count-out at 8:49 after sending the champion into the steel ring post with an atomic drop on the floor; after the bout, the challenger continued to attack the champion when Moolah reentered the ring and then posed with the title belt (*Best of the WWF Vol. 13*, *The Women of the WWF*)
Demolition defeated B. Brian Blair & Jim Brunzell at 16:09 when Ax, the illegal man, pinned Brunzell with a forearm to the back of the head as Brunzell had Smash in a roll up cover
Prime Time Wrestling - 5/30/88: Ron Bass pinned Jose Luis Rivera at 9:37 with the Pedigree; prior to the bout, Bass had a verbal confrontation with Gorilla Monsoon, with Bass challenging Monsoon to fight him in the ring after Monsoon knocked his hat off
Ken Patera (sub. for Jake Roberts) defeated the Honky Tonk Man (w/ Jimmy Hart) via disqualification at 9:56 when Hart interfered as Honky was caught in the bearhug; after the contest, Patera locked both Honky and Hart in the move at the same time; on commentary after the bout, Gorilla Monsoon said Patera had won the match via submission (Patera's MSG return after a 2-year absence) (*The Ken Patera Story*)

WWF @ New York City, NY - Madison Square Garden - June 14, 1987 (14,246)
Televised on the MSG Network - included Gorilla Monsoon & Lord Alfred Hayes on commentary; included Monsoon conducting backstage interviews with WWF World Champion Hulk Hogan, Outback Jack about their matches later in the card; included Monsoon interviewing NY Yankees player Dave Winfield at ringside about being in attendance for the show:
Prime Time Wrestling - 6/22/87: Rick Martel & Tom Zenk defeated the Shadows at 18:56 when Martel scored the pin with a crossbody; Bobby Heenan did guest commentary for the match and after the bout, Heenan left the commentary table and confronted Martel & Zenk, saying they wouldn't have won the match had they been wrestling the Islanders; Martel then told Heenan to bring the Islanders out then and there but as Haku & Tama tried to come to the ring, they were held back by officials and referees; once the Islanders had being taken out, Martel asked Heenan to sign the Islanders a contract to face them as they wouldn't be able to read or write to do it themselves, with Heenan saying they could have them anytime; later in the card a match was confirmed between the two teams for the following month's card during a backstage interview by Lord Afred Hayes with Martel & Zenk
Prime Time Wrestling - 8/10/87: Hercules fought Billy Jack Haynes to a 20-minute time-limit draw at 22:55
Prime Time Wrestling - 6/22/87: The Islanders (w/ Bobby Heenan) defeated Paul Roma & Jim Powers at 19:02 when Tama pinned Powers with a splash off the top after a backbreaker from Haku (*Best of the WWF Vol. 13*)
Paul Orndorff (w/ Bobby Heenan) pinned the Junkyard Dog at 9:47 after dropping JYD across the top rope
WWF World Champion Hulk Hogan pinned King Harley Race (w/ Bobby Heenan) in a Texas Death Match at 9:56 after hitting him with the title belt after Race accidentally delivered a diving headbutt onto the belt (*Even More Unusual Matches*)
Prime Time Wrestling - 7/13/87: Outback Jack pinned Jose Estrada with a bulldog at 4:47
Prime Time Wrestling - 6/22/87: Billy Jack Haynes (sub. for Koko B. Ware), Davey Boy Smith, & the Dynamite Kid defeated Danny Davis, WWF Tag Team Champions Bret Hart & Jim Neidhart at 18:08 when Dynamite pinned Bret with a diving headbutt after being thrown by Smith

Rick Martel and Tom Zenk at MSG. While Zenk's NYC appearances were few,
Martel was an on-again, off-again fixture from the early 1980s through the mid 1990s.

Wrestling encounters

"Unlike other arenas, Madison Square Garden is situated right in the middle of the city. Fans can line up on the sidewalk out in front and watch the talent enter the building. Some choose to enter through the underground garage by car, but others routinely stroll right into the VIP entrance on 33rd Street. Over the years, I've waited with hundreds of other fans to catch a glimpse of wrestlers getting ready for a night of work. I've seen Jeff Hardy smoke a cigarette, Sika hobble across the street to a parking garage, Chris Benoit rapidly walk, head down, while ignoring chants and pleas for autographs. I've seen a cowboy-hat wearing brute exit a taxi and said taxi driver leave his car bragging to all outside, "That was Outlaw Ron Bass in my cab!"

The most interesting encounter I had outside The Garden was seeing the Honky Tonk Man strut across the street, guitar case in one hand, gym bag in the other. People ran up to him. I pulled on the sleeve of his hot pink sports coat and he took a very real swing at my head. I quickly moved away, thinking nothing of it. Back in the day, there were no lawsuits every time someone was touched. But I was mad, so in my angry 11-year old voice, and being the diehard Macho Man fan I was, I yelled, "If Macho Man was a good guy he'd kick your butt and be Intercontinental champion!" Just two months later, Macho Man tuned good and started a heated feud with the Honky Tonk Man. To this day, I like to think Honky heard my idea, ran to Vince McMahon and made it happen. At least it puts a smile on my face thinking I helped set the stage for Macho Man's incredible face turn and world title run."

Mike Goldberg, *Brooklyn, NY*

WWF @ New York City, NY - Madison Square Garden - July 25, 1987 (18,100)
Televised on the MSG Network - included Gorilla Monsoon & Lord Alfred Hayes on commentary; included Monsoon conducting backstage interviews with Ricky Steamboat & WWF Intercontinental Champion the Honky Tonk Man & Jimmy Hart after their match, with Steamboat saying he would go out later to publicly challenge Honky to a rematch, with Honky saying in his interview that Steamboat didn't deserve a rematch; included Monsoon interviewing Tito Santana about his match with Nikolai Volkoff later in the show:
Prime Time Wrestling - 8/3/87: Dino Bravo (w/ Johnny V) pinned Brady Boone at 10:46 with the side suplex
Rick Martel pinned Tama (w/ Haku) at 19:47 when the momentum of a crossbody from Tama put Martel on top; after the bout, Martel was double-teamed until several referees were able to keep the Islanders away; the bout was originally scheduled as a tag team match with the Islanders vs. Martel & Tom Zenk
Prime Time Wrestling - 8/10/87: Butch Reed pinned Hillbilly Jim at 10:58 with a flying clothesline and using Hillbilly's overalls for leverage during the cover
Ricky Steamboat defeated WWF Intercontinental Champion the Honky Tonk Man (w/ Jimmy Hart) via count-out at 11:39 when Steamboat tried to drag Honky back into the ring before the 10-count but Honky held onto the apron to prevent it; after the bout, Steamboat attacked Honky on the floor and chased Hart from the ring when Hart was parading around the ring with the belt
Prime Time Wrestling - 8/3/87: Tito Santana pinned Nikolai Volkoff at 8:21 with the flying forearm; after the bout, Ron Bass attacked Santana and whipped and choked him with Miss Betsy until Outback Jack made the save leading straight into their scheduled match
Ron Bass pinned Outback Jack at around the 6-minute mark with the pedigree; after the bout, Ricky Steamboat came to the ring and announced that he had being granted a rematch with WWF Intercontinental Champion the Honky Tonk Man for the following month's card and said there would be wrestlers around the ring making this a lumberjack match so that Honky couldn't get himself counted out again
Brutus Beefcake defeated Greg Valentine via disqualification at 13:11 when Dino Bravo interfered as Beefcake had the sleeper on Johnny V when Johnny had attempted to interfere moments earlier; after the bout, Davey Boy Smith & the Dynamite Kid made the save as Valentine made a start cutting Beefcake's hair as Bravo held him up
Prime Time Wrestling - 8/3/87: Rick Rude defeated Jerry Allen via submission with a backbreaker at 7:12 (Rude's MSG debut)
Prime Time Wrestling - 8/10/87: WWF Tag Team Champions Bret Hart & Jim Neidhart (w/ Jimmy Hart) defeated Davey Boy Smith & the Dynamite Kid at 10:26 when Bret pinned Smith after Neidhart swept Smith's legs out from under him as the challenger attempted to suplex Hart into the ring; after the bout, the Bulldogs cleared the ring of the champions and Jimmy Hart

WWF @ New York City, NY - Madison Square Garden - August 22, 1987 (18,000)
Televised on the MSG Network - included Gorilla Monsoon & Lord Alfred Hayes on commentary, with Pete Doherty joining the commentary team for the Martel / Haku, Steamboat / Honky, and Graham / Reed matches; included Howard Finkel introducing Andre the Giant who came halfway down the aisle before returning backstage, unhappy with the reception he had received; included Gorilla Monsoon conducting backstage interviews with Pete Doherty about being the newest member of the WWF broadcast team; included Monsoon interviewing Superstar Billy Graham, Butch Reed & Slick and George Steele & the Junkyard Dog about their matches later in the show; included Lord Alfred Hayes conducting a backstage interview with Demolition prior to their match:
Prime Time Wrestling - 9/7/87: Tama pinned Scott Casey at 11:23 with a splash from the middle turnbuckle
All American Wrestling - 9/6/87: Tito Santana fought Ron Bass to a 20-minute time limit draw at 19:45; the bell rung moments after Santana hit the flying forearm knocking Bass out of the ring; after the bout, Santana challenged Bass to 5 more minutes to decide a winner with Bass going back to the locker room instead
WWF Women's Champion Sensational Sherri pinned Velvet McIntyre at 14:21 with a back suplex after the challenger argued with the referee over a slow count
Haku pinned Rick Martel at 9:19 after Tama came ringside and hit Martel with a chair; after the bout, Tito Santana made the save; prior to the bout, Martel went back and brought Santana to ringside with him after the Islanders refused to let Martel enter the ring, with the referee ordering both Santana and Tama backstage before the match could begin
Prime Time Wrestling - 2/1/88: WWF Intercontinental Champion the Honky Tonk Man (w/ Jimmy Hart) pinned Ricky Steamboat in a lumberjack match at 11:06 after hitting the challenger with Hart's megaphone when the referee was distracted putting George Steele out of the ring after he had counted Steamboat's pinfall attempt on Honky himself when the referee was distracted by Hart on the apron; lumberjacks included: the Islanders, Tito Santana, George Steele, the Junkyard Dog, Scott Casey, Lanny Poffo, Ron Bass, and Jose Estrada; after the bout all the lumberjacks brawled until the babyfaces cleared the heels from the ring
Superstar Billy Graham fought Butch Reed (w/ Slick) to a double disqualification at 8:56 when Slick interfered and hit Graham with his cane as Reed was caught in the bearhug; after the bout, Graham reapplied the hold and it took a ring-full of officials - among them Pat Patterson, Terry Garvin, Arnold Skaaland and Gorilla Monsoon (who left the commentary table) - to convince him to release the hold; during the melee Monsoon elbowed Slick, knocking him to the mat; Graham would have won the match via disqualification due to Slick's interference but because he refused to release the bearhug after the bout, he was also disqualified (Graham's MSG return after a 4-year absence)
Wrestling Spotlight - 9/5/87: Lanny Poffo (sub. for Chavo Guerrero Sr.) pinned Jose Estrada at 7:42 with a somersault splash off the top
Prime Time Wrestling - 9/17/87: Demolition defeated the Junkyard Dog & George Steele via disqualification at 6:10 when Steele hit Smash with a steel chair after the JYD was relentlessly double teamed (*George 'The Animal' Steele*)

Once headliner Superstar Billy Graham returned to the MSG ring in 1987 for a series of matches against Butch Reed.

WORLD WRESTLING FEDERATION®
MONDAY, SEPTEMBER 21, 1987
MADISON SQUARE GARDEN
NEW YORK, NY

MAIN EVENT: FOR THE WWF HEAVYWEIGHT TITLE

HULK HOGAN Venice Beach, CA...302 lbs. **(WWF CHAMPION)**	vs	**ONE MAN GANG** Chicago, IL...450 lbs. **(CHALLENGER)**
HONKY TONK MAN Memphis, TN...255 lbs.	vs	**JAKE "THE SNAKE" ROBERTS** Stone Mountain, GA...248 lbs.
RICK MARTEL Quebec City...245 lbs. & **TITO SANTANA** Tocula, Mexico...244 lbs. (STRIKE FORCE)	vs	**HAKU** South Pacific...275 lbs. & **TAMA** South Pacific...235 lbs. (ISLANDERS)
GEORGE "THE ANIMAL" STEELE Detroit, MI...288 lbs.	vs	**SIKA** Samoa...299 lbs.
MAGNIFICENT MURACO Sunset Beach, HI...275 lbs.	vs	**COWBOY BOB ORTON** Kansas City...248 lbs.
JACQUES ROUGEAU Montreal...238 lbs. & **RAYMOND ROUGEAU** Montreal...234 lbs. (ROUGEAU BROTHERS)	vs	**DINO BRAVO** Montreal...255 lbs. & **GREG "THE HAMMER" VALENTINE** Seattle, WA...248 lbs. (THE DREAM TEAM)
HILLBILLY JIM Mud Lick, KY...286 lbs.	vs	**KING HARLEY RACE** Kansas City...253 lbs.
BRAD RHEINGENS Appleton, MN...231 lbs.	vs	**TIGER CHUNG LEE** Korea...275 lbs.

WORLD WRESTLING FEDERATION®

WATCH WWF WRESTLING:

Saturdays 10:00 am WNYW-TV Ch. 5 WWF Wrestling Challenge
Saturdays 11:00 am WWOR-TV Ch. 9 WWF Wrestling Spotlight
Saturdays 5:00 pm WWOR-TV Ch. 9 WWF Superstars of Wrestling
Lucha Libre—Martes, 11:30 pm WNJU-TV Ch. 47 WWF Superstars of Wrestling
Lucha Libre—Jueves, 11:30 pm WNJU-TV Ch. 47 WWF Wrestling Challenge

WWF @ New York City, NY - Madison Square Garden - September 21, 1987 (19,745; sell out)
Televised on the MSG Network - included Gorilla Monsoon & Lord Alfred Hayes on commentary, with Bobby Heenan doing guest commentary for the first two matches; included Monsoon conducting a backstage interview with Hillbilly Jim his match later in the card against King Harley Race; included Craig DeGeorge conducting a backstage interview with Andre the Giant & Bobby Heenan, with Heenan saying he had a plan to take out WWF World Champion Hulk Hogan; included DeGeorge interviewing the One Man Gang & Slick following Gang's match with Hogan, with Slick demanding a rematch; included Monsoon interviewing Randy Savage about his upcoming match with the Honky Tonk Man:
Prime Time Wrestling - 10/8/87: Scott Casey pinned Steve Lombardi with a bulldog at 11:32
Don Muraco pinned Bob Orton Jr. at 11:42 by reversing a piledriver into a backdrop
The Islanders (w/ Bobby Heenan) defeated Rick Martel & Tito Santana at 13:58 when Haku pinned Martel with a diving headbutt after switching places with Tama
Prime Time Wrestling - 10/8/87: Tiger Chung Lee pinned Brad Rheingans with a shoulderbreaker at 5:01
WWF World Champion Hulk Hogan fought the One Man Gang (w/ Slick) to a double count-out at 9:09 when both men began brawling on the floor after Slick had distracted Hogan from making the pinfall following a powerslam and the legdrop on Gang; after the bout, Hogan cleared Gang from the ring with a backdrop (Gang's MSG debut)
Prime Time Wrestling - 10/8/87: Jacques & Raymond Rougeau fought Greg Valentine & Dino Bravo (w/ Johnny V) to a time-limit draw at 17:07; the bell rang as Valentine had the figure-4 applied on Jacques; after the bout, the Rougeaus cleared the ring of their opponents
Prime Time Wrestling - 10/1/87: George Steele defeated Sika (sub. for Kamala) (w/ Mr. Fuji & Kimchee) via disqualification at the 3-minute mark after Sika used a steel chair as a weapon; after the match, Steele chased his opponent backstage with the chair before chasing Kimchee back into the ring and clearing him from the ring (*George 'the Animal' Steele*)
Prime Time Wrestling - 10/1/87: King Harley Race (w/ Bobby Heenan) pinned Hillbilly Jim with a diving headbutt off the top at 8:37; after the bout, Heenan introduced Andre the Giant to the crowd
Randy Savage (sub. for Jake Roberts) (w/ Miss Elizabeth) pinned WWF Intercontinental Champion the Honky Tonk Man (w/ Jimmy Hart) at 11:56 in a non-title match with the flying elbowsmash

WWF @ New York City, NY - Madison Square Garden - October 16, 1987 (19,700; sell out)
Televised on the MSG Network - featured Gorilla Monsoon & Nick Bockwinkel on commentary:
Prime Time Wrestling - 11/12/87: Outback Jack pinned Jose Estrada at 9:44 with a powerslam; Bobby Heenan provided commentary for the bout and afterwards introduced Nick Bockwinkel to fill in for him for the remainder of the show
B. Brian Blair & Jim Brunzell defeated Dino Bravo & Greg Valentine (w/ Johnny V) when Blair pinned Valentine with a sunset flip from the top at 10:57 after an illegal double switch by using their masks
Prime Time Wrestling - 10/29/87: Ivan Putski pinned Iron Mike Sharpe at 5:34 with the Polish Hammer
Rick Rude (w/ Bobby Heenan) defeated Paul Orndorff (w/ Oliver Humperdink) via count-out at 10:41 after Heenan hit Orndorff with a chair while Orndorff was climbing back in the ring; Orndorff had punched Heenan off the apron moments earlier, with Nick Bockwinkel leaving the broadcast position to help Heenan back to his feet; prior to the bout, Orndorff won a prematch posedown over Rude
All American Wrestling - 11/8/87: Don Muraco pinned Sika (w/ Mr. Fuji) at 8:20 after ramming his knee into Sika's head as Muraco fell from the top
Randy Savage (w/ Miss Elizabeth) pinned Killer Khan (w/ Mr. Fuji) at 10:14 with the flying elbowsmash after blocking Khan's green mist with his hands, rubbing it in Khan's face and hitting a powerslam; after the bout, Savage cleared Fuji from the ring with an atomic drop after he attempted to sneak attack Savage
Superstar Billy Graham defeated Butch Reed in a steel cage match at 10:59 by escaping the cage through the door after hitting Reed with his own brass knuckles
Prime Time Wrestling - 10/22/87: Billy Jack Haynes pinned Nikolai Volkoff at 5:27 with a roll up
Prime Time Wrestling - 5/30/88: Rick Martel & Tito Santana defeated the Islanders in a Best 2 out of 3 falls match, 2-1; fall #1 - Haku pinned Santana at 7:11 after a double set of headbutts; fall #2 - Santana pinned Tama at 8:07 with a small package, which Martel had reversed behind the referee's back to put Santana on top; fall #3 - Martel pinned Tama with a roll up at 10:27 after Tama collided with Haku on the ring apron

WWF @ New York City, NY - Madison Square Garden - November 24, 1987 (17,000)
Televised on the MSG Network - included Gorilla Monsoon, Lord Alfred Hayes, & Nick Bockwinkel on commentary:
Prime Time Wrestling - 12/10/87: The Ultimate Warrior pinned Frenchy Martin (sub. for Bob Orton Jr.) following a series of clotheslines at 4:38 (Warrior's MSG debut)
Prime Time Wrestling - 12/14/87: WWF Women's Tag Team Champions Judy Martin & Leilani Kai (w/ Jimmy Hart) defeated the Jumping Bomb Angels at 13:59 when Kai scored the pin following a powerbomb from Martin; after the bout, the challengers cleared the Glamour Girls and Hart from the ring (*The Women of the WWF*)
Rick Rude (w/ Bobby Heenan) pinned Paul Orndorff (w/ Sir Oliver Humperdink) at 8:44 with a roll up and using the tights for leverage after Heenan distracted Orndorff from ringside; after the bout, Orndorff attacked Rude and cleared him from the ring (Orndorff's last MSG appearance)
Prime Time Wrestling - 12/14/87: B. Brian Blair & Jim Brunzell defeated Boris Zhukov & Nikolai Volkoff (w/ Slick) at 20:26 when Blair, under a mask, pinned Zhukov with a flying bodypress
WWF Intercontinental Champion the Honky Tonk Man (w/ Jimmy Hart) defeated Randy Savage (w/ Miss Elizabeth) via count-out at 13:24 after Savage hit the champion with Hart's megaphone, knocking him back inside the ring; after the bout, Savage cleared both men from ringside, even hitting Honky in the back with his own guitar as he made his way back to the lockerroom
Prime Time Wrestling - 12/14/87: Jake Roberts pinned Danny Davis with the DDT at 7:22; after the bout, Jake placed Damien on top of Davis and left ringside; moments later, Jimmy Hart came out and helped carry Davis backstage along with several officials
WWF Tag Team Champions Tito Santana & Rick Martel defeated Bret Hart & Jim Neidhart (w/ Jimmy Hart) via disqualification at 18:18 after Bret hit Martel with Jimmy Hart's megaphone as Martel attempted the Boston Crab on Neidhart; after the bout, Santana used one of the title belts to clear the opposition from the ring
Ted DiBiase (w/ Virgil) pinned Ivan Putski with a powerslam at the 3-minute mark; prior to the bout, DiBiase cut an in-ring promo, saying he was in negotiations to buy MSG but opted not to after realizing he would also get the New York Knicks and Rangers; he then said both teams were useless and all the MSG fans were losers (DiBiase's return to MSG after nearly 8 years)
Prime Time Wrestling - 5/23/88: Bam Bam Bigelow (w/ Sir Oliver Humperdink) pinned King Kong Bundy (w/ Bobby Heenan) with a splash at 3:22 after Bundy missed a splash of his own

Dec. 18, 1987: Depeche Mode performed at MSG for the first time.

WWF @ New York City, NY - Madison Square Garden - December 26, 1987 (sell out)
Televised on the MSG Network - included Gorilla Monsoon & Lord Alfred Hayes on commentary, with Bobby Heenan also providing commentary for the first four matches:
Prime Time Wrestling - 1/4/88: Iron Mike Sharpe pinned SD Jones at 7:33 after hitting him in the head with his forearm support
Prime Time Wrestling - 1/4/88: Jacques & Raymond Rougeau defeated the Conquistadors at 13:07 when Jacques scored the pin following a double team move off the top
Prime Time Wrestling - 1/4/88: Jim Duggan pinned Sika with the running clothesline at 9:16
Prime Time Wrestling - 1/18/88: WWF Women's Champion Sensational Sherri pinned Rockin Robin at 7:30 after Sherri blocked a splash from the middle turnbuckle by lifting her knees
Greg Valentine (w/ Jimmy Hart) defeated Brutus Beefcake via count-out at 11:53 after Beefcake chased Hart backstage; after the bout, Beefcake returned to the ring but was attacked by Valentine; moments later, Beefcake chased Valentine backstage with his scissors after blocking Valentine's attempts to apply the figure-4
Ricky Steamboat fought Rick Rude (w/ Bobby Heenan) to a 20-minute time-limit draw at 20:28; after the bout, Heenan grabbed the microphone and told Steamboat he was lucky the match didn't last another 5 minutes, otherwise Rude would have easily won, and that he himself could beat Steamboat in 5 minutes; Rude then attacked Steamboat from behind but Steamboat eventually cleared both he and Heenan from the ring (Steamboat's last MSG appearance for more than 3 years) (*WWE's Top 50 Superstars of All Time*)
Dino Bravo (w/ Frenchy Martin) pinned Koko B. Ware at 6:38 with the side suplex
Prime Time Wrestling - 3/14/88: The Islanders (w/ Bobby Heenan) defeated B. Brian Blair & Jim Brunzell at 10:45 when Haku pinned Brunzell after Tama hit a diving headbutt off the middle turnbuckle on Brunzell and placed his partner on top
Cowboy Lang & Chris Dube defeated Little Tokyo & Lord Littlebrook at 3:19 when Lang pinned Littlebrook with a sunset flip
Randy Savage (w/ Miss Elizabeth) defeated WWF Intercontinental Champion the Honky Tonk Man (w/ Jimmy Hart & Peggy Sue) via disqualification at 9:29 after the champion shoved Savage into the referee; the referee was knocked down for several moments and didn't come to his senses and ring the bell until after Savage was knocked to the floor after being hit with the title belt, as a result was unclear until the winner was announced; during the match, Jimmy Hart was suspended above the ring in a cage; after the bout, Savage attacked Honky and Hart, then stole the wig off of Peggy Sue before all three ran backstage (*Macho Madness*)

The Honky Tonk Man fended off challenges at MSG from Ricky Steamboat and Randy Savage before ultimately losing the belt to the Ultimate Warrior at the inaugural SummerSlam.

WWF @ New York City, NY - Madison Square Garden - January 25, 1988 (19,750; sell out)
Televised on the MSG Network - included Vince McMahon doing guest commentary, substituting for Gorilla Monsoon who had suffered a mild heart attack, alongside Bobby Heenan and Lord Alfred Hayes (McMahon's return to MSG commentary after an absense of 5 years); during the intermission, McMahon conducted several interviews at ringside with the Islanders & Bobby Heenan, Jim Duggan, Butch Reed & Slick:
Prime Time Wrestling - 2/11/88: Scott Casey pinned Jose Estrada with a shoulder breaker at 10:06
Prime Time Wrestling - 3/14/88: Sam Houston pinned Danny Davis with a small package at 8:08
Butch Reed (w/ Slick) pinned the Junkyard Dog with a roll up and holding the tights for leverage at 5:26 after JYD chased Slick into the ring
Prime Time Wrestling - 2/11/88: Omar Atlas pinned Dusty Wolfe at 7:29 with a reverse roll up
The One Man Gang (w/ Slick) pinned Don Muraco (w/ Superstar Billy Graham) after Butch Reed interfered and hit Muraco with Slick's cane as the referee was busy breaking up a confrontation between Graham and Slick; after the bout, Muraco was thrown to the floor as Graham was triple teamed in the ring, with OMG hitting one splash and preparing to hit a second until Muraco made the save and cleared the ring
WWF World Champion Hulk Hogan & Bam Bam Bigelow (w/ Oliver Humperdink) defeated Ted DiBiase & Virgil (w/ Andre the Giant) when Bigelow pinned Virgil with a splash at 9:26 after Hogan hit the legdrop; after the bout, Hogan and Bigelow cleared the ring before the champion taunted Andre with the world title belt; Andre had to be held back by DiBiase and Virgil during the confrontation (*Hulkamania 3*)
Paul Roma & Jim Powers defeated Steve Lombardi & Barry Horowitz when Powers pinned Lombardi after a powerslam at 13:33; early in the bout, Heenan left the broadcast table, claiming King Harley Race wanted to speak with him in the dressing room
Jim Duggan pinned King Harley Race (w/ Bobby Heenan) at 10:50 by reversing a crossbody off the top (*'Hacksaw' Jim Duggan*)
Prime Time Wrestling - 2/19/88: Ron Bass pinned Hillbilly Jim at 5:32 with the Pedigree
The Islanders defeated Davey Boy Smith & the Dynamite Kid via disqualification at 15:35 when the Bulldogs used a leash on their opponents that was originally brought to the ring by Bobby Heenan

---

A very stressful day

"I stayed at the Marriott at the Newark Airport. For us, we'd come in around 5 o'clock. We'd take two hours from the hotel, but it was OK because everybody was coming out of New York and we were going into New York. We were not facing traffic that much. There was no leisure time. In New York, you didn't want to get caught in an accident of the freeway. We all knew that Madison Square Garden was Vince's little baby. Every time we went, Vince was there. It was a very stressful day. You knew you had to go in there and perform, and perform to your best, and you knew the New York fans had seen many matches. You had to seduce them, the fans. And if you did that, you seduced Vince."
Jacques Rougeau, *TheHistoryofWWE.com interview, 2014*

WWF @ New York City, NY - Madison Square Garden - February 22, 1988 (less than 10,000)

Televised on the MSG Network - included Gorilla Monsoon & Lord Alfred Hayes on commentary, with Bobby Heenan joining the commentary team beginning with the third match; this was the first MSG card in which there were mats on the floor surrounding the ring; included Craig DeGeorge conducting backstage interviews with Dino Bravo & Frenchy Martin, Jake Roberts, Bam Bam Bigelow & Oliver Humperdink, and Jim Duggan about their matches later in the card and with Slick about Butch Reed facing Don Muraco & the Ultimate Warrior in a tag match:

Prime Time Wrestling - 3/14/88: Jacques & Raymond Rougeau defeated King Harley Race & Iron Mike Sharpe (sub. for Hercules) at 9:26 when Raymond pinned Sharpe after the Rougeau Bomb from Jacques (Race's last MSG match)

Prime Time Wrestling - 2/29/88: George Steele pinned Sika at 2:49 after Sika hit himself with a chair that bounced off the ring ropes, moments after Steele threw three chairs into the ring; after the bout, Steele grabbed hold of Lord Alfred Hayes' headset and put it on before quickly throwing it off and breaking it

Prime Time Wrestling - 2/29/88: Demolition Ax (w/ Mr. Fuji) pinned Ken Patera at 7:27 with a running knee to the back after Demolition Smash came ringside and distracted Patera as the full nelson was applied; after the bout, Patera was double teamed until the Junkyard Dog made the save

Prime Time Wrestling - 2/29/88: The Junkyard Dog (sub. for Billy Jack Haynes) (w/ Ken Patera) pinned Demolition Smash (w/ Mr. Fuji & Demolition Ax) at 3:44 by hitting him with his steel chain after Patera tripped Smash and attacked Ax, distracting the referee

Prime Time Wrestling - 3/7/88: Jake Roberts fought Dino Bravo (w/ Frenchy Martin) to a 20-minute time-limit draw at 19:23; after the bout, Jake was able to wrap Bravo in the ring ropes and was about to put Damien on him but instead put the snake on Martin when he sneaked up behind Roberts; Bravo then quickly ran from the ring when he was able to escape as Roberts went towards him again with the snake

Ted DiBiase (w/ Virgil) defeated Bam Bam Bigelow (w/ Sir Oliver Humperdink) via count-out at 11:04 after sending Bigelow into the steel ring post after Bigelow was chasing Virgil on the floor after Virgil tripped Bigelow from the outside as he was attempting the slingshot splash; Bigelow used Vince McMahon's "Stand Back" song as his entrance music for the bout; after the bout, Craig DeGeorge interviewed DiBiase & Virgil backstage, with DiBiase saying that was a tuneup for WrestleMania IV

Prime Time Wrestling - 3/7/88: Jim Duggan fought Ron Bass to a double count-out at 15:16 when Bass left ringside after Duggan hit him with the 2X4 when Bass was choking him out with his whip Miss Betsy; after the bout, Craig DeGeorge interviewed Bass backstage with Duggan interrupting the interview pushing Bass out of the way saying he wanted another piece of Bass

Don Muraco & the Ultimate Warrior defeated Butch Reed (w/ Slick) & King Kong Bundy (sub. for the One Man Gang) when Warrior pinned Bundy with a crossbody at 14:48, with Bundy falling backwards over Muraco who was on all fours; during the match, Slick briefly joined the commentary team of Gorilla Monsoon and Lord Alfred Hayes at ringside (Bundy's last appearance for 6 and a 1/2 years)

March 3-5, 1988: Michael Jackson performed at MSG for the first time as a solo act, with three consecutive sold-out shows during his Bad World Tour.

WWF Women's Champion Sensational Sherri

WWF @ New York City, NY - Madison Square Garden - April 25, 1988 (17,000)
Televised on the MSG Network - included Gorilla Monsoon & Lord Alfred Hayes on commentary; the card was to have included Ricky Steamboat vs. Greg Valentine but the match was cancelled due to Steamboat leaving the WWF:
Prime Time Wrestling - 5/9/88: Brady Boone pinned Steve Lombardi with a German suplex at 14:57
Dino Bravo defeated Ken Patera via forfeit after Bravo attacked Patera during an arm-wrestling contest as Bravo was about to lose; as a result of the attack, Patera was unable to compete; Patera had already won the arm-wrestling contest once, but Bravo said Patera had cheated and so it was restarted
Bret Hart fought Bad News Brown to a 20-minute time-limit draw
The One Man Gang defeated Bam Bam Bigelow via disqualification at 9:12 after Bigelow rammed OMG's head into the top turnbuckle for longer than the referee's 5-count

Ted DiBiase (w/ Virgil) defeated WWF World Champion Randy Savage (w/ Miss Elizabeth) via count-out at the 12-minute mark after Virgil pushed the champion from the top rope to the floor; after the bout, Savage chased DiBiase and Virgil away with a chair
Prime Time Wrestling - 5/2/88: Barry Horowitz pinned Jose Luis Rivera at 10:39 with a Russian leg sweep
Prime Time Wrestling - 5/9/88: WWF Women's Champion Sensational Sherri pinned Desiree Peterson at 7:29 by reversing Peterson's Irish whip and throwing her down by the hair (*The Women of the WWF*)
The Ultimate Warrior pinned Hercules with the gorilla press slam at 12:48 (*The Self Destruction of the Ultimate Warrior* FYE version)
WWF Tag Team Champions Demolition (w/ Mr. Fuji) defeated Rick Martel & Tito Santana at 7:22 when Smash pinned Santana after Fuji interfered and hit the challenger with his cane as Santana prepared to put Smash in the figure-4

The One Man Gang

WWF @ New York City, NY - Madison Square Garden - May 27, 1988 (16,000)

Televised on the MSG Network - included Rodger Kent & Superstar Billy Graham on commentary (Graham's debut as a commentator); included Bobby Heenan coming to the ring saying he had signed an open contract to face anyone and he didn't care who it was, gloating over his victory over Koko B. Ware earlier in the night and at WrestleMania IV; later in the show when announcing the following month's card, Howard Finkel announced that Heenan would face the Ultimate Warrior and that Warrior would be bringing a weasel suit he had made and would stuff Heenan inside it; the announcement caused Heenan to return the ring:

Prime Time Wrestling - 6/6/88: The Conquistador pinned SD Jones at 9:13 when the momentum of a flying crossbody put the Conquistador on top

Greg Valentine defeated George Steele via disqualification at 5:54 when Steele brought the timekeeper's hammer into the ring and pushed the referee down; Steele then chased Valentine backstage before returning to the ring and chasing the referee away after the decision was announced

Prime Time Wrestling - 6/6/88: Jacques & Raymond Rougeau defeated Jim Powers & Paul Roma at 14:26 when Jacques pinned Powers with a small package after Raymond reversed Powers' small package behind the referee's back

Prime Time Wrestling - 6/20/88: Brutus Beefcake fought the One Man Gang to a double count-out at 10:20 when both men fell over the top to the floor as Beefcake was on Gang's back with the sleeper applied; after the bout, Beefcake was able to cut part of Gang's hair

Haku, High Chief Afi (sub. for Tama) & Bobby Heenan defeated Koko B. Ware, Davey Boy Smith, & the Dynamite Kid at 14:10 when Heenan pinned Koko after hitting him with brass knuckles

Prime Time Wrestling - 6/6/88: Iron Mike Sharpe pinned Jerry Allen at 6:26 with an elbow drop

WWF World Champion Randy Savage (w/ Miss Elizabeth) defeated Ted DiBiase (w/ Virgil) via disqualification at 11:55 when Virgil interfered and prevented the pinfall after the challenger hit an unprotected turnbuckle head-first; after the match, Savage was double teamed and thrown to the floor but later cleared the ring with his title belt; as Savage celebrated with Elizabeth on his shoulder, DiBiase & Virgil returned to the ring and attacked Savage from behind until several referees pulled them off, when Savage came to he ran backstage to look for DiBiase & Virgil (*Macho Madness*)

Prime Time Wrestling - 5/30/88: Jim Neidhart pinned Don Muraco (w/ Superstar Billy Graham) at 6:22 after reversing a roll up attempt by sitting on Muraco's chest; Lord Alfred Hayes did guest commentary for the match, subbing for Graham

Dino Bravo (w/ Frenchy Martin) pinned Ken Patera at 7:15 with the side suplex after Patera became distracted by Frenchy Martin on the ring apron (*Best of the WWF Vol. 17*)

Prime Time Wrestling - 8/8/88: The Junkyard Dog pinned Ron Bass at 8:15 by reversing a powerslam attempt into a cover

WWF @ New York City, NY - Madison Square Garden - June 25, 1988 (18,300)
Televised on the MSG Network - included Rodger Kent, Superstar Billy Graham, & Lord Alfred Hayes on commentary (Kent's last appearance):
Prime Time Wrestling - 6/27/88: The Big Bossman pinned Scott Casey at 7:45 with the sidewalk slam; after the bout, Bossman handcuffed Casey to the ropes and beat him with the nightstick
Prime Time Wrestling - 6/27/88: Jacques & Raymond Rougeau defeated the Conquistadors at 11:35 when Raymond scored the pin following a double team move from the top
Prime Time Wrestling - 7/11/88: Don Muraco defeated Danny Davis via disqualification when Greg Valentine interfered as Muraco had Davis up for the tombstone; after the bout, Valentine confronted Superstar Billy Graham at the announce table, pushed him, and kicked him in the leg
Prime Time Wrestling - 7/25/88: Andre the Giant pinned Bam Bam Bigelow with an elbow drop at 9:09 after kicking Bigelow in the face as he charged the corner; prior to the match, Andre was escorted to the ring by Bobby Heenan; after the bout, Jim Duggan made the save with his 2x4 after Andre began choking Bigelow with the strap from his tights
Prime Time Wrestling - 7/4/88: George Steele defeated Greg Valentine via count-out in a No DQ match at 6:35 after Steele chased Valentine around the ring after Valentine stole Steele's Mine doll
Prime Time Wrestling - 6/27/88: Bad News Brown defeated Jim Neidhart via count-out at 16:23 after Neidhart sustained the Ghetto Blaster, fell to the floor, and could not return to the ring before the 10-count; after the bout, Neidhart sent Bad News out of the ring
Prime Time Wrestling - 6/27/88: Jim Duggan pinned the One Man Gang at 9:49 with the running clothesline after the Gang missed a splash in the corner
The Ultimate Warrior defeated Bobby Heenan via submission with a sleeper in a Weasel Suit match at 5:30; after the bout, Warrior stuffed the unconscious Heenan in the suit (*The Greatest Wrestling Stars of the 80s*)
WWF World Champion Randy Savage (w/ Miss Elizabeth) defeated Ted DiBiase (w/ Virgil) in a steel cage match at 12:20 by escaping over the cage after ramming the challenger's head into that of an interfering Virgil at the top of the cage; moments prior to the finish, a fan climbed onto the cage but was quickly pulled down (*Macho Madness, Best of the WWF Vol. 18, WWF Wrestling's Greatest Steel Cage Matches Ever!, Macho Madness: The Ultimate Randy Savage Collection*)

Where you aspire to be
"As a young wrestler, that's where you aspire to be.
If you made it to Madison Square Garden, you made the big time.'"
Shawn Michaels,
'The Best of WWE at Madison Square Garden,' 2013

WWF @ New York City, NY - Madison Square Garden - July 25, 1988 (11,500)
Televised on the MSG Network - included Sean Mooney, Lord Alfred Hayes, &
Superstar Billy Graham on commentary:
Prime Time Wrestling - 8/15/88: Terry Taylor defeated Lanny Poffo via submission at 9:52 with the Scorpion Deathlock
Prime Time Wrestling - 8/8/88: Jacques & Raymond Rougeau defeated Shawn Michaels & Marty Jannetty at 14:59 when Raymond pinned Michaels after Michaels was shoved off the top by Jacques; after the bout, Davey Boy Smith & the Dynamite Kid made the save (*Best of the WWF Vol. 17*)
Prime Time Wrestling - 8/8/88: Bret Hart pinned Danny Davis with the piledriver at 9:35
Don Muraco fought Greg Valentine to a time-limit draw at 18:41; after the bout, Valentine knocked Muraco out of the ring, with Superstar Billy Graham pulling Valentine out as well; moments later, Valentine attacked Graham with Muraco making the save and both clearing the ring with a steel chair
WWF Tag Team Champions Demolition (w/ Mr. Fuji) defeated Davey Boy Smith & the Dynamite Kid at 20:25 when Smash pinned Smith after Jacques & Raymond Rougeau appeared and Jacques hit Smith with Fuji's cane
The Powers of Pain defeated Nikolai Volkoff & Boris Zhukov at 7:37 when the Barbarian pinned Zhukov with the running powerslam / diving headbutt double team
Prime Time Wrestling - 8/1/88: King Haku (w/ Bobby Heenan) pinned SD Jones at 7:06 with a side kick to the face
Andre the Giant (w/ Bobby Heenan) defeated Jim Duggan in a lumberjack match at 12:38 with an elbow drop; lumberjacks included Bret Hart, Don Muraco, Shawn Michaels & Marty Jannetty, SD Jones, the Dynamite Kid, Lanny Poffo, Jacques & Raymond Rougeau, Danny Davis, Terry Taylor, King Haku, Greg Valentine, and WWF Tag Team Champions Demolition; after the bout, all the lumberjacks began brawling after Andre attacked a few of them, with Duggan eventually clearing the heel lumberjacks from the ring with his 2x4

SUMMERSLAM
Madison Square Garden – August 29, 1988

Refining the matches

"My brother, Raymond, and I, we were comfortable anywhere in the world. We were hard workers, we were good workers. We would give 100 percent any night. There was never a doubt we wouldn't get the crowd. We had the chance to work with great workers. Most of the time, with the exception of the British Bulldogs, we had a chance to work with the guys two months, three months ahead of time. So by the time we came to Madison Square Garden, our match was refined. It was total, total perfect."
Jacques Rougeau, *TheHistoryofWWE.com interview, 2014*

Summer Slam 88 - New York City, NY - Madison Square Garden - August 29, 1988
Pay-per-view bouts - featured Gorilla Monsoon & Superstar Billy Graham on commentary; included the announcement Brutus Beefcake was too injured to compete against WWF Intercontinental Champion the Honky Tonk Man as originally scheduled; featured a video package recapping the attack by Ron Bass on Beefcake from the 8/27/88 WWF Superstars, during which Bass cut Beefcake's forehead with his spurs until Shawn Michaels & Marty Jannetty, Koko B. Ware, and others came out to make the save; during the segment, a giant X covered the screen to censor the blood; included Gene Okerlund conducting a backstage interview with WWF World Champion Randy Savage, Hulk Hogan, & Miss Elizabeth regarding their upcoming match against Andre the Giant & Ted DiBiase; featured Okerlund conducting a backstage interview with Honky Tonk & Jimmy Hart regarding Beefcake's injury at the hands of Bass and being replaced by another wrestler in the title match later in the show; during the segment, Honky repeatedly told Okerlund not to tell him who the replacement was because he wanted it to be a surprise; included an in-ring segment of the Brother Love Show in which Brother Love said the WWF promised him a special guest, with Brother Love then saying the only thing that made his guest special was the fact he was a guest on his show; Love then introduced Jim Duggan, with Duggan then coming out to the ring and telling Brother Love he was a phoney; Brother Love then said Duggan had no love, with Duggan eventually threatening to attack Brother Love with his 2x4 if he didn't leave the ring by the count of 5; Duggan got to 4 and then began swinging at Love, with Love then jumping out of the ring and running backstage; featured several minutes of highlights from the 1987 Survivor Series to promote the 2nd Annual Survivor Series; included Sean Mooney conducting a backstage interview with Jesse Ventura regarding his being the guest referee for the main event and his recent controversial dealings with DiBiase; featured a backstage segment in which Okerlund conducted an interview with Honky, alongside Hart, during which Jacques & Raymond Rougeau, Hercules, Dino Bravo, and Nikolai Volkoff tried to console Honky after his title loss; moments later, Honky said he would wrestle anyone but he never said he would wrestle the Ultimate Warrior and that he would get the title back; included Mooney conducting a backstage interview with the Warrior regarding his IC

title win, with Warrior celebrating with Duggan, Davey Boy Smith & the Dynamite Kid, Don Muraco, the Junkyard Dog, and Ken Patera, during which Warrior said he would face Honky anytime he wanted
Prime Time Wrestling - 9/20/88: Davey Boy Smith & the Dynamite Kid fought Jacques & Raymond Rougeau to a 20-minute time-limit draw at 19:03; the bell rang as Dynamite had Jacques covered after hitting a headbutt after being thrown by Smith; after the match, Smith & Dynamite cleared the Rougeaus from the ring and chased them backstage
Prime Time Wrestling - 10/11/88: Bad News Brown pinned Ken Patera with the Ghetto Blaster at 6:33 after Patera hit his shoulder on the ringpost
Prime Time Wrestling - 10/18/88: Rick Rude (w/ Bobby Heenan) defeated the Junkyard Dog via disqualification at 6:18 when Jake Roberts attacked Rude and knocked him out of the ring after Rude pulled down his tights to reveal another pair underneath, with Cheryl Roberts' face on the front

Brother Love

232

The Powers of Pain (w/ the Baron) defeated Boris Zhukoff & Nikolai Volkoff (w/ Slick) at 5:27 when Barbarian pinned Zhukov following the running powerslam / headbutt off the top combo (the TV debut of Baron Von Raschke as the Baron)

The Ultimate Warrior (sub. for Brutus Beefcake) pinned WWF Intercontinental Champion the Honky Tonk Man (w/ Jimmy Hart) with a flying shoulder block and splash at the 27-second mark to win the title (*The Ultimate Warrior, The Brains Behind the Brawn, The Self Destruction of the Ultimate Warrior, History of the Intercontinental Championship, Ultimate Warrior: The Ultimate Collection*)

Prime Time Wrestling - 9/27/88: Dino Bravo (w/ Frenchy Martin) pinned Don Muraco with a reversal into the side suplex at 5:28; Bobby Heenan joined the commentary team for the match; prior to the contest, Heenan said Andre the Giant was reading the Wall Street Journal backstage and Ted DiBiase was counting his money while Hulk Hogan & WWF World Champion Randy Savage were screaming and begging to be let out of their match

WWF Tag Team Champions Demolition (w/ Mr. Fuji & Jimmy Hart) defeated Bret Hart & Jim Neidhart at 9:49 when Smash pinned Hart after Ax hit Hart with Jimmy Hart's megaphone as Bret had Smash prepared for the piledriver; Jimmy Hart came out with the champions but was sent backstage early in the match by the challengers only to return during the final moments of the contest

Prime Time Wrestling - 10/4/88: The Big Bossman (w/ Slick) pinned Koko B. Ware with the sidewalk slam at 5:57

Jake Roberts pinned Hercules with the DDT at 10:06

Hulk Hogan & WWF World Champion Randy Savage (w/ Miss Elizabeth) defeated Ted DiBiase (w/ Virgil) & Andre the Giant (w/ Bobby Heenan) at 13:57 when Hogan pinned DiBiase with the legdrop after Savage hit the flying elbowsmash; late in the bout, Elizabeth distracted the opposing team by climbing on the ring apron and taking off her skirt, with Savage then knocking Andre to the floor leading to the finish; Jesse Ventura was the guest referee for the bout (Hogan's first TV match in 3 months) (*Summer Slam's Greatest Hits, Macho Madness, Macho Madness: The Ultimate Randy Savage Collection, The Top 25 WWE Rivalries*)

Warrior wins the belt

"When The Ultimate Warrior defeated the Honky Tonk Man for the Intercontinental title in 30 seconds at the first SummerSlam, I with about 5,000 other people in my section jetted out of our seats straight to the souvenir stand to buy an Ultimate Warrior shirt. The sting of disappointment still feels fresh to this day of hearing his shirt was sold out."
Mike Goldberg, *Brooklyn, NY*

On being replaced on pay-per-view

"I was supposed to get the (IC) title then. And back then, winning the IC belt was their way of grooming you for the world title. But Warrior said he was going to quit and he threw his hands up so they had to placate him, give him the belt, and make him happy. It still worked out fine, it didn't really hurt me any. It would have been nice to get the IC belt but I made the best of it."
Brutus Beefcake, *TheHistoryofWWE.com interview, 2005*

Spoilers

"Seeing Hogan and Macho Man out there together, it was a pretty cool thing. I always liked Randy Savage and Elizabeth. If you saw Randy Savage going to the gym to work out, you could take a photo. But if he was with Elizabeth, you couldn't go near him. ...The show had a different look. They rearranged the camera angles, they added more lights. Whereas if you look at WrestleMania 1, it looks like the regular Garden show the month before and the month after. It's much more well lit, the atmosphere is different. ...Being the fan that I was, I used to go, if they were in New Haven, I'd go for the TV tapings. They're doing an angle with the Ultimate Warrior; the Honky Tonk Man lost the belt in a dark match with the Warrior. But at the end of the night, he gets his belt back. Why did they do all those interviews with Warrior and the belt? Because they're going to air after SummerSlam. It kinda ruined it for me. I shot myself in the foot. By 1988, now I'm getting the (Wrestling) Observer newsletter. Now i really know what's going on"
Charlie Adorno, *Brooklyn, NY*

The Mega Powers vs. The Mega Bucks

WWF @ New York City, NY - Madison Square Garden - September 29, 1988 (13,500)

Televised on the MSG Network - included Rod Trongard, Superstar Billy Graham, & Lord Alfred Hayes on commentary; included Sean Mooney conducting a backstage interview with Dino Bravo following his win earlier in the night and possibly facing Jim Duggan next; included Mooney interviewing Shawn Michaels & Marty Jannetty about earning a title shot against WWF Tag Team Champions Demolition following their win earlier in the night; included Mooney interviewing Andre the Giant & Bobby Heenan about Andre's match earlier in the show with WWF World Champion Randy Savage, with Andre forcing Mooney to introduced him as the new WWF World Champion; included Mooney interviewing Brutus Beefcake about his upcoming match with Ron Bass; included Mooney interviewing the Honky Tonk Man & Jimmy Hart about Honky's upcoming match with WWF IC Champion the Ultimate Warrior.

Terry Taylor defeated Sam Houston via referee's decision at 8:19; when the referee stopped the match, Taylor was trying to get Houston in a cradle as Houston fought back with punches

Prime Time Wrestling - 3/13/89: Shawn Michaels & Marty Jannetty defeated the Conquistadors at 14:30 when Michaels scored the pin with a splash from Jannetty's shoulders

Prime Time Wrestling - 10/25/88: The Junkyard Dog defeated King Haku (w/ Bobby Heenan) via disqualification at 14:45 when Heenan prevented the pinfall after JYD hit the powerslam, JYD was then double teamed until he chased Heenan and Haku off with his chain (JYD's final MSG appearance)

Prime Time Wrestling - 10/4/88: Dino Bravo pinned B. Brian Blair at 13:45 with the side suplex

WWF World Champion Randy Savage (w/ Miss Elizabeth) fought Andre the Giant (w/ Bobby Heenan) to a double count-out at 9:57 when Savage attacked Andre on the floor after Andre grabbed Elizabeth by her ankle; after the bout, Savage carried Elizabeth backstage as Andre posed with the title belt; Andre then roughed up the referee in the corner after he said Savage was still the champion, with the referee getting Howard Finkel to announce he was giving Andre a heavy fine; early in the bout, Heenan was ordered back to the locker room other wise he would be suspended and fined and the match awarded to Savage after he kept chasing after Elizabeth around the ring and not staying in a neutral corner with Pat Patterson ordering the referee to make the call (*WWF Greatest Champions, Legends of Wrestling: Andre the Giant and the Iron Sheik*)

Prime Time Wrestling - 10/11/88: Scott Casey pinned Sandy Beach at 6:06 with a bulldog; after the bout, WWF World Champion Randy Savage came back to the ring where he said he had an open contract that he wanted Andre to sign and whenever he faced Andre again he would "kick his ass"

Brutus Beefcake pinned Ron Bass with a crossbody at 10:50; after the bout, Bass attacked Beefcake with his whip Miss Betsy, wrapped it around Beefcake's neck and dragged him around the ring; Bass was then going to cut open Beefcake again with his spurs until Shawn Michaels & Marty Jannetty made the save

Bad News Brown pinned Tito Santana with the Ghetto Blaster at 7:44

The Honky Tonk Man (w/ Jimmy Hart) defeated WWF IC Champion the Ultimate Warrior via count-out at 3:48 after Hart jumped on the champion's back as he was on the arena floor when Honky distracted him and Honky made it back in the ring just before the 10-count; after the bout, Warrior attacked Honky until Honky was able to escape after Hart ran into the ring to distract Warrior; Warrior then destroyed Honky's guitar

---

An honorary Rosatti Sister

"From that point on, I was hooked. I actually met Gorilla Monsoon and the Rosatti sisters after the show. I became friendly with them (Rosattis) and got to sit with them every month, which was so fun. They adopted me as an honorary Rosatti."

Mary-Kate (Grosso) Anthony, *Tampa, Fla.*

WWF @ New York City, NY - Madison Square Garden - October 24, 1988 (12,500)
Televised on the MSG Network - included Rod Trongard, Superstar Billy Graham, & Lord Alfred Hayes on commentary; featured Sean Mooney conducting a backstage interview with Ted DiBiase, with Virgil, about Hercules and Virgil's match with him earlier in the show; included Mooney conducting a backstage interview with Jim Duggan about his upcoming match with Dino Bravo; featured Mooney conducting a backstage interview with Jacques & Raymond Rougeau about their upcoming match with Bret Hart & Jim Neidhart, with the Rougeaus saying they love when the Harts win because Jimmy Hart still owns half of their contract; included Mooney conducting a backstage interview with Rick Rude, with Bobby Heenan, about facing Jake Roberts later in the night, with Rude saying he would beat Roberts and take Cheryl Roberts out after the show:
Prime Time Wrestling - 11/1/88: Paul Roma pinned Danny Davis at 12:22 with a dropkick off the top to the back of Davis' head
Prime Time Wrestling - 11/15/88: The Big Bossman (w/ Slick) pinned Koko B. Ware with the sidewalk slam at 7:03; after the bout, Bossman handcuffed his opponent to the middle rope and assaulted him with the nightstick
Prime Time Wrestling - 11/1/88: WWF Tag Team Champions Demolition (w/ Mr. Fuji) defeated Shawn Michaels & Marty Jannetty at 12:24 when Smash pinned Jannetty after falling backwards with Jannetty caught in a bearhug and Axe hitting a clothesline from the apron
Hercules defeated Virgil (w/ Ted DiBiase) via submission with the full nelson at 2:15; before the match, DiBiase took the mic and cut a promo, saying he bought Hercules; moments later, Hercules ran out and fought with DiBiase as the match began; after the bout, DiBiase attacked Hercules in an attempt to break the full nelson without success; DiBiase eventually tried choking Hercules with his own chain but Hercules quickly cleared him from the ring and stalked him all the way backstage
The Blue Blazer pinned Steve Lombardi with a moonsault off the top at 8:09 (Owen Hart's MSG debut)
WWF World Champion Randy Savage (w/ Miss Elizabeth) defeated Andre the Giant (w/ Bobby Heenan) via disqualification at 6:59 when Heenan ran around the ring and grabbed Savage's boot; prior to the match, Pat Patterson informed Howard Finkel that both Heenan and Elizabeth must remain in their corner and if they left the corner their wrestler would be disqualified; stipulations stated if Savage was counted-out he would lose the title; after the bout, Savage fought off Andre and Heenan; moments later, Andre threw a fit at ringside and scared off the commentary team
Dino Bravo (w/ Frenchy Martin) defeated Jim Duggan via count-out at 8:16 after Duggan fought off Bravo on the floor and started stalking Martin around the ring as Bravo slid back in; after the bout, Duggan twice hit Martin with the 2x4, scared Bravo from the ring, and waved the American flag in the ring
Bret Hart & Jim Neidhart fought Jacques & Raymond Rougeau to a time-limit draw at 22:32; the match initially ended as a time-limit draw at 19:28 after, behind the referee's back, Jacques rang the bell as Raymond was about to sustain the Hart Attack inside the ring, with the referee then believing the time limit had expired; after the initial ruling, Neidhart took the mic and challenged the Rougeaus to 5 more minutes; the Rougeaus acted like they would accept but then left ringside; Howard Finkel then announced that there were 3 minutes left in the match and the Rougeaus, while arguing with Pat Patterson on their way down the aisle, had to return to the ring
Jake Roberts (w/ Cheryl Roberts) pinned Rick Rude (w/ Bobby Heenan) with the DDT at 12:24; after the bout, Roberts held Rude up so Cheryl could slap him twice; moments later, Roberts laid Damien on top of Rude until Rude could roll out of the ring; pre-match stipulations stated that the participants could only make the pin after they hit their respective finishing hold; prior to the bout, Howard Finkel announced that Bobby Heenan would accompany Rude but Heenan never appeared (*Jake 'The Snake' Roberts: Pick Your Poison*)

WWF @ New York City, NY - Madison Square Garden - November 26, 1988 (19,700; sell out)
Televised on the MSG Network - included Rod Trongard, Superstar Billy Graham, & Lord Alfred Hayes on commentary; included Sean Mooney conducting a backstage interview with WWF Tag Team Champions Demolition following their match with the Powers of Pain, saying they wanted a return match; featured Mooney interviewing the Big Bossman & Slick about Bossman's match with Hulk Hogan later in the show; included Mooney interviewing the Powers of Pain & Mr. Fuji, with Fuji saying he wanted a no DQ match with Demolition; included Mooney conducting interviews with Sensational Sherri, WWF Women's Champion Rockin Robin, the Big Bossman & Slick and Hulk Hogan to close the program:
Lanny Poffo pinned Barry Horowitz at 12:33 with a sunset flip
Prime Time Wrestling - 12/5/88: Mr. Perfect pinned Paul Roma with the Perfect Plex at 8:35; after the bout, Mr. Fuji came to the ring and announced he was the new manager of the Powers of Pain before kicking Roma; Roma retaliated with a dropkick which brought out the Powers of Pain who attacked him until he had to be taken from ringside on a stretcher (Curt Hennig's MSG return after a 5+ year absence)
Ted DiBiase (w/ Virgil) pinned Hercules at 9:06 after hitting him with a foreign object; after the bout, Hercules fought off DiBiase and Virgil and chased them backstage
Akeem (w/ Slick) pinned SD Jones at 4:42 with the splash
WWF Tag Team Champions Demolition fought the Powers of Pain (w/ Mr. Fuji) to a double disqualification at 5:59 when Fuji got into the ring and used his cane as a weapon on Smash, with Ax then taking the cane and also using it
Prime Time Wrestling - 12/5/88: Nikolai Volkoff pinned Iron Mike Sharpe at 5:27 with a roll up
Prime Time Wrestling - 12/5/88: Tito Santana fought Greg Valentine to a time-limit draw at 18:13; the bell rang as the referee reached a count of nine almost counting out Santana after Valentine had just got back in the ring; prior to the match, Freddie Blassie was introduced to the crowd and refused Valentine's offer to shake his hand and gave him a thumbs down sign instead; Blassie did guest commentary for the bout, subbing for Superstar Billy Graham; after the bout, Santana cleared Valentine from the ring
WWF Women's Champion Rockin Robin pinned Sensational Sherri at 8:25 with a sunset flip from the middle turnbuckle
Hulk Hogan defeated the Big Bossman (w/ Slick) via count-out at 10:57 after Hogan handcuffed his opponent to the ring ropes and clotheslined him over the top when it was Bossman who was attempting to handcuff Hogan to the ropes; after the bout, Hogan cornered Slick in the corner with the Bossman's nightstick until Bossman was able to escape and make the save before he and Slick quickly left the ring

WWF @ New York City, NY - Madison Square Garden - December 30, 1988 (16,000)
Televised on the MSG Network - included Rod Trongard, Hillbilly Jim, & Lord Alfred Hayes on commentary; featured an appearance by Rick Rude in which he closed his eyes to allow a female audience member to kiss him, only for Hillbilly Jim to enter the ring and then kiss and hug the woman instead; Rude then attacked Jim from behind but Hillbilly eventually chased him from the ring:
The Blue Blazer fought the Red Rooster to a 20-minute time-limit draw; after the bout, Bad News Brown came to the ring and cut a promo on how everyone can remember this day as the day he won the world title
Mr. Perfect pinned Koko B. Ware at 11:42 with the Perfect Plex
The Bushwhackers defeated Nikolai Volkoff & Boris Zhukov at 9:23 following the battering ram and a double gutbuster on Zhukov after Zhukov accidentally clotheslined his partner to the floor (the Bushwhackers' MSG debut) (*SuperTape*)
Jim Duggan pinned Dino Bravo (w/ Frenchy Martin) in a flag match at 7:26 after Martin accidentally hit Bravo with the French flagpole (*'Hacksaw' Jim Duggan*)
Tim Horner pinned Barry Horowitz at 8:20 with a reverse roll up
The Powers of Pain (w/ Mr. Fuji) defeated WWF Tag Team Champions Demolition via count-out at 6:55 in a No DQ match; after the bout, the champions cleared the POP from the ring after the challengers began posing with the belts
Greg Valentine pinned Ron Garvin at 17:09 with a roll up and grabbing the tights for leverage as Garvin argued with the referee after the referee took Valentine's shinguard from him when Garvin attempted to use it as a weapon; after the bout, Garvin used the weapon to clear Valentine from the ring (Garvin's MSG debut)
WWF World Champion Randy Savage (w/ Miss Elizabeth) pinned Bad News Brown at 9:54 by reversing a powerslam attempt into an inside cradle; after the bout, Brown returned to the ring and attacked Savage with a garbage can until the champion cleared him from the ring

Being recognized as a superfan

"I met Vlad in probably '84. We'd meet at the Garden. Then by '85, we'd be around ringside in the first two rows. Now they're airing on the MSG Network, and now everybody's getting cable. Everybodys seeing it. Me, I'm quiet. Sitting next to Vladimir all those years got me noticed. Going to the hotels and going every month, the wrestlers get to know who you are. After Summerslam '88, we met somebody who worked at the Garden. They approached us and said, 'You guys are here every month.' They set it up, until 2008, to get the same exact seats across from the hard camera for 20 years. If you go back and watch any Garden show from '88 until the end when they broadcast it, we were there. Now, anytime you're watching the Garden show, we're right there. By that time, me and Vladimir were such wrestling fans we'd go to other shows; independent shows, NWA at the Philadelphia Civic Center. Back in like '85-86, when the NWA and AWA combined for Pro Wrestling USA at the Meadowlands, we went to all those shows. It wasn't just about the Garden. We were going to the Meadowlands, Nassau Coliseum, Philly. If you went to the Garden, you'd see a show. If you went to the Spectrum, you'd see different matches. We even took the Greyhound bus up to the Boston Garden. I went there to see Roddy Piper vs. Bruno in a steel cage match. They didn't have that at MSG."
Charlie Adorno, *Brooklyn, NY*

238

WWF @ New York City, NY - Madison Square Garden - January 23, 1989 (14,000)
Televised on the MSG Network - featured Rod Trongard & Lord Alfred Hayes on commentary:
Prime Time Wrestling - 1/30/89: Sam Houston (sub. for Rick Martel) pinned Danny Davis at 9:39 with a bulldog
Prime Time Wrestling - 2/13/89: Mr. Perfect defeated Brutus Beefcake via count-out at 9:29 when Perfect came off the apron with a double axe handle as Beefcake was distracted by Ron Bass at ringside, who attempted to steal Beefcake's scissors (*Best of the WWF Vol. 19*)
Prime Time Wrestling - 1/30/89: Tim Horner pinned Jose Estrada at 8:15 with a reverse roll up into a bridge
Bret Hart fought the Honky Tonk Man (w/ Jimmy Hart) to a double count-out at 12:04 when both men began brawling on the floor
Arn Anderson & Tully Blanchard defeated Shawn Michaels & Marty Jannetty at 16:14 when Blanchard pinned Jannetty after Anderson swept Jannetty's foot out during an attempted suplex and held the laces of his boot down during the cover (Anderson & Blanchard's MSG debut) (*Shawn Michaels: Heartbreak & Triumph*)
Prime Time Wrestling - 2/13/89: Rick Rude pinned Hillbilly Jim with the Rude Awakening at the 8-minute mark
Hercules defeated Ted DiBiase (w/ Virgil) via reverse decision; DiBiase originally won the match via pinfall at 12:41 with his feet on the ropes but the referee overruled the call and gave the win to Hercules after Virgil, who was barred from ringside for the duration of the contest, attacked Hercules after the bout; prior to the decision being made, Hercules cleared DiBiase & Virgil out of the ring after DiBiase accidentally clotheslined Virgil when Hercules moved out of the way
Prime Time Wrestling - 1/30/89: Tito Santana pinned Ron Bass at 6:35 with a roll up after Bass became distracted by Brutus Beefcake at ringside and brawled with him on the floor before Beefcake pushed him back inside the ring
The Big Bossman (w/ Slick) defeated Hulk Hogan via disqualification at 9:29 when Hogan brought Bossman's nightstick into the ring and shoved referee Dave Hebner after twice hitting the legdrop but opting not to make the cover; early in the bout, Hogan handcuffed Slick to the ringpost but Bossman later uncuffed his manager

Costume girl
"It was the anniversary of Hulkamania. I got front row seats for the first time ever. I used to bring different costumes. Security would get me the line up sheet and the order of the matches. And so, with every match, I would put on a different costume depending on who was coming out. A lot of the wrestlers knew me as the costume girl. Jimmy Hart comes out and here's this girl, all of 14 years old, dressed as him on the front row. ...From then on, every month. And every month was a family reunion. It's like when people have season tickets for baseball games. You would get to know these people and know their families and know their birthdays. I was very fortunate, the time that it was, I got to meet wonderful, wonderful people that I'm still friends with today."
Mary-Kate (Grosso) Anthony, *Tampa, Fla.*

WWF @ New York City, NY - Madison Square Garden - February 20, 1989 (20,000; sell out)
Televised on the MSG Network - featured Rod Trongard & Lord Alfred Hayes on commentary (Trongard's last appearance):
Jim Powers pinned Iron Mike Sharpe with a small package at 12:14; during the ring introductions, Howard Finkel accidentally referred to Sharpe as "Canada's strongest man" instead of "Canada's greatest athlete"
The Brooklyn Brawler (w/ Bobby Heenan) pinned the Red Rooster at 14:40 when Heenan grabbed Rooster's foot and held his leg down as he attempted a suplex into the ring, with Brawler falling on top for the win; after the match, Rooster cleared Brawler from the ring; later in the show, Brawler returned ringside and challenged Rooster to a rematch anytime and any place, noting how easy it was to beat him
Big John Studd fought Akeem to a double count-out at 7:49 when both men began brawling on the floor; after the match, Studd challenged Akeem to come back out so he could slam him, which he did after pulling Akeem into the ring while he was on the apron (Studd's MSG return after more than a 2-year absence; his final MSG appearance)
The Bushwhackers defeated Jacques & Raymond Rougeau at 12:15 when Butch pinned Jacques after Luke hit Jacques with an axe handle behind the referee's back as Jacques had Butch covered after being tripped from the floor by Raymond (*The Most Powerful Families of Wrestling*)
Brutus Beefcake pinned Rick Rude (w/ Bobby Heenan) at 18:48 with a reverse roll up; after the match, Rude threw Beefcake out of the ring, with Beefcake chan chasing Rude out of the ring using his scissors

Prime Time Wrestling - 2/27/89: Rick Martel fought King Haku (w/ Bobby Heenan) to a 20-minute draw as Martel attempted to apply the Boston Crab; after the bout, Martel cleared Haku from the ring with two dropkicks

Prime Time Wrestling - 6/26/89: Greg Valentine pinned Jim Neidhart at 8:06 after pulling off his shinguard and hitting Neidhart with it after Neidhart shoved the referee down

WWF World Champion Randy Savage defeated WWF Intercontinental Champion the Ultimate Warrior via count-out at 9:34 in a non-title match when Savage came off the top with a double axe handle as the Warrior was attacking Rick Rude on the floor, who came ringside mid-way through the contest; after the match, Savage and Rude shook hands and hugged before Warrior tossed the world champion to the floor and hit the gorilla press slam on Rude (*Wrestling Super Heroes*)

The Ultimate Warrior and Randy Savage began their storied rivalry with a champion vs. champion series that included a stop at MSG.

WWF @ New York City, NY - Madison Square Garden - March 18, 1989 (matinee) (20,000; sell out)
Televised on the MSG Network - included Tony Schiavone & Lord Alfred Hayes on commentary; featured Lanny Poffo reading a poem about WrestleMania V in which he praised WWF World Champion Randy Savage and said he would beat Hulk Hogan; Poffo then left the ring, opting not to throw his trademark frisbee into the crowd:
Prime Time Wrestling - 4/10/89: Paul Roma & Jim Powers defeated the Conquistadors at 13:19 when Roma scored the pin with a missile dropkick
WWF Women's Champion Rockin Robin pinned Judy Martin at 9:59 with a roll up after Martin missed a splash in the corner
Mr. Perfect pinned Ron Garvin at 12:21 when the momentum of a crossbody off the top by Garvin put Perfect on top for the pin
Hulk Hogan defeated the Big Bossman (w/ Slick) in a steel cage match at 11:14 by escaping over the top after handcuffing Bossman to the cage bars, and barely getting to the floor before Bossman escaped out the door; after the bout, Hogan hit Bossman in the head with a chair on the outside, then attacked Slick inside the cage and threw him into the bars (*Hulkamania 4, Best of the WWF: Steel Cage Matches, Best of Hulkamania*)
Shawn Michaels & Marty Jannetty defeated Arn Anderson & Tully Blanchard via disqualification at 13:53 when Anderson pulled the referee out of the ring as Michaels had Blanchard covered following a Rocket Launcher (*Allied Powers*)
The Red Rooster pinned the Brooklyn Brawler at 11:50 with a backslide; stipulations stated Bobby Heenan was barred from ringside for the match
Prime Time Wrestling - 4/17/89: Hercules fought Bad News Brown to a double count-out at 14:48 when both men began brawling on the floor and News prevented Hercules from getting back in the ring
Jim Duggan & the Bushwhackers defeated Dino Bravo (w/ Frenchy Martin), Jacques, & Raymond Rougeau at the 15-minute mark when Butch pinned Jacques after Duggan hit him with the 2x4 from the floor as Jacques was on the apron

Fan interactions
"The March 1989 show featured a 400+ lb. fan sitting next to me who had made signs for all of the babyface wrestlers on the card. Right before the national anthem he yelled out, 'Let the bullshit begin!'"
Eric Melniczek, *High Point, NC*

The style of wrestling
"Montreal's crowd was much more serious wrestling. Hardcore, old fashioned. A lot of people were sitting in the stands and going, 'That's fake. But that move they just did must be real.' In New York, it was more entertaining. It was Koko B. Ware and his bird, Jake the Snake and his snake. It became more comedy, less serious wrestling. Although the wrestling was still great, the credibility of the seriousness went down when all these comedians came in. It took a lighter side. In southern wrestling, that was really hardcore stuff. Ole Anderson, Wahoo McDaniel, Tommy Rich. You made them believe what was happening was real. New York was more Cyndi Lauper, Lou Albano. More entertaining. Even Brutus Beefcake cutting the hair. I remember working with the Bushwhackers so many times. They'd bite your ass and lick your face, but the guys knew how to wrestle."
Jacques Rougeau, *TheHistoryofWWE.com interview, 2014*

WWF @ New York City, NY - Madison Square Garden - April 24, 1989 (16,000)
Televised on the MSG Network - included Tony Schiavone & Lord Alfred Hayes on commentary:
Prime Time Wrestling - 6/12/89: Greg Valentine (w/ Jimmy Hart) pinned the Blue Blazer at 10:57 by catching him coming off the top rope and slamming him to the mat (Owen Hart's final MSG appearance for 3 and a half years)
Hillbilly Jim defeated the Honky Tonk Man (w/ Jimmy Hart) via disqualification at the 24-second mark after Honky attacked Jim from behind with Hart's megaphone after Jim became distracted by Hart, with Honky & Hart then further attacking Jim before leaving ringside; after Hillbilly got to his feet, he grabbed the mic and said he didn't want that type of victory and challenged Honky to come back out and continue the match, but the challenge went unanswered
Prime Time Wrestling - 10/30/89: Dino Bravo pinned Hercules at 16:26 by sitting on Herc's chest and then holding onto the ropes for leverage; after the bout, Hercules applied the full nelson on Bravo (*WWF Strong Men*)
Prime Time Wrestling - 5/8/89: Paul Roma pinned Boris Zhukov at 12:21 with a powerslam; after the bout, Hillbilly Jim returned to the ring and said he said he wanted to fight the Honky Tonk Man anywhere he could get a match with him; later in the show, Howard Finkel announced a rematch had been signed for 5/8 at the Meadowlands
Jake Roberts pinned Ted DiBiase (w/ Virgil) at 16:16 with a roll up as DiBiase played to the fans; after the bout, DiBiase & Virgil attacked Jake until they knocked him out of the ring, as DiBiase & Virgil then began to leave ringside, Jake pulled Virgil back inside the ring, where he was about to lay Damien across him, but DiBiase returned to ringside and pulled Virgil away before Jake could do anything (*SuperTape*)
Mr. Perfect fought Bret Hart to a 20-minute time limit draw at 19:05; after the bout, Hart challenged Perfect to 5 more minutes, with the two briefly brawling until Hart sent his opponent to the floor (*The Life and Times of Mr. Perfect*)
The Bushwhackers defeated Arn Anderson & Tully Blanchard at 10:02 when Butch pinned Anderson after Luke headbutted Anderson in the mid-section when he was attempting to powerslam Butch, with Butch falling on top for the pin
Randy Savage (w/ Sensational Sherri) defeated WWF World Champion Hulk Hogan via count-out at 10:36 after Sherri jumped on Hogan's back to prevent him from reentering the ring, and Savage attacked Hogan from behind after Hogan he got Sherri off him and then quickly reentered the ring on the 9-count; after the bout, Sherri put the world title belt around Savage's waist and raised his hand in victory until Hogan snuck up behind them, rammed their heads together and reclaimed his title belt before chasing both from the ring

WWF @ New York City, NY - Madison Square Garden - September 30, 1989 (20,000; sell out)
Televised on the MSG Network - featured Tony Schiavone & Hillbilly Jim on commentary:
Prime Time Wrestling - 11/20/89: The Genius pinned Koko B. Ware at 13:01 with a roll up
Prime Time Wrestling - 11/20/89: Jimmy Snuka pinned the Honky Tonk Man (w/ Jimmy Hart) at 10:27 with a bodyslam and diving headbutt off the top after Honky collided with Hart on the ring apron (Snuka's MSG return after a 4 1/2 year absence) (*World Tour*)
Mr. Perfect pinned the Red Rooster after reversing a small package at 9:38
Prime Time Wrestling - 12/4/89: Mark Young pinned Barry Horowitz with a reverse sunset flip at 10:58 (Young's MSG debut)
WWF Intercontinental Champion the Ultimate Warrior defeated Andre the Giant (w/ Bobby Heenan) via disqualification at 9:28 after Andre pulled referee Danny Davis in front of a charge by the Warrior; after the bout, Warrior repeatedly hit Andre with the title belt on the floor, knocking him down
Demolition defeated WWF Tag Team Champions Arn Anderson & Tully Blanchard (w/ Bobby Heenan) via disqualification at 12:51 when Blanchard pulled the referee out of the ring as Smash had Anderson covered following a double team Hot Shot; after the bout, Howard Finkel accidentally announced Anderson & Blanchard as the winners before then correcting himself and saying Demolition won (Anderson & Blanchard's last MSG appearance)
Greg Valentine pinned Ron Garvin at 17:05 by blocking a sunset flip and grabbing the ropes for leverage
Roddy Piper fought Rick Rude to a double count-out at 11:00; moments later, Piper brought Rude out from backstage and threw him back into the ring, then hitting him in the head with a steel chair and punching referee Danny Davis; Rude then hit Piper with the chair and fled the ring (Piper's MSG return after a 2 1/2 year absence)

On wrestling Andre the Giant

"He was unbelievably gracious toward me. I'll never forget what he did for my character. During one match at Madison Square Garden, he told me to put him in a bear hug. So I did, and he squealed like a fucking pig, man. That's how you sell the power, and he did that for me to convince the people that the Ultimate Warrior was that powerful. Then he told me to slam him. He was a really great guy."
The Ultimate Warrior, *Sports Illustrated, 2014*

WWF @ New York City, NY - Madison Square Garden - October 28, 1989 (16,000)
Televised on the MSG Network 10/29/89 - featured Gorilla Monsoon & Hillbilly Jim on commentary; included Sean Mooney conducting backstage interviews with Mr. Perfect, the Bushwhackers, and Andre the Giant & Bobby Heenan prior to their matches; included Mooney conducting separate interviews with Jim Duggan and Randy Savage & Sensational Sherri about their rematch on the 11/25 MSG card with two referees signed for the match:
Prime Time Wrestling - 11/27/89: Tito Santana pinned Boris Zhukov (sub. for Barry Windham) at 12:46 with the flying forearm
Prime Time Wrestling - 11/27/89: Al Perez pinned Conquistador #1 (Jose Luis Rivera) at 10:15 with a spinning crucifix powerbomb (Perez' MSG debut)
Prime Time Wrestling - 3/19/90: Bret Hart fought Dino Bravo to a 20-minute time-limit draw at 18:22
Prime Time Wrestling - 11/27/89: The Brooklyn Brawler pinned Jose Luis Rivera at 7:34 after sending Rivera face-first to the mat from the middle rope
Randy Savage (w/ Sensational Sherri) pinned Jim Dugagn at 16:04 after Sherri held Savage's leg on the ropes for leverage; after the bout, Duggan cleared Savage from the ring with the 2X4 (*Mega Matches*)
Prime Time Wrestling - 11/27/89: Hercules defeated Akeem via count-out at 11:19 after Akeem fell to the floor when Hercules ducked a clothesline
Prime Time Wrestling - 12/18/89: Mr. Perfect pinned Jimmy Snuka at 10:36 with the Perfect Plex
WWF Intercontinental Champion the Ultimate Warrior pinned Andre the Giant after a with three clotheslines and a splash; no bell could be heard to start the match and Warrior's music never stopped playing after his entrance. If the bell had rung upon the initial contact; the time of the fall would have been 18 seconds; prior to the bout, Bobby Heenan was order backstage by a count of 10 or he would be suspended; after the bout, Andre grabbed the microphone, protesting the decision to referee Danny Davis saying there was no bell rung to start the match so how could he make a 3-count (Andre's only pinfall loss at MSG) (*Ultimate Warrior: The Ultimate Collection*)
The Bushwhackers defeated the Powers of Pain (w/ Mr. Fuji) via disqualification at 7:55 when Fuji interfered and hit Luke with the cane; after the bout, Butch cleared the POP from the ring with the cane after Fuji dropped it when fleeing the ring

WWF @ New York City, NY - Madison Square Garden - November 25, 1989 (8,200)

Televised on the MSG Network - featured Gorilla Monsoon & Hillbilly Jim on commentary; included Sean Mooney conducting a backstage interview with Randy Savage & Sensational Sherri about Savage's match with Jim Duggan later in the show; included an in-ring segment of the Brother Love Show, with Brother Love introducing Sensational Sherri as a "lady" before the two spoke about the definition of "jezebel;" moments later, Love introduced Miss Elizabeth as matching that description, with Love and Sherri saying Elizabeth was not worthy being in the presence of the Queen with Love cutting Elizabeth off as she attempted to answer his questions; Sherri eventually slapped Elizabeth and called her a commoner when Elizabeth said she wasn't afraid of Sherri with Love blocking Elizabeth from retaliating, Jim Duggan then came out and chased Sherri to the back with Love then cornering Miss Elizabeth and telling her he loved her until Duggan came back out and hit Love with the 2X4 and threw him out of the ring before shaking Elizabeth's hand; included Mooney interviewing Ted DiBiase & Virgil about DiBiase's rematch with Virgil signed for the following month's card; included Mooney introducing Event Center promos from Rick Rude, Roddy Piper, WWF Tag Team Champions Demolition, and Andre the Giant, Haku & Bobby Heenan about their scheduled matches on next month's card:

Prime Time Wrestling - 12/18/89: Haku pinned Paul Roma at 10:08 with a side kick to the face after Roma ran into the corner when Haku moved out of the way

Bret Hart & Jim Neidhart fought Shawn Michaels & Marty Jannetty to a 20-minute time-limit draw at 19:39 when Neidhart and Jannetty, the illegal men, began shoving each other in the ring; after the bout, the two teams continued brawling until several officials as well as Hercules, Tito Santana, and Paul Roma came in to break them apart (*Shawn Michaels: His Journey, Shawn Michaels vs. Bret Hart*)

Prime Time Wrestling - 1/1/90: Al Perez pinned the Brooklyn Brawler with a spinning vertical suplex at 8:33

Jake Roberts defeated Ted DiBiase (w/ Virgil) via disqualification at 15:09 when Virgil interfered as Jake was about to hit the DDT on DiBiase; after the bout, Jake was double-teamed until he was able to clear DiBiase from ringside and then hit the DDT on Virgil and put Damien on him

Prime Time Wrestling - 12/25/89: Tito Santana fought Bad News Brown to a double count-out at 15:53 when both men began brawling on the floor, with both men trying to grab hold of a steel chair

Prime Time Wrestling - 4/2/90: Dino Bravo pinned Hercules with an elbow drop at 9:11 after the referee messed up the count following the side suplex

Jim Duggan defeated Randy Savage (w/ Sensational Sherri) via count-out at 7:33 after hitting him with Miss Elizabeth's loaded purse after Elizabeth had come to ringside moments earlier and threw it to Duggan in the ring while the two referees assigned for the match were distracted by Sherri on the ring apron; the King's Crown was on the line for the match but did not change hands due to the count-out victory

Sensational Queen Sherri holds the ropes open for the Macho King Randy Savage.

WWF @ New York City, NY - Madison Square Garden - December 28, 1989 (13,500)
Televised on the MSG Network - included Gorilla Monsoon & Hillbilly Jim on commentary; included Sean Mooney conducting backstage interviews with Demolition, Rick Rude & Bobby Heenan prior to their matches; included Mooney introducing promos from the Powers of Pain & Mr. Fuji and Shawn Michaels & Marty Jannetty about their match on the 1/15 MSG card; included Mooney interviewing Jake Roberts about his return match with DiBiase on the 1/15 card also, with the announcement DiBiase would be putting his Million $ Belt on the line for the first time; included Mooney introducing promos from Mr. Perfect & the Genius and WWF World Champion Hulk Hogan about their title match on the 1/15 MSG card:
Prime Time Wrestling - 1/22/90: Tito Santana pinned Bob Bradley (sub. for Barry Windham) with the flying forearm at 14:24
Little Cocoa & Karate Chris Dube defeated Cowboy Cottrell & Little Tokyo at 11:55 when Cottrell & Tokyo were both pinned by Dube & Cocoa in a pile on
Rick Martel pinned Brutus Beefcake at 14:48 by blocking a sunset flip into the ring and holding onto the ropes for leverage; after the bout, Beefcake put Martel in the sleeper but Bobby Heenan revived Martel and he was able to retreat backstage before having his hair cut (*WrestleFest 90*)
Tugboat Thomas pinned Dale Wolfe at 2:28 with a splash (Tugboat's MSG debut)
Jake Roberts pinned Ted DiBiase at 18:37 with the DDT in a No DQ match; Virgil was barred from ringside for the match but later prevented Roberts from stealing the Million $ belt (*Battle of the WWF Superstars, WWE's Top 50 Superstars of All Time*)
Koko B. Ware pinned Iron Mike Sharpe at 12:07 with the Ghostbuster
WWF Tag Team Champions Andre the Giant & Haku (w/ Bobby Heenan) defeated Demolition via count-out at 11:12 when Smash was counted out after Andre headbutted Smash in the back of the head and threw him out of the ring; after the bout, Demolition clotheslined Andre out of the ring and hit the Decapitation on Haku with Smash making his own 3-count as Ax pinned Haku (Andre's last MSG match)
Roddy Piper defeated Rick Rude (w/ Bobby Heenan) in a steel cage match at 12:55 by knocking Rude out with brass knuckles, which were thrown to Rude by Heenan, and leaving through the door; both men simultaneously hit the floor by escaping over the top at 8:09 but the match was ordered to continue (*Wrestling Super Heroes, SuperTape 2; Best of the WWF: Steel Cage Matches, Born to Controversy: The Roddy Piper Story, Legends of Wrestling: Roddy Piper and Terry Funk*)

The strange fans
"At the time, what I would notice, is you would see the 'goofies.' These were the fans where wrestling completely epitomized their lives. They'd show up with binders upon binders of photos they took the month before. Not to sell them, but just to show them to fans they didn't even know. There were fans you would see often wearing the same shirts. You would see people just waiting to say hello to the Big Bossman, just to say hello. I saw Lord Alfred Hayes shove past so many fans, making a beeline to the building. Obviously, watching the show on television every month, you're thinking who the hell is this orange guy with the glasses and this guy with the pony tail? Little did 9, 10, 11-year-old Mike Johnson know, one would be my best man at my wedding and the other would be one of my best friends in the world. Who are these wacky guys and how do they always have these same seats?"
Mike Johnson; *Glendale, NY*

WWF @ New York City, NY - Madison Square Garden - January 15, 1990 (11,500)
Televised on the MSG Network - featured Gorilla Monsoon & Hillbilly Jim on commentary; Regis Philbin was shown in the crowd watching the show; included Sean Mooney conducting backstage interviews with Ted DiBiase & Virgil, Jimmy Snuka & Ron Garvin, Greg Valentine, the Honky Tonk Man, & Jimmy Hart about their matches later in the card; included Mooney interviewing the Powers of Pain & Mr. Fuji about their scheduled match the following month with the Rockers & Jim Duggan; included Mooney conducting separate interviews with Mr. Perfect & the Genius and WWF World Champion Hulk Hogan about the scheduled handicap championship match for the following months card where it was announced that if Perfect or Genius got the decision over Hogan they would become the new champion:
The Genius pinned Jim Neidhart at 9:21 after Mr. Perfect interfered and hit Neidhart with the Genius' scroll (*1st Annual Battle of the WWF Superstars*)
The Powers of Pain (w/ Mr. Fuji) defeated Shawn Michaels & Marty Jannetty at 9:59 when the Barbarian pinned Michaels with an elbow drop after Fuji tripped Michaels from the ring apron; after the bout, Michaels dropkicked Fuji but was then thrown to the floor and Jannetty sustained a brutal triple teaming before Michaels eventually cleared the ring with a steel chair; Jannetty was then carried out on a stretcher (*SuperTape 2*)
Prime Time Wrestling - 2/12/90: Al Perez pinned Paul Roma at 11:18 when the momentum of a flying crossbody by Roma put Perez on top
Mr. Perfect (w/ the Genius) defeated WWF World Champion Hulk Hogan via disqualification at 13:36 after Hogan hit the challenger with his own pair of brass knuckles, moments after Perfect used them behind the referee's back; the bell did not ring until after the champion hit the legdrop and made the cover (*WrestleFest 90, The Life and Times of Mr. Perfect*)
Prime Time Wrestling - 2/19/90: Akeem (sub. for Bob Orton Jr. who was to have returned) pinned Bret Hart at 8:30 by blocking a sunset flip and hitting a sit-down splash
Prime Time Wrestling - 2/12/90: Jimmy Snuka & Ron Garvin fought the Honky Tonk Man & Greg Valentine (w/ Jimmy Hart) to a 20-minute time-limit draw at 19:39
Ted DiBiase (w/ Virgil) defeated Jake Roberts via count-out at 20:31 when Roberts attacked Virgil on the floor after Virgil had tried to stop Jake from getting back in the ring; the referee didn't call for the bell to end the match until Jake got back in the ring and hit the DDT on DiBiase; after the bout, Jake threw Damien on the referee; the Million $ belt was at stake in the match

WWF @ New York City, NY - Madison Square Garden - February 19, 1990 (13,800)

Televised on the MSG Network - featured Gorilla Monsoon, Bobby Heenan, & Hillbilly Jim on commentary; included Sean Mooney conducting separate backstage interviews with the Powers of Pain & Mr. Fuji, and the Rockers & Jim Duggan about their match later in the card; included Mooney showing an Event Center promo from Roddy Piper about his scheduled match with Rick Martel on the following month's card, with Mooney also conducting a live backstage interview with Martel about the match; included Mooney showing an Event Center promo from WWF IC Champion the Ultimate Warrior about his match scheduled for the following month against Mr. Perfect, with Warrior saying he would pin Perfect which Hulk Hogan couldn't do, with Mooney conducting a live backstage interview with Perfect & the Genius about the match with Perfect promising to destroy Warrior and keep his perfect record:

Prime Time Wrestling - 3/5/90: Tito Santana pinned Buddy Rose at 16:55 with the flying forearm (Rose's MSG return after a 5-year absence)

Earthquake pinned Ron Garvin at 7:35 with the sit-down splash; after the bout, Garvin sustained three more sit-down splashes before being taken backstage on a stretcher (Earthquake's MSG debut)

Prime Time Wrestling - 3/12/90: Rick Martel defeated the Red Rooster via submission with the Boston Crab at 21:00

WWF World Champion Hulk Hogan & Brutus Beefcake defeated Mr. Perfect & the Genius at 15:27 when Hogan pinned the Genius with the legdrop; after the bout, Perfect left ringside as the Genius was put in Beefcake's sleeper and had some of his hair cut; the bout was originally announced to be a handicap match with Hogan against Perfect & the Genius (*SuperTape 2*)

Bad News Brown pinned Jim Brunzell (sub. for Jimmy Snuka) at 14:39 with the Ghetto Blaster

Dusty Rhodes (w/ Sapphire) defeated Akeem (w/ Slick) via count-out at 9:04 after Slick accidentally hit Akeem with a running knee on the floor when Rhodes moved out of the way (Rhodes' MSG return after a 6+ year absence) (*1st Annual Battle of the WWF Superstars*)

Jim Duggan, Shawn Michaels, & Marty Jannetty defeated Mr. Fuji & the Powers of Pain at 16:38 when Jannetty pinned Fuji after Duggan used his 2X4 as a weapon as Fuji was preparing to throw salt in Jannetty's eyes

The return of the Dream

"When they brought Dusty Rhodes in doing the American Dream thing, I hated that. Him and Sapphire. I quickly turned on Dusty Rhodes, and you can see me booing the hell out of him. 'You're breaking my heart.' It was really bad, and I love Dusty. One of my favorite things when I was a kid was Dusty and Billy Graham."
Charlie Adorno, *Brooklyn, NY*

Topeka, KS was my Madison Square Garden

"I wrestled in Madison Square Garden 30 times, and two of them were main events. That's a lot less than Bruno Sammartino. I have to say I was more nervous the first time. By the time I had been there 30 times… I don't mean to sound blase, I'm not saying it was just another building. But I was more interested in what Hulk and Beefcake were doing than what the building was doing. I'm thinking, 'OK, what's tomorrow? I've been on the road two weeks.' I'm very grateful that I had the chance to do it. I know people with more ability than me who have never been to Madison Square Garden. For example, Magnum TA. My Madison Square Garden was Topeka, KS because that's where I fought Hulk Hogan on NBC. NBC is better than Madison Square Garden."
Lanny Poffo, *TheHistoryofWWE.com interview, 2014*

WWF @ New York City, NY - Madison Square Garden - March 19, 1990 (9,500)
Televised on the MSG Network - featured Gorilla Monsoon, Lord Alfred Hayes, and Hillbilly Jim on commentary; included Sean Mooney conducting a backstage interview with Bret Hart about his upcoming match against Rick Martel; featured Mooney conducting a backstage interview with Martel about his upcoming bout with Hart; included Mooney conducting a backstage interview with Brutus Beefcake about facing Dino Bravo; featured Mooney conducting a backstage interview with Mr. Perfect about facing WWF IC Champion the Ultimate Warrior, with Perfect saying he would prove Warrior was just another man and his perfect winning streak would stay intact; included Howard Finkel announcing Earthquake would face WWF World Champion Hulk Hogan at the 4/30/90 MSG event; moments later, Earthquake and Jimmy Hart came out, with Earthquake taking the mic and saying he would put Hogan out of wrestling:
Jim Powers pinned Iron Mike Sharpe with a powerslam at 13:00
Prime Time Wrestling - 4/9/90: Hercules defeated Black Bart via submission to a backbreaker at 12:06
Prime Time Wrestling - 4/9/90: Koko B. Ware pinned Frenchy Martin with the Ghostbuster at 12:40
The Orient Express (w/ Mr. Fuji) defeated Demolition via count-out at 10:58 after Sato threw salt into Ax' eyes as Ax attempted to hit Fuji with his own cane on the floor (*SuperTape 2*)
Earthquake (w/ Jimmy Hart) pinned Jim Duggan with a splash in the corner and elbow drop at 6:30 after Hart grabbed Duggan's leg from the floor; after the match, Earthquake hit another elbow drop and tossed Jim Powers and Koko B. Ware from the ring when they tried to intervene; Duggan then chased Earthquake and Hart backstage with his 2x4
Bret Hart (sub. for Roddy Piper) fought Rick Martel to a time-limit draw at 21:36; the match ended as both men fought on the floor; after the bout, Hart fought off an attack from Martel and hit a clothesline to the floor (*SuperTape 2*)
Dino Bravo (w/ Jimmy Hart) defeated Brutus Beefcake via count-out at 11:27 when, as Hart distracted the referee while Beefcake had Bravo in the sleeper, Earthquake came out, pulled Beefcake to the floor, and rammed him into the ringpost; after the contest, Earthquake twice hit an elbow drop on Beefcake inside the ring; two referees then came out and ordered Earthquake out of the ring
Prime Time Wrestling - 4/9/90: Tugboat pinned Pez Whatley with a splash at 5:51
WWF IC Champion the Ultimate Warrior pinned Mr. Perfect with the gorilla press slam and splash at 10:02 (Perfect's first TV loss) (*Ultimate Warrior: The Ultimate Collection*)

WORLD WRESTLING FEDERATION®
MONDAY, APRIL 30, 1990
MADISON SQUARE GARDEN
NEW YORK, NY

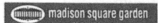
madison square garden

MAIN EVENT: ONE FALL, ONE-HOUR TIME LIMIT

HULK HOGAN	VS	**EARTHQUAKE**
Venice Beach, CA...303 lbs.		Vancouver, B.C., Canada...468 lbs.
BIG BOSS MAN	VS	**MILLION DOLLAR MAN TED DiBIASE**
Cobb County, GA...357 lbs.		Palm Beach, FL...260 lbs.
JAKE "THE SNAKE" ROBERTS	VS	**BAD NEWS BROWN**
Stone Mountain, GA...249 lbs.		Harlem, NY...271 lbs.
BUSHWHACKERS		**RHYTHM AND BLUES**
BUTCH		**GREG "THE HAMMER" VALENTINE**
&	VS	&
LUKE		**HONKY TONK MAN**
Combined Weight...499 lbs.		Combined Weight...497 lbs.
SUPERFLY JIMMY SNUKA	VS	**BARBARIAN**
Fiji Islands...245 lbs.		Parts Unknown...300 lbs.
HERCULES	VS	**HAKU**
275 lbs.		Isle of Tonga...273 lbs.
RED ROOSTER	VS	**DINO BRAVO**
Vero Beach, FL...240 lbs.		Montreal, Quebec, Canada...260 lbs.

PLUS ONE OTHER MATCH

WORLD WRESTLING FEDERATION®

WATCH WWF WRESTLING:

Saturdays	10:00 am	WNYW-TV	Ch. 5	WWF Superstars of Wrestling
Sundays	12 noon	WNYW-TV	Ch. 5	WWF Wrestling Challenge
Lunes	11:00 pm	WNJU-TV	Ch. 47	WWF Superstars de Lucha Libre

WWF @ New York City, NY - Madison Square Garden - April 30, 1990 (9,500)
Televised on the MSG Network - featured Gorilla Monsoon & Lord Alfred Hayes on commentary; included Greg Valentine, the Honky Tonk Man, & Jimmy Hart performing their new song "Hunka, Hunka, Hunka, Honky Love" in the ring; included Sean Mooney conducting backstage interviews with Ted DiBiase, the Big Bossman, and Earthquake & Jimmy Hart about their matches later in the show; included Howard Finkel announcing the card for the next show in the Metropolitan area on 5/11 at the Nassau Coliseum as MSG would be temporarily closed due to renovation; included Mooney interviewing Earthquake & Jimmy Hart following the match with Hulk Hogan, saying they would put Hogan in the hospital next time; included Mooney introducing Event Center promos from Mr. Perfect and WWF World Champion the Ultimate Warrior about their matches at the 6/8/90 Meadowlands show, with footage also shown of Rick Rude preparing in the gym with Bobby Heenan for his match with the Warrior:
Hercules pinned Haku (w/ Bobby Heenan) at 11:51 after reversing Haku's pinfall attempt by sitting on Herc's chest into a roll up
Prime Time Wrestling - 5/7/90: Paul Diamond pinned Jim Powers at 9:53 by reversing a powerslam into a small package; during the bout, Bobby Heenan joined Gorilla Monsoon & Lord Alfred Hayes in the broadcast booth and provided guest commentary for the next few matches
Jake Roberts pinned Bad News Brown with the DDT at 12:55; after the bout, Brown was just able to escape when Jake threw Damien into the ring after Brown had hit the snake bag under the ring earlier in the bout; later in the show, Bad News Brown came back out and promised the next time we see him he would bring his own bag with him after he had got the biggest sewer rat he could find to take care of Damien
Nikolai Volkoff pinned Jose Luis Rivera at 5:23 with a clothesline to the back of the head
Greg Valentine & the Honky Tonk Man (w/ Jimmy Hart) defeated the Bushwhackers via count-out at 13:01 when Luke chased Honky backstage with a steel chair after Honky threw Butch into the ringpost, leaving only Valentine in the ring; after the match, Valentine threw Butch back inside the ring and continued to attack him but was hit by Luke wielding a chair as he attempted to put Butch in the figure-4; the Bushwhackers then knocked Valentine to the floor with the battering ram (*1st Annual Battle of the WWF Superstars, WWF's Funniest Moments*)
Prime Time Wrestling - 5/21/90: Dino Bravo (w/ Jimmy Hart) pinned the Red Rooster at 4:45 with the side suplex
The Big Bossman pinned Ted DiBiase (w/ Virgil) at 11:18 with a small package after DiBiase put his head down for a backdrop attempt; after the bout, Bossman was double-teamed until he was able to stop an attack with his own nightstick and chase DiBiase & Virgil away from ringside with it; prior to the bout, Bobby Heenan left the broadcast booth saying he didn't want to watch the Big Bossman
The Barbarian (w/ Bobby Heenan) pinned Jimmy Snuka at 6:40 with a boot to the face and both feet on the ropes for leverage
Hulk Hogan defeated Earthquake (w/ Jimmy Hart) via disqualification at 8:39 when Hart broke the pinfall after Hogan's legdrop; after the bout, Hogan fought off Earthquake before dropping him with a bodyslam (*Hulkamania Forever, Hulk Hogan: The Unreleased Archives*)

Putting on the working boots

"In the years that would pass, every now and then, we'd go and see a show. A lot of times we'd go to the Nassau Coliseum because my aunt worked at the box office. The way the guys wrestled when they worked in Nassau was not the way they worked in The Garden. Vince wasn't there, and they weren't on television. It was built into the DNA of everyone. Even with the wrestlers, it became this self-fulfilling prophecy."
Mike Johnson*; Glendale, NY*

WWF @ New York City, NY - Madison Square Garden - September 21, 1990 (11,000+)
Televised on the MSG Network - featured Gorilla Monsoon & Bobby Heenan on commentary; Lord Alfred Hayes subbed for Heenan for Tito Santana vs. the Barbarian, Jim Duggan vs. Rick Rude, and the six-man tag team match; included Sean Mooney introducing Event Center promos from Mr. Perfect & Bobby Heenan, Tugboat, Ted DiBiase, & WWF Tag Team Champions Bret Hart & Jim Neidhart about their matches on the next MSG card on 10/19:
Prime Time Wrestling - 10/29/90: Dustin Rhodes pinned Paul Diamond at around the 13:04 with a flying forearm and an elbow drop; Rhodes used the "Crank it Up" song by Jimmy Hart as his theme song (Dustin's MSG debut)
Sgt. Slaughter defeated Nikolai Volkoff via submission with the Camel Clutch at 8:40 (Slaughter's MSG return after a 6-year absence)
Prime Time Wrestling - 11/5/90: The Barbarian (w/ Bobby Heenan) pinned Tito Santana at 13:28 when the momentum of a crossbody off the top by Santana put the Barbarian on top for the win
Paul Roma (w/ Hercules) pinned Marty Jannetty at 13:43 when Hercules swept Jannetty's feet from under him as Jannetty attempted to slam Roma and held the leg down during the pin; Jannetty's opponent was determined via a coin toss before the match (*SuperTape 3*)
Prime Time Wrestling - 11/5/90: Ron Garvin pinned Bob Bradley at 12:21 with a roll up (Garvin's final MSG appearance)
Prime Time Wrestling - 10/22/90: Jim Duggan defeated Rick Rude (w/ Bobby Heenan) via disqualification at 9:10 after Rude pushed the referee to the mat (Rude's last MSG appearance for 7 years)
WWF World Champion Ultimate Warrior & the Legion of Doom defeated Demolition Ax, Smash, & Crush when Warrior pinned Smash at 12:59 with the shoulderblock / splash combo; before the bout, Bobby Heenan left the commentary table and cut an in-ring promo on the Big Bossman's mother until Jim Duggan ran out and cleared Heenan from the ring with his 2x4 (LOD and Crush's MSG debuts; Demolition Ax's final MSG appearance) (*SuperTape 3*)

The accessible Garden

"Even though I lived in New Jersey, it was actually easier to attend MSG shows because it was a simple 30 minute New Jersey train ride, directly into Penn Station, which is actually downstairs from Madison Square Garden, as opposed to a 30-40 minute drive down the congested New Jersey Turnpike.
Now for fans outside of NY/NJ, just think about the convenience of that train ride for a minute. A 10-minute walk down the street or a 5-minute car ride to my local train station and, in about 30 minutes, the train pulls into Penn Station. Penn Station is one of the largest and busiest train stations in the world, and is right in the heart of New York City's entertainment area, and is located downstairs from the most famous arena in the world. Once you depart the train and walk up the stairs to Penn Station, you walk another set of stairs and simply enter into Madison Square Garden. The convenience of access to the most famous arena in the world, and a stage for so many great WWE moments over the years, is something that I will always have very fond memories of.
Walking up the stairs from Penn Station provided a rush of adrenaline. You can literally feel and sense the change of atmosphere, as you reach the top of the steps or escalator. Once you've reached the top, you have now entered into the mecca of all entertainment....New York City. There you are met with thousands of people coming and going, big huge buildings, which at night time look amazing lit up...the streets filled with cars and buses, different sounds and noises, vendors selling all kinds of food. It's a really unique and intense feeling. You go from suburban New Jersey and a typically quiet train ride, to the entertainment mecca of the world in just a matter or 30 minutes. It's amazing. The fact that MSG is right in the center of all this, just makes it that much more awesome."
Michael Berlinski, *Edison, NJ*

WWF @ New York City, NY - Madison Square Garden - October 19, 1990 (9,000)

Televised on the MSG Network - featured Gorilla Monsoon & Bobby Heenan on commentary; included an in-ring performance by Greg Valentine & the Honky Tonk Man of "Hunka Hunka Honky Love;" featured Sean Mooney hosting an Event Center segment with promos by Earthquake & Jimmy Hart, Hulk Hogan, Sgt. Slaughter & Gen. Adnan, and Jim Duggan regarding their matches for the 11/24/90 MSG event; included Lord Alfred Hayes conducting a backstage interview with Dusty Rhodes, with Rhodes challenging Ted DiBiase & Virgil to a tag team match against he and his son Dustin; featured Hayes conducting a backstage interview with DiBiase, alongside Virgil, in which he accepted Rhodes' challenge:

Prime Time Wrestling - 11/26/90: Shane Douglas pinned the Brooklyn Brawler with a sunset flip at 10:19

Prime Time Wrestling - 11/12/90: The Warlord pinned Koko B. Ware at 8:07 after dropping him throat-first across the top rope

Mr. Perfect (w/ Bobby Heenan) fought WWF IC Champion Kerry Von Erich to a double count-out at 8:50; after the match, Perfect cut a promo in the ring regarding the bad officiating in the match and demanded a rematch with a referee that knew what he was doing; Lord Alfred Hayes provided guest commentary for the bout (Von Erich's MSG return after a 10 and a half year absence)

Prime Time Wrestling - 11/12/90: Iron Mike Sharpe pinned SD Jones at 10:56 after hitting him with the loaded forearm

Ted DiBiase (w/ Virgil) defeated Dusty Rhodes via disqualification at 8:46 after Rhodes hit DiBiase with the timekeeper's bell, brought into the ring by Virgil; after the match, DiBiase knocked Rhodes out with the weapon

Davey Boy Smith pinned Haku (w/ Bobby Heenan) at 19:34 with the running powerslam (*Mega Matches*)

Tugboat defeated Dino Bravo via disqualification at 8:28 after Bravo continuously prevented Tugboat from reentering the ring

Prime Time Wrestling - 11/26/90: WWF Tag Team Champions Bret Hart & Jim Neidhart defeated Greg Valentine & the Honky Tonk Man at 6:10 when Bret pinned Honky after Valentine accidentally hit Honky with his guitar

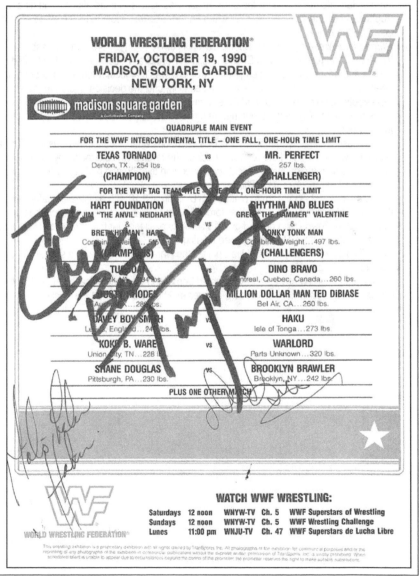

WWF @ New York City, NY - Madison Square Garden - November 24, 1990 (15,700 paid)
Televised on the MSG Network - featured Sean Mooney, the Honky Tonk Man, & Jimmy Hart on commentary; included Lord Alfred Hayes conducting separate backstage interviews with Earthquake, Dino Bravo, & Jimmy Hart and Hulk Hogan & Tugboat, with Hogan & Tugboat wanting a tag match with Earthquake & Bravo on the next MSG card; included Hayes conducting separate interviews with Mr. Perfect and Roddy Piper, with Perfect challenging Roddy Piper to a match and Piper saying he wanted Perfect here in MSG; both matches were confirmed later in the show for the next months card on 12/28:
Prime Time Wrestling - 12/24/90: Davey Boy Smith pinned Buddy Rose at 8:48 with the running powerslam; prior to the match, Rose took issue with being announced at 317lbs., then took out a weight scale, stood on it, and claimed he was only 217lbs, and got Howard Finkel to announce that it read 217 even though Rose had the scale in his hands
Prime Time Wrestling - 1/7/91: Tugboat pinned Boris Zhukov at 5:57 with the splash
Earthquake (w/ Jimmy Hart) defeated Hulk Hogan via count-out at 8:33 after Dino Bravo came to ringside and prevented Hogan from getting back in the ring before the 10-count after Hogan had threw Earthquake and also Jimmy Hart into the ring; after the bout, Hogan was double-teamed after he had hit a bodyslam on Earthquake until Tugboat made the save with a chair when Earthquake was about to hit the sit-down splash as Bravo held Hogan down on the mat
Prime Time Wrestling - 1/7/91: Shane Douglas pinned Haku at 7:48 with a crossbody off the middle turnbuckle
WWF IC Champion Kerry Von Erich pinned Mr. Perfect at 11:38 when Von Erich lifted his shoulder following a back suplex and bridge by the challenger; Roddy Piper was the guest referee for the bout; after the bout, Perfect celebrated with the title belt, believing he had won, until the decision was announced; moments later, Perfect repeatedly hit both Von Erich and Piper with the title belt until referees swarmed the ring; Piper eventually struggled to his feet, went after Perfect, but then returned to the ring to raise Von Erich's hand in victory (*The Life and Times of Mr. Perfect*)
Ted DiBiase & Virgil defeated Dusty & Dustin Rhodes when Virgil pinned Dustin at 8:51 after DiBiase dropped Dustin with a powerslam behind the referee's back as the referee was distracted by Dusty and the Honky Tonk Man arguing at the announce table; after the bout, Honky went in the ring and performed "Hunka, Hunka, Hunka, Honky Love" (*American Dream: The Dusty Rhodes Story*)
Sgt. Slaughter (w/ Gen. Adnan) pinned Jim Duggan at 9:10 with a clothesline after Adnan hit Duggan with the Iraqi flag pole; prior to the bout, Slaughter forced Howard Finkel to make the announcement that it was Veteran's Day in Iraq and that crowd stand up and give 10 seconds of silence for the Iraqi soldier who died during the invasion of Kuwait; after the bout, Duggan cleared the ring
WWF Tag Team Champion Bret Hart pinned the Barbarian at 4:09 with a sunset flip (*2nd Annual Battle of the WWF Superstars, Mega Matches*)
Shawn Michaels & Marty Jannetty defeated Demolition via disqualification at 10:53 when Crush pulled the referee outside the ring as Smash was being covered by Michaels following the Rocket Launcher

WWF @ New York City, NY - Madison Square Garden - December 28, 1990 (13,700)

Televised on the MSG Network - included Gorilla Monsoon & Lord Alfred Hayes on commentary; featured a segment in which the Goobledy Gooker danced with Howard Finkel in the ring:

Prime Time Wrestling - 1/14/91: Koko B. Ware pinned Black Bart at 10:07 with the Ghostbuster

Prime Time Wrestling - 1/14/91: Jimmy Snuka defeated the Warlord via disqualification at 8:28 when the Warlord refused to stop choking Snuka on the ropes; after the bout, Snuka eventually cleared Warlord from the ring

Shawn Michaels & Marty Jannetty fought Paul Roma & Hercules to a time-limit draw at 21:11; late in the bout, the middle rope broke as Hercules attempted a superplex on Michaels; after the bout all four men continued brawling until Herc & Roma escaped the ring

Prime Time Wrestling - 1/7/91: Saba Simba defeated Greg Valentine (w/ Jimmy Hart) via disqualification at 8:29 after Valentine pushed the referee; after the bout, Hart hit Valentine with his own guitar when Simba moved out of the way, busting him open in the process; when Valentine came around, he almost attacked Hart after the crowd began cheering Valentine to do so but Hart was able to escape before anything could happen (Tony Atlas' first MSG appearance in 4 and a half years and his final MSG appearance)

Hulk Hogan & Tugboat defeated Earthquake & Dino Bravo (w/ Jimmy Hart) at 9:24 when Hogan pinned Bravo with a roll up following a boot to the face; after the bout as Hogan & Tugboat were posing, Earthquake & Jimmy Hart returned to the ring, with Hart throwing salt into Tugboat's eyes, and Earthquake attacking Hogan with a chair and hitting the sit-down splash; after the bout, Hogan refused to be stretchered out of the ring

Kerry Von Erich pinned Virgil (sub. for Ted DiBiase who underwent knee surgery) at 7:55 following the Tornado Punch; after the bout, Virgil shook Tornado's hand; following this bout, Jimmy Hart came to the ring, and said what happened to Hulk Hogan earlier, was only the beginning, he then went on to say that the Honky Tonk Man had challenged Greg Valentine to a match and that Valentine had refused to accept, it was announced later in the show however that Valentine had accepted the match and it would take place the following month, but it didn't due to Honky leaving the WWF

Sgt. Slaughter & Gen. Adnan defeated Dusty Rhodes & Jim Duggan at 9:10 when Rhodes submitted to Slaughter's Camel Clutch after Duggan chased Adnan backstage (Rhodes' final MSG appearance)

Roddy Piper defeated WWF IC Champion Mr. Perfect via count-out at 12:38 after Piper crotched the champion on the top rope by shaking it as Perfect was about to jump from it; after the bout, both men continued brawling with Piper eventually hitting Perfect in the head with his own title belt (*Legends of Wrestling: Roddy Piper and Terry Funk*)

Hercules and Paul Roma comprised the team of Power & Glory.

WWF @ New York City, NY - Madison Square Garden - January 21, 1991

Televised on the MSG Network - featured Sean Mooney & Bobby Heenan on commentary, with Brother Love replacing Heenan beginning with the Greg Valentine / Dino Bravo match after the Big Bossman had chased Heenan away after making his entrance for his match; included a promo for WrestleMania VII at the Los Angeles Memorial Coliseum; included Mooney introducing Event Center promos from the Nasty Boys & Jimmy Hart, the Rockers WWF IC Champion Mr. Perfect & Bobby Heenan, and Kerry Von Erich about their matches for the 2/16/91 Nassau Coliseum card; included Lord Alfred Hayes conducting a backstage interview with the Big Bossman about Bossman's ball & chain match with Bobby Heenan on the 2/16 Nassau Coliseum card; included Hayes interviewing Randy Savage & Sensational Sherri about Savage's upcoming steel cage match with the Ultimate Warrior:

Prime Time Wrestling - 1/28/91: Paul Roma pinned Shane Douglas at 10:01 with a powerslam; the bout seemed to have ended moments earlier at 9:16 when Roma pinned Douglas by reversing a crossbody off the top but they continued to wrestle even after the bell sounded; the referee gave a fast count for the powerslam cover and Roma refused to have his hand raised in victory following the win

Davey Boy Smith defeated the Warlord via disqualification in an arm wrestling contest after Warlord pushed the table up into Smith's face as it looked Smith was about to win; Warlord then attacked Smith and applied the full nelson until he was forced to break the hold by several referees

Prime Time Wrestling - 2/4/91: Tito Santana pinned Koko B. Ware following the flying forearm at 10:10; Koko played the heel for the contest (*SuperTape 4*)

The Undertaker (w/ Brother Love) pinned Jimmy Snuka with the tombstone at 7:14 after catching Snuka in mid-air (Taker's MSG debut)

The Legion of Doom defeated Demolition (w/ Mr. Fuji) at 2:58 when Road Warrior Animal pinned Smash after Road Warrior Hawk hit the flying clothesline as Smash attempted a piledriver on Animal

Prime Time Wrestling - 3/26/91: The Big Bossman defeated Hercules via disqualification at 7:16 when Paul Roma interfered and hit a missile dropkick; after the bout, Bossman was double teamed by Power & Glory and eventually tied up with Hercules' chain; moments later, Bobby Heenan came out and began slapping Bossman in the face until the Legion of Doom made the save

Prime Time Wrestling - 4/2/91: Greg Valentine pinned Dino Bravo (sub. for the Honky Tonk Man) (w/ Jimmy Hart) with a small package at 8:53 after reversing Bravo's attempt at the figure-4

The Nasty Boys (w/ Jimmy Hart) defeated the Bushwhackers at 7:49 when Brian Knobbs pinned Butch after Jerry Saggs hit an elbow off the middle turnbuckle behind the referee's back as Butch had Knobbs covered (the Nasty's MSG debut) (*2nd Annual Battle of the WWF Superstars*)

Randy Savage (w/ Sensational Sherri) defeated the Ultimate Warrior in a steel cage match at 10:33 by escaping over the top while the Warrior was distracted by an interfering Sensational Sherri, who entered through the door and climbed the cage to choke Warrior with her clothing; after the bout, Savage was able to escape the cage after a number of referees and the Nasty Boys restrained Warrior; moments thereafter, Warrior hit the gorilla press slam on Sherri (*Best of the WWF: Steel Cage Matches, Mega Matches, The Greatest Cage Matches of All Time*)

WWF @ New York City, NY - Madison Square Garden - March 15, 1991 (14,500)
Televised on the MSG Network - featured Gorilla Monsoon, Bobby Heenan, & Lord Alfred Hayes on commentary:
Prime Time Wrestling - 4/2/91: Marty Jannetty pinned Pat Tanaka (w/ Mr. Fuji) at 10:52 by reversing a tombstone piledriver attempt and hitting his own for the win (*WrestleFest 91*)
Prime Time Wrestling - 4/2/91: The Mountie (w/ Jimmy Hart) pinned Koko B. Ware at 4:43 with a two-handed chokeslam; after the bout, the Mountie handcuffed his opponent to the bottom rope and assaulted him with the shock stick
Davey Boy Smith pinned the Warlord at 10:34 with a roll up after Warlord ran into the corner; after the bout, Warlord applied the full nelson on Smith, until he was pulled off by two referees
The Undertaker (w/ Paul Bearer) pinned Tugboat at 3:23 with an elbow drop off the top
Prime Time Wrestling - 3/26/91: WWF Tag Team Champions Bret Hart & Jim Neidhart defeated Earthquake & Dino Bravo (w/ Jimmy Hart) at 10:24 when Bret pinned Bravo after Neidhart powerslammed his partner onto Bravo; after the bout, Earthquake hit the sit-down splash on Bret until Neidhart cleared the ring with a chair
Prime Time Wrestling - 4/2/91: The Barbarian pinned Jim Brunzell with a boot to the face at 7:13
Kerry Von Erich (w/ Virgil) pinned Ted DiBiase at 4:50 after Virgil tripped DiBiase, with Von Erich falling on top for the win; prior to the bout, Kerry introduced Virgil as a surprise corner man
Prime Time Wrestling - 3/26/91: Kato (w/ Mr. Fuji & Pat Tanaka) pinned Shawn Michaels (w/ Marty Jannetty) with a backslide at 12:50 after Tanaka interfered and hit Michaels with Mr. Fuji's cane while the referee was distracted by Jannetty trying to get Fuji off the ring apron
Jim Duggan (w/ Hulk Hogan) defeated WWF World Champion Sgt. Slaughter (w/ Gen. Adnan) via disqualification in a flag match at 14:12 when Adnan prevented the pinfall after Hogan interfered and hit the champion in the back with Duggan's 2x4; after the bout, Slaughter and Adnan attacked Duggan and Hogan with both Duggan's 2x4 and the Iraqi flag until referees swarmed the ring; moments later, as Gen. Adnan returned ringside to grab Slaughter's title belt, he was attacked by Hogan and Duggan and quickly sent to the floor (*2nd Annual Battle of the WWF Superstars*)

<u>Rocker three-way?</u>
"My sister worked for a cable company. Somehow, someway she got us into a meet and greet. I remember that one of the PR directors grabbed Shawn (Michaels) and Marty (Jannetty) and pulled them into a room. I'm a little older now. I ask my dad, 'What do you think she's doing?' 'She's probably blowing both of them.'"
Matt Striker, *TheHistoryofWWE.com interview, 2014*

WWF @ New York City, NY - Madison Square Garden - April 22, 1991 (12,200)
Televised on the MSG Network - featured Gorilla Monsoon, Bobby Heenan, & Jim Neidhart on commentary; included a segment in which Lord Alfred Hayes discussed visiting Roddy Piper and Ted DiBiase backstage earlier in the night, with Piper refusing to speak and DiBiase saying he would send Piper out of the ring on a stretcher.
Ricky Steamboat pinned Haku with the crossbody off the top at 9:35 after Haku missed a charge into the corner
Paul Roma & Hercules defeated the Bushwhackers when Roma pinned Butch at 8:34 after Hercules and Luke took turns dropping elbows on Roma and Butch behind the referee's back and putting their partner on top
The Big Bossman pinned the Mountie at 7:56 with the sidewalk slam; during the Mountie's entrance, Lord Alfred Hayes questioned him at ringside as to if he had any law enforcement authority in the United States, with the Mountie saying he had jurisdiction in the WWF and would prove Bossman was just a hick cop; late in the match, Mountie took the mic and said, "I'm going to show you who the real boss is" to the fans; after the bout, Mountie jumped Bossman from behind and repeatedly shocked him with his cattle prod until several referees came to the ring
Sgt. Slaughter (w/ Gen Adnan) defeated WWF World Champion Hulk Hogan via disqualification at 16:00 when referee Joey Marella came to, saw Hogan with a steel chair, and believed Hogan had been the one that twice hit him with the weapon as he was knocked down; Hogan was double teamed by both men to start the match, before quickly tossing them both to the floor; Hogan's head was bandaged until Slaughter removed the bandage early in the contest, exposing a bloody gash underneath; during the contest, Hogan used a steel chair on the floor and Slaughter hit Hogan with the title belt outside the ring, both in clear view of the referee; late in the bout, Adnan gave Slaughter the chair, with Slaughter missing Hogan before Hogan stole it away and attacked Adnan with it; after the match, Slaughter and Adnan attempted to throw a fireball at Hogan but Hogan avoided it and chased them backstage with the chair; Hogan then brought a young fan in the ring with him to pose and wave the American flag
IRS pinned Jimmy Snuka at 6:33 by grabbing the tights for leverage after the momentum of a reverse crossbody from the middle turnbuckle by Snuka put IRS on top; IRS wore black trunks that read "IRS" on the back, and brown leggings for the match; prior to the contest, IRS cut an in-ring promo in which he said most tax cheats lived in New York City (Mike Rotunda's MSG return after more than a 4-year absence)
Kerry Von Erich fought the Warlord to a double count-out at 9:15 when both men began brawling on the floor
(*Rampage 91*)
Prime Time Wrestling - 5/14/91: Shawn Michaels, Marty Jannetty, & Virgil defeated the Orient Express & Mr. Fuji at 10:33 when Virgil applied the Million $ Dream on Tanaka
Ted DiBiase (w/ Sensational Sherri) defeated Roddy Piper via referee's decision at 7:33 when referee Danny Davis stopped the match as Piper was caught in the figure-4 to prevent further injury to Piper's leg; Piper used bagpipe music for his entrance but not his WWF theme song; DiBiase came to the ring in possession of a crutch; during the match, DiBiase hit Piper with a steel chair; after the annoucement of the ruling, Piper stripped Sherri of her dress, cleared DiBiase from the ring, and knocked Davis from the ring

WWF @ New York City, NY - Madison Square Garden - June 3, 1991
Televised on the MSG Network - featured Gorilla Monsoon, Bobby Heenan, & Jim Neidhart on commentary; Jim Quinn of the World Bodybuilding Federation was shown in attendance; included Sean Mooney conducting a backstage interview with Mr. Fuji about the Barbarian's loss earlier in the show and Bobby Heenan being upset with him, with Fuji challenging a team of Heenan's against a team of his own; featured Mooney conducting a backstage interview with the Big Bossman about his upcoming match with the Mountie; included Mooney conducting a backstage interview with Sgt. Slaughter, with Gen. Adnan, about his attack on Jim Duggan earlier in the show and facing WWF World Champion Hulk Hogan later in the show in a Desert Storm match; featured Mooney conducting a backstage interview with Hogan about the upcoming match with Slaughter:
Prime Time Wrestling - 6/24/91: Ricky Steamboat pinned Demolition Smash with the flying bodypress at 10:14 (*Rampage 91*)
Prime Time Wrestling - 6/24/91: The Warlord pinned Koko B. Ware at 10:33 after dropping Koko throat-first across the top rope
Col. Mustafa (w/ Gen. Adnan) defeated Jim Duggan via count-out at 5:47 after Duggan chased Adnan backstage and was attacked by Sgt. Slaughter in the hallway; Slaughter assaulted Duggan with the 2x4 and Adnan also stomped him until the two were forced away by officials
Bret Hart pinned the Barbarian (w/ Mr. Fuji - sub. for Bobby Heenan) at 12:09 after Fuji accidentally hit the Barbarian with his cane; prior to the match, Howard Finkel announced that Heenan, due to his broadcast obligations, had agreed to allow Fuji to manage Barbarian for the contest; after the bout, Heenan and Barbarian argued with Fuji regarding the loss
Prime Time Wrestling - 6/10/91: Jimmy Snuka pinned Bob Bradley at 4:02 with the splash off the top
Earthquake defeated Jake Roberts via disqualification at 10:56 when, after Roberts tripped Earthquake as Earthquake attempted the sit-down splash on the snake bag, Roberts took Lucifer out of the bag and scared Earthquake to the floor
Tugboat pinned the Brooklyn Brawler at 2:40 with the splash
The Mountie pinned the Big Bossman at 5:50 after using his shock stick as a weapon behind the referee's back; after the match, Mountie continued to shock Bossman until referees swarmed the ring; the Mountie then took the mic and said he was the only law and order
Prime Time Wrestling - 6/24/91: Road Warrior Animal pinned Paul Roma (w/ Hercules) with a powerslam at 5:00 after Roma accidentally hit an interfering Hercules with a missile dropkick; prior to the bout, a coin toss was held to see which of Roma and Hercules would compete (*Rampage 91*)
WWF World Champion Hulk Hogan defeated Sgt. Slaughter (w/ Gen. Adnan) in a Desert Storm match at 15:34 when Adnan threw in the towel as Hogan had Slaughter in the Camel Clutch after throwing a fire ball in his face; after the bout, Hogan cleared Slaughter from the ring and celebrated with a young fan (*WWF Greatest Champions, WWF Champion Hulk Hogan's Greatest Matches*)

WWF @ New York City, NY - Madison Square Garden - July 1, 1991 (8,800)
Televised on the MSG Network - featured Gorilla Monsoon & Bobby Heenan on commentary; included Randy Savage as a guest of the Barber Shop in which Savage admitted he was planning on proposing to Miss Elizabeth on the coming week's edition of WWF Superstars and if she said yes the two would marry at Summer Slam; featured Sean Mooney conducting a backstage interview with Earthquake & Jimmy Hart regarding Earthquake's upcoming match against Jake Roberts, with Andre the Giant in Roberts' corner; included Mooney conducting a backstage interview with Roberts & Andre regarding the upcoming match; featured Mooney conducting a backstage interview with the Barbarian & Haku regarding their upcoming match against the Orient Express, during which Barbarian blamed Mr. Fuji for his previous loss at MSG; included Mooney conducting a backstage interview with the Undertaker & Paul Bearer regarding Taker's upcoming bodybag match against the Ultimate Warrior.
Prime Time Wrestling - 7/15/91: Dino Bravo pinned Shane Douglas at 5:32 with the side suplex
Prime Time Wrestling - 8/5/91: Ricky Steamboat pinned Paul Roma with the crossbody off the top at 11:05 after Roma hit the opposite corner chest-first
The Berzerker (w/ Mr. Fuji) pinned Jimmy Snuka at 7:16 after catching him in mid-air and dropping him throat-first across the top rope
Prime Time Wrestling - 7/29/91: WWF Tag Team Champions the Nasty Boys (w/ Jimmy Hart) defeated Bret Hart & Jim Neidhart via disqualification at 13:46 after referee Joey Marella caught Bret intercept Jimmy Hart's motorcycle helmet and hit both champions with it (Hart & Neidhart's last match as a team for 6 years)
Prime Time Wrestling - 7/29/91: The Warlord pinned Greg Valentine at 10:19 with a powerslam after Valentine hit the corner
Jake Roberts (w/ Andre the Giant) pinned Earthquake (w/ Jimmy Hart) at 10:30 with the DDT after Earthquake became distracted by Andre while attempting the sit-down splash; both men were down about 30 seconds before Roberts was able to make the cover; after the contest, Earthquake knocked Roberts to the floor, grabbed a steel chair, and faced off with Andre until Roberts used Lucifer to chase him backstage
Haku & the Barbarian defeated Mr. Fuji (sub. for Pat Tanaka whose father had passed away) & Kato when Haku pinned Kato at 7:32 with an elbow drop after Bobby Heenan tripped Kato from the floor; prior to the match, Fuji did a ceremonial throwing of salt and threw some at Heenan at the commentary table, with Heenan then climbing up the ring steps to confront Fuji until Haku & Barbarian made their appearance; after the match, Fuji threw salt in the eyes of Haku, Barbarian, & Heenan as Heenan tried to get at Fuji in the ring; moments later, Heenan led his men backstage to find Fuji & Kato
The Ultimate Warrior defeated the Undertaker (w/ Paul Bearer) in a bodybag match at 9:29 following a series of clotheslines and hitting Taker with his own urn; Gorilla Monsoon & Lord Alfredy Hayes called the match without Bobby Heenan; after the contest, Bearer unzipped Taker from the bodybag (*The Undertaker's Most Dangerous Matches*)

Jimmy Hart
"This Monday night at Summer Slam, I want the LOD completely destroyed."
Jerry Saggs
"No problem, Jimmy. The pleasure's all ours."
Brian Knobbs
"LOD, I hope you come on your baddest day. Because the Nasty Boys don't want no excuses. This is your last trip to Nastyville."
=======================================
Road Warrior Animal
"Nasty Boys, you don't have to worry about us being at our baddest, because we're bad every day. Right Hawk?"
Road Warrior Hawk
"That's right. And don't forget something else. This ain't our first trip to Nastyville. We own the stinking town."
SummerSlam 91 Report

<u>SUMMERSLAM</u>
Madison Square Garden – August 26, 1991

"I've always had some great fans around the world, but my hardcore greatest wrestling fans were always in New York."
Bret Hart, *WrestleMania Rewind*, WWE Network

Bret and Curt steal the show

"I can watch the Bret Hart-Curt Hennig match again and again. That was a great show. I enjoyed it so much. It's 1991, I know that (Randy Savage and Elizabeth) are married in real life. But it was cool. The main event, it was what it was. The Bret Hart-Curt Hennig match, that's the match that stands out to me. And the wedding at the end. You see the production values, they're getting better and better."
Charlie Adorno, *Brooklyn, NY*

Going to jail

"It was totally awesome. We pretaped that day, during the day of the show. I was arrested by police, thrown into the wagon. We got all those pretapes before the show so they could show it on the big screen. After every match, you had them going back."
Jacques Rougeau, *TheHistoryofWWE.com interview, 2014*

Summer Slam 91 - New York City, NY - Madison Square Garden - August 26, 1991 (20,000)
Koko B. Ware pinned Kato at 7:15 with a missile dropkick
Pay-per-view bouts - included Gorilla Monsoon, Roddy Piper, and Bobby Heenan on commentary; featured Bobby Heenan going backstage to confront WWF World Champion Hulk Hogan at his dressing room door and challenging him to a match against Ric Flair, with Hogan quickly slamming the door in Heenan's face; Heenan had the NWA World Title in his hands during the segment; Hogan was not featured on camera in the segment; included the in-ring wedding of Randy Savage & Miss Elizabeth:
Ricky Steamboat, Davey Boy Smith, & Kerry Von Erich defeated the Warlord, Hercules, & Paul Roma (w/ Slick) at 10:42 when Steamboat pinned Roma with the crossbody off the top
Bret Hart defeated WWF IC Champion Mr. Perfect (w/ the Coach) at 18:02 via submission with the Sharpshooter to win the title; during the bout, Stu, Helen, and Bruce Hart were seen in the audience; after the contest, Bret hugged his parents at ringside (*Summer Slam: The Greatest Hits, The Bret Hart Story: The Best There Is, Was, and Ever Will Be, The Life and Times of Mr. Perfect, History of the Intercontinental Championship*)
The Natural Disasters (w/ Jimmy Hart) defeated the Bushwhackers (w/ Andre the Giant) at 6:27 when Earthquake pinned Luke with the sit-down splash; during the contest, Bobby Heenan left the commentary position to go backstage and confront Hulk Hogan; after the bout, the Natural Disasters made their way toward the injured Andre on the floor until the Legion of Doom came to the ring, scaring Earthquake & Typhoon from ringside
Virgil pinned Million $ Champion Ted DiBiase (w/ Sensational Sherri) at 10:53 to win the title after DiBiase hit his head on an unprotected turnbuckle; during the opening moments of the bout, Heenan returned ringside; the bell originally rung when Sherri interfered early on but referee Earl Hebner opted to continue the bout and order Sherri backstage, with the stipulation that if she didn't go she would face permanent suspension
The Big Bossman pinned the Mountie (w/ Jimmy Hart) at 8:38 in a Jailhouse Match after the Bossman reversed a piledriver attempt into a throw-down slam; late in the match, the Mountie kicked out of the Bossman's sidewalk slam; pre-match stipulations stated the loser would spend the night in jail; after the bout, the Mountie was handcuffed at ringside by police officers and taken into a NYPD vehicle backstage (*Best of the WWF: Most Unusual Matches*)
The Legion of Doom defeated WWF Tag Team Champions the Nasty Boys (w/ Jimmy Hart) at 7:44 to win the titles in a No DQ, No Count-Out match when Road Warrior Animal pinned Jerry Saggs following the Doomsday Device after both champions were hit with Hart's motorcycle helmet (*Best of WWF Tag Team Champions, The Life & Death of the Road Warriors, The Best of the WWF: Summer Slam*)
IRS pinned Greg Valentine at 7:07 with an inside cradle and grabbing Valentine's hair for leverage as Valentine attempted the figure-4
WWF World Champion Hulk Hogan & the Ultimate Warrior defeated Sgt. Slaughter, Col. Mustafa, & Gen. Adnan at 12:38 in a handicap match when Hogan pinned Slaughter with the legdrop after throwing powder in his face; Sid Justice was the guest referee for the bout; after the bout, Hogan invited Sid back to the ring where the two men posed for the fans (Sid's MSG debut) (Warrior's last appearance for 7 months)

During the Ultimate Warrior's legal battle with the WWF in the mid 1990s, specifically regarding his contract to be paid equal as Hulk Hogan, these documents went public regarding the pay the wrestlers received for SummerSlam 91. You'll notice that the documents were made so far after the fact that Kato is referenced as "Max Moon."

```
DATE   MONDAY  , 08/26/91        07:45PM    GROSS          $404150.00
NAME   MADISON SQUARE GARDEN                Less TAXES     $ 22228.25
LOCATION  NEW YORK, NY          NYC01       OFFICIALS      $  3050.00
TEMPERATURE      CONDITIONS                 OTHER          $     0.00
  TENDANCE 17474    COMPS          1731     NET            $378871.75
  IL    90 %                                TALENT NET     $724150.00
                                            TALENT PCT           191 %
                                            EST TRAVEL     $ 11457.65
```

```
        ORIGINAL CARD: HULK/WARRIOR VS. SLAUGHTER/MUSTAFA/ADNAN
                        *MARRIAGE*
                    SAVAGE VS. ELIZABETH
                     *TAG-TITLE*
                    LEGION OF DOOM VS. NASTY BOYS
                    (NO DQ AND NO COUNT-OUT)
                       *TITLE*
                    HART B. VS. MR. PERFECT

                     *MILLION $ BELT*
                    VIRGIL VS. DIBIASE
                     *JAIL MATCH*
                    BIG BOSS MAN VS. MOUNTIE
                    (LOSER SPENDS THE NIGHT IN JAIL)
                    BUSHWHACKERS VS. NATURAL DISASTERS
                    (ANDRE)
                    VALENTINE VS. I.R.S.
                    DRAGON/TEXAS TORNADO/BULLDOG VS. POWER & GLORY
                                                   WARLORD
```

	MATCH	TALENT NAME	#	PAY	DRAW	BONUS	TYPE	COMMENTS
1	1	000458 HULK		75000		15000 0		
2		000563 Z WARRIOR		75000				
3		000495 SGT. SLAUGHTE		50000				
4		000367 Z COLONEL MUS		25000	200			
5		000464 Z GENERAL ADN		10000	200			
6	2	000676 SAVAGE, RANDY		75000				
7		000602 Z ELIZABETH		50000				
8	3	000492 Z HAWK		25000				TAG
9		000493 Z ANIMAL		25000				
10		011728 KNOBBS, BRIAN		17500	200			
11		011731 SAGS, JERRY		17500	200			
12	4	000588 HART B,		17500				
13		000524 PERFECT, MR.		20000	200			

	MATCH	TALENT	NAME	#	PAY	DRAW	BONUS	TYPE	COMMENTS
	5	000522	VIRGIL		10000	200			
15		000521	DIBIASE, TED		20000	200			
16	6	000507	BIG BOSS MAN		15000	200			
17		000690	Z MOUNTIE		20000				
18	7	000421	MILLER, BUTCH		5000	200			
19		000422	WILLIAMS, LUK		5000	200			
20		000466	TYPHOON		7000				
21		000468	EARTHQUAKE		7000	200			
22	8	000348	Z VALENTINE		5000	200			
23		000584	I.R.S.		5000	100			
24	9	000643	Z DRAGON		5000	200			
25		000490	Z TEXAS TORNA		5000	200			
26		000653	Z BULLDOG		6000	200			

	MATCH	TALENT	NAME	#	PAY	DRAW	BONUS	TYPE	COMMENTS
7		000639	Z GLORY		5000	200			
28		000634	Z HERCULES		5000	200			
29		000413	Z WARLORD		5000	200			
30	10	000633	HART J		8000	200			MANAGERS
31		000450	SHERRI		5000	200			
32		000307	Z ANDRE		7500	500			
33		000349	FUJI		2000	200			
34		001473	Z COACH		3000				
35		000672	SLICK		3000	200			
36		000474	PAUL BEARER		3500	200			
37	11	000504	MICHAELS, SHA		2000	200			STAND BY
38		000635	Z KOKO		1000	200			
39		000487	Z MAX MOON		1000	200			

MATCH		TALENT	NAME	#	PAY	DRAW	BONUS	TYPE	COMMENTS
		012720	Z BERZERKER		1500	200			
41		013282	BEAU BEVERLY		1000	200			
42		000472	UNDERTAKER		5000	200			
43		000471	KIMCHEE/BRAWL		1000	200			
44		000505	JANNETTY, MAR		2000	200			
45		000484	Z TANAKA		1000	200			
46		000414	Z BARBARIAN		2000	200			
47		000359	Z SNUKA, JIMM		2000	200			
48		013281	BLAKE BEVERLY		1000	200			
49		000497	Z SNAKE		5000	200			
50		000570	DUGGAN, JIM		2000				
51	12	000459	MATADOR		1000				
52		000716	WHITE, TIM		750				

MATCH		TALENT	NAME	#	PAY	DRAW	BONUS	TYPE	COMMENTS
		000629	Z NEIDHART		1000				
54		000350	BEEFCAKE		1000				
55		000476	Z SID JUSTICE		25000				
56		000999	LOCAL						
57		000999	LOCAL						
58		000999	LOCAL						
59		000999	LOCAL						
60		000999	LOCAL						
61	13	000708	LANZA, JACK		3500				AGENTS
62		000463	GAREA, TONY		1200	100			
63		000442	GOULET, RENE		1200				
64		000547	Z GARVIN, TER		1000	500			
65		000357	STRONGBOW, JA		3500				

MATCH		TALENT	NAME	#	PAY	DRAW	BONUS	TYPE	COMMENTS
66		000655	HEBNER, DAVE		2000				
67		000309	SKAALAND		1000				
68		000475	MYERS, JIM		2000				
69	14	000743	D'AMICO, JOHN		0				RING CREW
70		013002	SUSI, JOE		0				
71		000535	YEATON, MARK		0				
72		001085	COLLERTON, CR		0				
73	15	000539	MARELLA, JOEY		2000	200			REFEREE
74		000538	HEBNER, EARL		3500				
75		000537	Z SPARTA, FRE		1500				
76		000325	DAVIS, DANNY		1000				

43050 05792

WWF @ New York City, NY - Madison Square Garden - October 28, 1991 (9,000)
Televised on the MSG Network - included Gorilla Monsoon, Bobby Heenan, & Lord Alfred Hayes on commentary, with Heenan leaving the commentary team for the Ric Flair vs. Roddy Piper match; featured Sean Mooney conducting a backstage interview with Ric Flair and Bobby Heenan about Flair's win over Roddy Piper earlier in the show, with the two then challenging WWF World Champion Hulk Hogan; included Howard Finkel announcing Flair would face Hogan and WWF IC Champion Bret Hart would face the Mountie at the following month's show:
Prime Time Wrestling - 11/18/91: Kerry Von Erich pinned Big Bully Busick with the Tornado Punch at 7:47
Prime Time Wrestling - 11/11/91: Davey Boy Smith fought IRS to a 20-minute time-limit draw at 20:05; Smith did not have theme music during his entrance; late in the bout, IRS and Smith took turns choking each other with one of the tag ropes, in plain view of referee Danny Davis, and IRS hit a low blow; the match ended as Smith had IRS covered with an inside cradle
Prime Time Wrestling - 12/9/91: The Mountie (w/ Jimmy Hart) pinned Jim Neidhart at 11:19 by using the tights for leverage after Neidhart missed a running kneelift into the corner
Ric Flair (w/ Bobby Heenan) pinned Roddy Piper at 11:59 by sliding in the ring and putting his feet on the ropes for leverage after punching Piper in the face; after the match, Piper hit the referee with a steel chair before repeatedly hitting Flair with the chair - knocking him to the floor; Flair came out in possession of the "real world's title" (Flair's MSG return after a 15-year absence) (Piper's first pinfall loss at MSG) (*Nature Boy Ric Flair: The Definitive Collection*)
The Big Bossman pinned Col. Mustafa with a standing sidewalk slam at 4:52 following a gutwrench suplex; prior to the bout, IRS came ringside and demanded the match be stopped, claiming Bossman was a tax cheat; the distraction allowed Mustafa to attack Bossman from behind
WWF IC Champion Bret Hart pinned the Berzerker with a crucifix at 10:17
Prime Time Wrestling - 11/18/91: Tito Santana pinned Hercules with the flying forearm at 9:11
WWF Tag Team Champions the Legion of Doom defeated the Natural Disasters (w/ Jimmy Hart) via disqualification at 8:02 when Typhoon threw the referee to the floor; after the bout, Road Warrior Hawk hit the clothesline off the top, made the save for Road Warrior Animal, and cleared the opponents from the ring

Flair in The Garden?
"The idea of Flair, who epitomized Jim Crockett Promotions, working for the WWF. In Madison Square Garden? Mind exploding. It was one thing for Tully (Blanchard) and Arn (Anderson) to work there, but Flair? I can remember seeing Flair wrestle the Undertaker there. Hogan vs. Flair in The Garden, when Flair hit him with the brass knuckles and pinned him. There were people jumping up and down. The hardcore fans were happy; the WWF-centric fans were like, 'How could this happen?' It was one of those dream matches that we'll never see today. The impact of an AJ Styles of Samoa Joe or Michael Elgin going to the WWF today does not have nearly the same importance of a WCW/NWA guy coming to the WWF back then."
Mike Johnson; *Glendale, NY*

Flair bad for business?
"And then they brought in Ric Flair, which I was so excited about, loving heels and loving NWA wrestling, I loved Ric Flair. I couldn't wait for him to get here. Ric Flair vs. Roddy Piper followed by Hulk Hogan vs. Ric Flair did not sell out. I was so surprised. How could Hulk Hogan vs. Ric Flair not sell out the Garden? How did Roddy Piper vs. Ric Flair not sell out the Garden? People didn't really care that much about the NWA guys back then. So when Ric Flair came here, it didn't mean that much. It did to me."
Charlie Adorno, *Brooklyn, NY*

Hulk Hogan and Ric Flair had a historic showdown at MSG in November 1991. Despite years of hype, the show was not a sell out.

WWF @ New York City, NY - Madison Square Garden - November 30, 1991 (15,000)
Televised on the MSG Network - featured Vince McMahon, Bobby Heenan, & Lord Alfred Hayes on commentary:
Prime Time Wrestling - 12/30/91: Tito Santana pinned Kato with the flying forearm at 10:04
Kerry Von Erich defeated the Berzerker via count-out at 2:00 after ramming Berzerker's head into the ring steps and sliding back into the ring
Prime Time Wrestling - 1/6/92: Virgil pinned Skinner with a sunset flip at 6:07
Hulk Hogan defeated Ric Flair via reverse decision at 9:25; Flair originally won the match via pinfall after hitting Hogan with a pair of brass knuckles, handed to him by Mr. Perfect; Perfect appeared ringside late in the contest; after the initial decision, Dave Hebner came out, caught Flair with the weapon, and the call was changed; Hogan then cleared Flair and Perfect from ringside as the decision was changed; moments later, Hogan brought a young fan into the ring and posed with him (*Greatest Wrestling Stars of the 90s*)
Prime Time Wrestling - 12/23/91: Jim Duggan pinned the Barbarian with the running clothesline at 7:51; after the match, the Barbarian knocked Duggan to the floor, with Duggan then attacking Barbarian with his 2x4 and sending him to the floor
WWF IC Champion Bret Hart pinned the Mountie at 12:58 with an elbow drop off the middle turnbuckle; prior to the bout, Hart refused to get in the ring until the referee took the Mountie's shock stick away, with the Big Bossman then running out, attacking the Mountie, and taking the weapon backstage
IRS pinned the Big Bossman at 13:46 after hitting him over the back with his briefcase as the referee was distracted by the Mountie at ringside; late in the bout, the Mountie came ringside and attacked Bossman on the floor behind the referee's back; after the contest, the Bossman ran backstage in search of the Mountie
Prime Time Wrestling - 1/6/92: The Nasty Boys defeated Shawn Michaels & Marty Jannetty when Jerry Saggs pinned Jannetty with a small package at 16:20; Brian Knobbs initially reversed Jannetty's move behind the referee's back, with Jannetty then reversing it back; without noticing, Michaels accidentally put Saggs back on top; after the contest, Michaels apologized to Jannetty before Jannetty left the ring

Seeing the dream match
"I was there for the first Hogan vs. Flair match. It was in Pro Wrestling Illustrated as a dream match. And it was all right. Watching it now, you go, 'Oh this is all right.' Watching it then you go, 'This is real. this is happening.'"
Mary-Kate (Grosso) Anthony, *Tampa, Fla.*

Hogan vs. Flair
"Pat (Patterson) was on hiatus for a while. And I was directly involved with (WrestleMania VIII). Vince would take a match and put it out to kind of get a feel for it before he would build it. It's a different time now. You can't do that now because of the Internet, everything is instantaneous. There were a series of matches between Hulk and Flair. And, to everybody's surprise, I think, box office-wise, it didn't do what we thought it would. That was the reason the Hulk / Flair match didn't take place at WrestleMania."
JJ Dillon, *The Place to Be Nation, 2013*

WWF IC Champion Bret Hart prepares to face Ted DiBiase.

WWF @ New York City, NY - Madison Square Garden - December 29, 1991 (matinee) (11,000)
Televised on the MSG Network 12/31/91 - featured Gorilla Monsoon & Bobby Heenan on commentary; included an in-ring promo by Col. Mustafa & Gen. Adnan in which they insulted Sgt. Slaughter.
Prime Time Wrestling - 2/3/92: Davey Boy Smith pinned the Berzerker with a small package at 5:05
Prime Time Wrestling - 2/3/92: Sgt. Slaughter defeated Gen. Adnan & Col. Mustafa in a handicap flag match at 3:27 by pinning Mustafa with a clothesline; after the bout, Slaughter led the crowd in saying the Pledge of Alliegence
Prime Time Wrestling - 1/20/92: Hercules pinned Greg Valentine by lifting his shoulder out of a back suplex into a bridge at 7:44
Prime Time Wrestling - 1/27/92: The Nasty Boys defeated the Bushwhackers when Knobbs pinned Butch at around 9:45 with a clothesline; after the bout, the Nastys continued to assault their opponents until Sgt. Slaughter made the save
Prime Time Wrestling - 1/27/92: Skinner pinned Jim Powers with the reverse DDT at 6:51
Prime Time Wrestling - 1/20/92: Chris Walker pinned the Brooklyn Brawler with a flying bodypress at 4:02
Virgil defeated Repo Man via disqualification at 9:35 when Repo began choking Virgil with his rope
Prime Time Wrestling - 1/20/92: WWF IC Champion Bret Hart fought Ted DiBiase (w/ Sensational Sherri) to a 20-minute time-limit draw at 19:06 as Hart chased Sherri around ringside and into the ring; late in the bout, as DiBiase had Hart in the Million $ Dream, Sherri ran over and rang the time keeper's bell which resulted in the match pausing until referee Earl Hebner ordered the match to continue; after the bout, DiBiase attempted to attack Hart with the title belt but was clotheslined to the floor
Hulk Hogan defeated Ric Flair (w/ Mr. Perfect) via count-out at 10:09 after ramming Flair's head into the ringpost on the floor; after the match, Flair jumped Hogan from behind but Hogan fought him off and sent him to the floor (*Hulk Hogan: The Unreleased Archives*)

Miss Elizabeth returned to Randy Savage's corner during Savage's feud with Jake Roberts.

Bret Hart prepares to face the Undertaker in their first singles match. The two would go on to have a rivalry through Hart's WWF departure in 1997.

WWF @ New York City, NY - Madison Square Garden - January 31, 1992 (9,000)
Televised on the MSG Network - included Gorilla Monsoon & Bobby Heenan on commentary:
Prime Time Wrestling - 2/24/92: Rick Martel pinned Kerry Von Erich at 9:39 with his feet on the ropes; after the bout, Von Erich chased Martel backstage (Von Erich's last MSG appearance)
Prime Time Wrestling - 3/2/92: Shawn Michaels pinned Jimmy Snuka with the Teardrop suplex at 12:17 following a superkick (Snuka's last MSG apperance as a full-time wrestler)
Sid Justice pinned the Mountie at 4:26 with the powerbomb
Prime Time Wrestling - 2/17/92: The Warlord (w/ Harvey Wippleman) pinned Hercules at 5:39 with a running powerslam
Sgt. Slaughter & Jim Duggan defeated the Nasty Boys via count-out at 10:26 after Duggan assaulted Knobbs on the floor with his 2x4 and Slaughter shoved Saggs into the ringpost
Chris Walker pinned Kato at 9:44 with a flying bodypress
The Undertaker (w/ Paul Bearer) pinned Bret Hart at 12:27 with a double axe handle and hitting Hart in the face with the urn, moments after Hart released the Sharpshooter to go after Bearer, who was holding down referee Danny Davis (*Bret Hitman Hart: The Dungeon Collection*)
Prime Time Wrestling - 5/11/92: Repo Man pinned Virgil with a back elbow at 11:04
Randy Savage (w/ Miss Elizabeth) pinned Jake Roberts at 6:07 with the flying elbowsmash; early in the bout, Elizabeth was escorted backstage (Roberts' last MSG appearance for 4 years; Elizabeth's last MSG appearance)

WWF @ New York City, NY - Madison Square Garden - February 23, 1992 (matinee) (14,000)
Televised on the MSG Network 2/29/92 - featured Gorilla Monsoon, Bobby Heenan, & Lord Alfred Hayes on commentary:

Prime Time Wrestling - 4/20/92: The Berzerker pinned Jim Brunzell with a falling slam at 8:44

Prime Time Wrestling - 5/25/92: The Nasty Boys (w/ Jimmy Hart) defeated the Bushwhackers at 12:38 when Brian Knobbs pinned Butch after Saggs hit Butch with the ring bell behind the referee's back

Prime Time Wrestling - 3/9/92: The Warlord pinned Chris Walker at 11:14 with a powerbomb

Prime Time Wrestling - 3/23/92: Sid Justice (w/ Harvey Whippleman) pinned Hercules with a powerbomb at the 25-second mark; prior to the bout, Justice allowed Hercules to leave the ring and forfeit the match but Herc attacked him from behind

WWF IC Champion Roddy Piper pinned Repo Man at 3:31 with an elbow drop after hitting the challenger with his own steel hook; prior to the bout, Repo stole a watch from a woman at ringside only for Piper to return it to her after the conclusion of the match

The Undertaker (w/ Paul Bearer) pinned Davey Boy Smith at 5:19 after dropping him throat-first across the top rope

Prime Time Wrestling - 4/20/92: Rick Martel pinned the Big Bossman at 13:49 after hitting him with Bossman's own nightstick behind the referee's back as the referee prevented Bossman from using Martel's atomizer can as a weapon

Sid Justice won a 20-man battle royal by last eliminating Hulk Hogan at 16:37; Hogan originally elimiated Justice at 15:50 but the referee inside the ring had been knocked to the floor by Justice; moments later, Sid returned to the ring, hit Hogan with Harvey Wippleman's doctor's bag, rolled Hogan to the floor underneath the bottom rope, and woke the referee up to tell him he threw Hogan over the top; other participants included: WWF IC Champion Roddy Piper, Chris Walker, Rick Martel, WWF World Champion Ric Flair, the Big Bossman, Davey Boy Smith, the Berzerker, Hercules, the Bushwhackers, Skinner, Repo Man, the Warlord, Kato, Jim Brunzell, the Nasty Boys, and the Undertaker; order of elimination: Butch by the Nasty Boys (2:31); the Berzerker by Hogan (5:30); Skinner after Piper ducked a clothesline (5:49); Kato by Piper (6:00); Brunzell by Martel (6:38); Hercules by Hogan (7:09); Martel by Bossman (7:18); Saggs by Hogan (8:25); Luke by the Undertaker (8:36); Walker by the Warlord (8:48); Flair & Repo by Piper (9:45); Piper by Sid (10:06); Taker by Bossman (11:42); Smith by Sid (12:32); Knobbs by Hogan (13:10); Warlord by Hogan (13:33); Bossman by Sid (13:41); the Legion of Doom were to have competed in the match but were replaced

WWF @ New York City, NY - Madison Square Garden - March 23, 1992 (9,000)

The last MSG card televised on the MSG Network for 5 years; featured Gorilla Monsoon & Bobby Heenan on commentary; included Lord Alfred Hayes conducting a backstage interview with Shawn Michaels & Virgil about Michaels' upcoming match with Virgil; included Hayes conducting a backstage interview with Hulk Hogan & WWF IC Champion Roddy Piper about their upcoming match with WWF World Champion Ric Flair & Sid Justice:
Tatanka pinned Col. Mustafa at 8:45 with the Samoan Drop (Tatanka's MSG debut)
Prime Time Wrestling - 5/4/92: WWF Tag Team Champion IRS fought Tito Santana to a 20-minute time-limit draw at 20:34; after the match, Santana hit the flying forearm on IRS
Prime Time Wrestling - 4/13/92: Rick Martel pinned JW Storm with a roll-up and holding the tights at 9:33
Prime Time Wrestling - 5/4/92: Bret Hart & the Bushwhackers defeated the Mountie & the Nasty Boys at 12:46 when Bret pinned the Mountie with a roll-up at 13:05
Prime Time Wrestling - 4/13/92: The Warlord pinned Jim Brunzell at 10:18 with the running powerslam (Warlord's final MSG appearance)
Prime Time Wrestling - 4/27/92: Shawn Michaels (w/ Sensational Sherri) pinned Virgil with the side suplex at 12:13 after Virgil hit the corner; during the bout, Virgil wrestled with a face mask to protect his broken nose but took it off late in the match (*WrestleFest '92*)
Hulk Hogan & WWF IC Champion Roddy Piper defeated WWF World Champion Ric Flair & Sid Justice (w/ Harvey Wippleman) at 18:02 when Hogan pinned Flair with a clothesline (Hogan's last MSG appearance for 10 years; Sid's last MSG appearance for 3 years; Piper's last MSG appearance for 2 years)

WWF @ New York City, NY - Madison Square Garden - September 11, 1992 (9,000)
Owen Hart & Koko B. Ware defeated Skinner & Barry Horowitz when Koko pinned Horowitz
The Mountie pinned Tito Santana
WWF Tag Team Champions Natural Disasters defeated the Beverly Brothers
Shawn Michaels pinned Virgil
Razor Ramon pinned Randy Savage after Ric Flair came ringside (Razor's MSG debut)
Bret Hart pinned Papa Shango
The Undertaker defeated WWF World Champion Ric Flair via disqualification

WWF World Champion Ric Flair prepares to face the challenge of the Undertaker.

WWF @ New York City, NY - Madison Square Garden - November 28, 1992 (12,300)
Lance Cassidy pinned the Brooklyn Brawler
Crush defeated Repo Man via submission with the head vice
Bob Backlund pinned Rick Martel with a small package (Backlund's MSG return after more than an 8 year absence)
The Nasty Boys defeated WWF Tag Team Champions Ted DiBiase & IRS via disqualification when DiBiase shoved Jerry Saggs off the top
The Big Bossman pinned Kamala after Kamala accidentally hit Kimchee; after the bout, Kamala chased Harvey Wippleman and Kimchee backstage
Max Moon defeated Terry Taylor
The Undertaker pinned Nailz at the 12-minute mark with the chokeslam

WWF @ New York City, NY - Madison Square Garden - January 29, 1993 (12,000)
Headlock on Hunger benefit show; included a 10-bell toll in tribute to the passing of Andre the Giant; the show lasted 3:45 and featured a 15-minute segment where WWF World Champion Bret Hart, flanked by all the heels and faces, presented the Red Cross with a giant $100,000 check
Tito Santana pinned Skinner at 8:38 with the flying forearm
Randy Savage pinned WWF Tag Team Champion Ted DiBiase (w/ Jimmy Hart) at the 14-minute mark with the DDT
Tatanka pinned Damien Demento at 9:02 with a tomahawk chop
WWF World Champion Bret Hart pinned Bam Bam Bigelow at 11:42 with a victory roll after kicking Bigelow as he ran into the corner
Mr. Perfect defeated Ric Flair (w/ Bobby Heenan) via disqualification at the 17-minute mark when Razor Ramon interfered; Heenan was sent backstage during the bout by Sgt. Slaughter after Heenan gave Flair brass knuckles to use as a weapon (Flair's last MSG appearance for more than 9 years; Perfect's MSG return following Summer Slam 91)
The Headshrinkers defeated Virgil & Jim Powers (sub. for Jim Duggan) at 6:20 when Powers was pinned (the Headshrinkers' MSG debut)
Typhoon pinned the Berzerker at the 6-minute mark with a splash
Razor Ramon pinned the Big Bossman with a roll up after Ramon moved when Bossman charged at him in the corner
The Undertaker (w/ Paul Bearer) pinned IRS (w/ Jimmy Hart) at 4:30 with the tombstone
Rick & Scott Steiner defeated the Beverly Brothers at 10:00 when Scott pinned Blake with the Frankensteiner (the Steiners' MSG debut)
Bob Backlund defeated WWF IC Champion Shawn Michaels via count-out at the 18-minute mark

Headlock on Hunger
"It was like a 4-hour show. They did like 11 or 12 matches, plus they did a ceremony with the Red Cross. That was a really unique show. Every top talent was on that show - Undertaker, the Steiners, Tatanka. They treated it like it was a step up from even a normal Garden house show."
Mike Johnson; *Glendale, NY*

WWF @ New York City, NY - Madison Square Garden - March 21, 1993 (10,400)
Included Rob Bartlett conducting an in-ring interview with Harvey Wippleman and Giant Gonzalez
Terry Taylor pinned Jim Brunzell
Virgil pinned Repo Man with a roll up
Randy Savage fought Doink the Clown to a no-contest when Doink attacked Savage on the floor before the bell; as a result, the scheduled match between the two was postponed until later in the card
Jerry Lawler pinned Tito Santana at 12:59 by blocking a sunset flip into the ring and holding onto the ropes for leverage; after the match, Santana battled Lawler into the crowd (Lawler's MSG debut)
Rick Steiner pinned WWF Tag Team Champion IRS with a roll up at 10:18 after Scott Steiner came ringside and prevented IRS from using a steel chair; Scott escorted his brother to ringside before the match began but was eventually sent backstage; the match was initially advertised as a non-title bout between the Steiners and IRS & Ted DiBiase
Randy Savage defeated Doink the Clown via disqualification at around 7:30 after Doink sprayed Savage in the eyes; after the bout, Savage had to be restrained by officials in the aisle as he attempted to get at Doink (Doink's MSG debut)
Tatanka pinned Reno Riggins (sub. for Papa Shango) with the Samoan Drop
WWF World Champion Bret Hart & Mr. Perfect defeated Razor Ramon & Lex Luger at around 19:12 when Hart pinned Razor with an inside cradle after both Luger and Perfect reversed the pin attempt behind the referee's back; after the bout, Luger, Razor, and Giant Gonzalez won a brawl over Hart, Perfect, and Savage (Luger's MSG debut)

> ### On Giant Gonzalez
> "He just couldn't get it. He just couldn't get it. I drove him around. I was like his babysitter. He was a really nice guy. We became really good friends. He wasn't a dumb guy by any means, he just couldn't get the hang of it."
> **Harvey Wippleman,** *The Place to Be Nation, 2013*

WWF @ New York City, NY - Madison Square Garden - June 12, 1993 (9,100)
Tito Santana pinned Papa Shango with a roll up at 10:14 (Santana's last MSG match)
Razor Ramon defeated WWF IC Champion Shawn Michaels via count-out at 8:51 when Diesel pulled the champion out of the ring and helped him backstage immediately after the challenger hit the Razor's Edge; after the bout, Razor grabbed the microphone and challenged Michaels to bring Diesel and the belt back out, with Michaels and Diesel returning briefly before leaving ringside (Diesel's MSG debut)
Bret Hart pinned Bob Backlund with a roll over at 32:21; prior to the bout, the two shook hands; during the bout, Hart sustained an injured ankle; after the bout, the two shook hands and Backlund raised Hart's arm in a showing of respect (Backlund's first pinfall loss at MSG)
The Undertaker defeated the Giant Gonzalez via disqualification at 4:34 when Gonzalez hit Taker in the back with a steel chair as Taker grabbed Harvey Wippleman on the ring apron; after the match, Taker sat up in the ring as Gonzalez & Wippleman attempted to use Chloroform on him, with Taker then using the rag on Gonzalez instead (Gonzalez' only MSG match)
Tatanka defeated Bam Bam Bigelow via count-out at 11:21 after hitting the Samoan Drop on the floor; after the bout, Bigelow attacked Tatanka in the ring and hit the diving headbutt
The Headshrinkers & Afa defeated the Smoking Gunns & Kamala at around the 9-minute mark when Kamala was pinned with a roll up as he was distracted by Afa in the ring (Afa's in-ring return to MSG after a nearly 9-year absence, the Gunns' MSG debut, Kamala's last MSG match)
Lex Luger pinned Mr. Perfect at 14:02 after taking his forearm pad off behind the referee's back and knocking Perfect out while the referee was distracted by Shawn Michaels and Diesel at ringside; prior to the bout, Luger was forced to wear the pad or he would be fined $25,000 and be suspended for 6 months

WWF @ New York City, NY - Madison Square Garden - August 13, 1993 (13,000)
The original line up for this card included Marty Jannetty vs. Doink, Bret Hart vs. Yokozuna, and WWF IC Champion Shawn Michaels vs. Mr. Perfect in a steel cage match
Owen Hart pinned Blake Beverly with a crucifix as Blake made a lazy cover attempt (Blake's last MSG appearance)
The 1-2-3 Kid pinned Doink the Clown at the 14-minute mark with a roll up (the Kid's MSG debut)
The Smoking Gunns defeated the Headshrinkers at the 13-minute mark when Billy pinned Samu with a sunset flip
Jerry Lawler defeated Randy Savage (w/ the Macho Midget) via disqualification when Bret Hart interfered
WWF World Champion Yokozuna defeated Bret Hart in a steel cage match at 25:00 by escaping through the door after Jerry Lawler interfered and threw salt into Hart's eyes
Bastion Booger pinned the Brooklyn Brawler with the sit-down splash at the 80-second mark (Booger's MSG debut)
WWF IC Champion Shawn Michaels, Diesel, & Bam Bam Bigelow defeated Mr. Perfect, Marty Jannetty, & Tatanka in an elimination match at 22:36; Diesel pinned Jannetty at 12:42 with a punch to the back of the head; Tatanka and Bigelow fought to a double count-out at 18:20; Perfect pinned Michaels with the Perfect Plex at 22:26 after throwing Michaels into the corner; Diesel pinned Perfect with a punch to the back of the head; after the contest, Perfect was double teamed by Michaels and Diesel and thrown to the floor; moments later, Perfect came back and knocked both men out of the ring

WWF @ New York City, NY - Madison Square Garden - September 25, 1993 (11,500)
Included an in-ring segment in which WWF Tag Team Champions the Quebecers protested having to face Bam Bam Bigelow & Adam Bomb instead of Rick & Scott Steiner
Bastion Booger (sub. for WWF IC Champion Shawn Michaels) pinned the 1-2-3 Kid by blocking a sunset flip and hitting a sit-down splash
Men on a Mission defeated Well Dunn when Mabel pinned Dunn (MOM and Well Dunn's MSG debuts)
Tatanka fought IRS to a 20-minute time-limit draw
WWF World Champion Yokozuna pinned the Undertaker with a legdrop after hitting the challenger four times in the head with his salt bucket as the referee was knocked down; late in the bout, Paul Bearer and Mr. Fuji went backstage; after the match, Yoko went to hit the Bonzai Drop on Taker, with Bearer and Fuji then returning ringside; moments later, Taker fought Yoko off and cleared him from the ring; Taker then attacked Yoko on the floor until the champion retreated backstage; moments later, Taker returned to the ring and posed with the title belt
WWF Tag Team Champions the Quebecers (sub. for Rick & Scott Steiner) defeated Adam Bomb & Bam Bam Bigelow via count-out at 12:56 when Bigelow and Bomb began arguing on the floor; Johnny Polo appeared ringside late in the bout and shoved Luna Vachon after Luna interfered; moments later, as Bigelow had Pierre covered following the headbutt off the top, Bomb began arguing with Luna causing Bigelow to go out to the floor and argue with his tag team partner; after the contest, Polo got down on his knee to apologize to Bigelow, with Bigelow then throwing him into the corner; Bomb and Bigelow then fought with Bigelow eventually gainging the upper hand and knocking Bomb to the floor (Jacques Rougeau's MSG return after a year absence; Pierre Oulette's MSG debut; Bomb's MSG debut; Johnny Polo's MSG debut)

Jimmy Snuka pinned Brian Christopher at 7:26 with the splash off the top; prior to the bout, Christopher cut an in-ring promo in which he introduced himself and insulted the New York crowd before issuing an open challenge (Snuka's surprise MSG return after a year absence; Christopher's MSG debut)
Razor Ramon pinned Rick Martel with the Razor's Edge
Mr. Perfect defeated Diesel via disqualification when Rick Martel interfered as Diesel was caught in the Perfect Plex; prior to the contest, Paul Bearer appeared and said the Undertaker would bury Yokozuna in their casket match rematch; moments later, Rick Martel appeared and protested his loss earlier in the show, leading to Martel and Perfect having a scuffle; after the bout, Razor Ramon made the save

WWF World Champion Yokozuna faced the challenge of Bret Hart, the Undertaker, and Tatanka at MSG before losing his title at WrestleMania X.

WWF @ New York City, NY - Madison Square Garden - November 27, 1993 (12,600)

Included the announcement that a 30-man Royal Rumble match would take place at the next show on Jan. 17, featuring Shawn Michaels, the Bushwhackers, Diesel, Doink the Clown, Bastion Booger, the Smoking Gunns, Greg Valentine, Owen Hart, Bret Hart, the Heavenly Bodies, Scott Steiner, Ivan Putski, Scott Putski, IRS, Bob Backlund, Men on a Mission, Virgil, the Headshrinkers, Rick Martel, Adam Bomb, Ricky Morton & Robert Gibson, Crush, and Randy Savage

The Headshrinkers defeated the Smoking Gunns at 11:54 when Samu pinned Billy Gunn after he and Fatu dropped Gunn throat-first across the top rope behind the referee's back

Tiger Jackson pinned Little Louie with a leap off the top at 5:51 (the first midget match at MSG in 4 years; Jackson's MSG return after a 9-year absence; Louie's MSG return after a 17-year absence)

Shawn Michaels pinned Doink the Clown with the superkick at 8:18 after Doink became distracted by Bam Bam Bigelow at ringside; Michaels came out in possession of his own WWF IC Title belt, with him then telling ring announcer Howard Finkel that he should be referred to as champion but that this is a non-title bout; late in the bout, Luna Vachon came ringside, with Doink kissing her leading to Bigelow coming out; after the bout, Bigelow & Luna double teamed Doink for several minutes; moments later, Bigelow went to hit the headbutt off the top only for Doink to trip Luna and Bigelow hit Luna with the headbutt instead; Doink then returned to the ring and doused her with a pail of water to revive her, with Bigelow then tripping over himself to try to get at Doink as Doink left ringside

Rick & Scott Steiner defeated WWF Tag Team Champions the Quebecers via disqualification at 12:37 when Pierre jumped on referee Danny Davis to prevent Jacques from being pinned after sustaining the Frankensteiner; after the bout, the Steiners celebrated with the title belts; moments later, Scott took the mic and challenged the Quebecers to get back in the ring and try to take the belts from them; Jacques then said they would think about giving the Steiners 5 more minutes, with he, Pierre, and Johnny Polo then returning backstage

WWF IC Champion Razor Ramon pinned Diesel at 12:05 with an inside cradle; late in the match, referee Earl Hebner was knocked down, leading to shawn Michaels running out and hitting the champion with his fake IC title belt; Michaels and Diesel then tried to revive Hebner, leading to Razor hooking the inside cradle, Michaels pulling Hebner out of the ring, and a replacement referee sliding in to count the pinfall; after the match, Michaels and Diesel double teamed Razor until they were sent backstage by referees; after they went backstage, Howard Finkel announced Michaels had been fined $5,000 for his actions

Owen Hart defeated Marty Jannetty via submission with the Sharpshooter at 8:14 after Jannetty injured his ankle attempting a leapfrog

The Undertaker defeated WWF World Champion Yokozuna in a non-title casket match at 9:05 after hitting Yoko in the head with his own salt bucket

WWF @ New York City, NY - Madison Square Garden - January 17, 1994 (9,000)
Ricky Morton & Robert Gibson and the Heavenly Bodies were both advertised but did not appear due to transportation problems
Scott Putski pinned Iron Mike Sharpe with the Polish Hammer
Rick Steiner fought Ludvig Borga to a double count-out; it was during this match that Borga sustained an ankle injury that not only kept him off the Royal Rumble card but also WrestleMania and eventually led to his leaving the WWF
WWF IC Champion Razor Ramon defeated Jeff Jarrett via disqualification when Shawn Michaels interfered (Jarrett's MSG debut)
WWF World Champion Yokozuna pinned Tatanka with the Bonzai Drop; after the bout, Tatanka sustained a second Bonzai Drop and was taken from ringside on a stretcher
The Quebecers defeated WWF Tag Team Champions Marty Jannetty & the 1-2-3 Kid at 21:24 to win the titles following the Tower of Quebec on the Kid after Johnny Polo interfered and caused the Kid to crotch himself on the top rope
Owen Hart won a 30-man Royal Rumble match at 1:10:06 by last eliminating Fatu; order of entry: Diesel (00:00), Mo (00:00), Bushwhacker Butch (2:25), the 1-2-3 Kid (4:20), Scott Steiner (6:47), Iron Mike Sharpe (8:26), Samu (10:42), Bob Backlund (12:25), Jeff Jarrett (14:35), Virgil (16:35), Bam Bam Bigelow (17:58), Randy Savage (20:45), Adam Bomb (23:03), Sgt. Slaughter (24:53), Crush (27:13), Mabel (29:22), Jim Powers (31:07), Bastion Booger (33:12), Bushwhacker Luke (35:16), Owen Hart, Rick Martel (39:18), Bret Hart (41:20), IRS (43:30), Johnny Polo (44:56), Scott Putski (46:53), Fatu (49:00), Marty Jannetty (51:02), Bart Gunn (53:22), Shawn Michaels (56:05), and Doink the Clown (57:18); order of elimination: Mo by Diesel (1:54), Butch by Diesel (3:16), the Kid by Diesel; during the elimination, the Kid sustained a leg injury that kept him sidelined for 2 months (5:53), Sharpe by Scott (8:46), Diesel by Savage after Diesel failed a boot to the face and landed across the ropes (21:18), Jarrett by Savage after ducking a clothesline (21:36), Bomb by Slaughter, Backlund, & Steiner (25:06), Scott by Crush (27:55), Savage by Crush (29:27), Bigelow by Crush (30:07), Slaughter by Crush after being thrown into the corner (30:43), Powers by Mabel after a splash in the corner (31:50), Mabel, Virgil, & Backlund by everyone else as they attempted to eliminate Mabel (33:47), Booger by Crush via a clothesline (34:26), Samu by Luke (35:32), Luke by Crush (36:16), Crush by Bret via a dropkick to the back (43:26), Jannetty by Michaels via a backdrop (57:14), Polo by Owen after knocking him off the top (58:08), Putski by Fatu via a backdrop (58:23), Martel by IRS via a backdrop (59:02), Bart by Doink via a clothesline (1:00:12), Doink by Michaels via a clothesline (1:00:29), IRS by Bret via an atomic drop (1:01:09), Bret by Michaels as Bret attempted to eliminate Fatu (1:02:55), Michaels after Owen hit a spinning heel kick to Fatu and Fatu collided with Michaels, knocking him over the top; Michaels was distracted by Razor Ramon on the floor which led to the elimination; after the elimination, Razor and Michaels brawled to the back (1:05:35); once the match was down to two, Samu returned ringside to help Fatu while Bret Hart came out to support Owen; Fatu by Owen after crotching him on the top and hitting a clothesline; after the bout, Bret and Owen fought off both Headshrinkers

WWF IC Champion Razor Ramon makes his entrance at MSG.

March 18-20, 1994: The WrestleMania X Fan Festival was held at the Rotunda at Madison Square Garden.

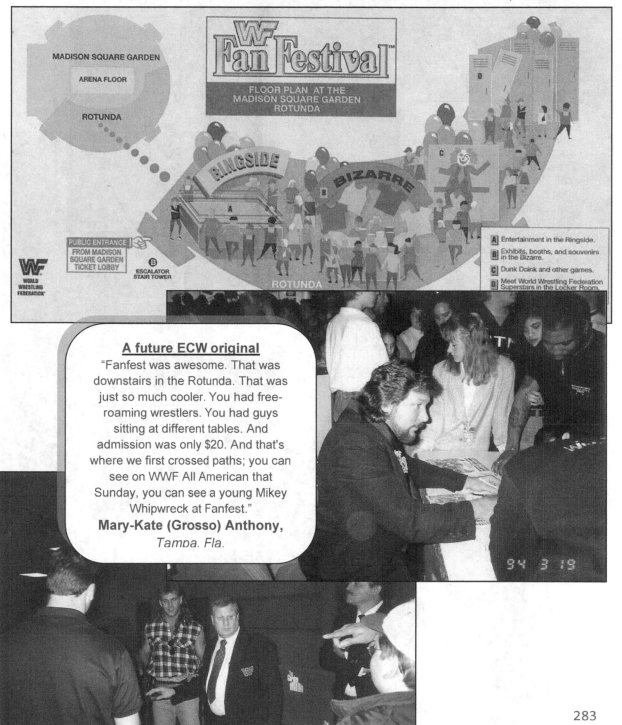

A future ECW original

"Fanfest was awesome. That was downstairs in the Rotunda. That was just so much cooler. You had free-roaming wrestlers. You had guys sitting at different tables. And admission was only $20. And that's where we first crossed paths; you can see on WWF All American that Sunday, you can see a young Mikey Whipwreck at Fanfest."

Mary-Kate (Grosso) Anthony,
Tampa, Fla.

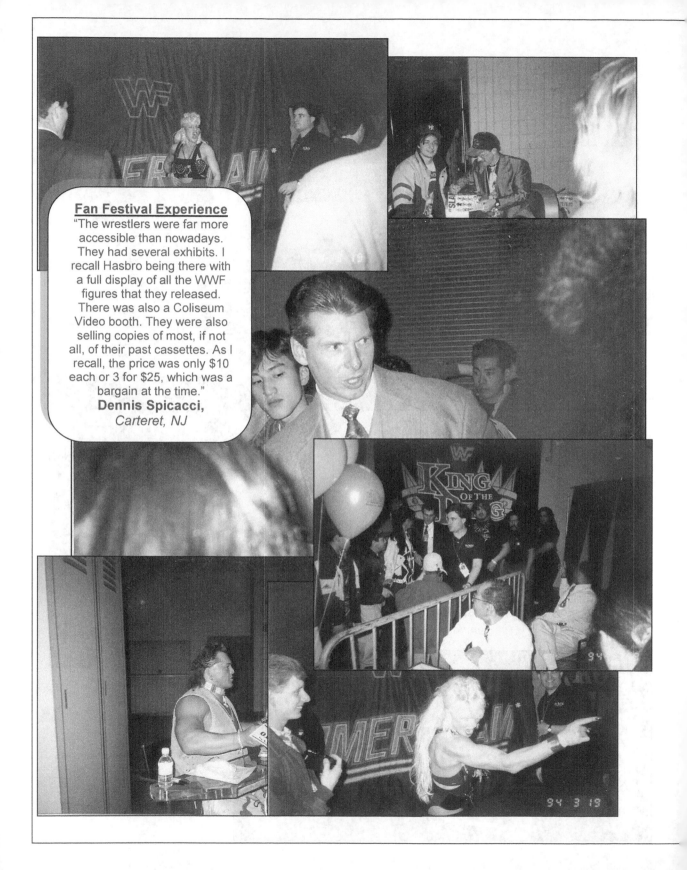

Fan Festival Experience
"The wrestlers were far more accessible than nowadays. They had several exhibits. I recall Hasbro being there with a full display of all the WWF figures that they released. There was also a Coliseum Video booth. They were also selling copies of most, if not all, of their past cassettes. As I recall, the price was only $10 each or 3 for $25, which was a bargain at the time."

Dennis Spicacci,
Carteret, NJ

WRESTLEMANIA X
Madison Square Garden – March 20, 1994

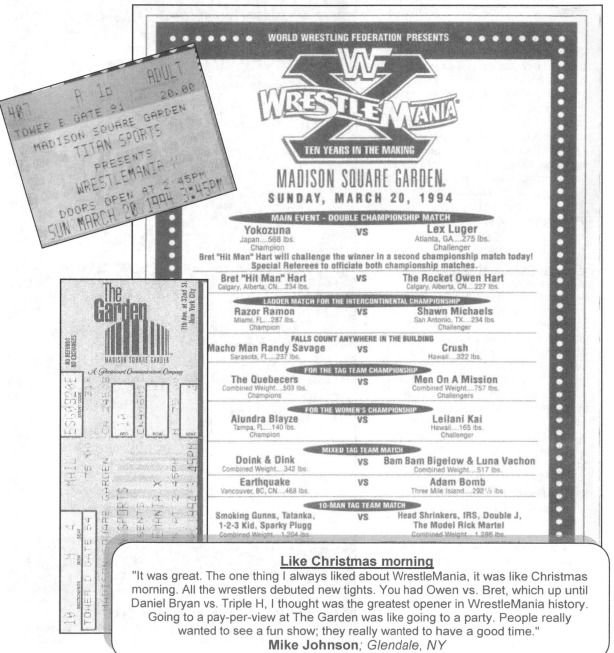

WORLD WRESTLING FEDERATION PRESENTS

WWF WRESTLEMANIA X
TEN YEARS IN THE MAKING

MADISON SQUARE GARDEN.
SUNDAY, MARCH 20, 1994

MAIN EVENT - DOUBLE CHAMPIONSHIP MATCH

Yokozuna	VS	Lex Luger
Japan....568 lbs. Champion		Atlanta, GA....275 lbs. Challenger

Bret "Hit Man" Hart will challenge the winner in a second championship match today!
Special Referees to officiate both championship matches.

Bret "Hit Man" Hart	VS	The Rocket Owen Hart
Calgary, Alberta, CN....234 lbs.		Calgary, Alberta, CN....227 lbs.

LADDER MATCH FOR THE INTERCONTINENTAL CHAMPIONSHIP

Razor Ramon	VS	Shawn Michaels
Miami, FL....287 lbs. Champion		San Antonio, TX....234 lbs. Challenger

FALLS COUNT ANYWHERE IN THE BUILDING

Macho Man Randy Savage	VS	Crush
Sarasota, FL....237 lbs.		Hawaii....322 lbs.

FOR THE TAG TEAM CHAMPIONSHIP

The Quebecers	VS	Men On A Mission
Combined Weight....503 lbs. Champions		Combined Weight....757 lbs. Challengers

FOR THE WOMEN'S CHAMPIONSHIP

Alundra Blayze	VS	Leilani Kai
Tampa, FL....140 lbs. Champion		Hawaii....165 lbs. Challenger

MIXED TAG TEAM MATCH

Doink & Dink	VS	Bam Bam Bigelow & Luna Vachon
Combined Weight....342 lbs.		Combined Weight....517 lbs.

Earthquake	VS	Adam Bomb
Vancouver, BC, CN....468 lbs.		Three Mile Island....292½ lbs.

10-MAN TAG TEAM MATCH

Smoking Gunns, Tatanka, 1-2-3 Kid, Sparky Plugg	VS	Head Shrinkers, IRS, Double J, The Model Rick Martel
Combined Weight....1,204 lbs.		Combined Weight....1,286 lbs.

Like Christmas morning

"It was great. The one thing I always liked about WrestleMania, it was like Christmas morning. All the wrestlers debuted new tights. You had Owen vs. Bret, which up until Daniel Bryan vs. Triple H, I thought was the greatest opener in WrestleMania history. Going to a pay-per-view at The Garden was like going to a party. People really wanted to see a fun show; they really wanted to have a good time."
Mike Johnson; *Glendale, NY*

MSG on the big stage

"I think everybody has that expectation of the Garden. And when you see it you go, 'OK, it's kinda cool.' And then you walk in, and take the elevator to where the dressing rooms are. We had to park across the street. Everything in New York is kinda dirty and small, it seemed to me. It's not that (the Garden) wasn't impressive, but it wasn't as shiny and glittery as I thought it would be. It was more nuts and bolts. But it was still a cool atmosphere. They had pictures of Hulk Hogan and Elvis. And our first show was WrestleMania 10, that was pretty cool in itself, with the exception that we were (the dark match) against the Bushwhackers. ...We got there early in the morning, they had catering for us. We were there all day."

Tom Prichard,
TheHistoryofWWE.com interview, 2014

Giving notice at WrestleMania

"When you start talking about WrestleMania 10, it's the 640lb. double suplex. That was the first time Mabel ever left his feet. I enjoyed working with those guys, very very much. But it was a turning point in the relationship between me and Vince McMahon that night. We had been getting beat every night for months. And we were supposed to beat them. Pat Patterson comes up to us before the match and says, 'If you win this match tonight, if you beat them, who are you going to work with after?' That night, I gave my notice. I told Pat, 'No problem. We'll do that, no problem. Tell Vince to look into my bookings. Two months, three months, whatever it is. And after that, I'm finished.' He changed the plan and took away all our credibility by having us lose all the time. If you're in a winning situation most of the time, you have merchandise value. For six months, we were beat every night and we lost our value."

Jacques Rougeau,
TheHistoryofWWE.com interview, 2014

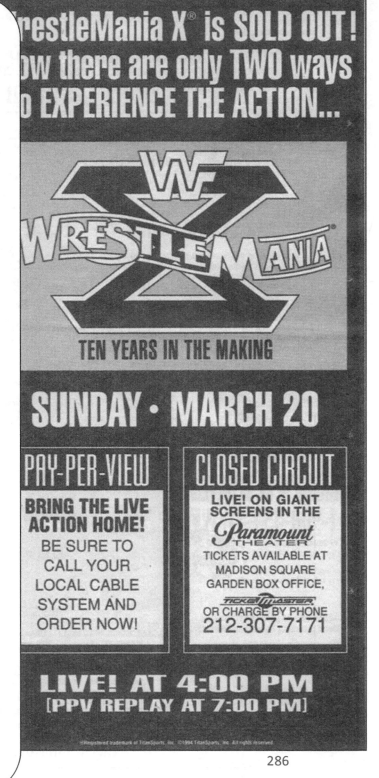

WrestleMania X® is SOLD OUT! Now there are only TWO ways to EXPERIENCE THE ACTION...

WWF WrestleMania X

TEN YEARS IN THE MAKING

SUNDAY · MARCH 20

PAY-PER-VIEW
BRING THE LIVE ACTION HOME!
BE SURE TO CALL YOUR LOCAL CABLE SYSTEM AND ORDER NOW!

CLOSED CIRCUIT
LIVE! ON GIANT SCREENS IN THE
Paramount THEATER
TICKETS AVAILABLE AT MADISON SQUARE GARDEN BOX OFFICE, *TICKETMASTER* OR CHARGE BY PHONE
212-307-7171

LIVE! AT 4:00 PM
[PPV REPLAY AT 7:00 PM]

®Registered trademark of TitanSports, Inc. ©1994 TitanSports, Inc. All rights reserved.

286

WrestleMania X - New York City, NY - Madison Square Garden - March 20, 1994 (18,065; sell out; 4,200 in Felt Forum)

Countdown show - hosted by Todd Pettengill and Johnny Polo; featured Pettengill in the Paramount speaking with Jeff Jarrett; included a video package promoting Little Richard's appearance; featured Polo outside Jeannie Garth's dressing room before showing a video package promoting the Randy Savage vs. Crush match; included Polo outside of Rhonda Shear's dressing room, mocking that Tony Garea and Mike Chioda were shown walking out of the room; Polo then showed Tom Prichard & Jimmy Del Ray preparing to go out for their match and then walking through the tunnel; moments later, Polo reported live from ringside during the Bushwhackers vs. Prichard & Del Ray match; featured a video package hyping the WWF IC Champion Razor Ramon vs. Shawn Michaels ladder match; included Polo conducting a backstage interview with Diesel about the Razor vs. Michaels match; featured a pretaped WrestleMania rap video from Men on a Mission; moments later, Jerry Lawler was introduced to the crowd, with Pettengill interviewing Lawler at ringside about his return and Lawler saying he couldn't wait to see Bret Hart be humiliated; Lawler then joined McMahon at the commentary table (Lawler's surprise return after a 4-month absence); Pettengill then got in the ring, took a video camera from a cameraman and filmed the crowd himself during the final moments of the countdown show:

Tom Prichard & Jimmy Del Ray (w/ Jim Cornette) defeated the Bushwhackers at 5:39 when Del Ray pinned Butch after Prichard hit a knee drop to the back of the head, moments after Del Ray sustained the battering ram and was covered (Prichard, Del Ray, & Cornette's MSG debut)

Pay-per-view bouts - featured an opening in-ring introduction by Vince McMahon in which he welcomed the fans to WrestleMania and then introduced Little Richard, who performed "America, the Beautiful;" included McMahon & Jerry Lawler on commentary; featured a WrestleMania Moment focusing on the WrestleMania II battle royal; included an in-ring segment, following the opening match, in which Bill Dunn introduced Hair Club for Men President Sy Sperling, who then introduced Howard Finkel, with a full head of hair; featured a segment in which "Bill Clinton" was shown in the crowd, with IRS and WWF President Jack Tunney sitting beside him; included Todd Pettengill conducting an interview with "Clinton" in the crowd about how he was enjoying the show; moments later, IRS shook "Clinton's" hand and congratulated him for raising taxes; featured a video package recapping the weekend's Fanfest activities; included Savage going into the Paramount to celebrate his victory; featured a WrestleMania Moment focusing on Savage's WWF World Title tournament win at WrestleMania IV; included a WrestleMania Moment focusing on Roddy Piper using a fire extinguisher on Morton Downey Jr.; featured a WrestleMania Moment focusing on the Ultimate Warrior vs. Hulk Hogan match at WrestleMania VI; the Smoking Gunns, Tatanka, Sparky Plugg, & the 1-2-3 Kid vs. Headshrinkers, IRS, Jeff Jarrett, & Rick Martel did not take place due to time constraints; featured Gorilla Monsoon & Chet Coppock on commentary for Radio WWF (the last pay-per-view to be broadcast on radio):

Owen Hart pinned Bret Hart by blocking an attempted victory roll at 20:21; after the bout, Todd Pettengill conducted a backstage interview with Owen regarding his victory, with Owen bragging that he was now the best there is, the best there was, and the best there ever will be; Owen went on to say Bret had no chance in his WWF World Title match later in the show; Bill Dunn was the ring announcer for the bout (*1994 Year in Review, The Bret Hart Story: The Best There Is, Was, and Ever Will Be, Greatest Wrestling Stars of the 90s*)

Bam Bam Bigelow & Luna Vachon defeated Doink & Dink the Clown at 6:11 when Bigelow pinned Doink with several headbutts and the headbutt off the top after Doink failed a back suplex attempt and Bigelow landed on top; after the bout, Luna attacked Dink and slammed him, with Doink eventually clearing Luna from the ring after tripping up Bigelow (*1994 Year in Review*)

Randy Savage defeated Crush (w/ Mr. Fuji) in a falls count anywhere match at 9:44; fall #1: Crush pinned Savage at the 46-second mark after dropping Savage with a press slam onto the ringside barricade; after the fall, Fuji struck Savage with the Japanese flag pole; fall #2: Savage pinned Crush at 4:31 after hitting the flying elbowsmash and then pushing Crush out to the floor so he could pin him there; fall #3: Savage pinned Crush at 8:09 after assaulting Crush backstage and ramming his head into a door; after the fall, Savage tied Crush upside down before then returning to the ring and assaulting Fuji; stipulations stated the loser of the fall would have to get back into the ring within 60 seconds or the match would end (*1994 Year in Review, Falls Count Anywhere: The Greatest Street Fights and other Out of Control Matches*)

WWF Women's Champion Alundra Blayze pinned Lelani Kai with the German suplex into a bridge at 3:26; after the bout, the Fabulous Moolah, Mae Young, Nikolai Volkoff, Capt. Lou Albano, and Freddie Blassie were shown sitting in the crowd (Kai's MSG return after a 6-year absence) (*1994 Year in Review*)

Men on a Mission (w/ Oscar) defeated WWF Tag Team Champions the Quebecers (w/ Johnny Polo) via count-out at 7:43 after Pierre sustained a bulldog / splash double team outside the ring; prior to the Quebecers' entrance, Todd Pettingill conducted a backstage interview with Rhonda Shear, of USA Up All Night; moments later, Shawn Michaels walked in for a photo with Rhonda, with Burt Reynolds then walking in and running off Michaels; the champions used an instrumental version of "Oh Canada" instead of their "We're Not the Mounties" theme song for their entrance; after the match, MOM celebrated with the title belts in the ring

WWF World Champion Yokozuna (w/ Jim Cornette & Mr. Fuji) defeated Lex Luger via disqualification when Luger pushed special referee Mr. Perfect, after Perfect was reluctant in making the count on the unconscious champion after Luger pulled both Cornette and Fuji into the ring and knocked them out; after the match, Luger and Perfect had a confrontation backstage; Donnie Wahlberg was the special ring announcer while Rhonda Shear was the special time keeper (Perfect's surprise return after a 5-month absence) (Cornette's MSG debut) (Luger's first appearance with new theme music) (*1994 Year in Review*)

Earthquake pinned Adam Bomb (w/ Harvey Wippleman) with a powerslam and the sit-down splash

WWF IC Champion Razor Ramon defeated Shawn Michaels in a ladder match at 18:49 after Michaels had his foot and later his arm entangled in the ring ropes; Diesel was in the challenger's corner for the early moments of the bout but was sent backstage after attacking Razor on the floor; (voted Match of the Year by the Wrestling Observer Newsletter, Pro Wrestling Illustrated, and Pro Wrestling Torch) (the first televised WWF ladder match) (*1994 Year in Review, Razor Ramon, Most Unbelievable Matches, Shawn Michaels: From the Vault, History of the Intercontinental Championship, The True Story of WrestleMania, Ladder Match 2: Crash & Burn*)

Bret Hart pinned WWF World Champion Yokozuna (w/ Jim Cornette & Mr. Fuji) to win the title at 10:33 after the champion lost his balance while attempting the Bonzai Drop; mid-way through the match, Piper knocked out Cornette with a punch after Cornette tried to interfere; after the match, Yokozuna chased surprise guest referee Roddy Piper backstage while Hart was congratulated by Lex Luger, WWF IC Champion Razor Ramon, Sparky Plugg, Tatanka, Piper, Randy Savage, the 1-2-3 Kid, Burt Rynolds, Rhonda Shear, Donny Whalberg, Pat Patterson, Gorilla Monsoon, and Vince McMahon; before the show went off the air, Owen Hart came ringside and stared at his brother inside the ring; Rynolds was the special guest ring announcer while Jeanie Garth was the special time keeper (Piper's surprise return after a 2-year absence) (*Bret "The Hitman" Hart, 1994 Year in Review, The Greatest Superstars of WrestleMania*)

'It was win-win'

"I was sitting upstairs a bit but the atmosphere was awesome. Owen vs. Bret still holds up today as one of my favorite WrestleMania matches of all time. The Ironman match is awesome but that match just symbolized so much to me. I loved them both, and to see Owen win was awesome. And then Bret wins the title, so it was win-win."
Mary-Kate (Grosso) Anthony, *Tampa, Fla.*

Witnessing history

"I personally loved the Bret Hart-Owen Hart match that opened the show. Owen, one of the nicest guys you'd ever meet. The middle was so-so. The main event with Bret and Yoko, the ending was really good. I was happy that Bret Hart won the belt. The ladder match, if it's on a DVD, I'm watching. I'm not skipping over it. Heel Shawn Michaels back then? Forget it. He's great."
Charile Adorno, *Brooklyn, NY*

The crowning

"This capacity crowd has come to Madison Square Garden. They have witnessed WrestleMania 10. They have seen a new World Wrestling Federation Champion crowned. They have witnessed, ladies and gentlemen, a brand new era. They are witnesses to the blastoff of the next decade in the World Wrestling Federation. ...Somehow, 'The Hitman' Bret Hart has done it. Unquestionably, fate on the side of Bret 'The HItman' Hart. ...He's done it. Somehow, he's done the impossible"
Vince McMahon, *WrestleMania X*

Double duty

"(Owen) was so excited, so happy. And for him, that was finally his breakthrough moment. ...He got that chance that he long deserved and finally got to show everybody that he was a real good talent. I think we surprised everybody, including my parents, as to how good it was. ...The thing I remember most about WrestleMania X and winning the title from Yoko was the moment after, when all the wrestlers came to the ring and hoisted me up on their shoulders.
I think that was all very spontaneous."
Bret Hart, *WrestleMania Rewind*, WWE Network

WWF @ New York City, NY - Madison Square Garden - May 20, 1994 (matinee)
Annual Mayor's Benefit Show - tickets were free and the card was held for handicapped children
Doink the Clown defeated Johnny Polo
WWF Tag Team Champion Samu defeated Jacques Rougeau
Jeff Jarrett defeated Sparky Plugg (Sparky Plugg's MSG debut)
WWF Tag Team Champion Fatu defeated Quebecer Pierre
Mabel defeated Kwang (Kwang's MSG debut)

The Fink vs. Harvey
"That was a lot of fun. Howard is one of my dearest friends in the business and we had a blast."
Harvey Wippleman, *The Place to Be Nation, 2013*

WWF @ New York City, NY - Madison Square Garden - May 20, 1994 (15,000)
Kwang pinned Sparky Plugg
WWF Woman's Champion Alundra Blayze pinned Luna Vachon with a roll up after sending Luna into Bam Bam Bigelow on the apron
WWF Tag Team Champions the Headshrinkers & Afa defeated the Quebecers & Johnny Polo
Bam Bam Bigelow pinned Mabel with the flying headbutt
Jeff Jarrett pinned Doink the Clown
Howard Finkel defeated Harvey Wippleman in a tuxedo match; Finkel came out to Hulk Hogan's "Real American" theme song
Razor Ramon fought WWF IC Champion Diesel to a double count-out
Lex Luger pinned Crush with the running forearm at 16:53 after Crush tried to hit Luger with a steel chair
WWF Champion Bret Hart pinned Owen Hart with a roll over at 25:00

On the heels of their classic at WrestleMania X, Owen Hart and Bret Hart would continue to square off at MSG events through 1994 and 1995.

WWF @ New York City, NY - Madison Square Garden - August 25, 1994 (4,300)
Sparky Plugg defeated Quebecer Pierre
Adam Bomb pinned Kwang with a series of clotheslines and a DDT at 9:53
The Heavenly Bodies defeated the Bushwhackers at 11:33; prior to the bout, the Bushwhackers were escorted to the ring by a fan
WWF Women's Champion Alundra Blayze pinned Bull Nakano (w/ Luna Vachon) with a German suplex into a bridge at 8:15 after avoiding a clothesline; Nakano used Kamala's theme song for her ring entrance; after the bout, Luna accidentally clotheslined Nakano when the champion moved out of the way
Shawn Michaels & WWF IC Champion Diesel defeated WWF Tag Team Champions the Headshrinkers via disqualification at 18:04 when Fatu assaulted both challengers with one of the title belts after Michaels brought the belt into the ring as the referee was knocked out
Jeff Jarrett & Bam Bam Bigelow defeated Mabel & Doink the Clown at 5:42 when Bigelow pinned Mabel with a clothesline after Jarrett made a blind tag
IRS defeated Tatanka in a strap match at 7:39 when Tatanka knocked IRS into the fourth and final corner
WWF World Champion Bret Hart & Razor Ramon defeated Owen Hart & Jim Neidhart at 15:14 when Bret pinned Owen after Neidhart shoved Bret as the champion had Owen in a bodyslam position with Owen falling on top and the momentum putting Bret on top

WWF @ New York City, NY - Madison Square Garden - October 29, 1994 (9,646)
Adam Bomb defeated Bam Bam Bigelow via disqualification
Jim Powers defeated Abe Schwartz
Jerry Lawler & Queezy defeated Doink & Dink the Clown
IRS defeated Duke Drose
WWF World Champion Bret Hart defeated Jim Neidhart via submission with the Sharpshooter at 8:31 after avoiding a splash off the top
Billy Gunn defeated Tom Prichard
Lex Luger fought Tatanka to a double count-out at 12:36 when both men began fighting on the floor; prior to the match, Tatanka cut an in-ring promo on the fans and Luger; after the bout, Luger took the mic and challenged Tatanka to get back in the ring with him; when Tatanka did, Luger hit the powerslam and then put Tatanka in the Torture Rack until referees intervened
The Undertaker defeated Yokozuna in a casket match at around the 12-minute mark after a flying clothesline and chokeslam; IRS was in Yokozuna's corner but was ejected from ringside mid-way through after closing the casket as Taker attempted to roll Yoko inside

WCW @ New York City, NY - Madison Square Garden - November 26, 1994
Cancelled; the show was initially scheduled to feature WCW World Champion Hulk Hogan vs. Ric Flair

Balancing MSG and the ECW Arena
"Once I started going to ECW, it was harder to balance the two. 'This is awesome (ECW). This is kid's stuff now (WWF).' But I still wanted to see everybody."
Mary-Kate (Grosso) Anthony, *Tampa, Fla.*

WWF @ New York City, NY - Madison Square Garden - November 26, 1994 (7,300)
Included a segment in which Howard Finkel introduced the new WWF World Champion Bob Backlund to the ring; Backlund stood in the ring for several minutes without speaking as the crowd booed, with Backlund eventually turning to leave before taking the mic and cutting a promo on the crowd; featured an announcement by Finkel that Bret Hart would not appear as scheduled later in the show but would return Jan. 16, 1995; he went on to say, despite Backlund's protest, he would face Diesel in a non-title match later in the show; moments later, an official came ringside and corrected Finkel that the title would be on the line, prompting Backlund to confront Finkel and protest before returning backstage; included an in-ring promo by Diesel on his title win earlier in the show
The Bushwhackers defeated Well Dunn
Aldo Montoya pinned Kwang at 7:03 with a hurricanrana into a roll up (Montoya's MSG debut)
WWF IC Champion Razor Ramon pinned Jeff Jarrett with the Razor's Edge at 20:13 after blocking a backdrop attempt; prior to the bout, Jarrett cut an in-ring promo; Jarrett initially won the match via count-out at 16:23 after sending Razor into the ringpost as the two fought on the floor; after the decision was announced, Jarrett took the mic and said he came to win the belt and wouldn't let Razor sneak out of getting beat for it, then challenging the champion to continue the bout
Mabel pinned Quebecer Pierre with a crossbody from the middle turnbuckle at 10:01
Action Zone - 11/27/94: Diesel (sub. for Bret Hart) pinned WWF World Champion Bob Backlund in a No DQ, no count-out, no time-limit match to win the title at the 9-second mark following a boot to the midsection and a powerbomb; Diesel's involvement in the match was not announced until *WWF Superstars* aired that morning; it was announced on local TV during the Nov. 5-6 weekend that Randy Savage would be the guest referee for the originally scheduled Hart vs. Backlund match but that announcement was never mentioned again
The New Headshrinkers defeated the Executioners (sub. for Shawn Michaels & Diesel) at 12:43 when Fatu scored the pin with one foot after hitting the splash off the top; a fan was the guest ring announcer for the match (the Barbarian's MSG return after a 3-year absence)
Davey Boy Smith fought King Kong Bundy to a double count-out at 6:53, moments after Smith hit the powerslam on Bundy as the two fought on the floor (Bundy's MSG return after a nearly 7-year absence)
The Undertaker pinned IRS with the tombstone at 8:06 after catching IRS in mid-air

Going backstage

"I was home from college for winter break, so what better way to take it easy and relive my childhood then heading to The Garden to catch some action. The times, they certainly had changed. It was 1995 and business was down. My best friend and I were able to get pretty decent seats ringside for face value. The upper deck was all but empty. We sat behind an older gentleman with a bushy blond mustache, and his wife, who looked as out of place at Madison Square Garden as Hulk Hogan would look sitting in a classroom of kindergarteners. The man turned to us a few matches into the card and asked if we liked "rasslin." Um, I was certainly not here to scope out any chicks.

We told him yes, we've been fans for years and we noted this was the closest we ever sat to ringside. He said that it was a good thing, because he could take us backstage. He claimed to be Jeff Jarrett's brother. I did not believe him; I smiled and said, "Umm, OK." Every match would end, and I would wait, but nothing. Finally, an hour or so later, he turns to us and says to follow him. We walk down the railing to the side of The Garden and proceed to the backstage area right behind the side of the "gorilla position." My friend and I were in awe. There was Billy Gunn, one of the Smoking Gunns talking on a pay phone! And he was wearing his cowboy hat and chaps! Finally, Jeff Jarrett came over and introduced himself to us. After years of watching this stuff, even following Smoky Mountain, USWA and knowing Double J from these promotions, we had absolutely nothing to say other than a soft "Hi" back. And that was that. We went back up to our seats and our chance to interact and talk with the superstars was over as quick as King Kong Bundy defeating SD Jones."

Mike Goldberg, *Brooklyn, NY*

WWF @ New York City, NY - Madison Square Garden - January 16, 1995 (7,500; 5,400 paid)
Included Jeff Jarrett as a guest of Shawn Michaels' 'Heartbreak Hotel'
Aldo Montoya pinned Steven Dunn
Duke Drose (w/ Dick Murdoch) defeated Timothy Well (w/ Steven Dunn); prior to the match, Murdoch cut an in-ring promo about being in MSG and his plans to win the Royal Rumble; moments later, Well insulted him; after the contest, Murdoch beat up both Well & Dunn
Henry Godwinn pinned Bob Holly
WWF Women's Champion Bull Nakano pinned Alundra Blayze with the legdrop off the top
The Undertaker pinned Tatanka with the tombstone; after the bout, King Kong Bundy and Bam Bam Bigelow attacked Taker
Bret Hart defeated Owen Hart in a no holds barred match via submission to the Sharpshooter; after the bout, Bret kept the hold applied until several referees came out to pull him off; after releasing the hold, Bret then briefly reapplied it
Lex Luger & Davey Boy Smith defeated King Kong Bundy & Bam Bam Bigelow via disqualification
WWF World Champion Diesel pinned Jeff Jarrett (sub. for Bob Backlund) (w/ Shawn Michaels) with the powerbomb; after the bout, Michaels hit the superkick on Diesel, threw the world title belt down on him and spat at him

WWF @ New York City, NY - Madison Square Garden - March 19, 1995 (matinee) (15,000; 10,000 paid)
Included an in-ring segment in which Bam Bam Bigelow was interviewed by Todd McDonald for Sports Extra on FOX Channel 5 regarding his upcoming WrestleMania match against Lawrence Taylor
Erik Watts & Chad Fortune defeated Jimmy Del Ray & Tom Prichard when Watts pinned Prichard
Henry Godwinn pinned Barry Horowitz
WWF Tag Team Champions the Smoking Gunns defeated Tatanka & Kama (sub. for IRS) when Bart pinned Tatanka after Kama was knocked to the floor
Bob Backlund defeated Adam Bomb in an I Quit match with the Crossface Chicken Wing
WWF World Champion Diesel & Razor Ramon defeated Shawn Michaels & WWF IC Champion Jeff Jarrett via disqualification the 17-minute mark when Psycho Sid interfered; during the bout, the Roadie clipped Razor, forcing Diesel to continue the match alone; moments later, Jarrett & Michaels were counted-out, with Michaels then facing Diesel in a singles match; after the bout, the Undertaker made the save for Diesel against Michaels and Sid
The Undertaker defeated Bam Bam Bigelow via count-out when Bigelow left ringside
Hakushi pinned the 1-2-3 Kid with a headbutt off the top; Kid sustained a concussion days earlier
Bret Hart & Davey Boy Smith defeated Owen Hart & Jerry Lawler when Smith pinned Lawler with the powerslam

06   A   12   ADULT
SECTION/BOX   ROW   SEAT
OWER A GATE 71   20.00
MADISON SQUARE GARDEN
TITAN SPORTS. INC.
PRESENTS
W W F
DATE SUBJECT TO CHANGE
SAT JUN 10, 1995 8:00PM

Psycho Sid battles Shawn Michaels inside a steel cage. The following year, the two would return to MSG to battle for the world title.

WWF @ New York City, NY - Madison Square Garden - June 10, 1995 (8,340)

Included an in-ring promo by WWF IC Champion Jeff Jarrett in which he said Razor Ramon was too injured to compete in a scheduled tag team match and Jarrett would beat Adam Bomb later in the show; featured an in-ring promo by Savio Vega, in Spanish, in which he talked about his and Razor's feud with Jarrett & the Roadie; included an in-ring promo by Ted DiBiase in which he challenged WWF World Champion Diesel & Shawn Michaels to face Psycho Sid & Tatanka at the Aug. 12 MSG return; Robin Leach was in attendance for the show

Skip pinned Aldo Montoya with a Frankensteiner off the top

Men on a Mission defeated the Smoking Gunns when Mabel pinned Bart with a belly to belly suplex

Jean Pierre Lafitte defeated Doink the Clown with the cannonball off the top

Adam Bomb defeated WWF IC Champion Jeff Jarrett via count-out after Jarrett was knocked to the floor; earlier in the match, Jarrett attempted to walk out of the match but was blocked by Savio Vega, who threw him back into the ring

Hearst Helmsley pinned Duke Drose at the 7-minute mark with the Pedigree (Helmsley's MSG debut)

Shawn Michaels (sub. for an injured WWF World Champion Diesel) defeated Psycho Sid in a steel cage match by escaping over the cage after sending Sid face-first into the cage; immediately after Michaels escaped, Tatanka attacked in at ringside and then put him back in the cage where he and Sid double teamed Michaels after Ted DiBiase locked the cage door; Sid then dropped Michaels with the powerbomb until Aldo Montoya, Savio Vega, and Billy Gunn ran out to try to open the door; Bam Bam Bigelow then scaled the cage and helped clear the ring before the four tended to Michaels

Man Mountain Rock pinned Bob Backlund at the 8-minute mark with a roll up as Backlund argued with ringside fans; after the match, Backlund applied the Crossface Chicken Wing on Rock

Savio Vega pinned WWF Tag Team Champion Owen Hart (w/ WWF Tag Team Champion Yokozuna) with a roll up after throwing Hart into the corner; the match was originally scheduled for Vega & Razor Ramon vs. Hart & Yokozuna; prior to the bout, Hart and Yokozuna flipped a coin to see which would face Vega; after the contest, Vega fought off an interfering Yokozuna before escaping the ring

Tatanka pinned Bam Bam Bigelow after, as the referee was knocked down, Ted DiBiase shoved Bigelow off the top as Bigelow attempted the moonsault

Amateur photographer

"The lot crew, that was a whole other crew that I would hang out with outside. I would bring a backpack on wheels filled with photo albums, my photos, if people wanted to buy my pictures and get signatures. There would be times i would leave with $300-400 in cash."

Mary-Kate (Grosso) Anthony, *Tampa, Fla.*

WWF @ New York City, NY - Madison Square Garden - August 12, 1995 (8,800)
Included the announcement of the following matches for the Oct. 6 return: Bret Hart (w/ George Steele) vs. Isaac Yankem DDS (w/ Jerry Lawler), WWF Women's Champion Alundra Blayze vs. Bertha Faye, the Undertaker vs. King Mabel, and a WWF World Title match; Bill Watts attended the show as a ticketholder, without knowledge of WWF management, and reportedly took notes and asked questions of fans around him
Skip pinned Bob Holly when the momentum of a flying bodypress by Holly put Skip on top
Fatu pinned King Kong Bundy with a bodyslam after Bundy missed a charge
Henry Godwinn pinned Adam Bomb at the 15-second mark with the Slop Drop
Jacob & Eli Blu defeated Lex Luger & Davey Boy Smith when Luger was pinned after Smith walked out of the match; prior to the bout, Smith took the mic and told the fans not to chant USA because it offended him
Savio Vega pinned Rad Radford (sub. for IRS) with a spin wheel kick
WWF World Champion Diesel & WWF IC Champion Shawn Michaels defeated Men on a Mission when Diesel pinned Sir Mo with a boot to the face; prior to In Your House 2, the bout was set for Diesel & Micheals vs. Psycho Sid & Jeff Jarrett; prior to that show, it was Sid & Tatanka; after the match, Davey Boy Smith and Razor Ramon made the save for the champions
Razor Ramon defeated Psycho Sid via disqualification when Ted DiBiase interfered as Sid was set up for the Razor's Edge
Hunter Hearst Helmsley pinned the 1-2-3 Kid with the Pedigree
Tatanka defeated Bam Bam Bigelow in an Indian strap match
Bret Hart pinned Jean-Pierre Lafitte by kicking off the turnbuckle while caught in a sleeper

WWF @ New York City, NY - Madison Square Garden - October 6, 1995 (9,000; 7,900 paid)
Benefit Show for the handicapped and underpriviledged; included a segment in which powerlifter Mark Henry was introduced to the crowd, with Skip & Sunny interrupting him, with Sunny claiming any of the fat, out of shape New Yorkers in attendance could make it to the Olympics; Skip then said he was tired of being treated like trash and tried pushing Henry, leading to Henry shoving him across the ring; Henry then cornered Sunny before she escaped the ring and ran backstage with Skip (Henry's MSG debut)
Hakushi pinned Skip at 9:09 with a hurricanrana into a roll up after knocking Skip into Sunny, who was on the ring apron, with a dropkick; prior to the match, Sunny cut an in-ring promo
Barry Horowitz pinned Sir Mo at 7:34 with a roll over after Mo collided with an interfering Skip on the apron; Skip & Sunny appeared ringside at the 3-minute mark
WWF Women's Champion Bertha Faye pinned Alundra Blayze at 7:26 with the sit-down powerbomb after pushing the challenger off the middle turnbuckle
The 1-2-3 Kid pinned Bob Backlund with an inside cradle at 11:24; prior to the bout, Backlund took the mic and told the fans to be responsible for their actions and he was looking forward to controlling their lives; after the bout, Backlund applied the Crossface Chicken Wing on the Kid; after the decision was announced, Backlund applied the hold on the ring announcer, with Howard Finkel, in street clothes, then taking over announcing duties for the remainder of the show; Savio Vega eventually ran out to make the save
Savio Vega pinned Kama with a spin wheel kick at 8:20; after the match, Kama attacked Vega before Vega sent him to the floor; Kama then again attacked Vega leading to Vega again sending him to the floor
WWF Tag Team Champions the Smoking Gunns defeated Jacob & Eli Blu at 8:37 when Billy Gunn scored the pinfall after hitting the Sidewinder
Bret Hart (w/ George Steele) defeated Isaac Yankem DDS (w/ Jerry Lawler) via submission with the Sharpshooter at 10:07; prior to the match, Lawler cut an in-ring promo on NYC; after the contest, Hart fought off Lawler and knocked Yankem to the floor, with Steele then biting Yankem; after the bout, Steele threw referee Earl Hebner out of the way to destroy a turnbuckle pad (Yankem's MSG debut)
WWF IC Champion Shawn Michaels defeated Davey Boy Smith via disqualification at around the 17-minute mark when Jim Cornette hit the champion in the back with his tennis raquet as Michaels punched Smith in the corner; Smith then immediately hit the running powerslam on Michaels and held up the IC title with Cornette as Michaels was announced the winner
The Undertaker pinned King Mabel with the chokeslam at 11:18; after the match, Taker dropped Sir Mo with the chokeslam as well

Davey Boy Smith
"I don't know who's more stupid, Big Daddy Cool Diesel or all those people in New York City. I beat Bret Hart (at the Meadowlands), Diesel, so what does that tell you and all those morons in New York City?"

Paul Bearer
"Oh yes, tonight. Madison Square Garden. The most historical arena in the world. My Undertaker, Bret Hart, for the WWF Championship."

The Undertaker
"Your quest to be the best, Bret Hart, has led you right into the dragon's layer. You must come face-to-face with the reaper. For a championship? I don't think so. For your soul? Possibly. To find out who's the best, for sure. Tonight, Bret Hart, you come face-to-face with all that you fear."

WWF World Champion Bret Hart
"Redemption, the greatest of all human qualities. You know, I've been champion for all of a week and it doesn't suit me that I'm going to walk into Madison Square Garden tonight and lose my championship belt to anybody, let alone the Undertaker. Undertaker, I've got nothing but infinite respect for you. But you're coming into my house, Madison Square Garden. And when you step into the ring with me, you're going to find out what everybody else already knows. That I'm the best there is, the best there was, and the best there ever will be. And you and Paul Bearer have no choice in it; you're going down."
Localized TV promos

WWF @ New York City, NY - Madison Square Garden - November 25, 1995 (7,400)
Included an in-ring segment in which Bob Backlund attempted to speak but then told the fans he would leave if they wouldn't be quiet, with Backlund eventually leaving when they got louder
Barry Horowitz, Hakushi, & Fatu defeated Skip, Isaac Yankem DDS, & Kama at 8:52 when Horowitz pinned Kama with a sunset flip and an assist superkick from Fatu behind the referee's back
Goldust pinned Bob Holly with the bulldog at 6:24; after the match, Goldust took the mic, stood on the middle turnbuckle, and cut a promo saying the fans would never forget the name of Goldust (Goldust's MSG debut; Dustin Rhodes' MSG return after a nearly 5-year absence)
Ahmed Johnson pinned Rad Radford with the Pearl River Plunge; after the match, Skip and Radford double teamed Johnson before he cleared them from the ring (Johnson's MSG debut)
The 1-2-3 Kid pinned Marty Jannetty with a kick to the back at 5:00 after Ted DiBiase distracted Jannetty from the floor; prior to the bout, DiBiase cut an in-ring promo mocking how poor the NYC fans were and, as he was in the Christmas spirit, he had some cash to give away; he then found a woman in the crowd to bark like a dog for $100 and found another to kiss his foot; after the match, Jannetty attacked the Kid and knocked him to the floor; Jannetty then confronted DiBiase before Psycho Sid ran out and dropped him with the powerbomb
Psycho Sid defeated WWF IC Champion Razor Ramon via count-out at 5:03 after, behind the referee's back, the 1-2-3 Kid ran ringside and threw the champion into the ringpost; after the bout, Ramon fought off the Kid, attacked Sid and hit Sid with the bulldog from the middle turnbuckle before he was attacked from the Kid; Razor was then triple teamed before sustaining the powerbomb from Sid
Hunter Hearst Helmsley pinned Henry Godwinn in a slop match at 12:53 with a roll over and grabbing onto the top rope with both hands for leverage; stipulations stated the loser would be slopped; after the match, Godwinn knocked Helsmley to the floor with a clothesline, grabbed his slop bucket, and chased Helmsley around ringside before eventually dumping the slop on him after he tripped and fell
Savio Vega pinned Isaac Yankem DDS (sub. for an injured Dean Douglas) with the spin kick at 6:11; prior to the bout, Douglas took the mic and said the New York State Athletic Commission wouldn't let him compete due to a slipped disc, then introduced Yankem as his replacement (Douglas' MSG return after more than 4 years; his last MSG appearance)
Davey Boy Smith defeated Diesel via disqualification at 4:51 when Diesel dropped Smith with Snake Eyes onto an exposed turnbuckle; after the bout, Diesel came back into the ring and twice dropped Smith with the powerbomb
WWF Tag Team Champions the Smoking Gunns defeated Owen Hart & Yokozuna at 9:03 when Billy Gunn pinned Hart with a roll up after Hart and Yoko collided
The Undertaker defeated WWF World Champion Bret Hart via disqualification at 22:17 when Diesel attacked the challenger as Taker had Hart up for the tombstone; after the match, Diesel and Undertaker squared off, with Hunter Hearst Helmsley, Owen Hart, and Yokozuna coming out and attacking the two; Diesel, Hart, and Undertaker eventually cleared them from the ring before Hart knocked Diesel to the floor with a clothesline and dove onto him outside the ring; other wrestlers then came out to hold Diesel back as Hart celebrated with the belt in the ring

WWF @ New York City, NY - Madison Square Garden - January 26, 1996 (15,000; 12,800 paid)
Included the announcement of the March 17 return main event - WWF World Champion Bret Hart & the Undertaker vs. Diesel & Shawn Michaels
Tatanka & Isaac Yankem DDS defeated Bob Holly & Fatu when Tatanka pinned Fatu with the Samoan Drop
Duke Drose (sub. for Razor Ramon) defeated the 1-2-3 Kid; after the bout, Drose put Kid in a trash can
Owen Hart pinned Hakushi with an enziguri
Ahmed Johnson pinned Jeff Jarrett with the Pearl River Plunge
Steve Austin defeated Henry Godwinn via submission with the Million $ Dream at 11:20 after a knee to the back when DiBiase distracted Godwinn from the apron (Austin's MSG debut)
The Undertaker pinned Yokozuna at 4:22 with a boot to the face after causing Yoko to collide with an interfering Owen Hart on the ring apron; Hart appeared ringside early in the match and interfered as referee Earl Hebner was knocked down; after the bout, Owen and Yoko argued, leading to Yoko shoving Hart to the mat and chasing him backstage
WWF Tag Team Champions Smoking Gunns defeated Skip & Zip when Billy pinned Zip with a sunset flip
Savio Vega defeated WWF IC Champion Goldust via count-out when the champion left ringside following the spin wheel kick
Shawn Michaels pinned Hunter Hearst Helmsley with the superkick after avoiding a Pedigree attempt; Michaels initially won the match via disqualification when Owen Hart interfered but Michaels took the mic and said he wanted the bout to continue
WWF World Champion Bret Hart defeated Diesel in a steel cage match at around the 13-minute mark by escaping the cage as Diesel attempted to leave through the door; after the bout, Diesel attacked Hart, threw him back in the cage, and attempted the powerbomb until the Undertaker's music began; Taker then confronted Diesel, leading to Hart jumping Diesel before Shawn Michaels ran out and leapt off the cage, leading to Hart and Michaels and Diesel and Taker having to be pulled apart by officials, as well as Hakushi, Henry Godwinn, WWF Tag Team Champions the Smoking Gunns, Ahmed Johnson, and others; Diesel eventually gave Hart the finger before returning backstage

Going during the down years

"It was awesome because you could buy a $12 ticket for the upper level and sit in the third row. As long as you quietly made your way around, you could make your way all the way down. At WrestleMania 10, we get there and go, 'These seats suck.' As Little Richard was singing his song, my buddy and I, we quietly made our way around the circle, then down to the next level. Then to the hard camera. We just went and sat at the end of the row and stayed there for the whole pay-per-view. If you were cute and smart and were slick, you could move around and get a great seat. The shows weren't great, but it was still going to see wrestling at The Garden with your friends. But, during the Attitude Era, if you didn't know someone or didn't buy a ticket right away, you weren't going to that show."
Mike Johnson*; Glendale, NY*

WORLD WRESTLING FEDERATION®

SUNDAY, MARCH 17, 1996
MADISON SQUARE GARDEN
NEW YORK, NY

TAG TEAM MATCH

BRET "HIT MAN" HART	VS	**DIESEL**
(FEDERATION CHAMPION)		**& SHAWN MICHAELS**
& UNDERTAKER		Combined Weight...544 lbs.
Combined Weight...562 lbs.		

RETURN BOUT: FOR THE INTERCONTINENTAL CHAMPIONSHIP...NO COUNT OUTS

GOLDUST	VS	**SAVIO VEGA**
Hollywood, CA...260 lbs.		South Bronx, NY...254 lbs.
(CHAMPION)		(CHALLENGER)

JAKE "THE SNAKE" ROBERTS	VS	**BRITISH BULLDOG**
& YOKOZUNA		**& OWEN HART**
Combined Weight...895 lbs.		Combined Weight...480 lbs.

JIM CORNETTE WILL BE HANDCUFFED TO GEORGE "THE ANIMAL" STEELE.

NO DISQUALIFICATION MATCH

DUKE "THE DUMPSTER" DROESE	VS	**HUNTER HEARST-HELMSLEY**
Mt. Trashmore, FL...305 lbs.		
		Greenwich, CT...246 lbs.

AHMED JOHNSON	VS	**1-2-3 KID**
Pearl River, MS...305 lbs.		Minneapolis, MN...214 lbs.

RETURN MATCH

THE GODWINNS	VS	**THE BODY DONNAS**
Combined Weight...573 lbs.		**SKIP & ZIP**
		Combined Weight...454 lbs.

BARRY HOROWITZ	VS	**STONE COLD STEVE AUSTIN**
St. Petersburg, FL...231 lbs		252 lbs.

ALDO MONTOYA	VS	**TATANKA**
PORTUGUESE MAN O" WAR		Pembroke, NC...252 lbs.
Luzoa, Portugal...225 lbs.		

PLUS ONE OTHER EXCITING BOUT FEATURING AVATAR VS. JUSTIN "HAWK" BRADSHAW.

Apply For Yours Today
CALL 1-800-440-0989

TUNE IN AND CATCH THE ACTION!
Saturdays 12:00 pm WNYW-TV Ch. 5 World Wrestling Federation Superstars™

WWF @ New York City, NY - Madison Square Garden - March 17, 1996 (17,000; sell out; 14,824 paid)
Matches advertised for the May 19 return included WWF world Champion Shawn Michaels vs. Diesel in a steel cage match, Razor Ramon vs. WWF IC Champion Goldust, Vader vs. Yokozuna, and Ahmed Johnson vs. Davey Boy Smith
Aldo Montoya pinned Isaac Yankem DDS with a small package
Justin Bradshaw pinned Avatar with the lariat
Henry & Phinneas Godwinn defeated Skip & Zip
Steve Austin defeated Barry Horowitz with the Million $ Dream
WWF World Champion Bret Hart & Undertaker defeated Diesel & Shawn Michaels via disqualification when Diesel hit the Undertaker with a steel chair as Taker had Michaels set up for the tombstone; Dok Hendrix was the guest ring announcer for the bout; after the match, Diesel hit Hart with the chair before doing the same to Michaels; moments later, as Michaels was helped from the ring, WWF TV cameras picked up him saying, "I'm going to kick his seven-foot ass"
Hunter Hearst Helmsley pinned Duke Drose in a No DQ match following the Pedigree onto a trash can lid
WWF IC Champion Goldust pinned Savio Vega after hitting him with the title belt; earlier in the match, Goldust attempted to walk out of the match but was threatened by the referee that he would lose the title if he did
Ahmed Johnson pinned the 1-2-3 Kid with the Pearl River Plunge
Jake Roberts & Yokozuna (w/ George Steele) defeated Davey Boy Smith & Owen Hart when Yoko pinned Hart after a DDT from Roberts and a legdrop; during the match, Jim Cornette was handcuffed to Steele at ringside for the duration of the bout; after the match, Steele ripped open one of the turnbuckles (Roberts' return to MSG after more than a 4-year absence)

The uptick in business
"It was getting better, but I think there was a change in the air. Razor (Ramon) was near his end and he got popped on the (drug) test. When we first got there, it was coming off the trial and the scandals and it was down. It started picking up. You had Shawn and Razor and Diesel. You could tell there was a change in the air because WCW was kicking ass."
Tom Prichard, *TheHistoryofWWE.com interview, 2014*

WWF @ New York City, NY - Madison Square Garden - May 19, 1996 (18,800; 16,564 paid; sell out)
The Bushwhackers defeated Marty Jannetty & Leif Cassidy (the Bushwhackers' last MSG match)
Savio Vega pinned Bob Backlund
Ahmed Johnson defeated Davey Boy Smith via disqualification at 10:34 when Owen Hart interfered and attacked Johnson as Johnson attempted the Pearl River Plunge; Hart and Smith briefly double teamed Johnson before Hart returned backstage, with Johnson then hitting the Pearl River Plunge on Smith and leaving the ring
Steve Austin pinned Jake Roberts at 13:54 with a clothesline and grabbing the tights for leverage after Ted DiBiase grabbed Roberts' foot from the floor; after the match, Austin punched Roberts before Roberts took Revelations out of his snake bag and cleared the ring (Roberts' MSG return after a 4-year absence)
The Ultimate Warrior pinned Owen Hart at 7:17 with two hands on his chest after landing three clotheslines and a flying shoulderblock (Warrior's MSG return after a 5-year absence)
Vader pinned Yokozuna at 7:02 after hitting him in the face and knee with Jim Cornette's tennis raquet behind the referee's back; after the bout, Vader hit the Vader Bomb on Yoko before leaving the ring
Henry & Phinneas Godwinn defeated WWF Tag Team Champions Skip & Zip to win the titles at 10:56 when Phinneas pinned Skip with a kick to the midsection and the Slop Drop after kissing Sunny on the ring apron; after the bout, the champions, Hillbilly Jim, Howard Finkel, and a young fan danced in the ring
Hunter Hearst Helmsley pinned Razor Ramon with the Pedigree moments after referee Tim White was knocked down as Ramon lifted Helmsley up for the Razor's Edge; after the bout, Ramon attempted to say goodbye to the fans but his mic was cut off (Scott Hall's last MSG match; his last WWE match for 6 years)
WWF World Champion Shawn Michaels defeated Diesel in a steel cage match at around the 20-minute mark by escaping out the door after hitting the challenger with a steel chair and following with the superkick; late in the bout, Davey Boy Smith briefly interfered and prevented the champion from escaping over the top; moments later, as Diesel was still knocked out and Michaels was posing with the title belt, Razor Ramon came out, hugged the champion and raised his hand; Michaels then revived Diesel and waved for someone else to join them in the ring; Hunter Hearst Helmsley then appeared and hugged Michaels before all four men embraced and held each others arm in the air (Kevin Nash's last MSG match for 7 years; his last WWE match for 6 years)

The Curtain Call

"Curtain Call was pretty awesome. I wasn't very Internet at that point, so I didn't know they were leaving. I had no idea. 'Oh this is nice, they're friends and they're doing this.'"
Mary-Kate (Grosso) Anthony, *Tampa, Fla.*

"I knew they were leaving. I was writing for the Wrestling Lariat. Hall went to take the house mic, the crowd was chanting 'You sold out.' And I sitting close enough that I could read his lips. He went, 'Say goodbye...' He was going to say 'Say goodbye to the Bad Guy.' They literally cut the mic on Scott Hall. And then, later on, Shawn kisses Diesel on the cheek like Sleeping Beauty. They're all hugging, everyone's clapping. Then Hunter comes out, and everyone's like, 'What the fuck?' Some people knew, but not the general populous. I remember being there, going 'Holy crap. I cannot believe this happened.'"
Mike Johnson*; Glendale, NY*

"I was in attendance for the most memorable night in all of Madison Square Garden history – the infamous curtain call. And it pains me to this day that, despite being there that night, I missed the entire thing. Something my dad instilled in me at an early age at wrestling shows was the art of the quick exit. Looking back, it was probably his way to not be subjected to this stuff for so long, but at the time he stated it was our plan of attack to beat the crowds and get to the subway first. It is something I also do at concerts and sporting events. So on this ill-fated night, before the main event cage match was even over, I was standing next to the exit. As soon as Shawn Michaels connected with his patented "Sweet Chin Music" on "Big Daddy Cool" Diesel, I grabbed my then-girlfriend by her hand and ran out the exit towards the staircase. I'm sure she was thrilled to leave too, as I dragged her in the first place. We know the rest of the story by now, but little did I know that the industry was about to change forever as I was hurrying down the steps to get to the subway."
Mike Goldberg, *Brooklyn, NY*

"I didn't even stay for the Curtain Call, and then the next day we heard about it.. I believe, especially knowing what I know now about Vince, Vince knew it was going to happen. But the agents weren't smart to it. Vince, in his position, he has to deny he knew. Vince knew he had to do something to save his ass. The agents were more upset. By that time, (the industry) was already what it was. Hunter's the one that had to eat the shit but he knew he would make up for it later on."
Tom Prichard, *TheHistoryofWWE.com interview, 2014*

WWF @ New York City, NY - Madison Square Garden - August 9, 1996 (14,000; 11,314 paid)

Included Jim Ross conducting an in-ring interview with Mark Henry regarding the Olympics which was eventually interrupted by Hunter Hearst Helmsley; Henry quickly scared Helmsley out of the ring; the announced card for the next month's return was WWF World Champion Shawn Michaels & the Undertaker vs. Mankind & Goldust, Farooq vs. Yokozuna, and Vader vs. Psycho Sid in a lumberjack match

Justin Bradshaw pinned Aldo Montoya with the lariat at 5:01

Henry & Phinneas Godwinn defeated Marty Jannetty & Leif Cassidy at 10:42 when Henry pinned the illegal man with the Slop Drop

Marc Mero pinned Hunter Hearst Helmsley with a leg roll up at 9:02

Mankind defeated Jake Roberts via submission with the Mandible Claw at the 37-second mark after attacking Roberts on the floor before the match began (Mankind's MSG debut)

Vader fought Psycho Sid to a double count-out at 10:16 when the two began fighting on the floor

Yokozuna (sub. for WWF IC Champion Ahmed Johnson) pinned Owen Hart with a leg drop and the Bonzai Drop at 6:37

WWF World Champion Shawn Michaels pinned Goldust with an elbow drop off the top and the superkick at 17:05; immediately after the match, Mankind attacked the champion until the Undertaker made the save

WWF Tag Team Champions the Smoking Gunns defeated Skip & Zip when Bart scored the pin at 7:23 after hitting the Sidewinder behind the referee's back

Savio Vega pinned Davey Boy Smith at 7:32 by lifting his shoulder out of an abdominal stretch into a roll up

The Undertaker defeated Steve Austin via disqualification at 9:23 when Mankind interfered after Austin sustained the tombstone; after the bout, Goldust and WWF World Champion Shawn Michaels also involved themselves in the brawl

Psycho Sid as a chicken

"I was on hand for what had to be one of the great moments in WWE history, when Mr. McMahon was watching Psycho Sid wrestle Vader. (Vader) had trouble finding his way as a character. There were some suggesting his character needed to be cowardly. Psycho Sid chased Vader around the ring and then Sid got in the ring and did a little bit of this (flapping his arms), the universal symbol for chicken. Mr. McMahon wasn't aware that was the international symbol. He turned around to Gerald Brisco, "Did Psycho Sid just flap his arms like a chicken?" and Gerald Brisco says, "Yes, he did." "I dont think I ever want to see that again."
Mick Foley, *WWE.com video diary, 2013*

Broken neck

"Chris (Candido) actually broke his neck. He was sitting outside the dressing room, I asked him if he was OK and he said he hurt himself. We finally talked him into going to the emergency room. Tammy (Sytch) took him to a place in downtown Manhattan. I was riding with Bradshaw and Dutch (Mantell) at the time, and we went to see the Statue of Liberty."
Tom Prichard, *TheHistoryofWWE.com interview, 2014*

WWF @ New York City, NY - Madison Square Garden - September 29, 1996 (matinee) (6,747; 3,917 paid)
Included a segment in which Brian Pillman came out, insulted New York City, and interviewed Sunny; Sunny then talked about Livewire and went on to insult Henry & Phinneas Godwinn; Phinneas then appeared and went to slop her before Billy Gunn attacked him from behind; Phinneas then chased the two backstage (Pillman's MSG debut)
Salvatore Sincere defeated Bob Holly with the Sincerely Yours
Justin Bradshaw pinned Alex Porteau with a lariat
Jake Roberts pinned TL Hopper with the DDT
Barry Windham pinned the Goon with the superplex
WWF Tag Team Champions Owen Hart & Davey Boy Smith defeated Henry & Phinneas Godwinn, the Smoking Gunns, and the Grimm Twins in an elimination match; Bart Gunn pinned one of the Grimm Twins with a forearm to the back, a roll up, and grabbing the tights for leverage; Smith pinned Henry after Owen came off the top behind the referee's back onto Henry and put Smith on top; Owen pinned Bart as Sunny distracted Billy
Vader pinned Psycho Sid in a lumberjack match with the moonsault after Steve Austin interfered and hit the Stunner on Sid; after the bout, Sid dropped several of the heel lumberjacks with the chokeslam
Hunter Hearst Helmsley pinned Freddie Joe Floyd with the Pedigree
Steve Austin pinned Savio Vega with the Stunner
WWF IC Champion Marc Mero defeated Farooq via disqualification after Farooq hit the champion with the title belt; the match was initially advertised as Farooq vs. Yokozuna
WWF World Champion Shawn Michaels & the Undertaker defeated Mankind & Goldust at around the 30-minute mark when Michaels pinned Goldust with the superkick after kissing him

SURVIVOR SERIES
Madison Square Garden – November 17, 1996

Bret Hart
"Madison Square Garden. It's not a church, but it's holy ground.
And Steve Austin, Stone Cold. We'll see who kicks whose ass."
Monday Night Raw, Oct. 21, 1996

Survivor Series 96 - New York City, NY - Madison Square Garden - November 17, 1996 (18,647; 16,266 paid)
Free For All:
Bart Gunn, Jesse James, Aldo Montoya, & Bob Holly defeated Billy Gunn, Justin Bradshaw (w/ Zebakiah), the Sultan (w/ the Iron Sheik), & Salvatore Sincere in an elimination match at around 9:45; the Sultan defeated Aldo via submission with the Camel Clutch at 2:59; Bart pinned Salvatore with a side slam at around 5:50; Bradshaw pinned Holly with the lariat at around 7:30; James pinned Bradshaw with a roll up at around 7:40, even though Bradshaw's shoulders were clearly not down for 3; James pinned the Sultan with an inside cradle at 8:41; Billy pinned James with the Rocker Dropper at 8:56; Bart pinned Billy with a forearm to the face after Billy missed a splash in the corner and hit his head on the turnbuckle; during the bout, Vince McMahon & Jim Ross announced that the winner of the Bret Hart / Steve Austin match later in the show would face the WWF World Champion at In Your House "It's Time"; moments later, Dok Hendrix attempted to interview Austin backstage but was chased out (*Free For All*)
Pay-per-view bouts - featured Vince McMahon, Jim Ross, & Jerry Lawler on commentary; included Kevin Kelly conducting an interview with Mankind & Paul Bearer in the lower level of the arena regarding Mankind's upcoming match with the Undertaker and the fact Bearer would be suspended above the ring in a cage for the duration of the bout; featured a look at Doug Furnas & Phil LaFon fielding questions on the WWE AOL website following their debut win; included Dok Hendrix conducting a backstage interview with WWF IC Champion Hunter Hearst Helmsley, Goldust, Marlena, Jerry Lawler, & Crush regarding the recent injury to Mark Henry and facing only three opponents instead of four; featured Todd Pettingill conducting a backstage interview with Steve Austin regarding his upcoming match with Bret Hart and the fact the winner would challenge the WWF World Champion at In Your House; Austin recieved a mixed reaction during his promo; included Hendrix conducting a backstage interview with Psycho Sid regarding his upcoming match against WWF World Champion Shawn Michaels, during which he said he would do anything in his power to win the title:
Doug Furnas, Phil LaFon, Henry & Phinneas Godwinn (w/ Hillbilly Jim) defeated Marty Jannetty, Leif Cassidy, WWF Tag Team Champions Owen Hart & Davey Boy Smith (w/ Clarence Mason) in an elimination match at 20:42; Henry pinned Jannetty with the Slop Drop at 8:12; Hart pinned Henry with a leg lariat at 8:19; Smith pinned Phinneas with the running powerslam at 9:04 after Owen made the blind tag and was then knocked to the floor; LaFon pinned Cassidy with a reverse suplex off the top at 13:43; LaFon pinned Smith with a crucifix at 17:22; after the fall, Smith clipped LaFon in the leg before leaving the ring; Furnas pinned Hart with a release German suplex; Harvey Wippleman served as the second ringside referee for the bout (Furnas & LaFon's debut)

WWF Tag Team Champions Davey Boy Smith & Owen Hart found their new challenge at Survivor Series 96 in the debuting Phil LaFon & Doug Furnas.

The Undertaker made his return from In Your House: Buried Alive to face Mankind.

The Undertaker pinned Mankind (w/ Paul Bearer) with the tombstone at 14:54; Bearer was suspended above the ring in a cage for the duration of the bout; during his entrance, Taker was lowered down from the ceiling, then scaring Bearer into the cage; after the bout, Taker waited in the ring as Bearer's cage was lowered; moments later, the Executioner ran out and attacked Taker, allowing Bearer to escape the ring; Taker quickly sent the Executioner to the floor after a flying clothesline (Taker's first TV appearance in a month; his first appearance in all leather, rather than his traditional wardrobe; Terry Gordy's one-time return to MSG after a 12-year absence)

Marc Mero (w/ Sable), Barry Windham, Rocky Maivia, & Jake Roberts (sub. for Mark Henry) defeated WWF IC Champion Hunter Hearst Helmsley, Goldust (w/ Marlena), Crush, & Jerry Lawler in an elimination match at 23:44; Sunny provided guest commentary for the bout, subbing for Lawler; during Helmsley's entrance, the commentary team noted he was without an escort and Jim Ross added, "He's more than perfect," subtly referring to the fact Mr.

Perfect was no longer with Helmsley; after Mero's team made their entrance, Mero took the mic and introduced Roberts as the replacement for Henry; during the match, Sunny said HHH was tired of Perfect taking all the credit, explaining why Perfect wasn't ringside; it was also noted Don Muraco was in attendance; Harvey Wippleman served as the second ringside referee for the bout; Roberts pinned Lawler at 10:01 with the DDT after avoiding a slam attempt; Goldust pinned Windham with the Curtain Call at 12:44; Mero pinned Helmsley at 19:19 with a moonsault onto a standing Helmsley; Crush pinned Mero with the heart punch at 20:30 after Mero missed a crossbody to the floor when Goldust pushed Crush out of the way; Crush pinned Roberts with the heart punch at 20:53; Maivia pinned Crush with a crossbody at 23:12 after Crush accidentally hit the heart punch to Goldust; Maivia pinned Goldust with a running shoulderbreaker (Maivia's TV in-ring debut; Roberts' return after a month absence) (*The Epic Journey of Dwayne The Rock Johnson*)

Jake Roberts earned revenge on Jerry Lawler after months of insults.

Bret Hart pinned Steve Austin at 28:34 by kicking off the top turnbuckle as he was caught in the Million $ Dream; following Austin's entrance, Todd Pettingill conducted a backstage interview with Hart regarding his return, with Hart noting MSG wasn't a church but it's holy ground and that he wasn't greedy for money but for respect and Austin would respect him; stipulations stated the winner would challenge the WWF World Champion at the following month's In Your House; during the bout, it was noted Austin would face Vader the next night on Monday Night Raw in a toughman contest; both men were heavily cheered during the bout; after the match, Hart spent several moments greeting ringside fans, during which time he was congratulated by Vince McMahon at the commentary table (Hart's in-ring return after a 2-month absence; his TV in-ring return after an 8-month absence) (*The Legacy of Stone Cold Steve Austin*)

Bret Hart returned to the ring to face Steve Austin, launching what would be arguably the top feud of 1997 in the WWF.

Savio Vega, Yokozuna, Flash Funk, & Jimmy Snuka (mystery partner) fought Farooq (w/ Clarence Mason), Vader (w/ Jim Cornette), Razor Ramon II, & Diesel II to a draw in an elimination match at 9:45; prior to the bout, Capt. Lou Albano came out to provided guest commentary at the Spanish announce table; Farooq was escorted to the ring by the Nation of Domination, including PG-13; Funk was escorted to the ring by the Funkettes; Cornette provided guest commentary for the match; Vader was legit injured early in the bout after sustaining a uranage from Yoko; Jack Doan served as the ringside referee for the bout; Diesel pinned Savio with the powerbomb at 8:32 after Farooq rammed Vega into the ringpost on the floor; Snuka pinned Razor at 9:28 with a knee drop and the top rope splash; the remaining participants were disqualified when Diesel repeatedly struck Snuka with a steel chair, prompting the other wrestlers to brawl in the ring and Vega to return to the ring and hit Diesel with his own steel chair; moments later, Vega's team cleared their opponents from the ring (Farooq's first appearance with the 'Nation of Domination' theme music and with an entourage; PG-13's surprise return after a year absence; Flash's debut; Snuka's one-match return after a 3-year absence; Yokozuna's last appearance)

Psycho Sid pinned WWF World Champion Shawn Michaels (w/ Jose Lothario) to win the title at 20:00 with the powerbomb after hitting the champion with a video camera on the floor; moments prior, Sid hit Lothario with the same video camera; after the match, Lothario was taken backstage on a stretcher with Michaels close behind; Sid was heavily cheered and Michaels booed during the match (*Shawn Michaels: The Heartbreak Express Tour*)

After years of failed attempts in the WWF and WCW, Psycho Sid won his first world title, at the expense of Shawn Michaels.

Sid beats Shawn

"You can see me in the front row falling over and crying. I died. I was sitting with Vlad and Charlie in the front row. We sat there and looked up and saw the scaffolding for the Sid pyro. 'Oh no, Sid has pyro. He's going to win.' And then, of course, Vlad is fistpumping with Sid after. 'Really? It's Shawn.'"

Mary-Kate (Grosso) Anthony, *Tampa, Fla.*

**WWF @ New York City, NY - Madison Square Garden -
January 25, 1997 (matinee) (16,634; 13,480 paid)**
*Included an opening announcement from Howard Finkel in
which he noted the injury to WWF Tag Team Champion Davey
Boy Smith and noted the passing the night before of Dr. Jerry
Graham, leading to 10 seconds of silence in his memory;
featured a segment in which Howard Finkel went to announce
the matches for the March 16 return, with Savio Vega
interrupting him and saying he wanted to face Ahmed Johnson
on the show*

Henry & Phinneas Godwinn defeated WWF Tag Team
Champion Owen Hart & Bob Holly (sub. for an injured WWF
Tag Team Champion Davey Boy Smith) when Phinneas pinned
Hart after Holly and Henry reversed the pin attempt behind the
referee's back; during the match, Hart and Holly argued; after
the contest, Hart attacked Holly before Holly threw Hart to the floor

Rocky Maivia pinned Salvatore Sincere with the shoulderbreaker

Steve Austin pinned Goldust with the Stunner after avoiding the Curtain Call

WWF IC Champion Hunter Hearst Helmsley (w/ Curtis Hughes) pinned Jake Roberts with the Pedigree after Hughes
interfered

WWF World Champion Shawn Michaels pinned Mankind with the superkick; after the match, Psycho Sid appeared
and congratulated Michaels on his win at the Royal Rumble; he went on to say that NYC was his town and Michaels
should defend the title against him in his town as he did to Michaels in San Antonio, with Michaels agreeing

Bret Hart defeated Vader via disqualification when Steve Austin interfered; prior to the bout, Hart cut a promo before
Vader took the mic and said Hart was "full of shit;" after the match, Austin hit the Stunner on Hart in the ring, then
stomped him until referees and officials broke it up

Farooq & Crush defeated Ahmed Johnson & Savio Vega when Farooq pinned Johnson with the Dominator after
Vega dropped Johnson throat-first across the top rope; after the match, Johnson was attacked by Vega and the
Nation before Vega cut a quick promo in Spanish over the mic

Psycho Sid defeated the Undertaker via count-out after Vader attacked the Undertaker at ringside; after the bout,
Taker and Sid took turns assaulting Vader

*Photos clockwise from top:
Ahmed Johnson, Owen Hart,
and Shawn Michaels.*

313

WWF @ New York City, NY - Madison Square Garden - March 16, 1997 (8,513)
Shown on the MSG Network - featured Jim Ross & Jim Cornette on commentary; included Dok Hendrix conducting an in-ring interview with Bret Hart, who claimed WWF World Champion Psycho Sid had lucked out everytime they had faced each other, and that Bret would change the face of WrestleMania 13 by defeating Sid in a steel cage match to become a 5-time WWF World Champion; included Hendrix conducting an in-ring interview with Ken Shamrock, who stated he would be impartial at WrestleMania 13, would not be swayed by the words of Hart or Steve Austin, and that he would let them go until one man submitted or could not defend himself; featured Hendrix conducting an in-ring interview with Sid, who stated he would defeat Hart on Raw, and that he smelled fear on the Undertaker (the first event on the MSG Network in 5 years; the final MSG show on the MSG Network):
The Sultan (w/ the Iron Sheik & Bob Backlund) defeated Flash Funk via submission with the Camel Clutch at 7:42; Sultan's music accidently began playing right before the hold was applied
Blackjack Windham & Blackjack Bradshaw defeated Henry & Phinneas Godwinn at 8:13 when Windham pinned Henry with a double axe handle to the back of the head after switching places with Bradshaw
Crush (w/ Savio Vega, PG-13, Clarence Mason, and D-Lo Brown) pinned Aldo Montoya at 1:46 with the heart punch; after the match, the Nation attacked Montoya until Ahmed Johnson cleared the ring with a 2x4
Ahmed Johnson defeated Savio Vega (w/ Crush, PG-13, Clarence Mason, and D-Lo Brown) via disqualification at 8:56 when the Nation interfered as Johnson had Vega covered following the Pearl River Plunge; after the match, the Nation, joined by Faarooq, beat down Ahmed until officials broke it up
WWF Tag Team Champions Davey Boy Smith & Owen Hart defeated Phil LaFon & Doug Furnas at 13:33 when Smith pinned Furnas after Hart tripped up the challenger as he attempted to suplex Smith into the ring
Hunter Hearst Helmsley (w/ Chyna) defeated WWF IC Champion Rocky Maivia via disqualification at 14:45 when Goldust interfered as Helmsley had Maivia covered following the Pedigree; moments later, Goldust clotheslined Helmsley to the floor, with Marlena then running out and jumping on Chyna's back until referees broke it up
Faarooq (w/ PG-13, Savio Vega, Crush, Clarence Mason, & D-Lo Brown) pinned Goldust at 8:26 with a piledriver after Crush tripped Goldust, with Crush pushing Goldust's foot off the bottom rope during the count; Sunny was the guest ring announcer for the bout; moments after the opening bell, Faarooq stated he had been forced to wrestle dead men, colored boys, and white boys, but drew the line at wrestling a "fag" like Goldust
Vader (w/ Paul Bearer) defeated the Undertaker in a casket match at 7:26 when Mankind came out of the casket, applied the Mandible Claw on Taker, forced him into the casket, and Bearer closed the lid; after the bout, Vader & Bearer left ringside, with Taker then coming out of the casket, assaulting Mankind in the ring, and dropping him with a chokeslam and the tombstone; Taker then rolled Mankind into the casket, shut the lid, and went backstage, with referees pushing the casket alongside him
Dark match: WWF World Champion Psycho Sid defeated Bret Hart in a steel cage match at 9:56 by crawling through the cage door to the floor before Hart touched the floor by climbing over the top, moments after Hart hit a superplex to the champion

WWF @ New York City, NY - Madison Square Garden - May 17, 1997 (15,000; 10,702 paid)

Bret Hart, Vader, and Psycho Sid did not appear due to injuries; included an in-ring promo by Mankind in which he noted it being the anniversary of when Bruno Sammartino beat Buddy Rogers for the WWWF World Title at (the previous) Madison Square Garden and said history would repeat itself later in the night; Mankind then insulted the NYC crowd before having the bell rung 10 times for the injured Paul Bearer

Leif Cassidy pinned Bob Holly with a powerbomb

Crush (sub. for the Sultan) pinned Jesse Jammes with the heart punch

Henry & Phinneas Godwinn defeated Doug Furnas & Phil LaFon when Henry pinned Furnas with the Slop Drop

Rockabilly pinned Flash Funk with a tornado DDT

Savio Vega pinned Rocky Maivia with a spin kick after Maivia became distracted by Crush on the ring apron

WWF World Champion the Undertaker defeated Mankind in a lumberjack match with the tombstone; the bout was advertised as Undertaker & Psycho Sid vs. Mankind & Vader; lumberjacks included: the Nation, Leif Cassidy, Bob Holly, Henry & Phinneas Godwinn, Jesse Jammes, Doug Furnas, Phil LaFon, and Rocky Maivia; Ken Shamrock was initially pegged to replace Sid but the match was changed to a singles bout due to Vader's injury

Hunter Hearst Helmsley pinned Goldust while Chyna held Goldust's legs down from outside the ring; prior to the match, Goldust introduced both Marlena and their daughter Dakota; after the bout, Goldust and Chyna faced off, with Goldust kissing Chyna before Chyna landed a low blow

Farooq (w/ the Nation) pinned Ahmed Johnson after Savio Vega interfered while the referee was knocked down and repeatedly hit Johnson with a chair

Steve Austin & the Legion of Doom defeated Brian Pillman (sub. for Bret Hart), WWF Tag Team Champions - WWF IC Champion Owen Hart & WWF European Champion Davey Boy Smith when Austin pinned Owen with the Stunner (Pillman's MSG debut)

Goldust and his daughter Dakota.

MONDAY, SEPTEMBER 22, 1997
MADISON SQUARE GARDEN
NEW YORK, NY

presented by

PlayStation.

WORLD WRESTLING
FEDERATION®

MAIN EVENT: TRIPLE THREAT MATCH FOR THE WORLD WRESTLING FEDERATION CHAMPIONSHIP

BRET "HIT MAN" HART	VS.	UNDERTAKER	VS.	SHAWN MICHAELS
CHAMPION				
Calgary, Alberta, Canada...234 lbs.		Death Valley...328 lbs.		San Antonio, TX...227 lbs.

• OVER THE TOP ROPE BATTLE ROYAL •
WINNER MEETS THE WORLD WRESTLING FEDERATION CHAMPION AT
MADISON SQUARE GARDEN ON SATURDAY, NOVEMBER 15!

PLUS LOTS MORE EXCITING ACTION!

NEW TIME...NEW ATTITUDE!
Watch RAW IS WAR™ at 9PM and WAR ZONE™ at 10PM
Back to Back, on USA NETWORK!

TUNE IN AND CATCH THE ACTION!

Mondays	9:00 pm	USA	RAW IS WAR™
Saturdays	10:00 am	USA	LIVE WIRE™
Sundays	11:00 am	USA	World Wrestling Federation Superstars™
Saturdays	11:00 am	WPXN-TV Ch. 31	World Wrestling Federation New York™

After 4 years, the WWF's flagship show Monday Night Raw was finally hosted at Madison Square Garden. The broadcast did not outscore WCW Monday Nitro in the ratings war, but it did provide the WWF with a shot in the arm to set them up for a historic 1998. Additionally, it was backstage at this event that Vince McMahon told WWF World Champion Bret Hart that he would not be able to financially afford Hart's new 20-year deal, a discussion that would eventually lead to the infamous Montreal Screwjob 6 weeks later.

316

Vince McMahon interviews the Undertaker about the upcoming debut of Hell in a Cell.

WWF @ New York City, NY - Madison Square Garden - September 22, 1997 (14,615; 10,672 paid; sell out)

It was prior to this show Vince McMahon told WWF World Champion Bret Hart he wouldn't be able to afford Hart's new 20-year contract; the show was originally announced as a house show for Sept. 13 but was moved to this date for the Raw TV taping

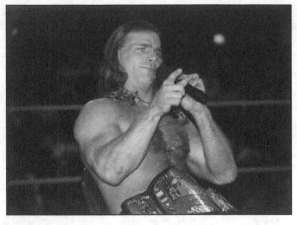

Steve Corino defeated Jimmy Cicero

The Brooklyn Brawler won a 20-man battle royal to earn a world title shot during the Nov. 15 return date; other participants included: Los Boricuas, DOA, the Truth Commission, Brian Christopher, Scott Taylor, the Headbangers, and Blackjack Windham & Blackjack Bradshaw, among others

Raw is War - included Vince McMahon, Jim Ross, & Jerry Lawler on commentary; featured an opening segment showcasing many of the historic MSG moments with clips of Hulk Hogan, Roddy Piper, Bruno Sammartino, Gorilla Monsoon, Jimmy Snuka, Superstar Billy Graham, Andre the Giant, Bret Hart, Shawn Michaels, Randy Savage & Miss Elizabeth; NY Athletic Commission Chairman Floyd Patterson was in attendance for the show; included a segment in which Steve Austin appeared in the crowd with a mic and said someone would get their ass whipped later in the show; featured an ad promoting Lazer Tag featuring Sable, Howard Finkel, Freddie Blassie, and Tim White; included the showing of still photos from the Shawn Michaels vs. Davey Boy Smith European title match at One Night Only detailing how Michaels won the title; featured McMahon conducting an in-ring interview with the Undertaker regarding his upcoming Hell in a Cell match against Michaels, during which it was announced the winner would face the WWF World Champion at the Survivor Series; Taker then said WWF World Champion Bret Hart would soon have his judgement day, but he would first deal with Michaels at Hell in a Cell; moments later, Michaels came out on the stage to interrupt, with his newly won European title, complained about the WWF stacking the deck against him; Michaels then argued that the WWF should just go ahead and give Taker the title shot since that was their ultimate plan anyway; Michaels then said he doesn't lay down for anyone and would be one step ahead of McMahon, Taker, and the fans again at Badd Blood; included an ad promoting the One Night Only home video; featured a clip recapping Jimmy Snuka's splash off the top of the cage onto WWF IC Champion Don Muraco in October 1983; included an ad promoting Stridex WWF trading cards; featured a tribute to the passing of Dick "Bulldog" Brower; included an ad promoting the Survivor Series Super Supper Sweepstakes; featured a clip of the Andre the Giant vs. Big John Studd bodyslam challenge at WrestleMania 1; included an in-ring promo by Michaels, sitting in a chair, in which he challenged Taker to "bring your dead ass" out to face him; following the commercial break, Taker walked out, fought off Triple H who attempted to attack him from behind, but fell victim to an assault from Michaels with the chair; moments later, Rick rude and Chyna also appeared, with the four assaulting Taker until Taker rose to his feet, grabbed the chair, and scared the four backstage:

WWF IC Championship Tournament Quarter-Finals: Ahmed Johnson pinned Rocky Maivia at 4:58 with the Pearl River Plunge; Farooq, D-Lo Brown, & Kama escorted Rocky to the ring but were ordered backstage by Sgt. Slaughter before the match began; prior to Ahmed's introduction, it was announced Ken Shamrock was injured and would be replaced in the tournament by Farooq; during the match, Capt. Lou Albano briefly appeared at ringside; Ahmed appeared to injure his hand during the contest; Maivia bled from the mouth late in the match (Ahmed's TV return match after a several month absence)

Shawn Michaels won the WWF European Title two days earlier from Davey Boy Smith in Birmingham, England.

The Legion of Doom defeated Farooq & Kama via disqualification at 2:32 when Rocky Maivia and D-Lo Brown interfered as the LOD attempted to hit the Doomsday Device on Farooq; Sunny was the guest ring announcer for the bout; prior to the match, footage was shown of the LOD and Steve Doocey giving the weather report earlier in the day on Fox News and of Farooq's injury to Ken Shamrock the previous week; during the bout, it was announced the LOD & Ahmed Johnson would face the Nation at Badd Blood; after the bout, Johnson attempted to make the save for the LOD but was beaten down as well until Gerald Brisco, Tony Garea, Sgt. Slaughter, and referees intervened

WWF IC Championship Tournament Semi-Finals: Owen Hart defeated Brian Pillman (w/ Marlena) via disqualification at 7:12 when Goldust interfered, punched Owen in the face, and then went after Pillman until he was held back by referees, with Pillman then escorting Marlena backstage; Hart was escorted to the ring by police officers to protect him from Steve Austin; prior to the match, Pillman came out with his arm in a sling and said he broke his arm while he was making Marlena squeal like a pig in the bathtub; Pillman then said he would have to forfeit; moments later, Sgt. Slaughter came out and - after proving the injury was a fake - threatened Owen and Pillman with never again wrestling in the WWF unless they had their scheduled match; moments later, the commentary team announced that Marlena and Goldust would renew their wedding vows during the Oct. 6 Raw from Kansas city; the two shook hands to start the match; after the bout, Owen cut an in-ring promo dedicating his win to his brother WWF World Champion Bret Hart, with Austin then coming out and attacking Hart until he was tackled by police and then cornered; moments later, Vince McMahon left the broadcast table and grabbed the mic to calm Austin down and prevent him from going to jail; McMahon told the officers to give him a minute and yelled at Austin to control himself; he then told Austin that if he competed now he could end up paralyzed and the WWF wouldn't let him do that to himself and end up in a wheelchair; he went on to say that the WWF cared about Austin and he needed to work within the system; Austin responded by saying wrestling was all he did and he was the best in the world, and he appreciated that Vince and the WWF cared; he then said Vince could kiss his ass before dropping him with the Stunner; Austin was quickly handcuffed by police as McMahon was tended to by referees and officials, with Austin turning around to give McMahon two middle fingers before he was led to the back; the show continued with just Jim Ross & Jerry Lawler on commentary

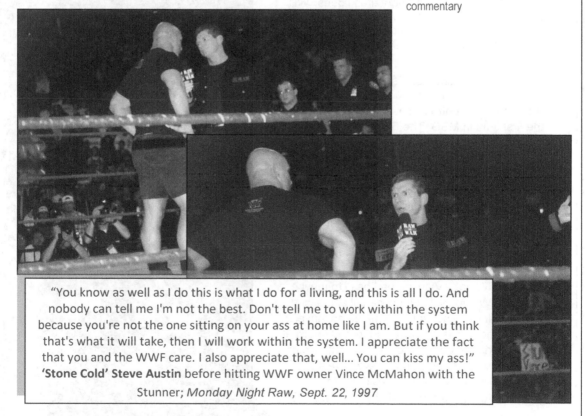

"You know as well as I do this is what I do for a living, and this is all I do. And nobody can tell me I'm not the best. Don't tell me to work within the system because you're not the one sitting on your ass at home like I am. But if you think that's what it will take, then I will work within the system. I appreciate the fact that you and the WWF care. I also appreciate that, well... You can kiss my ass!"
'Stone Cold' Steve Austin before hitting WWF owner Vince McMahon with the Stunner; *Monday Night Raw, Sept. 22, 1997*

The surprise debut of the Cactus Jack character in the WWF.

Cactus Jack (sub. for Dude Love) pinned Hunter Hearst Helmsley (w/ Chyna) in a streetfight at 13:40 following a piledriver through a wooden table; before the match, Jerry Lawler spoke with Rhonda Shear, host of of USA Up All Night, who sat behind the commentary table for the show; prior to the contest, Dude Love appeared on the Titantron, saying that streetfights just weren't his thing; after inviting out Mankind as a possible substitute in the pretaped video, Mankind said that he had an idea for the perfect replacement - Cactus Jack (Cactus' surprise debut) (*Mick Foley: Greatest Hits & Misses, Falls Count Anywhere: The Greatest Street Fights and other Out of Control Matches*)

'Will you shut up about the ECW cap?'
I was in the front row. It was the last time Bret wrestled in The Garden. The thing I remember the most, there was a female fan wearing an ECW cap. Owen says after talking to this girl, 'Bulldog, she's gonna get me a ECW cap.' Bret's got somebody in the Sharpshooter and goes, 'Will you shut up about the ECW cap?' I saw it. I was right there.
Mike Johnson; *Glendale, NY*

Owen wants a hat
"The night Vince talked to Bret about getting out of the 20-year contract. You had Cactus Jack for the first time in MSG. The Stunner, oh my gosh, how did i forget the Stunner? That had to be one of my five favorite moments. They teased that for so long and finally the Stunner happened. Bret against Goldust was awesome. Owen and Davey were at ringside. And Davey was a huge ECW fan, to the point where Davey would turn to us and start a ECW chant from the ring. And that was actually the night where Owen turned to Vladimir and goes, 'So when are you going to get me a ECW hat?' Vladimir had been to maybe three ECW shows. I pulled one out and asked, 'When are you going to get me a Vancouver Canucks hat?' The day i was supposed to give it to him, he had to go. He died a few months later. I still have that hat. I would never give it up because of who it was designated for."
Mary-Kate (Grosso) Anthony, *Tampa, Fla.*

WWF World Champion Bret Hart defeated Goldust via submission with the Sharpshooter at 12:50 in a non-title match after grabbing Goldust's foot as Goldust held it in the air to block a top rope elbow; prior to the bout, Hart cut an in-ring promo regarding facing either the Undertaker or WWF European Champion Shawn Michaels at the Survivor Series, telling both men that their days were numbered, he was the best there is, the best there was, and the best there ever will be "and New York City, you know it;" after the bout, Michaels - who appeared mid-way through the bout - and Triple H attacked Bret, with Davey Boy Smith, Owen Hart, Jim Neidhart and Rick Rude then coming out and joining in the bawl; moments later, Taker appeared, helped clear the ring, and then hit a double chokeslam on Hart and Michaels to end the show (Neidhart's return after a 2-month absence)

Shotgun - 9/27/97 - included the same opening segment from the previous Monday's Raw is War showing historic moments from MSG, as well as the main highlights from Raw; hosted by Jim Ross & Jim Cornette; included the showing of still photos from the Shawn Michaels / Davey Boy Smith European title match at One Night Only:

Savio Vega & Miguel Perez defeated Blackjack Windham & Blackjack Bradshaw at around the 6-minute mark when Perez pinned Bradshaw following a spinning heel kick from Savio after he and Windham were distracted when Jesus Castillo & Jose Estrada Jr. came to ringside also

Crush & Chainz (w/ Skull & 8-Ball) defeated Recon & Sniper (w/ the Jackyl & the Interrogator) via disqualification at around the 4-minute mark when Jackyl interfered and shoved Crush off the top rope; after the bout, DOA cleared the Truth Commission out of the ring (Jackyl's debut)

Jesse Jammes pinned Flash Funk at 5:37 with the pumphandle side slam after Jerry Lawler, who was doing guest commentary for the match, interfered and shoved Funk off the top so that he crotched himself on the top rope

Vader & the Patriot defeated Henry & Phinneas Godwinn (w/ Uncle Cletus) at around 7:30 when Vader pinned Phinneas with the Vader Bomb after Phinneas almost collided with Cletus on the apron when Vader moved out of the way of a charge from Phinneas

Dark match after the taping: WWF World Champion Bret Hart defeated the Undertaker and WWF European Champion Shawn Michaels by pinning Michaels after the Undertaker hit the tombstone on Michaels but was pulled out of the ring by the interfering Hart Foundation

The night's untelevised dark match pitting the Undertaker, Shawn Michaels, and Bret Hart against one another.

WWF @ New York City, NY - Madison Square Garden - November 15, 1997 (matinee) (15,479; 12,525 paid)
Prior to Bret Hart's leaving the WWF, the main event was scheduled to be a title defense for Hart pitting him against the Undertaker, Steve Austin, and Shawn Michaels in a four-way match; also originally scheduled was WWF Tag Team Champions the Legion of Doom vs. Owen Hart & Davey Boy Smith, Vader (w/ George Steele) vs. Triple H, and Dude Love vs. Miguel Perez Jr.; Bret, Smith, and Owen did not appear as advertised but no refunds were offered; included an in-ring promo by Goldust in which he said he "dumped the bitch" (Marlena), said the cast on his hand was her fault, admitted to wearing women's panties and told the men in the crowd to seek their feminine side
Billy Gunn & the Road Dogg defeated the Headbangers when Road Dogg pinned Mosh after Gunn came off the top behind the referee's back
Farooq (w/ D-Lo Brown) pinned Ahmed Johnson in a streetfight after Kama interfered as D-Lo distracted the referee
Crush & Chainz defeated D-Lo Brown & Kama when Crush pinned D-Lo with a belly to belly suplex
WWF World Champion & WWF European Champion Shawn Michaels pinned the Brooklyn Brawler at the 15-minute mark with the superkick after interference from Chyna and distraction from Triple H; Brawler came to the ring to the tune of Frank Sinatra's "New York, New York"
WWF Tag Team Champions Legion of Doom defeated Savio Vega & Miguel Perez Jr. (sub. for Owen Hart & Davey Boy Smith) when Road Warrior Hawk pinned Miguel following the Doomsday Device
Kane (sub. for Triple H) pinned Vader with a chokeslam; the match was wrestled under red lights
Max Mini, Nova, & Mosaic defeated Torito, Piratita Morgan, & Tarantula when Max Mini scored the pin
Dude Love (w/ George Steele) pinned Jim Neidhart at around the 4-minute mark in a No DQ match with the double arm DDT after Steele punched a blinded Neidhart fron the ring apron
Ken Shamrock defeated Rocky Maivia (w/ Farooq, Kama, & D-Lo Brown) via submission with the ankle lock in a no holds barred match after fending off Kama and D-Lo
The Undertaker & Steve Austin defeated WWF World Champion Shawn Michaels & Hunter Hearst Helmsley when Taker pinned Michaels with the chokeslam and tombstone; after the bout, Chyna twice slapped Austin before Austin gave her two middle fingers and, eventually, the Stunner

WWF @ New York City, NY - Madison Square Garden - January 10, 1998 (19,259; 15,712 paid; sell out)
$3 tickets were made available through co-sponsors
Included a segment in which an MTV camera crew taped Steve Austin cutting an in-ring promo regarding the Super Bowl half-time special 'Celebrity Deathmatch' which would be used to hype the program; originally scheduled for the show was Austin & the Undertaker vs. WWF World Champion Shawn Michaels & WWF European Champion Triple H in a steel cage match, WWF IC Champion the Rock vs. Ken Shamrock, Dude Love vs. Jeff Jarrett, and the Legion of Doom vs. WWF Tag Team Champions the Road Dogg & Billy Gunn; featured an in-ring promo by Jim Cornette promoting the NWA
WWF Light Heavyweight Champion Taka Michinoku pinned Brian Christopher at the 6-minute mark with a roll up
Henry & Phinneas Godwinn defeated the Headbangers in a Country Whipping match at the 3-minute mark when Henry pinned Thrasher after hitting him with the whip as Thrasher came off the top
Tom Brandi defeated Marc Mero via disqualification after Mero hit a low blow after Brandi attempted several near falls
Ken Shamrock pinned Farooq (w/ Kama) with a powerslam after throwing Farooq into Kama, who was on the ring apron; after the bout, Farooq argued with Kama and D-Lo Brown
The Undertaker & the Legion of Doom defeated WWF World Champion Shawn Michaels, WWF Tag Team Champions Billy Gunn & the Road Dogg in a steel cage match at around the 11-minute mark when Taker pinned Michaels with the tombstone after Owen Hart interfered and repeatedly hit the champion as he attempted to climb out of the cage (Michaels' last MSG match for more than 4 years)
Vader pinned TAFKA Goldust with a splash after Luna was knocked off the ring apron
Kane pinned Chainz in less than 2 minutes
Steve Austin & Cactus Jack (sub. for Dude Love) defeated WWF IC Champion the Rock & D-Lo Brown in a falls count anywhere match when Austin pinned the Rock with the Stunner after hitting him with a trash can and broom; prior to the match, Howard Finkel said Dude Love would not be competing and then introduced his replacement; after the bout, Austin fought off other Nation members with the Stunner

WWF @ New York City, NY - Madison Square Garden - March 22, 1998 (18,199; 15,297 paid)
WWF Light Heavyweight Champion Taka Michinoku pinned Brian Christopher
Henry & Phinneas Godwinn defeated Skull & 8-Ball in a country whipping match
Marc Mero pinned TAFKA Goldust
Cactus Jack pinned WWF Tag Team Champion Billy Gunn in a falls count anywhere match
Ken Shamrock defeated WWF IC Champion the Rock via disqualification
NWA Tag Team Champions the Headbangers defeated the Quebecers
Bradshaw pinned Barry Windham
Steve Austin pinned WWF European Champion Triple H in a non-title match

WWF @ New York City, NY - Madison Square Garden - June 5, 1998 (19,506; 16,814 paid; sell out)
Included an in-ring segment in which Pat Patterson introduced Vince McMahon to the ring to answer the Undertaker's challenge from earlier in the show; Taker then chased Patterson out of the ring and went to chokeslam McMahon after McMahon insulted him; moments later, Mankind ran out to make the save for McMahon, with Taker chasing both men away
The Headbangers defeated Brian Christopher & Scott Taylor when Thrasher pinned Taylor
Farooq fought Mark Henry to a no contest at the 4-minute mark when the Undertaker came to the ring and hit a chokeslam on both men, later calling Vince McMahon out on the microphone and stating that if his request was not answered he would keep interfering in matches
Scorpio pinned D-Lo Brown with a moonsault
Dustin Runnels & Terry Funk defeated Savio Vega & Jose Estrada Jr. when Dustin pinned Estrada with a DDT
Ken Shamrock defeated Owen Hart in a submission match by reversing an attempt at the Sharpshooter into the ankle lock
WWF Tag Team Champions the Road Dogg & Billy Gunn (w/ X-Pac) defeated the Legion of Doom when Road Dogg pinned Road Warrior Hawk after X-Pac interfered and hit Hawk with one of the title belts
Bradshaw pinned Kama with the lariat
Jeff Jarrett pinned Steve Blackman after Tennessee Lee held Blackman's leg during an attempted suplex
WWF European Champion Triple H pinned Vader with the Pedigree after Chyna interfered and hit a low blow on the challenger as X-Pac distracted the referee
WWF World Champion Steve Austin & the Undertaker defeated Kane & Mankind in a no holds barred match when Austin hit the Stunner on Mankind

WWF
WORLD WRESTLING FEDERATION

FRIDAY, JUNE 5, 1998
MADISON SQUARE GARDEN
NEW YORK, NY

MAIN EVENT: NO HOLDS BARRED NON-SANCTIONED ONE FALL TO A FINISH

STONE COLD STEVE AUSTIN & UNDERTAKER	vs	DUDE LOVE & KANE
Combined Weight...580 lbs.		Combined Weight...613 lbs.

SUBMISSION MATCH

KEN SHAMROCK	vs	OWEN HART
Sacramento, CA...235 lbs.		Calgary, Alberta, Canada...227 lbs.

FOR THE TAG TEAM CHAMPIONSHIP

NEW AGE OUTLAWS	vs	LOD 2000
Combined Weight...504 lbs. (CHAMPIONS)		Combined Weight...568 lbs. (CHALLENGERS)

FOR THE EUROPEAN CHAMPIONSHIP

HUNTER HEARST-HELMSLEY	vs	VADER
Greenwich, CT...246 lbs. (CHAMPION)		Rocky Mountains...456 lbs. (CHALLENGER)

STEVE BLACKMAN	vs	DOUBLE J
Annville, PA...245 lbs.		Nashville, TN...230 lbs.

TERRY FUNK & DUSTIN RUNNELS	vs	LOS BORICUAS SAVIO & JOSE
Combined Weight...505 lbs.		Combined Weight...484 lbs.

FAAROOQ	vs	MARK HENRY
270 lbs.		400 lbs.

HEADBANGERS MOSH & THRASHER		TOO MUCH
Combined Weight...492 lbs.		Combined Weight...486 lbs.

PLUS: SCORPIO vs. D-LO BROWN

SIGN ON TO THE WORLD WRESTLING FEDERATION OFFICIAL WEB SITE www.wwf.com
FOR EXCLUSIVE PHOTOS, LATEST NEWS AND YOUR CHANCE TO CHAT WITH THE SUPERSTARS OF THE
WORLD WRESTLING FEDERATION AT EACH PAY-PER-VIEW EVENT.
www.wwf.com

TUNE IN AND CATCH THE ACTION!

Mondays	8:57 pm	USA	RAW IS WAR™
Saturdays	10:00 am	USA	LIVE WIRE™
Sundays	11:00 am	USA	World Wrestling Federation Superstars™
Saturdays	11:00 am	WPXN-31	World Wrestling Federation New York™

This wrestling exhibition is a proprietary exhibition, with all rights owned by TitanSports, Inc. All photographs of the exhibition for commercial purposes and/or the reporting of any photographs of the exhibition in commercial publications without the express written permission of TitanSports, Inc. is strictly prohibited. When scheduled talent is unable to appear due to circumstances beyond the control of the promoter, the promoter reserves the right to make suitable substitutions. Printed in the USA.

SUMMERSLAM
Madison Square Garden – August 30, 1998

The Highway to Hell
"I remember walking into that show and thinking it was the coolest thing, to see the big poster with Steve Austin and the Undertaker and they're battling over New York City. I remember watching that show and they tried to do everything they could to make it a spectacle."
Mike Johnson; *Glendale, NY*

Summer Slam 98 - New York City, NY - Madison Square Garden - August 30, 1998 (19,066; 15,274 paid; sell out; 2,522 in Theatre; 1,816 paid)

Sunday Night Heat - shown live; featured an opening segment in which Shawn Michaels came out to the ring, posed, and then joined Jim Ross & Shane McMahon on commentary; included a backstage shot of WWF World Champion Steve Austin with a sledgehammer awaiting the Undertaker and Kane's arrival; featured an ad promoting Summer Slam to the tune of AC/DC's "Highway to Hell;" included Michaels conducting an in-ring interview with Sable about who her mystery tag team partner would be later in the night, with Sable only saying it wouldn't be one of the Oddities before having Michaels dance with her; featured Michael Cole conducting a backstage interview with Triple H, with Chyna, X-Pac, the Road Dogg & Billy Gunn, about DX's future after Summer Slam; included an ad promoting the WWF on the Home Shopping Network following Summer Slam at Madison Square Garden; featured a video package recapping Mario Lopez's recent altercation with Val Venis, with Lopez commenting from the set of 'Pacific Blue' and Venis commenting while surrounded by several scantily-clad women; included Cole conducting a backstage interview with Vince McMahon in which he said he needed to protect the main event and may have to physically take Austin's sledgehammer away from him himself; featured an in-ring segment in which Jeff Jarrett & Southern Justice grabbed Howard Finkel, stuck him in a chair, and shaved Finkel's hair; Jarrett then took the mic and gave a warning to the crowd and X-Pac not to piss him off; included a backstage segment in which Sgt. Slaughter, Pat Patterson, and Gerald Brisco attempted to take the sledgehammer away from Austin; featured an ad promoting the STOMP 2 line of WWF action figures; included a backstage segment with Vince, Patterson, Brisco, and Slaughter in which Vince said he would take away the sledgehammer; featured Cole and Brian Collard, of HSN, backstage discussing the WWF merchandise that would be on sale by HSN after Summer Slam; included a look at the Lion's Den cage at the Theater; featured a backstage segment in which Vince pleaded with Austin to get rid of his weapon, with Austin saying he wouldn't be jumped from behind by Kane and he wasn't losing his belt; Anthony Mason of the Charlotte Hornets was shown in attendance; included an in-ring segment in which Dok Hendrix introduced the "Highway to Hell" Summer Slam music video, with cameramen showing shots of fans singing along in the crowd; featured a backstage shot of WWF IC Champion the Rock and Mark Henry arriving to the arena; included a video package recapping the history between Triple H and the Rock; featured an in-ring promo by the Rock, with Henry, WWF European Champion D-Lo Brown, and Kama, with DX quickly running out, attacking the Nation and clearing them from the ring; included a backstage shot of a hearse arriving to the arena, with Austin yanking out the driver before smashing the windows with his sledgehammer; moments later, Austin used a forklift to lift the hearse into the air as the show ended:

WWF IC Champion The Rock.

Brian Christopher & Scott Taylor defeated the Legion of Doom at 2:14 when Taylor pinned Road Warrior Animal after Road Warrior Hawk fell off the top rope and hit Animal in the back with his LOD helmet; prior to the bout, Darren Drozdov came out with Road Warrior Animal for the match, with Road Warrior Hawk eventually staggering out to the ring and convincing Droz to let him take his place in the ring; Edge was shown in the crowd during the bout; Hawk worked the entirety of the match wearing his LOD helmet

Gangrel pinned Dustin Runnels at 2:32 with the DDT; during the bout, a backstage camera showed Kevin Kelly & Tom Prichard at the Byte This table (Gangrel's MSG debut)

Skull & 8-Ball (w/ Paul Ellering) defeated Bradshaw & Vader when Skull pinned Vader at 2:56 with a roll up after Bradshaw punched Vader from the apron, moments after Vader accidentally collided with Bradshaw; prior to the contest, Bradshaw and Vader argued over which would start the match; Tony Chimel was the ring announcer for the match, replacing Howard Finkel; after the bout, Vader and Bradshaw brawled before several referees broke up the fight; moments later, the fight continued in the ring before Vader knocked Bradshaw to the floor with a clothesline

Pay-per-view bouts - featured Jim Ross & Jerry Lawler on commentary:

WWF European Champion D-Lo Brown defeated Val Venis via disqualification at 15:22 when Val knocked down the referee after the ref inadvertently crotched the challenger on the top rope

Kurrgan, Golga, & the Giant Silva (w/ Luna & the Insane Clown Posse) defeated WWF Light Heavyweight Champion Taka Michinoku, Mens Teioh, Sho Funaki, & Dick Togo (w/ Yamaguchi-San) at 10:11 when Kurrgan and Silva hit double chokeslams on the opposition

X-Pac (w/ Howard Finkel) pinned Jeff Jarrett at 11:10 in a Hair vs. Hair match after Southern Justice' outside interference backfired, with X-Pac hitting Jarrett with his own guitar for the win; after the match, Droz, the Headbangers, and the Road Dogg & Billy Gunn held Jarrett down as he had his head shaved

Edge & Sable defeated Marc Mero & Jackie in a mixed tag team match at 8:25 when Sable pinned Mero following Edge's Downward Spiral (Edge's MSG debut)

Ken Shamrock defeated Owen Hart (w/ Dan Severn) at 9:14 via submission in a Lion's Den match by reversing a Dragon sleeper into the ankle lock; this match was held at the Theater at MSG, adjacent to the arena (*The Attitude Era*)

Billy Gunn & the Road Dogg defeated WWF Tag Team Champion Mankind at 5:16 in a handicap No disqualification falls count anywhere match to win the titles following a spike piledriver onto one of the title belts; after the match, Mankind's missing partner Kane appeared out of a dumpster at ringside and attacked Mankind with a sledgehammer

Triple H (w/ Chyna) defeated WWF IC Champion the Rock (w/ Mark Henry) at 26:03 in a ladder match to win the title after Chyna hit a low blow on the champion as he climbed the ladder; prior to the bout, the Chris Warren Band performed the DX theme song to bring the challenger and Chyna to the ring; late in the match, Henry threw powder in Triple H's face, blinding him; after the contest, X-Pac and WWF Tag Team Champions the Road Dogg & Billy Gunn appeared to celebrate and help Triple H to the back (*The Ladder Match, The Epic Journey of Dwayne The Rock Johnson*)

WWF World Champion Steve Austin pinned the Undertaker at 20:50 following a low blow and Stunner after avoiding the challenger's trademark arm attack off the top rope (*Greatest Wrestling Stars of the 90s, Stone Cold Steve Austin: The Bottom Line on the Most Popular Superstar of All Time*)

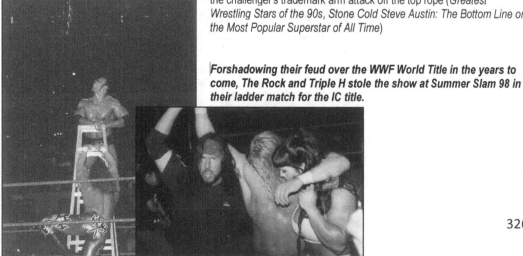

Forshadowing their feud over the WWF World Title in the years to come, The Rock and Triple H stole the show at Summer Slam 98 in their ladder match for the IC title.

326

Stone KO'd

"In that timeframe, there was just as much emphasis on Raw the next night as there was on Summer Slam. It was all about Raw, it was all about the TV show. ...The famous story, which is true, is that (Steve) Austin got KO'ed in the opening spot and forgot everything in the match and Earl Hebner basically had to remember everything for that match and recite it back to him for the entire rest of the way. If that concussion was perhaps just slightly more severe, and he's out cold, now what do you do?"

Kevin Kellv. *The Place to Be Nation. 2011*

WWF @ New York City, NY - Madison Square Garden - October 25, 1998 (18,086; 15,226 paid; sell out)
The Headbangers defeated Matt & Jeff Hardy when Thrasher pinned Matt after a legdrop off the top (Matt & Jeff's MSG debut)
Edge pinned the Godfather with the Downward Spiral
Marc Mero & WWF Women's Champion Jackie defeated Sable & Val Venis when Jackie pinned Sable as Mero held Sable down; prior to the bout, Goldust attacked Venis
Golga & Kurrgan (w/ Luna Vachon) defeated Brian Christopher & Scott Taylor when Golga pinned Taylor with the sit-down splash
Steve Austin defeated the Undertaker, Kane, and the Rock in a steel cage match by pinning Rock with the Stunner; Sgt. Slaughter was the guest referee for the bout but another referee made the pinfall for Austin after Austin hit Slaughter with the Stunner; after the contest, Vince McMahon wheeled himself ringside in his wheelchair and argued with Austin, still in the cage; McMahon then went to climb the cage, distracting Austin as the Big Bossman snuck in the cage and attacked him; after Bossman assaulted Austin, he took McMahon backstage in his wheelchair
Gangrel pinned Goldust with the DDT after Val Venis distracted Goldust
WWF European Champion X-Pac defeated Jeff Jarrett via disqualification after Jarrett smashed his guitar over X-Pac's head
Road Warrior Animal & Darren Drozdov (w/ Road Warrior Hawk) defeated Skull & 8-Ball when Droz scored the pin after Paul Ellering accidentally struck one of his own men with his briefcase
WWF IC Champion Ken Shamrock defeated Mankind and Vader when Vader submitted to Shamrock's ankle lock; after the bout, Mankind put the Mandible Claw on Shamrock (Vader's last WWE appearance for 14 years)
WWF Tag Team Champions the Road Dogg & Billy Gunn defeated Mark Henry & D-Lo Brown

WWF @ New York City, NY - Madison Square Garden - December 27, 1998 (16,282; sell out)

Included an opening segment in which Howard Finkel introduced Shane McMahon, who then introduced Vince McMahon, with Pat Patterson and Gerald Brisco; Vince then cut a promo saying he was glad Steve Austin couldn't appear and that Christmas was over; he went on to say he would prove his strength by beating Mankind in an arm wrestling contest later in the show and would have Kane destroy the Undertaker, then wished everyone a Happy New Year

Edge pinned Headbanger Mosh by reversing a powerbomb into a sunset flip

Goldust pinned Tiger Ali Singh with a powerbomb in less than 3 minutes

Al Snow & Scorpio fought Skull & 8-Ball to a no contest when Edge, Gangrel, & Christian interfered

Vince McMahon defeated Mankind in an arm wrestling

match; the stipulation said that the winner would receive a kiss from Sable; Sable was introduced as the guest official but Dave Hebner officiated the contest; prior to the contest, Vince was escorted to the ring by Shane McMahon, Pat Patterson, & Gerald Brisco; after the contest, Shane, Patterson, & Brisco returned, with Vince allowing Mankind to kiss Sable in his place; moments later, Test ran out and attacked Mankind; Shane joined in attacking Mankind as well before Vince kissed Sable; McMahon and his group then left the ring, with Sable then giving Mankind a kiss

The Acolytes defeated Road Warrior Animal & Darren Drozdov in less than 1 minute when Farooq pinned Animal with an inside cradle after Droz tripped his partner; after the match, Animal and Droz had to be held apart by officials

WWF World Champion the Rock (w/ Test) pinned Triple H with the Corporate Elbow after Test attacked the challenger; Triple H initially won the match and title earlier in the bout after using the title belt as a weapon but the match was forced to continue by Pat Patterson after sending Chyna backstage

Mankind defeated Test via submission with the Mandible Claw

Val Venis & the Godfather defeated Mark Henry & D-Lo Brown when Val pinned D-Lo with an inside cradle after Brown missed the Lo Down

WWF European Champion X-Pac defeated Jeff Jarrett in a Guitar on a Pole match with the X-Factor and a guitar shot to the head

Billy Gunn & WWF Hardcore Champion Road Dogg defeated WWF Tag Team Champions Big Bossman & WWF IC Champion Ken Shamrock via disqualification when Shamrock attacked the referee as Gunn had Bossman covered

The Undertaker (w/ Paul Bearer) pinned Kane in a streetfight with the tombstone after Shane McMahon accidentally hit Kane with a chair; after the match, the Undertaker beat up Vince McMahon while Kane hit a chokeslam on both Gerald Brisco and Pat Patterson until Shane threatened to send Kane back to the insane asylum if he didn't stop

WWF @ New York City, NY - Madison Square Garden - February 7, 1999 (16,399; sell out)
Edge & Christian defeated the Blue Meanie & Bob Holly
Al Snow defeated Goldust
WWF Tag Team Champions Owen Hart & Jeff Jarrett defeated Val Venis & the Godfather after WWF IC Champion Ken Shamrock interfered
WWF IC Champion Ken Shamrock defeated Steve Blackman and Dan Severn
The Undertaker & the Acolytes defeated WWF European Champion X-Pac, WWF Hardcore Champion the Road Dogg, & Billy Gunn when Taker pinned Road Dogg; late in the contest, Road Dogg injured his neck after falling through the ropes to the floor; after the bout, he was taken backstage on a stretcher; due to the severity of the injury, he was taken out of the St. Valentine's Day Massacre card the following week
Jackie, Matt, & Jeff Hardy defeated Mark Henry, D-Lo Brown, & Luna Vachon after WWF Women's Champion Sable appeared ringside and distracted Luna
Kane (w/ Chyna) defeated Triple H
Steve Austin & WWF World Champion Mankind defeated the Rock & the Big Bossman in a Rattlesnake Rules match

WWF @ New York City, NY - Madison Square Garden - April 24, 1999 (16,821 paid; sell out)
Included Howard Finkel hosting a 10-bell salute to the recent passing of Rick Rude; featured an in-ring promo by Shane McMahon, with the Mean Street Posse, in which he said Backlash would be Steve Austin's last night as WWF World Champion and that the Corporation would win in the night's main event
The Acolytes defeated Skull & 8-Ball at the 3-minute mark when Farooq scored the pin following a powerslam
Jerry Lawler pinned Darren Drozdov after hitting him with his crown
WWF Tag Team Champions X-Pac & Kane defeated Big Bossman & Test when Kane pinned Test with the tombstone after Bossman walked out of the match
WWF Hardcore Champion Hardcore Holly pinned Val Venis after Al Snow interfered and hit Venis with Head
The Road Dogg & Billy Gunn defeated Owen Hart & Jeff Jarrett and Gangrel, Christian, & Edge in an elimination match; Jarrett pinned Edge; Gunn pinned Hart with the Fameasser after Owen had Road Dogg caught in the Sharpshooter
Al Snow & Tori defeated D-Lo Brown & Ivory when Tori pinned Ivory; after the match, Terri Runnels & Jackie ran out and Jackie attacked Tori
The Undertaker & Mideon defeated Ken Shamrock & Mankind when Undertaker pinned Mankind with the tombstone after Mideon attacked Mankind as Mankind had the Mandible Claw applied on Taker
WWF IC Champion the Godfather defeated Goldust (w/ the Blue Meanie) with the Pimp Drop after a blinded Goldust hit the Shattered Dreams on Meanie
WWF World Champion Steve Austin & the Big Show defeated the Rock & Triple H when Austin pinned Rock with the Stunner after Rock collided with the Mean Street Posse on the ring apron

WWF @ New York City, NY - Madison Square Garden - June 26, 1999 (16,543 paid; sell out)
Included an in-ring promo by Vince McMahon in which he apologized for the poor performance of the New York Knicks and New York Rangers, and went on to apologize for Steve Austin since Austin wouldn't beat WWF World Champion the Undertaker in the main event
Edge & Christian (w/ Gangrel) defeated D-Lo Brown & Mark Henry when Christian pinned Henry
The Godfather pinned Mideon after a backdrop
WWF Hardcore Champion Al Snow defeated Hardcore Holly and Steve Blackman by pinning Blackman after Blackman was put through a table
Ken Shamrock defeated WWF IC Champion Jeff Jarrett via count-out after Debra McMichael took her top off to distract Shamrock, allowing Jarrett to flee the ring; after the bout, Shamrock chased Jarrett back into the ring and applied the ankle lock before then chasing Howard Finkel backstage
The Rock pinned the Big Bossman in a nightstick match with the People's Elbow after using the nightstick as a weapon; earlier in the bout, Test came out and briefly fought with Bossman
The Big Show pinned Triple H with the chokeslam
Viscera pinned Val Venis with a splash after Nicole Bass distracted Venis from ringside
Billy Gunn pinned Road Dogg with the Fameasser after Chyna came out and hit a low blow on Road dogg
WWF Tag Team Champions the Acolytes defeated Kane & X-Pac when Bradshaw pinned X-Pac
Steve Austin defeated WWF World Champion the Undertaker via disqualification when Paul Bearer pulled referee Earl Hebner from the ring after Austin hit the champion with the Stunner

Tony Garea and Pat Patterson, acting as agents, backstage at MSG. The two were regulars at WWE MSG events in the 1970s and 80s.

World Wrestling Federation

SATURDAY, AUGUST 28, 1999
MADISON SQUARE GARDEN
NEW YORK, NY

MAIN EVENT: FOR THE WORLD WRESTLING FEDERATION CHAMPIONSHIP

HHH	vs.	THE ROCK
Greenwich, CT ...246 lbs.		Miami, FL ...275 lbs.
(CHAMPION)		**(CHALLENGER)**

FOR THE TAG TEAM CHAMPIONSHIP

THE UNDERTAKER & THE BIG SHOW	vs.	X-PAC & KANE
Combined Weight...828 lbs.		Combined Weight...530lbs.
(CHAMPIONS)		**(CHALLENGERS)**

MANKIND	vs.	MR.ASS
287 lbs.		265 lbs.

FOR THE INTERCONTINENTAL CHAMPIONSHIP

JEFF JARRETT	vs.	D'LO BROWN
Nashville, TN...230 lbs.		Chicago, IL...268 lbs.
(CHAMPION)		**(CHALLENGER)**

KNOCK OUT OR SUBMISSION WINS THE MATCH

KEN SHAMROCK	vs.	STEVE BLACKMAN
San Diego, CA...235 lbs.		Annville, PA...245 lbs.

THREE TEAM TAG TEAM MATCH

CHRISTIAN & EDGE	vs.	HARDY BOYZ	vs.	THE ACOLYTES
Combined Weight..462 lbs.		Combined Weight...430 lbs.		Combined Weight...567 lbs.

TEST	vs.	BIG BOSSMAN
275 lbs.		Cobb County, GA...305 lbs.

MIXED TAG TEAM MATCH

AL SNOW & TORI	vs.	HARDCORE HOLLY & IVORY

VAL VENIS	vs.	MIDIAN
Las Vegas, NV ...242 lbs.		306 lbs.

CHAZ	vs.	GANGREL
Cherry Hill, NJ....320 lbs.		252 lbs.

PLUS A SPECIAL APPEARANCE BY CHRIS JERICHO

TUNE IN AND CATCH THE ACTION!

Y2J's MSG debut

"The show opened with Chris Jericho coming to the ring at MSG for the first time ever to cut a promo. While he was talking, the microphone kept cutting out. As he wrote about in his book, this was not part of the show, but I thought he did an excellent job in covering that up by throwing a temper tantrum, kicking the ropes and pouting. Several microphones later, Jericho finally got his point across and left the ring.

Mankind came to the ring for his match with Billy Gunn. He grabbed the microphone and told everyone that he had ordered the same pair of tights that Gunn was wearing in the masculine pink color and lips all over them. He said that we were lucky that he didn't wear them because then New York City would see what a real bad ass looks like."

Dennis Spicacci, *Carteret, NJ*

WWF @ New York City, NY - Madison Square Garden - August 28, 1999 (16,452 paid; sell out)

Following the national anthem, Chris Jericho came out and cut an in-ring promo saying he was there to save the crowd from boredom (Jericho's MSG debut)

WWF IC Champion Jeff Jarrett pinned D-Lo Brown at the 10-minute mark with a small package immediately after Brown hit a superplex

Gangrel pinned Chaz with the Impaler

The Big Bossman pinned Test after choking him with his nightstick as Shane McMahon distracted the referee

Val Venis pinned Mideon with the Money Shot

The Acolytes defeated Matt & Jeff Hardy and Edge & Christian in an elimination match; Edge pinned Jeff with the spear; Bradshaw pinned Edge after Gangrel interfered and hit Edge with the Impaler

Mankind defeated Billy Gunn via submission with the Mr. Socko Mandible Claw

Al Snow & Tori defeated Hardcore Holly & WWF Women's Champion Ivory when Tori pinned Ivory after Ivory was tripped by Snow

Steve Blackman defeated Ken Shamrock in a submission or knock out match with a head scissors after, as the referee was knocked out, Chris Jericho ran out and hit Shamrock with a steel chair

WWF Tag Team Champions the Undertaker & the Big Show defeated X-Pac & Kane when Show pinned X-Pac (Taker's last MSG appearance for 10 months)

WWF World Champion Triple H defeated the Rock with the Pedigree after hitting him with the title belt; late in the bout, Chyna dragged the referee out of the ring after the challenger hit the Rock Bottom and People's Elbow, with Shane McMahon then coming out with a referee shirt; McMahon gave a fast count during the pinfall

In 1999, pro wrestling was at the forefront of pop culture. And few names drew a bigger reaction than The Rock, who made his WWF TV debut at MSG just 3 years prior.

WWF @ New York City, NY - Madison Square Garden - October 30, 1999 (16,678 paid; sell out)

The Godfather pinned Viscera after Viscera became distracted by the hos at ringside

D-Lo Brown pinned Mideon with the Lo Down

The Big Show fought the Big Bossman to a double count-out in less than a minute; after the bout, Albert ran out and sustained the chokeslam from Show, with Show then doing the same to Tony Garea and Earl Hebner

WWF Tag Team Champions Crash & Hardcore Holly defeated the Road Dogg & Billy Gunn after Bubba Ray & D-Von Dudley interfered (Crash's MSG debut)

Mankind pinned Val Venis with a DDT onto his copy of 'Have a Nice Day;' prior to the bout, Mankind cut an in-ring promo about his new book

WWF European Champion Davey Boy Smith defeated Test

X-Pac pinned Kane after the Road Dogg & Billy Gunn came out, with Road Dogg distracting the referee as Gunn hit Kane with a chair; after the match, WWF World Champion Triple H came out and aided in attacking Kane

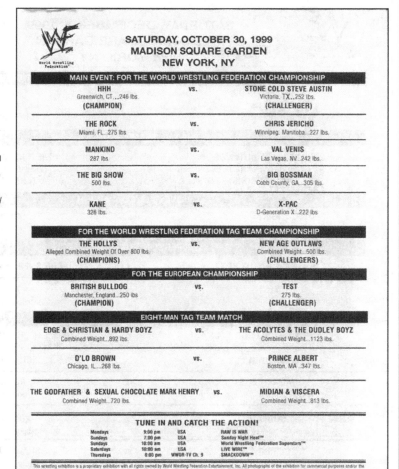

SATURDAY, OCTOBER 30, 1999
MADISON SQUARE GARDEN
NEW YORK, NY

MAIN EVENT: FOR THE WORLD WRESTLING FEDERATION CHAMPIONSHIP		
HHH Greenwich, CT...246 lbs. (CHAMPION)	vs.	STONE COLD STEVE AUSTIN Victoria, TX...252 lbs. (CHALLENGER)
THE ROCK Miami, FL...275 lbs.	vs.	CHRIS JERICHO Winnipeg, Manitoba...227 lbs.
MANKIND 287 lbs.	vs.	VAL VENIS Las Vegas, NV...242 lbs.
THE BIG SHOW 500 lbs.	vs.	BIG BOSSMAN Cobb County, GA...305 lbs.
KANE 326 lbs.	vs.	X-PAC D-Generation X...222 lbs.

FOR THE WORLD WRESTLING FEDERATION TAG TEAM CHAMPIONSHIP		
THE HOLLYS Alleged Combined Weight Of Over 800 lbs. (CHAMPIONS)	vs.	NEW AGE OUTLAWS Combined Weight...500 lbs. (CHALLENGERS)

FOR THE EUROPEAN CHAMPIONSHIP		
BRITISH BULLDOG Manchester, England...250 lbs (CHAMPION)	vs.	TEST 275 lbs. (CHALLENGER)

EIGHT-MAN TAG TEAM MATCH		
EDGE & CHRISTIAN & HARDY BOYZ Combined Weight...892 lbs.	vs.	THE ACOLYTES & THE DUDLEY BOYZ Combined Weight...1123 lbs.
D'LO BROWN Chicago, IL...268 lbs.	vs.	PRINCE ALBERT Boston, MA...347 lbs.
THE GODFATHER & SEXUAL CHOCOLATE MARK HENRY Combined Weight...720 lbs.	vs.	MIDIAN & VISCERA Combined Weight...813 lbs.

TUNE IN AND CATCH THE ACTION!

Mondays	9:00 pm	USA	RAW IS WAR
Sundays	7:00 pm	USA	Sunday Night Heat™
Sundays	10:00 am	USA	World Wrestling Federation Superstars™
Saturdays	10:00 am	USA	LIVE WIRE™
Thursdays	8:00 pm	WWOR-TV Ch. 9	SMACKDOWN™

This wrestling exhibition is a proprietary exhibition with all rights owned by World Wrestling Federation Entertainment, Inc. All photographs of the exhibition for commercial purposes and/or the reprinting of any photographs of the exhibition in commercial publications without the express written permission of World Wrestling Federation Entertainment, Inc. is strictly prohibited. When scheduled talent is unable to appear due to circumstances beyond the control of the promoter, the promoter reserves the right to make suitable substitutions. Printed in the USA.

WWF European Champion Davey Boy Smith (w/ the Mean Street Posse) pinned Test after one of the Posse members hit the challenger with a chair; Debra McMichael was the guest ring announcer for the bout; after the contest, Smith left the ring as the Posse attacked Test; moments later, Shane McMahon ran out and helped Test clear the ring (Smith's MSG debut after a 2-year absence)

The Rock pinned Chris Jericho with the Rock Bottom after WWF IC Champion Chyna appeared ringside and distracted Jericho; after the match, WWF World Champion Triple H, Billy Gunn & the Road Dogg attacked the Rock (Jericho's MSG in-ring debut)

Edge, Christian, Matt & Jeff Hardy defeated the Dudley Boyz & the Acolytes

Steve Austin defeated WWF World Champion Triple H via disqualification when X-Pac, the Road Dogg, & Billy Gunn interfered; earlier in the match, the champion attempted to leave ringside but was stopped by Kane; after the bout, the Rock and Kane helped make the save, with Austin, Rock, and Kane then drinking beers to end the show

---

The ladies on 42nd Street.

"Mankind came out for his match with Val Venis and grabs the microphone. He said the Big Valbowski reminds him of the ladies on 42nd Street - he sucks. The crowd ate that line up and almost gave Mick a standing ovation."

Dennis Spicacci, *Carteret, NJ*

World Wrestling Federation

SATURDAY, DECEMBER 4, 1999
MADISON SQUARE GARDEN
NEW YORK, NY

FOR THE WORLD WRESTLING FEDERATION CHAMPIONSHIP

THE BIG SHOW	vs.	HHH
500 lbs.		D-Generation X...260 lbs.
(CHAMPION)		**(CHALLENGER)**

FOR THE TAG TEAM CHAMPIONSHIP

NEW AGE OUTLAWS	vs.	THE ROCK & MANKIND
Combined Weight...500 lbs.		Combined Weight...562 lbs.
(CHAMPIONS)		**(CHALLENGERS)**

ONE FALL TO A FINISH

KANE	vs.	VISCERA
326 lbs.		508lbs.

SIX PERSON TAG TEAM MATCH

CHYNA & HARDY BOYZ	vs.	CHRIS JERICHO & TOO COOL

TEST	vs.	X-PAC
282 lbs.		D-Generation X... 222 lbs.

FOR THE EUROPEAN CHAMPIONSHIP

BRITISH BULLDOG	vs.	CHRISTIAN
Manchester, England...250 lbs.		Toronto, Canada...217 lbs.
(CHAMPION)		**(CHALLENGER)**

VAL VENIS	vs.	AL SNOW
Las Vegas, NV... 242 lbs.		Lima, OH...246 lbs.

THE GODFATHER	vs.	KURT ANGLE
Red Light District... 320 lbs.		Pittsburgh, PA...228 lbs.

RAKISHI	vs.	SHAWN STASIAK
401lbs.		Tampa, FL...250 lbs.

16 MAN TAG TEAM BATTLE ROYAL, FEATURING:

THE ACOLYTES	DUDLEY BOYZ
MEAN STREET POSSE	HEAD BANGERS
TAKA MICHINOKU & FUNAKI	BIG BOSSMAN & PRINCE ALBERT
THE HOLLYS	D'LO BROWN & SEXUAL CHOCOLATE MARK HENRY

TUNE IN AND CATCH THE ACTION!

My first house show

"My Mom was the one that took us to my first house show, live show. We were up in the nosebleeds. At that time it wasn't renovated. It was section 427. So you could tell the weather from up there and we didn't care. It was me, my mom and my brother and we were excited to be there. I learned you can wait outside for them to walk in and get autographs, which was mind boggling to me. She took us and we waited outside the side entrance, and learned that if you got there late you would get the referees, which I was still excited to see. If you really wanted to get the good people you had to get there early. It started off, we probably got there 2 hours before. But after that, it went as far as 8 hours."

Reny Amoros, *Bronx, NY*

WWF @ New York City, NY - Madison Square Garden - December 4, 1999 (16,510 paid; sell out)
Tickets for the 2000 Royal Rumble went on sale during the show; Taz was backstage
Crash & Hardcore Holly won a 16-man tag team battle royal also involving the Acolytes, Mean Street Posse, Taka Michonoku & Sho Funaki, Dudley Boyz, Headbangers, WWF Hardcore Champion Big Bossman & Albert, and D-Lo Brown & Mark Henry
Kane (w/ Tori) pinned Viscera (w/ Mideon) with the chokeslam
Kurt Angle pinned the Godfather with the Angle Slam
WWF European Champion Davey Boy Smith pinned Christian with the running powerslam after the Mean Street Posse interfered
Rikishi pinned Shawn Stasiak
Matt & Jeff Hardy defeated Chris Jericho, Grandmaster Sexay & Scotty 2 Hotty in a handicap match when Jeff pinned Scotty with a Swanton after Chyna interfered and gave Jericho a low blow; the match was to have included Chyna as part of a 6-person tag team bout but she was too injured to compete; after the bout, Jericho attacked Sexay & Scotty until Rikishi made the save
WWF World Champion Big Show pinned Triple H with the chokeslam
X-Pac pinned Test with a low blow and the X-Factor
Al Snow pinned Val Venis with a roll up
The Rock & Mankind defeated WWF Tag Team Champions the Road Dogg & Billy Gunn via disqualification after Al Snow interfered

It didn't take long for Chris Jericho to connect with the MSG crowd, upon his arrival to the WWF in August 1999.

Mankind and WWF IC Champion Chyna.

339

ROYAL RUMBLE
Madison Square Garden – January 23, 2000

WWF @ New York City, NY - Madison Square Garden - January 23, 2000 (19,231; 16,629 paid; sell out)
Sunday Night Heat - featured live backstage interviews from MSG; included numerous Rumble participants drawing their entry numbers, with the Mean Street Posse and Kaientai being excluded since they were denied spots in the match; featured a segment on the opening of WWF New York, with footage from the Sugar Ray concert as well as comments by many of the WWF superstars in attendance; included footage from seperate Radio WWF interviews conducted over the weekend with Steve Austin and Triple H as well as the Road Dogg and Bradshaw fighting in the studio during a broadcast; featured an in-ring promo by the Big Show regarding the Royal Rumble match Pay-per-view bouts - included Jim Ross & Jerry Lawler on commentary; featured the Miss Rumble contest, with participants including WWF Women's Champion Miss Kitty, Jackie, BB, Terri, and Luna, in which Mae Young came out unannounced and took off her shirt to reveal prosthetic breasts; moments later, Mae was announced as the winner; judges for the contest included Sgt. Slaughter, Tony Garea, Johnny Valiant, Freddie Blassie, the Fabulous Moolah, and Andy Richter from "Late Night with Conan O'Brien"; Jerry Lawler was the MC for the segment; included Jonathan Coachman interviewing Linda McMahon at WWF New York regarding the McMahon-Helmsley Era:
Tazz (mystery opponent) defeated Kurt Angle at 3:14 with the Tazzmission; after the bout, Angle was attended to by medics and taken backstage on a stretcher; later in the broadcast, Angle claimed because he was choked out - which is illegal - his undefeated streak still stood (Tazz' surprise debut; Angle's first TV singles loss)
Matt & Jeff Hardy defeated the Dudley Boyz in a tables match at 10:17; Bubba Ray was put through a table at ringside at 4:12 following a legdrop off a ladder by Matt and a top rope splash by Jeff; Matt was powerbombed off the top through a table in the ring, on top of two sets of ring steps, by Bubba Ray at 6:31; D-Von was eliminated by a Swanton from Jeff after both teams began brawling into the crowd; Michael Cole conducted a backstage interview with the Hardyz & Terri prior to the bout in which Matt & Jeff told Terri she was staying backstage because it would be too violent for her to be at ringside; moments later, the Dudleyz cut an in-ring promo saying the NYC fans were ass-backwards for cheering the Hardyz and booing Atlanta Braves pitcher John Rocker (*Twist of Fate: The Matt & Jeff Hardy Story*)
WWF IC Champion Chris Jericho defeated WWF IC Champion Chyna and Hardcore Holly at 7:30 by pinning Chyna with a bulldog and Lionsault after Chyna applied a Boston Crab on Holly; due to the decision, Jericho became the sole holder of the IC title
WWF Tag Team Champions Billy Gunn & the Road Dogg defeated the Acolytes at 2:37 when Gunn pinned Bradshaw with the Fameasser after X-Pac interfered as referee Tim White was knocked down on the floor and hit a spin wheel kick on the challenger
WWF World Champion Triple H pinned Cactus Jack at 26:49 with the Pedigree followed by a second Pedigree onto a pile of thumb tacs inside the ring; Stephanie McMahon escorted the champion ringside prior to the match before going backstage; mid-way through the bout, the Rock interfered and hit the champion over the head with a steel chair as both participants were near the entrance; late in the contest, Stephanie returned ringside after the challenger poured a bag of thumb tacs over the ring; after the match, Cactus knocked over the champion's stretcher as he was being helped backstage, dragged him back inside the ring, and hit him with a 2x4 wrapped in barbed wire (*Most Memorable Matches of 2000, Triple H: The Game, Mick Foley's Greatest Hits & Misses, The History of the WWE Heavyweight Championship*)
The Rock won the 30-man Royal Rumble match by last eliminating the Big Show at 51:47; due to pre-match stipulations, Rock earned a WWF World Title match at WrestleMania
Order of entry: D-Lo Brown (00:00); Grandmaster Sexay (00:00); Headbanger Mosh (1:41); Taka Michinoku & Sho Funaki, who were not legal participants, ran to the ring and were quickly thrown out; Christian (3:23); Rikishi (5:05); Scotty 2 Hotty (6:40); Steve Blackman (8:42); Viscera (10:32); the Big Bossman (14:23); Bossman refused to get in the ring with Rikishi until Test came out and threw him in; Test (14:28); Davey Boy Smith (15:30); Gangrel (17:30); Taka & Funaki came out again and were again thrown to the floor; Taka hit his face on the floor after being thrown out and was taken to the hospital; Edge (19:07); Bob Backlund (21:03); WWF IC Champion Chris Jericho (22:49);

Crash Holly (24:27); Chyna (26:02); Farooq (27:36); WWF Tag Team Champion the Road Dogg (29:02); Al Snow (30:35); WWF European Champion Val Venis (32:13); Funaki came out again and was quickly thrown out of the ring; Albert (33:49); Hardcore Holly (35:28); the Rock (37:02); WWF Tag Team Champion Billy Gunn (38:38); the Big Show (40:39); Bradshaw (41:53); Kane (escorted to the ring by Tori) (43:50); Funaki came out a final time and was thrown out by Snow; the Godfather (46:09); X-Pac (46:52)

Order of elimination: Mosh by Rikishi (5:18); Christian by Rikishi following a belly to belly suplex (5:32); D-Lo by Rikishi following the Rikishi Driver (6:09); Grandmaster & Scotty by Rikishi after all three men danced together in the ring (7:43); after the elimination, Too Cool & Rikishi showed there were no hard feelings; Blackman by Rikishi following the Rikishi Driver (9:27); Viscera by Rikishi via a shoulderblock after three superkicks (11:57); Rikishi by Edge, Gangrel, Backlund, Bossman, Smith, & Test (21:27); Backlund by Jericho via a dropkick (23:04); after his elimination, Backlund left through the crowd; Jericho by Chyna following a suplex from the apron to the floor (26:36); Chyna by Bossman after being shoved off the apron (26:40); Farooq by the Bossman after Rodney, Pete Gas, & Joey Abs came out and attacked Farooq (27:53); Smith by Road Dogg (30:51); Edge by Snow & Venis via a double backdrop (33:55); Bossman by Rock via a punch (37:11); Crash by Rock following a floatover DDT (39:22); Test by Show via a boot to the face as Test was straddled on the top rope (40:45); Gangrel by Show (40:50); Bradshaw by Gunn & Road Dogg after Bradshaw fought off an interfering Mean Street Posse and threw all three men to the floor (42:17); moments later, Farooq joined Bradshaw in battling the Posse backstage; Venis by Kane via a choke throw (44:00); Albert by Kane via a clothesline (45:12); Hardcore by Kane via a clothesline (47:16); Godfather by Show (47:41); Snow by Rock via a clothesline (47:52); Road Dogg by Gunn (48:04); Gunn by Kane following two uppercuts (48:16); moments later, Kane brawled with the New Age Outlaws outside the ring, distracting referees as the Rock threw X-Pac over the top; Kane by X-Pac via a spin kick after Kane bodyslammed Big Show (50:01); X-Pac by Show via a press slam to the floor (50:24); Show by Rock when Rock held onto the top rope as Show had him on his shoulder and ran toward the ropes to throw him out, with the momentum sending Show over the top to the floor; after the elimination, Rock cut an in-ring promo on going to WrestleMania but was eventually interrupted by Show, who ran back out to the ring and threw Rock to the floor

The MSG Rumble

"I wasn't big into the Internet at that time, so I didn't know for sure that Taz was going to debut. Taz was the face of ECW, so his WWE debut was a pretty big deal. It was common knowledge he was leaving ECW for the WWE, and there were rumors he would make his debut at the Rumble, but I didn't know for certain it would be at this event. As soon as the orange and black appeared on the TitanTron, the place popped huge. Rumble matches always come across as exciting to watch on TV, but it's true that they really are even better in person. The most memorable part of this match for me was Rikishi and Too Cool dancing. That's not a knock on the match, it's just that it was such a unique and entertaining part. The best part of this entire night didn't happen on the show....although the show was really great and fun. But the best part of the night came after the show. There is an area on the side of MSG where most of the wrestlers enter and exit the building. This area is very visible to the street, and lots of fans line up outside of the barricades to see the wrestlers exit and enter. After all the times at MSG, this was the first time I found out about this. We stood with the rest of the crowd and saw quite a few of the wrestlers come and go, and remember....this is January....late at night and it was freezing cold, so it seemed like forever waiting for each guy to come out. Most of the wrestlers were coming out of the arena and quickly getting into fancy SUVs or fancy town cars and being chauffeured off. All of a sudden there is a commotion away from exit area, and people are screaming and cheering, so I turn around and it's Mick Foley walking directly past us, and in traditional Foley fashion he gets into the back of a taxi cab! This was a main event guy, at the highest level of his career, and he just struts out of MSG in sweatpants and hops in a taxi. A lot of us were chanting "Foley, Foley, Foley" as he drove off. It was a really cool moment, and he was one of only a few of the wrestlers who acknowledged the fans as they left the building. People started to head off as it looked like most of the wrestlers were done leaving, but out of no where, literally stomping down the street, heading towards the Times Square area was Bob Backlund. He was in the stands for the show that night, but it was a surprise to see him after the show marching down the street like that. It was pretty funny, and capped off a really entertaining night."
Michael Berlinski, *Edison, NJ*

RAW IS WAR
MONDAY FEBRUARY 28, 2000
MADISON SQUARE GARDEN

GET READY FOR THE WARZONE!

LAST NIGHT AT "NO WAY OUT", TRIPLE H DEFEATED CACTUS JACK INSIDE "HELL IN A CELL" TO RETAIN THE WWF CHAMPIONSHIP AND END CACTUS' CAREER. TONIGHT, THE WWF PAYS TRIBUTE TO MICK FOLEY WITH A STIRRING VIDEO TRIBUTE!

ALSO LAST NIGHT, SHANE MCMAHON RETURNED AND SHOCKED THE WORLD BY ASSISTING THE BIG SHOW IN DEFEATING THE ROCK! THE BIG SHOW IS NOW THE NUMBER ONE CONTENDER AND IS HEADING TO WRESTLEMANIA!

WORD IS THE ROCK IS HERE TONIGHT AND UPSET!

IN ACTION TONIGHT:

THE NEW WWF TAG TEAM CHAMPIONS, THE DUDLEY BOYS HAVE BEEN CHALLENGED BY DX TO DEFEND THE GOLD!

THE NEW INTERCONTINENTAL CHAMPION, KURT ANGLE HAS ISSUED AN OPEN CHALLENGE TO ANYONE WHO FEELS THEY ARE WORTHY OF A SHOT AT ONE OF HIS TWO TITLES!

TALK ABOUT A DREAM MATCHUP!
TAZZ GOES ONE ON ONE AGAINST CHRIS BENOIT!

EDGE AND CHRISTIAN FACE
AL SNOW AND STEVE BLACKMAN

THE HARDCORE CHAMPIONSHIP IS ON THE LINE WHEN CRASH HOLLY DEFENDS AGAINST MARK HENRY

ALSO HERE TONIGHT: CHRIS JERICHO AND CHYNA, THE RADICALS, THE HARDY BOYZ, THE ACOLYTES AND MORE!
CARD SUBJECT TO CHANGE

WWF @ New York City, NY - Madison Square Garden - February 28, 2000 (12,256; sell out)

Joey Abs pinned an unknown

Jakked: Test pinned Mideon with an elbow drop off the top at 4:10

The Headbangers defeated Kevin Landry & the Inferno Kid at 2:17 following the Stage Dive

WWF Light Heavyweight Champion Essa Rios (w/ Lita) pinned Sho Funaki at 3:11 with a moonsault

The Godfather & D-Lo Brown defeated the Big Bossman & Albert at 4:33 when D-Lo pinned Albert following a leg lariat

Raw is War - included WWF World Champion Triple H, with Stephanie McMahon, cutting an in-ring promo on the previous night's Hell in a Cell match against Mick Foley in which he said he had more respect for Foley than anyone and played a tribute video to Foley's career; the video began with classic images of Mick but then cut to embarrassing clips in which Foley was beaten down to the tune of the DX theme; moments later, Shane McMahon & the Big Show interrupted, with Shane cutting a promo on Stephanie running Vince out of the WWF, then stating that the Big Show would be the future world champion; the Rock then came out onto the stage and said he would be the WWF Champion at WrestleMania despite what happened at No Way Out; Triple H then stated that since Rock was no longer the #1 contender, he would have to start off at the bottom of the roster and face the Brooklyn Brawler later in the show; featured a backstage segment in which Billy Gunn complained to DX about not being involved in the tag team title shot against the Dudley Boyz, despite the fact he had his arm in a sling; after telling Triple H off, Triple H, X-Pac, and the Road Dogg attacked Gunn and threw him out of the dressing room; included a musical tribute to the career of Mick Foley to the tune of Sarah McLachlan's "I Will Remember You":

Matt & Jeff Hardy defeated the Acolytes at 3:57 when Matt pinned Bradshaw with a kick to the midsection and the Twist of Fate after Jeff made the blind tag

Rikishi defeated WWF IC & European Champion Kurt Angle via count-out at 1:39 when Angle left the ring after sustaining the Stinkface; prior to the bout, Angle made an open challenge in the ring for anyone to face him, which Rikishi accepted; immediately after the bout, Chris Jericho came out with Chyna and threw Angle back inside the ring where Rikishi hit the Rikishi Driver and Bonzai Drop; moments later, Chris Benoit, Eddie Guerrero, Dean Malenko, and Perry Saturn attacked Jericho, Rikishi, and Chyna, with Too Cool eventually coming out to make the save; moments later, Rikishi, Too Cool, Jericho, and Chyna danced in the ring; only the Euro title was on the line

Edge & Christian (w/ Terri) defeated Al Snow & Steve Blackman at 3:23 when Edge pinned Blackman with the spear after Christian hit a missile dropkick while Blackman was distracted by Terri wearing the Head Cheese hat on the floor; prior to the bout, Terri came down to be in Edge & Christian's corner and do guest commentary; during their entrance, Snow debuted Blackman's entrance music, which was put together to better portray his personality

The Rock pinned the Brooklyn Brawler with the Rock Bottom at the 31-second mark after an Irish whip; after the bout, the Rock grabbed a microphone and called Triple H out; Shane & Stephanie McMahon, Triple H, and the Big Show then came out, with Stephanie saying Rock could get a WrestleMania world title shot if he could pin either Triple H or Show in a handicap match later in the night

Chris Jericho (w/ Chyna) pinned Perry Saturn (w/ Dean Malenko) with the Lionsault at 3:03 after Chyna interfered behind the referee's back and hit a low blow on Saturn (Saturn and Malenko's MSG debut)

Mark Henry (w/ Mae Young) fought WWF Hardcore Champion Crash Holly to a no contest at around the 1:50 mark after Mae hit a splash on Crash inside the ring and doubled over in pain; moments later, EMTs came to the ring along with Pat Patterson, Gerald Brisco, and the Fabulous Moolah and helped Mae onto a stretcher and to the back; later in the show, Mae gave birth to her baby, which turned out to be a hand

Tazz defeated Chris Benoit via disqualification at 2:03 when the Big Bossman and Albert attacked Tazz as Benoit was caught in the Tazzmission; Eddie Guerrero was in Benoit's corner at the beginning of the match but was ejected by the referee mid-way through the bout; after the match, Tazz was double teamed by Bossman & Albert, eventually sustaining the Baldo Bomb and then a torture rack into a neckbreaker from Albert; moments later, Bossman cut a promo on the microphone as officials came in the ring to check on Tazz (Benoit & Guerrero's MSG debut)

WWF Tag Team Champions the Dudley Boyz fought X-Pac & the Road Dogg (w/ Tori) to a no contest at around 4:30 when Kane and Paul Bearer came to the ring, with Kane hitting the chokeslam on Road Dogg, D-Von, and Bubba Ray as a sign to what he planned to do to X-Pac

The Rock defeated WWF World Champion Triple H (w/ Stephanie McMahon) & the Big Show (w/ Shane McMahon) in a handicap match via disqualification at 6:53 when Shane broke Rock's cover on Triple H after hitting the People's

343

Elbow; after the bout, Rock sustained a low blow from Shane, was beaten down by Triple H, and took a chokeslam from Big Show; pre-match stipulations stated that had Rock earned the pinfall, he would have received a world title match at WrestleMania

WWF @ New York City, NY - Madison Square Garden - April 15, 2000 (16,925 paid)
WWF Light Heavyweight Champion Dean Malenko pinned Scotty 2 Hotty
WWF European Champion Eddie Guerrero pinned ECW World Champion Tazz after Chyna interfered and hit a DDT on the challenger; only the European title was at stake; Tazz was not announced as the ECW World Champion nor did he appear with the title belt
The Big Bossman & Bull Buchanon defeated the Headbangers when Buchanon pinned Thrasher with a legdrop off the top; after the contest, Kane appeared and dropped both Buchanon and one of the Headbangers with a chokeslam; Kane then dropped the other Headbanger with the tombstone
WWF Hardcore Champion Crash Holly pinned Perry Saturn; during the match, ECW World Champion Tazz ran out with a second referee in an attempt to win the title; after the match, Tazz and Saturn brawled
WWF Tag Team Champions Edge & Christian defeated Matt & Jeff Hardy and the Dudley Boyz in an elimination match; D-Von pinned Matt with the 3D; Edge pinned Bubba with the spear; after the contest, the Dudleyz set up a table, with the Hardyz returning ringside, brawling with them, and then putting Christian through the table themselves
Test & Albert defeated Al Snow & Steve Blackman when Test pinned Snow
Kurt Angle pinned Val Venis with a roll up and grabbing the tights for leverage
WWF IC Champion Chris Benoit pinned Chris Jericho with his feet on the ropes for leverage
The Big Show fought Rikishi to a double count-out when both men brawled on the floor; prior to the match, the two had a dance contest; after the bout, the two faced off in the ring before dancing together
WWF World Champion Triple H, Road Dogg, & X-Pac defeated the Rock & the Acolytes

WWF @ New York City, NY - Madison Square Garden - June 24, 2000 (16,975 paid)

Included Jerry Lawler interviewing Donald Trump, who sat ringside for the event

The Godfather pinned D-Lo Brown with a roll up after hitting the Ho Train

WWF Light Heavyweight Champion Dean Malenko defeated Crash Holly via submission with the Texas Cloverleaf; after the bout, Holly raised Malenko's hand

Kane pinned Gangrel at the 90-second mark with the chokeslam

Terri defeated the Kat in an arm wrestling match; Jerry Lawler was the official for the contest; after the match, Kat gave Terri the Bronko Buster and, after he asked, did the same to Lawler

WWF European Champion Eddie Guerrero pinned Perry Saturn with a hurricanrana after Chyna interfered

The Rock & the Dudley Boyz fought WWF World Champion Triple H (w/ WWF Women's Champion Stephanie McMahon), X-Pac, & Road Dogg to a no contest at around the 16-minute mark; following DX's entrance, Triple H

took the mic and confronted referee Earl Hebner and threatened to kick his ass if he screwed with them in the match and leave him as bloody and beaten as he did Mick Foley at the Royal Rumble; late in the bout, Bubba Ray Dudley was put through a table at ringside; moments later, Rock hit the Rock Bottom and People's Elbow on Triple H, only for Vince McMahon to run out and yank Hebner out of the ring to prevent the pinfall; Rock was then triple teamed and sustained the Pedigree until Kane came out; Kane was then triple teamed as well until the Undertaker drove his motorcycle to the ring and dropped Shane McMahon, X-Pac, and Triple H with the chokeslam (Undertaker's MSG return after a 10-month absence)

The Acolytes defeated the Big Bossman & Bull Buchanon after Buchanon walked out of the match

WWF IC Champion Rikishi pinned Kurt Angle with a belly to belly suplex; after the match, WWF Tag Team Champions Grandmaster Sexay & Scotty 2 Hotty came out and danced with Rikishi

Chris Benoit defeated Chris Jericho, Hardcore Holly, and Val Venis after hitting Holly over the head with a chair and applying the Crippler Crossface; stipulations stated the winner would be the #1 contender for the WWF IC Title

WWF Tag Team Champions Grandmaster Sexay & Scotty 2 Hotty defeated Edge & Christian, Matt & Jeff Hardy, and Test & Albert in an elimination match; Matt Hardy pinned Test; Christian pinned one of the Hardyz with the Impaler; Scotty pinned Christian

---

The Donald at ringside

"Jerry Lawler interviewed Donald Trump, who was sitting at ringside. Lawler asked why is he is there and Trump says that he is a personal friend of Vince McMahon. The fans don't like that and boo loudly. As the 2013 Hall of Fame would prove, it wouldn't be the last time that Trump was booed in the Garden. Trump redeems himself by telling the King that The Rock is his favorite wrestler."

Dennis Spicacci, *Carteret, NJ*

WWF @ New York City, NY - Madison Square Garden - August 7, 2000

The Dupps defeated Charlie & Russ Haas
The Mean Street Posse defeated Low-Ki & Vince Goodnight
Jakked:
The Big Bossman pinned Taka Michinoku with the sidewalk slam at 3:29
WWF Hardcore Champion Steve Blackman pinned Mideon at 3:36 after kicking a trash can into the challenger's chest
D-Lo Brown & Chaz defeated Gangrel & Crash Holly at 3:21 when D-Lo pinned Crash with the frog splash after the Big Bossman interfered
WWF Light Heavyweight Champion Dean Malenko defeated Essa Rios via submission with the Texas Cloverleaf at 4:21
Raw is War:
Rikishi defeated X-Pac via disqualification at 2:57 when Road Dogg interfered and hit a low blow on Rikishi; after the bout, the two double teamed Rikishi
The Dudley Boyz defeated Bull Buchanon & the Goodfather (w/ Steven Richards) via disqualification at 3:24 when Richards prevented a pinfall on Buchanon following the 3D; after the bout, the Goodfather powerbombed one of his former hoes through a table
Too Cool & Chyna (sub. for Eddie Guerrero) defeated Test, Albert, & WWF IC Champion Val Venis (w/ Trish Stratus) at 3:50 when Chyna pinned Venis after Guerrero interfered and hit a frogsplash on the champion; Chyna took over for Guerrero before the bout began after Venis hit a piledriver on the floor
WWF World Champion the Rock pinned Chris Benoit (w/ Shane McMahon) with the Rock Bottom in a No DQ match at 8:12 after Chris Jericho interfered, hit two powerbombs on Benoit onto a steel chair, and chased Shane through the crowd
The Acolytes & Matt Hardy defeated the Big Show (w/ Shane McMahon) & WWF Tag Team Champions Edge & Christian via disqualification at 1:38 when Show hit the Acolytes with one of the tag title belts; after the match, the Undertaker made the save and took out Show, Shane, Edge, and Christian
Kurt Angle and Triple H (w/ WWF Women's Champion Stephanie McMahon) pinned Chris Jericho in a #1 contenders match at 6:46 following a double superplex; after the bout, the Rock - who was doing guest commentary - hit a Rock Bottom on Triple H, Angle, and Stephanie

Raw's return to MSG in August 2000 helped set up several of the top matches for Summer Slam later that month.

<u>All day in NYC</u>
"You would go to WWF New York, go for a signing in the morning, and go straight from there to Madison Square Garden. Got to meet Lilian Garcia. Then Chris Jericho, Christian, Test, JBL. ...There were plenty of homeless people sleeping outside. Give somebody a dollar or two while you're waiting. Make friends."
Reny Amoros, *Bronx, NY*

WWF @ New York City, NY - Madison Square Garden - September 23, 2000 (19,530; 16,952 paid; sell out)

Included an in-ring promo by William Regal before he was interrupted by Naked Mideon, with Regal then leaving the ring disgusted; featured an in-ring promo by Shane McMahon

Grandmaster Sexay & Scotty 2 Hotty defeated D-Lo Brown & Chaz when Scotty pinned D-Lo after Sexay hit the Hip Hop Drop

WWF European Champion Al Snow pinned Perry Saturn after hitting him with Head

Test, Albert, & Jackie (sub. for an injured Trish Stratus) (w/ Trish Stratus) defeated WWF Women's Champion Lita, Matt & Jeff Hardy when Jackie pinned Lita; prior to the match, Trish cut an in-ring promo noting she couldn't compete

WWF Tag Team Champions Edge & Christian defeated the Dudley Boyz after Edge hit Bubba with one of the title belts

Jerry Lawler & the Kat defeated Tazz & Ivory when Kat pinned Ivory

WWF Hardcore Champion Steve Blackman defeated Gangrel

The Goodfather & Val Venis defeated the Acolytes after Val Venis interfered; after the match, the Dudley Boyz ran out and aided the Acolytes in clearing the ring

Chris Jericho & Rikishi defeated WWF IC Champion Eddie Guerrero & X-Pac

WWF World Champion the Rock, Triple H (w/ Stephanie McMahon), & the Undertaker defeated Kurt Angle, Chris Benoit, & Kane when Rock pinned Angle with the Rock Bottom; Triple H's ribs were heavily taped in the match; late in the contest, Angle accidentally suplexed Stephanie, thinking she was someone else

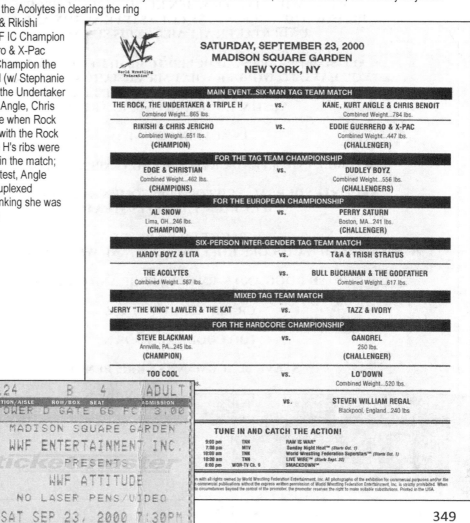

SATURDAY, SEPTEMBER 23, 2000
MADISON SQUARE GARDEN
NEW YORK, NY

MAIN EVENT...SIX-MAN TAG TEAM MATCH		
THE ROCK, THE UNDERTAKER & TRIPLE H Combined Weight...865 lbs.	vs.	KANE, KURT ANGLE & CHRIS BENOIT Combined Weight...784 lbs.
RIKISHI & CHRIS JERICHO Combined Weight...651 lbs. (CHAMPION)	vs.	EDDIE GUERRERO & X-PAC Combined Weight...447 lbs. (CHALLENGER)
FOR THE TAG TEAM CHAMPIONSHIP		
EDGE & CHRISTIAN Combined Weight...462 lbs. (CHAMPIONS)	vs.	DUDLEY BOYZ Combined Weight...556 lbs. (CHALLENGERS)
FOR THE EUROPEAN CHAMPIONSHIP		
AL SNOW Lima, OH...246 lbs. (CHAMPION)	vs.	PERRY SATURN Boston, MA...241 lbs. (CHALLENGER)
SIX-PERSON INTER-GENDER TAG TEAM MATCH		
HARDY BOYZ & LITA	vs.	T&A & TRISH STRATUS
THE ACOLYTES Combined Weight...567 lbs.	vs.	BULL BUCHANAN & THE GODFATHER Combined Weight...617 lbs.
MIXED TAG TEAM MATCH		
JERRY "THE KING" LAWLER & THE KAT	vs.	TAZZ & IVORY
FOR THE HARDCORE CHAMPIONSHIP		
STEVE BLACKMAN Annville, PA...245 lbs. (CHAMPION)	vs.	GANGREL 250 lbs. (CHALLENGER)
TOO COOL	vs.	LO'DOWN Combined Weight...520 lbs.
	vs.	STEVEN WILLIAM REGAL Blackpool, England...240 lbs

TUNE IN AND CATCH THE ACTION!

9:00 pm	TNN	RAW IS WAR® *(Starts Oct. 1)*
7:00 pm	MTV	Sunday Night Heat™ *(Starts Oct. 1)*
10:00 am	TNN	World Wrestling Federation Superstars™ *(Starts Oct. 1)*
10:00 am	TNN	LIVE WIRE™ *(Starts Sept. 30)*
8:00 pm	WOR-TV Ch. 9	SMACKDOWN™

SG0923E 124 B 4 ADULT
EVENT CODE SECTION/AISLE ROW/BOX SEAT ADMISSION
$ 43.00 TOWER D GATE 66 FC 3.00
7.10
SECTION/AISLE MADISON SQUARE GARDEN
124 WWF ENTERTAINMENT INC.
VI 100X PRESENTS
ROW SEAT
B 4 WWF ATTITUDE
2VS7054 NO LASER PENS/VIDEO
16AUG00 SAT SEP 23, 2000 7:30PM

WWF SMACKDOWN
TUESDAY DECEMBER 5, 2000
MADISON SQUARE GARDEN

LAYIN THE SMACKDOWN ON THE BIG APPLE!

AT ARMAGEDDON, LIVE THIS SUNDAY ON PAY PER VIEW, SIX MEN WILL COLLIDE INSIDE HELL IN A CELL FOR THE WORLD WRESTLING FEDERATION CHAMPIONSHIP! IT'S THE MOST DANGEROUS MATCH IN FEDERATION HISTORY AND WHAT WILL HAPPEN WHEN KURT ANGLE, TRIPLE H, RIKISHI, THE ROCK, STONE COLD STEVE AUSTIN AND THE UNDERTAKER ALL MEET THIS SUNDAY?

ALL SIX MEN ARE SCHEDULED TO BE HERE TONIGHT AND YOU HAVE TO WONDER WHAT MR MCMAHON IS THINKING ABOUT FOLLOWING THE ASSAULT ON HIM LAST NIGHT BY AUSTIN, ROCK AND UNDERTAKER!

IN ACTION TONIGHT!

BILLY GUNN AND CHYNA VS VAL VENIS AND IVORY

#1 CONTENDERS MATCH FOR THE WOMEN'S CHAMPIONSHIP MOLLY HOLLY VS TRISH STRATUS

TAG TEAM WARFARE
Y2J AND HARDCORE HOLLY VS KANE AND WILLIAM REGAL

ROAD DOGG AND K-KWIK VS EDGE AND CHRISTIAN

CRASH HOLLY VS TAZZ

TOO COOL VS LO DOWN

STEVE BLACKMAN VS CHRIS BENOIT

... MORE MATCHES!

... CT TO CHANGE

WWF @ New York City, NY - Madison Square Garden - December 5, 2000 (11,945 paid)
The Dupps defeated Charlie & Russ Haas
Sho Funaki pinned Chris Chetti
Sunday Night Heat - 12/10/00 - only shown internationally - hosted by Jonathan Coachman & Michael Hayes:
Chris Benoit pinned WWF Hardcore Champion Steve Blackman in a non-title match at 4:33 by reversing a roll up and using the ropes for leverage Perry Saturn (w/ Terri & Eddie Guerrero) pinned Taka Michinoku (w/ Sho Funaki) at 4:37 with the Death Valley Driver
Tazz defeated Crash Holly via submission with the Tazzmission at 3:28
D-Lo Brown & Chaz (w/ Tiger Ali Singh) defeated Grandmaster Sexay & Scotty 2 Hotty at 6:00 when Chaz pinned Sexay after Sexay sustained D-Lo's Sky High
Smackdown! - featured Vince McMahon telling Linda he wanted a divorce:
Val Venis & WWF Women's Champion Ivory defeated WWF IC Champion Billy Gunn & Chyna when Venis pinned Chyna after Ivory hit Chyna with the Women's title belt as Gunn was distracted by Chris Benoit at ringside
Molly Holly defeated Trish Stratus via disqualification when Trish hit Molly with a trash can lid; due to pre-match stipulations, Molly became the #1 contender to the Women's title
Chris Jericho & Hardcore Holly defeated Kane & WWF European Champion William Regal when Regal submitted to a sleeper by Holly
The Road Dogg & K-Kwick defeated Edge & Christian when Road Dogg pinned Edge after Edge sustained a spin kick from Kwick
WWF World Champion Kurt Angle, Steve Austin, the Rock, and the Undertaker fought to a no contest when Triple H and Rikishi interfered and a brawl ensued involving all six men, with Triple H remaining as the last man standing (*WWE's Top 50 Superstars of All Time*)

Howard Finkel caught outside MSG. Note the XFL jacket.

WF
World Wrestling
Federation®

SATURDAY, JANUARY 27, 2001
MADISON SQUARE GARDEN
NEW YORK, NY

FOR THE WORLD WRESTLING FEDERATION CHAMPIONSHIP

KURT ANGLE	vs.	CHRIS JERICHO
Pittsburgh, PA... 229 lbs.		Winnipeg, CN... 227 lbs.
(CHAMPION)		(CHALLENGER)

EIGHT MAN TAG TEAM MATCH

STONE COLD STEVE AUSTIN, THE ROCK, THE UNDERTAKER & KANE vs. TRIPLE H, RIKISHI, CHRIS BENOIT & HAKU

THREE TEAM ELIMINATION MATCH FOR THE TAG TEAM CHAMPIONSHIP

DUDLEY BOYZ	vs.	HARDY BOYZ	vs.	THE ACOLYTES
(CHAMPIONS)				

FOR THE EUROPEAN CHAMPIONSHIP

TEST	vs.	CHRISTIAN
Toronto, CN....282 lbs.		Toronto, CN...217 lbs.
(CHAMPION)		(CHALLENGER)

"THE ONE" BILLY GUNN	vs.	STEVEN RICHARDS
265 lbs.		Right To Censor...235 lbs.

FOR THE HARDCORE CHAMPIONSHIP

RAVEN	vs.	STEVE BLACKMAN
The Bowery...237 lbs.		Annville, PA...245 lbs.
(CHAMPION)		(CHALLENGER)

K-KWIK	vs.	PERRY SATURN
Charlotte, NC...223 lbs.		Boston, MA...241 lbs.

HARDCORE HOLLY	vs.	ALBERT
Mobile, AL...235 lbs.		Boston, MA...347 lbs.

TOO COOL	vs.	BULL BUCHANAN & THE GOODFATHER
Combined Weight...431 lbs.		Combined Weight...617 lbs.

FOR THE WOMEN'S CHAMPIONSHIP

IVORY	vs.	MOLLY HOLLY
(CHAMPION)		

TUNE

Mondays	9:00 p
Sundays	7:00 p
Sundays	10:00 a
Saturdays	10:00 a
Thursdays	8:00 p

6G0127E 222 B 4 ADULT

EVENT CODE	SECTION/AISLE	ROW/BOX	SEAT	ADMISSION
$33.00	TOWER C GATE 76	FC		3.00

6.85

SECTION/AISLE
222

A 145X
ROW   SEAT
B   4

VS714A
9DEC00

MADISON SQUARE GARDEN
WWF ENTERTAINMENT INC.
PRESENTS
"COME GET SOME!"
NO LASER PENS/VIDEO
SAT JAN 27, 2001 7:30PM

WWF @ New York City, NY - Madison Square Garden - January 27, 2001 (19,448; 17,238 paid)
Grandmaster Sexay & Scotty 2 Hotty defeated the Goodfather & Bull Buchanon when Sexay pinned Buchanon with the Hip Hop Drop; Debra was the guest ring announcer for the bout
WWF Hardcore Champion Raven pinned Steve Blackman with a DDT onto a steel chair
WWF Women's Champion Ivory defeated Molly Holly (sub. for Jackie) after Steven Richards aided in blocking a sunset flip attempt
Billy Gunn defeated Steven Richards (sub. for Val Venis) with the cobra clutch slam
WWF Tag Team Champions the Dudley Boyz defeated Matt & Jeff Hardy and the Acolytes in an elimination match; Bradshaw pinned Matt with the Clothesline from Hell as Matt came off the top; Bradshaw was pinned with the 3D
WWF World Champion Kurt Angle (w/ Trish Stratus) pinned WWF IC Champion Chris Jericho with a low blow and the Olympic Slam
Perry Saturn pinned K-Kwick with the Death Valley Driver
Albert defeated Hardcore Holly
WWF European Champion Test pinned Christian with a boot to the face, despite interference from William Regal; prior to the match, Regal cut an in-ring promo on the crowd and then sat ringside for the match
The Undertaker, Kane, Steve Austin, & the Rock defeated Triple H (w/ Stephanie McMahon), Chris Benoit, Rikishi, & Haku when the Rock pinned Benoit with the Rock Bottom; after the match, Austin twice hit the Stunner on Triple H

"Ivory and Lilian Garcia, it would take them hours to get inside because they would stop to sign autographs and meet every single person on the way in to the arena. The same when Matt Striker was with the WWE."
Mary-Kate (Grosso) Anthony, *Tampa, Fla.*

Stephanie McMahon was often ringside in 2000 and 2001, supporting the likes of Triple H or Kurt Angle.

SATURDAY, MARCH 24, 2001
MADISON SQUARE GARDEN
NEW YORK, NEW YORK

MAIN EVENT - SIX-MAN TAG TEAM MATCH

STONE COLD STEVE AUSTIN, THE UNDERTAKER & KANE	vs.	TRIPLE H, KURT ANGLE & BIG SHOW
Combined Weight... 808 lbs.		Combined Weight... 989 lbs.

FOR THE INTERCONTINENTAL CHAMPIONSHIP

CHRIS JERICHO	vs.	EDDIE GUERRERO
Winnipeg, Manitoba...227 lbs.		El Paso, TX... 215 lbs.
(CHAMPION)		(CHALLENGER)

SPECIAL CHALLENGE MATCH

CHRIS BENOIT	vs.	PERRY SATURN
Edmonton, Alberta...229 lbs.		Boston, MA... 241 lbs.

FOR THE TAG TEAM CHAMPIONSHIP

DUDLEY BOYZ	vs.	BULL BUCHANAN & THE GOODFATHER
Combined Weight: 567 lbs.		Combined Weight: 617 lbs.
(CHAMPIONS)		(CHALLENGERS)

FOR THE EUROPEAN CHAMPIONSHIP

TEST	vs.	VAL VENIS
Toronto, Ontario...282 lbs.		Right To Censor...242 lbs.
(CHAMPION)		(CHALLENGER)

HARDY BOYZ	vs.	X-PAC & JUSTIN CREDIBLE
Combined Weight: 441 lbs.		Combined Weight... 449 lbs.

FOR THE HARDCORE CHAMPIONSHIP

RAVEN	vs.	"THE ONE" BILLY GUNN
The Bowery...235 lbs.		265 lbs.
(CHAMPION)		(CHALLENGER)

FOR THE LIGHT HEAVYWEIGHT CHAMPIONSHIP

CRASH	vs.	DEAN MALENKO
Mobile, AL...215 lbs.		Tampa, FL...218 lbs.
(CHAMPION)		(CHALLENGER)

THE ACOLYTES	vs.	EDGE & CHRISTIAN
Combined Weight:..567 lbs.		Combined Weight: 462 lbs.

FOR THE WOMEN'S CHAMPIONSHIP

IVORY	vs.	MOLLY HOLLY
(CHAMPION)		(CHALLENGER)

TUNE IN AND CATCH THE ACTION!

Mondays	9:00 pm	TNN	RAW IS WAR
Sundays	7:00 pm	MTV	Sunday Night Heat™
Sundays	10:00 am	TNN	World Wrestling Federation Superstars™
Saturdays	10:00 am	TNN	LIVE WIRE™
Thursdays	8:00 pm	UPN-9	SMACKDOWN™

Lita, in the ring, and Trish Stratus, ringside. The two would go on to have a feud that would help redefine the women's division.

WWF @ New York City, NY – Madison Square Garden - March 24, 2001 (17,311 paid)
WWF Light Heavyweight Champion Crash Holly pinned Dean Malenko with a la magistral cradle
WWF Hardcore Champion Raven pinned Billy Gunn with the DDT onto a trash can lid
WWF Women's Champion Ivory pinned Molly Holly after constant interference from Trish Stratus; after the bout, Lita and Molly held off Ivory and Steven Richards
Edge & Christian (w/ Rhyno) defeated the Acolytes when Edge pinned Bradshaw after Rhyno interfered and hit the Gore
WWF IC Champion Chris Jericho defeated Eddie Guerrero via submission with the Walls of Jericho
X-Pac & Justin Credible (w/ Albert) defeated Matt & Jeff Hardy when Credible pinned Jeff after Albert interfered and hit the Baldo Bomb as Jeff came off the top
WWF European Champion Test pinned Val Venis with a boot to the face; after the match, Venis and Steven Richards argued but eventually left ringside together
Chris Benoit defeated Perry Saturn via submission with the Crippler Crossface
WWF Tag Team Champions the Dudley Boyz defeated the Goodfather & Bull Buchanon following the 3D on the Goodfather after Spike Dudley interfered
Steve Austin, the Undertaker, & Kane defeated Kurt Angle, the Big Show, & Triple H when Austin pinned Triple H with the Stunner; late in the contest, Shane McMahon interfered on behalf of Austin's team

Undertaker's birthday
"Had my best-ever seats for this show – right in the front row. Austin got the biggest reaction of the night. Mind-boggling that they turned him heel the following week at WrestleMania X-Seven, but that's another story. A gigantic brawl on the outside left Austin and HHH alone in the ring. HHH had Austin set up for the Pedigree, but Shane McMahon came out and speared HHH to a huge pop. A Stunner later and Austin got the three-count. There was a big victory celebration as Austin twice drenched our section with beer from the top turnbuckle. Austin also announced that it was Undertaker's birthday, so they toasted to that and Taker celebrated by giving HHH a tombstone and a huge chokeslam to send everyone home happy."

Dennis Spicacci, *Carteret, NJ*

Steve Austin hosts a beer bash, just a week before turning heel at WrestleMania X-7.

RAW IS WAR!
MADISON SQUARE GARDEN
NEW YORK CITY
MONDAY JUNE 25, 2001

ON THE HEELS OF KING OF THE RING, THE WWF RETURNS
TO THE WORLD'S MOST FAMOUS ARENA TONIGHT!!!

THE DUDLEY BOYZ WILL SQUARE OFF AGAINST THE
UNDERTAKER AND KANE, IN A TABLE MATCH FOR THE TAG
TEAM CHAMPIONSHIP!!!

WITH WARS WAGED LAST NIGHT ACROSS THE RIVER, AND
THE APPEARANCE OF BOTH WCW SUPERSTARS DIAMOND
DALLAS PAGE AND BOOKER T AT KING OF THE RING, WILL
THERE BE A FIRST-EVER WCW PRESENCE HERE IN THE
GARDEN TONIGHT???

IN A RETURN MATCH FROM LAST NIGHT'S KING OF THE
RING, JEFF HARDY WILL DEFEND THE LIGHT-
HEAVYWEIGHT CHAMPIONSHIP AGAINST X-PAC.....

THE "ERA OF AWESOMENESS" KICKS OFF IN HIGH STYLE,
WITH THE OFFICIAL CELEBRATION / CORONATION OF THE
NEW KING OF THE RING, EDGE.....

CHRIS JERICHO SEES ACTION AGAINST COMMISSIONER
REGAL'S CHARGE, TAJIRI

TEST PUTS THE HARDCORE CHAMPIONSHIP ON THE LINE
AGAINST THE FORMER HARDCORE TITLIST, RHYNO...

PLUS OTHER G[...]

CARD SUBJECT[...]

WWF @ New York City, NY - Madison Square Garden - June 25, 2001 (13,763; sell out)
Guido Maritato & Tony Mamaluke defeated Danny Doring & Roadkill (the MSG debuts of all four men)
Raw is War - included an opening in-ring promo by Vince McMahon in which he addressed the rumor the night before that Chris Jericho or Chris Benoit were planning to defect to WCW should they have won the WWF World Title the night before; McMahon then bragged about the win by Steve Austin, despite the interference of WCW World Champion Booker T; he went on to say the T in Booker T stood for terrible, trash, and temporarily employed; McMahon went on to say it was still his goal to put WCW and Shane McMahon out of business, adding that no WCW star should be in the building because it was hallowed ground and the house the WWF helped build; McMahon then showed the WWF Hall of Fame tribute video to Vince McMahon Sr., with comments from Freddie Blassie and Gorilla Monsoon; McMahon then guaranteed the fans more memorable moments at MSG later in the night; featured a backstage segment with Vince, Austin, and Debra in which McMahon complained about the two being late, and allowing a WCW wrestler to steal one of his belts; Austin then told Vince he didn't care, and said Vince wasn't there when he needed him the night before when his back was against the wall; after Austin told Vince that Vince didn't really care about him, the two ended up hugging; included a video tribute to Bruno Sammartino for his accomplishments at MSG; featured a backstage segment with the Big Show and Trish Stratus, with Show noting he was challenging for the WWF European Title later and asked if Trish wanted to take a european vacation with him after he wins it; included a backstage segment with Kurt Angle, Austin, McMahon, and Debra in which McMahon congratulated Angle on beating his son Shane McMahon; Austin then mocked Angle's concussion, and said he had to deal with worse the night before and he won; Vince then invited Angle to join them, with Austin staring at Angle; featured a video tribute to Superstar Billy Graham and his accomplishments at MSG; included a backstage segment with Austin, Angle, Vince, and Debra in which Austin quietly asked Vince if they could get rid of Angle, with Vince saying he was concerned about Angle since the King of the Ring ceremony was coming up and he needed to be around someone; Angle then brought up all the similarities between he and Austin before joking they could be related; featured an in-ring ceremony in which Commissioner William Regal and Tajiri awarded the 2001 King of the Ring trophy to Edge; moments later, Billy Gunn interrupted, bitter over having won the tournament himself two years prior but never having the opportunity to defend it, and having to spend the previous night at WWF NY; after trading insults, the two agreed to a match for later in the night; included Shane McMahon introducing WCW World champion Booker T to the crowd at WWF NY, with Booker then challenging Austin; Austin agreed to the challenge and brought Angle with him but by the time they arrived at WWF NY, Booker and Shane had already left the building; moments later, Shane came ringside to interrupt Vince's promo, distracting Vince just long enough for Booker T to come into the ring from behind; once Vince saw Booker, he took a punch; Booker responded with a flurry of blows, ending with the scissors kick; seconds later, the Acolytes, Kaientai, Raven, Justin Credible, K-Kwick, Dean Malenko, and several others ran to the ring as Booker escaped through the crowd (Booker T's MSG debut):
Rhyno pinned WWF Hardcore Champion Test to win the title at 4:33 after hitting the Gore backstage; seconds later, Mike Awesome ran down the hall, hitting Rhyno with a lead pipe and then powerbombing him onto a steel ladder to win the title (Rhyno's MSG debut; Awesome's surprise debut)
X-Pac pinned WWF Light Heavyweight Champion Jeff Hardy to win the title at 3:11 with a backslide and putting his feet on the ropes for leverage after the champion failed a Swanton
Tazz defeated Steven Richards at the 13-second mark via submission with the Tazzmission
WWF Tag Team Champions the Dudley Boyz defeated the Undertaker (w/ Sara) & WWF IC Champion Kane at 4:51 when D-Von pinned Kane after Albert interfered and hit the Baldo Bomb; Kane then chased Albert backstage while Diamond Dallas Page knocked Taker out with a chair before ripping out a lock of Sara's hair (DDP's MSG debut)
The Big Show (w/ Trish Stratus) defeated WWF European Champion Matt Hardy (w/ Lita) via disqualification at 3:12 when Lita hit a low blow on the challenger to prevent the chokeslam
Edge (w/ Christian) pinned Billy Gunn at 6:18 with the DDT after Christian interfered
Chris Jericho pinned Tajiri (w/ William Regal) with the bulldog and Lionsault at 5:11 after Tajiri accidentally sprayed mist into Regal's face (Tajiri's MSG debut)
Jakked - 6/30/01: Crash & Hardcore Holly defeated Sho Funaki & Taka Michinoku at 3:15 when Hardcore pinned Funaki with the Alabama Slam
Raven pinned Low-Ki with the DDT at 3:58
Jerry Lynn pinned Essa Rios at 5:33 with a tornado DDT (Lynn's MSG debut)
K-Kwik pinned the Inferno Kid at 4:04 with the Hat Rack Cracked

Edge, just a day after winning the 2001 King of the Ring tournament.

Christian with the 2001 King of the Ring trophy.

WWF @ New York City, NY - Madison Square Garden - June 26, 2001 (11,772; sell out)
Essa Rios defeated Jerry Lynn
Low-Ki pinned Mike Sullivan with the Tidal Krush
Smackdown! – 6/28/01 - featured an opening in-ring promo by Vince McMahon in which he said Madison Square Garden stunk after the invasion of several WCW stars during Monday Night Raw, then adding it now might as well be the Nassau Coliseum; as Vince continued to vent, Linda McMahon eventually walked out and said she knew how important MSG was to the WWF, then introducing a clip of Vince at MSG months earlier in which he said he wanted a divorce and didn't care about the WWF fans; Linda then said Vince would allow WCW matches to be part of Raw and Smackdown beginning the following week out of fairness; after Vince protested, Linda said that Fully Loaded was coming up in July and would be the perfect time for a WCW vs. WWF showdown, then asking whether Vince was afraid of competition before Vince eventually accepted, saying the event would now be called Invasion; included a backstage segment in the WWF locker room in which Farooq spoke to Godfather, Bull Buchanon, Haku, Dean Malenko, K-Kwick, Justin Credible, Test, Jerry Lynn, Al Snow, and more about getting payback on the WCW wrestlers; featured a backstage segment with WWF World Champion Steve Austin and Debra talked about Booker T showing up at MSG during Raw, with Vince walking in moments later and Austin suggesting WCW matches should happen on WWF TV, then whispering his plan to Vince and Vince agreeing with the idea; included a backstage segment with Spike Dudley and Molly Holly, with Perry Saturn walking in and ranting before walking off; moments later, Crash Holly interrupted and said he and Jackie wanted to challenge them to a match later in the show; featured Jim Ross conducting a pre-taped sit-down interview with the Undertaker & Sara regarding Diamond Dallas Page attacking Taker during Raw and taking a lock of Sara's hair; after Sara got done talking, Taker walked off; included a backstage segment in which Vince spoke with Austin and Debra about WCW World Champion Booker T, with Kurt Angle then walking in and asking what would happen if Austin faced Booker; Austin quickly chimed in that he would beat Booker and would welcome the chance; featured a backstage segment with Vince, Austin, Debra, and Angle in which Vince said it was Taker's fault Kane lost the WWF IC title because Taker wanted Diamond Dallas Page to have an all-access pass; included a backstage segment with Vince, Austin, Debra, and Angle in which Angle discussed who would have the advantages between Austin vs. Booker; moments later, Dave Hebner walked in and said someone from WCW wanted to see Vince in another dressing room; working under the assumption it was Booker, Vince, Angle, and Austin left together; featured a backstage segment with Vince in which he walked into the other dressing room only to find Torrie Wilson instead; Torrie then said she wanted to see whether she could get a contract with the WWF, with Vince saying they should meet in private (Torrie's surprise debut); included a backstage segment with William Regal and Tajiri, with Regal still showing green paint on his face as a result of Chris Jericho; moments later, Jericho appeared in Regal's office and said Regal & Tajiri should face he and another partner; Regal joked that Chris Benoit was out of action for six months, with Jericho saying he could find someone; featured a shot of the WWF wrestlers keeping watch for WCW stars at the entrance; included a backstage segment with Vince, Austin, Debra, and Angle in which Austin said he would go out to the ring and call out Booker; featured a closing in-ring segment in which Austin came out to the ring, took the mic, and called out Booker; after Booker didn't show, Tazz joined Austin in the ring and said Austin should worry less about Booker T and should instead apologize for attacking Michael Cole the previous week during Smackdown, causing Cole to be taken backstage on a stretcher; after Austin said he wouldn't apologize, Tazz said he would beat an apology out of him and take the title in the process; moments later, Austin said he would accept the challenge but it wouldn't be tonight, then hitting Tazz with the title belt and continuing to assault him at ringside before throwing him onto Cole at the commentary table and repeatedly hitting him with a steel chair; the crowd then chanted "Booker T" and "Asshole" as Cole went to check on Tazz; Austin then said Cole was next and told Cole to get in the ring if he had any guts; moments later, Booker came through the crowd, hit Austin with the WCW Title, and escaped through the audience as the WWF lockerroom sprinted out and chased him; moments later, Booker was shown running into Shane McMahon's black limo backstage and the limo drove off as hte WWF wrestlers watched on:
Edge & Christian defeated WWF Light Heavyweight Champion X-Pac & Billy Gunn when Edge pinned X-Pac with the DDT at 3:53 after knocking Gunn to the floor; following Edge & Christian's entrance, Edge took the mic and introduced Gunn as "Billy Bitchcakes;" Christian came out to the ring carrying Edge's King of the Ring trophy
Albert pinned WWF IC Champion Kane to win the title in a No DQ match at 5:53 with the Baldo Bomb after Diamond Dallas Page came through the audience and hit the Diamond Cutter on the champion before leaving through the crowd

WWF Tag Team Champions the Dudley Boyz fought Matt & Jeff Hardy (w/ Lita) to a no contest in a tables match at around the 5-minute mark when WCW Tag Team Champions Sean O'Haire & Chuck Palumbo interfered, attacking both teams and O'Haire hitting the Swanton on Matt; after the bout, O'Haire & Palumbo escaped into the crowd but were attacked in the crowd and in the ring by Rhyno, the Acolytes, Kaientai, the Goodfather, Bull Buchanon, Raven, K-Kwick, Hardcore & Crash Holly; moments later, O'Haire & Palumbo were sent through tables; during the commercial break, the WWF wrestlers physically threw O'Haire & Palumbo out of the building (O'Haire & Palumbo's surprise debuts)

Spike Dudley & Molly Holly defeated Crash Holly & Jackie at 3:32 when Molly pinned Jackie with the Molly-Go-Round after Spike caused Crash to crotch Jackie on the top rope; after the bout, Crash and Jackie argued, with Crash shoving Jackie and Jackie responding by decking Crash and walking off

The Big Show (w/ Trish Stratus) pinned Perry Saturn (w/ Terri) with the chokeslam at 3:22 after Terri and Trish began fighting on the floor; during Show's entrance, footage was shown from the commercial break of Saturn interrupting Show backstage, with Show snapping Saturn's mop in half

Chris Jericho & Scotty 2 Hotty (mystery partner) defeated William Regal & Tajiri at 4:22 when Scotty pinned Tajiri with the bulldog and the Worm; during Jericho's entrance, he took the mic and introduced his mystery partner (Scotty's surprise return after a 3-month absence)

Sunday Night Heat – 7/1/01 - the live broadcast from WWF NY featured WWF Tag Team Champions the Acolytes being attacked by WCW Tag Team Champions Sean O'Haire & Chuck Palumbo:

Justin Credible pinned K-Kwick with the superkick at 4:35

Hardcore Holly defeated Test via disqualification at 4:04 after Test used the ring bell as a weapon, moments after Holly brought the weapon into the ring

Rhyno pinned Raven with the Gore at 3:42

Sunday Nigh Heat - 7/1/01 (international version): Dean Malenko defeated Taka Michinoku (w/ Taka Michinoku) via submission at 3:59 with the Texas Cloverleaf

SUNDAY, OCTOBER 14, 2001
MADISON SQUARE GARDEN
NEW YORK, NY

MAIN EVENT.....TITLE –VS– TITLE

STONE COLD STEVE AUSTIN	-VS-	**THE ROCK**
Victoria, TX...252 lbs.		Miami, FL...275 lbs.
(WORLD WESTLING FEDERATION CHAMPION)		(WCW CHAMPION)

KURT ANGLE	-VS-	**WILLIAM REGAL**
Pittsburgh, PA...237 lbs.		Blackpool, UK...240 lbs.

THE UNDERTAKER	-VS-	**BOOKER T**
305 lbs.		251 lbs.

KANE	-VS-	**TEST**
326 lbs.		282 lbs.

FOR THE WORLD WRESTLING FEDERATION TAG TEAM CHAMPIONSHIP

DUDLEY BOYZ	-VS-	**A.P.A.**
Combined Weight: 556 lbs.		Combined Weight: 567 lbs.
(CHAMPIONS)		(CHALLENGERS)

MIXED TAG TEAM MATCH

MATT HARDY & LITA	-VS-	**THE HURRICANE & MIGHTY MOLLY**

FOR THE WORLD WRESTLING FEDERATION LIGHT HEAVYWEIGHT CHAMPIONSHIP

X-PAC	-VS-	**TAJIRI**
Minneapolis, MN...215 lbs.		Japan...206 lbs.
(CHAMPION)		(CHALLENGER)

JEFF HARDY	-VS-	**KANYON**
Cameron, NC...218 lbs.		Queens, NY...248 lbs.

"THE ONE" BILLY GUNN	-VS-	**JUSTIN CREDIBLE**
269 lbs.		225 lbs.

PERRY SATURN	-VS-	**TOMMY DREAMER**
Boston, MA...241 lbs.		245 lbs.

MSG debut

"I remember being at (Tommy) Dreamer's debut at The Garden. Sitting in the front row, all the crew that had followed him were also front row Garden fans. He came out and was supposed to be a heel. Everyone treated him like he was babyface and (Perry) Saturn was heel. After the match, he high-fived and hugged those fans, even though he was heel. When guys debut at The Garden, I see that as a check on their checklist. As far as I'm concerned, if you want to wrestle in the WWE, your goal is to wrestle in Madison Square Garden. That's the biggest show, other than a pay-per-view or TV taping."

Mike Johnson; *Glendale, NY*

SG101
EVENT CO
$ 48.
7.
SECTION/AISLE
123
CA 99X
ROW SEAT
D 12
ZVS700A
9SEP01

"THE INVASION OF THE WORLDWRESTLINGFEDERATION"
MADISON SQUARE GARDEN
SUN OCT 14, 2001 2:00PM

Somber atmosphere

"The usual excitement and adrenaline rush I would get when walking through Penn Station and heading upstairs to MSG was replaced by a very eerie feeling and somewhat somber atmosphere. Walking through Penn Station, people still seemed on edge about the attacks from a month prior. Police presence was huge. The eeriest part of it all was that a short distance before the steps leading upstairs to MSG, there were walls on both sides that were covered with pictures of people who had died in the 9/11 attacks. People were usually in such a rush coming up and down the stairs or coming in and out of the stores in Penn Station, but this time, hundreds of people were literally standing in front of these walls and staring at the pictures. Even the people walking by were not rushing like usual. They too, were looking at the pictures of these people on the wall. Some of the pictures were "In Memory Of" and some were labeled "Missing" with a picture of the person. Well, we all knew they really weren't missing. Their bodies were just so severely burned they weren't able to be identified yet. It was a sight I will never forget. Once we finally entered MSG and took our seats, it felt good to be in NYC and MSG again, surrounded by WWE fans. The show did feel different though, obviously. Many members of the NYPD and FDNY were honored at this show, which was nice. Something really cool about this show was the fact that "Classy" Freddie Blassie was in attendance. He must have been visiting backstage and at some point requested to watch the show from the stands, because he wasn't there for the entire show. He came and sat for about 30 minutes and then left. It was really cool though, because he was seated directly across from me, and he stood out with his dark tan and white hair. People were coming up and shaking his hand. Blassie was like the grandfather to WWE, so to have him there in attendance at this special event, watching parts of the show, was a really cool moment."

Michael Berlinski, *Edison, NJ*

Post 9/11

"The first MSG show after 9/11. A rare Sunday afternoon show. Prior to the show, The Garden had a different vibe than the usual before a WWE show for obvious reasons. I remember the show starting with Jim Ross coming out and talking about the terrorist attacks.He then introduced some "first responders" that were in attendance in the front row which got a huge ovation from the crowd. He then introduced Lilian Garcia who sang our National Anthem. Now Lilian Garcia has always done one thing different that nobody else does when singing the anthem. When she gets to the part that says "Gave proof through the night, that our flag was still there", when she sings the "that our flag was still there" part she does it in an upbeat way hitting a high note where everyone else does it low key. I always like that about her rendition. When she hit that part that afternoon it was just so perfect and of course it brought a huge ovation from the MSG crowd. Whenever I think about it, it gives me goosebumps. It was just such an emotional, awesome moment. That moment set the tone for the rest of the night. The crowd was its usual self from that point on. The card that night was stacked with all the top talent including a main event of the Rock vs. Stone Cold Steve Austin, which speaks for itself. Even though it ended in a DQ finish, it was an awesome match. A great ending to a great afternoon at Madison Square Garden that I am sure helped a lot of people forget about their troubles that afternoon if only for a few hours."

Lou Spadone, *Queens, NY*

WWF @ New York City, NY - Madison Square Garden - October 14, 2001 (matinee) (11,098)

Included an opening in-ring promo by Jim Ross, addressing the terrorist attacks of Sept. 11 and noting that members of the New York City police, fire, and emergency services were in attendance

Billy Gunn pinned Justin Credible with the Fameasser

Perry Saturn pinned Tommy Dreamer with a catapult into the turnbuckle and the swinging fisherman's suplex

WCW Tag Team Champion Matt Hardy & Lita defeated WWF European Champion Hurricane Helms & Molly Holly when Matt pinned Helms with the Twist of Fate

Test pinned Kane with the boot to the face after Booker T came ringside; after the match, the Undertaker made the save

The Undertaker pinned Booker T with the powerbomb in under 10 minutes

Kurt Angle pinned William Regal via submission with the ankle lock in a No DQ match after Mick Foley countered the outside interference of Tazz and put Tazz in the Mr. Socko Mandible Claw

WCW Tag Team Champion Jeff Hardy pinned Kanyon with the Swanton after reversing a top rope Samoan Drop into a powerbomb

WWF Light Heavyweight Champion X-Pac pinned Tajiri with a low blow and the X-Factor

WWF Tag Team Champions the Dudley Boyz defeated the Acolytes when D-Von pinned Farooq after hitting him with one of the title belts, as Stacy Keibler distracted referee Nick Patrick

WCW World Champion the Rock defeated WWF World Champion Steve Austin via disqualification when WWF Tag Team Champions the Dudley Boyz interfered as Austin was trapped in the Sharpshooter; after the match, Rock cleared the Dudleyz from ringside and hit the People's Elbow on Austin

X-Pac and Tajiri battle for the Light Heavyweight title.

Bubba Ray Dudley arrives to MSG.

*The WWF's Undertaker vs.
The Alliance's Booker T.*

369

Native North Carolinians The Hurricane and Matt Hardy face off in a mixed tag team match.

WWF World Champion Steve Austin, representing the Alliance, prepares to face WCW World Champion The Rock, representing the WWF.

It was like a family reunion

"Test was walking in with Stacy Keibler one day. We were waiting outside. There was some girl, I don't know what she said but he fired back, "Will you get the hell away from me you dirty ring rat?" She sorta just walked away. ...The fans that would wait out there sometimes became celebrities themselves. It was like a family reunion that you're dreading, but you knew the people there. You had the guy that always dressed like Hurricane. You had the guy with the kendo stick, wanting signatures on the stick. Tye Dye Guy was always there. We used to look for him. There's always those groups of fans that sit in certain places. The drunk fans who are just there because they're drinking. You have the european fans in section 200. You have the boyfriend explaining to the girlfriend every move. You have all these different fans you know you're going to see."

Reny Amoros, *Bronx, NY*

WWF @ New York City, NY - Madison Square Garden - January 7, 2002 (13,978)
Brock Lesnar defeated Rico Constantino
Randy Orton defeated Ron Waterman
Jakked:
The Hurricane pinned Sho Funaki with a flying crossbody at 4:55
Crash Holly pinned Prince Nana with a Tornado bulldog at 4:13
Perry Saturn defeated John Jirus (Xavier) via submission to the Rings of Saturn at 4:56
Christian pinned Lo-Ki with the Unprettier at 3:24
Raw is War - featured a closing segment in which Triple H made his much-hyped return to the ring after being on the DL since 5/21/01:
Rob Van Dam pinned Test with the Van Daminator and the five star frog splash at 3:44
Billy Gunn & Chuck Palumbo defeated Scotty 2 Hotty & Albert at 3:43 after Gunn hit the Fameasser on Scotty
WWF IC Champion Edge pinned Lance Storm with the DDT at 1:10 (Storm's MSG debut)
Steve Austin & the Rock defeated Booker T & the Big Bossman when Austin pinned Bossman with the Stunner at 8:21
WWF World Champion Chris Jericho pinned Rikishi in a non-title match at 4:27 after hitting him with the title belt; Rikishi kicked out of the cover but referee Nick Patrick made the three count anyway as payback for receiving the Stinkface earlier in the bout
Tazz & Spike Dudley defeated WWF Tag Team Champions the Dudley Boyz (w/ Stacy Keibler) in a hardcore match to win the titles at 3:45 when Spike pinned Bubba Ray with the Dudley Dog through a table
WWF Women's Champion Trish Stratus fought Terri to a no contest in a wet t-shirt contest when Jazz interfered and attacked Trish; Jerry Lawler was the guest host for the contest

WWF RAW
MADISON SQUARE GARDEN
NEW YORK, NY
MONDAY, JANUARY 7, 2002

TONIGHT MARKS THE RETURN TO RAW OF THE GAME, TRIPLE H!

AMONG THE MATCHES ON TONIGHT'S CARD:

STONE COLD STEVE AUSTIN JOINS FORCES WITH THE ROCK, AND THEY TAKE ON THE COMBINATION OF BOOKER T AND THE BIG BOSSMAN.....

ROB VAN DAM GOES ONE ON ONE WITH TEST..

EDGE DEFENDS THE WORLD WRESTLING FEDERATION INTERCONTINENTAL CHAMPIONSHIP AGAINST LANCE STORM...

ANOTHER TAG MATCH FINDS SCOTTY 2 HOTTY AND ALBERT OPPOSE THE COMBINATION OF "THE ONE" BILLY GUNN AND CHUCK PALUMBO...

G FEDERATION TAG TEAM
HE LINE, AS THE DUDLEY BOYZ DEFEND
AZZ ANS SPIKE DUDLEY, IN A TABLE

NGE.....

SG0107E 127   F   5   ADULT
EVENT CODE   SECTION/AISLE   ROW/BOX   SEAT   ADMISSION
$ 48.50 TOWER D GATE 66 FC   3.50
7.75   NO LASER PENS/VIDEO
SECTION/AISLE
127   WORLDWRESTLINGFEDERATION
CA 108X   PRESENTS
ROW   SEAT
F   5   "RAW"
ZUS700A MADISON SQUARE GARDEN
2DEC01   MON JAN 7, 2002 7:45PM

The return of The Game

"Months before this date when I purchased tickets for this event a live Monday Night Raw from the World's Most Famous Arena, I was already looking forward to the show. Any event from The Garden is a fun time, but a live Monday Night Raw is always one of the best. Then maybe a few weeks prior to the show, it was rumored and then confirmed that Triple H would be making his long awaited return after being sidelined for 8 months with a torn quad. Once this was confirmed, I knew that this was going to be a can't-miss show. Outside MSG that night, it was cold with snow and rain coming down. Inside The Garden was hot. Prior to the show starting, Triple H chants were coming from all over The Garden. A cool side note: the two dark matches prior to this Raw included Brock Lesnar and Randy Orton. When Raw finally did start, they aired the awesome "Triple H Returns Tonight" video package to U2's "Beautiful Day" on the Titantron and the crowd went nuts. The anticipation kept building throughout the night. Then after a disappointing "wet t-shirt" contest between Trish Stratus and Terri Runnels, the graphic displayed on the Titantron stating "Triple H Returns, NEXT!"

From this point on I don't think one person remained in their seat. When Raw came back from commercial and Triple H's theme song hit, as the cliché goes, "The roof blew off Madison Square Garden!" The crowd was insane. Then, when Triple H finally appeared onto the ramp, the MSG Crowd erupted. The Garden was deafening. Now I have been going to MSG since 1990. I have heard ovations for Hulk Hogan, Bret Hart, Shawn Michaels, the Undertaker, Stone Cold and the Rock. I can honestly say I have never heard The Garden louder than it was that night. Maybe when Hogan beat the Sheik in January 1984 could give it a run, but I myself could not tell you. All I know was this crowd was insane and it was not a quick pop either. This was a long, sustained pop that was unbelievable. To this day, this is my favorite memory at any live event I have been to. To top it off, my cousin and I got on TV holding three neon green H's during his entrance. That was a night I will never forget."

Lou Spadone, *Queens, NY*

"Amazing. If someone asked me to sum up my experience of MSG from January 7, 2002... that is the word I would use. I rode the train from New Jersey into New York City for WWE events over 10 times prior to this show, but this night the train ride was a different experience that would set the tone for the rest of the night. Typically, a train ride to a WWE event at The Garden, was a calm experience. Most of the passengers were commuters and people visiting the city. You might have come across a handful of wrestling fans wearing some kind of merchandise, but nothing over the top. This night was different. First, at our local train station, we instantly noticed more WWE fans than usual. Boarding the train, there were more people than usual, so we had to stand for the duration of the ride. As the train stopped at more stations along the way, more fans entered the train and the chatter and excitement picked up. As we were about 10 minutes from arriving at Penn Station, we heard fans loudly chanting "Triple H, Triple H, Triple H." My buddy and I were huge wrestling fans and very much looked forward to this show, so we were pleasantly surprised that people were just as excited about Triple H's return as we were. The Triple H chants actually continued as we got off the train and entered Penn Station. The video package promoting Triple H's comeback was one of the best videos WWE ever produced. To be fortunate enough to attend this event made it even more exciting, and it goes down as one of my favorite memories of WWE. Equally cool is, to this day, Triple H still speaks fondly of this night and talks about how special it was to him. The chants from the train and Penn Station, most certainly carried into MSG. The chants of "Triple H, Triple H" went from a few dozen on the train, to about a hundred in Penn Station, to thousands inside MSG. Shortly before his return segment, they played the U2 'Beautiful Day' video that was used to promote his return, but the coolest part about this video was that at the end, it said "Triple H returns....Next" There were no more weeks of waiting, this was it. Nobody sat during that commercial break. It was 2 minutes of eager anticipation, and Triple H chants. When his music finally hit.....amazing. One of my favorite memories of being a WWE fan. Seeing that many people cheer, chant and be so excited about his return was awesome."

Michael Berlinski, *Edison, NJ*

"That monster, monster, monster pop that I haven't heard much louder ever in that building."

Mary-Kate (Grosso) Anthony, *Tampa, Fla.*

'I was crying'

"I was there when Triple H came back. I'm getting goosebumps right now just talking about it. I was crying. The feeling of just everyone cheering and screaming, and grown men getting emotional that he was back. And him not talking for a long time. It's one of the few moments that still elicits emotion from me today."

Reny Amoros, *Bronx, NY*

SMACKDOWN!
MADISON SQUARE GARDEN
NEW YORK, NY
JANUARY 8, 2002

AMONG THE MATCHES ON TONIGHT'S CARD:

THE TAG TEAM OF THE ROCK AND ROB VAN DAM TAKE
ON THE COMBINATION OF CHRIS JERICHO AND TEST...

NEW WORLD WRESTLING FEDERATION TAG TEAM
CHAMPIONS TAZZ AND SPIKE DUDLEY MAKE THEIR
FIRST TITLE DEFENSE AGAINST THE CHALLENGE OF
CHRISTIAN AND LANCE STORM...

INTERCONTINENTAL CHAMPION EDGE DEFENDS HIS
TITLE AGAINST THE BIG BOSSMAN...

TAJIRI WILL SQUARE OFF AGAINST "THE ONE" BILLY
GUNN...

WWF @ New York City, NY - Madison Square Garden - January 8, 2002 (12,175)
Brock Lesnar pinned Randy Orton with a powerslam
Ron Waterman defeated Rico Constantino via submission with a Torture Rack backbreaker
Sunday Night Heat:
Albert & Scotty 2 Hotty defeated Crash Holly & Sho Funaki at 5:20 after Scotty hit the Worm on Crash
Bily Gunn pinned Tajiri at 4:31 with the Fameasser
The Dudley Boyz defeated Perry Saturn & Sgt. Slaughter via disqualification at 5:08 when Slaughter used his belt as a weapon
Smackdown!:
WWF Tag Team Champions Tazz & Spike Dudley defeated Christian & Lance Storm when Christian submitted to the Tazzmission at 4:57
WWF IC Champion Edge pinned the Big Bossman with the DDT at 3:55
The Rock & Rob Van Dam defeated WWF World Champion Chris Jericho & Test at 9:30 when the Rock used the Sharpshooter to make Jericho submit
Jazz & Terri defeated WWF Women's Champion Trish Stratus & Jackie; the match was cut from the show and was not televised
Rikishi fought Booker T to a no contest when Booker vomitted on the announce table after recieving the Stinkface
Steve Austin fought Kurt Angle to a no contest when Kane interfered and hit the chokeslam on both men

One time MSG headliner Sgt. Slaughter teaming with Perry Saturn.

Brock Lesnar prepares to face Ric Flair.

WWE (Raw) @ New York City, NY - Madison Square Garden - June 29, 2002
WWE European Champion William Regal & Christopher Nowinski defeated Bubba Ray & Spike Dudley when Nowinski pinned Spike; after the match, Nowinski was powerbombed through a table
D-Lo Brown pinned Justin Credible
Shawn Stasiak pinned WWE Hardcore Champion Bradshaw to win the title after Steven Richards interfered
Spike Dudley pinned WWE Hardcore Champion Shawn Stasiak to win the title with the Dudley Dog
Steven Richards pinned WWE Hardcore Champion Spike Dudley to win the title with the Steven Kick
Bradshaw pinned WWE Hardcore Champion Steven Richards to win the title with the Clothesline from Hell
WWE Women's Champion Molly Holly pinned Trish Stratus with her feet on the ropes for leverage after reversing an attempt at the Stratusfaction
Matt Hardy pinned Raven
Brock Lesnar (w/ Paul Heyman) pinned Ric Flair with the F5
Steven Richards pinned Tommy Dreamer with the Steven Kick
WWE IC Champion Rob Van Dam defeated Eddie Guerrero in a ladder match
Booker T & Goldust defeated X-Pac & the Big Show when Booker pinned X-Pac
WWE World Champion the Undertaker pinned Hulk Hogan with the chokeslam after Vince McMahon distracted Hogan from ringside; Jim Ross was the ring announcer for the match (Hogan's MSG return after a 10-year absence)

WWE IC Champion Rob Van Dam vs. Eddie Guerrero

Ladder war

"Rob Van Dam wrestled Eddy Guerrero in a ladder match that was better than their excellent TV match from the month before. It might have been the best match I've ever seen live."
Dennis Spicacci, *Carteret, NJ*

*Ric Flair
vs. Brock
Lesnar*

Hulk Hogan vs. WWE World Champion The Undertaker

385

WWE RAW
MONDAY, AUGUST 26TH, 2002
MADISON SQUARE GARDEN
NEW YORK CITY

A NEW WWE CHAMPION REIGNS TODAY. BROCK LESNAR..AND TONIGHT, YOU CAN EXPECT TO SEE HIM HERE IN THE GARDEN….

AMONG THE MATCHES ON TONIGHT'S CARD:

BOOKER T GOES ONE-ON-ONE WITH TAG TEAM TITLE CO-HOLDER CHRISTIAN…

JEFF HARDY GOES ONE-ON-ONE WITH CHRIS JERICHO…

BUBBA RAY AND SPIKE DUDLEY SEE TAG TEAM ACTION AGAINST WILLIAM REGAL AND CHRISTOPHER NOWINSKI…

TRISH STRATUS FACES VICTORIA…

ALSO IN THE HOUSE TONIGHT ARE SUCH WWE SUPERSTARS AS THE UNDERTAKER….ROB VAN DAM…TRIPLE H…. BRADSHAW…AND BOOKER T……

CARD SUBJECT TO CHANGE

DON'T FORGET TO CHECK OUT THE WWE SOUVENIR STANDS WHERE WE HAVE MANY GREAT ITEMS FROM YOUR FAVORITE SUPERSTARS INCLUDING THE NEW WWE MADE IN USA SHIRT. GET THERE QUICK. SUPPLIES ARE LIMITED.

WWE @ New York City, NY - Madison Square Garden - August 26, 2002

Shelton Benjamin pinned Shawn Stasiak with a spin kick to the face

Raw:

Booker T (w/ Goldust) pinned WWE Tag Team Champion Christian (w/ Lance Storm) with the scissors kick after Goldust sent an interfering Storm out of the ring

Bubba Ray & Spike Dudley defeated William Regal & Christopher Nowinski (w/ Molly Holly) when Bubba pinned Regal with the Bubba Bomb; after the match, Nowinski saved Molly from going through a table but Regal sustained a Dudley Dog onto and then a Bubba Ray powerbomb through the wooden table

Jeff Hardy defeated Chris Jericho via disqualification when Jericho failed to release the Walls of Jericho after Hardy reached the ropes; after the match, several referees forced Jericho to break the hold

WWE IC Champion Rob Van Dam pinned WWE Hardcore Champion Tommy Dreamer with the Five Star Frog Splash in a unification match following a modified Van Terminator as Dreamer was tied up in the Tree of Woe, with his legs trapped in a ladder; the match was fought under hardcore rules; after the match, the two embraced out of respect

Triple H prepares to face The Undertaker.

Lillian Garcia (w/ Trish Stratus) defeated Howard Finkel in an Evening Gown vs. Tuxedo match, after both Trish and Stacy Keibler helped in attacking and stripping Finkel; due to pre-match stipulations, Lillian became the permanent ring announcer for Raw

Triple H pinned the Undertaker after Brock Lesnar interfered and hit Taker in the face with the world title belt; due to pre-match stipulations, Triple H became the #1 contender to the world title

Sunday Night Heat - 9/1/02 - hosted by Jonathan Coachman & D-Lo Brown:

Goldust pinned Johnny Stamboli with the Curtain Call at 5:21

Steven Richards pinned Crash Holly with the Steven Kick at 3:52

Bradshaw pinned Justin Credible with the Clothesline from Hell at 3:27

D-Lo Brown pinned Raven with the Sky High at 5:30

Making history on RAW

"Me and Rob Van Dam unified the Hardcore title and the IC title. After that, I went down the steps, I cried a little bit. It was very emotional. My father was very, very sick. I called him."

Tommy Dreamer,

TheHistoryofWWE.com interview, 2014

SURVIVOR SERIES
Madison Square Garden – November 17, 2002

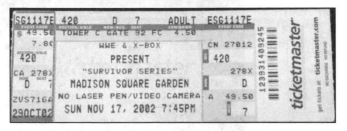

Survivor Series 02 - New York City, NY - Madison Square Garden - November 17, 2002 (17,930; 15,500 paid)

Matt Striker was in attendance for the show

Sunday Night Heat - shown live:

Lance Storm & William Regal defeated Goldust & the Hurricane at 3:02 when Storm pinned Goldust with a cradle after Regal hit Goldust from behind; after the bout, Tommy Dreamer assaulted both Storm & Regal with his Singapore cane, clearing them from the ring (*Survivor Series 02*)

Pay-per-view bouts - included Jim Ross & Jerry Lawler on commentary for the Raw matches and Michael Cole & Tazz on commentary for the Smackdown! matches; featured Saliva performing "Always," the show's theme song, at The World; during the performance, clips were shown promoting the WWE Women's Title, Smackdown! Tag Team Title, WWE World Title, and World Heavyweight Title matches later in the show; Stacy Keibler introduced the band at The World; included Kurt Angle speaking with Chris Benoit backstage, with Angle saying if Billy Kidman could win the Cruiserweight title then there was no doubt they could regain the Smackdown! Tag Team Titles; featured a backstage camera showing Victoria looking in the mirror, before the smashed it and then tore the head off a cardboard cutout of Trish Stratus; included Jonathan Coachman interviewing Eric Bischoff backstage until the Big Show interrupted and said Bischoff would be sorry for trading him since he would be leaving MSG with the WWE World Title; featured Paul Heyman speaking with WWE World Champion Brock Lesnar backstage about the match against Show later in the night; Al Wilson & Dawn Marie were shown sitting in the crowd; included an in-ring segment by Christopher Nowinski in which he insulted the crowd for not being as smart as him, with the crowd chanting "Shut the fuck up;" moments later, Matt Hardy appeared as well and said New Yorkers were not stupid, but losers; after both continued to insult the crowd, debating as to whether the fans were stupid or losers, Scott Steiner appeared and easily beat down both men, eventually gorilla pressing Hardy onto Nowinski on the floor before doing push ups in the ring and then cutting his own in-ring promo (Steiner's surprise debut after a 9-year absence); featured Terri interviewing Shawn Michaels backstage regarding the Elimination Chamber, which was interrupted by a pre-taped RNN segment in which Randy Orton discussed his road to recovery and urged fans to continue sending well wishes to GetwellRandy@wwe.com; included Coachman interviewing World Heavyweight Champion Triple H, with Ric Flair, regarding his Elimination Chamber title defense later in the night:

Jeff Hardy, Bubba Ray & Spike Dudley defeated Rosey, Jamal, & Rico in an elimination tables match at 13:53; Spike was eliminated following a double flapjack through a table by Rosey & Jamal at 4:23; Hardy eliminated Rosey with a Swanton off an EXIT ramp through a table set up underneath at 7:42; Jamal eliminated Hardy with a splash off the top through a table on the floor at 10:31; Bubba eliminated Jamal with a powerbomb off the top through a table at 11:42; after the elimination, Rosey & Jamal attacked Bubba until D-Von Dudley made the save and cleared them from the ring; Bubba eliminated Rico following the 3D through a table by Bubba & D-Von (Bubba & D-Von's surprise reunion after 7 months)

Billy Kidman pinned WWE Cruiserweight Champion Jamie Noble (w/ Nidia) with the Shooting Star Press at 7:29 to win the title after kicking Nidia off the apron and knocking Noble off the middle turnbuckle; after the bout, Kidman left through the crowd (the debut of Kidman's "You Can Run" theme song)

Victoria pinned WWE Women's Champion Trish Stratus in a hardcore match to win the title at 7:01 with a suplex after spraying a fire extinguisher in the champion's face

The Big Show pinned WWE World Champion Brock Lesnar (w/ Paul Heyman) to win the title at 4:19 after hitting the champion in the midsection with a chair followed by a chokeslam onto the chair; moments before the finish, Heyman turned on Lesnar by pulling the referee out of the ring and knocking him out after Lesnar hit the F5 on the challenger; immediately after the match, Heyman & Show drove out of the arena (Lesnar's first TV pinfall loss) (*The Big Show: A Giant's World*)

Eddie & Chavo Guerrero Jr. defeated WWE Smackdown! Tag Team Champions Edge & Rey Mysterio Jr. and Kurt Angle & Chris Benoit in an elimination match to win the titles at 19:20; Edge pinned Benoit with the spear at 13:04 after avoiding a clothesline; after the elimination, Angle & Benoit attacked their opponents and then argued with one another as they left ringside; Eddie forced Mysterio to submit to the El Paso Lasso after Chavo hit Rey in the leg with one of the title belts as the champion attempted the West Coast Pop (*Cheating Death, Stealing Life: The Eddie Guerrero Story*)

Shawn Michaels defeated World Heavyweight Champion Triple H, Booker T, Rob Van Dam, WWE Raw Tag Team Champion Chris Jericho, and Kane in an Elimination Chamber match to win the title at 39:21; Booker pinned RVD with a missile dropkick at 13:38 immediately after RVD hit the Five Star Frog Splash off the top of one of the chambers, with one of RVD's knees landing across Triple H's throat as he landed; Jericho pinned Booker with the Lionsault at 17:41; Jericho pinned Kane with the Lionsault after Kane sustained both Michaels' superkick and the Pedigree at 22:54; Michaels pinned Jericho with the superkick at 30:43 as Jericho had the Walls of Jericho applied on Triple H; Michaels pinned Triple H with the superkick after reversing the Pedigree into a backdrop; prior to the bout, Eric Bischoff came out and cut an in-ring promo inside the chamber, detailing what the chamber was created of and the rules of the match; during Jericho's entrance, Saliva performed "King of My World" live from The World; Ric Flair escorted Triple H to the ring prior to the match (Michaels' in-ring return to MSG after a 4 year absence) (debut of the Elimination Chamber) (*Satan's Prison: The Anthology of the Elimination Chamber*)

WWE (Raw) @ New York City, NY - Madison Square Garden - February 1, 2003
Steven Richards pinned Spike Dudley with the Steven Kick
Sean O'Haire pinned Rico with the Razor's Edge
Rob Van Dam pinned D-Lo Brown with the Five Star Frog Splash
Booker T pinned Christian with the scissors kick onto a steel chair
Scott Steiner pinned Batista with a powerbomb
WWE Women's Champion Victoria defeated Jackie and Molly Holly by pinning Jackie after Steven Richards interfered
Chris Jericho (w/ Christian) defeated Test after Christian interfered
WWE Raw Tag Team Champions Lance Storm & William Regal defeated the Dudley Boyz after Regal hit Bubba Ray with brass knuckles while Chief Morley distracted the referee
Brock Lesnar defeated WWE World Champion Kurt Angle, Shelton Benjamin & Charlie Haas (sub. for World Heavyweight Champion Triple H) in a gauntlet match; Lesnar pinned Benjamin with the F5 after 6 minutes; Lesnar pinned Haas with the F5; Lesnar defeated Angle via disqualification when Benjamin & Haas interfered; prior to the match, Stephanie McMahon appeared and slapped Paul Heyman; after the bout, Lesnar hit the F5 on all three opponents

WWE @ New York City, NY - Madison Square Garden - June 23, 2003 (announced at 14,451)

Aaron Stevens defeated Primo Carnera III with a roll up

Mark Jindrak pinned Spike Dudley with a modified powerbomb

Raw - featured Lance Storm as a guest of the Highlight Reel; included an in-ring tribute to Mick Foley during which a music video set to Staind's "So Far Away" was shown; later in the broadcast, Foley was confronted backstage by Randy Orton, assaulted, and kicked down the stairway:

WWE IC Champion Christian & Test defeated Booker T & Scott Steiner (w/ Stacy Keibler) when Test pinned Steiner with the boot to the face after Steiner clotheslined Christian to the floor; moments prior to the finish, Test pushed Steiner into Stacy - knocking her off the ring aprong

Maven pinned Christopher Nowinski (w/ Teddy Long) by avoiding a suplex and using a roll up at the 30 second mark

The Dudley Boyz defeated Chris Jericho & Lance Storm in an impromptu match when D-Von pinned Storm with the 3D after Storm collided with Jericho on the ring apron

WWE Raw Tag Team Champions Sylvian Grenier & Rene Dupree defeated the Hurricane & Sgt. Slaughter in a non-title match when Dupree pinned Slaughter after hitting him with one of the title belts, moments after Slaughter applied the Cobra Clutch on both opponents

Shawn Michaels & Kevin Nash defeated Ric Flair & Randy Orton when Michaels pinned Flair with the flying elbowsmash and superkick

Bill Goldberg pinned Rodney Mack (w/ Teddy Long) with the Jackhammer at the 26 second mark of the 5-minute White Boy Challenge; during Goldberg's entrance, Mack attempted to attack his opponent on the stage but was knocked through the pyro and down the ramp

World Heavyweight Champion Triple H (w/ Ric Flair) pinned Kane with the Pedigree at around the 11-minute mark after Randy Orton came out of the crowd and hit a low blow and the RKO as Kane prepared to chokeslam the champion; moments earlier, Kane fought off a double team from Triple H and Flair, eventually hitting Flair with a chokeslam; due to pre-match stipulations, Kane was forced to unmask; after the bout, Eric Bischoff came out and ordered Kane to unmask but, before he could, Evolution attacked him which brought out Rob Van Dam to make the save; after clearning the ring, Kane eventually did unmask before hitting a chokeslam on RVD (*The Greatest Superstars of the 21st Century*)

Sunday Night Heat - 6/29/03 - hosted by Al Snow & Jonathan Coachman; included a backstage segment with Rico scolding his off-camera assistant Jan for appearing on camera, then introducing Jackie Gayda who modeled an evening dress; featured a home video promo for 'From the Vault: Shawn Michaels;' included exclusive footage of Mick Foley being stitched up on Monday following his backstage assault at the hands of Randy Orton & Ric Flair; featured Rico & Gayda salsa dancing backstage until Rico became aggrivated by Jan attempting to dance with them; included Terri Runnels in the men's room attempting to interview Steven Richards & Victoria, with Richards hopping out of a stall and revealing his new "Stevie Night Heat" trunks; featured a PPV promo for Vengeance:

Garrison Cade pinned Rosey at 2:19 with a high knee

Val Venis pinned Roman Zachako at 1:58 with the Money Shot; after the bout, Venis kisses a female in the front row

Rico (w/ Jackie Gayda) pinned Tommy Dreamer at 2:36 with a spinning kick as Dreamer was about to DDT the interfering Gayda

Steven Richards & Victoria defeated Goldust & Trish Stratus in an at 5:17 when Richards pinned Trish with a roll up as she prepared to hit Stratusfaction on Victoria; the bout was mistakenly announced as a mixed tag team match

---

Those steps

"I still remember those steps, while you're filing out. Mick Foley and Randy Orton. Those stairs, I'm sure Mick legit fell because everyone has fallen down those stairs. It's still a great memory to have."

Reny Amoros, *Bronx, NY*

392

WWE @ New York City, NY - Madison Square Garden - June 24, 2003

Roman Zachako defeated Aaron Stevens with a roll up

Smackdown! - 6/26/03 - Billy Kidman sat ringside for the show after not appearing on WWE TV for four months:

John Cena pinned Orlando Jordon by rolling through on a flying bodypress and using the tights for leverage; after the bout, Cena hit the FU on his opponent before leaving ringside as the Undertaker made his way to the ring; in a show of respect, Taker gave Jordon a pat on the ribs for a good showing (Jordon's TV debut)

The Undertaker & the Acolytes defeated Nunzio, Chuck Palumbo, & Johnny Stamboli when Bradshaw pinned Stamboli with the Clothesline from Hell after Stamboli clotheslined Taker to the floor

WWE US Title Tournament Quarter Finals: Matt Hardy pinned Rikishi with the Twist of Fate after Rikishi missed a splash in the corner, hitting an unprotected turnbuckle back-first

WWE Smackdown! Tag Team Champions Eddie Guerrero & Tajiri defeated Roddy Piper & Sean O'Haire when Guerrero pinned Piper with the frog splash after Tajiri sprayed green mist into Piper's eyes (Piper's last appearance for 2 years; Piper's last MSG match for 3 years)

The Ultimo Dragon pinned Shannon Moore with a standing Dudley Dogg into a reverse DDT; Rey Mysterio Jr. did guest commentary for the bout and helped celebrate the win with Dragon after the match (Dragon's TV debut)

The Big Show, Shelton Benjamin, & Charlie Haas defeated WWE World Champion Brock Lesnar, Kurt Angle, & Mr. America when Show pinned Mr. America with the chokeslam after Mr. America became distracted by Vince McMahon and an injured Zach Gowen at ringside; after the bout, McMahon ordered a handicap match for the following week pitting the Big Show against Zach Gowen & Stephanie McMahon with the stipulation that if Gowen's team is able to win, he would earn a WWE contract (Mr. America's last appearance; Hulk Hogan's last apperance for 2 years)

Velocity - 6/28/03 - hosted by Josh Matthews & Ernest Miller:

Billy Gunn (w/ Torrie Wilson) pinned Kanyon with the Fameasser at 5:24

Spanky pinned John Xavier at 6:24 with Sliced Bread #2

Albert pinned Kevin Knight at 2:40 with the backbreaker

Chris Benoit & Rhyno defeated Doug & Danny Basham (w/ Shaniqua) at 6:58 when Doug submitted to Benoit's Crippler Crossface after Rhyno hit the Gore

WWE @ New York City, NY - Madison Square Garden - September 20, 2003 (less than 12,000)

Chris Benoit defeated the Big Show via submission with the Crippler Crossface at 4:41

Matt Hardy & Shannon Moore defeated Spanky & Paul London at 7:35 when Hardy pinned London with the Twist of Fate (Spanky & London's MSG debuts)

Sho Funaki pinned Nunzio with a roll up at 5:22

Doug & Danny Basham defeated the Ultimo Dragon & Jamie Noble at 8:23 when Danny pinned Noble (the Bashams' MSG debuts)

Albert pinned Orlando Jordan with a boot to the face at 5:09

WWE Cruiserweight Champion Rey Mysterio Jr. pinned Tajiri following the 619 and West Coast Pop at 8:31

Charlie Haas pinned Billy Kidman at 6:40 with a roll up after Kidman failed the Shooting Star Press

WWE US & Smackdown! Tag Team Champion Eddie Guerrero defeated John Cena and Rhyno by pinning Cena with the frog splash at 6:45 after Rhyno hit the Gore on Cena who held up the title belt, knocking out both challengers; after the bout, Cena insulted NYC which prompted Tazz to come to the ring and apply the Tazzmission on Cena

Torrie Wilson defeated Dawn Marie and Sable in a tiny teddy contest; Sho Funaki was the guest MC

WWE World Champion Brock Lesnar defeated the Undertaker in a steel cage match at 18:20 by escaping over the top after Vince McMahon interfered and prevented the challenger from leaving the cage

WWE (Raw) @ New York City, NY - Madison Square Garden - December 12, 2003

Included Jonathan Coachman as the guest ring announcer for the night after Coachman ordered Howard Finkel to take the night off

The Hurricane pinned Test at 7:02 after Stacy Keibler prevented Test from using a steel chair, with Test then shoving Stacy into the corner and missing a chair shot to his opponent and the chair then bouncing off the top rope and hitting Test in the head

Mark Henry pinned Tommy Dreamer at 3:21 with a powerslam as Dreamer attempted to use his Singapore cane

WWE Women's Champion Molly Holly defeated Trish Stratus, Lita, and Jazz in an elimination match at 8:24; Lita sustained an injury at around 1:20 while attempting a flip out of the corner and was helped backstage by Fit Finley and officials at the 4-minute mark; Trish pinned Jazz with a roll up at 6:31; after the elimination, Jazz continued to attack Trish until guest referee Victoria threw her out of the ring; Molly pinned Trish with a side roll after Victoria kicked Trish in the mid section as the challenger attempted the standing hurricanrana off the top

Mark Jindrak & Garrison Cade defeated Lance Storm & Val Venis at 8:57 when Jindrak pinned Storm after Cade pulled Storm from the ring, after he and Venis hit the Hart Attack, and threw him into the steel ring post

Matt Hardy pinned Maven with the Twist of Fate at 5:46 after Maven narrowly avoided colliding with the referee in the corner

WWE Raw Tag Team Champions the Dudley Boyz defeated Chris Jericho & Christian in a tables match at 14:48 when Christian was put through a table with the 3D moments after he accidentally knocked Jericho to the floor; late in the bout, both Trish Stratus and Lita interfered on behalf of the champions, hitting a simultaneous Wazzup Drop off the top

Shawn Michaels pinned Ric Flair at 21:17 with the superkick; the bout originally ended in a 20-minute time-limit draw, at 16:26, as Michaels was caught in the figure-4 but a bloody Flair challenged his opponent to 5 more minutes

WWE IC Champion Rob Van Dam & Booker T defeated Randy Orton & Batista at 11:03 when RVD pinned Orton with the Five Star Frog Splash after Booker hit the scissors kick

World Heavyweight Champion Bill Goldberg pinned Kane with the spear at 6:52; after the bout, Goldberg fought off Batista, Randy Orton, and Mark Henry, throwing Batista out of the ring and hitting the spear on the other two

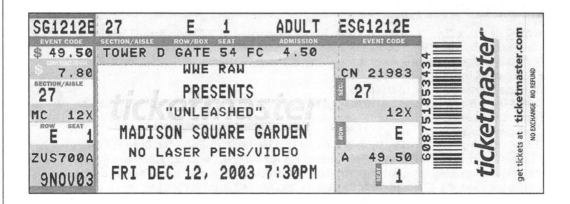

WRESTLEMANIA XX
Madison Square Garden – March 14, 2004

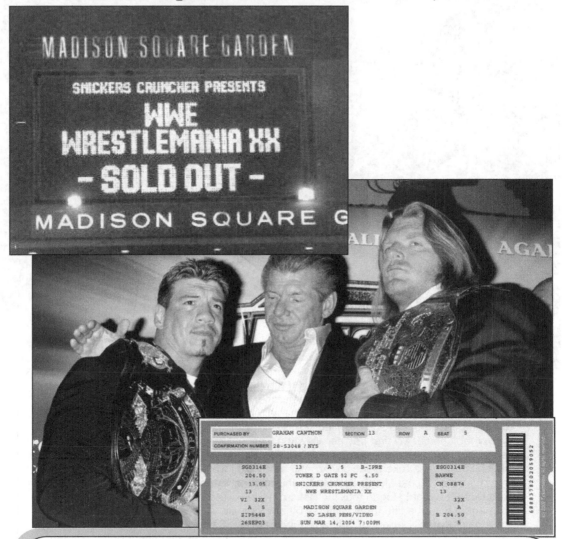

It was the best childhood memory

"When my father and I were trying to find our seats for WrestleMania XX, we got off at the wrong section. There was a guard that was very nice and was just like, 'No, you guys aren't here, you guys are all the way up there (pointing to the top level).'
I remember it was just the saddest thing ever. When we finally sat in our seats, that was the moment he was, 'I'm sorry. I did my best.' 'It's fine. I'm going to be in that ring one day.' ...No matter what our seats were, it was the best childhood memory ever was my dad sacrificing and to give me that moment. It was the best thing that ever happened to me."
AJ Lee, *WWE.com video diary, 2013*

The crowd makes its way in prior to WrestleMania XX.

Here I was
"As a WWF/E fan for as long as I can remember, living in Northern Ireland, it was always my dream to one day attend Wrestlemania. I grew up with the fantastic history and amazing image of MSG in my mind, as to where the important shows and moments of history took place. My first pay-per-view trip was to WrestleMania XX and of course with that, MSG. I entered MSG that Sunday night in awe, the building where I had watched so much importance take place on TV, and now here I was, living my dream, many miles from home on a cold March day. Upon entering the arena I imagined what it was like to be there the night Hogan took the belt from Shiek. The night Bret overcame Yoko to once again hold the title and countless other moments. Also what it must have been like, to witness Bruno, Backlund, Graham, Piper, Hogan, Savage, an endless list, all in their prime, light up such a historic venue. The famous image of the interior of the Garden itself took my breath away for a second. Here I was."
Gordon Elliot, *Northern Ireland*

WrestleMania XX - New York City, NY - Madison Square Garden - March 14, 2004 (18,500 paid; sell out)
Zack Ryder, Curt Hawkins, and AJ were in attendance for the show
Pay-per-view bouts - included a Hall of Fame segment showcasing Bobby Heenan, Harley Race, Superstar Billy Graham, Don Muraco, Greg Valentine, the Junkyard Dog, Tito Santana, Big John Studd, Sgt. Slaughter, Pete Rose, and Jesse Ventura; featured an interview by Ventura with Donald Trump, who sat ringside for the event; the Harlem Boys Choir performed 'America the Beautiful' to begin the broadcast; included Jim Ross & Jerry Lawler on commentary for the Raw matches, with Michael Cole & Tazz commentating the Smackdown! Bouts
John Cena pinned WWE US Champion the Big Show to win the title at 9:13 with the FU after hitting the champion with a pair of brass knuckles
WWE Raw Tag Team Champions Rob Van Dam & Booker T defeated Mark Jindrak & Garrison Cade, the Dudley Boyz, and Rene Dupree & Rob Conway at 7:55 when RVD pinned Conway with the Five Star Frog Splash after Booker hit the scissors kick
Christian pinned Chris Jericho at 14:56 with a roll up and using the tights for leverage after Trish Stratus accidentally raked Jericho in the eyes; after the bout, Trish slapped Jericho and left ringside with Christian
WWE IC Champion Randy Orton, Ric Flair, & Batista defeated the Rock & Mick Foley in a handicap match at 17:09 when Orton pinned Foley with the RKO as Foley prepared to apply the Mandible Claw (Foley's first match in 4 years; Rock's first match in 11 months) (*Randy Orton: The Evolution of a Predator*)
Torrie Wilson & Sable defeated Stacy Keibler & Jackie Gayda in a Playboy Evening Gown Match when Torrie pinned Jackie with a roll up at 2:41; prior to the bout, all four women disrobed to their bra and panties
WWE Cruiserweight Champion Chavo Guerrero Jr. (w/ Chavo Guerrero Sr.) defeated Nunzio, Shannon Moore, Rey Mysterio Jr., Sho Funaki, the Ultimo Dragon, Jamie Noble, Billy Kidman, Tajiri, and Akio in a gauntlet match at 10:38; Dragon pinned Moore with the Asai DDT at 1:18; Noble defeated Dragon via submission with a guillotine; Noble pinned Funaki with an inside cradle; Nunzio was counted-out at 4:15; Kidman pinned Noble at 6:08; Mysterio pinned Kidman at 7:35; Mysterio pinned Tajiri at 8:38; Akio couldn't pariticpate after Tajiri accidentally blew mist into his face; Chavo pinned Rey by holding onto Chavo Sr. outside the ring
Bill Goldberg pinned Brock Lesnar at 13:48 with the spear and Jackhammer; after the bout, guest referee Steve Austin hit the Stunner on Lesnar before doing the same to Goldberg (Lesnar and Goldberg's last match in the WWE) (*Goldberg: The Ultimate Collection*)
WWE Smackdown! Tag Team Champions Rikishi & Scotty 2 Hotty defeated the Acolytes, Shelton Benjamin & Charlie Haas, and Doug & Danny Basham when Rikishi pinned Danny with a sit-down splash at 6:05
WWE Women's Champion Victoria pinned Molly Holly at 4:56 by reversing a neckbreaker submission hold into a backslide; due to prematch stipulations, Molly had her head shaved bald after the bout
WWE World Champion Eddie Guerrero pinned Kurt Angle at 21:30 with an inside cradle and using the ropes for leverage after avoiding the ankle lock by unlacing his boot
The Undertaker (w/ Paul Bearer) pinned Kane with the tombstone at 6:56; prior to the bout, druids holding torches lined each side of the aisle as Taker walked to the ring (Taker's return after a 4-month absence) (Bearer's surprise return after a nearly 4-year absence) (*Tombstone: The History of the Undertaker*, *The Undertaker: 15-0*)
Chris Benoit defeated World Heavyweight Champion Triple H and Shawn Michaels to win the title at 24:07 when Triple H submitted to the Crippler Crossface; after the bout, WWE World Champion Eddie Guerrero came out to congratulate Benoit; following the telecast, Benoit's family came out to celebrate the victory as well; voted Pro Wrestling Illustrated Match of the Year (*Hard Knocks: The Chris Benoit Story*)

John Cena celebrates winning his first WWE title, the US championship.

Disappointed
"I had come back after four years out of the ring and I kind of let myself down. I had the perfect opportunity in Madison Square Garden teaming up with the Rock against Evolution, and I just kind of dropped the ball. I didn't give the performance that I should have, and the next month I came back (at Backlash) and redeemed myself."
Mick Foley, *USA Today, 2014*

A happy ending

"(Chris) Benoit's stuff was awesome. And the first time really, since WCW, seeing him with Nancy. It was a beautiful beautiful moment. People should still see that moment for what it meant for the two of them, not for what what happened to Chris Benoit and Eddie Guerrero. (Benoit) was a funny person and a good man."

Mary-Kate (Grosso) Anthony, *Tampa, Fla.*

Chris Benoit celebrates his World Heavyweight title win as confetti falls from above.

WWE (Raw) @ New York City, NY - Madison Square Garden - June 26, 2004 (10,000)

WWE Raw Tag Team Champions Rob Conway & Sylvian Grenier defeated Rhyno & Tajiri when Tajiri was pinned following the Aur Reviour

Eugene pinned Jonathan Coachman with the Rock Bottom and People's Elbow, moments after William Regal countered the interference of Eric Bischoff; after the bout, Eugene dropped Bischoff with the Stunner

Kane pinned Matt Hardy with the chokeslam

The Hurricane & Maven defeated Garrison Cade & Test when Hurricane pinned Test with a roll up

Chris Jericho pinned Batista at 9:35 by reversing the sit-down powerbomb into a roll up and grabbing the tights for leverage

WWE IC Champion Randy Orton pinned Edge at 13:25 with a roll up and putting both feet on the top rope for leverage after dropping the challenger head-first onto the top turnbuckle

WWE Women's Champion Trish Stratus (w/ Tyson Tomko) pinned Victoria at 7:21 by putting her feet on the ropes for leverage after Tomko pulled her out of the way of the challenger's moonsault; after the bout, Tomko attempted to press slam Victoria until Lita came out and gave Tomko a low blow from behind

WWE Raw World Champion Chris Benoit defeated Triple H via submission with the Crippler Crossface after reversing an attempt at the Pedigree at 24:42, moments after the champion hit an interfering Ric Flair and Batista with a steel chair

WWE @ New York City, NY - Madison Square Garden - October 4, 2004

Val Venis defeated Muhammad Hassan (w/ Shawn Davari)

Raw - included WWE IC Champion Chris Jericho interrupting an in-ring promo by Triple H, admitting that it was Jericho who suggested the idea for Taboo Tuesday and that Triple H would have several challengers for the fans to choose from:

Shawn Michaels pinned Christian at 13:21 with the superkick

Batista defeated Chris Benoit via disqualification at 4:54 when Randy Orton interfered

WWE Raw Tag Team Champions Rob Conway & Sylvian Grenier defeated the Hurricane & Rosey at 2:16 following the Aur Reviour

Stacy Keibler pinned Molly Holly with a roll up at 2:51

World Heavyweight Champion Triple H pinned WWE IC Champion Chris Jericho in a non-title lumberjack match at 5:20 after Rhyno interfered and hit the Gore on Jericho

Sunday Night Heat - 10/10/04 - hosted by Todd Grisham & Al Snow:

Victoria pinned Gail Kim with the Widow's Peak at 4:19

Rhyno & Tajiri defeated Danny Doring & Arch Kinkaid at 5:52 when Tajiri pinned Kincaid with the kick to the head after the Tarantula

Maven pinned Steven Richards at 4:09 with a roll over

Shelton Benjamin pinned Rodney Mack (w/ Jazz) with the Exploder suplex at 5:22 after Mack collided with Jazz on the ring apron

406

WWE (Smackdown!) @ New York City, NY - Madison Square Garden - December 5, 2004 (matinee) (5,821)
WWE Cruiserweight Champion Spike Dudley defeated Nunzio, Shannon Moore, and Sho Funaki by pinning Moore with a roll up at 7:17
The Big Show defeated Kurt Angle, Luther Reigns, and Mark Jindrak in a handicap match by placing one hand on both Reigns and Jindrak following a double chokeslam at 5:54
Jesus pinned Charlie Haas at 6:43 with a roll up and putting his feet on the ropes for leverage after lifting his knees to block a Vader Bomb off the ropes (Jesus' only MSG appearance)
Chavo Guerrero Jr. pinned Billy Kidman with the Gory Bomb at 9:14 after crotching Kidman on the top as he attempted the Shooting Star Press
WWE World Champion John Bradshaw Layfield (w/ Orlando Jordan) defeated Eddie Guerrero and Booker T at 8:54 by pinning Booker after hitting him with the title belt; moments prior to the finish, Orlando crotched Guerrero on the top rope as Eddie attempted the frog splash but was then kicked off the apron by Booker as JBL grabbed for the title belt
WWE Smackdown! Tag Team Champions Rene Dupree & Kenzo Suzuki defeated Rob Van Dam & Rey Mysterio Jr. at 14:41 when Suzuki pinned Mysterio with the STO after Dupree threw salt into Mysterio's eyes after Mysterio leap frogged over Suzuki
Jackie Gayda pinned Dawn Marie at 5:42 with a sunset flip; after the bout, Torrie Wilson made the save for Jackie against Dawn and helped in clearing the ring of both Dawn and an interfering Hiroku
The Undertaker pinned John Heidenreich (w/ Paul Heyman) with the chokeslam and tombstone at 16:04; after the bout, John Bradshaw Layfield and Orlando Jordan double teamed the Undertaker inside the ring; moments later, Eddie Guerrero and Booker T came to ringside, distracting JBL & Orlando just long enough for Taker to get back to his feet and hit chokeslams on both men; Heyman was then thrown into the ring where he also sustained a chokeslam

'Get your programs!'

"There was a man that worked there for years that was the distributor of the programs. Had to be well into his 70s. His voice would carry into the outside. He would have this really nasally shout, "Programs, get your programs!" Any time going to a show, we would just say it along with him."

Reny Amoros, *Bronx, NY*

WWE (Raw) @ New York City, NY - Madison Square Garden - February 25, 2005 (12,000 paid; 14,000)
Featured a WrestleMania music video to the tune of Kid Rock's "Lonely Road of Faith;" included an appearance by
Superstar Billy Graham in which he cut a promo on Ivan Putski and hit Jonathan Coachman after Coachman insulted
him; Vince McMahon, in a wheelchair recovering from a double quad tear, was backstage for the show
WWE IC Champion Shelton Benjamin pinned Christian with the Exploder suplex at around the 12-minute mark
Chris Masters defeated Val Venis via submission with the full nelson at 9:31 (Master's MSG debut)
WWE Raw Tag Team Champions William Regal & Tajiri defeated Rob Conway & Sylvian Grenier at 7:08 when
Regal pinned Grenier with a running knee to the face
WWE Women's Champion Trish Stratus defeated Victoria and Molly Holly at 4:36 by pinning Molly after Molly
sustained Victoria's Widows Peak, with Victoria then being hit with the champion's Chick Kick immediately thereafter
Muhammad Hassan pinned Rhyno with the Flatliner at 6:43 after Rhyno failed the Gore
Kane pinned Gene Snitsky with the chokeslam at 8:18; Christy Hemme was the guest ring announcer for the bout
Chris Benoit defeated Chris Jericho in a submission match with the Crippler Crossface at 12:07 after Jericho spent
nearly 50 seconds in the hold; after the match, the two men shook hands out of respect and held each other's arm in
the air
Shawn Michaels pinned Edge with the superkick at 14:18 as Edge attempted the spear
Batista & Randy Orton defeated World Heavyweight Champion Triple H & Ric Flair in a steel cage match at 19:58
when Batista pinned Triple H with a spinebuster and the sit-down powerbomb; both Flair and Orton were deemed
unable to continue and helped backstage at around the 8-minute mark after Orton dropped Flair with an RKO on the
floor and Triple H hit Orton over the head with a steel chair seconds later

411

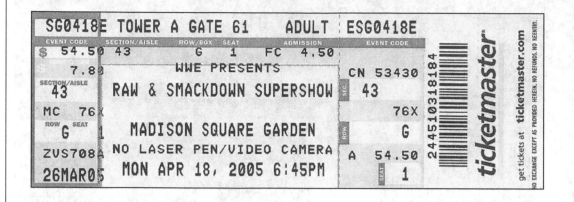

WWE @ New York City, NY - Madison Square Garden - April 18, 2005 (17,258; 13,000 paid; sold out)
WWE Cruiserweight Champion Paul London & Nunzio defeated Billy Kidman & Spike Dudley at 5:24 when London pinned Kidman with a DDT off the top

Raw - featured Jonathan Coachman doing guest commentary alongside Jerry Lawler; included an in-ring confrontation between Trish Stratus and Lita, where the crowd loudly and repeatedly chanted "You screwed Matt" towards Lita, before Kane eventually came out to stalk Trish; moments later, Viscera came out to make the save, assaulting Kane inside the ring as the crowd chanted "Let's go, Mabel"; featured Chris Masters challenging a fan out of the crowd by the name of Roman to escape his Masterlock full nelson, and if he succeeded he would win $1,000; Roman failed; included an in-ring promo from Christian, with Tyson Tomko, in which Christian was interrupted by Vince McMahon who then announced that in approximately a month a new draft would take place to shake up the rosters of Raw and Smackdown!; Christian later made mention of going to Smackdown! and facing John Cena saying, "I would kick Marky Mark's ass and take his WWE title because that's how I roll"; moments later, McMahon stated Christian would face Batista for the world title the next week on Raw (Vince's surprise return to TV following his injury sustained at the Royal Rumble):
Chris Benoit fought Edge to a no contest when the two men fought their way backstage at around the 4:50 mark; following the commercial break, the two fought their way into the Divas' locker room before Eric Bischoff had them separated and ordered a Last Man Standing match to take place at Backlash
WWE Raw Tag Team Champions William Regal & Tajiri defeated the Heart Throbs in a non-title match when Tajiri pinned Romeo at 4:41 with a modified sunset flip after Regal dropped Romeo throat-first across the top rope; after the bout, the champions were attacked from behind, with Tajiri eventually sustaining a double STO (the Heartthrobs' surprise Raw debut)
Shawn Michaels defeated Muhammad Hassan (w/ Daivari) via disqualification at 10:06 when Daivari, who was thrown into the ring moments earlier by Michaels, began stomping Michaels after Hassan hit the Flatliner; moments later, Hulk Hogan came out to make the save, with Hogan and Michaels eventually throwing both Hassan & Daivari from the ring before posing to "Real American" (Hogan's surprise return to MSG after an absence of 2 years)
WWE IC Champion Shelton Benjamin pinned Simon Dean with the Exploder suplex in a non-title match at 3:17; prior to the bout, Chris Jericho came out and told Benjamin that he would get a title shot at Backlash, with Jericho then bringing out Rich Ward from Fozzy to help him perform Fozzy's latest single, "Shelton's a Little Bitch"; Jericho remained on the stage for the duration of the match
Jim Ross pinned Triple H (w/ Ric Flair) in a No DQ match at 11:33 after Batista interfered, beat down Flair, hit Triple H with a steel chair, and hit the Batista Bomb before placing JR on top of Triple H; earlier in the bout, Jerry Lawler came to the ring to check on JR but was also beaten down; Batista was to have been in JR's corner for the duration of the match but showed up late after Triple H paid off his limo driver to get lost

Smackdown! - included WWE Smackdown! Tag Team Champion Eddie Guerrero as a guest of Carlito's Cabana in which Rey Mysterio Jr. came out; moments later, the two shook hands and buried the hatchet for their issues over the previous few weeks; they were then interrupted by MNM on the big screen, shown backstage next to Guerrero's low rider; to goad Guerrero & Mysterio into granting them a title shot, MNM vandalized Guerrero's car; featured John Heidenreich inviting out his 'friend' the Brooklyn Brawler, with Heidenreich then reading a poem he wrote about the

Brawler; moments later, Brawler ran down the poem, disowned New York, took off his Yankees' shirt and hat and put on a Red Sox shirt and hat instead; Heidenreich then attacked the Brawler, eventually hitting the sidewalk slam:
#1 Contender's Tournament Opening Round: The Big Show fought Booker T to a double disqualification at 5:19 when Kurt Angle and John Bradshaw Layfield, who were both doing guest commentary, attacked Show and Booker on the outside to make sure neither man advanced in the tournament; Booker's wife Sharmel was at ringside for the match; after the bout, Show and Booker cleared the ring of the opposition; moments later, Teddy Long came out and ordered that a four-way match take place the following week in England between Angle, JBL, Booker, and Show to determine Cena's top contender and that Booker & Show would face Angle & JBL later in the show

Matt Morgan pinned Brett Matthews at 1:18 with a suplex into a sidewalk slam (Morgan's TV return after an absence of over a year)

Booker T & the Big Show defeated Kurt Angle & John Bradshaw Layfield at 13:11 when Show pinned JBL with the chokeslam after Booker hit the scissors kick; moments prior to the finish, Angle walked out on his partner

Johnny Nitro & Joey Mercury (w/ Melina) defeated WWE Smackdown! Tag Team Champions Eddie Guerrero & Rey Mysterio Jr. to win the titles when Mercury pinned Mysterio at 10:26 after hitting the elevated double team DDT as Melina jumped on Guerrero on the floor to distract him; after the bout, Guerrero & Mysterio argued in the ring over the outcome with Guerrero shoving Mysterio to the mat; moments later, Mysterio confronted Guerrero on the floor and shoved him to the floor before walking backstage alone (Guerrero's last MSG appearance)

WWE World Champion John Cena pinned WWE US Champion Orlando Jordan in a non-title match with the FU at 7:06 after Jordan collided with an interfering Danny Basham on the ring apron

The first visit as 'talent'

"When you're working the Garden, you go in to the side entrance and you go up the elevator. I remember riding up in that elevator ...When I was younger and got nervous I used to twitch. Those things didn't reemerge in my adult life, those little OCDs that I had. I remember I was fidgeting so much. I had to tell myself to relax, slow down. I remember walking around the dressing rooms. The dressing rooms were tiny, tiny tiny. I stepped through the curtain into the empty arena and I walked to the floor. They have all the banners up top. You know when you can kinda feel someone's beside you? I turn around and there's Vince. 'It never gets old here does it?' 'No, it doesn't.' 'Have a good day.' And then he walked away. When is a new, low-level talent going to stand next to Vince and be equal on something? For that moment, Madison Square Garden was so powerful that it was able to join generations and economic backgrounds; the connection between Vince and I at that moment."

Matt Striker, *TheHistoryofWWE.com interview, 2014*

WWE @ New York City, NY - Madison Square Garden - September 11, 2006 (17,298; sell out)

The return to MSG after an absence of 17 months

Jim Duggan & Eugene defeated Charlie Haas & Viscera when Duggan pinned Haas with the running clothesline (Duggan's MSG return after a nearly 15-year absence)

ECW - 9/12/06 - the MSG debut of Joey Styles; featured an opening in-ring segment in which Paul Heyman, with his two bodyguards in riot gear, cut a promo saying his recent comprimise with Vince McMahon brought ECW from a bingo hall to the Garden and all the fans owed him a thank you; moments later, Sabu appeared, rushed the ring, attacked the bodyguards with a steel chair, and cleared them from the ring; Heyman, from the floor, then ordered Sabu to face ECW World Champion the Big Show in an extreme rules match later in the show, with Sabu then leaping from the top rope onto the bodyguards on the floor; included a look at Robert Patrick's role in the John Cena film "The Marine;" featured a brief backstage confrontation between CM Punk and Mike Knox after Kelly Kelly started hitting on Punk; included a backstage promo by Matt Striker regarding the Sandman:

Rob Van Dam defeated Hardcore Holly via disqualification at 4:50 when Test, Mike Knox, and Stevie Richards interfered as Van Dam attempted the Five Star Frog Splash; after the bout, Tommy Dreamer and the Sandman came through the crowd to make the save, with RVD eventually hitting the Five Star Frog Splash on Richards (Sandman and Knox' MSG debuts; Dreamer's MSG return after a 3-year absence; Richards' MSG return after a 2-year absence; Holly's MSG return after a 5-year absence; RVD's MSG return after a 2-year absence)

CM Punk defeated Shannon Moore via submission with the Anaconda Vice following a uranage at 1:51 (Punk's MSG debut; Moore's ECW TV debut; Moore's MSG return after a 2-year absence)

Rene Dupree pinned Balls Mahoney at 3:24 after Kevin Thorn, who was at ringside for the duration of the match with Ariel, knocked Mahoney off the ring apron and onto the steel ring steps (Dupree's ECW TV debut)

ECW World Champion the Big Show (w/ Paul Heyman & his two bodyguards) pinned Sabu in an extreme rules match after a chokeslam through a table, a cobra clutch backbreaker and the Showstopper (Sabu's MSG debut)

Raw - featured a moment of silence in honor of those lost on Sept. 11, 2001, the presentation of the American flag by the USMC Color Guard 2nd Battalion 25th Marine Regiment, and Lillian Garcia singing "America, the Beautiful" to open the show; included clips from the Triple H / Mick Foley, Shawn Michaels / Undertaker, Triple H / Chris Jericho, and Triple H / Kevin Nash Hell in a Cell matches to promote the upcoming Hell in a Cell at Unforgiven; featured the announcement that Sabu would face ECW World Champion the Big Show in an extreme rules match the following night on ECW TV; included a backstage confrontation between Jeff Hardy and WWE IC Champion Jeff Hardy in which Hardy doused Nitro with buckets of paint; Anthony Michael Hall and Toby Keith sat ringside for the event; featured a vignette promoting the debut of Cryme Tyme; included a look at Robert Patrick's role in the John Cena film "The Marine;" featured a "This Week in Wrestling" segment focusing on the 9/13/01 live Smackdown! from Houston, the first show held in the aftermath of the Sept. 11 attacks:

Umaga (w/ Armando Allejandro Estrada) defeated Ric Flair via disqualification at 1:06 when Flair began repeatedly hitting Umaga over the head with a steel chair, with Umaga seemingly not being affected by the blows; after the bout, Umaga attacked Flair and hit a Samoan Drop on the floor; moments later, Kane appeared, fought off Umaga, repeatedly hit him over the head with the chair, knocking him to the floor, threw the ring steps into Umaga's face, and then rammed the steps into Umaga on the floor, knocking him into the front row (Umaga & Estrada's MSG debuts)

Roddy Piper, Robbie & Rory McAllister defeated WWE Raw Tag Team Champions the Spirit Squad in a non-title impromptu match at around the 8-minute mark when Piper scored the pin after the Highlanders hit the Scot Drop behind the referee's back; the match came about when the Spirit Squad interrupted Piper & the Highlanders' in-ring promo, in which Piper put over the fact he was named the #1 heel of all time in the new "51 Worst Offenders" WWE magazine; the NYPD Pipes and Drums Emerald Society played Piper & the Highlanders to the ring (the bout began during the commercial break) (Piper's first match back in MSG after more than a 3-year absence)

John Cena, Jeff Hardy, & Carlito Caribbean Cool defeated WWE World Champion Edge (w/ WWE Women's Champion Lita), WWE IC Champion Johnny Nitro (w/ Melina), & Randy Orton at 17:47 when Nitro submitted to Cena's STFU after sustaining the FU; during the bout, the crowd had dueling chants directed to Cena - "Let's go, Cena" / "Cena sucks" and "Go to Smackdown!" / "Stay on Raw" (Hardy's MSG return after an almost 4-year absence; Carlito's in-ring MSG debut)

Super Crazy pinned Chris Masters at 2:58 with a reversal (Super Crazy's MSG debut)

Trish Stratus pinned Mickie James with the Stratusfaction at 3:14 after kicking an interfering WWE Women's Champion Lita off the ring apron; after the bout, Trish and Mickie shook hands and hugged; moments later, Trish took the microphone and thanked the fans for their support (Trish's last match on Raw)

Vince McMahon pinned Triple H in a no holds barred match at 7:00 after hitting Triple H with his own sledgehammer after the outside interference of Shane McMahon, ECW World Champion the Big Show, and Shawn Michaels; prior to the bout, Lance Cade, Trevor Murdoch, Show, and Shane attacked DX backstage, during which Triple H had McMahon's limo door slammed against his head causing him to bleed from the ear (*Unforgiven 06, The New & Improved DX*)

'Of course I want to be there'

"When I got to WWE, anytime we were in the area my dad would always come. The one time we were going to be at the Garden, I didn't know if I would be wrestling or not. So I didn't know if I should leave tickets for him. (long pause) He said to me, 'Just knowing that you're in the building is enough for me. Of course i want to be there.' I did get to work that night."

Matt Striker, *TheHistoryofWWE.com interview, 2014*

'We almost lost Evander'

"One of best stories ever from commentary was at Madison Square Garden with Evander Holyfield. I had met Evander before and he was a total jerk, complete jerk to both me and Ron (Simmons). He used the religious image while he was an absolute reprehensible creature. He's had a ton of kids by a ton of women and professes to be a model Christian. I don't mind people being what they are, but I abhor fakes. I can't stand Evander Holyfield. Soooooo……. On to MSG. Evander is to box Matt Hardy in a 'boxing match' as MVP's replacement in a Madison Square Garden event. I am doing commentary and the whole show I am putting over Evander as this great guy, blah blah blah. By the end of the show I am sick of myself. So during commercial I tell Michael Cole a true story of Evander and my wife at Fox News. My wife had called me and told me she was in the 'Green Room' with a famous boxer but not being a sports fan she didn't know who he was., she told me it was Evander Holyfield. I explained to her he was one of greatest boxers of all time and told her the whole story of his career which I knew by heart as a huge boxing fan. She told me that he was 'very nice'. I said, "Of course, he has had 9 kids by 9 women of course he is nice, leave now!" and of course I was joking, but half serious. During the break, I tell Michael this story, but of course I go further. I totally tear down Evander as a hypocrite and piece of garbage that I think he is. I have no idea this is being broadcast into his dressing room, I still had my headphones and mic on. Every word I say Evander hears. Matt Hardy and MVP were in the room, ask them how tense it got. A spokesperson for Evander went to Vince and threatened to have him leave the show. More importantly, how would you like to be Matt Hardy? He is facing the former heavyweight champion in what he hopes is a work and he now knows this guy is furious. While I was saying this Evander had one of his kids on his lap listening, and from Matt's story he just got very quiet. Evander ended up doing business which I am sure Matt was thankful. My headset was ringing to tell me to shut up. After the show, I went to Evander's dressing room, not to apologize for what I said. I meant it and still do, but it was totally inappropriate for me to treat a guest of our show like that, I shouldn't have let my personal feelings potentially screw up a show. At his dressing room I encountered a security guard. I was expecting anything from a fight to him accepting my apology. I had no idea, but I had made my bed and I would lie in it. I never apologized for what I said but for the venue I said it in as he was our guest. I meant what I said, but shouldn't have said it to a guest of the WWE. The security guard looked at Evander who was less than five feet away and Evander shook his head, so I never spoke to him direct though that was my intention and he heard every word I said. And, I never apologized for calling him what I did, I apologized for doing it on a WWE show. As I walked by the boys to Evander's dressing room, no one knew what would happen. Ron Simmons told me, "Leg dive him!' which was my plan. It was a tense moment. I have seen him since, I have no respect for him, but I do hate he is getting 'punch drunk' as no one deserves that. He is a great boxer but a rotten human being. The next day I apologized to Vince, I was wrong to attack a guest like that. Vince said, "We almost lost him." And I responded, "We almost lost Matt." And we both laughed."

John Bradshaw Layfield, *The Layfield Report blog, 2012*

WWE @ New York City, NY - Madison Square Garden - August 13, 2007 (sell out; announced as 16,827)
D-Lo Brown pinned Ryan O'Reilly at 3:48 with the Lo Down
Raw - featured an opening in-ring promo by Vince McMahon, as the ring was surrounded by dozens of talent from Raw, Smackdown!, and ECW, regarding the news he has an illegitimate child - with the crowd chanting "Who's Your Daddy;" moments later, Stephanie McMahon appeared, berated him for what he put the rest of the family through, and said the illegitimate child is a WWE superstar; as Vince left the ring, he stared at both Ken Kennedy and Mark Henry, wondering if they could be his son; included a vignette of Bobby Lashley in Birmingham, AL recovering from his shoulder injury sustained weeks earlier at the hands of Kennedy; featured footage backstage of McMahon and Jonathan Coachman in which McMahon vented about the news that his child works for WWE, with Ric Flair then appearing and repeatedly going "Whoo" towards McMahon; included a series of vignettes throughout the show detailing Randy Orton's attacks on Shawn Michaels, Rob Van Dam, Dusty Rhodes, and Sgt. Slaughter; featured a backstage segment with William Regal, preparing for his hosting WWE Idol later in the show, in which Michael Cole & John Bradshaw Layfield dressed as Hall & Oates and sang "Private Eyes;" moments later, Maria and Ron Simmons appeared with Regal sayiing Maria would be one of the judges for the contest later in the show and she and Simmons date would be next week; Santino Marella then appeared and objected, saying he would sing a romantic song during WWE Idol to melt Maria's heart but Regal said there weren't any more spots open in the contest; Simmons then stared at JBL & Cole, with them asking Simmons what his favorite 80s band was, with Simmons sayinig "Wham!;" included two ads for Saturday Night's Main Event the following weekend; featured a vignette promoting the return of Triple H at Summer Slam; included a backstage segment with Vince and Coachman with Coachman saying he would cross reference all of McMahon's "indescretions" with the WWE superstars; moments later, Cody Rhodes appeared, said he knew who his father was, and gave McMahon a condom, saying he thought he could use it; the Boogeyman then appeared behind McMahon, singing Harry Chapin's "Cats in the Cradle;" featured WWE Idol, judged by William Regal, Maria, and Mick Foley; Jillian Hall sang "Memories" from Cats, with her own lyrics; Nikolai Volkoff, with Howard Finkel and the Iron Sheik, singing the Russian National Anthem; after the performance, Regal and Sheik got into an argument until Regal had the three removed by security; Lilian Garcia sang "New York, New York" until she was interrupted by Santino Marella, who said Lilian was dressed as a "filthy prostitute" before himself singing a modified version of "Amore;" after Santino pressured Maria to leave with him, Simmons appeared, with Santino calling him Cookie Monster because he rhymes and Simmons throwing him into the stage; Simmons was then declared the winner and said "Damn" over the mic; included an in-ring segment in which Jerry Lawler was scheduled to officially crown Booker T, with Sharmell, as the sole king in wrestling; after Booker demanded Lawler to crown him, Lawler said Booker wasn't the only king in wrestling and at Summer Slam - by order of William Regal - he would be facing Triple H, "the King of Kings;" Booker and Lawler then traded blows with Booker gaining the advantage thanks to Sharmell and busting Lawler open after hitting him with a TV monitor; Todd Grisham filled in for Lawler for the remainder of the show; featured a closing backstage segment with McMahon and Coachman in which Linda McMahon appeared and said Vince no longer had a home:
Ken Kennedy pinned the Sandman with a fireman's carry into a forward roll at 2:23
WWE Raw Tag Team Champions Lance Cade & Trevor Murdoch defeated Cryme Tyme via disqualification in a non-title match at around the 4-minute mark when Shad hit Murdoch over the back with a steel chair after the champions hit the High-Low behind the referee's back; prior to the bout, Cryme Tyme appeared ringside, took Lilian Garcia's chair, autographed it, and then offered to sell it to fans in the crowd, with one fan buying it for $1,000; the same chair was used in the finish of the bout (the bout began during the commercial break)
Snitsky pinned Robbie McAllister (w/ Rory McAllister) with the pumphandle slam at the 20-second mark; after the bout, Rory attempted to make the save but was kicked in the face and also sustained the pumphandle slam
Cody Rhodes pinned Charlie Haas (w/ Shelton Benjamin) with an inside cradle at 5:04
WWE World Champion John Cena & WWE IC Champion Umaga defeated Randy Orton & Carlito Caribbean Cool at 13:54 when Cena pinned Carlito with the FU after Umaga avoided Carlito's Back Stabber; prior to the bout, Orton cut an in-ring promo on Cena being the longest reigning champion in nearly two decades and his match with Cena at Summer Slam; the crowd chanted in unison during the bout, "Let's Go, Cena" and "Cena Sucks"
Saturday Night's Main Event #35 - 8/18/07 - featured an opening backstage segment with Vince McMahon and Jonathan Coachman in which Coachman said he has cross referenced all the WWE superstars and is confident he could name the identity of McMahon's child later in the show; included Michael Cole, Jim Ross, & John Bradshaw

Layfield on commentary; featured a backstage segment where McMahon saw an early 80s version of himself in the mirror; moments later, Ron Simmons walked over to the mirror, stared at it, and said "Damn;" included a vignette promoting the return of Triple H at Summer Slam; featured WWE US Champion MVP backstage with Evander Hollyfield and his entourage talking about Hollyfield's fight with Matt Hardy later in the show; included an in-ring segment with McMahon and Coachman regarding McMahon's mystery child in which Coachman introduced Eugene as the man he believed to be McMahon's son, then Melina who he thought to be McMahon's daughter, with Melina saying she would take McMahon for every cent that he has if it turns out she is his daughter; moments later, Coachman brought out a third option, Steve Austin; Austin then talked about McMahon possibly being his father and all the things he missed out on growing up without McMahon and then said he wanted to help McMahon control his "overactive grapefruits" and then kicked and punch McMahon in the groin before dropping Coachman with the Stunner; moments later, as McMahon struggled to his feet, Austin offered McMahon a beer to celebrate Austin's return to Madison Square Garden; as McMahon went to drink it, Austin dropped him with the Stunner; featured backstage footage of MVP hyping Hollyfield up for his fight against Hardy later in the show; included a closing music video highlighting the night's events:

Batista & Kane defeated World Heavyweight Champion the Great Khali (w/ Runjin Singh) & Finlay at 8:25 when Batista pinned Finlay with the spear and sit-down powerbomb, despite interference from WWE Cruiserweight Champion Hornswaggle, after Batista & Kane hit Khali with a double chokeslam

WWE World Champion John Cena defeated Carlito Caribbean Cool via submission with the STFU in a non-title match at 5:37; after the bout, Randy Orton attacked Cena, throwing him into the steel ringsteps, and dropping Cena with an RKO onto a steel chair set up at ringside; the crowd chanted back and forth "Randy Orton" and "Sucks" as Orton stood over Cena's body; after the commercial break, Todd Grisham conducted a backstage interview with Orton regarding the attack and Orton's upcoming match against Cena at Summer Slam

Evander Hollyfield (w/ WWE US Champion MVP) fought Matt Hardy to a no contest in a boxing fight at the 44-second mark of Round 2 when Hollyfield knocked out MVP with a punch after MVP repeatedly tried to tell Hollyfield what to do in the fight and climbed into the ring; Michael Buffer was the guest ring announcer for the bout

CM Punk & the Boogeyman defeated ECW World Champion John Morrison & Big Daddy V (w/ Matt Striker) at 6:40 when Punk pinned Morrison with an inside cradle; Tazz did guest commentary for the bout

ROYAL RUMBLE
Madison Square Garden – January 27, 2008

Royal Rumble 08 - New York City, NY - Madison Square Garden - January 27, 2008 (announced at 20,798; 19,000; sell out)

Jimmy Wang Yang & Shannon Moore defeated Deuce & Domino (w/ Cherry) in under 5 minutes

Pay-per-view bouts - the first pay-per-view to air in HD; included Jim Ross & Jerry Lawler on commentary for Raw, Michael Cole & Jonathan Coachman on commentary for Smackdown!, and Joey Styles & Tazz on commentary for ECW; featured a backstage segment with Vince McMahon and Hornswoggle in which McMahon discussed the upcoming Royal Rumble match and told Hornswoggle he couldn't trust anyone else in the match; moments later, Finlay appeared and McMahon suggested Hornswoggle could turn on him in the bout; included the debut of Mike Ademle as a new broadcaster, who introduced a video package on the Chris Jericho / John Bradshaw Layfield feud; featured a backstage segment with Ashley and Santino Marella in which Santino said Maria was too busy to talk with Ashley about Playboy and slammed the door in her face; included a backstage segment with Ric Flair - wearing a towel after getting out of the shower - and Ken Kennedy in which Kennedy congratulated Flair on his win until Shawn Michaels appeared, just as Kennedy implied he wanted to retire Flair, with Kennedy then walking off; Michaels then congratulated Flair on his win and Flair gave Michaels a pep talk before his participation in the Rumble; Batista and Triple H then appeared, with those two and Michaels chiming in on who would win the Rumble; featured an in-ring HD Kiss Cam, hosted by Maria, with Ashley then appearing and asking if Maria would be interested in posing for Playboy; Santino Marella then appeared with a person cloaked in black, insulted the crowd, especially the New York Giants by saying they were going to choke in the Super Bowl, and tried to take Maria backstage with him; after Ashley asked Maria again, Santino said they would discuss it more later and then brought the cloaked person into the ring, unveiling it as Big Dick Johnson wearing a Tom Brady Patriot's jersey and thong; Ashley, who laughed outloud throughout the segment, then knocked Johnson to the floor; included a 'Baywatch' themed WrestleMania 24 ad with Kelly Kelly and Mae Young; featured Ademle introducing a Randy Orton / Jeff Hardy video package, accidentally calling Hardy 'Harvey' before correcting himself; the segment featured Hardy's portion to the tune of Lostprophets' "Rooftops":

Ric Flair defeated WWE US Champion MVP via submission with the figure-4 in a non-title match at 7:50; prior to the match, Flair cut an in-ring promo on his career and thanked the MSG crowd for the respect they had shown him over the years; MVP originally won the match at the 4-minute mark following a boot to the face but referee Charles Robinson had the bout continue after noticing Flair's foot was on the bottom rope during the cover; pre-match stipulations stated Flair would have to retire if he lost the match; Michael Cole & Jonathan Coachman provided commentary for the match

John Bradshaw Layfield defeated Chris Jericho via disqualification at 9:24 when Jericho hit JBL in the head with a steel chair as both men brawled on the floor; after the match, a bloody Jericho threw the chair into JBL's face in the ring and choked him with a TV cable until he was pulled away by referees

World Heavyweight Champion Edge (w/ Vickie Guerrero) pinned Rey Mysterio Jr. at 12:36 by hitting the spear as Mysterio attempted a springboard into the ring, moments after hitting both Edge and an interfering Guerrero with the 619; Zack Ryder & Curt Hawkins were in the champion's corner early on but were ejected at the 3-minute mark as they attempted to attack Mysterio on the floor; after the bout, Ryder, Hawkins, and Edge tended to Guerrero outside the ring and helped her back into her wheelchair (*Edge: A Decade of Decadence*)

WWE World Champion Randy Orton pinned WWE IC Champion Jeff Hardy at 14:06 by reversing the Twist of Fate into the RKO (*Jeff Hardy: My Life My Rules*)

John Cena won the 30-man Royal Rumble match at 51:30 by last eliminating Triple H; due to pre-match stipulations, Cena earned a world title match at WrestleMania 24; Michael Buffer was the guest ring announcer for the match; Jim Ross, Jerry Lawler, Michael Cole, Jonathan Coachman, Joey Styles, & Tazz did commentary for the bout (Cena's surprise return after a 3-month absence)

Order of entry: The Undertaker (0:00); Shawn Michaels (0:00); Santino Marella (1:39); the Great Khali (w/ Runjin Singh) (3:34); upon Khali's appearance, the crowd chanted "You can't wrestle;" WWE Raw Tag Team Champion Hardcore Holly (5:06); WWE Smackdown! Tag Team Champion John Morrison (6:42); Tommy Dreamer (8:00); Dreamer received several chants of his name upon his appearance; Batista (9:36); Hornswoggle (36:49); Hornswoggle hid under the ring upon his entrance where he remained until much later; Chuck Palumbo (12:34); Jamie Noble, with his ribs taped (14:04); CM Punk (15:27); WWE Raw Tag Team Champion Cody Rhodes (17:00); Umaga (18:35); Snitsky (20:04); Mike Mizanin (21:32); Shelton Benjamin (22:49); Jimmy Snuka (24:17); Roddy Piper (25:59); Kane (26:53); Carlito Caribbean Cool (28:11); Mick Foley (29:28); Ken Kennedy (30:56); Big Daddy V (32:46) (not shown on camera); Mark Henry (34:13); ECW World Champion Chavo Guerrero Jr. (35:47); Finlay (36:59); Finlay appeared before his number to save Hornswoggle from Henry & Big Daddy V, with Finlay laying out several men with the shillalagh before leading Hornswoggle backstage; Elijah Burke (38:47); Triple H (40:08); John Cena (43:02)

Order of elimination: Marella by Taker following Michaels' superkick (2:05); Khali by Taker (4:43); Dreamer by Batista after fighting off a DDT attempt (10:10); Noble by Palumbo via a kick as Noble was on the apron (14:32); after the elimination, Noble was helped backstage by referees; Palumbo by Punk via a running knee to the head as Palumbo stood on the apron (16:34); Holly by Umaga via the thumb strike to the throat (18:52); Benjamin by Michaels via the superkick (23:07); Piper by Kane (27:00); Snuka by Kane (27:02); Snitsky by Taker via a clothesline (32:31); Taker by Michaels via the superkick (32:36); Michaels by Kennedy (32:42); after Taker's elimination, Taker hit a legdrop onto Snitsky while he was laid atop the commentary table; Mizanin by Hornswoggle by pulling him down from the floor as Mizanin tried to keep himself on the top rope (34:39); Morrison by Kane via a boot to the face (36:06); Hornswoggle left ringside (38 minute mark); Finlay was disqualified for using a weapon (38 minute mark); Punk by Guerrero via a suplex (39:20); Rhodes by Triple H (40:16); Big Daddy V by Triple H following a kneelift (40:33); Foley & Burke by Triple H (40:58); Carlito by Cena (43:19); Guerrero by Cena (43:22); Henry by Cena (43:26); Kennedy by Batista via a clothesline (44:28); Umaga by Batista via a clothesline (44:41); Kane by Batista & Triple H (44:53); Batista by Triple H via a clothesline (47:18); Triple H by Cena via an FU to the floor

"What the Fuck?!?!"

"Twenty nine men had entered the Rumble and we were all waiting on #30. At this point usually all the surprises are usually done and I think everyone in The Garden, myself included, did not expect anything spectacular for #30. Boy was I glad I was wrong. The crowd counts down the final 10 seconds and after a brief few seconds of silence, whose entrance music hits but John Cena. Cena had legitimately torn his pectoral muscle months prior and was expected to be out for possibly up to one year. Nobody expected him back. What made it even a more of a surprise is usually the online wrestling newsboards or "dirt sheets" pick up when someone will be making a "surprise return" and announce it. However, none of the online sources had even mentioned Cena at all for a couple weeks prior to the show. So when John Cena's music hit and he appeared in front of The Garden crowd as #30 the response was something I honestly never heard before from an MSG crowd. Especially for John Cena. There were none of the usual boos or cheers. When Cena came out as #30 it was more like 20,000 people going, "What the Fuck!?!?" Everybody including myself was totally caught off guard and were just in total shock. It was actually pretty cool. Then about 10 minutes later when Cena dumped Triple H over the top rope to win the Royal Rumble, the MSG crowd went back to its normal reaction for John Cena. Incessant booing."

Lou Spadone, *Queens, NY*

The roof was going to come off

"I have attended Madison Square Garden only one time, but it was an experience I will never forget. I sat 7th row ringside on the entrance ramp for the Royal Rumble 2008 and what a show that was. Leading up to the event that night, I was super excited to finally for the first time experience MSG live. The day of the show, we took a tour of the arena and, I kid you not, right when you first step foot on the hallowed ground that so many legendary superstars have walked before, you get goosebumps. When the event started that night, there was just a buzz in the air that can't be described, the atmosphere in that building is unlike any other facility I have ever attended a WWE event at. The show was amazing and it was topped off by the surprise and down right awesome return of John Cena. I literally felt like the roof was going to come off MSG that night when he returned, the biggest ovation I have ever experienced live. Every year they do a video package for the Rumble and it always includes that return and I can see myself going bonkers for the return as he walks by me and slaps my hand."

Nick Zablocki, *Finlay, Ohio*

The best 2 minutes of my life

"To my dying day, the greatest 2 minutes of my life was the Madison Square Garden Royal Rumble. I probably got one of the biggest ovations there. Undertaker was there, Shawn Michaels was there. The chant went from 'ECW' to 'Tommy Dreamer' and I'm in there with all those big stars. It didn't die. I was only there for 2 minutes. Batista came out and eliminated me and the place was fucking pissed. Right after that, I'm in the back. I walked around. 'Fuck, that's a great moment.' I like to take in big moments like that. And here comes Darryl Strawberry. 'Holy shit, you're Darryl Strawberry. Whats going on?' He was there with his family and we just sat and watched the rest of the Royal Rumble in the back."

Tommy Dreamer,
TheHistoryofWWE.com interview, 2014

WWE @ New York City, NY - Madison Square Garden - August 23, 2008 (19,068; sell out)

Primo Colon pinned William Regal with a backslide at 8:42 (Colon's MSG debut)

Lance Cade pinned D-Lo Brown at 8:30 with the sit-down spinebuster

WWE Women's Champion Beth Phoenix pinned Mickie James at 8:47 with the double chickenwing into the facebuster

Jamie Noble defeated Snitsky via submission at 6:45 with a front headlock chokehold

WWE Raw Tag Team Champions Cody Rhodes & Ted DiBiase Jr. defeated Cryme Tyme at 8:48 when DiBiase pinned Shad after Rhodes hit an elbow drop onto Shad behind the referee's back as Shad had DiBiase covered

WWE IC Champion Santino Marella pinned Kofi Kingston at 9:34 with a roll up after WWE Women's Champion Beth Phoenix interfered

John Cena & Batista defeated Chris Jericho & Kane at 17:28 when Cena pinned Kane with the FU (Cena's last match for 3 months)

World Heavyweight Champion CM Punk defeated John Bradshaw Layfield in a steel cage match at 16:35 when JBL accidentally punched the champion out of the door as the two were fighting on the apron; before the bout, Punk hugged ROH owner Cary Silkin, who sat ringside with Larry Sweeney

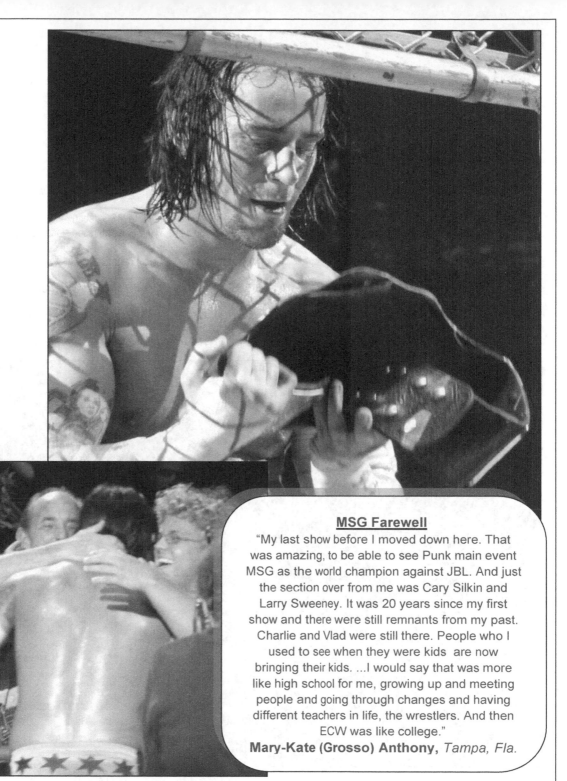

MSG Farewell

"My last show before I moved down here. That was amazing, to be able to see Punk main event MSG as the world champion against JBL. And just the section over from me was Cary Silkin and Larry Sweeney. It was 20 years since my first show and there were still remnants from my past. Charlie and Vlad were still there. People who I used to see when they were kids are now bringing their kids. ...I would say that was more like high school for me, growing up and meeting people and going through changes and having different teachers in life, the wrestlers. And then ECW was like college."

Mary-Kate (Grosso) Anthony, *Tampa, Fla.*

World Heavyweight Champion CM Punk celebrates with Cary Silkin and Larry Sweeney, from Ring of Honor.

Nov. 12, 2008: John Cena and Vince McMahon were among those in attendance for AC/DC's performance at MSG.

WWE (Raw) @ New York City, NY - Madison Square Garden - December 28, 2008
Howard Finkel was the ring announcer for the show; featured an in-ring promo by Santino Marella which was interrupted by the Boogeyman, with the Boogeyman then chasing Marella backstage
Finlay pinned Mark Henry after hitting him with the shillelagh as the referee was distracted by Tony Atlas and Hornswoggle
Melina & Kelly Kelly defeated WWE Women's Champion Beth Phoenix & Jillian Hall when Melina pinned Hall with a modified legdrop
ECW World Champion Matt Hardy pinned Jack Swagger with the Twist of Fate (Swagger's MSG debut)
WWE Raw Tag Team Champions John Morrison & Mike Mizanin defeated Cryme Tyme when Morrison pinned Shad with the Moonlight Drive
Shawn Michaels pinned Kane with the superkick; late in the bout, John Bradshaw Layfield appeared ringside, distracting both men
WWE IC Champion William Regal pinned CM Punk with a low blow and the knee to the head after Layla distracted the challenger as he attempted the Go To Sleep
Rey Mysterio Jr. & Kofi Kingston defeated Randy Orton & Cody Rhodes (w/ Manu) when Mysterio pinned Rhodes with a splash off the top after hitting a simultaneous 619 on both opponents
World Heavyweight Champion John Cena pinned Chris Jericho in a steel cage match with an FU off the top rope

WWE @ New York City, NY - Madison Square Garden - April 28, 2009 (announced at 17,294; 13,000 paid; sell out)

Mike Knox defeated Ricky Ortiz

ECW - 4/28/09 - featured an opening video package recapping Christian beating ECW World Champion Jack Swagger for the title at Backlash 2009, set to The Veer Union's "Seasons;" included an in-ring promo by Christian regarding his title win, during which he said it was the greatest moment in his career; moments later, Tommy Dreamer, in a suit and tie, came out, congratulated Christian, and said finally ECW had a champion that truly represented the company; he then said he had less than six weeks before his contract expired and had to win the championship one more time or he would walk away; after Dreamer challenged Christian to a title match, Christian offered to put the title up later in the show; moments later, Jack Swagger appeared at the entrance stage, said Christian's win was a fluke, and Dreamer was a joke; Swagger then said he had a rematch coming to him at Judgment Day and that no one should get a title shot before him; Tiffany then appeared and said Swagger would get his shot at Judgment Day and Dreamer would get his shot later in the broadcast; featured a promo by Vladimir Kozlov, decked out in a Russian military uniform, at the entrance stage in which he said there was no one in ECW that could compete with him and he would achieve global domination; included Gregory Helms conducting a backstage interview with Evan Bourne in which Bourne said he wanted a title shot; moments later, Paul Burchill & Katie Lea interrupted, with Paul saying he would be facing Bourne later in the week on WWE Superstars (Helms' ECW debut); featured an ad promoting Rey Mysterio Jr. vs. Chris Jericho vs. Jeff Hardy vs. Kane to take place Friday on Smackdown!, with the winner earning a title shot against World Heavyweight Champion Edge; the same match was advertised the previous night on Raw as featuring John Morrison and the Great Khali, instead of Kane, in a scramble match:

Tyson Kidd (w/ Natalya Neidhart) pinned Finlay at 10:36 after hitting Finlay in the back of his knee with his own shillelagh as Natalya distracted the referee; prior to the match, it was announced the show would move back to its original timeslot of Tuesday at 10 p.m. EST the following week

ECW World Champion Christian fought Tommy Dreamer to a no contest at 13:50 when Jack Swagger interfered and attacked both men after the challenger put Christian in the Tree of Woe; after the bout, Swagger dropped Christian with the gutwrench powerbomb

WWE Superstars - 4/30/09 - featured a vignette on Mark Henry; included an ad for "The Greatest Stars of the 90s;" featured a "Did you know" graphic which read the recent European tour saw sell outs in Germany, France, Austria, Ireland, Switzerland, and the UK; included a video package recapping the European tour; featured Josh Matthews conducting a backstage interview with Cody Rhodes & Ted DiBiase Jr. regarding Shane McMahon facing WWE World Champion Randy Orton the following week on Raw and DiBiase facing WWE Unified Tag Team Champion Carlito later in the broadcast, during which DiBiase said they wanted the tag team titles; included the DiBiase vs. Carlito match taped 4/27/09 in Bridgeport, CT:

Michelle McCool & Alicia Fox defeated Gail Kim & Maria at 4:34 when McCool pinned Kim with a kick to the face as Kim came off the top; Todd Grisham & Jim Ross provided commentary for the match

Evan Bourne pinned Paul Burchill (w/ Katie Lea) at 10:36 with the Shooting Star Press after knocking Burchill off the top; Josh Matthews & Matt Striker provided commentary for the match

430

Smackdown! - 5/1/09 - featured an opening in-ring promo by Chris Jericho in which he said he was the biggest name to ever be drafted to Smackdown! and that he was the logical #1 contender and shouldn't have to fight for that right later in the show; World Heavyweight Champion Edge then interrupted and argued he was better than Jericho because while Jericho could never beat John Cena, Edge did so at Backlash in a last man standing match; as the two shared words, CM Punk then appeared and aired a clip from his beating Edge to win the World Heavyweight Title the previous year; Jericho then repeatedly told Punk to leave the ring and then left the ring himself when Punk ignored him; when Edge then told Punk to leave, Punk said he would be facing Edge later in the show in a non-title match but when that match was over, he was cashing in his Money in the Bank briefcase; included a "Did you know?" graphic which read WWE.com was ranked #1 for entertainment websites for males under 34, beating out AOL TV, CBS.com, Fox.com, Oprah.com, TMZ.com, and MTV.com; featured a video package recapping the history between WWE US Champion MVP, Dolph Ziggler, and Sherry Shepherd; included a backstage segment with Jericho and Teddy Long in which Jericho argued he shouldn't have to compete in the #1 contender match later in the show; moments later, the Great Khali & Runjin Singh interrupted, with Khali reportedly telling Jericho to get over himself; featured a backstage segment with Jericho and Maria in which he demanded to see Long after claiming to be screwed in the elimination match; Edge then appeared also asking for Long, complaining that he shouldn't have to face Punk later in the show; included Cryme Tyme hosting an in-ring dance contest between Layla and Eve, set to the Black Eyed Peas' "Boom Boom Pow;" after Eve was named the winner, Layla attacked her with both women then fighting until Cryme Tyme pulled them apart as the crowd chanted "Let them fight;" featured a backstage segment with Shepherd and MVP in which Shepherd, dressed in a Ric Flair-like robe, said she wanted MVP to be on "The View" Monday; included a "Did you know?" graphic which read WWE programs can be seen in 465 million homes worldwide, more than the NBA, MLB, and NFL combined; featured a backstage segment with Jericho and Long in which Jericho insulted Long before John Morrison appeared, with Jericho slapping Morrison before the two men brawled; moments later, Charlie Haas, Tony Garea, and R Truth pulled the two men apart as Punk walked by on his way out for the main event:

John Morrison pinned Shelton Benjamin at 2:46 with a springboard kick to the face and the Moonlight Drive

Jeff Hardy defeated WWE IC Champion Rey Mysterio Jr., Kane, and Chris Jericho in an elimination match at 17:31; stipulations stated the winner would earn a World Heavyweight Title match at Judgment Day; Jericho pinned Kane at 7:00 after Hardy hit the Whisper in the Wind and Swanton on Kane and was then pulled out to the floor by Jericho; after the fall, Kane attacked the three other men and threw a steel chair into the ring; Jericho was disqualified at 8:18 by blocking a springboard into the ring by Mysterio with raising the chair to block the move; Hardy pinned Mysterio with a roll up immediately after Mysterio hit a springboard senton; after the match, Hardy and Mysterio shook hands

WWE US Champion MVP (w/ Sherry Shepherd) pinned Dolph Ziggler with the Playmaker at 3:53; prior to the bout, Ziggler cut an in-ring promo stating he would win the US title "right here in New Jersey;" late in the bout, Shepherd slapped the challenger in the face

CM Punk pinned World Heavyweight Champion Edge in a non-title match at 11:35 with the Go To Sleep; after the match, Punk called to cash in his Money in the Bank title shot but Umaga came out of the crowd and laid Punk out before then leaving through the audience; moments later, Edge attempted to assault Punk with the Money in the Bank briefcase but Jeff Hardy made the save and hit the Swanton on the champion

Dark match after the taping: John Cena, Batista, & WWE IC Champion Rey Mysterio Jr. defeated World Heavyweight Champion Edge, WWE World Champion Randy Orton, & Chris Jericho at the 15-minute mark when Batista pinned Jericho with the sit-down powerbomb

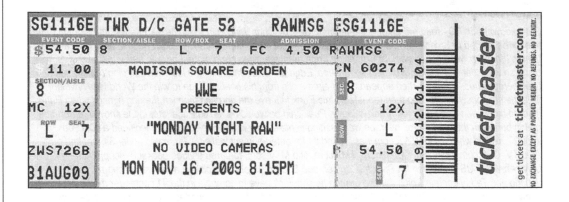

WWE @ New York City, NY - Madison Square Garden - November 16, 2009 (announced at 20,538; 17,000 paid; sell out)

The recently departed Lilian Garcia sang the National Anthem before the show went live
Raw - featured an opening backstage segment of Piper's Pit in which Roddy Piper, the host of the episode, introduced Luis Guzman and spoke about his upcoming film "Old Dogs," with Seth Green, John Travolta, and Robin Williams; Piper stated Mr. T was in the film too, which Guzman corrected; moments later, Piper said he arranged for "Iron Chef" Bobby Flay to be part of the show but the Iron Sheik, with Brie & Nikki Bella, came out instead; Guzman told Sheik he remembered when he fought Hulk Hogan, with Sheik then going into a tirade about Hogan and eventually using an Iron Sheik LJN action figure to beat up a Hogan LJN action figure and put him in the Camel Clutch; Piper, Guzman, and Sheik then said "Live, from New York, it's Monday Night Raw;" included a new show opening to the tune of Nickelback's "Burn it to the Ground;" featured a new entrance way; included an in-ring promo by Triple H & Shawn Michaels in which they shilled "The Unauthorized History of DX" and noted Sherri Shepherd, of "The View," was in the crowd with her own copy; Triple H then said he and Michaels agreed that they weren't going to implode and it didn't matter which of them beats WWE World Champion John Cena at Survivor Series; they then brought up the fact Hornswoggle was continuing to use their gimmick and asked for him to come out to the ring to see if he was a good fit to join DX; moments later, Triple H dropped Hornswoggle with the Pedigree and Michaels led the crowd in saying "Suck it;" Triple H & Michaels then pulled a backboard out from under the ring, which already had DX written on it, and took Hornswoggle backstage on it; featured a video package highlighting the history of WWE at Madison Square Garden, to the tune of "Empire State of Mind" by Jay-Z feat. Alicia Keys; included a backstage segment with Piper and WWE Unified Tag Team Champion Chris Jericho, with Jericho insulting Piper until Piper brought over Chris Masters and had him flex his pecs to the tune of the Black Eyed Peas' "Boom Boom Pow;" moments later, Brie & Nikki Bella walked in, were impressed by Masters, and walked off with him; moments later, TABOO and apl.de.ap of the band were shown in attendance; featured a "Did you know?" graphic which read the WWE just completed a 22 show, 2-week tour of Europe which drew more than 170,000 fans; included the announcement that Raw would remain on the USA Network through 2014; featured an in-ring promo by Piper in which he talked about his history at MSG with Cyndi Lauper, Hogan, Andre the Giant, Bruno Sammartino, and Capt. Lou Albano and said if you faced Piper at MSG, you either ended up dead or bald; Piper then said he's the reason Hogan has no hair; Piper then said he wanted a match with Vince McMahon and noted McMahon fired him in that arena after Piper appeared on "Real Sports with Bryant Gumbal;" moments later, McMahon came out, complimented Piper on his hair dye job and said Mother Nature hadn't been kind to him; Piper responded by saying there were many things Vince should be ashamed of and said his pinstripe suit was bought by Mr. Gotti; McMahon then noted his wins over Triple H, the Undertaker, the Rock, and Steve Austin and said he was officially retired; moments later, Piper said he had beaten cancer, he could beat McMahon, and he wanted it later in the show; included the announcement Jamie Noble had told WWE.com he was retired following the injuries sustained weeks earlier at the hands of Sheamus; featured an in-ring promo by Sheamus in which he made an open challenge to anyone backstage; when no one answered the challenge, Sheamus went to the floor and beat up a crew member before laying out Jerry Lawler with the kick to the face; moments later, referees tended to Lawler at ringside and he was

432

helped backstage; following the commercial break, Matt Striker replaced Lawler on commentar; included a "Did you know?" graphic which read fans from 50 states and 22 countries purchased WrestleMania 26 tickets the previous week; featured an in-ring segment in which Piper called for McMahon to come out and accept his challenge to a streetfight; moments later, Randy Orton appeared instead of McMahon, to chants of "Randy Orton," and said he wanted to lay Piper out to relive some stress; Orton then punched Piper, with Piper punching him back; Orton then assaulted Piper and prepared to kick him in the head until Kofi Kingston made the save and cleared the ring; after Orton went to go backstage, Kingston jumped him from behind and threw him into the front row; the two continued to brawl in the crowd, at ringside, and in the ring for several minutes until they were eventually pulled apart by referees; the fight continued until Kingston hit Orton across the face with a storage case near the technical table and attempted to jump from the stands through the table until he was forced down by referees; Kingston eventually broke free and hit the Boom Drop through the table Orton was laid out on; included a backstage promo by Cena regarding his teaming with World Heavyweight Champion the Undertaker in the night's main event; moments later, Cena was handed a piece of paper that clarified his match against DX at Survivor Series was a triple threat match and not a handicap match, with Cena then ranting that he would still win, during which he noted the Ghostbusters once saved NYC from a giant marshmellow man; featured an ad for "Hulk Hogan's Unreleased Collector's Series":
WWE US Champion Mike Mizanin pinned MVP with the Skull Crushing Finale at 3:46 after blocking a move in the corner and kicking the challenger; prior to the bout, Mizanin cut an in-ring promo about being the US champion while the New York Yankees had to buy their World Series championship; Sherri Shepherd, of "The View," was shown in attendance prior to the match; the challenger wore a Yankees hat to the ring
Santino Marella pinned Chavo Guerrero Jr. with a roll up at 2:50 after Guerrero became distracted by Hornswoggle, dressed in DX gear, on the apron; Marella wore a New York Rangers jersey to the ring but then took it off to reveal a New York Giants jersey underneath, then taking that off to reveal a New York Knicks jersey under that; Marella continued to take off his shirts, revealing jerseys of the New York Jets, New York Mets, Philadelphia Phillies, and finishing with the New York Yankees (*The Best of Raw: 2009*)
WWE Divas Champion Melina pinned Alicia Fox in a lumberjill match at 1:39 with the sunset flip / powerbomb; Judah Friedlander, of "30 Rock," was the guest ring announcer for the match; his intro claimed he was master of the martial arts, a bodybuilder, and a former player of the Brazilian National Soccer Team where he scored 15 goals in one game as the goal keeper, and is the greatest athlete in the world; the match was scheduled as a regular singles match; the added stipulation wasn't announced until after both participants made their entrance; lumberjills around ringside included Jillian Hall, Mickie James, WWE Women's Champion Michelle McCool, Layla, Beth Phoenix, Kelly Kelly, Gail Kim, and Eve; after the contest, all the divas brawled with the babyfaces eventually clearing the ring and dancing with Judah in the ring
Jack Swagger pinned Evan Bourne at around the 4-minute mark with the gutwrench powerbomb after ramming Bourne into two consecutive corners (the bout began during the commercial break)
WWE World Champion John Cena & World Heavyweight Champion the Undertaker defeated Triple H & Shawn Michaels and WWE Unified Tag Team Champions Chris Jericho & the Big Show in a non-title match at 7:07 when Cena pinned Triple H with the FU after Triple H knocked Taker to the floor; Taker's entrance featured druids appearing with torches, during which the crowd chanted "Undertaker;" immediately after the match, Taker slid back into the ring and dropped Cena with the tombstone before posing with his own belt as Cena lay nearby (*The Best of Raw: 2009*)
WWE Superstars - 11/19/09: Mark Henry pinned Cody Rhodes with the powerslam at 11:08; prior to the match, footage was shown of MVP beating Ted DiBiase Jr. during the previous week's show; Michael Cole & Jerry Lawler provided commentary for the match

WWE (Raw & Smackdown!) @ New York City, NY - Madison Square Garden - June 19, 2010 (sell out)
WWE IC Champion Kofi Kingston pinned Drew McIntyre; after the bout, Matt Hardy ran out of the crowd, assaulted McIntyre, and left through the crowd; moments later, as McIntyre made his way backstage, Hardy attacked him a second time
Christian & MVP defeated Luke Gallows & the masked man
Kane defeated CM Punk
WWE US Champion Mike Mizanin defeated R-Truth, Evan Bourne, and Mark Henry by pinning Truth after Bourne hit the Shooting Star Press on Truth but Miz knocked him to the floor and made the cover himself
World Heavyweight Champion Jack Swagger pinned the Big Show in a No DQ match after Kane interfered and dropped Show with the chokeslam; after the bout, Kane dropped Swagger with the chokeslam as well; moments later, after Show recovered, he knocked out Swagger with a punch
WWE Divas Champion Eve, Brie & Nikki Bella defeated Maryse, WWE Women's Champion Michelle McCool, & WWE Women's Champion Layla when Eve pinned Maryse with a neckbreaker; Santino Marella was the guest referee for the bout
Randy Orton pinned Edge with the RKO
WWE World Champion John Cena pinned Sheamus with the FU; after the bout, Wade Barrett, David Otunga, Heath Slater, Justin Gabriel, Skip Sheffield, and Darren Young attacked Cena until Randy Orton, Evan Bourne, Mark Henry, WWE IC Champion Kofi Kingston, R-Truth, and Edge made the save

WWE (Smackdown!) @ New York City, NY - Madison Square Garden - September 25, 2010 (13,500)
Bret Hart Appreciation Night - video clips of Hart vs. Mr. Perfect at Summer Slam 91, vs. Yokozuna at WrestleMania X, vs. Steve Austin at Survivor Series 96, and an overall package aired during the show; Howard Finkel was the guest host of the show
Kofi Kingston pinned WWE IC Champion Dolph Ziggler in a non-title match with the spin kick to the face
WWE Tag Team Champions Drew McIntyre & Cody Rhodes defeated MVP & Chris Masters when Rhodes pinned Masters after hitting the Crossroads
Alberto Del Rio defeated Chavo Guerrero Jr. via submission with the armbar; Guerrero worked the match as a babyface (Del Rio's MSG debut)
Melina & Kelly Kelly defeated WWE Divas Champion Michelle McCool & WWE Divas Champion Layla when Melina pinned Layla with a roll up after Hornswoggle distracted Layla
Mark Henry pinned Jack Swagger with the powerslam
Bret Hart, Tyson Kidd, & David Hart Smith defeated Justin Gabriel, Heath Slater, & Michael Tarver in an impromptu match when Gabriel submitted to Hart's Sharpshooter
The Big Show pinned CM Punk after hitting the chokeslam and punch; prior to the bout, Howard Finkel introduced Hart, Lawler, and the Hart Dynasty and gave Hart three framed photos - one of him with Martha Hart, one with Owen Hart, and one with him and his father and brothers; Hart also received a New York Rangers jersey with #10 on the back; moments later, Nexus interrupted to offer Hart a spot with them to survive the night; after the contest, Nexus laid out Kidd & Smith, with Hart and Lawler then fighting them off and Hart locking Slater in the Sharpshooter
World Heavyweight Champion Kane pinned the Undertaker in a streetfight with the chokeslam; after the bout, Taker avoided being hit with a steel chair and dropped Kane with the chokeslam

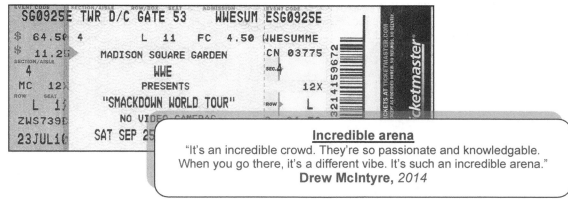

Incredible arena
"It's an incredible crowd. They're so passionate and knowledgable. When you go there, it's a different vibe. It's such an incredible arena."
Drew McIntyre, *2014*

Bret Hart made his MSG in-ring return after a 13-year absence to face members of the Nexus.

WWE (Raw) @ New York City, NY - Madison Square Garden - December 26, 2010 (14,500; 11,000 paid but many didn't show up due to weather)

The show took place during a snowstorm; Sgt. Slaughter, Heath Slater, Gail Kim, and Alicia Fox could not make it to the arena due to weather, with ring announcer Justin Roberts arriving late and a local having to announce the opening matches; referee duties alternated between Charles Robinson and Nuzio, who was there visiting and asked to help out; included a segment in which Michael Cole announced the Raw GM made him the guest host of the show; featured an in-ring segment of Piper's Pit in which Roddy Piper discussed 'The Top 50 WWE Superstars of All Time' DVD before introducing his guest as Tito Santana, subbing for Slaughter; after the two had words, Cole interrupted, said the Raw GM wanted them out of the ring, and that they were hasbeens; moments later, the Raw GM had Jimmy & Jey Uso escort Piper and Santana from the ring, with Piper and Santana attacking the Usos and clearing them from the ring

Zack Ryder won a battle royal by last eliminating Mark Henry and Michael McGillicutty at the same time; other participants included: WWE Tag Team Champions Santino Marella & Vladimir Kozlov, Primo Colon, Alex Riley, Darren Young, Yoshi Tatsu, William Regal, David Otunga, and David Hart Smith; stipulations stated the winner would challenge WWE US Champion Daniel Bryan later in the show; after the bout, Ryder cut an in-ring promo saying he would win Bryan's title

Tyson Kidd pinned David Hart Smith with a roll up after avoiding the running powerslam

Brie & Nikki Bella defeated Maryse & Melina when Melina was pinned after a facebuster; Eve picked a guest time keeper from the crowd before the bout; Nunzio was the guest referee for the match

WWE Tag Team Champions Santino Marella & Vladimir Kozlov defeated Justin Gabriel & Husky Harris when Santino pinned Gabriel with the Cobra; prior to the bout, Michael Cole announced the Raw GM wanted the teams to have a dance contest first, with the challengers attacking the champions after the champions danced

WWE World Champion Mike Mizanin pinned Randy Orton with the Skull Crushing Finale after Alex Riley interfered; after the bout, the Raw GM stated Riley would face Orton in a No DQ match and that Miz would have to leave ringside or he would be suspended

Randy Orton pinned Alex Riley in a No DQ match with the RKO after about 2 minutes

WWE US Champion Daniel Bryan defeated Zack Ryder via submission with the LeBell Lock at the 2-minute mark

John Morrison pinned Sheamus in a streetfight with a knee to the face as Sheamus was sitting in a chair in the ring

John Cena pinned Wade Barrett in a steel cage match following an FU from the second turnbuckle

Nor'easter ends streak
"I made every single Garden show from January 1994 through the fall of 2010, without missing even one show. The Nor'easter snowstorm, the day after Christmas 2010, is why my streak of shows ended (thanks, Mother Nature!). For most of those shows, I'd be at the Garden by noon, even though the shows started after 7. I was one of the 'Garden Gang' regulars, hanging out, getting autographs of the wrestlers coming in, etc."
Keith Lagasse, *New Britain, CT*

WWE (Raw) @ New York City, NY - Madison Square Garden - March 19, 2011 (18,500; 15,000 paid)

Included an in-ring contest officiated by R-Truth in which two men and two women had a dance off, per the Raw GM, for four tickets to the next MSG show; one of the men won

Randy Orton defeated WWE World Champion Mike Mizanin via disqualification at the 8-minute mark when CM Punk interfered; after the bout, the Raw GM ruled that, based on the fans, Orton would have a rematch later in the show or Orton would team with John Cena to face Miz & Punk; the fans chose for the tag team match

Evan Bourne, Santino Marella, & Vladimir Kozlov defeated Zack Ryder, Primo Colon, & Tyson Kidd when Bourne pinned Ryder with Air Bourne

The Great Khali pinned Alex Riley in under a minute; prior to the bout, Riley cut a promo and said the Raw GM said he could be back on the Raw roster and accompany WWE World Champion Mike Mizanin to WrestleMania but all he had to do was win a match on Raw; moments later, the Raw GM sent an e-mail that read Riley could get his opportunity right now

John Morrison pinned Dolph Ziggler (w/ Vickie Guerrero) with Starship Pain; Ziggler initially won the bout with his feet on the ropes but the match was ordered to continue

Daniel Bryan defeated Ted DiBiase Jr. via submission with the LeBell Lock

Triple H pinned WWE US Champion Sheamus in a streetfight with the Pedigree after 20 minutes

John Cena & Randy Orton defeated WWE World Champion Mike Mizanin & CM Punk when Orton pinned Miz with the RKO as Cena had Punk pinned with the FU

SURVIVOR SERIES
Madison Square Garden – November 20, 2011

Survivor Series 2011 - New York City, NY - Madison Square Garden - November 20, 2011 (16,749; 13,000 paid; sell out)

Santino Marella pinned Jinder Mahal with the Cobra

Pay-per-view bouts - featured Michael Cole, Jerry Lawler, & Booker T on commentary; included an opening segment in which John Laurinaitis walked out and noted it was the 25th anniversary of Survivor Series and his 10th anniversary with WWE; featured an ad promoting WWE 12; included a backstage segment with CM Punk and David Otunga in which Otunga said Laurinaitis ordered Punk to apologize to Michael Cole before his WWE World Title match later in the show, with Punk responding he would think about it after he wins the belt; featured a backstage promo by the Rock in which he talked about being in the crowd in 1977 to see Peter Maivia face Superstar Billy Graham, then hanging out with Andre the Giant years later as his dad Rocky Johnson defended the WWF (instead of WWE) tag team titles; Rock then noted his 1996 TV debut, despite his haircut and outfit, and said it started a legacy before running down his classic catchphrases; Rock continued by saying he would put boots to asses in regards to Mike Mizanin & R-Truth before then discussing John Cena, prompting massive boos and chants of "Cena sucks;" Rock went on to rant about Cena, prompting a chant of "lady parts" from the crowd, and then led the crowd in singing Frank Sinatra's "New York, New York;" included a backstage segment with ADR speaking with Nikki & Brie Bella, with Laurinaitis walking in and reminding ADR of the importance of his title defense; after ADR said it would be one of his many MSG title defenses and walked off, Laurinaitis was shown texting on his phone; featured anti-bullying comments from Ariel Winter, Miz, Cena, David Arquette, Chelsie Hightower, Alicia Fox, Jordin Sparks, Sheamus, Eve, WWE Tag Team Champion Evan Bourne, and Angus T. Jones; included Matt Striker conducting a backstage interview with Wade Barrett in which he said he wanted to be World Heavyweight Champion, with Miz & Truth interrupting and Barrett walking off; Miz then said not enough people were paying attention to Miz & Truth, with Truth complaining about Cena and Rock getting a billboard and then ranting about pigeons he saw earlier in NYC; they then said Cena and Rock were a load of crap and were about to get got; several National Guard soldiers were shown on camera, prompting a "USA" chant; featured an ad promoting 'Stone Cold Steve Austin: The Bottom Line from the Most Popular Superstar of All Time':

WWE US Champion Dolph Ziggler pinned John Morrison at 10:44 with the Zig Zag after avoiding the Starship Pain; Vickie Guerrero was in Ziggler's corner until she was ejected from ringside late in the bout; there were numerous chants of "We want Ryder" and "Woo woo woo" during the bout; Morrison was noticably booed during his entrance and the match; after the contest, Vickie ran back out to the ring and Ziggler took the mic, responding to the "We want Ryder" chants, saying Ryder wasn't there; Ziggler went on to say he wasn't a show off because he was just really, really good at what he does; Ryder then ran out to the ring, hit the Rough Ryder on Ziggler, and cleared Ziggler from the ring

WWE Divas Champion Beth Phoenix (w/ Natalya Neidhart) pinned Eve with a Glam Slam off the top at 4:34 in a lumberjill match; lumberjills for the match included Natalya, Kelly Kelly, AJ, Alicia, Kaitlyn, Aksana, Nikki & Brie Bella, Tamina, Rosa Mendes, and Maxine

Wade Barrett, Jack Swagger, WWE US Champion Dolph Ziggler, Hunico, & WWE IC Champion Cody Rhodes defeated Randy Orton, Sheamus, Sin Cara, Mason Ryan, & WWE Tag Team Champion Kofi Kingston in an elimination match at 22:11; Orton pinned Ziggler at 1:34 with the RKO; Sin Cara was eliminated at around the 3-minute mark when he injured himself doing a move to the floor, with trainers then tending to him on the floor and taking off his boot; following the injury, the crowd chanted "We want Ryder;" Rhodes pinned Ryan with the Beautiful Disaster and Crossroads at 8:52 after Hunico made the blind tag; after the fall, the crowd chanted "Cody;" Barrett pinned Kingston with a boot to the face and Wasteland at 14:06; Sheamus was disqualified at 18:26 when he didn't abide by the referee's 5-count while assaulting Swagger in the corner; after the decision, Sheamus kicked Swagger in the head; Orton pinned Swagger after the boot from Sheamus at 19:34; Orton pinned Hunico with a RKO as Hunico came off the top at 21:39; Barrett pinned Orton with the Wasteland after Orton dropped Rhodes with an RKO; late in the match, it was noted by the commentary team that Sin Cara sustained a torn patella (Rhodes' debut wearing knee pads; Kingston's tights featured the Stay Puff Marshmallow Man from Ghostbusters)

The Big Show defeated World Heavyweight Champion Mark Henry via disqualification at 13:04 when Henry kicked Show in the groin after avoiding the punch to the face; prior to the bout, crew members were shown reinforcing the ring; the crowd chanted "Boring," "Daniel Bryan," and "Undertaker" during the bout; late in the match, Henry knocked Show through the timekeeper's barricade with a tackle; Show later hit a superkick, prompting a "HBK" chant, and an elbow drop off the top, prompting a "Randy Savage" chant; after the bout, Henry locked Show's ankle in a steel chair but missed a bomb off the ropes, with Show then knocking Henry out with a punch; as Henry was knocked out, the crowd chanted "Daniel Bryan," with Show then locking Henry's ankle in the chair and hitting a legdrop onto it; Henry was then tended to by medics as Show left the ring, with Henry later yelling at the medics not to touch him

CM Punk defeated WWE World Champion Alberto Del Rio to win the title at 17:16 via submission with the Anaconda Vice; Ricardo Rodriguez served as ADR's ring announcer for the bout while Howard Finkel served as Punk's ring announcer; early in the bout, the crowd chanted "We want ice cream" and "Colt Cabana" at Punk; at the 16-minute mark, Punk hit an elbow drop off the top, prompting a "Randy Savage" chant; after the contest, and Finkel announcing him as the new champion, Punk jumped into the crowd to celebrate

John Cena & the Rock defeated Mike Mizanin & R-Truth at 21:33 when Rock pinned Miz with the People's Elbow; prior to his entrance, the crowd chanted "Cena sucks;" following the ring entrances, Cena gave his shirt to Arnold Skaaland's widow at ringside; early in the bout, after Rock outwrestled Miz & Truth by himself, the crowd chanted "You've still got it;" moments later, the crowd chanted "Fruity Pebbles," "You can't wrestle," and "You still suck" at Cena; a dueling chant later broke out of "Let's go, Cena" and "Cena sucks;" Rock's mom was shown in the crowd

following the finish; after the contest, Rock celebrated in the ring as Cena watched from the aisle, with Rock then calling for Cena to get back into the ring and pose for the fans, which Cena did to loud boos; Rock then posed again to loud applause, then dropped Cena with the Rock Bottom as he went to leave the ring (Rock's first match after a 7-year absence)

The Fink's return

"The highlight of that show, to me, was CM Punk bringing out Howard Finkel as the ring announcer. When Howard came out, there was this huge reaction of, 'This is our guy.' For Howard to come back out, and obviously it was mean to parody Ricardo (Rodriguez) and Alberto (Del Rio), but it was great stuff. I remember Punk winning the title and jumping into the crowd. The Zack Ryder phenomenon was incredible. His hometown is going nuts for him like he's as big as anyone."

Mike Johnson; *Glendale, NY*

WWE @ New York City, NY - Madison Square Garden - December 27, 2011 (14,000; 11,000 paid)

Featured an opening segment in which Mike Mizanin cut an in-ring promo, stating he would beat WWE World Champion CM Punk later in the show; moments later, R-Truth ran out and attacked Miz; after Miz left, John Laurinaitis appeared and ordered Truth to leave since he wasn't supposed to be at the show; Laurinaitis then introduced the opening match

Dolph Ziggler won a 12-man battle royal by last eliminating WWE Tag Team Champion Kofi Kingston; stipulations stated the winner would challenge WWE US Champion Zack Ryder later in the show

Alex Riley pinned Leo Kruger with the TKO

WWE Divas Champion Beth Phoenix pinned Eve with the Glam Slam; Brie Bella was the guest referee for the bout and Nikki Bella was the guest timekeeper; after the bout, Kelly Kelly made the save for Eve against Beth and the Bellas

Jerry Lawler pinned Jack Swagger with a fist drop from the middle turnbuckle in an impromptu match; prior to the bout, Mick Foley came out, spoke about being back at MSG, and noted his seeing Jimmy Snuka vs. Don Muraco there in 1983; Swagger then interrupted and challenged Foley to a match, with Foley then bringing out Lawler as Swagger's opponent instead; after the contest, Foley put the Mandible Claw on Sawgger

Santino Marella pinned Michael McGillicutty with the Cobra

WWE US Champion Zack Ryder pinned Dolph Ziggler with the Rough Ryder; Ziggler initially won the match and title but referee Charles Robinson restarted it after noticing Ryder's foot on the ropes during the cover

WWE Tag Team Champions Kofi Kingston & Evan Bourne defeated Primo Colon & Epico when Bourne pinned Epico with the Air Bourne

John Cena defeated Kane via disqualification when Kane used a steel chair as a weapon; after the bout, Kane dropped Cena with a chokeslam; moments later, Cena fought off an attempt at a tombstone and dropped Kane with the FU

WWE World Champion CM Punk pinned Mike Mizanin in a steel cage match with the Go To Sleep

WWE (Raw & Smackdown!) @ New York City, NY - Madison Square Garden - March 18, 2012 (17,000; 13,500 paid; sell out)

Zack Ryder pinned Mike Mizanin with the Rough Ryder after avoiding the Skull Crushing Finale

WWE Tag Team Champions Primo Colon & Epico defeated R-Truth & Kofi Kingston when Primo pinned Kingston with the Back Stabber after the challenger became distracted by John Laurinaitis; the challengers initially won the match and titles when Kingston pinned Primo with the spin kick to the face but Laurinaitis had the match continue since Primo's foot was on the ropes during the cover

WWE US Champion Santino Marella pinned Jack Swagger (w/ Vickie Guerrero) with the Cobra after Hornswoggle interfered; Swagger initially won the match and title by grabbing the ropes for leverage but Teddy Long came out and had the match continue; late in the bout, John Laurinaitis came out and argued with Long; after the bout, Marella, Long, and Hornswoggle celebrated in the ring

Alberto Del Rio defeated Mason Ryan via submission with the armbar within several seconds

WWE World Champion CM Punk, Triple H, & Randy Orton defeated Chris Jericho, WWE IC Champion Cody Rhodes, & Dolph Ziggler when Triple H pinned Ziggler with the tombstone, then sticking his tongue out like the Undertaker during the cover

WWE Divas Champion Beth Phoenix & Natalya Neidhart defeated Kelly Kelly & Tamina when Phoenix pinned Kelly with the Glam Slam after Eve, from ringside, tripped Kelly; prior to the bout, Eve cut an in-ring promo regarding the chants of "Hoeski" that the crowd was giving her

World Heavyweight Champion Daniel Bryan defeated the Big Show and Mark Henry at 9:34 by pinning Henry after Show dropped Henry with the chokeslam and Bryan clipped Show in the knee; after the bout, Show again punched Henry in the face

John Cena defeated Kane in a last man standing match after hitting a FU through a table

WWE (Raw) @ New York City, NY - Madison Square Garden - December 27, 2012 (14,500)
Included an opening in-ring introduction by Vickie Guerrero
The Road Dogg & Billy Gunn defeated Cody Rhodes & Damien Sandow when Gunn pinned Rhodes with the Fameasser
Brodus Clay pinned David Otunga with the splash; after the bout, Jack Swagger came out and challenged Clay to a match
Brodus Clay pinned Jack Swagger with the splash
WWE Divas Champion Eve pinned Kaitlyn
Santino Marella pinned Tensai; after the match, per stipulations, Tensai had to sing "Rudolph the Red Nosed Reindeer"
Seth Rollins, Dean Ambrose, & Roman Reigns defeated Mike Mizanin, WWE Tag Team Champions Daniel Bryan & Kane after Miz sustained the triple powerbomb
Jimmy & Jey Uso defeated Darren Young & Titus O'Neil after both men hit the splash off the top
WWE US Champion Antonio Cesaro pinned Zack Ryder with the Neutralizer
Ryback pinned Paul Heyman with Shellshocked in a streetfight; early in the match, Seth Rollins, Dean Ambrose, & Roman Reigns attacked Ryback, with Mike Mizanin, WWE Tag Team Champions Daniel Bryan & Kane then making the save; after the bout, Ryback hit a spear on Heyman through a table set up in the ring
John Cena pinned Dolph Ziggler (w/ AJ & Big E Langston) in a steel cage match with the FU

449

- 4/6/13: Bruno Sammartino, Bob Backlund, Trish Stratus, Mick Foley, Booker T, and Donald Trump were inducted into the WWE Hall of Fame during a ceremony at Madison Square Garden.

Message board brought to life

"I will always remember the 2013 WWE Hall of Fame Induction Ceremony because I got to attend it with one of my best friends. As soon as Wrestlemania 29 weekend was announced for NJ and NY, a group of us planned to get tickets for the big show. But it was with one of my closest friends that I choose to go to the Hall of Fame event with. You probably know him as the guy that got into a fight with Michael Cole and Tazz on a satellite radio show. If not, Google it. We were able to get tickets as soon as they went on sale because we knew they would sell out fast if the rumored main inductee became a reality (spoiler alert: he did). The day of the event, we both dressed in formal wear because we had seen the audiences at previous HOF events do the same and we wanted to show our respect to the inductees. Not everyone was dressed up but we didn't care, although the train ride in on the Long Island Rail Road was interesting as we were dressed in suits while the majority of passengers were headed to the city to party on a Saturday night. One of the highlights of the event that didn't air was CM Punk grabbing a sign from a fan before the event began that mentioned he was going to beat the streak. Punk held the sign up high and received a huge ovation for it. Finally, as anyone from Long Island that has attended a WWE event at the Garden knows, the train ride home is one big wrestling message board thread come to life. Being with my good friend and surrounded by everyone else to discuss the Hall of Fame ceremony is one of the biggest and best memories of my life."

Mike Abitabile. *Long Island. NY*

$1,800 airfare to make a dream reality

"I have been a wrestling fan since 1980, when one afternoon it came on after the Moscow Olympics. I was fascinated by what I saw before, and have been an avid fan ever since, never losing interest, even in times of it being a stale product, my favorites retiring or whatever. One of the big things that made me a fan in the 80s was MSG shows, how Gorilla Monsoon and Jesse Ventura used to put it over as The Mecca of Professional Wrestling. Even though I was in my early teens at the time and literally half a world away, I got the feeling that this was the place to be. I wondered what it would be like to walk into The Garden, so full of history and wonder.

I finally got that chance as part of a wrestling holiday I took with friends in 2013. We had previously flown to the U.S. for WrestleMania 27 in 2011. So when WrestleMania 29 was announced for NY/NJ with the Hall Of Fame being held at MSG, we knew we had to go again. We touched down in the U.S. the Sunday before WrestleMania, giving us time to see the sights of the city. When arriving at MSG, we stood there in wonder, looking up at all the posters on the wall and noticed a few wrestling ones. There was also a big banner promoting the Hall of Fame' it featured Bruno Sammartino and Mick Foley. To have flown 22 hours, and spent $1,800 on an airfare, none of that mattered, because a dream I'd had for nearly 20 years was now reality."

Steve Campbell, *Brisbane, Australia*

'Thank you, Bruno'

"Madison Square Garden is a special place to me. Being a longtime hockey fan, I grew up attending New York Rangers games all the time as a kid. But once I discovered professional wrestling, The Garden was a special place all over again. I've attended many house shows, but one night that will stand higher above the rest was when me and my girlfriend attended the WWE Hall of Fame ceremony. I've loved wrestling since the early age of 12 years old, and once I heard that the hall of fame was coming to the Garden, I couldn't let the opportunity slip away. I remember hoping on the bus eagerly staring at my watch. I never imagined I would get this chance before. We literally ran off the bus to the Garden, not letting anything get in our way. Not tonight. We were out of breath and starving, but I was too excited to not just keep running till we got to our seats. The lights dimmed. Applause and cheers rang in my ears as the screen showed the legends that made this great sport what it is today. It was a great night. Seeing the men and women who worked all their careers to make it to this one night was special. And I was there. I'll never get the moment when time froze, as the entire building stood when Bruno Sammartino took the stage. 'Thank you, Bruno' chants ran wild, as the audience young and old gave their respect to the living legend. It was quite a night I will never forget. Thank you WWE for making a fan out of me. Thank you MSG for bringing more memories."

Kyle Marsden, *South Hackensack, NJ*

WWE @ New York City, NY - Madison Square Garden - December 26, 2013 (14,000)

Included a segment in which Booker T introduced Michael Hayes to the ring, with the two strutting and doing Spinaroonies; during Booker's intro, he claimed Hayes sold out MSG "dozens of of times;" before the show, Bob Backlund took photos with fans in the lobby; DMC was in attendance for the show

Rey Mysterio Jr. pinned Alberto Del Rio with the 619 and splash off the top

Zack Ryder pinned Brodus Clay with a roll up at the 3-minute mark

The Big Show pinned Kane with the punch to the face after Kane briefly fought with guest referee Booker T

Nikki & Brie Bella, Cameron & Naomi defeated Kaitlyn, Alicia Fox, Rosa Mendes, & Aksana when one of the Bellas pinned Fox with the facebuster; prior to the bout, the Bellas, Cameron & Naomi defeated the other team in a dance off, with Brad Maddox then appearing and making it a tag team match as well

Sin Cara pinned Curtis Axel with the swanton; after the match, Axel took the mic and made an open challenge, saying he wouldn't end 2013 with a loss

The Great Khali pinned Curtis Axel with a chop to the head in an impromptu match

WWE Tag Team Champions Cody Rhodes & Goldust defeated Antonio Cesaro & Jack Swagger in a steel cage match when Rhodes pinned Cesaro with a moonsault off the top of the cage

El Torito & Los Matadores defeated Ricardo Rodriguez (sub. for Heath Slater), Jinder Mahal, & Drew McIntyre when Torito pinned Rodriguez; 3MB came out dressed as reindeer (Torito's MSG debut)

John Cena defeated WWE World Heavyweight Champion Randy Orton via disqualification at the 22-minute mark when Orton hit a low blow; after the match, Cena hit the FU to Orton

The Fans

"They've renovated it as of late. Going in there now, it actually doesn't have the same feel. I think the people make it. I think there was a certain scent to it. It was the smell of the city, mixed in with beer and popcorn. "What's that smell? Oh, it's us." It is a building but I think the fans really make it that electric feeling. Even if I go now, the fans make it that MSG crowd."

Reny Amoros, *Bronx, NY*

TITLE CHANGES AT THE GARDEN

WWE-WWF-WWWF WORLD HEAVYWEIGHT TITLE

May 17, 1963: Bruno Sammartino defeated WWWF World Champion Buddy Rogers via submission with a backbreaker at the 48-second mark to win the title

January 18, 1971: Ivan Koloff pinned WWWF World Champion Bruno Sammartino with a bodyslam and knee drop off the top rope to win the title at 14:55 after kicking the champion in the face as he charged into the corner

February 8, 1971: US Champion Pedro Morales pinned WWWF World Champion Ivan Koloff to win the title at 23:18 kicking off the top turnbuckle as Koloff had him in a waist lock, with both men falling backwards and having their shoulders down, but Morales lifting his at the count of 2; after the bout, Bruno Sammartino came out to congratulate Morales on his win

December 10, 1973: Bruno Sammartino pinned WWWF World Champion Stan Stasiak at 12:35 to win the title after three consecutive bodyslams; prior to the bout, Sammartino was escorted to the ring by Arnold Skaaland and the Grand Wizard escorted the champion

February 20, 1978: Bob Backlund pinned WWWF World Champion Superstar Billy Graham to win the title at 14:51 with the atomic drop, even though the champion's foot was on the bottom rope during the pinfall; voted Pro Wrestling Illustrated's Match of the Year

December 17, 1979: Bob Backlund defeated Bobby Duncum in a Texas Death Match to win the vacant WWF World Title at 17:18; Backlund did not come to the ring with the belt, rather WWF President Hisashi Shima was in possession of it and was introduced to the crowd before the match; Backlund was not introduced as champion however the title being vacant was not mentioned to the US audience but was known by the Japanese audience since the title controversy took place there; in commentary, Vince McMahon continued to refer to Backlund as the title holder

November 23, 1981: Bob Backlund (w/ Arnold Skaaland) pinned Greg Valentine to win the vacant WWF World Heavyweight title at 15:36 with a German suplex into a bridge after avoiding a punch; in a move that was only recognized in the NYC area, the championship was vacated the previous month when the referee accidentally handed Valentine the title following his loss to Backlund; prior to the bout, the Grand Wizard escorted Valentine to the ring

December 26, 1983: The Iron Sheik (w/ Freddie Blassie) defeated WWF World Champion Bob Backlund (w/ Arnold Skaaland) at 11:50 to win the title when Skaaland threw in the towel as Backlund was trapped in the Camel Clutch; moments prior to the finish, Backlund attempted his roll up into a bridge but was unable to keep it applied due to his injured neck

January 23, 1984: Hulk Hogan (sub. for Bob Backlund) pinned WWF World Champion the Iron Sheik (w/ Freddie Blassie) at 5:40 with the legdrop to win the title after ramming the champion back-first against the turnbuckle to escape the Camel Clutch; during his entrance, Hogan was seen walking past Vince McMahon in the backstage hallway; after the bout, Gene Okerlund interviewed the new champion backstage in which he was congratulated by Andre the Giant, Rocky Johnson, and Ivan Putski (Hogan's return to MSG after a nearly 3-year absense)

March 20, 1994: Bret Hart pinned WWF World Champion Yokozuna (w/ Jim Cornette & Mr. Fuji) to win the title at 10:33 after the champion lost his balance while attempting the Bonzai Drop; midway through the match, Piper knocked out Cornette with a punch after Cornette tried to interfere; after the match, Yokozuna chased surprise guest referee Roddy Piper backstage while Hart was congratulated by Lex Luger, WWF IC Champion Razor Ramon, Sparky Plugg, Tatanka, Piper, Randy Savage, the 1-2-3 Kid, Burt Rynolds, Rhonda Shear, Donny Whalberg, Pat Patterson, Gorilla Monsoon, and Vince McMahon; before the show went off the air, Owen Hart came ringside and stared at his brother inside the ring; Rynolds was the special guest ring announcer while Jeanie Garth was the special time keeper (Piper's surprise return after a 2-year absence)

November 26, 1994: Diesel (sub. for Bret Hart) pinned WWF World Champion Bob Backlund at the 8-second mark to win the title following a boot to the midsection and a powerbomb; Diesel's involvement in the match was not announced until *WWF Superstars* aired that morning; it was announced on local TV during the Nov. 5-6 weekend that Randy Savage would be the guest referee for the originally scheduled Hart/Backlund match but that announcement was never mentioned again

November 17, 1996: Psycho Sid pinned WWF World Champion Shawn Michaels (w/ Jose Lothario) to win the title at 20:00 with the powerbomb after hitting the champion with a video camera on the floor; moments prior, Sid hit Lothario with the same video camera; after the match, Lothario was taken backstage on a stretcher with Michaels close behind; Sid was heavily cheered and Michaels booed during the match

November 17, 2002: The Big Show pinned WWE World Champion Brock Lesnar (w/ Paul Heyman) to win the title at 4:19 after hitting the champion in the midsection with a chair followed by a chokeslam onto the chair; moments before the finish, Heyman turned on Lesnar by pulling the referee out of the ring and knocking him out after Lesnar hit the F5 on the challenger; immediately after the match, Heyman & Show drove out of the arena (Lesnar's first TV pinfall loss)

WWE-WWF INTERCONTINENTAL TITLE

April 21, 1980: Ken Patera defeated WWF Intercontinental Champion Pat Patterson to win the title at 20:48 with a knee drop off the middle turnbuckle to the champion's back; the referee, still groggy from a collision with Patterson moments prior, did not notice that the champion's foot was on the bottom rope during the cover; prior to the bout, the Grand Wizard escorted Patera to ringside before returning backstage when the match began

December 8, 1980: Pedro Morales defeated WWF Intercontinental Champion Ken Patera to win the title at 18:51; Pat Patterson was the guest referee for the bout

November 23, 1981: Pedro Morales pinned WWF Intercontinental Champion Don Muraco in a Texas Death Match to win the title after hitting Muraco with his own foreign object at 13:36

January 22, 1983: Don Muraco pinned WWF Intercontinental Champion Pedro Morales to win the title at 11:34 when the champion's injured knee gave out as he attempted a slam, with Morales falling on top for the pin (Morales' first pinfall loss at MSG in 18 years)

August 29, 1988: The Ultimate Warrior (sub. for Brutus Beefcake) pinned WWF Intercontinental Champion the Honky Tonk Man (w/ Jimmy Hart) with a flying shoulder block and splash at the 27-second mark to win the title

August 26, 1991: Bret Hart defeated WWF IC Champion Mr. Perfect (w/ the Coach) at 18:02 via submission with the Sharpshooter to win the title; during the bout, Stu, Helen, and Bruce Hart were seen in the audience; after the contest, Bret hugged his parents at ringside

August 30, 1998: Triple H (w/ Chyna) defeated WWF IC Champion the Rock (w/ Mark Henry) at 26:03 in a ladder match to win the title after Chyna hit a low blow on the champion as he climbed the ladder; prior to the bout, the Chris Warren Band performed the DX theme song to bring the challenger and Chyna to the ring; late in the match, Henry threw powder in Triple H's face, blinding him; after the contest, X-Pac and WWF Tag Team Champions the Road Dogg & Billy Gunn appeared to celebrate and help Triple H to the back

January 23, 2000: WWF IC Champion Chris Jericho defeated WWF IC Champion Chyna and Hardcore Holly at 7:30 by pinning Chyna with a bulldog and Lionsault after Chyna applied a Boston Crab on Holly; due to the decision, Jericho became the sole holder of the IC title

June 26, 2001: Albert pinned WWF IC Champion Kane to win the title in a No DQ match at 5:53 with the Baldo Bomb after Diamond Dallas Page came through the audience and hit the Diamond Cutter on the champion before leaving through the crowd

August 26, 2002: WWE IC Champion Rob Van Dam pinned WWE Hardcore Champion Tommy Dreamer with the Five Star Frog Splash following a modified Van Terminator as Dreamer was tied up in the Tree of Woe, with his legs trapped in a ladder, to unify both title belts; the match was fought under hardcore rules; after the match, the two embraced out of respect

WWE-WWF-WWWF WORLD TAG TEAM TITLES

December 6, 1971: Karl Gotch & Rene Goulet defeated WWWF Tag Team Champions Luke Graham & Tarzan Tyler to win the titles in a Best 2 out of 3 falls match, 2-0, at 17:20

May 22, 1972: Chief Jay Strongbow & Sonny King defeated WWWF Tag Team Champions Baron Mikel Scicluna & King Curtis to win the titles in a Best 2 out of 3 falls match, 2-0

June 26, 1978: The Yukon Lumberjacks defeated WWWF Tag Team Champions Dino Bravo & Dominic DeNucci to win the titles at 15:21 when Pierre pinned DeNucci following a double chop behind the referee's back

October 22, 1979: Ivan Putski & Tito Santana defeated WWF Tag Team Champions Johnny & Jerry Valiant at 13:39 to win the titles when Santana pinned Johnny, the illegal man, with a crossbody after the champions collided in the ring, with Jerry being knocked to the floor

June 28, 1982: Chief Jay & Jules Strongbow defeated WWF Tag Team Champions Mr. Fuji & Mr. Saito to win the titles at 9:48 when Jules pinned Fuji after Fuji missed a dive in the ring; the decision was later overturned when the replay showed Fuji's foot on the bottom rope during the pin and the titles were declared vacant; Ivan Putski was the guest referee for the bout; prior to the match, Fuji & Saito were escorted to the ring by Capt. Lou Albano

March 31, 1985: Nikolai Volkoff & the Iron Sheik (w/ Freddie Blassie) defeated WWF Tag Team Champions Mike Rotundo & Barry Windham (w/ Capt. Lou Albano) to win the titles at 6:56 when Volkoff pinned Windham after Sheik hit Windham in the back with Blassie's cane; after the bout, Gene Okerlund conducted a backstage interview with Blassie and the new champions

August 26, 1991: The Legion of Doom defeated WWF Tag Team Champions the Nasty Boys (w/ Jimmy Hart) at 7:44 to win the titles in a No DQ, No Count-Out match when Road Warrior Animal pinned Jerry Saggs following the Doomsday Device after both champions were hit with Hart's motorcycle helmet

January 17, 1994: The Quebecers defeated WWF Tag Team Champions Marty Jannetty & the 1-2-3 Kid at 21:24 to win the titles following the Tower of Quebec on the Kid after Johnny Polo interfered and caused the Kid to crotch himself on the top rope

May 19, 1996: Henry & Phinneas Godwinn defeated WWF Tag Team Champions Skip & Zip to win the titles at 10:56 when Phinneas pinned Skip with a kick to the midsection and the Slop Drop after kissing Sunny on the ring apron; after the bout, the champions, Hillbilly Jim, Howard Finkel, and a young fan danced in the ring

August 30, 1998: Billy Gunn & the Road Dogg defeated WWF Tag Team Champion Mankind at 5:16 in a handicap No disqualification falls count anywhere match to win the titles following a spike piledriver onto one of the title belts; after the match, Mankind's missing partner Kane appeared out of a dumpster at ringside and attacked Mankind with a sledgehammer

January 7, 2002: Tazz & Spike Dudley defeated WWF Tag Team Champions the Dudley Boyz (w/ Stacy Keibler) in a hardcore match to win the titles at 3:45 when Spike pinned Bubba Ray with the Dudley Dog through a table

WWE-WWF WOMEN'S TITLE

July 23, 1984: Wendi Richter (w/ Cyndi Lauper) pinned WWF Women's Champion the Fabulous Moolah (w/ Capt. Lou Albano) to win the title at 11:20 after lifting her right shoulder out of a bridged roll up; David Wolfe did guest commentary for the bout; after the bout, Moolah & Albano attacked the referee after hearing the decision

February 18, 1985: Leilani Kai (w/ the Fabulous Moolah) pinned WWF Women's Champion Wendi Richter (w/ Cyndi Lauper & David Wolff) with a roll up to win the title at 11:49 after Moolah hit the champion with a forearm to the face as Richter was trying to help Lauper on the floor after she was attacked by Moolah; after the bout, Richter and Lauper scared Moolah and Kai from the ring

March 31, 1985: Wendi Richter (w/ Cyndi Lauper) pinned WWF Women's Champion Leilani Kai (w/ the Fabulous Moolah) to win the title at 6:14 when the momentum of a crossbody off the top by Kai put Richter on top for the win; after the bout, Gene Okerlund conducted a backstage interview with Richter and Lauper, with David Wolfe

November 25, 1985: Spider Lady pinned WWF Women's Champion Wendi Richter to win the title at 6:38 with a small package even though the champion clearly kicked out before 3; after the bout, Richter continued attacking the challenger and pulled her mask off to reveal her as the Fabulous Moolah, not realizing the match had ended and - once she did - she refused to give up the championship belt; the finish, which Richter was unaware, came as a result of contract disputes with the champion; moments later, Richter whipped Moolah out of the ring with the title belt (Richter's last appearance in the WWF)

November 17, 2002: Victoria pinned WWE Women's Champion Trish Stratus in a hardcore match to win the title at 7:01 with a suplex after spraying a fire extinguisher in the champion's face

WWE SMACKDOWN TAG TEAM TITLES

November 17, 2002: Eddie & Chavo Guerrero Jr. defeated WWE Smackdown! Tag Team Champions Edge & Rey Mysterio Jr. and Kurt Angle & Chris Benoit in an elimination match to win the titles at 19:20; Edge pinned Benoit with the spear at 13:04 after avoiding a clothesline; after the elimination, Angle & Benoit attacked their opponents and then argued with one another as they left ringside; Eddie forced Mysterio to submit to the El Paso Lasso after Chavo hit Rey in the leg with one of the title belts as the champion attempted the West Coast Pop

April 18, 2005: Johnny Nitro & Joey Mercury (w/ Melina) defeated WWE Smackdown! Tag Team Champions Eddie Guerrero & Rey Mysterio Jr. to win the titles when Mercury pinned Mysterio at 10:26 after hitting the elevated double team DDT as Melina jumped on Guerrero on the floor to distract him; after the bout, Guerrero & Mysterio argued in the ring over the outcome with Guerrero shoving Mysterio to the mat; moments later, Mysterio confronted Guerrero on the floor and shoved him to the floor before walking backstage alone (Guerrero's last MSG appearance)

WWE-WWF HARDCORE TITLE

April 15, 2000: WWF Hardcore Champion Crash Holly pinned Perry Saturn; during the match, ECW World Champion Tazz ran out with a second referee in an attempt to win the title; after the match, Tazz and Saturn brawled

June 25, 2001: Rhyno pinned WWF Hardcore Champion Test to win the title at 4:33 after hitting the Gore backstage; seconds later, Mike Awesome ran down the hall, hitting Rhyno with a lead pipe and then powerbombing him onto a steel ladder to win the title (Awesome's surprise debut)

June 29, 2002: Shawn Stasiak pinned WWE Hardcore Champion Bradshaw to win the title after Steven Richards interfered, Spike Dudley pinned WWE Hardcore Champion Shawn Stasiak to win the title with the Dudley Dog, Steven Richards pinned WWE Hardcore Champion Spike Dudley to win the title with the Steven Kick, and Bradshaw pinned WWE Hardcore Champion Steven Richards to win the title with the Clothesline from Hell

August 26, 2002: WWE IC Champion Rob Van Dam pinned WWE Hardcore Champion Tommy Dreamer with the Five Star Frog Splash following a modified Van Terminator as Dreamer was tied up in the Tree of Woe, with his legs trapped in a ladder, to unify both title belts; the match was fought under hardcore rules; after the match, the two embraced out of respect

WWE CRUISERWEIGHT TITLE

November 17, 2002: Billy Kidman pinned WWE Cruiserweight Champion Jamie Noble (w/ Nidia) with the Shooting Star Press at 7:29 to win the title after kicking Nidia off the apron and knocking Noble off the middle turnbuckle; after the bout, Kidman left through the crowd (the debut of Kidman's "You Can Run" theme song)

WWF LIGHT HEAVYWEIGHT TITLE

June 25, 2001: X-Pac pinned WWF Light Heavyweight Champion Jeff Hardy to win the title at 3:11 with a backslide and putting his feet on the ropes for leverage after the champion failed a Swanton

WWF JR. HEAVYWEIGHT TITLE

January 23, 1978: Tatsumi Fujinami pinned WWWF Jr. Heavyweight Champion Jose Estrada to win the title at 11:31 with a Dragon suplex into a bridge; after the bout, Fujinami was interviewed in the ring by the Japanese TV announcer

December 28, 1984: The Cobra pinned the Black Tiger to win the vacant WWF Jr. Heavyweight Title at 12:29 with a tombstone and senton bomb off the top; after the bout, the Black Tiger attacked the Cobra after Cobra offered to shake hands; moments later, the Cobra retaliated by hitting Tiger with a steel chair

WWF INTERNATIONAL TITLE

August 30, 1982: Tatsumi Fujinami pinned WWF International Champion Gino Brito with a suplex at 11:34 to win the title; prior to the bout, WWF President Hisashi Shinma was introduced to the crowd

WWF INTERNATIONAL TAG TEAM TITLES

December 9, 1969: Victor Rivera & Tony Marino defeated WWWF International Tag Team Champions Prof. Toru Tanaka & Mitsu Arakawa in a Best 2 out of 3 falls match, 2-0, to win the titles

June 15, 1970: Bepo & Gito Mongol defeated WWWF International Tag Team Champions Victor Rivera & Tony Marino to win the titles in a Best 2 out of 3 falls match (the Mongols' MSG debut)

WWWF UNITED STATES TAG TEAM TITLES

February 21, 1966: Johnny Valentine & Antonio Pugliese defeated WWWF U.S. Tag Team Champions Dan & Dr. Bill Miller to win the titles

MILLION $ TITLE

August 26, 1991: Virgil pinned Million $ Champion Ted DiBiase (w/ Sensational Sherri) at 10:53 to win the title after DiBiase hit his head on an unprotected turnbuckle; during the opening moments of the bout, Heenan returned ringside; the bell originally rung when Sherri interfered early on but referee Earl Hebner opted to continue the bout and order Sherri backstage, with the stipulation that if she didn't go she would face permanent suspension

LONGEST MATCHES IN GARDEN HISTORY

August 24, 1981: WWF World Champion Bob Backlund fought
WWF Intercontinental Champion Don Muraco to a 60-minute time-limit draw

February 19, 1979: WWF World Champion Bob Backlund (w/ Arnold Skaaland) fought Greg Valentine
to a 60-minute time-limit draw at 59:18; after the match, Skaaland saved Backlund from the figure-4
by hitting Valentine with the world title belt (Valentine's MSG return after a 4-year absence)

July 29, 1972: WWWF Tag Team Champions Prof. Toru Tanaka & Mr. Fuji
fought Chief Jay Strongbow & Sonny King to a 60-minute draw

July 12, 1965: WWWF World Champion Bruno Sammartino defeated Bill Miller via referee's decision
when the match was stopped due to the curfew at the 60-minute mark

May 20, 1968: WWWF World Champion Bruno Sammartino fought George Steele to a curfew draw at 50:51

SHORTEST MATCHES IN GARDEN HISTORY

November 26, 1994: Diesel (sub. for Bret Hart) pinned WWF World Champion Bob Backlund
at the 8-second mark to win the title following a boot to the midsection and a powerbomb

June 25, 2001: Tazz defeated Steven Richards at the 13-second mark via submission with the Tazzmission

August 12, 1995: Henry Godwinn pinned Adam Bomb at the 15-second mark with the Slop Drop

October 28, 1989: WWF Intercontinental Champion the Ultimate Warrior pinned Andre the Giant
after a with three clotheslines and a splash; no bell could be heard to start the match and Warrior's music
never stopped playing after his entrance. If the bell had rung upon the initial contact; the time of the fall
would have been 18 seconds; prior to the bout, Bobby Heenan was order backstage by a count of 10 or
he would be suspended; after the bout, Andre grabbed the microphone, protesting the decision to referee
Danny Davis saying there was no bell rung to start the match so how could he make a 3-count

August 13, 2007: Snitsky pinned Robbie McAllister (w/ Rory McAllister) with the pumphandle slam
at the 20-second mark; after the bout, Rory attempted to make the save
but was kicked in the face and also sustained the pumphandle slam

*(Note: On March 31, 1985: King Kong Bundy pinned SD Jones at the 24-second mark
with the Avalanche and a splash; the announced time of the match was 9 seconds)*

CREDITS

The Writer
Graham Cawthon is award-winning journalist, columnist and newspaper editor. He grew up in a military family and spent much of his childhood traveling from West Germany to Anchorage, Ak. His research on the wrestling industry has been cited by the Wrestling Observer Newsletter, Fighting Spirit Magazine, PWInsider.com and WWE publications. He is a lifetime member of the Cauliflower Alley Club and was part of the selection committee for the 2011 class of the Professional Wrestling Hall of Fame. A graduate of Radford University, he lives in North Carolina with his wife, dog and cat. Follow him on Twitter at @GrahamCawthon or @TheHistoryofWWE

The Editor
Grant Sawyer is a lifelong sports fan and obsessive statistician that attended the Savannah College of Art & Design as a video major before moving on to FOX television. Combining his loves for video and the professional wrestling industy, he went on to establish relationships with numerous independent wrestling organizations to tape, edit and produce their events. Today the majority of his production work can be seen at CWF Mid-Atlantic. Grant also enjoys comics, his smokin' hot wife & insane child, and NFL football where he obsessively loves and follows all things related to the Green Bay Packers. Follow him on Twitter at @Statmark

The Cover Designer
Kristen Allen is a physically-disabled, self-taught, freelance graphic and web designer with over ten years experience. She was an honors graduate of West Davidson High School, class of 2007. She attended Davidson County Community College for two years under the general education program. Some of her work has been featured in various wrestling promotions throughout the Mid-Atlantic. She currently resides in Lexington, North Carolina with her father and grandmother. You can follow her Spinebuster Studios on Twitter at @SBusterStudios

OTHER TITLES ALSO AVAILABLE IN THE "HISTORY OF PROFESSIONAL WRESTLING" SERIES! AVAILABLE AT AMAZON.COM AND ALL FINE BOOK RETAILERS WORLDWIDE! ALSO AVAILABLE ON KINDLE

WWF 1963-1989
806 pages
ISBN-10: 1492825972
ISBN-13: 978-1492825975

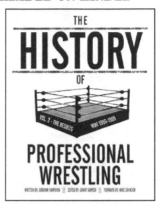

WWF 1990-1999
594 pages
ISBN-10: 149356689X
ISBN-13: 978-1493566891

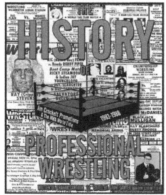

JIM CROCKETT PROMOTIONS
1983-1988
527 pages
ISBN-10: 149480347X
ISBN-13: 978-1494803476

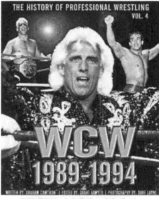

WCW 1989-1994
629 pages
ISBN-10: 1499656343
ISBN-13: 978-1499656

CPSIA information can be obtained at www.ICGtesting.com
Printed in the USA
LVOW05s1816280115

424741LV00021B/996/P

9 781505 229264